LAST GANG IN TOWN
THE STORY AND MYTH OF THE CLASH

MARCUS GRAY

Henry Holt and Company
New York

Henry Holt and Company, Inc.
Publishers since 1866
115 West 18th Street
New York, New York 10011

Henry Holt® is a registered trademark
of Henry Holt and Company, Inc.

Library of Congress Cataloging-in-Publication Data
Gray, Marcus.
Last gang in town: the story and myth
of the Clash / Marcus Gray.—1st American ed.
p.   cm.
Originally published: London: Fourth Estate, 1995.
Includes index.
1. Clash (Musical group)   2. Rock musicians—
England—Biography.   I. Title.
ML421.C57G73   1996   95-46937
782.42166'092'2—dc20   CIP
[B]   MN

ISBN 0-8050-4640-2

Henry Holt books are available for special promotions
and premiums. For details contact: Director, Special Markets.

First American Edition—1996

Typeset by SX Composing, Rayleigh, Essex

Printed in the United States of America
All first editions are printed on acid-free paper.∞

1   3   5   7   9   10   8   6   4   2

CONTENTS

ILLUSTRATIONS

ACKNOWLEDGEMENTS

A lot of people I'd never met before gave of their time and energy to benefit this project. None more so than Mark Woodley, who allowed me unrestricted access to his sizeable new wave archive, was generally more helpful than I had any right to expect and 'talked punk' over the phone with me for two years. Not, I hasten to add, non-stop.

Mark Gibson-White, John Holmes and Mark McDonald were swift to provide me with cuttings, tapes, videos and information when asked.

They who also served: Alan Anger, Hilary Arthur, Dougie Cameron, K. H. Carter (Head of Upper School, Dover Grammar School for Boys), Jonny Diamond, Peter Drum (College Secretary, Chelsea College of Art and Design), Graham Fraser, Daniel Gooding, David Haywood (Headmaster, City of London Freemen's School), R. E. Hough (Assistant Registrar, John Lewis plc), Alison Jinks, Sarah Kightley, Pattie Kleinke, Phillip McIllmurray, Iain McNay (of Cherry Red records), Joyce Moore (of Moore Management), Tami Peterson, Nicole Pickford, Joanne Richards, Pete Rippon, Haddon Smith, Gary Sutton, John Talbot, Sarah Talbot, Julien Temple, Gene Turbett, Kosmo Vinyl, Horst Weidermuller (of Studio K7), Thelma Winyard (Principal's Assistant, Byam Shaw School of Art) and Tim Young.

A big round of applause for the staffs of the National Sound Archive, the Gulbenkian Library, the London Records Office, the Central Reference Library and the Public Search Room at St Catherine's House.

Some of the people I interviewed went a good deal further out of their way than others, but lest special mentions lead to accusations of favouritism, I'll dispense my appreciation alphabetically: Steve Allen, Bill Barnacle, Gary Barnacle, Pete Barnacle, Steve Barnacle, Kelvin Blacklock, Brady, John Brown, Simon Cassell, Jack Castle, Terry Chimes, Sebastian Conran, Tom Critchley, Andy Czezowski, Matt Dangerfield, Alan Drake, Richard Dudanski, Vaughan Flood, Jerry Green, Johnny Green, Rob Harper, Simon Humphrey, Brian James, Alan 'Jiving Al' Jones, Wynn Jones, Keith Levene, Liz Lewis, Andrew Matheson, Glen Matlock, Mole, Mick Morris, Patrick Nother, Chris Parry, Tony Parsons, Alvaro Peña-Rojas, Mark Perry, Honest John Plain, Beryl Ritchie, Esperanza Romano, Rat Scabies, Pennie Smith,

Clive Timperley, Geir Waade, Stephen Williams and Jules Yewdall.

Photo credits: 1, 2 courtesy John Brown; 3, 4, 15, 16, 19 Erica Echenberg; 5, 6 photographers at present unknown, courtesy Nox Archives; 7 author; 8 courtesy David Haywood; 9, 10, 12 Alan 'Jiving Al' Jones; 11 Ray Eagle, courtesy Alvaro Peña-Rojas; 13 Jules Yewdall; 14 Ray Stevenson, Retna; 17 Adrian Boot, Retna; 18 photographer at present unknown, courtesy John Holmes; 20 Pennie Smith; 21, 22 Bob Savage; 23 Phillip McIllmurray; 24 Paul Slattery, Retna; 25 Paul Syrysko; 26 Neil Trotter, courtesy Mark Woodley.
　　Picture research by the author. It was not possible to trace the owners of the copyright for all the above photos, though every effort was made. Copyright owners who can prove ownership are invited to contact Marcus Gray c/o Fourth Estate Ltd.

Line illustrations: Vultures poster by Woody Mellor, courtesy Alan Jones; A Night of Pure Energy and 1977 Starts at the Roxy by Sebastian Conran; The Clash Sort It Out courtesy John Holmes; Bonds Casino courtesy Pattie Kleinke.

Allow me to be the first to admit that this book builds upon foundations laid by other journalists and writers. I have acknowledged my sources in the main text, but I'd also like to take this opportunity to doff my cap to the following stalwarts of the international press, music and otherwise: John Aizlewood, Billy Altman, Alan Anger, Stuart Bailie, Danny Baker, Lester Bangs, Robin Banks, Simon Banner, Jack Barron, Jack Basher, Will Birch, Chris Bohn, Lloyd Bradley, Chris Brazier, James Brown, Len Brown, Gordon Burn, Garry Bushell, Duncan Campbell, Roy Carr, Tom Carson, Brian Case, Robert Christgau, Jay Cocks, Mark Coleman, Andrew Collins, Richard Cook, Caroline Coon, Giovanni Dadomo, Stephen Dalton, Steve Daugherty, Adrian Deevoy, Stephen Demorest, Harold De Muir, Chas De Whalley, Dave DiMartino, Paul Du Noyer, Bruce Elder, Mick Farren, Bill Flanagan, Ross Fortune, Pete Frame, David Fricke, Graham Fuller, Vic Garbarini, Jane Garcia, Phil Gifford, Vivien Goldman, Richard Grabel, Granuaille, Mark Hagen, Ralph Heibutzki, Dave Henderson, James Henke, David Hepworth, Paolo Hewitt, Tom Hibbert, Geoff Hill, Mary Ann Hobbs, Bill Holdship, Barney Hoskyns, Patrick Humphries, Geoff Hutt, Jonh Ingham, Allan Jones, Jan Kaluza, Graham Kay, Danny Kelly, Nick Kent, Simon Kinnersley, Alan Lewis, Kurt Loder, Ian MacMillan, Stuart Maconie, Greil Marcus, Gavin Martin, Paul Mathur, John McCready, Dave McCullough, Don McLeese, Malcolm McSporran, Richard Meltzer, John Mendelssohn, Mick Mercer, Steve Mick, Ted Mico, Barry Miles, Robbi Millar, X. Moore, Paul Morley, Elliot Murphy, Charles Shaar Murray, Barry Myers, Kris Needs, Jeff Nesin, Mike Nicholls, Jimmy Nicol, Neil Norman, Richard North, Lucy O'Brien, Sean O'Hagan, Lesley O'Toole, Julie

Panebianco, Tony Parsons, Mike Pattenden, Mal Peachey, Deanne Pearson, Ian Penman, Mark Perry, Keri Phillips, John Piccarella, David Quantick, Paul Rambali, Graham Reid, Jim Reid, Roz Reines, Dave Rimmer, Lisa Robinson, Mark Roland, Clint Roswell, Ed St John, Chris Salewicz, Robert Sandall, Jon Savage, William Shaw, John Shearlaw, Pete Silverton, Jane Simon, Billy Sloan, Will Smith, Mat Snow, Jane Solanas, Tim Southwell, Neil Spencer, Caroline Sullivan, Phil Sutcliffe, Adam Sweeting, Paul Syrysko, John Tague, Neil Taylor, Adrian Thrills, Paul Tickell, John Tobler, James Truman, Steve Walsh, Steven Wells, Susan Whitall, Simon Williams and the Unknown Journalist.

Where would we all be without the *NME*, *Melody Maker*, *Q*, *Mojo*, *Rolling Stone*, *Creem* and *The Face*? Probably where we are without *Sounds*, *ZigZag* and *Sniffin' Glue*, only more so.

There is only one fairly perfunctory Clash biography in existence at the time of writing, and it gave me nothing I needed. More useful were *The Clash Songbook* (Wise Publications) and *The Clash Second Songbook* (Riva Music Ltd); Pennie Smith's unsurpassed rock'n'roll photo-book *The Clash: Before And After* (Eel Pie/Plexus); the booklet Kosmo Vinyl researched and edited to accompany the *Clash On Broadway* compilation (Epic Legacy); the sleevenotes 'Albert Transom' wrote for *The Story Of The Clash, Volume 1* compilation (CBS); and Mick Jones and Joe Strummer's version of 'The Story Of The Clash' as included in the 1980 tour programme, *The Armagideon Times*. As an introduction to the career of the 101ers, Jules Yewdall's snappily titled photo-book *Joe Strummer With The 101ers And The Clash 1974–1976* (Image Direct) was invaluable.

Although the Clash have been poorly served by the publishing industry, there are numerous books available on the Sex Pistols and punk in general. By far the best of these is Jon Savage's *England's Dreaming: Sex Pistols and Punk Rock* (Faber and Faber). Jon's book gave me something to work off and, on occasion, argue with, and I will consider it an honour if my humble effort is deemed to be its pale, but interesting, shadow.

Dusting down my knees, I must also acknowledge Lee Wood's simple but illuminating *Sex Pistols Day By Day* (Omnibus Press) and Fred and Judy Vermorel's pioneering *Sex Pistols: The Inside Story* (Omnibus Press). I consulted it at source, but Caroline Coon's punk era journalism is collected together in *1988: The New Wave Punk Rock Explosion* (Orbach and Chambers). Another early punk text is Julie Burchill and Tony Parsons's *The Boy Looked At Johnny* (Pluto Press), which has more porkies per page than *Animal Farm*, but still makes for an amusing read. Mention is also due to John Lydon's autobiography (with the help of Keith and Kent Zimmerman), *Rotten: No Irish, No Blacks, No Dogs* (Hodder and Stoughton). John's self-serving distortions really pulled my chain, but I suppose that's the point. Glen Matlock's autobiography (with the help of Pete Silverton), *I Was A Teenage Sex Pistol* (Omnibus Press), was useful, and would doubtless have been a lot more so had I not managed to talk to Glen in person.

Other helpful punk texts: Paolo Hewitt's *The Jam: A Beat Concerto* (Riot Stories/Omnibus Press); Bruce Foxton and Rick Buckler's autobiography (with the help of Alex Ogg); *The Jam: Our Story* (Castle Communications); Carol Clerk's Damned biography, *The Light At The End Of The Tunnel* (Omnibus Press); and Chris Twomey's booklet *The Stranglers: The Men They Love To Hate*. George Gimarc's *Punk Diary 1970–1979* (Vintage) arrived too late to act as anything other than a fact-checker, but did some good in that role.

Moving out of the punk arena, the following books were all consulted at some point, but not neccessarily in this order: Peter York's *Style Wars* (Sidgwick and Jackson); Barry Miles's *Ginsberg: A Biography* (Harper Perennial); Dave Rimmer's *Like Punk Never Happened: Culture Club And The New Pop* (Faber and Faber); *The Penguin Encyclopedia of Popular Music*, edited by Donald Clarke; my Old Faithful, *The New Musical Express Book Of Rock No 2* (Star), edited by Nick Logan and Bob Woffinden; *The Guinness Book Of British Hit Singles* and *The Guinness Book Of British Hit Albums*, edited by Jo and Tim Rice, Paul Gambaccini and Mike Read; my own *London's Rock Landmarks* (Omnibus Press); *Rolling Stone Rock Almanac* (Papermac); *The Time Out Film Guide* (Penguin), edited by Tom Milne; J. G. Ballard's *High-Rise* (Flamingo); George Orwell's *1984* (Penguin); Joseph Conrad's *Heart Of Darkness* (Penguin); Nick Kent's *The Dark Stuff* (Penguin); Nigel Fountain's *Underground: The London Alternative Press 1966–74* (Comedia-Routledge); *Music Master* (John Humphries).

Turning now to other media: I swore to myself that I wouldn't spend ridiculous amounts of time transcribing ancient radio interviews for this project, but felt obliged to break my own rule for a select few particularly memorable or revealing encounters. So consider your collective knuckles bumped Beacon Radio, Radio Hallam, Radio One's *Rock On*, Radio West, KCRW, KSJO and WHFS.

Useful television interviews, features, documentaries: the *London Weekend Show* punk documentary (ITV, November 1976); the Grundy–Sex Pistols encounter on *Today* (ITV, December 1976); the Clash tour feature on *Nationwide* (BBC1, 1980); the Joe Strummer interview on *Wired* (Channel 4, 1988); Joe's appearance on *Night Network* (1989); his interview on *Rapido* (Channel 4, 1989); the Mick Jones episode of *That Was Then, This Is Now* (BBC2 Def II, 1989); the Clash *Rockumentary* (MTV, 1991).

Video: *This Is Video Clash* (CMV); *Rude Boy* (Hendring); Don Letts's *Punk Rock Movie* (available from Studio K7, Kaiserdamm 7, D-1000 Berlin 15); *Punk In London '77* (also Studio K7; autumn 1977 German documentary on the London scene); *Punk* (Warners; compilation of appearances on Granada TV show *So It Goes*).

Time to get personal. My agent, Julian Alexander, pumped up my ego and protected me from big bad wolves both real and imaginary. My editor, Jane Carr, was cheerful in the face of my habitual deadline-crashing and never once turned up her nose at the smell of burning martyr. The alterations she suggested inspired me to make many more, all of which improved the book enormously. My good friend Jerry 'Jel-Boy' Scadden stepped in when it became clear I had no taste for accounting.

I am in the debt of Nick Beacock and Phil Jew at that most worthy of organisations, the Campaign for Bedsit Rights, for lending me their spare PC when mine started picking up coded messages from Uranus.

I'd like to thank my friends for sitting in my corner while I fought with the Clash, and for picking me up and dusting me down on those occasions when the Clash won. Sophie Talbot gave me the most time and encouragement and in return deserves and receives the most gratitude.

Nevertheless, there is much left over for Mark Scothern, Nick 'Dewey' Hogg, Trevor Wilkinson and Tracey Gauld. Thanks also – hey, for just being you – to Mark Wilkinson and Janette Atkinson; Pete Wills and Rosie Littlefair; and the Salisbury Contingent, including Jane, Colin, Sarah and Clive the Dog.

I wouldn't dream of forgetting Ma, Pa, Our Kid and Gail, but I think I'd better leave it there before I start thanking God and Anyone Else Who Knows Me.

FOREWARNING

This book is not an 'official' or 'authorised' project. I did try to gain access to the former members of the Clash via their record company, their management offices and a couple of their home addresses, but I was either ignored or actively discouraged.

By chance, wandering along Exhibition Road in a rainstorm one day, I happened to see Paul Simonon dodge out of a car and into the Victoria and Albert Museum. Not wanting to bother him while he was engaged in cultural pursuits, I dived into a nearby phone box to compose a note, which I tucked under his windscreen wiper. I received no reply. To this day, I don't know whether it was because the wind blew it away, the rain made it illegible, I put it on the wrong car or I was deemed to have made some unforgivable social gaffe by writing it on the back of a prostitute's calling card.

Not long afterwards, however, the following fax was sent to my editor from Clash overseer Kosmo Vinyl: 'The Clash have no objection to Marcus Gray's book, but this does not mean they have given the book any kind of official approval or are willing to contribute.' As a result, I thought it best to abandon my plans to stake out the dentist's where I'd heard Nick Headon was having his teeth fixed. (My friends, who were rooting for a chapter entitled 'Topper's Choppers', took the news badly.) In fact, I desisted from trying to make any further contact at all in case it should be construed as harassment.

Much later, a friend of mine bumped into Joe Strummer at Heathrow Airport, and told him about the book I had – by then – been working on for over two years. 'Well, he hasn't spoken to *me*,' was Joe's apparently somewhat bemused response. Later still, I sent some last-minute queries to former 101ers drummer Richard Dudanski, now resident in Spain. Although I didn't know it, Joe was staying with him at the time. The upshot of this coincidence was that he helped Richard with the replies. As they say in America: *go figure...*

While I was disappointed to be denied anything more than this most indirect and fleeting of contacts with the band, I was not heartbroken. I knew that a biography written without the Clash's co-operation would have to be very different, but I also knew it need not necessarily be inferior. I was aware that without the band pointing me in the right direction and supplying me with useful contacts a lot more detective work would be required; but I knew at least they wouldn't be attempting to influence my choice of interviewees, questioning my interpretation of events or demanding right of approval on the finished manuscript. When the word 'authorised' appears on a dust jacket, it is often a euphemism for 'sanitised'.

In the event, *Last Gang In Town* took two and a half years to plan, research and write. There were times when I felt like an intrepid private eye, relentlessly homing in on long-hidden truths; there were other times when I felt like a sad sack in an anorak, doggedly assembling a complicated jigsaw without reference to the picture on the box or, for that matter, even knowing whether I had all the pieces.

For the Clash's own words, I turned to a wide variety of secondary sources, both obvious and obscure: the music press, fanzines, style magazines, the arts sections of newspapers, radio and television interviews. I have included in the main text the name of each source, the date and, where known, the name of the interviewer. This is partly because I believe in giving credit where credit is due, but mostly because – as I soon found out – the medium, time and recipient of the message has a direct bearing on the content and reliability. The Clash's career has been subject to continual Orwellian revisionism. A 1986 version of events or attitudes will almost certainly contradict a 1984 version that will almost certainly contradict a 1982 version. . . and so on, all the way back to the original 1976 embellishment or half-truth. And that's before one factors in the hostility (perceived or actual) of the interviewer or the media outlet for which he or she works.

For my factual framework, I consulted the usual records: again, the music press, but also books, charts, telephone and street directories, electoral rolls, birth, marriage and death certificates and education and employment files.

For the kind of information that is not kept in archives and for a fresh perspective, I interviewed as many friends, associates and contemporaries of the band as possible. I made it clear in advance that I was not interested in propagating the Clash Myth. Many of those with whom I talked were happy enough to blow large holes in it, but I had to bear in mind that some of them were following their own agendas, and that we were discussing events of anything up to 30 years ago. I did my best to cross-check all information. Some conspiracy theories and accusations of moral turpitude had to be left out for want of proof. In other, less potentially litigious areas, rather than damage the book by omission, I have indicated where an anecdote is possibly apocryphal or have given a balancing argument.

Publishing is a far more flexible industry today than it was even five years ago. Nothing is written in stone. It is more than likely that, sometime in the not too distant future, a revised and, if necessary, updated second edition of this book will see the light of day. Anyone who disagrees with anything in the main text, or who can throw light on a previously dark area, or who has any relevant information of any kind – including archive materials, photographs, etc. – is invited to contact the author c/o Fourth Estate Ltd.

*

Lastly, I have to declare my own interests. It is both arrogant and insulting to the reader to pretend that any work of non-fiction is wholly objective. However hard authors try to keep their own voice out of their work, the very selection and sequencing of the material betrays their feelings and inevitably influences the response. Let me be upfront about it: in 1977, I was smitten by punk rock. It caught me at an impressionable age, and I believed much of what Tony Parsons calls the 'florid rhetoric' of the times. It would not be too melodramatic to confess that punk changed my life. Naturally, approaching this project as an adult who has had to live with the consequences of those changes, I was curious to understand what lay behind them.

I was also disappointed that punk did not achieve more, and that its most outspoken and – apparently – politically motivated exponents, the Clash, not only failed to deliver on so many of their promises, but ultimately failed to come to terms with their own inherent flaws and contradictions. As a result, I have judged them, and sometimes harshly; but mostly by their own words. Overall, let's just say I come not to bury the Clash, nor to praise them, but to take them apart and see how they work.

This book, however, is not just about the Clash, or even punk; it is also about the curious phenomenon of rock mythology, and about the spirit of activism and protest in popular music.

Nearly all our present-day forms of art and entertainment owe their genesis to our age-old fascination with myths and legends. Once upon a time, we mythologised gods, kings and great warriors. Then, as society became more straitlaced, we turned to mavericks and outlaws. Now it's serial killers and popular entertainers. We seem to have the need to make the people who intrigue us larger than life and more than human. For those with no interest in it, rock'n'roll must seem a strange medium to load with such expectation and deep feeling; and its young, sometimes inarticulate, selfish and two-dimensional exponents a peculiar breed of heroes.

Upon further examination, though, perhaps it is not quite so odd after all: more than any other contemporary means of expression, the popular song acts as a barometer of the times. To echo the words of Dennis Potter, in his final Channel 4 interview with Melyvn Bragg in April 1994: 'I wanted to write about the way popular culture is an inheritor of something else. You know that cheap songs, so called, actually do have something of the Psalms of David about them. They do say the world is other than it is. They do illuminate.'

During the writing of *Last Gang In Town* I grew sick of hearing about 'slackers' and the third 'Generation X' (a somewhat tired label, having already been affixed to a Sixties social document and a Seventies punk band), 'couch potatoes', 'new lads' and anything else that encouraged people to fiddle with syringes or themselves while London and the rest of the world burned. As well as creating a new poster-martyr for determined miserablists everywhere, Kurt Cobain's suicide gave a lot of people who make their living in or on the periphery of the music business pause for thought. It made me want to depict a punk rock that was not about the nihilist junky loser ethos as perpetuated by Kurt and his hero Sid Vicious, but something altogether more positive, outgoing, spirited and engaged.

Marcus Gray, 1995

Every generation must invent its own cure for the blues.
To give itself something to think about, something to do,
something to get involved in.
Joe Strummer, 1989

Like Richard Hell says, rock'n'roll is an arena
in which you recreate yourself.
Lester Bangs, *NME*, 1977

You don't need a leather jacket to be a rebel.
In fact, the more people look like rebels,
usually the less they are.
Ken Loach, *NME*, 1994

INTRODUCTION

Whether you grew up with the Clash or discovered them after they broke up, you probably think you have at least a rough idea of the Clash story. It is far more likely, however, that what you have is a rough idea of the Clash Myth. Over the years, the Myth has been revisited, retrodden and reworked numerous times by the band and by the music press that helped establish it in the first place. The real story has never been told; not even in the former Clash members' more confessional post-split interviews, or the liner notes to the band's posthumous compilation albums.

The very fact that this is the first in-depth biography to emerge in the ten years since the band disintegrated or the 20 since they first got together is not due to a lack of interest on the part of other writers. The Clash have always been uncooperative, because they don't want the story told. They prefer the Myth, which may not always have served them well in the past, but which now at least ensures them their place among the All Time Great Rock'n'Roll Bands.

The book breaks down into three sections. The first, Rock Dreams, explores the early lives and formative experiences of band members Mick Jones, Paul Simonon and Joe Strummer. Much of this information was deliberately obscured or substantially revised when they first established their punk personae, and a significant proportion of it has not been made public to this day.

The second section, Punk Myths, looks at the Clash's efforts to become key players in the UK punk scene, and at their major contribution to its development of a political consciousness. Along the way, it takes issue with the received wisdom regarding many of punk's supposed values, and offers the first detailed account of 1976 and All That from a perspective other than that of Malcolm McLaren or the Sex Pistols.

The third section, Star Turns, details the post-punk development of the Clash. It addresses their struggle to reconcile their punk-era outlook and rhetoric to the harsh realities of life as debtors to a major record company; the motives behind their efforts to break the American market; the development of their obsession with the world of cinema; and the reasons why the UK music press turned against them. It attempts a coherent account of the internecine wrangles that ultimately led to the Clash split, and – to make sure no stone is left unturned – it also examines the former band members' subsequent careers.

It would be unwise to claim that *Last Gang In Town* tells the truth, the whole truth and nothing but the truth; but it should take you considerably closer to the truth than you are now. Overall, the Clash story is very different to the Clash Myth, but no less fascinating. As it is necessary to go through the latter in order to reach the former, you, the reader, get two tales for the price of one. Also, a picture sleeve and illustrated inserts; but, alas, no unlisted extra chapter or free EP. . .

PART 1...

ROCK DREAMS

1... LONELY PLANET BOY

'**M**ick was always Rock'n'Roll Mick.' So says Keith Levene, who knew him well only for the six months or so they were both members of the Clash. As sweeping statements go, though, it turns out to be a remarkably accurate one. Michael Geoffrey Jones was born on 26 June 1955. '1955!' he crowed to *Blitz*'s William Shaw 33 years later. 'The birth of rock'n'roll!' His arrival at much the same time as the musical movement destined to establish the concepts of teenage and youth culture is a coincidence that Mick has devoted much of his life to making seem like an act of fate. This despite the inauspicious choice of venue for his début appearance: the South London Hospital for Women in Clapham.

Just over 18 months earlier, Thomas Gilmour Jones, then a 26-year-old taxi driver living with his Welsh parents, Evan and Gladys, at 66 Lynette Avenue in Clapham, had married Renee Zegansky, a 25-year-old fancy-jewellery saleswoman living with her mother, Stella, at 61 Christchurch House, Christchurch Road in neighbouring Streatham. Mick was their first and only child. By the time of his birth, Tommy and Renee had set up home together at 20 Fair Green Court, Mitcham, far enough to the south of London to qualify as part of Surrey. Mick's earliest recollection is a musical one: the Life Guards Band marching down Mitcham's main street. In *That Was Then, This Is Now*, a 1989 BBC2 Def II retrospective of his career to date, he said, 'I must have been very, very young then: two or three.'

Possibly even younger than that, because in 1957, Tommy, Renee and Mick moved briefly into what had been Renee's pre-marital residence, before being given their own flat at 109 Christchurch House. This late Thirties council block, located on the north-west corner of the crossroads where Brixton Hill meets Streatham Hill, was to remain Mick's home for the next ten years. Mick's memories of the early to mid Sixties are largely music-related. As was the case with many young kids at the time, his life was brightened considerably by the Beat Boom, and all the colour, style, noise and excitement that went with the burgeoning UK pop scene. Renee, still relatively young – and even younger at heart – was an ardent fan of Elvis Presley, so the radio was often tuned to the pirate stations, and Mick had little to overcome in the way of parental prejudice. On *That Was Then, This Is Now*, he said, 'I remember Len Barry's [autumn 1965 hit] "1-2-3" was a tune that I heard all the time. "One, two, three / It's so easy. . ." I thought that was what life was all about.'

Most of his contemporaries lost their hearts to the winning smiles, fluffy mop-tops and memorable melodies of the Beatles, but Mick joined the fan clubs of the Animals and the Kinks, displaying an early predilection for the kind of raucous showmanship that was to dominate his tastes well into the next decade. The Kinks were to remain a firm favourite, and in 1989, when recording Big Audio Dynamite's *Megatop Phoenix* at Ray Davies's Konk studios in Hornsey, north London, Mick confessed to his long-time musical hero that - after nearly 25 years – he still had his original Kinks fan club membership card at home.

Mick claims that his parents divorced when he was eight, but the split was not a sudden one. 'They kind of left home one at a time,' he told *Melody Maker*'s Caroline Coon in November 1976. Renee had always been fascinated with America, and decided to move there following the split. She opened a second-hand clothes shop, then met and married a copper mine engineer named George Tiitu before settling down in Armwood, Michigan. Tommy left Mick in the care of his nan, Stella, and continued to work as a taxi driver in south London.

Stella was no stranger to the vagaries of marital life. The daughter of a photographer, she was born Esther Stella Class on 7 December 1899 in Whitechapel. She became a milliner, and was courted by a Russian émigré named Morris Zegansky, the son of a master tailor. He himself was in the clothing trade, working as a furrier. They were married at Holborn Register Office on 30 May 1927. Morris claimed to be 22 at the time and, as was then considered to be a woman's prerogative, so did the 27-year-old Stella. Their relationship inspired the 1986 Big Audio Dynamite (BAD) song 'Beyond The Pale', in which, with the lyrical assistance of Joe Strummer, Mick trounces racism and English nationalism, and celebrates the Russo-Jewish half of his heritage.

Renee Zegansky was born in late 1928, by which time her parents had moved from Holborn to Kensington. The fate of Stella and Morris's marriage prefigured her own: the couple went their separate ways, then divorced. (Morris died in 1971.) During the Second World War, Stella and Renee took up residence in the newly built Christchurch House. On 17 December 1952, less than a year before her daughter took the plunge for the first time and in the same place, Wandsworth Register Office, Stella married again. Her new husband was Harry Marcus (né Hyman Markis), a 49-year-old divorced wireless salesman; Stella, a gowns saleswoman at the time of the wedding, once again knocked five years off her real age. Harry moved into 61 Christchurch House a matter of months before Renee left. He was in residence when she returned with her family in 1957, before moving into number 109. On 25 May 1961, Harry had a heart attack and died, leaving Stella on her own, and the Joneses moved back in with her to keep her company.

Renee and Tommy's separation shortly afterwards came when Mick was at an impressionable age. Although both parents maintained regular contact – Tommy called round to see him and Renee sent comics and magazines from the US – Mick has admitted that he felt abandoned, and that he found what he perceived as a double rejection 'pretty traumatic'. He told Caroline Coon, 'They decided I weren't happening, I suppose. Psychologically, it really did me in. Now I know it isn't that big a deal. But then at school, I'd sit there with this word "divorce, divorce" in my head all the time. But there was no social stigma attached to it because all the other kids seemed to be going through the same thing. Very few of the kids I knew were living a sheltered family life.'

No one could say he was starved of affection either prior to or following his parents' departure. If anything, he was a little spoiled. Despite the generation gap, a close relationship had already developed between grandson and grandmother which was to last until Stella's death in 1989. In his 'difficult' teenage years, the way Mick talked to Stella in front of his friends could be brusque to the point of unpleasant, but no one who witnessed it was ever in any doubt about his true feelings for her. In his early twenties, Mick occasionally lived apart from Stella for short periods, but even in the first days of the Clash, he still considered her flat to be his main home. In *That Was Then, This Is Now*, filmed shortly after her death, Mick declared, 'I always used to come back to my nan, because I loved her.' BAD's *Megatop Phoenix*, recorded that same year, is dedicated to her memory.

In September 1966, Mick began to attend Strand School, located towards the south-east end of Elm Park, off Brixton Hill, and just round the corner from Christchurch House. A bright boy, he did well for the first few years. 'I was really good at Religious Instruction and Oral English.' Before long, however, he started directing most of his energies into football and rock'n'roll, especially the latter.

In 1967, the R&B that had both inspired and provided the original repertoire for the Rolling Stones and the Yardbirds - as well as the Animals and the Kinks – was enjoying a new lease of life in what was then usually referred to as the British Blues Boom. At home, Mick commandeered the flat's mono radiogram to listen to the *Perfumed Garden* show on pirate station Radio London, where DJ John Peel mixed the new heavy blues with 'underground' music from both the UK and the West Coast of America. At the age of 12, he saved up the necessary 33s 3d and bought his first album, Cream's *Disraeli Gears*. It became close to impossible to prise him away from the radiogram. 'I used to stick my head to the oval-shaped speaker for hours,' he told *Blitz*'s William Shaw. He began reading the music press, and before long had become the music industry's dream consumer, spending the money he earned from his paper round on whatever the critics happened to be praising that week.

Talking to Jay Cocks of the US magazine *Time* in 1979, Mick described his upbringing thus: 'I stayed with me gran and a lot of wicked aunts!' The aunts came into the picture early in 1968, when Stella and her grandson moved north of the river to share their flat at 90 Park West, on Edgware Road between Kendal Street and Burwood Place. Cissie Class and Celia Green were great-aunts rather than aunts, of the same generation as Stella: Celia had been one of the witnesses at Stella's marriage to Morris Zegansky. For all the lack of wickedness on display, sharing his new home with three elderly women must have been a strange experience for the teenage Mick. He and the rest of the band would later get considerable mileage out of Mick's immediately pre-Clash address – a depressing Sixties high-rise – but, perhaps unsurprisingly, no mention would ever be made of the place where he lived for much of the remainder of his schooldays. A nine-storey, late Deco private mansion block with porterage and its own underground car park, Park West was and is considerably more upmarket than the average council high-rise. 'It was close to Hyde Park, very exclusive,' says Mick's schoolfriend Kelvin Blacklock. 'I only went there about two or three times, but it was really quite ultra-posh when you got inside as well. There was a swimming pool in the basement, and we used to sneak in.'

The central location also had its perks. It enabled Mick to attend his first live show in the summer of 1968: an open-air free concert in Hyde Park featuring Nice, Traffic and the Pretty Things. This was arranged by Blackhill, a young management organisation which, 11 years later, would briefly look after the affairs of the Clash. On 5 July 1969, just nine days after his 14th birthday, Mick attended a much larger free concert in the park, this time featuring the Rolling Stones. He was not about to let the fact that there were 250,000 other fans in attendance prevent him from getting as close as possible to one of his favourite bands. 'I spent all day worming my way through the crowd to the front of the stage just to see them,' he told William Shaw. 'I can show you which one's me on the pictures. And then they chucked all those butterflies up, and half of them died. Most of them landed on my head.' Founder Stones member Brian Jones had drowned in his swimming pool just two days earlier – the butterflies were intended as a tribute – and the emotionally charged occasion had a considerable effect on the starstruck teenager.

For his first three years at secondary school, Mick had, fairly typically, hung around with his contemporaries. That started to change in the autumn of 1969, the beginning of his fourth year. On turning up for one of his classes, he found himself sitting next to Robin Crocker, who ought to have been commencing his fifth year. Robin's loudmouthed, disruptive behaviour betrayed all the classic symptoms of the inveterate attention-seeker. 'He was just cocky, and trying to impress everybody' is Kelvin Blacklock's verdict. In the booklet accompanying the triple CD compilation *Clash On Broadway* (1991) Mick said of Robin, 'He was a wild one. Everybody used to get him to do the things they wished they could do themselves, so he always got into trouble.' One result of this was that he was required to resit a year, which is why he came to be sharing a desk with Mick.

'There's a marvellous story to be told about how we met,' says Robin. 'We had a fight in the maths class on the floor in front of everybody about who was better: Bo Diddley or Chuck Berry.' Once they had got over their disagreement about the relative merits of the two giants of R&B, they found they had a lot in common. Not least was a love of the Rolling Stones and, a little later, the Faces, a sloppy, good-time rock'n'roll band fronted by Rod Stewart and very much in the Stones tradition. It was another band, however, that was responsible for widening Mick's circle of friends and, ultimately, for encouraging him to pursue a musical career.

Mott the Hoople were formed when producer, manager and Svengali Guy Stevens teamed up Hereford band Silence with permanently shaded singer-songwriter Ian Hunter, renamed them after a Willard Manus novel and secured them a deal with Island records. The band's eponymous début album was released in 1969. They were discovered soon afterwards by a bunch of the Strand's sixth formers, among them Kelvin Blacklock, Jim Hyatt and John Brown. 'We thought Mott the Hoople were a great rock band,' says Kelvin, 'and accessible, because they were playing venues like the Roundhouse [in Camden's Chalk Farm Road] and wherever for the equivalent of 50 pence.' In the words of Kris Needs, who ran Mott the Hoople's fan club and went on to edit *ZigZag* magazine during its punk phase: 'They had the loudest amps, the longest hair, the hardest rock and the baddest attitude, although their ballads could have a whole hall in tears.' The band acknowledged their debt to the rock tradition with rock'n'roll medleys and cover versions of the Rolling Stones' 'Honky Tonk Women' and the Kinks' 'You Really Got Me'.

The Mott the Hoople craze spread amongst the school's musically aware pupils. The sixth formers were two to three years older than Mick, a considerable age gap at school. Nevertheless, his friendship with the older Robin went some way to bridging it, and Mick's home situation also proved to be an advantage. 'He had a lot more freedom than a lot of us, actually,' says Kelvin. 'His grandmother was quite loose.' When Kelvin and company planned outings to live concerts, Mick was usually able to tag along. 'I think the thing that brought everyone together,' says John Brown, 'was a general appreciation of Mott the Hoople. That and going down the Roundhouse on a Sunday afternoon to see Implosion with all the bands that used to be on. You used to pay your money, go in and spend the whole day there from midday on. Loads of bands all through into the evening.'

In addition to Sundays at the Roundhouse, there were numerous trips to see Mott the Hoople further afield. Once he began to recognise the Strand boys' faces, the band's road manager, Stan Tippins, let them in for free. This in turn encouraged them to attend every Mott concert they could, dodging the fares, distance no object. 'We did the craziest things,' recalls John. 'We'd wait until the train got into the station, get out the wrong side and run back along the lines with guys hopping up and down and shouting at us.' Among his memories is the occasion when one of the gang got his hair caught in barbed wire while trying to scale an overhead pedestrian walkway at Southampton. Kelvin remembers that another outing, which included Mick, took them as far as Liverpool and involved another chase along the tracks. 'It was well *A Hard Day's Night!*'

Kris Needs recollects seeing Mick 'at many of the 80 or so gigs I caught'. Together with other committed fans, the Strand boys helped keep up the Mott spirits through some hard times, and it was to them and their ilk that later band songs like 'Ballad Of Mott' and 'Saturday Gigs' were addressed. Even at the time, the band were appreciative of their dedicated followers, and generous with their time and attention. Particularly in Kelvin's case. 'Ian Hunter noticed me,' he says. 'He used to call me Jagger, because we'd never had any formal introduction. He used to get me up on-stage to join him, because they used to do a song called "Walking With A Mountain", which was a crossover with "Jumping Jack Flash", just repeating that line to get the audience singing. So I used to get up and do that with him. That was why I became a singer, really. It was so great, such a buzz up there.' 'Kelvin was always pushy, you know,' says John. 'He told Ian about his aspirations, what he wanted to be. The whole Mott thing had a vast and far-reaching impact on all of us. It changed our lives, everyone who got involved. It was very infectious.'

With Ian's encouragement, Kelvin and the others decided to form their own band. The initially nameless outfit first started playing together in June 1970. Instrumental duties were assigned by Kelvin, the most forceful personality. He played guitar and sang lead vocals, John played second guitar and also did some singing and Bob Goffman took up the bass. 'Jim Hyatt was very laid-back, the sort of guy who wouldn't create any waves,' says John. 'So he was told he was going to play drums, and he just accepted that.' Kelvin lived on a council estate in Battersea, and the band used to rehearse on Thessaly Road, sometimes in the youth club and sometimes in the church hall that the Who would shortly take over and convert into Ramport studios. According to Kelvin, the music was 'just straight-ahead blues, simple little riffs. That's all we could play.' Other people went along to sit in occasionally, including Robin and a guitarist from Mick's year named Paul Wayman. Mick used to go and watch. 'I don't think Mick had even been contemplating playing at that point,' says Kelvin.

Kelvin was wrong. There were two Micks in the gang: the other, being more extrovert, was known as Mad Mick, while Mick Jones, younger, and yet to shoot up to his not inconsiderable full adult height, was known as Little Mick. Although not cruelly meant, the diminutive gives some idea of Mick's status among the older boys, and he was as inhibited and full of self-doubt as might be expected under the circumstances. His true feelings spilled out, in somewhat melodramatic terms, in a September 1976 interview with Steve Walsh of punk fanzine *Sniffin' Glue*: 'I was the last kid on my block to pick up a guitar 'cause all the others were repressing me and saying, "No, you don't want to do that, you're too ugly, too spotty, you stink!", and I believed 'em. I was probably very gullible. And then I realised that they weren't doing too well, and I said, "Ah, fuck, I can do just as well!"'

It was to be another two years before he came to this realisation and acted upon it, but the desire to be actively involved in rock'n'roll dated from his first record purchase. Back in 1967, his interest had been signalled, if not realised, by a brief flirtation with the Stylophone. In addition to his deep love of the music itself, Mick was also attracted to the camaraderie of band life and the glamour of pop stardom. On *That Was Then, This Is Now* he declared, 'There's a time when you have a choice between football or music, or you just do what everybody does, and you ain't gonna get out.' Although keen on football, both as player and follower, his overriding ambition was to be part of a rock'n'roll band. 'That was it, really: be in a group.'

The 1978 Clash song 'Stay Free' was written entirely by Mick, and at the time of composition its apparently autobiographical subject matter encouraged much speculation about his past. It tells of a couple of friends who meet at school, mess around and get thrown out; it details a shared south London nightlife spent dancing, drinking, laughing, fighting and playing pool; but while one of the two devotes the rest of his time to learning the guitar, the other slips into a life of crime, as a result of which he and his cohorts end up serving a three-year sentence in Brixton Prison. In July 1978, Chris Salewicz of the *New Musical Express* (*NME*) asked Mick to verify that the song's other main protagonist was currently working as a 'dilettante journalist' for another music publication. He did not name him, but he meant Robin Crocker. 'It's not just about him,' answered Mick. 'It's about all my gang in Brixton. That guy's the lucky one: he's escaped. Two of the others work in butchers' shops and are in the National Front. Twenty-three, and they're in the Front. I don't not talk to them because of that, though. I go and see them. Show them what *I've* done. Show them the possibilities.'

Mick's explanation raises the question, among others, just what was it that had to be escaped? As he suggested on *That Was Then, This Is Now*, sport and, more recently, popular music are traditionally perceived to be the only two legitimate ways for working class people in inner city slum areas to throw off the shackles of poverty. For those unwilling to submit to the relentless drudgery of life as fodder for the factories or dole queues, the remaining option is crime. The story of East End boxers-turned-gangsters Ron and Reg Kray adds credence to this general picture. As Mick claims, some – though by no means all – of his schoolmates lived on the area's numerous council estates, and the pressures of urban life may well have resulted in a higher than average number of broken homes. Nevertheless, the pupils at Strand School had one passport to freedom that Mick has tended to gloss over in interviews, and comes close to denying in 'Stay Free': a privileged education.

Strand School was not some gang-dominated, drug-infested, anarchic hell-hole, the sole purpose of which was to keep the lid on its inmates until they reached minimum leaving age. It had been established in 1890 as an offshoot of King's College in the Strand, and had moved out to the Elm Park site 20 years later. 'It came, as a fairly snooty school, to Brixton, which at the time was a very prosperous suburb,' says John Brown. 'Of course, the area changed over the years.' The school refused to follow suit. By the early Seventies, the Strand was still an old-fashioned, boys-only grammar attended by fewer than 500 pupils. Situated next to two much larger comprehensive schools, it made a mockery of the very notion of comprehensive education, the original intention of which was to provide equal opportunities for all.

Grammar schools, supposedly rendered obsolete by the change to the comprehensive system at the turn of the decade, admitted only the more academically oriented pupils, as determined by the 11-plus, an examination taken in the final year of primary school. Such children were considered the most likely to go on to gain Ordinary (O) or even Advanced (A) level General Certificates of Education, and in order to realise this potential, they were afforded preferential treatment. Today's equivalent qualifications to O and A levels might not seem to be worth much in the current climate of high unemployment and cutbacks in government educational grants, but in the early Seventies O levels practically guaranteed a reasonably paid white collar job, and A levels either a well-paid one or the opportunity to go on to college.

John makes the perfectly valid point that children of 11 have next to no say in the matter of their education, and even when they get older and gain some understanding of the implications, they have relatively little power to effect any changes. 'There was never any looking down, though, although you were maybe aware that you were a bit privileged,' he says. 'Especially with 2,000 kids crammed into a skyscraper nearby, which is what Tulse Hill was.' 'Strand was a really uptight school, quite strict, actually,' recalls Kelvin. 'We could never grow our hair long. We used to try and get away with it and all that sort of bollocks, but we used to get in trouble for it. The tough nuts ended up with the school next door, Tulse Hill. There was never really any trouble. I had a few fights at school, but I think everybody has a few fights at some point.'

Both John and Kelvin say that any problems came from external rather than internal sources, as a direct result of inequalities that could be clearly perceived by the pupils of the neighbouring comprehensive schools: according to John's estimates, Dick Sheppard and Tulse Hill were both over 90 per cent black, while the Strand was just one or two kids away from being 100 per cent white. 'We were like a plantation, almost,' he says. 'We inherited this "They're the white kids, let's kill them" sort of thing. Every Friday they used to gather outside the school. Really heavy. We had to run the gauntlet.'

Right up until he left school, Mick was still a marginal figure on the school band scene, and the 'gang' he spent most of his time with consisted of Robin and his cohorts. John remembers that Robin used to be friendly with one particular skinhead who held racist views, and Kelvin recalls some members of Robin's social circle being involved in unprovoked attacks on local Asians, or 'Paki-bashing' as it was known at the time. Although the effective apartheid practised by the local school system did little to promote racial harmony, this type of behaviour could not be attributed to ignorance or stupidity, and was by no means typical of the Strand's pupils. There was an element of perversity in the indulgence of such moronic aggression, and if members of Mick's crowd did, as he claimed, end up joining the National Front and working in butchers' shops, then it was in spite of the opportunities they had been offered, rather than due to the lack of them.

The intelligent and highly articulate Robin was under no social or economic pressure to become a bad lot; he just chose to live that way, even when mixing with the less trouble-oriented school band circle. 'There'd be a gang of us who'd go to Leicester Square for fun,' says Kelvin. 'He was one of the outrageous ones. He'd hang out outside the girls' toilet. He'd chat girls up, and when their guy came along, go, "Fuck off!": just insult people. And one day, this one particular guy who was a lot older than us ran off and raised a whole gang of people, and they came down with bottles and everything, and we all ran off. Robin was a bit of a rebel. I used to go back to his place up near Crystal Palace, and he used to go into shops and thieve and do all the things you do. He was quite out there.' As 'Stay Free' suggests, Robin was indeed asked to leave the Strand. John Brown was standing next to him when he finally pushed his luck too far. He swung a keychain around his head shortly before baiting one of the school 'wimps', and was reported to the Head, who accused him of threatening the boy with a dangerous weapon. 'He was just looking for an excuse to get rid of Robin, and that was it: he got one,' says John. 'Robin was kicked out that very moment.'

For a couple of years after leaving school, Mick and Robin's friendship became, in the latter's words, 'hands on, hands off', and during this time Robin apparently extended the scope of his operations. 'He was in the *South London Press* for running a protection racket,' Mick told *The Story So Far* fanzine in 1980. 'He was the ringleader, he was the one that did it all. A kleptomaniac if ever I met one.' Sometime around 1974 or 1975, he was arrested for the offence that led to his incarceration as described in 'Stay Free'. Some artistic licence was used in the song, however: he was not sent to Brixton Prison. Although a young offender, he was made up to a senior prisoner and sent to Wormwood Scrubs, before being transferred to Albany on the Isle of Wight. There is some confusion among both his schoolfriends and the people who knew him later as to the exact nature of the crime committed, but, as the song says, he was sentenced to three years' imprisonment, of which he served two.

Not long after his release, in the spring of 1977, the Clash hired Robin as Mick's guitar roadie. While this move was partly motivated by Mick's highly developed sense of loyalty, some of the band's critics, including Julie Burchill and Tony Parsons in their 1978 book, *The Boy Looked At Johnny*, interpreted the Clash's employment of an ex-jailbird (not their first) as a bid for credibility by association. Certainly, the mawkish 'Stay Free' was not the only way in which Mick capitalised on Robin's past: he was not above hinting that he had been involved in some of his friend's lawless enterprises. 'The hooligans who never got caught make the best rock'n'roll,' he boasted to *Sounds'* Garry Bushell in November 1978. As the people who knew him at the time are quick to point out, the idea of Little Mick qualifying as a hooligan is laughable. But it seems that his desire to be taken seriously as a bad boy during the punk era was so great that he was prepared to exaggerate links with and – worse – mythologise a bunch of characters who were about as far from embodying the Clash ideal as it was possible to get.

Robin positively revelled in the attention. For several years after he was first hired by the Clash, he divided his time between acting as the band's all-purpose troublemaker and exploiting his inside contacts to write about punk for *ZigZag* magazine under the all too appropriate pseudonym Robin Banks.

Thus, 'Stay Free' and the story behind its inspiration he offered to the *NME*'s Chris Salewicz have created a misleading impression of Mick's teenage experiences. Rather than being one of the few who 'escaped', the 'dilettante journalist' was one of the very few friends or acquaintances of Mick who risked capture. Mick's own idea of escape was not from privation and poverty, but rather from what he saw as the boredom of everyday life as experienced by the majority of working stiffs. It was an escape into fantasy, which, employing a metaphor drawn from the euphoria engendered by the Mott expeditions, was summed up in the following lines from another 1978 Clash composition, 'The Prisoner': 'You're only free to dodge the cops / And bunk the train to stardom.'

In March 1979, a long way from home and a couple of years past the heyday of punk revisionism, Mick admitted to *Time*'s Jay Cocks that his school song had been 'Servants Of The State To Be'. 'It was the high hope that you would become a Civil Servant. That was the best you could do. But rock'n'roll changed the way I look at society.' For a would-be rock star the Civil Service might have appeared something to be avoided at all costs, but – when one considers some of the other career opportunities available – for most people the possibility of becoming a clerical assistant with prospects was scarcely a life sentence with hard labour.

A line in 'Stay Free', 'We got thrown out and left without much fuss', would seem to suggest that Mick's education was also curtailed prematurely, but he was still attending the Strand in June 1971, when he sat three O levels, Art, History and English Language. Music mania and fooling around with the gang had obviously taken its toll, though, because he failed all three. The members of the school band took their A levels at the same time. Bob Goffman went on to university, but the others chose to continue with their musical endeavours instead. Kelvin and John put long-term career plans on hold, taking whatever jobs would generate enough money to buy the band some reasonable equipment. Kelvin moved around, but John found steady, if dull, employment on the production line at the Wright, Layman and Umney factory (makers of Wrights' Coal Tar Soap) near London Bridge, where he also found a job for Robin. Having no similar immediate goals to aim for, Mick decided to go back to school for a further year and make another attempt at gaining some qualifications.

Jim Hyatt combined the best of both worlds, committing himself to the band, yet managing to find employment with the BBC's publishing department. Aside from the prospects offered by the job in its own right, it came with perks, not least of which was the opportunity to attend recordings of the chart-oriented BBC1 TV show *Top Of The Pops*. Over the next year or two, Jim and his friends got to see many of their idols up close.

There were some changes in the band. John switched to bass, and Kelvin began to concentrate on vocals. By January 1972, the line-up had been augmented by a guitarist named Glen and a saxophonist and guitarist called Pete. Rehearsals continued in Thessaly Road, or at John's parents' house at 3 Penry Street, just off the Old Kent Road. The repertoire had extended to include originals, and, perhaps conveniently, it is Jim Hyatt's early compositions that Kelvin and John choose to remember. 'He wrote a song called "The Teaser",' says John. '"You call her a teaser, teaser, teaser / You can't really please her, please her, please her. . ." Something like that. You're talking about some very young talent here!' 'There was one song that was called "Dairy Maid",' recalls Kelvin. '"Dairy maid, I love you. . ." As you can imagine, a bunch of crap! We used to just record on to a cassette player, and a tape that we put together at that time was actually played to Ian Hunter of Mott the Hoople.'

Having rehearsed for the best part of two years, amassed enough equipment and finally settled on the name Schoolgirl, the band started looking for gigs in March 1972. There was no manager or agent, and venues were selected for approach almost at random. 'It was just what we called hustling, really,' says John. 'It was usually through friends. Someone who lived nearby who knew someone. That's how most of the gigs came about.' Mad Mick and Little Mick volunteered their services as roadies, the latter with a special responsibility for the drums. 'He wanted to be involved,' says John. 'Hang out, be part of the band and all that stuff.'

Schoolgirl were as naïve and inexperienced as a young band can be, and the catalogue of setbacks and failures that dogged their brief career still causes John to lapse into fits of embarrassed giggles over 20 years later. Gigs mostly took place in local pub venues, and the band also entered a couple of talent shows with little success. They managed to persuade Mott the Hoople's Ian Hunter to come down and see them on two separate occasions, but he advised Kelvin to sack the others – apart from John – because they were 'shit'. For possibly the last time in his life, Kelvin neglected to heed this advice. An attempt to induce Guy Stevens to attend another show came to nothing. Between 10 March and 20 October 1972, Schoolgirl played a total of 15 times. They split up on the evening of what was supposed to be their 16th performance, when Glen offered his resignation in the time-honoured fashion of not bothering to turn up. During the next year, Kelvin, John and Jim got together to play another four one-off engagements, some of which also involved fellow Strand old boy Paul Wayman on guitar, but that, effectively, was that.

In January 1972, Mick retook his Art O level, and in June of that year he resat History and English Language and – for the first time – sat English Literature and Sociology. Having completed his courses, he left Strand School. While awaiting his results, he took a holiday job at what he later described to William Shaw as a warehouse where all the lads used to call him Alice because they said he looked like Alice Cooper. The erstwhile Vincent Furnier had begun to make an impact in the UK in the summer of 1972, and finally hit the number one spot in August with a song that was highly apposite for Mick, 'School's Out'.

By that time, glam rock was already well established. David Bowie had captured the hearts, minds and imaginations of teeny-boppers and 'serious' rock fans alike with his concept album *The Rise And Fall Of Ziggy Stardust And The Spiders From Mars*. Bowie and his guitarist and sidekick Mick Ronson had also produced Lou Reed's album *Transformer,* thus helping to revitalise the former Velvet Underground frontman's career. Indeed, Bowie had his fingers in everybody's pie that year: in March, after three years' effort and no commercial reward, Mott the Hoople had decided to call it a day. Learning of this, Bowie had made them a present of arguably the definitive glam anthem, 'All The Young Dudes', and offered to produce their next album. On the strength of this act of generosity, the band had agreed to give it another try, saying goodbye to Island and Guy Stevens, and hello in quick succession to MainMan (Bowie's management company), CBS and success.

One result of this glam-blitz was that Mick Ronson was now vying with Keith Richards for the honour of being Mick's ultimate guitar hero. Another was a distinctly effeminate bent to his clothing and accessories: all tight, flared trousers, fitted jackets, high-heeled boots and flowing Kensington Market scarves. He had pushed the Strand rule on hair length for much of his last year there, and since May had not been required to heed it at all, so his dark, curly locks were now a long way past shoulder-length. Although he bought a few Alice Cooper records – something he has since been reluctant to admit – Mick's hairstyle was more of a tribute to his enduring role model, the recently glammed up, but resolutely hirsute, Ian Hunter.

After several months as a roadie for the hapless Schoolgirl, Mick no longer stood quite so much in awe of their musical skills. Jim's were especially meagre. 'There was not a lot of technical talent there,' says John. 'He just muddled through. He never really pushed himself.' Perhaps because he was aware of Jim's shortcomings, Mick took every opportunity he could to get behind the kit and teach himself the basics. Growing in confidence, he quickly raised his musical sights: the first purchase he made with his wages from the warehouse was a second-hand Hofner guitar. 'I paid £16 for it, and I think I was ripped off,' he told Caroline Coon in 1976. 'But I tell you something: I sold it for £30 to a Sex Pistol!' While it was still in his possession, he practised on it diligently; that is, once Robin Crocker had shown him how to tune it and shape his first chords.

He began contemplating another step in the right direction that August, upon learning that he had passed all his exams. This meant he now had the educational qualifications to attend an art school, for which the usual entrance requirement was five O levels. Although artistically talented, Mick's main motivation was not to learn how to express himself on canvas, but rather to link up with like-minded rock'n'roll fans and form a band. Steeped in rock mythology, he was aware that the likes of Keith Richards, Pete Townshend and John Lennon had all gone to art school, and so presumed such institutions to be the natural place for embryonic rock stars to congregate. 'I thought if I went to art school, I'd meet people jamming in the toilets and things like that,' he told William Shaw.

Unfortunately, at 17, he was still a year short of the minimum age requirement of most colleges. With 12 months in which to work up a portfolio, Mick capitulated to the Strand School's conditioning, and decided to employ his five O levels in the temporary service of the state. Having signed on at night school to begin A levels as a security measure, he joined the Department of Health and Social Security (DHSS) as a clerical assistant in the Benefit Office at 5 Praed Street, Paddington. In such a conventional environment his appearance attracted even more attention than it had at the warehouse. 'They used to take the mickey out of me,' he told *That Was Then, This Is Now*. 'It didn't used to bother me, because I didn't care in those days.'

Other of his experiences there did bother him; or so he claimed during the early years of the Clash, when explaining the inspiration behind part of the lyric for 'Career Opportunities'. In the 1977 *NME* interview conducted by Tony Parsons that was partly responsible for establishing the Clash Myth, Mick – fizzing on amphetamine sulphate and Bernie Rhodes's team talks – went into it all in some detail: 'The Social Security made me open the letters during the letter bomb time [an IRA terrorist campaign that coincided with Mick's stint as most junior employee] because I looked subversive. Most of the letters the Social Security get are from the people who live next door saying their neighbours don't need the money. The whole thing works on spite. One day an Irish guy that they had treated like shit and kept waiting for three hours picked up a wooden bench and put it through the window into Praed Street . . . And they degrade the black youth even more. They have to wait even longer. No-one can tell me there ain't any prejudice.'

Sometime in early to mid 1973, Mick and Stella left Park West, and were rehoused by the council at 111 Wilmcote House, an early Sixties tower block on the Warwick Estate, just off the Harrow Road. Stella had not registered to vote at Park West, which makes the duration of their stay there difficult to pin down, but both she and Mick first appear on the electoral roll for their new home in 1974, meaning that they were in residence prior to October 1973, by which time Mick had attained his majority. Yellow panels intended to provide relief from the expanses of grey window and grey concrete lend the 20-storey monolith that is Wilmcote House the aspect of a particularly half-hearted prefab Mondrian. It may be debatable whether anyone should be made to live in such a soulless, community-destroying environment, but few would dispute that a flat on the 18th floor of a high-rise was hardly the ideal spot for a 73-year-old woman. 'It was really a kind of horrible place to live,' Mick told William Shaw. 'At the time I was living there I didn't think much about it, but I'm shocked when I go back there, because people are still living in it. It's worse than it was. It gets worse every year.'

The one consolation was the view, south-east over Bayswater, Knights-bridge and – in the foreground – the main route west out of central London, the A40(M), more commonly known as the Westway. A few years later, the strings of streetlights and streams of headlights as seen from the 18th-floor balcony would inspire a visiting Joe Strummer to write the lyric for 'London's Burning'; that one song would establish the Westway as one of the original bastions of Clash mythology and, albeit inadvertently, prepare the ground for the unpleasantness of tower block life to become one of the foremost clichés of punk. Even to this day, Wilmcote House is frequently employed by journalists to illustrate the humbleness of Mick's origins, though he was already an adult when he moved there and only stayed there on and off between 1975 and 1980, when Stella too moved out.

Certainly, neither his new job nor his new home appeared to cause Mick any immediate trauma. In fact, it was at this time that he started to come into his own. As he was no longer 'little' and was now earning his own living, people like John and Kelvin found they had to readjust their impressions of him. 'He had the best record collection, all these obscure records,' recalls Kelvin. 'And he always had good gear on. He was always dressed better than anybody else. That's what made us look up and notice him. When we were 19 and he was 17, he was getting into the Speakeasy [the favoured watering hole of London-based rock stars, at 48 Margaret Street, off Oxford Circus]. And I remember, we were all after some groovy, lovely-looking girl, and he got her. We were all like, "How's *that* possible? He's the young guy that hangs out with us!"'

One of the less endearing traits of the new Mick was a tendency to show off to his friends at Stella's expense. 'His nan put up with so much from Mick, honestly,' says John. 'He treated her like a slave at times. He was terrible. He was always bringing millions of people home. I used to feel sorry for the old lady.' 'I was pretty averagely brought up, couldn't be rude to the parents,' says Kelvin. 'And there was Mick's old grandmother, whom he loved dearly, and we used to go in and he'd say, "Where's my fuckin' dinner?" And you'd just go, "*Whaaat?*" Shock and horror! "And make a cup of tea for everyone, as well!" He was pretty soft, really. It was just his way.'

In September 1973, Mick commenced the Art Foundation course at the Hammersmith School of Art and Building at 40 Lime Grove, Shepherd's Bush. His hopes of lavatorial jamming sessions were quickly dashed. 'First day, I rushed to the toilets to see who was there,' he told *That Was Then, This Is Now*. 'And there was two guys having a fag.' Nor did the course itself offer much in the way of consolation. 'You had to be traditional. I spent a whole year just doing life drawing before I could do my own painting.'

After deciding it was time he found something a little less dead-end than the soap factory, John Brown had entered the Civil Service at much the same time as Mick. He got a job with the Property Services Agency at the Department of the Environment (DOE), based at St Christopher House, Southwark Street. 'I was in the section that bought and sold premises for the Post Office,' he says. He and Mick had grown increasingly close in the latter stages of Schoolgirl. Their friendship was cemented shortly after Mick started art school: still barely competent on guitar, he felt he would have a better chance of finding a band to join if he switched to bass, and asked John for some lessons. 'I gave him the rudiments, and he took it from there.' John also lent him a spare Vox Precision bass, until Mick got round to buying his own Ned Callan.

In return, Mick introduced John to the delights of Portobello Market and the Notting Hill scene. 'We used to go down the Portobello Road and hang out every Saturday, Mick and I,' says John. 'We used to go down the Duke of Clarence, and Hennekey's [now the Earl of Lonsdale, on the corner with Westbourne Grove]: that used to be the place to go. We were in each other's pockets all the time. We would see things like *Clockwork Orange* together, we'd go to concerts, we'd go and watch *The Night Porter*. We would go anywhere to see weird science fiction films. When I think about it, we had a great time!' Over the next couple of years, although they liked to get out and about and sample what London had to offer, the duo also spent a considerable amount of time in Mick's room at Wilmcote House, flicking through his by now sizeable collection of American superhero comics. A regular pair of popular culture vultures, they also read avidly and swapped books, and again science fiction was a particular love. 'We were into J. G. Ballard: *Concrete Island* - the Westway novel – *Crash, High-Rise*.' These books all deal in some way with the psychological damage inflicted by harsh urban environments. The actual concrete island of the 1974 novel's title – a roundabout on the Westway – was less than a mile from Wilmcote House. *High-Rise*, published in 1975, struck another chord with Mick, addressing as it does the alienating effect of living in a 40-storey tower block and documenting the breakdown of the social order in one such edifice.

Inevitably, though, music was the two friends' chief interest. In 1973, David Bowie continued to draw attention to his favoured artists, involving himself with the career of Iggy Pop and the Stooges. Represented by MainMan, the band came to London that year to record *Raw Power*, which quickly became a Mick Jones favourite and led to an extensive investigation of the Stooges' back catalogue. Pointed in the right direction by Iggy Pop and early Alice Cooper, he and John also picked up on that other infamous late Sixties Detroit band, the MC5. Although they had split the previous year, their original revolutionary political stance had been as left-field and unprecedented as their raucous free-jazz-tinged rock'n'roll, and their final record – 1971's *High Time* – had been a science fiction concept album.

For over a year, Mick and John had also been listening to the Flamin' Groovies, a San Franciscan band who – initially inspired by the mid-Sixties British Beat Boom – had remained faithful to the spirit of the classic upbeat three-minute pop song throughout the hippy era, recording their two cult garage punk albums, *Flamingo* and *Teenage Head,* in 1971. Mick went even further back, investigating all kinds of mid-Sixties obscurities, including comic agitprop jug band the Fugs (as in: the Fucks) and perhaps the quintessential garage band, the Standells, perpetrators of some of the period's most viciously basic teen anthems. The duo's awareness of such American underground acts was fed by their committed reading of the music press; not just the domestic papers, but also magazines like *Creem* – whose writers included Lester Bangs – which were dispatched from the States by Mick's mother, Renee. 'She sent some *Creem* T-shirts over,' says John. 'She seemed quite cool.'

At the time, left-field rock'n'roll bands were not well represented on television. The only real alternative to BBC1's chart-oriented *Top Of The Pops* was BBC2's late night rock show, *The Old Grey Whistle Test.* This attempted a magazine format, offering interviews, the odd album track accompanied by some antediluvian cartoon footage and a band playing a two- or three-song set live in the studio. Presenter Whispering Bob Harris made a trademark of his laid-back delivery, and as his own tastes leaned towards the West Coast and muso end of the rock spectrum, the *Whistle Test* was hardly compulsive viewing for those who liked their music with hairstyle and attitude. Even when a live act threatened to ignite, the lack of a studio audience to supply the necessary reaction tended to throw a bucket of cold water over proceedings.

Not so on one particular show on 28 November 1973, when the New York Dolls, visiting from the US, managed to secure a performance slot despite conforming to very few of the programme's 'quality music' criteria. Loud, lewd and outrageous in their habitual glam drag, the Dolls looked and sounded like transvestite hookers from hell as they preened and pouted their way through 'Jet Boy', a song from their recently released eponymous début album. Unusually for the programme, they were miming, but they did it with such total commitment it hardly showed or mattered. The Dolls prided themselves on living out the ultimate decadent rock star fantasy. They had been praised in *Melody Maker* as early as September 1972. Anglophile guitarist Johnny Thunders had taken his name from a Kinks album track. Original drummer Billy Murcia (since replaced by Jerry Nolan) had died from drug-related causes on their first visit to London, a fact that had been documented on Bowie's 1973 album, *Aladdin Sane* . . . All in all, they were the perfect band for Mick Jones.

Surprisingly, then, it took several months for the Dolls' influence to sink in. According to John, it wasn't until the band's second album, *Too Much Too Soon*, came out in June 1974 that his or Mick's interest was sufficiently aroused for them to dash down to a speciality record shop near Leicester Square and buy both albums – one each – on American import.

The boys might have had an ear for obscure cult classics, but their tastes were catholic, and encompassed commercially successful artists and some obscure cults who were not destined to become as retrospectively hip as the Dolls and the Stooges. John in particular was a big fan of Free. Bass player Andy Fraser left that band in late 1972 to form the Sharks with guitarist Chris Spedding and vocalist Snips. John and Mick were intrigued enough to investigate their 1973 début album, *First Water*. 'We loved the Sharks,' says John. 'We saw them whenever we could, the second incarnation of the band, after Fraser had left [later in 1973]. They were a big influence on Mick.' He goes on to draw attention to what is indeed a remarkable similarity between the stop-start riffs opening the Sharks' 'Sophistication', included on their late 1973 post-Fraser album, *Jab It In Yore Eye*, and Mick Jones's most famous and commercially successful Clash composition, 'Should I Stay Or Should I Go'.

In 1974, Panther published Ian Hunter's account of Mott the Hoople's late 1972 US tour under the title *Diary Of A Rock'n'Roll Star*. 'It was especially interesting to us, because we knew all the people involved intimately,' says John. There was enough name-dropping, rock'n'roll romanticism and vaguely decadent behaviour with girls and drugs to fire Mick's imagination. He devoured the book avidly, taking it as the blueprint for his own future. 'It was the brochure at the time, the brochure for how I wanted to be,' he admitted laughingly in 1989. 'It ain't how I want to be *now*, but it was then.'

The book's tales of touring America's pawn shops in search of cheap second-hand classic guitars brought back memories. 'Mott would come back and they'd have 20 to 25 guitars, Les Paul Juniors,' says John. 'Made us drool, you know. Us with our Hofners and nameless Japanese things.' In the summer of 1974, Mick decided it was about time he bought himself another guitar, and a name one at that. To make up the money, he took a stall at a science fiction convention at a hotel in Russell Square, and sold £80 worth of his rarer American comic books. Afterwards he took John along with him on a shopping expedition to the speciality instrument shops in the West End's Denmark Street–Charing Cross Road area. Mick chose a second-hand black Fender Telecaster with a maple neck. 'It wasn't cheap,' says John. 'He saw it and he just loved it. He wanted to buy it no matter what it sounded like. I advised him against it. I didn't like the tone on it: it was very thin. It never suited his playing.'

Despite being disappointed by what he believed to be the limited opportunities offered by his foundation year at Hammersmith Art School, Mick applied for and was accepted on the full-time Painting course commencing in September 1974. 'You get a grant, don't you?' To pay for those of his interests not covered by his grant, during the long summer vacation Mick took a job at the Economists' Bookshop, then at 106 Hampstead Road. Kelvin Blacklock, between bands at the time, worked there too. 'It's possible, actually, that Mick got me that job,' he says. 'It was like a warehouse. It had a shop front, but it wasn't open to the public. It was a mail-order book thing, you'd pack up the books and send them off.' Kelvin was as generously *coiffured* as Mick, but neither of them suffered any taunts about their appearances. 'Mick was well in with the guy who ran it, who had *really* long hair, and was probably in his forties. It was all like, Mick's wonderful. "How do you keep your hair dry, Mick, when you're having a bath?"' Kelvin was less popular, and before Mick returned to college was sacked for spending too much time on the phone trying to arrange auditions. Thereafter, he and Mick lost touch for a while.

By the time he commenced the Painting course that September, Mick's glam look had reached a level of excess worthy of the New York Dolls themselves, down to the leather trousers (decidedly rare in pre-punk days) and women's high-heeled sling-back shoes. Future Slits guitarist Viv Albertine was also attending the school. 'I thought he looked great, because he stood out a mile from the other students,' she told William Shaw in 1988. 'Half the college was like a builder's training college, and so when you went to the cafeteria, you used to walk past all these building students. It wasn't easy to walk past them if you were wearing leather trousers. Everyone knew who he was. He was always flamboyant. Always a bit of a star.' 'He got known as a bit of a poseur at that place,' says John. 'Because he used to do a bit of a Keith Richards, and just hang around. "Hanging out" was his main thing!'

The relationship between rock music and art, forged in the Sixties, had grown even stronger in the Seventies, as exemplified by the work of Belgian artist Guy Peellaert. He was responsible for the paintings adorning the covers of David Bowie's *Diamond Dogs* and the Rolling Stones' *It's Only Rock'n'Roll*, both released in 1974. That same year, he published *Rock Dreams*, a collection of fantasy illustrations depicting popular music luminaries as the inhabitants of a sleazy netherworld, willing slaves to drug abuse and sexual perversity. It was an accurate reflection of the current state of play in rock mythology: much of the music produced in the early Seventies betrayed the effects of a post-Sixties comedown, with ideals giving way to cynical self-interest, love and peace to fear, loathing and casual sex, and drug experimentation to oblivion-seeking and addiction. New and established acts alike projected a sense of ennui, or of barely suppressed disgust or violence. Some, not least David Bowie, even touched on the threat of imminent apocalypse. 'Decadence' was one of the key buzzwords of the era. Thus, the generation of music fans who had become teenagers in the late Sixties and early Seventies had been encouraged to believe that Peellaert's Burroughsian vision of a rock'n'roll parallel universe actually existed. It was a further reflection of the *Zeitgeist* that many of those fans found it appealing; some, like Mick, even aspired to dwell there.

His year of line drawing over, Mick was finally able to pursue his own artistic interests, producing paintings which, unsurprisingly, owed a great deal to the tradition of pop iconography, 'all razor blades and Marilyn Monroe and limousines and so on', as he told the *NME*'s Paul Rambali in 1981. 'He did some great work there,' says John. 'Some great photo-collages, but his heart wasn't really in art, I don't think.' Although art could take rock'n'roll as its subject, and hold a mirror up to popular culture, it was still at one remove from the experience itself. Mick didn't want to paint that kind of picture; he wanted to be in it. He had always thought of art school as a means to an end. 'It was all a bit disappointing,' he told William Shaw. 'I didn't manage to meet *anybody* at college to form a group with.'

In January 1975, in the second term of his first year on the Painting course, Hammersmith School of Art and Building became part of Chelsea School of Art, today known as Chelsea College of Art and Design. Current College Secretary Peter Drum consults Mick's files to discover that he 'had a good year's work in 1974–75, and a satisfactory year in 1975–76. The record shows that for 1976–77 he hardly attended during the first two terms.' In fact, Mick signalled his true intent early in 1976, at the beginning of the second term of his second year, when his entire grant cheque went towards the purchase of another new guitar. In *Diary Of A Rock'n'Roll Star* Ian Hunter remarked, 'Friends tell me some of the Jap copies are good, but to us in the band the old originals are the best, and finding an old Les Paul Junior in a junk shop is the equivalent of a stamp collector finding a Penny Black.' Mick's new guitar – the 'heart-attack machine' Joe Strummer later enthused about in the Clash's 1978 song 'All The Young Punks' – was a Fifties-vintage Les Paul Junior.

By the time his third year began, in September 1976, Mick was rehearsing and playing with the Clash. Although he occasionally still went along to 'hang out', his formal attendance at college was limited to turning up on the first day of term to collect his grant cheque, and his artistic output consisted of his part in decorating the band's rehearsal room, equipment and clothing. Towards the end of the year, on one of his infrequent visits to Lime Grove, Mick was accosted by a staff member and accused of not having produced any paintings the previous term. 'I said, "Hey, look at this!" and showed him my shirt,' Mick claimed on *That Was Then, This Is Now*. Quick thinking, maybe, but it failed to have the desired effect. 'It wasn't acceptable. I got chucked out in the end.' On 4 April 1977, the Head of Department advised the Inner London Education Authority that Mick had withdrawn from the course. 'I went back for the last day, when they have the show and you go up and get your diploma, and there was a space instead of my stuff. So I never got to have that.' Nor did he get to have that last term's grant cheque . . .

2... DIARY OF A ROCK'N'ROLL STAR

H e might not have met any prospective bandmates at art school, but it would be wrong to assume that Mick Jones was a non-performing musician prior to the formation of the Clash. Always selective with the information he is prepared to give the media about his life before the band, Mick has proved especially reticent about his early musical endeavours. When punk first broke, rumours began to circulate about a by then defunct band named the London SS. Apparently, it had included Mick in its line-up, along with – at one time or another - nearly every future punk star; and it had been managed by Bernie Rhodes, who was later to perform that task for the Clash. Questioned about it, Mick was invariably noncommittal. In January 1977, although he admitted the pre-Clash rehearsal band had existed, Bernie informed the short-lived music paper *National Rock Star* that the phrase 'London SS' had been nothing more than a slogan on a T-shirt worn by one of that rehearsal group's members.

At the time, going into detail about the London SS would have compromised the Clash Myth. For the duration of the Clash's existence, only odd snippets of information emerged from the band camp, it being left to various of the other people formerly involved with the London SS to supply their versions of events. In September 1977, *ZigZag* printed a Pete Frame Rock Family Tree entitled 'The Influence Of The New Wave Nine'. It included the most precise account of the London SS yet committed to print, tracing the band's origins back to the summer of 1975, and drawing its information from contemporary interviews with Brian James, Rat Scabies and, principally, one of the longest-serving members of the group, Tony James. A slightly expanded version was reprinted in the Christmas 1978 issue of *Sounds* under the title 'Children Of The Revolution 1976–78'.

Once the Clash split, Mick started to open up a little more about his previous band, particularly in the retrospective interviews he gave in 1988–9; but even in the booklet accompanying the 1991 CD compilation *Clash On Broadway* his version of events differed little from Tony's, while Bernie still avoided referring to the group by name and tried to give the impression that it had lasted for a couple of weeks at most. However, it would appear the name London SS was first thought up in March 1975, and was in use from October of that year (at the latest) to January 1976; and the roots of the band can be traced all the way back via Schoolgirl to Strand School and the Thessaly Road blues band.

Mick made the transition from bedroom strummer and part-time roadie to performer as early as May 1974. By that time, he had been playing bass for several months, and was already spending a lot of time with John Brown. Schoolgirl was long defunct, and John had abandoned what he describes as a second 'dodgy' band in October the previous year. Knowing that his older, slightly more experienced friend had no other irons in the fire, Mick made the tentative suggestion that the two of them should start a group of their own. 'I said, "We've got a fundamental problem here,"' says John. '"We've got two bass players!" And he said, "No, you can be bass. I'll switch to rhythm, and take it from there."' Hence the Telecaster purchase.

John recalls that the plan to form the band was hatched while he and Mick were attending a sci-fi film season at the National Film Theatre on the South Bank. The band name came along at the same time. 'He wanted to call it the Coca Cola Douche. He'd read in a weird and wacky publication that women used to do that,' laughs John. (In fact, 'Coca Cola Douche' is the title of a Fugs song.) 'I said, "I don't think we're going to get much record company interest with *that* one!" Then the Juvenile Delinquents came up. I said, "That's too much of a mouthful." So we ended up with the Delinquents.' The history of the London SS might have remained shadowy, but mention of the forerunning Delinquents has been almost non-existent: the band has only been referred to twice by name in the mainstream music press, and then only in the briefest of brief asides in the 1978 version of Pete Frame's punk Family Tree and a 1979 Clash interview by Pete Silverton of *Sounds*.

Luckily, John's diary covers the period in question, and he has also kept a Delinquents promotional leaflet which provides a rough outline of the band's history. First recruit, in late May 1974, was lead guitarist Paul Wayman, who had been in Mick's year at Strand School and also briefly involved with both the school blues band and Schoolgirl. Early the following month, wanting to find a drummer in a hurry, the trio placed a classified advertisement in *Melody Maker*. The paper had been the first non-underground music publication to drop the trite 'fave colour' approach of Sixties journalism and adapt its style to the more serious-minded progressive rock of the early Seventies. For that reason, despite the fact its layout was a nightmare and its tone pompous, earnest and dull – hence the punk era nickname *Monotony Maker* – its back pages had quickly established themselves as the traditional noticeboard for the UK's amateur and professional rock musicians.

The successful applicant was Mike Dowling, who lived in Dalston, north-east London, with his wife, the daughter of a Greek garment manufacturer. 'She was difficult, and she made things difficult for him,' says John. 'And he wasn't really totally the right guy.' There were compensations, however. 'His father-in-law had this terrace house near Dalston Lane somewhere that was basically a sweat shop full of machinery and knock-out clothing. Big bales of cloth on three floors, cutting tables and stuff like that. We used to rehearse there in the evening, two or three times a week; set our stuff up in the basement, and just play.' Additional weekend rehearsals were held at John's parents' house. 'Saturday morning, my dad would be upstairs watching the racing, and the gas fire would be bouncing along the wall with all the noise coming up from downstairs. They were very understanding, my mum and dad.'

The Delinquents rehearsed intensively, but allowed themselves remarkably little time to gel before they played their first gig on 19 June, in the Students' Union bar at Queen Elizabeth College, Campden Hill Road, Kensington. 'That was Mick's baptism of fire, really,' says John. 'It was the first gig of a new band, so everyone was pretty nervous, I'm sure. We didn't have a lot of our own material. That was the only time I know for sure that we played "Ohio" by Neil Young.' (The song is a response to the 1970 demonstration at Kent State University, where the National Guard fired into the crowd, killing four students.) Other than that, John can remember little about the evening, but it is telling that the band did not play another gig proper until the end of November. Rather than repeat Schoolgirl's experience of lurching from disappointment to disaster in the hope of the occasional small victory, they decided instead to adopt as businesslike an approach as possible.

The first step was to develop a band sound and work up a few original songs. 'The music played is in a Mott–Sharks vein, loud and punky,' claimed the Delinquents' promotional leaflet, first sent out in late September 1974. It estimated that, by then, only half the band's repertoire was made up of cover versions. John recalls these were relatively – and deliberately – obscure, and included 'World Park Junkies' and one other from the Sharks' début album, 'Second Cousin' by the Flamin' Groovies and a couple of songs from the MC5's *High Time*. Original material was composed by all three of the band's frontmen. 'Mick was really the songwriter in the band,' says John. 'I contributed a few ideas, as did Paul Wayman, but beyond that it was a showcase for Mick's writing.' That said, basic song ideas were further developed by the band as a whole. 'I don't think we ever actually sat down and said, "This is my song, that's your song."' All three frontmen shared the vocals, but again, Mick tended to dominate overall.

Still a fairly limited guitarist, Mick's ambition had nevertheless led him to begin experimenting with songwriting as soon as he could string a few rudimentary chords together. John cannot remember any titles, but says, 'He wrote some good stuff, even then.' In order to work on his compositions, Mick invested in a relatively sophisticated tape recorder. 'I think it was an Akai 4000 DS,' says John, 'which was the earliest reel-to-reel machine in this country that would do sound on sound. You could do overdubs, multi-tracking: you'd just bounce between tracks until the hiss got so loud you couldn't hear what you were doing.' Mick also used the machine to tape Delinquents rehearsals at the Dalston sweat shop. 'Mick must still have those recordings, if he's bothered to keep them,' says John. 'There'd be a lot of his early stuff on there, but he's quite close to his chest about stuff from the Delinquents days.'

According to the promotional leaflet, the next step to success was to obtain 'a good PA system courtesy of a friendly bank manager'. 'What happened was, because I was a civil servant, I got a loan quite easily,' says John. 'I got guarantees by quantity surveyors! My bank manager sort of interviewed me, gave us the dosh, and we went to a place in Goldhawk Road and kitted ourselves out with HH amplifiers, combos. They had quite a good sound, and they all lit up nicely on stage, so we looked good.' On 19 September, John registered 'the Delinquents' as a business name. 'We thought it was a good name, and we wanted a bit of protection, really. It cost a quid.'

Similar attention to detail was evident in the promotional package the band put together with the intention of approaching venue bookers and management companies. The leaflet outlined the Delinquents' history to date and listed the personnel, revealing that Mick was calling himself 'Michael J. Jones', though everyone – with the exception of Stella – had always known him as Mick. He was to experiment with several pseudonyms over the next couple of years, partly to avoid confusion with another guitarist named Mick Jones who had joined Spooky Tooth in 1973. Also, stage names were very much in vogue in the prevailing glam rock climate. 'At one point, I called myself Lance Rock, after the unfortunate guy in [the Russ Meyer cult film] *Beyond The Valley Of The Dolls*,' remembers John. 'Real kitsch stuff.'

September 1974 also saw the Delinquents arrange a photo-session to provide illustrations for the literature. They prepared themselves by taking some amateur snaps outside 3 Penry Street, posing with the old Austin Cambridge Estate in which Mike Dowling transported his drum kit to and from rehearsals. The promotional photos proper were taken not far away, at Butler's Wharf by the River Thames. Although this former warehouse district has since undergone gentrification, at the time it was largely derelict – 'a bombsite, basically' – and as such was perfectly suited to the Dead-End Kids image the band wanted to project. Although John still has in his possession two of the photographs the session produced, he gave a third – the best of them – to a former girlfriend. 'Someone had written "SPUNK" on this wall, and one of us stood in front of the "S" – me, in fact – so that it spelled the word "PUNK". Mick's got really long hair, and evening gloves on.'

There is still a general misconception regarding the history of the usage of the term 'punk' to denote a style of music. Since 1976, it has been closely associated with the movement of aggressive back-to-basics UK rock bands that was kick-started by the Sex Pistols. There is some recognition that the term had enjoyed a previous life. In the mid-Sixties, teenage American bands, inspired by the invasion of British bands like the Animals and the Rolling Stones, attempted with more enthusiasm than skill to emulate the music of their heroes. After getting together in the nation's suburban garages to bellow and whine about petty teen concerns over crude variations of the three-chord trick, the lucky ones went on to make a couple of records and enjoy 15 minutes of fame with a local hit before fading back into obscurity. Two derisory catch-alls were used to describe these bands: one, 'garage', is self-explanatory; the other, 'punk', was originally a piece of American prison slang for the passive partner in homosexual cell-pairing, from which it developed into a more widespread and general term of abuse meaning no good or worthless. Applied to rock bands, it was a sneer at musical standards and a comment on both the bratty protagonist of the typical song lyric and the posturing of the band members themselves. Such bands became less prevalent when the rock'n'roll world went psychedelic in 1966, and hopeful young musicians started to betray the influence of hallucinogens and hippy rhetoric.

It is incorrect to assume, as many do, that the term 'punk' disappeared in 1967, only to resurface nearly a decade later when the Sex Pistols reminded Caroline Coon of those long-ago American garage bands. In fact, some of the truly influential punk bands – the Stooges, the MC5, the Flamin' Groovies – did not make their impact until the Sixties were almost over. The spirit of the pre-Bowie Mott the Hoople (1969–72), was decidedly punk. In 1972, Elektra kept the flame burning with the release of *Nuggets*, Lenny Kaye's double album compilation of one-hit wonder classics from the original garage era. In 1973, David Bowie rehabilitated Iggy Pop, and the New York Dolls made their first record. In 1974, Lenny Kaye got together with Patti Smith to marry punk rock with poetry, the results of which would be brilliantly captured by the following year's album *Horses*. Thanks largely to Mick Jones's reading habits and extensive record collection, the Delinquents were a little hipper to this underground trend than most and, as their promotional leaflet and photos demonstrated, as far as they were concerned, 'punk' was in current usage in September 1974.

The most impressive part of the Delinquents' promotional package was its aural element. In the *Melody Maker* classifieds John found an advertisement for Budget studios, 'cheaper and better than the average studio. Professional recording from £3.50 per hour.' A session to record two original songs was booked for mid-September. 'It was like a mansion block fronting on to High Holborn, by the tube station,' says John. 'The crappy bit up at the top where the attic is, that's where we were. The thing that was quite unique about it was, it was a rare 3-track, from Philips's studio. They were so proud of it, this hi-tech machine! They said, "Dusty Springfield used this to record 'I Only Want To Be With You'!"'

The quality of the demo recording might have left a lot to be desired – 'they dampened the drums so much, they sounded like marshmallows!' – but nobody could fault its presentation: the band had it cut as a single, using the pressing service attached to Pye studios on Bryanston Street, off Edgware Road. 'You used to be able to bring in a tape, and they'd press it for you on acetate,' says John, 'and it cost something like £16 for five copies. And £16 in 1974 was a fair amount of money for aspiring musicians.' Mick held on to the original tape, and most of the acetates were sent out with the other promotional material (along with the obligatory advice to 'play loud'), but John still has one copy. Atypically, neither song was originated by Mick: John came up with the basic idea for the A-side, 'You Know It Ain't Easy', and Mick finished it off; the B-side, 'Hurry', was primarily Paul Wayman's song.

Both illustrate the band's marked Sharks influence, being based on sloppy stop-start guitar riffs in the style of Keith Richards, courtesy of Mick, overlaid with fluid but precise melodic lead guitar lines, courtesy of Paul. The B-side's lyric is unremarkable – boy advising girl she'd better hurry up and get somewhere, then taking the sting out of the warning by telling her he'll wait anyway – and Paul and Mick sing it dead straight, in unison. The A-side is a little more unusual. Its verses, sung clear and high by John, string together aspirational rock'n'roll clichés, charting the protagonist's progress from attending rock'n'roll shows to playing in the band. The chorus, sung by Mick, offers the observation 'You know it ain't easy, but it ain't hard / It could be so easy if you'd drive my car.' 'That's Mick's input,' says John. 'I did the rest of the lyric, he did the hook.' Beatles enthusiasts will recognise a subversion of the chorus from 'The Ballad Of John And Yoko', with a reference to 'Drive My Car' squeezed in for good measure. This, and Mick's sardonic, exaggeratedly yob Cockney delivery, work against the drift of the verses, and transform the song into a cynical observation on the rock star lifestyle. Despite Mick's dirty rhythm guitar work, Paul's aggressive lead guitar wig-out coda to 'Hurry' and Mike's inadvertently dampened drums, this is as 'punky' as either song gets. That said, the Clash would make regular use of similar marked contrast in vocal interplay, with Mick taking the high role and Joe Strummer the low.

Finally ready to go out into the world, the Delinquents paid for two classified ads in the 26 October 1974 issue of *Melody Maker*, which appeared in the shops at least two days earlier. (Although traditionally allotted the date of the coming Saturday, back in the mid-Seventies, the UK's weekly music press officially hit the newsagents' on a Thursday, and could usually be found on the capital's city centre news-stands on Wednesday.) The first ad, carried in the Groups section, read: 'THE DELINQUENTS, Raunch'n'roll, want gigs.' This was followed by a daytime number for John at the DOE and evening numbers for Paul at home and for Mick at Wilmcote House. The same numbers appeared in the second ad, in the Management Wanted section, which was a model of succinctness: 'THE DELINQUENTS want management/agency.'

The band's efforts brought some response. An agency invited them to audition in a rehearsal studio at 101 St John's Hill, Clapham. The Delinquents seemed to make a good impression. 'They were going to get us gigs in Sweden and stuff like that,' says John. 'We went to meet one of them. He had an apartment in the Barbican. It was all, "Oh, it's going to be great, wonderful!" And of course, it never came to anything.' Next to respond was a publishing company, still in existence, but nameless here for reasons that will become all too obvious: 'It was in this really plush office above Oxford Street. We went up there, and the guy listened to the record. The thing I remember is, he was talking to us about what we were after, and all this sort of stuff, and he walked over to the fire exit, pushed the doors open, got his todger out and started pissing out over the fire escape! "What the fuck's going on?", you know. One of us said, "What if you hit a ducting fan?" Because he'd short it, and it would go straight up his stream of urine and there'd be sparks coming out of his cock. I don't think he had an answer for that. He was a weirdo: one of those guys who's a bit of a paedophile on the quiet. There's a lot of those in the biz.' Needless to say, after having succeeded in exposing himself to the still mostly teenage band, he quickly lost interest.

Ironically, for all their determination to take a more professional route, the Delinquents' second live performance - and indeed, all subsequent gigs – came as a result of Schoolgirl-style hustling. John got things off to a start when he approached the landlord of his local pub rock venue, the Thomas à Beckett, 320 Old Kent Road, and was offered a gig on 25 November. Making the most of the opportunity, the Delinquents advertised their appearance on the Club Calendar page of *Melody Maker*, and ensured the gig was no secret to the members of their respective social circles. 'All our friends came, colleagues from work, my mum and dad, my sisters,' says John. 'I think Mick's dad might have popped in. Everybody we knew.' The partisan crowd reacted favourably, ensuring that the band was offered a return date on 9 December.

On 26 November, the Delinquents played the Woking Community Centre. 'I had a friend who lived in Woking,' is how John explains the band's trip to the Surrey home town of the Jam. (Paul Weller's band had already made their first ventures on to the local social club scene.) They hired a van, which Mike Dowling drove. The 20-mile journey discouraged any travelling support. 'It was playing in front of 14-year-old girls who didn't have a clue what we were about. They were much more interested in having the Archies on the disco.' (The Archies' twee bubblegum single, 'Sugar Sugar', had been a big hit in 1969.)

Three days later, the Delinquents played the Target pub in Reading, 30 miles west of London. Once again, the band were on their own; or almost. 'It was a real squaddies' pub: there was a barracks nearby, or something. It was a bad booking for us. We were all dressed up like the Dolls, knocking out all this fast stuff, and they weren't really into that. There was this one guy down the front, and we started playing "Second Cousin" by the Flamin' Groovies, and he was going, "Whoah! 'Second Cousin'! I've got it!" He was jumping up and down to it, and what he didn't realise was that all the crowd behind him had backed off and, like, *gone*. So he was at the front, bopping, and he turned around and realised he was in this huge empty area . . . He had a total nervous breakdown, then disappeared.'

Following the return engagement at the Thomas à Beckett, the

Delinquents played their sixth gig on 12 December at what was, for Mick, who arranged it, an even more familiar venue: Hammersmith College of Art. Although most of the audience knew him, his reputation as something of a poseur did not make for a particularly warm reception, and John remembers him being particularly self-conscious. 'It was a bit weird for Mick, playing that gig. You know the famous biblical quote about a prophet being without honour in his own country? He felt that very much, I think. We were all frontmen, but he was the mouthpiece, basically, and he was a bit unsettled about the whole thing.'

Thereafter, the band started to make inroads on the traditional pub rock circuit, but not everyone involved, however indirectly, considered this a good enough return for all the time, rehearsing, planning and expense that had gone into launching the Delinquents. Mike Dowling's wife had always believed he should be seeing more of her than of his bandmates. This conflict of loyalties led to his departure in mid-January after the band had played only three more gigs and were just beginning to get into their stride.

Hardly pausing for breath, Mick and John placed a classified ad in the Musicians Wanted section of the 25 January 1975 issue of *Melody Maker*. In addition to making pointed reference to the perceived shortcomings of their former drummer, it left no doubt as to their determination to continue in much the same musical vein: 'DRUMMER REQUIRED for ambitious together rock band, influenced by Rolling Stones, Free, Sharks etc. Must have view to turning professional in near future and have no commitments which might impede the band's development. No jokers.' It was accompanied by John's work number for days and Mick's home number for evenings. Shortly after it was placed, Paul Wayman found his own commitment wanting. Deciding he'd given rock'n'roll stardom a fair enough shot, he not only left the band, but also quit music altogether in order to devote himself to a career with the Post Office.

Any brief feelings of confusion or doubt Mick and John might have experienced were brushed aside in a matter of days, when they met Geir Waade. Geir and his keyboard-playing friend Casino Steel both hailed from Oslo, where they had first played together in 1966 in a band called Jane. They moved to London in 1971 to improve their chances of becoming rock stars. Success was not immediate. After a while, Geir went off to Amsterdam, then returned to discover that Casino had found himself a band for which the drum stool was already taken: the Queen. Andrew Matheson, the band's singer, frontman and, in his own words, 'mouthpiece and lead sex symbol' came over from Canada in 1971 with the same ambition as Casino and Geir, only more so. Via the inevitable *Melody Maker* ads, he recruited drummer Lou Sparks and Casino for what he envisaged as the ultimate in camp, sluttish trash glam bands. Early in 1973, following line-up changes and the emergence of Freddie Mercury's Queen, Andrew changed the band's name to the Hollywood Brats.

Originally from Dublin, committed Keith Richards fan Eunan Brady moved to London in 1969, also in search of the rock'n'roll dream. After a brief spell with Love Affair (of 'Everlasting Love' fame), he filled in his time with pub bands while waiting for his big break to come along. When it did – via Andrew's late 1972 *Melody Maker* advertisement for a guitarist 'drunk on scotch and Keith Richards' – Andrew decided that Eunan was far too un-rock'n'roll a name and decreed that the guitarist should henceforth be known simply as Brady. Finding a suitable bass player proved to be the greatest problem. Andrew finally settled for Brady's friend Derek, who was promptly rechristened Wayne Manor, 'after Batman's house'.

'We loved make-up, noise, aggression, outrageous clothes, and female tourists,' writes Andrew, now once again resident in his native Canada. 'We used to stop traffic on Oxford Street in the middle of the afternoon because we looked like we were from some planet you didn't want to visit.' 'Very streetwise and cool,' adds Brady. It is tempting to describe the Hollywood Brats as London's answer to the New York Dolls, but in spite of their similar dress, attitude and name, both Andrew and Brady insist no plagiarism was involved. The competition did not go unnoticed, however. 'We were deathly afraid of the Dolls because they seemed exactly like us and were apparently further up the ladder than we were,' Andrew reports. 'They made us extremely nervous right up until someone brought us their [début] record. We put it on and nearly died laughing in relief. We could have wiped the floor with them. In the end, and knowing that we were better than them, we ended up liking them. What the hell: there were only two of us in the world!'

The London-based group found the going even tougher than their New York counterparts, though perhaps not quite as tough as Andrew's highly embellished account would have it: 'We were hated everywhere we played, except by a tiny but ever-increasing minority in the audience. When I say hated, I don't mean mere ambivalence: there was always violence at our gigs. I once had a tooth knocked out by some deranged perspiring disco Don Juan. He screamed that I'd licked his girlfriend's hand, and smashed me in my lipsticked mouth. Brady booted him in the V of his Sergio Valentes, and all hell broke loose.' Record companies were simply uninterested. 'They kept saying that rock'n'roll music was dead, and that kind of raunchy music would never come back. They kept on talking about the Philadelphia Sound.'

The band's problems were exacerbated by its members' penchant for Dolls-style hard living, and Andrew's oversized ego, which tended to alienate potential allies. Despite this and despite signing with a legendarily suspect management company, the Brats finally landed a deal. Between December 1973 and January 1974, they recorded an album's worth of material for Arista. Within a month or two, however, the contract was cancelled, and after a few more months of 'backbiting and nasty words', the band disintegrated. Casino and Andrew retrieved the master tapes from the record company and Casino took them over to Norway. As a result, the eponymously titled record was released posthumously, at first only in the four Scandinavian countries.

It finally won a UK release on Cherry Red in 1980, whereupon *Record Mirror*'s Peter Coyne gave it an ecstatic five-star review. At least partly in response to enquiries made for this book, Cherry Red released the first CD version of the album in January 1994 with new sleevenotes by Andrew and Brady.

While his friend Casino was engaged with the Brats, Geir Waade had worked for Virgin records and, in the late spring of 1974, auditioned several times for eccentric glam rock outfit Sparks before being turned down. 'After that, I wanted a decadent band to play in,' he says. 'But that didn't exist in London at that time. Then I answered an ad in the *Melody Maker*. I remember talking to Mick Jones on the phone, and going up to see him in his grandmother's flat.' Conveniently, Geir was living just round the corner at the time, at 107 Elgin Avenue. 'I met Mick, and we sort of liked each other, I reckon. I didn't think he was rock'n'roll enough, myself, because he wore white silk gloves. Tiny Tim! He looked like a right twit, I'll tell you.' With his long blond tresses and classic Nordic good looks, Geir made a far better initial impression on Mick and John. He was also full of enthusiasm, and no mean talent at selling himself. 'He had a bit of the gift of the gab, did old Geir,' laughs John.

Egos in the rock'n'roll world being what they are, allowances usually have to be made for jealousy and spite whenever musicians appraise each other's talents. John, Brady, Kelvin Blacklock and Andrew Matheson all agree, however, that Geir was and is a personable enough human being, which gives some credibility to their individually volunteered claims that he was a terrible drummer. 'Apparently, he auditioned for Mick and John with the old drum kit that he bought from Lou of the Hollywood Brats,' says Brady. 'It was in such a bad state that – so John told me – the first time they played together, it collapsed. The bass drum went that way, and the snare drum went that way, and Mick and John just fell about in giggles. "Who *is* this guy?"' John confirms the story. 'But it always happened! He'd blame the snare drum every time. He was an excuse on legs, really, Geir. He had a great image, and we were swayed by good looks as much as anything. "We can *make* him a good drummer! We can work on him." But it never really happened. He had a couple of shining moments.'

It was as a motivator that Geir excelled. Not content to take a back seat (other than literally) with the band he had just joined, he was quick to suggest a candidate for the remaining gap in the line-up. 'He came in like a bullet,' says John. '"Oh, I got this guy, he's great. He used to be in the Hollywood Brats, you know. You must have heard of them?" "No!"' Nevertheless when Geir talked up Brady's talent and image, he aroused Mick's and John's interest. At the time, Brady was trying to extricate himself from the debris of the Brats, so a collaboration was at least theoretically possible. But things did not get off to a good start. 'Geir can't say the word "Eunan",' explains John. 'It sounds like "Junan". And we bumped into this guy in Portobello Road, I think it was two days later. Brady had been described to us as "looking more like Keith Richards than Keith Richards" and this guy did, so we said, "Excuse me, is your name Junan or Julian?" And he said, "No!" and walked off. Then, the next day, Geir brought him round!'

Geir had done a similar PR job with Brady, emphasising Mick's and John's fondness for the Stones, Alice Cooper, Mott the Hoople and the Dolls. Brady's diary entry for 9 February 1975 was: 'Had a blow, after much hassle, with Geir's guys. I might join.' Part of his initial lack of eagerness can be attributed to what he perceived as the others' musical shortcomings. He was already familiar with Geir's playing. 'The guy had no sense of rhythm! At the end of the day, he just couldn't hack it, you know. Mick was OK. He was a good rhythm player, but I think that's as far as it went. And John was steady on the bass: he wasn't exceptional.' He was similarly concerned by their lack of experience, especially Mick, whom he remembers as being 'very naïve'. Like Geir, he also thought Mick's look bordered on the ludicrous. 'He had long, black curly hair down to his arse! Like one of those Pre-Raphaelite paintings. And he used to wear black leather gloves.' All the same, Brady went along for a few more rehearsals and, having felt somewhat directionless since the Brats' collapse, he soon got caught up in the others' enthusiasm.

'Brady could plumb the depths of sheer crap, or hit the pinnacles of sheer genius,' says John. 'He was that sort of guitarist.' Such erratic brilliance being very much in vogue at the time, Mick and John were much taken with Brady's playing. Brady suspects that Mick in particular was even a little in awe of him. 'It's very hard to say. I mean, I don't want to sound pompous and arrogant, but I was very self-assured, and I had this lovely Gibson Firebird. I think it was the first time Mick had met some guy where, whenever he said, "Can you play this?" I could.'

Inevitably, the addition of the experienced Brady and the forceful Geir altered the balance of power in the group and influenced its direction. Previously, Mick and John had considered themselves strong enough singers to share the lead vocals, but both newcomers favoured the idea of recruiting a frontman in the tradition of the Stones' Mick Jagger, the Dolls' David JoHansen and the Brats' Andrew Matheson: someone who could both sing and provide the band with a focal point on-stage. On 22 February, a display ad was placed in the *Melody Maker* classifieds: 'DECADENT VOCALIST REQUIRED for newly formed contemporary rock'n'roll Band. Front man/personality essential.' Again, it was accompanied by Mick's home number and, to his subsequent regret, John's work number. 'Someone rang up the Sub-Permanent Under-Secretary for the State, or something, by mistake. He tried to get through on my number, and ended up somewhere else saying, "Yeah, I'm really decadent!" to this stuffed shirt Civil Service chap. And they traced where it was supposed to be going. I got hauled on the carpet for that one!'

The ad failed to produce a suitable singer, but it attracted the attention of someone who was possibly even more welcome, and who did manage to get through to John on the right extension. 'A guy called Tony Gordon answered,' says Geir. 'He was a sort of manager for Wedge records. He said he was interested in us.' Phoning up an unknown and incomplete band might seem an unlikely move for a management company, but Wedge records were keen to build up a roster of clients. (Two weeks later, they even placed their own *Melody Maker* ad for 'Together bands with image and original material'.) Tony Gordon – whom Brady describes as a 'dead ringer for Neil Sedaka' – listened to the band rehearse, made appreciative noises and said he would return once the line-up was complete.

Not having access to a regular practice room, the band split their rehearsal time roughly equally between Geir's flat in Elgin Avenue, Brady's squat at 28 Boundary Road in St John's Wood and 111 Wilmcote House. Brady chuckles when he recalls trying to work on ideas in Mick's bedroom while being told to keep the noise down by Stella. 'We spent more time looking for a lead singer than we did actually rehearsing,' he says. 'We did a lot of ligging and checking people out.'

After leaving the Economists' Bookshop, Kelvin Blacklock had joined a band called Overtown – 'named after a racehorse' – and had later brought in former Schoolgirl drummer Jim Hyatt. Although not a particularly stable group, they had managed to secure a residency at the Marquee club on Wardour Street, on alternate Wednesdays running from 15 January to 26 February. John and Mick took Geir and Brady along to see their old schoolmates play, and both of them were strongly impressed by the singer. 'We thought Kelvin looked brilliant,' says Brady. 'He was a tall, skinny guy with blond hair, and he leaped around.' 'I said I liked the guy,' says Geir. '"This is definitely a singer we should have."' Knowing Kelvin of old, neither John nor Mick was keen on the idea of poaching him, and Mick was especially vocal in his objections. 'He apparently said, "Kelvin's a breadhead"' is Kelvin's own explanation. Brady and Geir remember it slightly differently. 'Mick warned us that Kelvin was very unscrupulous, and only thought of number one,' says Brady. 'Mick said, "If you have him in the band, you'll get the sack,"' says Geir. '"He'll split the band up."' In Mick and Kelvin's relationship, the latter had always been the dominant party, and another likely reason for Mick's reluctance to consider him was fear of a further diminishing of his own status.

The search for a singer continued to prove unsuccessful, but the ligging helped strengthen the bonds between the band members. Both John's and Brady's diaries recorded the extent to which social activities were band-oriented: going to gigs together at the Windsor Castle on Harrow Road, the Marquee on Wardour Street and the Greyhound in Fulham, attending parties, hanging around at each other's homes and spending Saturday afternoons drinking down the Portobello Road. Mick borrowed Brady's clothes, and Brady even gave him a pair of tight flares he had worn with the Brats. There was a certain amount of sexual braggadocio and one-upmanship, and even longer-lasting relationships had an incestuous edge: earlier in the year, Mick had been seeing a girl called Jane Crockford; in

March, she started going out with John.

Andrew Matheson begs to differ, but Geir, Brady and John all insist that it was at this time that the London SS was first suggested as a band name, the Delinquents having been dropped almost immediately following Geir's arrival. Brady confirms his claim that it was Geir who came up with the replacement, but John insists it was the result of a general brainstorming session with a dictionary and thesaurus. Obviously, the London prefix was a nod in the direction of the New York Dolls and the Hollywood Brats, but there is some disagreement about the SS part. 'I didn't mean like a Nazi thing,' says Geir. 'It was because we all went on the dole, you see: Social Security.' John's and Brady's accounts suggest that Geir is guilty of indulging in face-saving revisionism. The pun may well have subsequently occurred to him and other original and later members of the band, but the Nazi reference was both deliberate and deliberately tasteless. It might seem incredibly irresponsible in today's post Anti-Nazi League world (as Geir is obviously well aware), but taken in context, it was merely another illustration of the mood of the times.

Luchino Visconti's 1969 film *The Damned* focuses on decadent behaviour in its portrayal of the rise of Nazism in the Thirties. Its dark mood quickly connected with the similar one developing in the rock'n'roll world: there is an infamous late Sixties photograph of the Rolling Stones' Brian Jones in an SS uniform, posing with one jackboot on the neck of a doll. The 1972 hit film *Cabaret* did much to strengthen the association between decadence, fascism and the theatrical rock'n'roll of the early Seventies. When, in 1973, *The Damned*'s stars Dirk Bogarde and Charlotte Rampling were reunited for Liliana Cavani's *The Night Porter*, they not only established the decadent Nazi movie as a genre, but also played up the S&M connotations of the uniforms and the dominant and submissive roles of oppressor and oppressed. All kinds of B movies jumped on the bandwagon, lending the Nazi theme schlock value and a certain humorous appeal: several of Russ Meyer's cult trash films feature a character dressed as Martin Boorman.

Guy Peellaert was indebted to the Nazi–S&M craze (and the earlier Brian Jones photograph) for his 1974 *Rock Dreams* painting of the Stones, which depicts most of the band – minus, for some reason, Bill Wyman – in SS uniforms and Mick Jagger in jackboots, stockings and suspenders, lounging around in a sumptuous suite in the company of several naked pre-pubescent girls. Peellaert was playing with the general public's media-fed image of the Stones as satanic outlaws, intent on breaking every possible social and sexual taboo. The Nazi trappings were not supposed to indicate the band's own political sympathies: the shock factor was everything. The same urge to provoke explains the swastika armband worn by Johnny Thunders in a 1974 Bob Gruen photograph of the New York Dolls. A year later, in thrall to such rock myth-making, the London SS were aspiring to appear just as decadent and amoral as their rock'n'roll heroes.

'I'll never forget,' says Brady, 'on his bedroom wall, Mick had this great poster of some terrible little cheap B movie about concentration camps. "Hitler did *this*!" We both just laughed about it.' 'On Portobello Road, across the road from Hennekey's, there used to be a guy selling Nazi memorabilia,' says John. 'We used to go and buy bits there. I'm not too proud about that, but it was the decadent thing, rather than the Nazi skinhead thing. More shock value than anything else. London SS was a name to slap you in the face. That was it, really. When it was suggested, we said, "Yeah, that's a great name!" and I started going away working out logos and stuff, as you do.' The decadent pose is a justification of sorts, but it should be remembered that Mick was half Jewish, and living with a Jewish grandparent. His flirtation with the visual symbols of Hitler's Germany might have been superficial and tongue-in-cheek, but his willingness to adopt them give some indication of just how naïve and apolitical he was at this time.

Approximately a year later, the Clash would adopt the stern political stance that permeated all their early interviews and helped set the agenda for what was and was not acceptable in punk. One issue would be the wearing of the swastika, which Malcolm McLaren promoted – and the likes of Sid Vicious and Siouxsie of the Banshees took up – for its annoyance value. One of the people annoyed was Bernie Rhodes, also Jewish, who felt that in the prevailing social climate, with the National Front steadily increasing its membership, it was potentially dangerous to flirt with fascist symbols. As a result, he argued with Malcolm and refused to allow Sid and Siouxsie to use the Clash's equipment at the 100 Club Punk Festival. In the circumstances, one can understand his reluctance to have revealed the extent of his or any of his charges' involvement with a band called the London SS.

Back in March 1975, making the final decision about a name was not of vital importance. The London SS was not officially adopted at this time, and appears to be just one of several possibilities under consideration. 'I remember Mick suggesting something like the Suicides,' says Brady. 'I'm sure we had loads of New York Dolls-type names, but we couldn't settle on one.' Brady also recalls Mick toying with adopting the pseudonym Mick Stabs. Everything was left very much up in the air while the band concentrated on more urgent matters. The Vocalists Wanted section of the *Melody Maker*'s 22 March issue carried another display ad, this time accompanied by just Mick's telephone number: 'DECADENT MALE VOCALIST. Must be exciting, pretty and passionately committed to the rock'n'roll lifestyle.'

Although much of the next week was given over to auditioning the various applicants, none of them had both the looks and the talent to stand out. Then, on 1 April, Tony Gordon sent John a letter: 'I have not heard from you for a few weeks and I wondered if you had yet acquired a singer? Perhaps you will let me know how things are going at your earliest opportunity?' Worried about losing Gordon's interest, the band felt compelled to take drastic measures: Mick's objections were overruled, and Kelvin was approached.

John's diary entry for 3 April noted: 'Kelvin is leaving Overtown and wants to join us. Dodgy!' The following day, Kelvin turned up two and a half hours late for a meeting at Wilmcote House, whereupon he was subjected to a probing aptitude test. A week later, on Friday, the 11th, he was given a proper audition, as a result of which he was offered the job. 'Could be so good with all of us in a band,' began John's diary entry for that day. If he sounded less than entirely convinced, it was because – inevitably, with Kelvin – there were complications, as the diary also recorded: 'He can't join for a month: a single and two gigs.' Kelvin's Overtown commitments took up most of the rest of April, but he managed a few covert rehearsals with his new band.

At the time, he was living in the first-floor flat at 22 Gladsmuir Road, Archway, and it was here that early rehearsals took place, 'with Geir on pads for drums, really quiet'. Someone moved out of one of the bedsits upstairs, and towards the end of the month, Mick moved in to live with his new girlfriend, Debbie. 'Just one room with a little grill in it,' remembers Kelvin. 'And for a while it was heaven, because we'd go and hang out at concerts and stuff.'

The band had only been together for six or seven weeks by this time, but had already gone a considerable way towards establishing a musical identity. The choice of covers reflected the band members' shared tastes. A feature was a version of Chuck Berry's 'Little Queenie' that owed much to the Rolling Stones' reading of the song as immortalised on their 1970 live album, *Get Yer Ya-Ya's Out*. 'We used to do an old Yardbirds song called "I'm Not Talking",' says Brady. 'I think we did a couple of the original Sixties American underground things from Mick's record collection, one called "Sometimes Good Guys Don't Wear White" [originally recorded by the Standells]. It was one of those tunes that was a bit like [Them's] "Gloria", with a very simple riff.'

Mick was by now a far more prolific composer than anyone else in the band. 'He'd write about ten songs, and nine would be crap, but one would be really good,' says Brady, who had quickly come to realise that Mick made up in other areas for his limitations as a guitarist: 'He was a good songwriter, and great at ideas and arranging.' The only song that he can recall is one of those that impressed him least, reminding him too much of Stones numbers like 'Wild Horses' and 'Dead Flowers'. It may or may not be the same Mick Jones composition that Kelvin also remembers from this time: 'I thought it was a really brilliant song. This real slow number. I can't remember what it was called, but the opening lines were "I guess I've reached an all-time low / There's nowhere else I wanna go", which I thought was pretty cool, for then.' It was a lyrical theme that Mick would return to – this time with far more life experience to back it up – in his 1979 Clash song 'I'm Not Down'.

When Kelvin signed up, he was by no means content to accept the band as it was. There were two reasons for this. Firstly, Kelvin's tastes were far more in the rock mainstream than the others'. 'I was a musical snob,' he acknowledges. 'I'd gone out and played with a bunch of musicians who'd had their trip together, which became a disadvantage in the punk days, but then I thought was fantastic.' 'Kelvin used to sing in an American voice,' says Brady. 'Paul Rogers [of Free and Bad Company], sort of thing.' Secondly, Kelvin had a typical frontman's ego, and could not accept Mick as the band's principal songwriter. 'After Kelvin joined, every time Mick came up with a song, it was rejected by Kelvin,' laughs Geir. 'There was a big argument: "Shut up, Mick, your songs are crap!", you know. . .' Kelvin confirms this: 'I was trying to monopolise the songs, but I wasn't really much of a songwriter, so I was also doing other people's songs. Mick was doing originals, and he had more songs than anybody else, so he probably got about four in, and I got about four in. And his were much better, actually. He had a way of writing lyrics that I hadn't sussed. My lyrics were dire, looking back.' According to Brady, Kelvin's songs were not even necessarily Kelvin's songs. 'Kelvin was so bad, he'd say, "I've written this great song", we'd rehearse it, and two months later he'd tell us that it was actually off this American album! Stuff like that.'

With the exception of Mick, no one considered Kelvin's pushiness to be particularly threatening: at the time, would-be rock'n'roll stars were *supposed* to be prima donnas. Besides, the band had other things on their mind. On 25 April, they arranged a showcase performance for Tony Gordon at a seedy rehearsal room near the Bell pub on Pentonville Road, King's Cross, as previously used on occasion by the Hollywood Brats. 'This guy had these terrible Marshall amps, and he'd nailed them to the floor because he kept getting his stuff nicked all the time,' says Brady. Despite the shabby surroundings and the limitations of the equipment, Gordon liked what he saw. He had only one proviso for taking on the band. 'He suggested calling it Little Queenie,' Brady reports with a wince, 'which I thought was *ridiculous*, because you already had Queen. But he said, "It's a great name, and you've got a great image", so we went along with that.' In fact, Queen had recently had a hit single with 'Now I'm Here', a song which included a lyrical quote from 'Little Queenie' over its closing bars, and, in retrospect, it would seem that Tony was hoping his flamboyant new discoveries would tap into the same market as the established glam rockers. If nothing else, he showed considerable astuteness in anticipating trends: just seven months later, Queen would begin an eight-week run at number one in the UK with their single 'Bohemian Rhapsody'.

On 7 May, a second showcase was arranged, this time at the slightly more salubrious Tracks studio in Acton. Tony Gordon had connections at Pye records, and he brought along a representative from the record company. 'I think he liked us,' recorded Brady's diary. This was indeed the case. The following day, the newly renamed Little Queenie were invited up to the Wedge records office at 13 Duke Street and offered a management contract which they read with mixed feelings. 'We signed to Tony Gordon,' Brady wrote in his diary, 'but Kelvin says it's a crap deal.' 'I remember the deal *was* very dodgy,' Brady says now, 'but we thought we might as well do it as we weren't doing anything else.'

With a management contract secured and a recording deal in the offing, certain members of the band felt it was time to take the musical side of things a little more seriously. 'Geir was a great bloke,' says Brady, 'but if you have a dodgy drummer, the whole band's dodgy.' Two days after the contract was signed, a meeting was called at Gladsmuir Road, and Geir was given the sack. Mick – upset at what he considered to be the betrayal of a friend – offered the only real objection, but he was partly mollified when it was decided that Geir's replacement should be another Strand School old boy, Jim Hyatt. The fact that Jim had always been particularly close to Kelvin supports Geir's belief that Kelvin was responsible for instigating his dismissal.

On 30 May, the new line-up of Little Queenie went into Pye's Bryanston Street 16-track studio to record a couple of demos with Tony Gordon producing. 'We were rehearsing in Acton, and they took us from there in cabs,' says John. 'We felt like royalty. Mick and I were together, and he was sitting back and he was *enjoying* it! It was the first taste of someone taking over, and providing for us. Treating us as though we were important, in a way.' Both John and Mick were in awe of the whole experience, Mick especially. 'He was like a little kid in the studio,' recalls Brady. 'Saying, "Oh, what does this do, and what does that do?" I thought it was a bit embarrassing.' The songs recorded were the inevitable 'Little Queenie' and Frankie Miller's 'Fool In Love', which Kelvin used to sing with Overtown. 'It came out quite well' is John's verdict. 'It was quite a good version of "Little Queenie", if I do say so myself.' Having been in a studio before, Brady was not so easily impressed, as his diary entry testified: 'Put two songs down. Ropy. Tony Gordon sucks!'

Kelvin was also feeling uneasy, and had been ever since signing the contract. He had spent the latter part of the month sounding out various of his contacts to see if he could come up with anything better. Having failed to entice Guy Stevens to come and watch Schoolgirl two and a half years previously, he now found him more approachable for reasons that had as much to do with Guy's own reduced circumstances as Kelvin's redoubtable powers of persuasion.

Charles Shaar Murray provided perhaps the most concise summary of Stevens's career in a December 1979 *NME* retrospective: 'Kingpin Mod DJ at the Scene Club in '64, Our Man in London for Sue Records, first house producer for Island Records, where he signed and produced Free and Spooky Tooth as well as inventing Mott the Hoople . . . the man who got Chuck Berry out of jail in 1964, the man who supplied the Who with the compilation tape that gave them most of their pre-original material repertoire, the man who introduced Keith Reid to Procol Harum and generated "Whiter Shade Of Pale" . . .' Quite some CV. Since losing Mott the Hoople in 1972, however, Guy's legendary fondness for speed and booze had taken its toll. 'I never really recovered from Mott the Hoople,' he told CSM. 'I never really got over working with Ian Hunter.'

Despite being something of a music industry joke by 1975, Guy was still well connected, and on a retainer from Warner Brothers head Mo Ostin in the US. For his part, when he heard that Kelvin's latest band was on the point of signing a contract, Guy thought it might just provide him with the opportunity to make a comeback. The day after the Pye session, Kelvin took the others along to meet him in a pub. Mick, John and Jim had been fascinated by him since their schooldays, and Brady was impressed by Guy's history, fund of anecdotes and fondness for a good time. 'Had drinks and lots of laughs,' he informed his diary. The Stevens charm was at work.

By the time Little Queenie turned up as scheduled for a meeting at the Wedge office on 2 June, Kelvin had decided to get the band out of its contract with Tony Gordon by any means necessary. 'He said, "I'll do it,"' Brady remembers: '"You guys just sit there, and don't laugh."' Kelvin's ploy was to leap on to the table in Tony's office, shout, 'I can't handle it!' and pretend to have a full-blown seizure. '*And he pulled it off!*' laughs Brady. 'That was the kind of guy Kelvin was in those days. In the end, I think Tony just said, "Oh, get out and leave me alone!" So we got out of the deal.' 'We got the contract back,' adds John, 'and we ran around the corner to the pub where Guy was, and we tore it into little bits and threw them into the air.' Perhaps unsurprisingly, Tony Gordon – who went on to manage Sham 69 and Culture Club – now claims to have no recollection of the band or any of its members.

The following day, Guy turned up at the Acton rehearsal room to watch Little Queenie run through a half-hour set. It must have been a glorious moment for Mick. Not only was he finally playing on equal terms with the older friends he'd once looked up to at school and roadied for in Schoolgirl, but he was also auditioning for the mentor and producer of his all-time favourite group. But what could have been a dream come true rapidly turned decidedly nasty. At the end of 1974, Mott the Hoople had split; Ian Hunter had gone off to team up with Mick Ronson and the rest of the band had commenced a long slide into oblivion under the truncated appellation Mott. The temptation to step into the breach and relive his heady days with the original band proved too strong for Guy, and he could not accept Little Queenie as they were. 'He took Kelvin aside,' says Brady, 'and said, "Well, I think you need keyboards. Brady can handle all the guitar." He didn't think Mick was very good, and he wanted a Mott the Hoople again.'

A band meeting was arranged for 5 June at Gladsmuir Road, and Kelvin gave Mick the bad news. 'A month after I got the sack, Mick got the sack,' says Geir Waade. 'He was right when he said, "As soon as you get that singer in, he'll split the band up." That's Kelvin!' Kelvin concedes the point. 'I made the cardinal sin of thinking, "I've got to listen to all these other people telling me what to do." I've always been a bit naughty like that. "You've got to get rid of Mick!" "But he's been my friend for years!" "Sorry, he's out."

"OK, fine."' Brady revealed his own attitude the next day. 'Mick was really, like, mega-depressed,' he says. 'He phoned me up and said, "I told you this would happen! How can you do this to me, Brady?" And I said, "Look, Mick, we've got a bit of a deal with the band now, and we might go places. *That's rock'n'roll*, you know?"'

As well as being hungry enough for success to sacrifice anything or anyone, Kelvin and, to a lesser extent, Brady had ulterior motives for acceding to Guy's demands. Although he was prepared to accept external control from a management figure, Kelvin wanted control within the group itself. For his part, in an era when musicians were supposed to exhibit rock'n'roll cool, Brady had been growing increasingly unhappy about what he perceived to be Mick's embarrassingly naïve behaviour. They both liked Mick – Brady in particular being much taken with the younger guitarist's ready wit – but at the time, their ambition allowed no room for sentiment.

Jim Hyatt was too new to the band and too easy-going to have much of a say. Only John showed any kind of loyalty at all. 'I voted against it. I said, "Fuck off! Mick and I formed this in the first place. This is *our* project." There was Guy Stevens saying, "I want to keep order in the band. Mick's excess baggage", and all this. Complete crap. I said, "I've had it!" Then I got people ringing me up and coming around, saying, "You can't do this! It's all going to happen. Stevens has got Warner Brothers in his pocket." And, eventually, they talked me around to it. I stayed on to see what was happening. Mick was completely nonplussed by the whole thing. Such a kick in the teeth! I went straight to him and said, "Look, this is what's happening", and he's never, as far as I know, held it against me.'

Looking back on it, John and Brady now agree that it was a mistake to allow Kelvin to get rid of the band's principal songwriter on the whim of the erratic Guy. 'Mick's was still the major writing input, and he was given the order of the boot, which was crazy,' says John. Kelvin has pulled too many similar stunts in his career to waste time worrying about one error of judgement in the distant past, but he is far more sensitive to the repercussions of his actions today than he was at the time. 'It must have hurt,' he acknowledges. 'Four friends who have all been schoolfriends, and three saying, "Sorry, goodbye." Mick was very responsible for getting it together. It was his energies.'

At Guy's suggestion, the band name was changed to Violent Luck. 'We started doing Mott the Hoople-type stuff,' says Brady. 'Which I thought was a bit dated then.' On 27 June, Violent Luck auditioned for a Warner Brothers representative at PSL rehearsal studios in Battersea. Thereafter, Jim Hyatt met a similar fate to his predecessor. The remainder of Violent Luck's career was to be dogged with difficulties in establishing a permanent line-up: they never did find either a full-time drummer or – even more ironically – a keyboard-playing replacement for Mick. On 21 August, the remaining trio went into Air studios on Oxford Circus to record some demos for Warner Brothers with Guy as producer and Bill Price as engineer. They were joined by a couple of guest session musicians: Leo Sayer's drummer, Theodore Thunder, and Mott the Hoople's original keyboard player, Verden Allen. Tracks recorded were the Flamin' Groovies' 'Slow Death', Ian Hunter's 'No Wheels To Ride' and Kelvin's 'That's Why My Baby (Let Me Go)'. The others later discovered it was pretty much a straight lift from a J. Geils Band song called 'Nightmare'.

Even while still with Overtown, Kelvin had kept his options open by attending auditions for several other bands. One of the *Melody Maker* ads he answered had been placed by bassist Tony James. Tony was reading Mathematics at Brunel University in Uxbridge, on the western outskirts of London, and living in Twickenham, a few miles to the south. Kelvin went down there four times before deciding against joining his band. 'He had all these really long songs with long lyrics.' After some initial hostility, Tony accepted Kelvin's decision, and a friendship of sorts developed; Tony became interested enough in Kelvin's new band to attend some of their rehearsals. In a vague effort to soften the blow of Mick's sacking, Kelvin suggested that he team up with the now bandless Tony. In Pete Frame's two Family Trees, the story of the London SS starts with this meeting. 'And I didn't get any credit for it,' complains Kelvin, with no hint of irony.

Geir too is very concerned that he should get full acknowledgement for his role in the pre-history of the Clash. ('I mean, he invented punk, you know!' laughs John.) He is familiar with Tony's account of the London SS as reported by Pete Frame, and is understandably annoyed to have been written out of the picture by someone who was originally little more than a hanger-on. He is now determined to even the score. 'The first time I saw Tony James, he came into the room and we said, "That guy looks like he comes from the country somewhere!" He just didn't fit the part. We were all very hip, a really stylish New York Dolls look-alike band, and here comes this hippy with jeans on that looked like Status Quo!'

On the surface Brady and John seem less bitter about being omitted from the London SS story, but, interviewed separately, they express their contempt for the guilty party with a relish that is even more startling than Geir's, coming as it does from two such generally easy-going men. Like Geir, they are also eager to undermine Tony's hip credentials. 'The first time I saw Tony James,' says John, 'he walked into the rehearsal studios that Violent Luck were using, and he had a copy of *Secret Treaties* under his armpit, the Blue Öyster Cult album.' 'We thought he was this wimpy sort of guy,' says Brady. '"What are you doing?" "Well," he says, "I work for one of the Beatles' associates." I think it was Neil Aspinall. What he did was, he used to look after his kids in the daytime! Everyone used to think, "Ah, Tony James: he's such a little wanker!" He really latched on to Mick. Mick was his idol. He was really infatuated with him, because he saw Mick had something.' According to John, Tony quickly abandoned his scruffy denims and greatcoat and began to dress like his new hero. 'Tony was a Mick clone,' he says. 'Mick would wear something, and the next day Tony would turn up in a replica. It was that bad.'

Since he had suddenly become an outsider himself, it is possible that Mick felt sympathetic to Tony's position. More probably, he enjoyed having his torpedoed self-esteem buoyed by Tony's attentions: after being denied by his friends in such a humiliating manner, the company of such an enthusiastic yes-man must have made for a pleasant change. Whatever, Mick decided to form another band in much the same vein as Little Queenie, only this time with himself as undisputed leader and Tony as trusty lieutenant. 'It was probably, "We'll show the bastards!"' says Brady.

The first step was for the duo to place a classified ad for further musicians in *Melody Maker*. Their notice, which appeared in the Musicians Wanted section of the 19 July 1975 issue, read: 'LEAD GUITARIST and drums to join bass player and guitarist/singer, influenced by Stones, NY Dolls, Mott etc. Must have great rock and roll image.' Hopefuls were asked to phone 'Michael' at Gladsmuir Road. Nothing much resulted, so a second ad was placed in the 9 August issue for the same two vacancies. The Stones and the Stooges were quoted as influences before the ad outlined its other key requirement: 'Decadent 3rd generation rock and roll image essential. New York Dolls style.'

The first caller was Brian James, a somewhat older – how much older he's not telling – lead guitarist with a passion for Iggy and the Stooges. A meeting was arranged at Gladsmuir Road. 'A dingy little flat,' recalls Brian. 'I came up, and I played them a tape of stuff I'd been doing in Brussels with a band called Bastard. It was rock'n'roll, and they liked it. Kindred spirits, you know.' The tape of Bastard's energetic material, inspired by the MC5 and the Stooges, did indeed impress Mick and Tony, but it was just the icing on the cake as far as they were concerned. 'As soon as we saw him, we said, "This is the guy!"' Tony told Pete Frame in 1977, 'because he had just the New York Doll image we wanted.' Although keen to throw in his lot with the other two, Brian first had to return to Belgium, break the news to Bastard and sort out his affairs.

At the end of August, Kelvin returned to Gladsmuir Road one night with a copy of Violent Luck's Warner Brothers demo tape. While living in the same house as Kelvin, Mick had tried to hide his bitterness and maintain a certain level of civility with his old schoolfriend, but the demos proved to be the last straw. 'I remember going upstairs to play them to Mick, and he was really, really upset,' says Kelvin. 'I'll never really forget that. I thought, "Maybe I'm a complete cunt", you know? He was saying, "I'm going to leave here!" He was really timid and everything else, but one thing he said was, "I'll be a better guitarist than Brady! I'll succeed!" Quite a statement . . .'

Mick moved back in with Stella at Wilmcote House, and his room at Gladsmuir Road was taken over by John. Shortly afterwards, Violent Luck finally began playing gigs, but the Warner Brothers deal did not materialise, and by the following spring Guy's erratic behaviour had made a parting of the ways inevitable. According to John, Kelvin was moved to write a song in Guy's honour entitled 'It's Not So Easy (When You Fall)', but it's worth noting that Ian Hunter's eponymous 1975 début solo album contains a track entitled 'It Ain't Easy When You Fall'. This, along with another of Kelvin's songs and a joint band composition, was demoed in June 1976 for the Electric Record Company (the recording arm of Chappell music publishing) with a session drummer. The producer was Keith Harwood, recently the Rolling Stones' engineer. On 22 June 1976, the band played their last gig as Violent Luck, supporting Eddie and the Hot Rods at the Marquee; a favourable review appeared in the very first edition of punk fanzine *Sniffin' Glue*.

Thereafter, the band was taken on by former David Bowie producer Tony Visconti, who renamed them Sister Ray – after the Velvet Underground song – and produced yet more demos at his home studio for Good Earth records: two of Kelvin's songs plus 'Slow Death'. Failing to hear a single, he then persuaded the band to record Garland Jeffries's 'Wild In The Streets'. Going along with the idea of a fresh start, the core band members adopted pseudonyms – Kelvin became Kelvin Colney, Brady became Billy James and John became John Belsen – and underwent an image make-over. The band were to play just three gigs in their new guise, however, the last of them on 26 July. By this time, Kelvin was getting that sinking feeling. When Ian Hunter, now dabbling in management with new wave band Tuff Darts, suggested the singer move to the States to front his new charges, he jumped ship without a second thought. Sister Ray fell apart.

Sometime before Mick's departure from the original line-up, Kelvin had made another useful musical connection. 'I met this guy Barry Jones, who used to work with [fashion designer] Zandra Rhodes,' he recollects. 'I'd gone up to her office for some reason, and I bumped into Barry, who said, "I've got a studio in Warrington Crescent." And I ended up going round there and meeting Matt.' Both northerners, Barry Jones and Matt Dangerfield had attended the Jacob Kramer School of Art in Leeds before moving to London in 1972. Soon afterwards, Matt had discovered a basement flat, 47A Warrington Crescent, recently vacated by a colony of hippies. He and Barry were guitarists and songwriters, and were attracted to the flat because it was large, bright, had lots of rehearsal space and, according to Matt, 'You could play really loud rock'n'roll without worrying about the neighbours.' There was also a coal storage area under the steps leading down from the street that was just large enough to house their studio. 'A 4-track, the first home studio that was available on the market, TEAC job,' says Matt. 'That was my connection with a lot of people at that time.'

Among the others who lived in the flat were 'Honest' John Plain, also ex-Jacob Kramer, and Barry's then girlfriend, Celia Perry, a fashion design student. In addition, number 47A was invariably packed with various musicians hoping to jam, form bands or record demos, and assorted friends and acquaintances who were there to hang out and play pool on the flat's own table, either before or after a night's drinking at the nearby Warrington pub. One such was Steve Hershkowitz, known as Fat Steve, whose father owned the Clearlake Hotel off Kensington Gore. Not being one to pass on an opportunity to network, Kelvin was soon a regular caller at the flat. One by one, he introduced all the members of Little Queenie/Violent Luck to the Warrington Crescent scene, which was made up of the like-minded and similarly attired. 'When Biba's was closing, Mick and I bought all this ocelot, leopardskin and tiger-striped velour material,' says John, 'and we all had trousers and tops made out of it by Celia.'

Matt remembers how Geir became a regular. 'I was doing some recording and I needed a drummer,' he says. 'This was in the days before drum machines. Kelvin just happened to be there and said, "There's a drummer lives round the corner, a Norwegian guy." I rang him up, he was round ten minutes later and did the drum track.' Since Wilmcote House was no more than a couple of hundred yards from Warrington Crescent, the flat also became a convenient hang-out and meeting place for Mick and his new shadow. It had the disadvantage of being frequented by members of his ex-band, whom he would have preferred not to see, but it offered the chance to make new alliances.

'Mick and I got on, started talking about getting a band together, pooling ideas. We had the same sort of influences, more or less,' says Matt. Although his main love was the Velvet Underground, he was also a fan of the New York Dolls, and had even heard the Hollywood Brats' album. 'I must admit, I didn't think much of Mick or Tony as musicians: I wasn't a great musician, but I definitely wasn't impressed by them. I thought Mick was a good songwriter. I remember one song called "Always the Bridesmaid, Never the Bride" which I thought was pretty good until, years later, I found there was an old country or blues song with the same title. That's the only one I can remember. Most of the time it was just jamming, fucking about.'

Things were so fluid at the Warrington Crescent Trainee Decadent Rock Stars' Workshop and Social Club that, over the late summer of 1975, there was no set band line-up. 'It was never a stable group. People were in and out,' says Matt. 'Whoever was available. Like Honest John, for instance, was only ever in it when we needed someone who could drum, or someone who could play guitar; just fill in, because he's a good all-rounder.' Matt recorded some of the sessions, but, unfortunately, the tapes have since been mislaid. Or, from Mick's point of view, fortunately: one song featured a Jones vocal ad lib that walked the fine line between sexual innuendo and obscenity for some considerable time before finally falling off on the latter side. 'Embarrassing!' grins Matt. '"Get down on your knees, baby . . ."' 'Definitely Blackmail Corner,' agrees Honest John, who played guitar on the session. 'I mean, I'm sure Mick Jones'd pay a *lot* to get hold of that. In fact, I think some record companies would pay a lot as well . . .'

September and October brought a number of key encounters that would encourage the resumption of a more businesslike approach. Mick had not ceased his regular gig-going activities, and it had become his habit to introduce himself to anyone he thought looked interesting enough to be potential band material. One night at the Nashville in West Kensington he bumped into a small, bespectacled man who was destined to have more of an influence on his musical future than anyone he had listened to or met thus far. 'I thought he was a piano player,' he told the *NME*'s Paul Rambali in 1981. 'He seemed like a really bright geezer. We got on like a house on fire.'

Bernard Rhodes objects to being called Bernie – 'I'm not a bloody taxi driver!' – but perhaps for that very reason almost everyone who has ever been associated with him refers to him by the diminutive. Neither a piano player nor a musician of any sort, Bernie was always more interested in popular music's associated culture than in the music itself. Originally from the East End of London he, like Mick, went to school in Brixton. One of the original early Sixties mods, he hung out on the Soho coffee bar scene, and went on the Bank Holiday scooter runs down to the south coast. As the Swinging Sixties progressed, so he claims, he went on to become an 'ideas person' for the Who, share a flat with Graham Bond, work in famed King's Road boutique Granny Takes a Trip, become 'ideas person' with T. Rex and get involved with Jerry Rubin and the Yippie movement. 'There was a very optimistic feeling,' he told Paul Rambali in 1980. 'The underground press was coming up, and together with that there was a lot of literature that one was consuming; knowledge, both from books and experience. Going abroad, checking it out. There was a lot of intake.'

In 1972, when the politically clueless Marc Bolan announced his intention of releasing a single entitled 'Children Of The Revolution', Bernie grew disillusioned with the pop and rock scene's potential for creating change. He opted out, and invested in a Renault garage in Camden Town. There proved to be limited scope for innovation and ideas in the motor trade, however, and a couple of years later he found himself drawn back to the cutting edge of pop culture. He returned to the fray via Malcolm McLaren's shop Sex, at 430 King's Road, Chelsea. Malcolm was an old friend from his mod days. As neither of them was there at the time, they did not, as one persistent and probably self-originated myth has it, meet during the Paris riots of 1968. Bernie became fascinated by the provocative designs Malcolm and his partner, Vivienne Westwood, were creating, and helped conceive and print some of the T-shirts that would soon make the shop notorious. Bernie's triumph was a late 1974 shirt that contrasted lists of cultural and political likes and dislikes beneath the slightly awkward would-be Situationist International/Class of '68 slogan 'You're gonna wake up one morning and *know* what side of the bed you've been lying on!'

As early as 1973, when Sex was known as Let It Rock and still sold rock'n'roll revival clothes, Malcolm had been pestered by a young regular named Steve Jones who wanted Malcolm to help out with the band for which he sang and his friend Paul Cook played drums. Malcolm linked Steve up with the shop's Saturday boy Glen Matlock, attended one or two rehearsals and eventually suggested the name Sex Pistols, but at the time, having no real interest in contemporary music, neglected to take matters any further.

Over the years, Bernie has proved himself to have a pretty fair lip (and, some would say, a penchant for improvisation) when it comes to blowing his own trumpet, but Glen Matlock supports his claim to have been the Pistols' real original motivator. At the time Bernie met them, the Pistols were still clumsily working their way through the Faces songbook. He would take the band - especially Glen, who was the most amenable to discussing ideas – down the road to the Roebuck pub (now the Dôme) and talk to them about the kind of music they should be playing, the way they should be dressing, the attitudes they should be expressing and, above all, what they wanted to achieve. From November 1974 to March 1975, Malcolm was in the US attempting to manage the New York Dolls, whom he had met and befriended on an earlier trip to New York. During this period, Bernie continued to work with the Pistols, encouraging them to rehearse and trying to convince the others to ditch original guitarist Wally Nightingale.

It has become something of a rock writer's cliché to say that, in terms of drink, drugs and ego, the Dolls were by this time intent on living up to the title of their second album, *Too Much, Too Soon*. In an attempt to revive their flagging career, Malcolm dressed them in red patent leather and made them a red hammer and sickle backdrop. This succeeded in alienating whatever audience they had left, and shortly afterwards the band began to disintegrate. Apparently unfazed by this failure, Malcolm returned to London with Sylvain Sylvain's guitar and his head buzzing with ideas. He promptly switched his attentions to the Pistols. Wally was summarily dispatched, Steve was given Sylvain's guitar to learn on and, after problems persuading former Television member Richard Hell to emigrate from New York, efforts were made to discover a more conveniently located vocalist. Although Glen makes the claim for Steve, and Malcolm makes the claim for Malcolm, it was Bernie who found Johnny Rotten. 'Bernie definitely influenced the start of the Pistols,' Johnny told Chris Salewicz for the *Face* in 1980. 'He got me in the band. Malcolm hated my guts, because of the way me and Sid used to take the piss out of him.' Not one to give credit unless it is due – and, usually, not even then – Johnny repeated this claim in his ghostwritten autobiography, *Rotten: No Irish, No Blacks, No Dogs*, published in 1994.

It was the last real contribution Bernie was allowed to make. Although considered by many to be a machiavellian manipulator in his own right, his friendship with Malcolm seemed to be constructed in such a way that the latter was always guaranteed the upper hand. Hardly unaware of this imbalance, Bernie asked Malcolm for what he felt he deserved, a partnership in both Sex and the Sex Pistols. He got what Malcolm felt he deserved: nothing. While it took Bernie some time to face up to the rejection – in fact, a strong case can be made for the theory that he never did – its initial voicing came as no real surprise to him. He later told Fred and Judy Vermorel as much for their book *Sex Pistols: The Inside Story*: 'I thought that together we could come up with something that was truly great . . . But I *knew* Malcolm would never give anyone half share. He'd always want to be in control.'

Melody Maker's early Seventies move from Sixties-type pop coverage to more serious muso-oriented rock journalism had left the other UK music papers behind. With the arrival of a new serious 'inky' in the shape of *Sounds*, it had looked as though the death-knell was about to sound for the *NME*. Then, suddenly, early in 1972, the paper had undergone a make-over. Editor Alan Smith had drafted in former underground press journalists Charles Shaar Murray and Nick Kent, and encouraged them to establish themselves as US-style larger-than-life personality rock writers in the Lester Bangs tradition. The new *NME* had promised intelligent, thought-provoking coverage of the early Seventies rock'n'roll scene. The usually more R&B-oriented CSM struck up a good relationship with Bowie, but it was Nick Kent who cornered the market in decadence and sleaze, and the kind of obscure bands beloved of the Warrington Crescent crowd.

Mick Jones had read Nick's *NME* rock'n'roll fashion feature of April 1974, 'The Politics Of Flash', and learned from it that Malcolm McLaren had supplied clothes to the New York Dolls. In July the following year, Malcolm, his shop and clothes had gained more mainstream notoriety when a regular customer was arrested and charged for wearing a provocative Sex T-shirt displaying a drawing of two extravagantly endowed cowboys naked from the waist down. The shop had been raided, and a further 18 shirts confiscated. These shenanigans had made the front page of the *Guardian*, and ensured that most of the Warrington Crescent crowd were aware of Malcolm as a face on the hip London scene. Mick duly visited Sex, and bought one of its less confrontational lines, a T-shirt bearing the legend that had also been the shop's previous name: 'Too Fast To Live, Too Young To Die'. That he was wearing this when he met Bernie, who furthermore claimed to have been involved in its design, proved to be the ice-breaker for their first conversation.

Even though the Sex Pistols had been taken away from him by Malcolm, Bernie was not yet thinking in terms of going into competition with a band of his own; but he was not averse to the idea of discovering a band that would impress his friend enough to make him reconsider the idea of a McLaren–Rhodes partnership. Bernie initially gave Mick the impression that such a partnership already existed, and as a result, the guitarist was happy to arrange another meeting. 'It was just me, Mick and Tony went along,' says Matt, who remembers that the encounter took place at a Rock'n'Roll Revival show. 'Bernie was Malcolm's partner, or so we thought, but in fact he'd just split with Malcolm. We didn't know about that. Bernie quite impressed me because he was weird, he had weird ideas. Bernie was very inspiring. He kind of gave you the feeling that, yeah, you could create something. McLaren doesn't listen to you, McLaren just talks at you. Bernie would somehow make you do your own thinking.'

Part of the reason Mick and Tony had not been pushing too hard to form a stable line-up from the 47A talent pool was that they were still waiting for Brian James to return from Belgium. Faced with what appeared to be a golden opportunity, however, they quickly pulled together the core of a band, with Matt on lead guitar and Geir once again behind the drums. (Thus, Kelvin might have stolen one band from Mick, but he was indirectly responsible for providing him with the bulk of the personnel for a new one.) Matt believes it was at this point that the band decided to call itself the London SS. Apparently, Bernie's principles were not yet quite so highly developed as they would become a year later. 'He said, "If you're going to have a name like that, you've got to go all the way. Are you prepared to do it?"' says Matt. 'We said, "Yeah, sure, why not?"'

Both Matt and Mick could sing, but the idea of a five-piece band with frontman was still very much in vogue. The first step towards filling the remaining vacancy, of course, was to chip in for another *Melody Maker* classified. The display ad which appeared in the 11 October Vocalists Wanted section gave 47A's phone number and made an oblique reference to the Tony Gordon interlude: 'UP FRONT ROCK AND ROLL VOCALIST, could be IGGY POP, required by pre-launched DECADENT 3rd GENERATION Rock Band.' 'We auditioned the singers with Bernie present as well,' recalls Matt. 'Bernie asking questions not about "Have you sung before?" or anything, but really abstruse questions that had nothing to do with being in a band or anything. Which quite impressed me, because it unnerved everybody. People didn't know how to behave.' Almost inevitably, the upshot of these mind games was that the band remained singerless.

With so many musicians hanging around the Warrington Crescent flat, perusing the *Melody Maker*'s classified ads pages was something of a weekly ritual. According to Tony, the Musicians Wanted section in the 27 September issue had made everyone sit up and take notice. In among the usual pop, cabaret and muso dross was a display ad reading: 'WHIZZ KID GUITARIST. Not older than 20. Not worse looking than Johnny Thunders. Auditioning: TIN PAN ALLEY.' The people present had believed themselves to be the only people in London apart from Nick Kent who even knew who the Dolls were. 'We couldn't believe it,' Tony told Pete Frame. 'So we phoned up straight away to find out which group it was. They were called the Sex Pistols.'

According to Glen Matlock, the main purpose of the Pistols' ad was to reassure drummer Paul Cook that everybody meant business, he being unconvinced that neophyte axe-hero Steve Jones could cope on his own. But Malcolm was still obsessed by the Dolls, and it is equally likely that he was also thinking in terms of emulating that band's two-guitar line-up. He had Steve Jones learning the rudiments by playing along to the Dolls' first album on Sylvain's old guitar, and having mentally cast him in Sylvain's role, he was seeking the appropriate musical complement.

Malcolm did not intend to devote himself exclusively to the Sex Pistols, who at that point must have seemed an extremely long shot indeed. Since his return to London he had been scouting around for other promising talent, and one of the exciting acts he kept hearing about was a Dolls-type band named the Hollywood Brats. He knew the Brats had also split up, but rumour had it that Andrew Matheson and Casino Steel were once more at large in London. He was interested in meeting them and, once contact had been made, expressed as much to the London SS camp. Geir knew Andrew and Casino were sharing a flat at 17 London Street, Paddington, and Mick and Tony took it upon themselves to pass on Malcolm's message. Mick's motive was not entirely altruistic. Keen to impress Malcolm, he was also not averse to getting on the right side of Andrew and Casino: it had not gone unremarked at Warrington Crescent that a merger with this duo would plug the gaps in the London SS line-up, add a certain amount of prestige and experience to the band, and almost certainly secure backing from McLaren.

'My memories of the era are as clear as a dry martini and twice as tart,' writes Andrew Matheson in his inimitable style. 'Well I recall the night that Mick Jones (who made up for in bottle what he lacked in chin) and Tony James (constantly blurring the edges between charming and unctuous) arrived at our sumptuous London Street dive to propose an alliance. The eagerness and optimism of Mick and Tony contrasted sharply to the negativity and disillusionment of the two of us – more so me than Cas – and when they left after expressing a desire to work with us, and after saying extremely flattering things about the Brats album, we found our passion somewhat rekindled.'

Andrew insists that it was during Mick and Tony's visit that the name London SS first came into being, and that it was the suggestion of Casino Steel. 'That is such complete rubbish!' splutters Geir in rebuttal. 'Andrew Matheson has got nothing to do with anything at all, whatsoever!' On balance, it does seem that Andrew is mistaken as to the original source of the name, but he and his songwriting partner were certainly intrigued by its possibilities. Andrew was a huge fan of *Cabaret* – 'I saw it eight times in a row over two days!' – and he and Casino were themselves flirting with Nazi chic as part of their own decadent pose. The London SS struck exactly the right note. 'We went on to design a stage set-up involving dry ice, blue lighting and barbed wire.'

Indeed, Andrew and Casino sported Nazi regalia for their visit, along with Mick and Tony, to the Pistols' newly acquired West End rehearsal rooms at 6 Denmark Street. 'Mick asked to borrow a Nazi armband of mine,' recalls Andrew. Sex Pistols' bassist Glen Matlock remembers the occasion well. 'It was only a titchy little place,' he says. 'There was like a downstairs rehearsal room, and an upstairs room which me and Steve Jones lived in. It was a little outbuilding. We was rehearsing downstairs, and we all had short hair, and the door squeaked open, and these blokes walked through, and it's like, "*What on earth* are these guys all about?" We just pissed ourselves laughing. Mick had snakeskin trousers on, stack-heel shoes, this flowery kind of chemise, hair down here with his earholes sticking out. And the others all looked exactly the same! Everyone else went sheepishly upstairs, but Mick clocked us. Me and Mick just looked at each other like that, *boom*, there was a buzz right away.'

All of which tallies with Andrew's version, except for which of the parties involved were behaving 'sheepishly': 'We walked in at the pre-arranged time (or not long thereafter), saw three guys with short hair dressed like off-duty bank tellers, and McLaren. There was an air of nervousness in the place, as though we'd caught them masturbating or something. McLaren was sort of jittery in slow motion. Hands gesticulating, wrists limp, and minimal eye-contact. He said that both his boys and the Dolls had spoken of us, and he alternately mumbled and ranted. Thoroughly peeved, I exited the scene, followed shortly by the other three, and that was it.' In truth, Mick exited quite some way behind. Any link-up with McLaren might have been off the agenda as far as Andrew was concerned, but Mick was keeping all his options open. Having made eye-contact with the three musicians in the Sex Pistols, he called back in downstairs to reinforce the connection in the time-honoured fashion of musicians the world over: 'He came and had a jam with us,' says Glen.

Back at Warrington Crescent, a rehearsal-cum-audition for the proposed new band went ahead anyway. Bernie was not present. He didn't miss much. 'I was in the London SS for exactly 14 minutes,' Andrew told *ZigZag*'s Alan Anger in 1978. 'Now, this is no reflection on those guys' talents today, but I class it as an absolutely disastrous musical encounter.' Going into more detail, he now writes: 'Mick Jones had a good sense of humour and a tenacity I quietly admired. His guitar style was non-existent, though he modelled himself closely on Brady: all the moves, just none of the chainsaw panzer sound. For obvious reasons, we kept his personal yodel well away from any of the microphones.' 'We did a Beatles song, "Bad Boy", which is a good little number,' he told Alan. (In fact, it is one of several Larry Williams songs of which the Beatles recorded cover versions.) 'After playing it once, we tried it again, and halfway through, I just walked out. It was terrible. That really is the sum total of my involvement with the London SS.'

Not quite. A few days later, both Matt and Geir received phone calls from the ex-Brats. 'Andrew and Casino said they wanted to get a band together with me,' says Matt, 'but not with Mick and Tony, basically. I kind of weighed up the odds, and I decided to go with the Hollywood Brats thing. At that time it was down to the fact that they had a good album and I thought Matheson was great; I didn't know what to think about Casino, but I knew he wrote good songs, which was a plus. I thought, "Why not?"' After he had broken the bad news to Mick and Tony, Matt received a visit from Bernie asking him to reconsider. 'But I'd made up my mind, for better or worse.' 'I left the band as well,' says Geir. 'I shouldn't have, but I did. I really got on with Mick and Tony at the time, and I think that was the beginning of the Clash, really.' Again, not quite.

At Andrew's suggestion, this breakaway band called themselves the

Choirboys. Inevitably, Geir did not last long, a fact he attributes to Andrew's 'unique personality' and Andrew attributes to Geir's drumming. The next to go was Andrew himself. 'He went back to Canada for the Christmas holidays or something,' says Matt, 'and just didn't come back for about six months, so we carried on without him.' Casino and Matt drafted in Honest John and some friends of his from Leeds, and shortened the band's name to the Boys. Their début album featured two re-recorded Hollywood Brats songs, one of which, 'Sick On You', had anticipated one of punk's major calling cards by four years.

While Warrington Crescent regular Fat Steve Hershkowitz was by no means obese, neither was he whippet thin, which seems to have ruled him out as a candidate for the London SS vocalist vacancy. Several interviewees for this book have suggested the reason guitarist Barry Jones was not considered as a potential recruit was because he was black, and that Barry – not unreasonably – developed something of a chip on his shoulder about this. (Barry was also asked to stand in as second guitarist at a couple of Violent Luck gigs without ever being invited to join.) If this is indeed the case, it seems both were victims of the prevailing cultural fascism which dictated that rock stars had to be long-haired, skinny, effeminate white boys. After Steve had dropped his unflattering prefix and instead adopted the surname Dior, he and Barry got their own back by forming their own band with a similarly Dolls-influenced name: the London Cowboys. Unfortunately, they became so enamoured of the Johnny Thunders lifestyle that it took them an age to get round to doing anything constructive.

When Kelvin Blacklock left Sister Ray, Brady and John Brown briefly formed a band called the Hitmen, whose sole retrospective claim to fame is the fact that their drummer was John Altman, later to portray ne'er-do-well Nick Cotton in the BBC1 TV soap opera *EastEnders*. When things fell through with Tuff Darts in spring 1977, Kelvin returned to London in time to join cash-in punk band the Tools. As its other members were Brady, John and Geir, it was effectively a made-over version of Little Queenie, minus Mick. That May, they recorded demos – one of the three songs was 'borrowed' by Kelvin from Tuff Darts, another from the nascent London Cowboys – for Virgin records at Pathway studios with Stiff house engineer Bazza producing. Virgin would only offer a singles deal, so the band took the tapes to Polydor. An album was recorded, but remained unreleased. Once again, Kelvin bailed out, leaving at the end of 1977 to join Rat Scabies's short-lived White Cats. That same year, as K. K. Black, he recorded a solo single, 'California Sun', for Aura, and another, 'I Don't Want Our Loving To Die', under his real name, for EMI, produced by Midge Ure. Following the dissolution of the Boys, he briefly paired up with Matt Dangerfield. He went on to pass in and out of bands too numerous to mention, most of them doomed by his own suggestibility and lack of commitment.

After a brief spell with the B52's (*not* the American band), who recorded some demos for MCA in May 1978 with ex-Animal Hilton Valentine producing, Geir and John teamed up yet again with Brady to become Last Orders, the backing band for Stiff recording artist Wreckless Eric. All three played on the 1978 album *The Wonderful World Of Wreckless Eric*, but Geir did not last long, and Brady left soon afterwards. John played with Eric on and off until 1984, when the needs of his family dictated that he take to a more stable line of work, computer programming. Geir returned to Norway, where he now hosts a radio programme which features a regular interview slot recorded in London by Matt.

Andrew Matheson pursued a career in Canada as a professional soccer player, before making a solo album for Ariola in 1979 entitled *Monterey Shoes*. Subsequent sporadic attempts to restart his musical career – including abortive Hollywood Brats reunions – have been hampered by his peculiarly negative brand of perfectionism. In 1993, however, MCA paid for him to visit Norway and record another solo album with Casino helping out on keyboards and production and Brady supplying occasional guitar. One of the songs recorded, 'Crushing The Doll', made reference to the Sixties photo of Brian Jones in Nazi uniform. Brady still plays on the London pub circuit, lately in the JCB Band. He is also writing lyrics for a local band he met while in Norway.

That none of their contemporaries was destined to enjoy the same recognition or commercial success as either Mick or Tony carries weight only in retrospect. In mid-October 1975, in addition to suffering from the inferiority complex that comes with being deemed not good enough, the duo were having to cope with the ignominy of having had their band stolen from them; and, in Mick's case, not once, but twice. Although they continued to visit Warrington Crescent, it was neither convenient nor comfortable for them to play there on anything other than a casual basis. Which meant that, as well as their drummer and lead guitarist, they had effectively lost their rehearsal room. It may well be that Tony was intent on taking his revenge when he talked Pete Frame through the London SS Family Tree two years later: Matt's not inconsiderable role was reduced to the same size as Casino's walk-on bit-part, and Andrew and Geir received no mention at all.

There is one last, wince-inducing postscript to the story of the abortive London SS/Hollywood Brats/Malcolm McLaren link-up. The only halfway suitable candidate for a second guitarist thrown up by the Sex Pistols auditions was 15-year-old Steve New. He attended a few rehearsals, but things didn't quite gel, and he faded out of the picture about the same time Matt and Geir were poached by Andrew and Casino. Glen Matlock had been quite taken with Mick Jones. 'I said, "Why don't we try that bloke that jammed with us?" And Malcolm said, "I don't know", and I said, "We could get his hair cut", and he said, "He might be like Samson: get his hair cut and he'll have nothing!"' Nevertheless, the two of them set out to track Mick down. 'We didn't really have a contact,' says Glen. 'All we had was this address on London Street [that is, Andrew's and Casino's flat]. Some bloke wouldn't let us in, so we were shouting through the letterbox, "We just want to get in touch with Mick Jones", and this bloke – I think he was Norwegian, might have been Casino Steel – goes, "Why should I tell you? What's in it for me?"' Mick remained unaware of the opportunity he had missed. Shortly afterwards, the Pistols abandoned the idea of taking on a second guitarist, and on 6 November 1975, they played their first gig at the art school where Glen had taken his Foundation year, St Martin's on Charing Cross Road.

It was following the loss of Matt Dangerfield and Geir Waade that Bernie first began to assert his influence. Despite his subsequent offhand comments about the band, it was he who became the main motivating force behind Mick's third post-Delinquents attempt to form a band, again under the name the London SS. Bernie's first move was to find a rehearsal room: a dingy basement under a café called the Paddington Kitchen, at 113–115 Praed Street, next to the Fountains Abbey pub on the corner of Norfolk Place. Ironically enough, it was no more than a hundred yards from Andrew and Casino's flat. Fortunately for the band, someone else proved more successful in tracing Mick than Glen and Malcolm were. Within days of the fateful Warrington Crescent audition - Tony claims it was the same night – Brian James phoned to say he was back in the UK and ready to go to work. That meant all that was needed was a drummer and a vocalist. Once again, the band turned to the *Melody Maker* classifieds in order to fill the vacancies, and gave Bernie's home phone number for what turned out to be a series of ads running up until 6 December.

By the end of 1975, glam had pretty much run its course as a musical genre, and even trash glam was old news. Bowie was flirting with 'plastic soul'; the New York Dolls now consisted of Sylvain Sylvain, David Johansen and some backing musicians; and following the split in the ranks of Mott the Hoople, neither the rump of Mott nor the Hunter–Ronson Band had made much of an impact. The situation with the other strand of the London SS's influence, Sixties punk rock, was equally unhealthy: the MC5 were long gone, the Flamin' Groovies did not have a secure recording contract and the Stooges had disintegrated early in 1974.

Luckily, the torch that these bands had set alight had been handed on to a new generation of New York bands, most of them regulars at a dingy club in the Bowery called CBGB's. They included the Patti Smith Group, Television, the Ramones and the Heartbreakers, the last of these being a band formed by ex-Television member Richard Hell, Johnny Thunders and fellow ex-Doll Jerry Nolan. None of the New York new wave bands sounded alike, but what they had in common was a no frills approach to raw rock'n'roll. Whether their hair was long or short, whether they wore ripped jeans, leather jackets and sneakers like the Ramones or torn T-shirts and cheap sunglasses like Richard Hell, the style of the New York bands was similarly back to basics.

Although next to nothing of this musical revolution had been captured on record during 1975, Bernie was full of it - thanks largely to the McLaren connection – and Mick had been following its development in his imported American magazines. The CBGB's summer festival of unsigned bands was also covered in both the *NME* and *Melody Maker*, and on 8 November, Charles Shaar Murray wrote a piece about the scene for the former paper entitled 'Are You Alive To The Jive Of The Sound Of '75?' Mid-December saw the release of the first fruits of the New York new wave, Patti Smith's instant classic, *Horses*. Mick and Tony approved of the musical trend, but – for a few more months – still preferred to hold on to the glam look of yesteryear.

The 25 October issue of *Melody Maker* carried a display ad for a 'YOUNG STOOGE VOCALIST' accompanied by a plain Musicians Wanted ad for a 'DRUMMER – YOUNG skinny psychopath'. In the issue of 1 November the request for a mentally disturbed percussionist was repeated, but a more populist appeal was made for a frontman: 'YOUNG JAGGER VOCALIST, VISCOUS [*sic*] skinny rock and roller wanted.' Two weeks later, a singer was no longer required, but the need for a drummer had grown urgent enough to warrant dropping the insanity qualification and investing in a display ad: 'THIN YOUNG DRUMMER REQUIRED – INTO Loud Punk Rock, MC5/DOLLS.' The last ad gave up on insider-speak, and took an altogether more formal approach: 'Wild young drummer wanted. Must be aware of current New York scene and MC5 thru to the Stooges. New energetic kids, 18–22, rather than seasoned pros with fixed ideals, although obviously ability essential. Immediate rehearsals based in central London. Must be dedicated and look great in the above terms.'

The frequency and number of the ads might suggest a lack of response, but in fact, the London SS found themselves deluged with replies. After an initial telephone vetting by Bernie, the band met hopefuls in the Paddington Kitchen, which had a jukebox loaded with London SS-approved singles. They then took them downstairs to the basement rehearsal room. Some of those put through their paces simply didn't have the ability. Most shared too few of the same influences and reference points, and either looked upon auditioning as a recreational pastime in its own right or just wanted to be in a group, any group. Even more disturbingly for aesthetes Mick and Tony, several candidates had facial hair, poor dress sense, receding hairlines and/or weight problems. 'I've never really been able to envisage rock musicians as anything but flash dressers,' an unrepentant Tony was still proclaiming to Nick Kent over three years later. 'It's always been an integral part of it for me . . . I could never imagine myself being in a group with some *fat* guy.'

A rabid Dolls and Mott fan and would-be singer called Steven Morrissey contacted Mick and started a brief correspondence, but as he was based in Manchester, it was not possible for him to contribute in a more practical way. Years later, he would team up with a young guitarist named Johnny Marr to form the Smiths. Pushed in front of the microphone for the first time ever, a visiting Paul Simonon was deemed to have the looks but not the presence to be a vocalist. Terry Chimes tried out as drummer, and thought he was in with a good chance, but was not called back. Nick Headon was offered the job, took it, but left after a week . . . Unfortunately, of the few that had the requisite ability, musical tastes, attitude and decadent appearance to join a Dolls-style band, several also had the *de rigueur* self-destructive bent. A 'fantastic' guitar player named George who looked a little like Ronnie Wood could have made room for himself in the line-up, but, according to Tony, 'he had no guitar and no amp. All he did was snort coke all day long.' Andy was 'the best drummer we'd heard in our lives. We offered him the job, but he felt he couldn't accept it as he had a pretty serious drug problem.' Even Roland Hot, who stayed behind the drum kit longer than most – 'probably because he had a leather jacket' – was deemed unsatisfactory because he 'used to get pissed a lot'.

It was Roland who accompanied the three official members of the band on the rough 'live in the rehearsal room' demo tapes recorded on Mick's reel-to-reel towards the end of the London SS's life, by which time they had given up the search for a singer – temporarily at least – and had Mick doing most of the vocals. 'And you ought to hear the music on those tapes!' Tony told Pete Frame in 1977. 'It drives like fuck. Raw rock'n'roll: it's really great!' Although bootlegs circulated during punk's heyday, they no longer seem to be available, thus denying the rest of the world the opportunity to judge for themselves. Tony, however, revealed that the band's repertoire included the hardy perennial 'Slow Death', the Strangeloves' 'Night Time' and the MC5's 'Ramblin' Rose'.

Shared influences also showed through in the sex and drugs pre-occupations of the trio's own compositions. Brian's were the most like the Stooges and the MC5, as is evidenced by his later contributions to the Damned's début album, *Damned, Damned, Damned.* That album also features 'Fish', a version of a London SS song he co-wrote with Tony as 'Portobello Reds'. Mick's songs betrayed his affection for the entire rock'n'roll tradition. They relied upon the conventional lyrical and structural devices, and took the vagaries of human relationships as their subjects, but like the best work of Mick's heroes, they always included some sort of thorn beneath the rose. The titles provide some idea of the songs' content: 'Ooh, Baby, Ooh (It's Not Over)', 'I'm So Bored With You' and 'Protex Blue'. The last of these was inspired by and named after the brand of contraceptives available from the machine in the toilets of the Windsor Castle music pub on the Harrow Road, just round the corner from Wilmcote House.

Mostly, though, night after night and week after week was devoted to jamming and trying out potential fourth members. Perhaps the quintessential London SS auditioning experience was enjoyed by a certain Chris Miller. In December 1975, Chris was based in Caterham, 20 miles south of London. For the previous six months, he had drummed for a would-be progressive band named Tor. A fan of the Who and Dr Feelgood, the ebullient Chris was less than happy with the 'arty-farty' music of the band he preferred to think of as Rot, and had long been attending auditions for other bands. At first, this had been with the genuine hope of finding some more sympathetic partners. Latterly, with such hopes dashed, it had been for the sheer anarchic joy of celebrating his incongruity. 'My favourite was a *Melody Maker* small ad for a jazz-funk-rock group who were after "a drummer with taste",' he told Pete Frame in 1977. 'So I went along and smashed the drums as hard as I could. Then I farted, belched, and waited for them to tell me to piss off. Which they did.'

Having monitored the London SS ads since October, Chris finally decided to respond to the 6 December one. Of his initial telephone conversation with Bernie, he says, 'That was pretty stormy. I knew they were obviously looking for somebody different, just because the ad had been running for so long. It was obvious that the run-of-the-mill approach wasn't the right one. Bernie was asking me what I knew about the New York scene, and I just said, "I live in the sticks, how on earth am I supposed to know what's going on in New York?" And we got into this, "Well, why did you bother to answer the advert, then?" "Because I knew you were looking for somebody special." And that kind of did it, because he said, "You obviously think you're really good", and I said, "Well, yeah." It was a bit of a showdown on the phone, but as soon as I'd copped some attitude, he gave me an address to go down and meet them in Praed Street.'

As was customary, he rendezvoused with the others in the Paddington Kitchen. 'We sat around and talked about what bands we were into. I liked the MC5 and stuff, and I knew the Stooges, so it was kind of like, "You got through part one." Then there was visual image . . .' As Chris was less than svelte, and not only had freckles, a large nose and unkempt sandy red hair, but was also attired in scruffy flared denims, his 'visual image' rating was not high. All the same, he was taken down to the rehearsal room. 'It was just this horrible old basement with this old drum kit in it, and these great big stacks. It was kind of, "Well, here you are: impress us." They were obviously so bored with trying people out they had a TV down there that they were watching while we were playing, which was really sensitive!'

As all those present knew all too well, auditioning was always a fairly brittle process, involving much ego-bruising and one-upmanship. Having quickly assessed the situation, Chris laid into the kit with even more than his usual ferocity. 'It was just one of those things where to get their attention, you had to be really aggressive.' Like the others, Brian had been devoting most of his attention to the war movie showing on the TV, but his interest picked up immediately. He and the drummer started to play off each other and show off their repertoire of tricks. At one point, Brian impressed Chris by soundtracking one of the movie's aeroplane dog fights with a screeching noise guitar solo.

Between songs, Chris was forced to down sticks and scratch himself energetically. Asked why, he admitted to having the contagious skin disease scabies, which prompted Bernie to run around covering the seats with newspaper. Despite this, it was decided that Chris was at least worth a second audition, this time on his own kit. Later that evening, after a visit to the pub, Mick and Tony returned to the rehearsal room. A mouse ran out across the basement floor, and, as one of them picked up a brick to kill it, Tony remarked on the rodent's startling resemblance to the recently departed drummer. When he next saw the band, a couple of days later, Chris found he had a new name: Rat Scabies.

'We played quite a few times,' says Rat. 'They came and picked up my kit, from Caterham, underneath this antique shop. I remember Mick was wearing parallel jeans instead of flares. It was, "Oh, wow, what are *they*?" We bundled the stuff into Bernie's old Renault, and we drove back and played some more.' One of the songs he remembers rehearsing was the Stones' 'You Can't Always Get What You Want'. After about a week, Mick, Tony and Bernie decided that Rat didn't have the right appearance after all, and Brian finally lost patience. He had never approved of Bernie's involvement – 'I was quite suspicious of him, to tell you the truth' – and after two months of trying out countless hopeless cases, he was disgusted that Mick and Tony had rejected what he considered to be the most exciting candidate thus far. 'It was all getting a little bit too much about looking for people who looked right, you know what I mean? I don't give a fuck what people look like as long as they can play!'

Just before Christmas, he informed the others that he was leaving, with the intention of getting a band together with Rat. Some of his irritation – exacerbated by the punk movement's then current trend for inter-band bitching – was still evident in the explanation he offered Pete Frame for the split some 18 months later: 'Mick and Tony are basically girls, and Rat and I wanted to play man's music.'

'In January 1976, Mick and I decided to call it a day,' Tony told Pete. 'It was back to the two of us after nine months of getting nowhere.' Although the duo remained close friends, and went on to share flats together, it seems that Tony did not have quite as much say in the dissolution of the partnership as he suggested. In the 1991 *Clash On Broadway* booklet Mick revealed that Bernie, presumably still intent on joining forces with Malcolm, brought the Pistols' manager down to Praed Street to watch the band rehearse. Malcolm's dismissal of what he saw might have been dubiously motivated, but it convinced Bernie that the London SS were not going to happen. (His claim to have already decided to scrap the band by then, also made in the booklet, is not particularly convincing.)

Thus, from Bernie's point of view, Rat and Brian's defection was a blessing in disguise, as it made winding up the London SS that much simpler a task. For Mick, it was the third time he had been rejected by a band he had been instrumental in forming, and, understandably, he took it less well. Dispirited, he offered no resistance to the termination of his partnership with Tony, in which he was the dominant figure, and instead formed another with Bernie in which he relied increasingly heavily on the older man's judgement. 'Bernie seemed to know more than me about what we were going to do,' he told Kosmo Vinyl for the *Clash On Broadway* booklet. 'Sometimes in the early days I lost heart, but he always saw a way through.' The basement rehearsal space was let go. Tony began attending auditions himself, including one for the Boys. Later in the year, he joined Gene October's Chelsea, before decamping with guitarist Billy Idol to form Generation X. He was still keeping true to the London SS's ideals in the mid-Eighties, when he launched his '5th Generation' futuristic trash glam rock'n'roll band, Sigue Sigue Sputnik.

Ironically, it was during this down and directionless period – immediately prior to or closely following the dissolution of the London SS – that Mick made his only post-Delinquents, pre-Clash live appearance. Even more ironically, it was thanks to the newly rechristened Steve Dior, who, in an attempt to kick-start his own career, arranged a one-off gig at Chiswick Polytechnic, Bath Road. In a way that was typical of the Warrington Crescent scene, the rest of the band was made up of whoever happened to be around the flat at the time. The songs rehearsed were all covers by the likes of the New York Dolls and Hollywood Brats, and Steve cheekily billed the concert under the latter name. As everyone who was not part of the fake Brats went along to watch, there is some confusion about who exactly took the stage, but Steve certainly sang, John Brown claims he played bass, Honest John Plain says that he played drums and, in view of his later partnership with Steve, it seems likely that Barry Jones was one of the guitarists. Everyone is agreed that Mick was the other one. 'I definitely remember Mick,' says Honest John. 'He had hair down to his waist, and black and white striped trousers: well MC5!'

It was that night at the poly that Mick met Glen Matlock again. Unaware that Celia Perry was – nominally, at least - going out with Barry, Glen had made a tentative date to meet her there. He arrived too late to see the band, but he, Celia, Mick and another girl decided to go on somewhere else in an ultimately fruitless search for after-hours fun. Thereafter, Celia and Glen began seeing one another (they eventually married) and Glen and Mick became good friends, both of which relationships helped bring the Warrington Crescent and Sex Pistols camps into the same orbit. Glen started accompanying Mick and various of the others on their ceaseless gig-going expeditions to places like the Royal College of Art in Kensington. 'We'd have nothing to do afterwards,' recalls Glen, 'and I'd say, "Let's go back and have a jam", because all the gear was set up. So people would come back.' Thus, the Pistols' rehearsal room in Denmark Street became another occasional haunt.

The Sex Pistols had followed up their first gig with a series of largely unannounced college gigs in and around the London area. By the end of 1975, the ever-ambitious Malcolm McLaren was harbouring fantasies of setting himself up as a latter-day Larry Parnes, the early Sixties manager who had run a stable of British rock'n'rollers including Billy Fury and Marty

Wilde. The end of the London SS was a godsend as far as he was concerned, releasing as it did a few more unattached musicians on to the market. Sniffing a way to resume working in cahoots with Malcolm, Bernie did not protest when his former associate attempted to poach his protégé. Nor did Mick object, having by this time had his first live exposure to the Pistols at a mutual friend's party. Reminiscing for an *NME* 'best gig ever seen' feature in 1994, he said, 'This was the most important. All kinds of things were going through my head; it was amazing. I basically felt like I'd seen the shape of things to come. Which I had.'

'There was this thing where Richard Hell was writing to Malcolm saying, "Honest, I'm not a junkie. I really want to come over to London,"' Mick told Nick Kent in 1978. 'So I was in line for that. Meanwhile, Malcolm or Bernie would be planning some new group or other, and I'd be sent over to some rehearsal. There was this pool of musicians that they'd have on tap, expecting us to form bands ultimately.' Others in the pool included Rat Scabies, biding time until he could begin rehearsals with Brian James, and Chrissie Hynde, former Sex shop assistant, *NME* journalist and girlfriend of Nick Kent, who returned from Paris to London in January 1976. Malcolm initially suggested that Chrissie team up with Nick Kent and Rat to form a band. After some consideration, Chrissie decided her history with Nick would make this too painful. There followed some talk of building a group around her to be known as the Love Boys, with Mick on guitar, but again, nothing came of it. Malcolm then put Rat and Chrissie together in a short-lived, deliberately ludicrous outfit known as Masters of the Backside. Chrissie played guitar, Rat's friend Ray Burns played bass and vocal duties were shared between Daves Zero and White. Rat and Ray were natural extroverts, Dave Zero – a gravedigger from Hemel Hempstead - liked to model himself on Dracula and Chrissie was supposed to dress as a boy to contrast with the effeminate mannerisms of the screamingly camp Dave White. Unfortunately, the predictable result was that nobody could take the venture remotely seriously, least of all Malcolm.

From the ashes of this quickly aborted outfit grew one of the first bona fide punk groups to follow the Pistols: after a brief season drumming for a Caterham pantomime production of *Puss In Boots*, Rat got back together with Brian James, Ray Burns – later to be known as Captain Sensible – and Dave Zero, who had already rechristened himself Dave Vanian. True to the band's origin in the London SS, they stuck with the 'Nazi decadence' theme, and named themselves after Visconti's film *The Damned*. (Interestingly, the name had previously been considered by Malcolm for the fledgling Sex Pistols.) Rat and Brian finally got to play their 'man's music' with a singer seldom seen out of make-up and a bassist with a penchant for taking the stage in a tutu.

When the Sex Pistols began to take off in February 1976, demanding more of Malcolm's attention, Bernie took over his mix'n'match policy and suggested that Mick and Chrissie form a band called Big Girl's Underwear.

The very name of this proposed outfit betrays just how much Bernie was still in thrall to Malcolm, and that he was willing to go along with the idea gives some indication of the blind faith Mick was by now showing in Bernie. Chrissie, however, although she was prepared to tolerate a certain amount of high-concept self-indulgence from Malcolm, was something of a rock'n'roll purist at heart. She was not prepared to play the fool at the bidding of a man she, like many others at the time, considered to be McLaren's pale shadow.

In October 1980, Chrissie told the *NME*'s Chris Salewicz that when she first met Mick, he was calling himself Brady, just Brady. 'But when I found out his real name was Mick Jones, I said, "What are you playing at? Mick Jones is a fantastic rock'n'roll name."' This interview was later used as the basis for Chris's 1982 book, *The Pretenders*, and established the Fake Brady Story as part of the Mick Jones myth. The most obvious explanation for it would be confusion of the two guitarists on Chrissie's part, but the real Brady insists that he never met her, which would seem to suggest that Mick adopted Brady's name for a brief spell. Having read *The Pretenders*, both Brady and Andrew Matheson are aware of the supposed impersonation. 'Verified and corroborated by many spiky, dyed-black-hair types over the years,' writes Andrew. 'I view this as not a black mark against Mick's character, but rather as further indication that the man had admirable large, clanking brass cojones during this period. Good for him.'

Although Andrew chooses to see Mick's adoption of the name as purely cynical, there are other possible interpretations. It was Brady who had rendered Mick obsolete in Little Queenie/Violent Luck. Following his outburst to Kelvin, when he vowed to become 'a better guitarist than Brady', Mick had tried to form a band with two ex-members of the Brats, in which he would have effectively taken over Brady's former role. (And, according to Andrew, he had by this time even taken to emulating Brady's playing style.) Mick had then performed a gig with a band attempting to pass itself off as the Hollywood Brats, in which he had again 'portrayed' Brady. If one chose to, one could construe this as being indicative of hero worship turned to identity crisis; obsession gone awry. Brady's own reaction to the impersonation – half flattered, half embarrassed – suggests that he for one holds this view.

The interpretation no one seems to have considered is both far less disturbing and far more likely. Calling the Chiswick Polytechnic band the Hollywood Brats was a Steve Dior in-joke, and calling himself Brady was a similar gesture by Mick Jones. It stuck as a Warrington Crescent scene nickname for a brief period, which happened to coincide with the time Chrissie first met Mick. Being unaware of both the real Brady's existence and the in-joke's origins, Chrissie was taken in by it.

While few of them are mentioned in the numerous accounts of the Sex Pistols' early days – punk era revisionism having dictated that long-haired, decadent types be expunged from the records – John Brown, Brady, Kelvin, Geir, Tony, Matt, Casino, Rat and Brian were all regulars at the Pistols' 1976 shows. Most of them attended the band's breakthrough gig of 12 February, supporting Eddie and the Hot Rods at the Marquee. 'We helped them move the gear on-stage,' says John. As well as representing the Pistols' graduation to club level, the Marquee gig was a key event for three other reasons. Firstly, Johnny Rotten damaged the Rods' monitors, which got the Pistols banned from the club, and set them off on the road to notoriety. Secondly, their performance won the band their first full-length live review in the *NME*, by Neil Spencer, entitled 'Don't look over your shoulder, but the Sex Pistols are coming'. It concluded with the soon to be legendary band quote 'Actually, we're not into music. We're into chaos', thus making the Pistols sound like the hottest ticket in town for anyone who preferred rock'n'roll to come spiced with a little danger.

Thirdly, the spectacle of the show combined with the subsequent music press reaction to it put a rocket up the collective backside of the audience. Although it was only a couple of dozen strong – in addition to the Warrington Crescent crowd, it was made up of former and current Sex sales assistants, Johnny Rotten's friends, a few Bowie and Roxy Music-cum-*Rocky Horror Show* types from Bromley (who shortly after became known as the Bromley Contingent) and one or two curious passers-by – that audience quickly realised the future was there for the taking. Together, the couple of dozen went on to form the bulk of the groups that turned punk from a one-band scene into a movement, so adding considerable weight to the challenge presented by the Sex Pistols. Even those who had not seriously contemplated the possibility of becoming performers were inspired to do so. People like Mick and Chrissie, both present, who had already been scratching around for a couple of years trying to get bands together, started to feel a renewed sense of urgency: a desire to be part of something vital and exciting, coupled with panic at the possibility of missing the boat.

A native of Akron, Ohio, Chrissie, just under four years older than Mick, had developed a similarly passionate love affair with the pop music of the mid-Sixties, especially Stax soul and the UK beat groups. Like Mick, she had a particular fondness for the Kinks; in fact, the development of her tastes roughly paralleled Mick's throughout the remainder of the Sixties and early Seventies, her favoured artists also including the Rolling Stones, heavy blues bands like Jeff Beck's, and punk outfits like Iggy and the Stooges. In 1973, the Anglophile Chrissie moved to London where she soon fell in with the World's Most Elegantly Wasted Rock Journalist, Nick Kent, another one of the country's extremely limited number of Stooges fans. It wasn't long before Chrissie's opinionated views on rock'n'roll, invariably expressed at top volume, secured her a job with the *NME*. From January 1974, she wrote reviews in a casual, yet scathingly witty, style which set something of a trend for the future 'hip young gunslingers' of punk journalism.

Out of step at the time, however, and increasingly bored by the kind of music she was being asked to write about, Chrissie left the paper in April 1974. Having developed a penchant for rubber miniskirts and other *outré* clothing, she went to work at Sex for a few months, during which period she became friends with Vivienne and Malcolm and got to know members of the Sex Pistols. A falling out with Nick prompted her to take an extended leave of absence – sandwiching a return visit to Akron between two lengthy stays in Paris, where she rehearsed and played with a variety of bands - and she arrived back in London just as the punk scene was beginning to get under way.

After all the talk of Love Boys and Big Girl's Underwear, it seemed fate was intent on pushing Mick and Chrissie together, so – almost despite the scheming of Malcolm and Bernie – they did form an uneasy sort of musical alliance following the Pistols' Marquee gig. It lasted, on and off, until April 1976. As Mick no longer had a proper rehearsal room of his own at his disposal and Chrissie didn't even have a fixed abode, the only opportunities to play as anything like a band occurred when both parties happened to be in the vicinity of the Pistols' Denmark Street rehearsal room. Glen remembers working up a song of Chrissie's entitled 'Get On Your Hynde Legs, Baby' that was strongly reminiscent of the Kinks' 'Sittin' On Your Sofa'. 'Chrissie was singing, Mick was playing guitar, I played bass and Steve Jones played drums. It was pretty good.' More often, though, Mick and Chrissie would get together in Mick's room at Wilmcote House to play and sing as a duo. With Stella ever on hand with the tea pot, they would work through such mutual favourites as the Kinks' 'I'm Not Like Anybody Else' and the Spencer Davis Group's 'Every Little Bit Hurts'. (The latter was written by Ed Cobb, who had also furnished the Standells with their more memorable songs.)

In spite of their many shared influences, their own compositions did not have much in common. Some of Chrissie's songs were tender soul ballads, but most were feisty rockers, often in idiosyncratic timings, with lyrics largely inspired by the junkie and biker subcultures she had encountered during her nomadic wanderings around London and the wider world. She remembers Mick's creations, by contrast, as 'rather dippy love songs'. The two of them continued to write separately, though Chrissie claims she changed a few lines of the lyric to 'Protex Blue' and Mick admits she helped him come up with the 'What a liar!' coda to a new song called 'Deny'.

Their differing writing styles were not the only obstacles to any long-term collaboration. Although mouthy, Chrissie was shy, and reluctant to perform on-stage, a problem that was exacerbated by her worries about living up to the harsh judgements she had handed out to others while with the *NME*. Having seen a bit of the world in her 24 years, she also felt keenly the age gap between herself and the relatively naïve 20-year-old Mick, as evidenced by her affectionate, but somewhat patronising, description of him as a 'really great kid'. Affecting a tough, leather-clad momma style herself, she also objected to his 'long hair and skinny, faggy little jackets'.

She decided to give him an image make-over. Round at Wilmcote House one day, under the pretext of trimming some split ends, she set about his lengthy Ian Hunter-like tresses with a pair of scissors and a vengeance. 'He was standing up, so it was hard for him to see what I was doing. But eventually, he started to see how all over him were these pieces of hair about four or five inches long,' she told Chris Salewicz. 'I can still remember how he reacted when he realised what I was doing. He clutched his stomach and was groaning, "*Oooooooh.* I've got to sit down. I've got butterflies . . ."' Later that night, Mick and Steve Dior went along to a Royal College of Art gig, a review of which appeared in one of the following week's music papers. 'It described how, in the front row, there was this perfect Keith Richards lookalike. So everything was all right after that.'

Not quite. From Mick's point of view, despite his penchant for dressing like a girl, forming a band with a bona fide female was a less than ideal proposition. Both Chrissie and Viv Albertine – by this time his girlfriend – testify that Mick was surprisingly sensitive and considerate for a mid-Seventies rock'n'roll guitarist, but the fact remained that rock was still a man's, man's, man's world. While his desire to emulate the debauched archetype consistently lost out to his inherent sense of decency, Mick had a very traditional idea of what a band should be: namely, a gang of guys dividing their time between playing, posing, doing drugs, pulling chicks, driving fast cars and indulging in miscellaneous other male bonding rituals. It was going to take a lot more than Patti Smith's *Horses* to change that mentality.

In the end, it was the Bernie factor that brought Mick and Chrissie's partnership to an end. Bernie might have lost the plot a little with his suggestion for Big Girl's Underwear, but the Sex Pistols' impact in the first four months of 1976 helped him regain it. He persevered with the notion of an underlying concept, but decided it should be provocative in a rebellious manner, rather than a smutty one. Initial criteria were the Look, Youth and Attitude. Chrissie had a cool rock'n'roll image, but, compared with the Pistols and Mick, was an old-timer. And although she had plenty of attitude, it didn't fit in with Bernie's: as she had already proved, she simply wasn't malleable enough to capitulate to his grand designs. Even while Mick was still rehearsing with her, Bernie was pushing his charge into forging new liaisons – with Paul Simonon and Keith Levene, among others – which were ultimately to squeeze Chrissie out of the picture.

Within a year, she was having to come to terms with having missed out on being in both the Damned and the Clash, who by then were enjoying coverage in the music press second only to the Pistols themselves. 'I wanted to be in a band so *bad*,' she told *Rolling Stone*'s Kurt Loder in 1980. 'All the people I knew in town were in bands. And there I was, the real loser.' By the time she gave that interview, however, she had bettered anything either the Damned or the Clash had so far achieved – in commercial terms, at least – by making it to number one in both the UK singles and albums charts with her own group, the Pretenders. Their eponymous début album included a Kinks cover version and several of the Hynde originals she and Mick had sung together, including an S&M biker song entitled 'Tattooed Love Boys'.

Having finally arrived, Chrissie could afford to look back with affection on time spent with Mick in Wilmcote House. 'His granny was starting to get a bit worried about him and his obsession with rock'n'roll, but I used to say to her, "Don't worry, he's great. He's really talented. He's going to make it . . ."'

3... JOHNNY TOO BAD

'**I** was the dark horse of the Clash,' Paul Simonon told *Melody Maker*'s Caroline Sullivan in October 1989. 'If anybody'd ever said to me, in an interview, "What do you do with your spare time?" maybe I'd have turned around and given them a big art lecture. But I think they thought I was an idiot.' A dumb blond? 'Something like that. A thicko from south London.'

On 6 August 1955, Gustave Antoine Simonon, of 94 Idmiston Road, West Norwood, married Elaine Florence Braithwaite of 1 Beulah Crescent in neighbouring Thornton Heath. He was a 20-year-old soldier, Private 22819801 in the Buffs Regiment; she was a 19-year-old librarian. Other available facts and figures go some way to explaining why they married at such a relatively early age: the venue for the wedding ceremony was Streatham's Church of the English Martyrs, a Roman Catholic place of worship; and Elaine was five months pregnant at the time. He preferred to call himself Antony, but Elaine's new husband celebrated his family's Gallic lineage by passing on the name Gustave to his son, as had his father and grandfather before him. Paul Gustave Simonon was born on 15 December 1955 at his mother's home in Beulah Crescent, three miles south of the Brixton he claims as his place of birth.

Before long, the young family moved even further away. Paul's brother, Nicholas Antony was born on 2 October 1959 at the Simonons' home at 3 George Street in Ramsgate, a Kentish coastal town 70 miles east of London. By the time of Paul's birth, his father had already completed his army service and taken a job as an insurance agent. By the time of Nick's, he had switched to a line of work more closely aligned to his wife's: running a book shop. Unfortunately, the arrival of another child did not make the marriage any more secure, and within another four years it was over; Paul's parents finally split up when he, like Mick Jones, was eight. Before the impasse was reached, however, the Simonons had moved back to south London.

Selling books was not the full extent of Antony's interest in the creative world, though Paul did not reveal this information until long after the Clash had split. 'Me dad used to paint a lot, and he'd leave them in my room to dry,' he told Caroline Sullivan. 'I'd be like all kids, trying to copy my dad, so I'd try and draw them.' In 1978, while still with the band, he told the *NME*'s

Chris Salewicz he owed his interest in painting to the fact that his father was always looking for some place to 'dump him' for a few days. Apparently, on one of these occasions, he was sent out to East Acton to stay with one of Antony's artist friends, who had a coffee-table book featuring the work of Henri Matisse. When his dad's friend was out of the room, Paul opened the book, and tried to copy the paintings in pencil. His confusion with artistic media was to last for some time. 'I used to try and copy Turner with water colours,' he said, while examining the Tate Gallery's collection of the landscape artist's work in 1989, 'but I could never get the same effect. I didn't know he used oils!'

When Antony and Elaine decided to go their separate ways, Paul and Nick stayed with their mother in the Brixton area. Paul attended Effra Primary School, on Barnwell Road, just off what was then the notorious Front Line, Railton Road. Much later, he found out Robin Crocker had been one of his slightly older co-pupils. Whereas Robin went on to cross paths with Mick Jones in the comparatively safe haven of Strand School, however, the next step on the educational ladder for Paul was one of Brixton's overcrowded comprehensives. In 1976, he told Caroline Coon that the school was 90 per cent black, much like those abutting Mick and Robin's grammar school. In an ideal world this figure would be irrelevant; what makes it worth noting is that the black population of the UK's inner cities has always been the most poorly served by the country's educational system.

Overcrowding and the other environmental pressures set such schools off to a poor start. The statistically proven fact that – due to prejudice as much as the state of the local economy – even blacks with equivalent qualifications were less likely than whites to be offered an opportunity to use them in a constructive manner quite understandably encouraged apathy towards education itself and resentment towards authority. Teachers bore the initial brunt of both, and so were less keen to work in such a depressing, sometimes threatening milieu. Which in turn meant that such schools could not always attract the more talented of their number. Even those individuals who felt they had something to offer, and took their posts for altruistic reasons, had to be extraordinarily committed, talented and charismatic to be able to make an impression. The result was a self-perpetuating downward spiral that, by the early Seventies, had resulted in what one contemporary Brixton headmaster summed up as 'an urban crisis of violence, truancy and maladjustment'.

An inner city secondary school that was 90 per cent black was not going to offer much in the way of opportunity to any but the most gifted and determined of its pupils, whatever their colour. 'All you done is played about and pissed on the teachers and that,' Paul told Caroline Coon in November 1976. 'There were 45 in our class, and we had a Pakistani teacher who didn't even speak English.' As he reached his teens, Paul got caught up in the working class skinhead youth cult, and hung around with a gang of friends who devoted their time to miscellaneous acts of mischief and vandalism.

The skinhead, or skin for short, emerged in the late Sixties as a more brutal and ascetic version of the early Sixties mod. There was as much obsessive attention to stylistic detail, but all hints of effete dandyism were rejected. The mod's hair had been short, but French-cut and styled; the skin's was either cropped to stubble or completely shaved. The mod had started out wearing tight Italian suits and gradually progressed to outlandish Regency ruffles and flares; the skin stuck to a basic uniform of highly polished DM boots, rolled Levi's jeans or tight Sta-Press trousers held up with thin, clip-on braces and plain T-shirts or button-down Ben Shermans worn under Harrington jackets or Crombie overcoats. Everything about the skinhead look was macho and uncompromising. While mid-period mods adopted the Union Jack as a Pop-Art symbol or celebration of Swinging London, they still prided themselves on their cosmopolitan tastes. Skins, however, used the flag to signal a confused patriotism that made many of their number easy pickings for the growing UK fascist movement, the National Front.

While hippies – their despised diametric opposites – were sitting in fields lauding the arrival of the Age of Aquarius and loving their fellow man, many skins were living in inner city council estates, absorbing the initial impact of the collapse of the Sixties dream and looking around for ways to vent their ill-focused dissatisfaction and frustration. Vandalism was one. Another was aggressive behaviour towards selected scapegoats, anyone alien to mainstream society or the skins' own subculture: hippies, supporters of rival football teams, gays, blacks and Asians. Not all skins were violent, homophobic or racist, by any means, but sufficient of their number were to shape history's view of the cult. Once extreme right-wing rhetoric was fed into the equation, unprovoked attacks on non-whites became commonplace, and Paki-bashing in particular was soon established as the skinhead's favourite recreational activity.

Racist skinheads displayed an almost incredible capacity for double-think: their preferred genre of music was ska – songs documenting life in Jamaica, written, performed and recorded by black Jamaicans – which was available to them only because of the immigrant West Indian communities in areas like Brixton and Notting Hill; and one theory even has it that the skinhead's very style was based on the cropped hair, big boots and rolled pants of the poor New World Negro agricultural worker.

Despite the near-the-knuckle comment about his Pakistani teacher, Paul was definitely not remotely racist in outlook by the time he met Mick Jones and helped form the Clash, and he denies that he was ever involved in any racially motivated unpleasantness. In 1978, he told Chris Salewicz that he had never gone Paki-bashing, and although he admitted to stealing from shops owned or run by Pakistanis, he claimed this was due more to demographics than design. Nor did he pick fights with blacks. 'When I was at school in south London I used to always want to be mates with the hardest kids in school,' he said. 'So I could get to figure 'em out. And most of those guys tended to be black.' Not the most 'right on' of remarks, maybe, but, if anything, all the more convincing for that. Certainly, Paul was not so disingenuous as to pretend race was never an issue for him while growing up. Discussing the song '(White Man) In Hammersmith Palais' in a 1988 *Melody Maker* retrospective marking the release of the compilation album *The Story Of The Clash, Volume 1*, he said it reminded him of 'Going to blues [i.e. Jamaican-style sound system] parties and being the only white boy there. When I was a kid, I wasn't so afraid of that, it's when I got to be a teenager that the feeling about race got to be a lot more powerful.'

Almost inevitably, Paul became involved with soccer violence. 'I used to go around to football matches with me mates from the street and be a nuisance,' he told *Creem*'s Stephen Demorest in May 1979. 'I remember once we'd just come from a football match and about 60 skinheads crossed over to where we was. We were skinheads as well, but we crossed over to the other side, and they crossed over again, and we ended up running down this road with them chasing us. In some ways, it's what "Last Gang In Town" is about. Stupid.'

It is not surprising that Paul's friendships at that time were motivated less by genuine liking than by expediency. Joining a gang could offer kicks and camaraderie, but it also appealed to the survival instinct: better to be part of something than an outsider and potential victim. In spite of gangs' supposedly rigid codes of honour, friendships developed within their confines tend to be flimsy and seldom encourage the development of true loyalty, as a casual remark made by Paul to *Melody Maker*'s Allan Jones in November 1978 would seem to illustrate: 'Friends turn against you quicker than anyone. Like at school, it's always your best mates that turn against you. You don't think anything of it. You just have to turn the other way and get on with what you're doing.' The nature of the friendships he had in his early teens helps to explain why the Clash era Paul Simonon appeared so self-reliant and yet - apparently paradoxically – was at his most open and outgoing when surrounded by the band's established entourage.

Living and attending school where he did, it was impossible for Paul not to have been exposed to ska, but his original allegiance to the music came as part of the cult experience: it was the soundtrack to nights spent at popular skin stomping ground, the Locarno on Streatham Hill. The attraction of the Locarno had as much to do with posing and fighting as music and dancing. Inevitably, the club got such a bad reputation for teenage violence that it closed in 1970, while Mecca gave it an overhaul prior to reopening it as the more adult-oriented Cat's Whiskers.

Ska had developed out of Jamaica's blues dances in the early Sixties, when rival sound system operators began to cut their own discs rather than compete to be the first to play blues and soul records imported from the US. Kingston was considerably tougher than Streatham, and there too the argy-bargy between the followers of the different sound systems did little to dispel the underlying threat of violence. Local hooligans dressed as sharply as the early UK mods, in tight suits and pork pie hats, and were known as rude boys, or rudies for short. The music caught on to a certain extent with the mods on the early Sixties London club scene, notably at the Flamingo in Wardour Street. It was not until 1967, however, when it was adopted by skinheads – who found its energetic, jerky rhythms perfect for stomping around in their DMs – that it began to make more than a token commercial impact in the UK. Some records were even tailored to this new market, such as Simaryp's 1970 single 'Skinhead Moonstomp'. By this time, back in Jamaica, ska had already slowed down and been rechristened rocksteady, though the terminology remained flexible for some time. Paul developed a genuine and abiding affection for the music, following it through its various changes over the coming years, but in the Clash's first ever interview with *Sniffin' Glue*'s Steve Walsh in September 1976 he was still citing the likes of the Ethiopians and the Rulers as his favourite artists.

When he was still in his early teens, he and his brother, Nick, went to live with their father in Notting Hill. They shared a room in what Paul, without ever being more specific, has implied was, like Mick's home, a flat in a high-rise block. The explanation Paul gave Caroline Coon in 1976 suggested that he chose to leave his mother: 'I felt it was getting a bit soft with her. I could do whatever I liked, and I wasn't getting anywhere, so I went to stay with my dad.' Reading between the lines, it is far more likely that the move came about because Elaine was finding it increasingly difficult to control the boys, especially her juvenile delinquent elder son.

Certainly, to hear Paul tell it, the regime at his father's was strict enough to qualify as punishment for crimes past, or at the very least to indicate the conscious deployment of a firm guiding hand. 'It was good training because I had to do all the launderette and that,' he told Caroline. 'In a way, I worked for him, getting money together.' One source of income was a Saturday job on Portobello Market. 'It used to get so cold in winter you had to stand with your feet in cardboard boxes.' The fullest account of his youthful labours appears in *The Clash Songbook*, edited by Paul and Mick Jones in 1977 and published the following year. Paul claimed he had to get up to do a paper round at six in the morning, and then make Antony his breakfast before heading off to school. During the midday break, he had to come home and make his father's lunch. After school, he would fit in another paper round before making the tea.

The school in question was Isaac Newton in Wornington Road, in the shadow of the giant high-rise block Trellick Tower, a west London landmark that would later adorn the covers of several Big Audio Dynamite albums, including one painted by Paul. Again, this school was mostly black, and again – or so he claimed in *The Clash Songbook* – the teachers were totally inept. 'It's a real sort of depressing school,' he told Janet Street-Porter on ITV's November 1976 *London Weekend Show* punk documentary. 'You go there, you don't learn nothing. All you're working for is to go into the factory that's around the corner. And, well, most of the mates I know are working in the factory.' Just over two years later, he told *Creem*'s Stephen Demorest that even school trips were geared towards introducing pupils to the army or merchant navy.

According to anecdotes freely – even gleefully – offered to a string of interviewers, Paul continued to vent his frustrations by stealing from the market stalls, vandalising phone booths, fighting, rolling cars down hills, throwing stones through rich people's windows and dropping bricks from the landings of his high-rise block. To sum up, then: the picture Paul chose to paint in the Clash's early interviews in particular, though not exclusively, was of an unremittingly bleak, repressive home life lacking any kind of female influence; a hopeless, dead-end educational life; and a recreational life that was little more than a violent reaction to both of these.

Closer examination reveals it to be an interpretation so free it borders on the abstract. The impression Paul gives is that his father forced him to double as the family's provider and housekeeper. Although Antony's character remains shifting and vague in these accounts, he invariably comes over poorly: as a penniless loser dependent on his son, a rigorous taskmaster driven solely by the work ethic, or a tyrant intent on exploiting his own flesh and blood. In fact, Antony was considerably more sensitive and sophisticated than any of these would suggest. At this stage he was not only an artist himself, but also a qualified art teacher, and one who, as Paul himself admitted in a rare lapse of consistency, was conscientious enough to set his son homework because he wanted him to 'get on'.

By the time Paul reached his mid-teens, Antony was involved in another steady relationship. Marion Clarke was 13 years Antony's junior, and just seven years older than Paul. This in itself may have caused some tension, though Paul has never made any mention of it, but she was a schoolteacher, which suggests a certain maturity and stability. In this educated, middle class domestic environment it is not beyond the realms of possibility that Paul was expected to help with various chores and work for his own pocket money, but to accept that he was treated like a slave or required to hand over his earnings to swell the family pot stretches credibility almost as far as *Monty Python*'s famous 'Four Yorkshiremen' sketch: 'You were *lucky* . . .'

As for his school experiences, by February 1981, when he gave Chris Salewicz a rare solo interview for the *Face*, Paul was prepared to be a little less scathing. He even recalled one particular teacher who was so keen for his pupils to do well that he abandoned all pretence of professional integrity. 'He was really good, this one bloke. He told us all the answers during the exam. Most still failed, though.' For all his earlier claims not to have anything to show for his formal education, Paul also revealed to Chris that he had two O levels, in Art and English, and further undermined the general public's view of him as barely literate by instigating a discussion on the work of Graham Greene. The author's *Brighton Rock*, it transpired, had been one of the texts on the Isaac Newton O level syllabus, and Paul's own experience of teenage gangs had sharpened his interest in the machinations of central character Pinkie.

Thus, it would seem Paul was not quite such an under-privileged, unloved child of the streets as both he and the Clash Myth would have it. Admittedly, parental break-ups can have long-reaching and damaging psychological consequences, but his teenage yobbishness appears to have been more a matter of lifestyle choice than something forced upon him by circumstance.

Pinkie might have made an impression, but most of the other heroes of Paul's mid-teenage years came from the silver screen, and particularly from films – predictably enough - involving war, gangsters, guns and hard men. His curiously amoral adult interest in weaponry and violence was shaped more by early Seventies movies like *Dirty Harry* than by his own skinhead activities. He grew out of the cult and its pastimes – 'Breaking things up gets a bit boring after a while. I started going out with girls. It's more fun' – but his fascination with the instant myth-making of Hollywood proved to be an enduring one. In 1978, he told *Negative Reaction* fanzine, 'I'd like to act in films like Clint Eastwood.' When he finally bought his own flat in Notting Hill, Paul decorated the walls with various rebel posters, man-shaped shooting gallery targets, holsters and six-guns. Chris Salewicz questioned him about a replica model of a German machine pistol propped up in the corner. 'It really seems like it's meant to be held' was the not entirely successful attempt at justification. 'I just look on it as a work of art.'

The cinema was where the various strands of his teenage interests came together: stimulating visuals, macho poses, cool styles, tough action and rebellion, yes, but also humour and creative expression. During an October 1977 *Sounds* interview Giovanni Dadomo eavesdropped on a fascinating Clash discussion about contemporary cinema, in which Paul switched, without a significant change in tone, from comparing the relative authenticity of the carnage depicted in two current war films, to an appreciation of Woody Allen, to enquiring whether anyone had yet seen *Fellini's Casanova*: 'What were the settings like? That's what I'm interested in.'

Back in his late teens, one film in particular was practically guaranteed in advance to appeal to Paul. The early Seventies saw a rash of movies targeted specifically at the urban black American population. They replaced white action heroes like Clint Eastwood's Dirty Harry with black action heroes like Richard Roundtree's Shaft, thereby earning the genre title 'blaxploitation'. As dirty as Harry, Shaft is also a less uptight superstud version of James Bond. The genre's morally ambiguous portrayal of black inner city life – especially in a film like *Superfly*, where the hero is a cocaine dealer – did little to redress the balance of mainstream Hollywood films, in which urban blacks were more than likely to be depicted as junkies, dealers, muggers or pimps.

Released in the UK during 1972, Perry Henzell's *The Harder They Come* rode the blaxploitation trend, but although it was violent and its central character, Ivan, was a gun-toting outlaw fighting corruption, it ran against the genre's grain in four key respects: it was a film with a serious sociological point to make; Ivan's glamorised self-image was regularly undermined; it was shot in Kingston, Jamaica; and the score was made up not of wah-wah funk, but of the indigenous popular music, reggae. Ivan (portrayed by veteran ska vocalist Jimmy Cliff), up against both Jamaica's notorious music business and the police, was – in his own mind, at least – a latter-day rude boy version of Robin Hood or Billy the Kid. In spite of being well outside the mainstream, the film's subject and music attracted healthy audiences in the UK's predominately West Indian immigrant inner city communities, and as a cult movie it became a hardy perennial on the arthouse and independent cinema circuits.

From the late Sixties, Jamaican music had continued to develop, further slowing down the tempo and beefing up the bass until rocksteady evolved into reggae, and devoting its lyrics more and more to Rastafarianism, black self-awareness and commentary on Jamaica's increasingly volatile sociopolitical climate. *The Harder They Come* was filmed at the turn of the decade, so the songs on its soundtrack – and on the soundtrack album, released in the UK by Island – were from the cusp period. Some, like Jimmy Cliff's title track, Desmond Dekker's '007 (Shanty Town)' and the Slickers' 'Johnny Too Bad', were still largely concerned with celebrating or admonishing the rude boy; others, such as Cliff's 'Many Rivers To Cross' and 'Sitting In Limbo' and the Melodians' 'Rivers Of Babylon', dealt with the black Jamaican struggle; and the Maytals' 'Pressure Drop' made clear what it was like to be on the receiving end of the forces of oppression.

Following the film's reissue in 1977, a little punk scene mini-cult developed around it: the poster can be seen on the wall of the Slits' rehearsal room in Don Letts's *Punk Rock Movie*. The Clash's first recorded reggae cover was a version of Junior Murvin's 1976 hit 'Police And Thieves', but thanks largely to Paul's unflagging love for the film and its music – which ultimately prompted him to purchase the video and the Michael Thelwell novel as well as the soundtrack – *The Harder They Come* was the band's true point of entry into reggae culture.

Like him, the other members of the Clash bought into the myth wholesale. 'Safe European Home' namechecks the film; the band covered 'Pressure Drop'; they appeared in a film called *Rude Boy*; the line 'rudie can't fail', which occurs in both the band's song of that title and 'Safe European Home', was borrowed from '007 (Shanty Town)' (the reason rudie can't fail in so many reggae songs of the period is that he has invariably just got out of jail, and it rhymes . . .); Mick and Joe also make reference to 'Johnny Too Bad' in 'The Prisoner'; and, of course, Paul himself transplants the film's basic storyline to his original south London skinhead moonstomping ground in his 1979 songwriting début, 'Guns Of Brixton'.

Isaac Newton School has now become part of Kensington and Chelsea College, and no records of Paul's time there survive. If he completed his O level courses on schedule, he should have left school at 16, in the summer of 1972. In *The Clash Songbook* Paul stated: 'When I left school, I got a job in John Lewis carrying carpets.' Providing some background on the song

'Clampdown' for the *Melody Maker* in 1988, he said, 'This was about shop-floor fascism, in so far as I worked in John Lewis carrying carpets, and not being a skilled worker, I did get the shit end of the stick.' By his own account, this dead-end job began to pall after a while, and so he decided to fall back on his one obvious talent, and apply to art schools. His lack of qualifications held him back, but he eventually found a college, the Byam Shaw, that judged applicants solely on the quality of their portfolios. He was granted a scholarship by the local council, and thus escaped from the daily grind to which he would otherwise have been condemned for life. In several interviews he claims to have been brought up chiefly by his father, so one is tempted to presume that he continued to live with Antony at least until he went to college.

Again, the little factual evidence available suggests the truth has been bent to improve Paul's street credibility rating. After Paul and Nick had taken up residence in Notting Hill, Elaine had moved into a privately owned top-floor flat at 18 Border Road, Lewisham, just two miles north-east of Paul's place of birth. The electoral roll also places Paul at this address for both 1974 and 1975, indicating that, by October 1973 at the latest, he had gone back south of the river to live with his mother once more, and that he continued to do so for much of the first year of his adulthood. This supposition is supported by the fact that, sometime in 1973, Antony and Marion (who was by now also using the surname Simonon, though the couple did not marry until November 1975) took up residence in a flat at 63 Ridge Road, Hornsey, a move that presumably either precipitated or was made possible by Paul's departure.

He did indeed work for John Lewis, but the personnel records show that his two periods of employment at the department store's warehouse, then situated on the corner of Draycott Avenue and Ixworth Place in Chelsea, lasted from July to August 1973 and from June to August 1974. These were too brief and too closely tied to traditional school and college summer vacations for his carpet-carrying to have been anything other than a temporary holiday job. It appears Paul continued to attend school until the summer of 1973, presumably resitting O levels, which in turn suggests that, however unsuccessful his efforts might have been, he was rather more serious about gaining the qualifications required by more conventional art schools than he has since chosen to admit.

In 1987, the Byam Shaw School of Art moved to 2 Elthorne Road, Archway, but in the early Seventies it was located at 2 Campden Street, Holland Park. Entry is still by portfolio and interview, rather than standard academic qualifications. Although several of the institution's staff remember Paul, once again the school's records do not go back far enough to provide any hard facts about his stay. It seems likely that his Foundation year was bookended by his two stints with John Lewis, and that he began the Fine Art diploma course in October 1974.

'I was just hanging around a posh art college because I didn't fancy working in a factory,' Paul told *Record Mirror*'s Jan Kaluza in March 1979. 'I spent a lot of time round rich girls' houses drinking wine with daddy.' Two years earlier, he told Chris Salewicz, 'It's great, because everybody there is rich. You can walk around the college, nick their paints, nick their canvases, and they don't really miss it because they can buy more. You don't get many working class kids like me and Mick going to art school. I used to draw blocks of flats and car dumps. I used to really hate Leonardo Da Vinci at first. I didn't understand him. Then I realised he'd do just a thumb and it would be the whole hand. That's what I tried to do.'

Wynn Jones, then as now a tutor at the Byam Shaw, and Stephen Williams, an established artist who was based at the college during Paul's stay, remember things somewhat differently. The closest they come to agreeing with Paul is in allowing that his motivation was not as strong as it might have been. 'He wasn't prolific,' recalls Stephen. 'He did large paintings, and kept at them, but the commitment was 60 per cent rather than 100 per cent. There was a lot of prevarication. If you said, "Let's get this done, then", he'd say, "Well, I've just got to do this first . . ." He wanted to finish the work, obviously, but put off doing so because he knew that meant having to start something else. My perception was that he was a "part-time student": he didn't really know what he wanted to do.' Wynn got the same impression. 'On reflection, I'm not sure that Paul was looking for anything as ambitious, demanding or as structured as a fine art course,' he writes. 'Perhaps, like many other young people who come to art school, he wanted a period of reflection, time to think about his life so far and to consider future options.' Nevertheless, Stephen originally struck up his acquaintance with Paul because both were among the first to arrive at the college each morning, which would suggest a degree of enthusiasm, and Wynn goes on to describe him as both 'clearly talented' and 'intense in his art'.

Stephen takes exception to the way Paul has portrayed the school over the years. He insists it was neither posh nor exclusive, Paul being by no means the only student on a scholarship. 'I remember reading some quote about the school being full of rich kids and him nicking their paints. There were some, sure, but there's some at every art school. The Byam Shaw had a very good cross-section of people from Newcastle, the East End, wherever, as well as the more aristocratic ones. A whole mixture of ages and social classes.' Paul had a relationship with one particular rich girl in which he might well have been cast as the Bit of Rough, but the role was hardly thrust upon him. 'I think he liked that,' comments Stephen, wryly. It was certainly not the last time Paul would play the part.

Contrary to the idea he gives of himself as a jack-the-lad working class scourge of the ineffectual posh twits, Paul was one of the more retiring pupils. 'I remember him as a quiet, modest young person,' writes Wynn. Stephen, who had more social contact with Paul, tends to concur: 'He was a very quiet, shy individual. Not at all extrovert, although he became more so. At parties, after a few jays [joints] and drinks, he'd come out with stuff in a group. He hung around with a rowdy crowd, but he was one of the quieter, more sensible ones. I find it hard to believe that the anger he expressed in the Clash was deeply felt.'

What little friction there was at college developed out of Paul's stubbornness regarding his work, which, according to both Wynn and Stephen, differed greatly in both subject matter and style from his subsequent description. 'He had early on developed a fascination for the Pre-Raphaelite painters, and everything he did was strongly influenced by this, which made him quite difficult to teach in the sense of introducing him to a wide range of issues and alternative ideas,' writes Wynn. 'I do think that his preoccupation with the Pre-Raphaelites made it difficult for some tutors to engage with him, and perhaps there was eventually an element of frustration on both sides.'

'Paul was very stylised,' says Stephen. 'Large composite paintings; very Romantic. I remember a Bayeux Tapestry-type painting in Pre-Raphaelite colours which told a story of a battle, or fighting a dragon, or something. He didn't want to be influenced in his work. He was very defensive, to keep the tutors away.' He offers the theory that anyone who is that determined to hold on to one idea at all costs is doing so to avoid sliding down a hole elsewhere in their character.

By the time of the Clash's first London gig on 13 August 1976, Paul had decorated the wall of the band's rehearsal studio with a mural depicting a car dump overlooked by tower blocks and the Westway: an image of urban decay more in keeping with punk's new brutalism than the pastoral romanticism of the Pre-Raphaelites. *This* was the kind of subject he later claimed to have been drawing when at art school. 'That might have been in his mind,' says Stephen, 'but the manifestation of it was hard to find at the time.'

The beginning of the end of Paul's time as an art student was a chance street meeting with Mick Jones one day towards the end of 1975, when Mick was still trying to complete the line-up of the final version of the London SS. 'We just sort of bumped into each other,' Paul told *Rolling Stone*'s James Henke in April 1980. 'I was going out with this girl, and she was friends with this drummer, and Mick invited this bloke to rehearsal.' Paul went along to provide moral support, but Mick persuaded him to audition for the vacant vocalist's job.

By his own admission, at that point Paul had never even seen a live rock'n'roll band, and he knew nothing about the New York Dolls or the MC5. Nor does Stephen Williams recall Paul being much of a dandy while he was at the Byam Shaw: 'It was just jeans, boots and a T-shirt, really. I remember I had some Texan [cowboy] boots which he liked, and they had got too small for me, so I sold them to him for a fiver. He wore them to death.' Thus, the invitation was extended on the strength of Paul's good looks and natural poise and not because he was a recognisable member of the glam trash subculture. For his part, while he still preferred to wear his hair short, Paul was considerably more tolerant of long-haired types than he had been in his skinhead days. Vaguely intrigued rather than wildly enthusiastic, he took up the London SS offer.

Instead of making it easy for him, the band put him through his paces on a couple of songs that were certainly unfamiliar to Paul, and would have qualified as obscure by anyone's standards. One of them was the Standells' 1967 garage classic 'Barracuda', which includes the immortal line, 'I'm a young barracuda, don't you mess with me.' The other was Jonathan Richman's 'Roadrunner'. Although Richman's band, the Modern Lovers, had recorded the song in 1972, it was not to be officially released until 1976; 'Roadrunner' might have been destined to become a rock classic, but at the time of Paul's audition it was available only on bootlegs. (According to Glen Matlock, the Sex Pistols were also covering the song in late 1975.) For both numbers, Paul – shy whenever in strange surroundings, and now completely out of his depth – just stood in front of the microphone and chanted the few words he had managed to pick up over and over again. The result was not a great success, even forgetting the obvious limitations of the Simonon singing voice. 'He didn't get the gig,' Tony James explained to Pete Frame for his Family Tree. 'Didn't really have enough stage presence.' Pausing long enough only to indulge in the obligatory verbal spat with Bernie Rhodes, Paul said what he thought was his goodbye to rock'n'roll and left.

He stayed in casual contact with Mick, and in late March of the following year – after the London SS had split – Mick got in touch and suggested that Paul consider learning an instrument in order to join the new band he was intending to put together. Paul later discovered that the overture was prompted by Bernie, who had been impressed enough by his looks and attitude to overlook his lack of any conventional musical talent. There was also the precedent set by Richard Hell, who had learned bass from scratch to join the Neon Boys, the forerunners of Television. Plans to bring Hell to London, pair him with Mick and build a band around them had only recently been scrapped. Paul was physically not dissimilar to the American, and with a look that, more by accident than design, combined elements of both the Pistols (cropped hair and intimidatory manner) and the New York Dolls (rail-thin physique and pretty-boy face), he was close to ideal raw material for Mick's and Bernie's dream bands.

It is perhaps not immediately obvious why Paul went along with Mick's idea, especially after his London SS auditioning experience. That had been a spur of the moment thing, not particularly serious and hardly successful enough to give him the rock'n'roll bug. He still had no real interest in the music, so why agree to put himself out in order to join a rock band? For a start, Paul was not unaware of the workings of pop culture, and he coveted the kind of attention that came with success in that field. In 1977, Joe Strummer told Caroline Coon, 'for Paul, the Clash is a chance for him to strut his stuff', and in his own contemporary NME feature Tony Parsons postulated that Paul was in the band because 'it gets him laid a lot'. While both observations might well have been correct, however, they did not represent the full extent of his interest.

It was accompanying Mick to see the Sex Pistols on 3 April at the Nashville that won Paul over to the idea of punk and hardened his resolve to team up with the guitarist. Like Mick and Bernie, and an increasing number of other regular attenders of Pistols shows, he saw the potential and felt the excitement of a scene in the making. It was not only about being famous and adored, but also about self-expression and self-realisation, and it was provocative to boot. Here was something that, to a physically oriented 20-year-old, was far more vital, dynamic and of the moment and would probably reach a far greater audience than anything that could be created with paint and canvas. 'You know, you'd do a painting, and people'd love you for a week,' he told Chris Salewicz. 'But you're just in a room playing with your own ego. You're not really communicating. That's why I started playing music.' On other occasions, his rejection of his former medium of expression was total. 'Art is dead,' he told Jan Kaluza in 1979. 'It's not the way to reach the kids, rock'n'roll is.'

Between them, the band that became the Clash and the punk scene in general also gave Paul somewhere to belong, another gang, another subculture, and one with a difference: they allowed a brooding James Dean figure to become a Rebel with a Cause. Whereas being a skinhead had been about destruction and negativity, what the Clash represented to him can best be summed up by two slogans that, in late 1976, he stencilled on to his instrument and his jacket sleeve respectively: 'POSITIVE' and 'CREATIVE VIOLENCE'. As well as providing a few pleasurable perks, then, joining the band enabled him to fill the hole that Stephen Williams had sensed in his life. There is no doubt that the hole was there, or that Paul was aware of it. In 1979, he told Stephen Demorest, 'I always wanted to be a guitarist, he's the one that looks really exciting. But when I met Mick, I couldn't sing. I couldn't do fuck all: I was useless. About all I could do was break things. But he encouraged me; I used to go round his house, and he played records to me.' He also attempted to teach Paul some simple guitar chord shapes, but after just one painfully trying session, they came to the mutual conclusion that it would be easier for Paul to take up bass. There were two strings fewer to worry about, and he would be able to play individual notes rather than have to learn chords.

Paul borrowed – and later bought – Tony James's spare bass, a cheap and not particularly convincing Fender copy. In order to help him find his way around it, he painted the more commonly used notes on the fretboard, under the relevant strings. In 1978, Mick laughingly told the *NME*'s Nick Kent that he gave Paul lessons 'for all of three days. Which meant that Paul got pissed off after those three days and would go away, and then return some days later to try again.' In addition to the sessions with Mick, he practised diligently on his own, playing along with reggae records and, following its 24 April release, the Ramones' eponymous début album. It did not come naturally: Paul was still using his Play As You Learn bass when the Clash signed with CBS in

February 1977; Mick often had to cross the stage at Clash gigs to tune it for him between numbers; and Paul continued to play basslines devised and taught to him by Mick until at least 1979.

Bill Barnacle – who guested on 1980's *Sandinista!* album, and whose sons Gary, Steven and Pete got to know the rest of the Clash in 1977 via Topper Headon – offers a possibly apocryphal anecdote as illustration. Apparently, halfway through one particular rehearsal, Mick preceded the next song on the list by yelling his customary '1, 2, 3, 4 . . .' while the bassist was taking a drag on his cigarette. Paul quickly moved his hands to his instrument. Even after he'd started to play, though, something still sounded horribly wrong. When the band made it to the end of the song, everybody stopped on time except Paul, who hit two extra notes. 'Why d'ya finish two bonks after everybody else?' demanded Joe. 'Because I fuckin' *started* two fuckin' bonks after every fucker else!' came the defiant retort.

Just because he could not hope to become technically proficient overnight, Paul saw no reason to assume the traditional British bassist's role of strong silent type, standing impassively off to one side and allowing the guitarists and vocalist to hog the limelight. He decided to be a grandstanding performer from the off, wearing his bass low on his thigh *à la* Dee Dee Ramone and jerking it around with a studiedly casual violence strongly reminiscent of none other than Richard Hell. When, in 1978, Paul told Chris Salewicz, 'I want to be able to stick the bass behind my neck and play it like Jimi Hendrix played the guitar', it was the showmanship and not the virtuosity to which he was referring, for his musical ambition was the rather more modest one of fluent simplicity. His conflation of the Ramone and Hell approaches to the bass was subsequently plagiarised by both his friend Sid Vicious and Joy Division/New Order's Peter Hook, who, while he has little respect for Paul's musical skills, is more than willing to give credit where it is due in other areas: 'What a strap length!'

Despite the rivalry between the New York and London scenes and the egos of the people involved, UK punk has always been happy to acknowledge the influence of the Ramones. Possibly because they portrayed themselves as such two-dimensional cartoon characters, they represented no artistic threat to the altogether more self-conscious and self-important London bands. Richard Hell, on the other hand, took himself equally seriously, and in order to discourage the media from identifying New York as UK punk's place of origin and Hell as the movement's nihilistic John the Baptist, his numerous contributions to its style and content were either played down or denied altogether.

As early as 1974, he was modelling the violently chopped hairstyle that was subsequently adopted by Johnny Rotten, Paul Simonon and Sid Vicious, taking the stage in ripped T-shirts and wearing safety pins and razor blades as jewellery. Johnny still refuses to admit an influence, and in his autobiography, *Rotten*, as elsewhere, made a credible enough case for having independently developed his own dyed spike-top and safety pin look. The jury remains out. In *his* autobiography, however, Glen Matlock admitted it was seeing the title of the Hell song 'Blank Generation' on a Television poster that prompted him to write 'Pretty Vacant', thereby introducing UK punk to the lyrical theme that would go hand in hand with its characteristic pose of studied indifference.

Paul teamed up with Mick in the last term of his second year of the Diploma course, but rehearsals began to demand all his time only at the start of the summer vacation. By October 1976, when he was due to commence his third year at Byam Shaw, the Clash had already played their first few gigs and received their first enthusiastic write-ups. This meant it was no great wrench for Paul to abandon his education. 'I was sorry to see Paul go as he was clearly talented, and an unusual and engaging personality,' writes Wynn. 'I was delighted to hear of his great success with the Clash, and also surprised, as he had given no hint of his musical activities whilst a student!'

Save for the mural, one or two similar contemporary paintings and the odd outrageous cartoon caricature of Bernie Rhodes, Paul effectively abandoned his painting and drawing for much of the first six or so years he was with the Clash. This lack of activity, along with his 'art is dead' pronouncements, goes a long way towards explaining why he was not offered the opportunity during that time to give that 'big art lecture' that might have convinced interviewers he was more than 'a thicko from south London'. Near the end of the band's career, however, he reversed his opinion of the relative merits of painting and playing rock'n'roll, and picked up his brushes again.

The distinctive style he developed in the mid to late Eighties quickly came to resemble the not wholly truthful description of his college work he had given to Chris Salewicz back in 1978. In its placing of members of various modern subcultures against inner city backdrops, it combined the urban realism of his 1976 Clash rehearsal room mural with the romanticism of his earlier Pre-Raphaelite-influenced style. One of these paintings is captured in the back cover photograph for the *Cut The Crap* sleeve, propped up against the wall in Paul's Ladbroke Grove flat. It depicts three girls – bearing a marked resemblance to the Supremes – dancing in the street to a ghettoblaster, with tower blocks in the background. The painting he provided for the front cover of Big Audio Dynamite's *Tighten Up Vol 88* captures a multiracial open-air blues dance in the shadow of Trellick Tower and the Westway. In his October 1989 *Melody Maker* interview with Caroline Sullivan he described a current work-in-progress thus: 'One I've done that I particularly like is called *The Last Supper*. It was obviously based on the Leonardo one, but I set it under the Westway with a bunch of characters on motorcycles, eating Colonel Sanders and drinking Special Brews.' He was interviewed for 1991's MTV Clash *Rockumentary* standing in front of this very same painting.

Back in April 1976, Paul's bass lessons by no means guaranteed him his place in Mick's new band. The day before the Ramones' album was released, the first substantial Sex Pistols interview, by *Sounds'* Jonh Ingham, hit the streets. In it Malcolm McLaren acknowledged that unusual new bands had a difficult time getting signed by record companies, but cited the example of the Rolling Stones and other early Sixties London R&B bands: 'No-one came to sign up the Stones, no-one wanted to know. But when they saw a lot of bands sounding like that with a huge following, they had to sign them. Create a scene and a lot of bands – because people want to hear it – and they'll have to sign them even though they don't understand it.' Mick had experienced more than his share of disappointments in the past, and both he and Bernie were keen to get a band up and running, and be part of that scene. Consequently, as Mick admitted in the *Clash On Broadway* booklet, they were trying out as many candidates as possible, and Paul, like Chrissie Hynde, was just one of them.

Mick's old schoolfriend John Brown, co-founder of both the Delinquents and Little Queenie/Violent Luck, believes he might have been another. 'I was still with Violent Luck, under Guy Stevens's patronage,' he says. 'It was looking good, and I was feeling pretty positive. Mick rang me up and said, "Look, let's spend some time together, I haven't seen you in ages. Come over and listen to what I'm doing." So I went over to Wilmcote House, and he ran through a load of stuff, including "Protex Blue": that's the one that really hit me. He started going on about the political edge to what he was going to do, digging around to see what my reactions would be to stuff like that.' It was then that John got the feeling the meeting was not purely social. 'Mick's a very proud guy. I don't think he could have asked me. I'd have to have said, "Look, I really want to get involved with this." And I think he perceived what I was giving out, really: I'm not interested in that. Not sloganeering. To me, it's "Fuck art, let's dance!"' John was subsequently approached separately by both Mick and Bernie and asked to help with Paul's bass lessons; although he agreed, the matter was not pursued.

Mick was also still approaching strangers at gigs. 'Viv and I met Mick at a Roxy Music concert,' recalls Alan Drake. 'We were standing together, and we always used to dress outrageously. He just came over and started talking to us, and we thought he was pretty cool, pretty crazy. After the gig we went off to this little café he told us about. He had an expression he kept using at the time: "Oh, it's great. It's really *rock'n'roll!*"' Viv Albertine had seen Mick walking around Chelsea School of Art, but apparently they hadn't talked to each other prior to this meeting. She and Alan had once been girlfriend and boyfriend, but were now simply friends sharing a squat together at 22 Davis Road, Shepherd's Bush, a few hundred yards west along the Uxbridge Road from the art school's Lime Grove site. 'It was a street of houses split into an upstairs flat and a downstairs flat,' says Alan. 'We had the upstairs flat. A friend lived next door, and told us about this house that had been empty for ages. I just broke into it. We lived there for nearly a year.'

Mick turned into a regular visitor. 'He just became a good friend, and used to come around all the time. Then he and Viv started an affair, so he practically lived at the place.' In spring 1976, Alan and Viv also began to attend Sex Pistols gigs. Inspired both by that band and by sightings of guitar-playing Chrissie Hynde, Viv bought her own instrument, and Mick found he had another pupil. 'Suddenly, from wanting to be an artist, she was thrown into this world of rock'n'roll and loved it, you know,' says Alan. 'She's a real perseverer. Whereas I would lose patience within five minutes and then throw the guitar across the room because I couldn't get the sound I wanted, she'd just stick at it and stick at it.'

Despite this commitment, it is unlikely that Viv was ever a serious candidate for Mick's band. Alan was in with a better chance, being another pretty boy with the Bowie fan's almost obligatory love of dressing up. 'I used to get a lot of people coming up to me and asking me if I would be the singer in their band just because of the way I looked. It might sound conceited, but that's just the way it was. Mick liked the way I looked and everything, and so we thought it'd be ideal for me to be a vocalist.' They rehearsed together at Davis Road. 'But Mick was just so intense: he'd stop every two minutes to tell me, "This is very important, duh da duh duh / duh da duh", and I'd say, "I *know* Mick, I know! Let's just get on with it and do it." I just couldn't handle his approach to it all. As far as I'm concerned, rock'n'roll, up to a certain point – I mean, I'm not an idiot – should just *happen*. He was so incredibly *fanatical*, it all had to be right. I used to say, "Well, it will be . . ." In the end, I just kind of slipped away and stopped doing stuff with him.'

Another regular visitor to the Davis Road squat was Alan's old friend and fellow Bowie fan, Keith Levene. 'We'd known each other since we were schoolkids,' says Alan. 'We were both from east London originally, then I moved to north London and so did he. He lived literally over the road from me. He was a few years younger, and when you're like 13, 14, just three or four years can make so much difference. I used to hang out more with his older sister, but Keith was pretty cool for his age, even when he was 11. He taught himself to play guitar. He's a genius, a really clever guy. He teaches himself things. He'll look at something, and the next minute he can work it out completely. Anyway, as he got older, we used to hang out together, and then we became inseparable.'

Keith claims to have been '17 going on 18' when he first encountered Mick, but in fact he was two years older than that. Pale, sharp-featured and edgy to the point of aggressive, his precocious talent as a guitarist was accompanied by an ambition almost as intense as that of his new acquaintance. 'I met Mick Jones, otherwise known as Rock'n'Roll Mick, got on really well with him,' says Keith. 'The main thing we had in common was, all we knew was we really, really wanted to get a band together. That was it.' In the *Clash On Broadway* booklet Mick revealed that it was again 'probably' Bernie who encouraged him to join forces with Keith, who might not have been such a glamour-puss as Paul, but certainly had attitude to spare.

Paul had been cycling over from Campden Road to Lime Grove to spend more and more of his time with Mick. As Davis Road became the focus of

Mick's life, Paul too became a fixture there. Early in May, a decision was made: Mick introduced Paul to Keith as the third member of their band. In spite of having little respect for conventional notions of musical proficiency, Keith was not exactly ecstatic to hear the news. 'He couldn't play bass, but he was a good artist,' he recalls, somewhat sardonically. 'He came across thick, but apparently wasn't.'

Paul had left home sometime the previous summer. Shortly afterwards, his mother had married for a second time, and her new husband, Michael Short, moved in with her at the Border Road flat. Although there seems to have been no bad feeling on his part, Paul's family ties slackened thereafter to the point where, in November 1976, he could tell Caroline Coon, 'I get on all right with my parents, but I don't see them very much.' In May of that year, the opportunity to live rent free with his new friends proved a tempting one, and he moved into the Davis Road squat's small front bedroom. Initially, rehearsals took place either there or in Mick's equally tiny bedroom in Wilmcote House. 'We used to show Paul where to put his fingers, and play the electric guitars acoustically, and that was a band rehearsal,' says Keith. 'Talk about a long shot, man!'

During waking hours, Alan's room was co-opted by Bernie for use as an office. He had not yet been officially instated as manager, but Bernie was taking his advisory role increasingly seriously. Alan maintains that, as the whole household were now on close terms with the Sex Pistols camp, it was transparently obvious where most of Bernie's ideas were coming from. 'Basically, Bernie Rhodes was an arsehole, and whatever Malcolm McLaren did, Bernie would be round in a flash, and he'd say, "We've got to do this, we've got to do that", because Malcolm had done the same thing like three hours before. He'd dash back sometimes at 12 at night to my place – knowing that most of them would be there – with another idea he'd nicked off Malcolm. Give him his due: he had enough suss to realise, and jump on the bandwagon quick.'

Davis Road soon turned into a meeting place for members of the nascent punk scene. Glen Matlock was not impressed – 'I went round there one time and there was fucking shit everywhere!' - but Johnny Rotten's friend John Beverley, shortly to be rechristened Sid Vicious, was less fastidious, became a frequent visitor and eventually moved in. The others got on well with him, especially Paul, but, according to Alan, 'Mick used to find Sid a bit too much.' In addition to members of the Pistols and their followers, the household also used to hang out with Rat Scabies. As ever for Mick, Saturday afternoons were spent on the Portobello Road.

One particular drinking session that May led indirectly to a moment of solidarity so memorable that it later entered Clash mythology as Significant Event One in the birth of the group. Mick has told the anecdote several times, most notably on the 1989 TV programme *That Was Then, This Is Now*. Paul recounted it in the *Clash On Broadway* booklet. Here is the Rat Scabies version: 'I always remember, we went down to the top of Portobello Road, and they were doing these really gaudy leather coats for about £1 each that someone had sprayed pink and bright yellow. And everyone bought one. And there was like, me and Keith and Mick and Paul Simonon, just walking down the road, and Mick said, "Oh, look: we're in a band!" And we all wore 'em together to some dreadful party that night.'

Hanging around together in matching day-glo leather carcoats might have increased everyone's sense of unity and purpose, but there were still a couple of gaps to fill in the line-up before it could be considered a proper band. Rat was already committed to working with Brian James, so his membership was nothing more than honorary. More immediately vital than finding a drummer, though, was the acquisition of a frontman and singer. 'There were several guys who came along to try out to be the vocalist,' remembers Alan. According to Keith, one of them was 'This awful singer that was like a Mick Jagger clone from High Wycombe. We did a few rehearsals with him, but he wasn't really working out.'

Unable to play at any volume at Davis Road – the line 'Complaints, complaints, what an old bag!' in the 1977 Clash song 'Garageland' refers to the legitimate tenant of the downstairs flat – the embryonic band would sometimes scrounge a couple of hours in the Sex Pistols' Denmark Street rehearsal room, but this was hardly satisfactory. Then Bernie remembered Wally Nightingale. Wally's father had the contract from Hammersmith Council to clear out the BBC's former Riverside studios in Crisp Road, Hammersmith. When Bernie had worked with the Pistols and Wally had still been in that band, they had taken advantage of this connection to use one of the Riverside's former soundtrack-dubbing rooms for rehearsals. Obviously, the arrangement had terminated at the same time as Wally's involvement in the Pistols, but when Bernie re-established contact, Wally proved happy enough to rent out the studio on a temporary basis. (In 1978, Wally would be briefly employed as a Clash roadie.)

It is the 'Jagger wannabe', whose name was Billy Watts, who appears with Mick, Keith, Paul and – to make up the numbers – Alan in some would-be promo photographs taken sometime in mid-May outside the Davis Road squat. One of these shots has all five posing with guitars and bass in the street. Much later, when the embarrassment it could cause was deemed to be minimal, it was used as a still in *That Was Then, This Is Now* (with Billy Watts cropped out) and as an illustration on page 22 of the *Clash On Broadway* booklet. A second snap shows the 'band', minus Keith, on the stairs leading down from the squat's back door. This photograph made its unsanctioned public début considerably earlier than the other, turning up in an August 1978 issue of the *NME* as that week's Blackmail Corner item.

As well it might, because, like the other photo, it captures its subjects in a period of transition not quite far enough advanced to justify their view of themselves as sartorial scene-setters. Alan is wearing a bomber jacket, T-shirt and baseball-boots in a vaguely Ramones style, but his hair is straight, centre-parted and shoulder-length, recently dyed blond in a way that is reminiscent of *Raw Power* era Iggy Pop, and his baggy jeans are gathered into his ankles with bicycle clips. Billy has on a tight black suit and a white shirt with a skinny tie in apparent emulation of Patti Smith on the *Horses* album cover; but while his white plimsolls and centre-parted curtain of long, wavy hair could possibly be ascribed to the Ramones influence, somehow they manage to look just plain naff. Keith is also sporting viciously tapered trousers, a skinny tie and a three-button Oxfam jacket – all of which pass the Patti test – but he too lets himself down at the extremities, this time with unstyled, shoulder-length hair and zip-sided stack-heeled boots.

Paul is the only one with a punk *coiffure* – a slightly less perfect version of his later spike-top – and is also wearing a skinny tie at half mast, plus a pair of granny-style sunglasses, as introduced to the rock'n'roll world in 1965 by the Byrds and subsequently adopted by the New York new wave and Johnny Rotten. Sadly, the remainder of his ensemble consists of a tight-fitting and tight-waisted bum-freezer jacket in a broad pinstripe, and a pair of commodious dark Oxford bags which totally obscure whatever he might be wearing on his feet. The ensemble as a whole appears to be a rough approximation of David Bowie's then current plastic soul look. Mick is by far the most coolly attired of all. Unfortunately, he is coolly attired for 1974: Keith Richards hair and Ian Hunter shades, waistcoat over collarless shirt and necklace, and – even though most people interviewed for this book remember him wearing drainpipes from late 1975 onwards – tight flared trousers.

One of the London SS ads had asked for a Jagger-style singer, and Keith maintains that Mick was happy enough with Billy, someone who fitted that description. Mick certainly fancied himself as a Keith Richards look-alike, and the photos suggest that it was hardest for him to let go of his past musical infatuations in order to move on; the others could be accused of being copyists too, but at least they were fumbling towards plagiarising something new. Interestingly, in spite of Keith's claims that the band was still nameless at the time, the photo that appeared in Blackmail Corner was captioned 'the Young Colts', which also suggests transition: somewhere between 'Wild Horses', *Horses* and the Sex Pistols.

Bernie having already annexed the ideas department, it was Paul who was the quickest to respond to the sartorial breakthroughs of both the New York new wave and the domestic punk scene. Acknowledging that Mick 'had a lot of good ideas himself', Alan nevertheless adds, 'he did a few things that he really didn't want to do. But he could see what was happening. Paul didn't need any telling how to look. He always knew how to look good.' Shortly after the photos were taken, Keith followed Paul's lead and had his hair cut short. Mick refused to go any further with his than Chrissie Hynde had already taken it, but it would appear that Billy too opted for some kind of trim: by the time Terry Chimes encountered the band in late May 1976, while the new look might not have taken over completely, it was dominant enough to make an impression on both him and the general public.

It was some six months after Terry's original audition for the London SS when he finally received the follow-up call. 'Bernie said that Mick had passed his apprenticeship, whereas the other members of the London SS hadn't,' he recalls. 'And he was now in a situation where he needed a drummer to complete this new set-up. So I went down to play with them, and this time it was at Riverside studios.' The audition was not a particularly lengthy one, and the only song Terry can remember rehearsing is 'I Can't Control Myself' by the Troggs, one of the few UK bands who could have claimed to be punks in the Sixties. As not much polite chat was forthcoming, Terry's perception of the band was based on visual information. The others kept their heads down, but even in rehearsal Billy Watts was an extrovert performer. 'He made some weird faces. Really weird contortions of his face, which was quite . . . *interesting*!'

Such Jaggeresque mannerisms were too old-school for what Bernie had in mind, and Billy's time was not to be long. A suitable replacement was found shortly after Terry's audition, whereupon Billy was sacked. He went on to form his own band called the Reds, which Bernie included on one or two of the bills for gigs he promoted in 1978 under the Club Left banner. Terry knew nothing of this upheaval as he did not hear from Bernie again for two or three weeks. What stuck in his mind while he was waiting for the call was not so much the band's music as the impact they had on passers-by in the street. 'When we walked from where we met – which was some caff or something – to the studio, it was quite a long walk across Hammersmith, everyone was looking at us, and that struck me at the time. Everyone was staring at this group of people. It was like your school, when you had a gang, and you could be identified as a member of that gang, sortathing.' Paul Simonon was already feeling right at home.

4... I GET AROUND

Mick Jones's rock dreams were shaped by a very early Seventies notion of rock'n'roll stardom, but Joe Strummer's had their origins in the mythology created by the lifestyles and lyrics of the blues, folk, R&B and rock'n'roll performers of between ten and 40 years earlier. All three of his self-originated nicknames bear testament to this fascination. Woody was the real-life Woody Guthrie, the hobo folksinger who travelled the USA in the Thirties, documenting Depression life and writing some of the most enduring songs in the folk canon, and who, many years later, provided the young Bob Dylan with the inspiration for his initial musical style and image. Johnny was a lyrical archetype: the outsider, the wild one, the doomed lover and, most famously, the poor, illiterate country boy whose ability to play his guitar 'like ringing a bell' was his escape route from a life of privation and drudgery. Joe was similarly ubiquitous, but always seemed to have a gun in his hand and to be making a more dramatic sort of getaway.

These names have romantic connotations, but the singers and songs from which they derive were born of poverty and hard times. For John Mellor, more commonly known as Joe Strummer, they were a means of distancing himself from his middle class British origins. He chose to live what Sebastian Conran describes as a 'sort of Orwellian *Down And Out In Paris And London* type lifestyle' because it was appropriate to his personal rock mythology, based on the folk culture of poor white and Negro Americans. Of Joe's real background Robin Crocker says, 'It caused Joe a lot of problems. In terms of his personality, it's been a big dilemma for him always. He's always been very torn, felt very guilty.'

The recent history of the Mellor family could stand as a microcosm of social change in 20th-century Britain. In the space of three generations it encompasses the end of Empire and the start of the counter-culture – from Raj to raga – and sees the urge to better oneself overtaken by the desire to express oneself. Joe's paternal grandfather, Frederick Adolph Mellor, was an official on the Indian Railway, based in Lucknow. It was there that Joe's father, Ronald Ralph Mellor, was born in December 1916. 'His father died when he was eight, so he went to an orphan school,' Joe told *Melody Maker*'s Caroline Coon in March 1977. By that time, Joe's street credibility was already coming under fire from some quarters, and in the interview with

Caroline he set out to validate his position. The most convincing lies bear a close relation to the truth and, while Joe gave the appearance of talking openly and frankly about his personal history, this was not always the case. When he spoke about his father, Joe made much of Ronald's humble origins and did his best to play down his subsequent achievements. In his version, Ronald was smart enough to win a scholarship to the 'poxy' University of Lucknow in India. He then came to London, where he worked his way up in the Civil Service from a 'junior bum' to a 'not-so-junior bum', before reaching his high point and becoming a 'diplomat going overseas'.

In fact, the Second World War insisted on a lengthy interruption to this sequence of events. Ronald served in HM Forces from 1942 to 1947, and it was not until the age of 30 that he joined the Foreign Office as a Clerical Officer. On 22 October 1949, he married Anne Girvan, known as Anna, the 34-year-old daughter of Scottish farmer David MacKenzie. Following her divorce from her first husband, Adam Girvan, she had been working in London as a State Registered Nurse. Ronald and Anna set up home together at 22 Sussex Gardens, Paddington, and on 17 March 1951, Anna gave birth to their first son, David Nicholas Mellor. That same year, Ronald received his first posting abroad, and the family set off for Ankara in Turkey.

It was here that John Graham Mellor was born on 21 August 1952. It is unlikely he has any clear memory of the place, however, as Ronald was transferred to Cairo in 1954. Two years later, the family went to Mexico City, and in 1957 they moved yet again, this time to Bonn. Although the description 'junior bum' does not do Ronald's position justice, it is true that his rise through the ranks was hardly meteoric and none of his early postings could be considered high-profile.

For his sons, the frequent moves established a pattern of withdrawal from a familiar environment followed by introduction to an alien one. Friendships were fleeting, and a sense of security based on the notion of a stable home was difficult to maintain. In such circumstances, the tendency is for children to become increasingly self-reliant or, conversely, introverted and insecure. It is not unreasonable to suppose that the manner in which the Mellor brothers coped with both their early nomadic existence and the next, equally traumatic stage of their upbringing had much to do with shaping their respective characters and fates.

In 1959, when David was eight and John six going on seven, Ronald brought the family back to Britain while he commenced another three-year stint at Foreign Office headquarters in Whitehall. Rather than return to the inner city with two youngsters, Ronald followed the trend of the times and elected to commute from suburbia. He bought a single-storey house at 15 Court Farm Road in Warlingham, a dormitory town 14 miles south of central London. It was to remain the Mellor family's UK base for the next 20 years, and it was this property which Joe described as 'a bungalow in south Croydon' when talking to Caroline Coon in 1977.

The boys were sent to the primary school in nearby Whyteleafe, but this was only a temporary measure. The nature of his chosen profession dictated that Ronald would soon be posted overseas again, and it was generally considered that, once the children of Foreign Office employees had reached a certain age, the best way to ensure they received a reasonably disruption-free education was to board them at public school. As such institutions are fee-paying and were originally intended to encourage leadership qualities in the male progeny of the aristocracy, attendance has traditionally been perceived to say more about the wealth and social standing of the parents than the academic merit of the pupil. For this reason, despite the fact the choice has nothing to do with the child, being educated at public school carries with it connotations of privilege which, while they might stand a person in good stead in the corridors of power and their minor tributaries, are downright embarrassing for would-be scourges of the establishment.

Punk era Joe was so concerned about the threat his schooldays represented to his credibility that he constructed an elaborate five-part defence against the suggestion that the nature of his education represented any sort of advantage. The first part questioned whether the school even qualified as 'public' in most people's perception of the meaning of that term: Joe stressed that it was co-educational and preferred to describe it as a 'boarding school (with girls)' or, on one occasion, as 'a kind of private comprehensive'. Part two of Joe's case was that his and David's attendance was not an accurate reflection of their father's income: the fees were paid by the Foreign Office as a perk of the job.

Part three addressed the school's, and young John's, lack of academic clout. According to Joe, this was no institution offering a fast lane for the intelligent and patient coaching for the less gifted; it was – he told Caroline in 1977 – a place where 'thick rich people sent their thick rich kids', and for Ronald in particular it represented something of a last resort. 'When I was eight, he made me sit all these exams for these flash public schools, but I failed the lot. Finally, I got into this other crummy school where they had this thing going, that if [one] brother [David] passed the entrance exam, his brother [John] was let in too.' Matters did not improve dramatically once he was in residence. 'I found that I was just hopeless at school,' he told *Rolling Stone*'s James Henke in 1980. 'It was just a total bore.' Just how hopeless was subject to some variation. 'First I passed in Art and English, and then just Art,' he told James. 'That was when I was 17; I left to go to art school.' The following year, the *NME*'s Paul Rambali was informed, 'If you got three O levels, you were top of the list. I got three: History, English and Art.' In a December 1980 interview for Radio Hallam, Joe said, 'I tried to do A levels, but I only got Art.'

Part four concerned the anguish he suffered as a result of being separated from his parents between the ages of nine and 17; and not just during term-time, as with other public school kids. In 1962, Ronald was posted to Tehran, and in 1966, after being promoted to Second Secretary of Information, he was sent to Blantyre, Malawi. Neither the Middle East nor southern Africa was close enough to make frequent visits realistic, and so for almost the entire duration of his schooldays John only saw Anna and Ronald in the long summer holidays, when the Foreign Office would pay for his and David's return aeroplane fares. In November 1976, Joe expressed his hurt at being thus abandoned as anger towards the parties he considered responsible. 'It's easier, isn't it? I mean, it gets kids out of the way,' he told Caroline Coon. 'And I'm really glad I went, because my dad's a bastard. I shudder to think what would have happened if I hadn't gone to boarding school. I only saw him once a year. If I'd seen him all the time, I'd probably have murdered him by now. He was very strict.' By 1980's *Rolling Stone* interview, such brittle defiance – typical of punk rhetoric – seemed to have given way to sadness at having missed out on a more family-oriented childhood: 'It's not a lot to go back to, if you know what I mean. My dad was working abroad, and my mother was tagging along. I don't think I really gave them a thought after a while.'

One thing that has remained constant over the years is Joe's portrayal of the bullying that went on at school, the fifth and final part of his defence against having received any kind of preferential treatment. 'On the first day I was surrounded and taken to the bathroom where I was confronted by a bath full of used toilet paper,' he told *Record Mirror* in 1977. 'I had to either get in or get beaten up. I got beaten up.' Nor was this a one-off initiation rite. 'I was a dwarf when I was younger, grew to my normal size later on,' the still fairly diminutive Joe informed *Melody Maker*'s Chris Bohn in 1979. 'But before then I had to fight my way through school.'

He mentioned regular beatings in several other interviews, and even after the Clash had split he continued to portray his schooldays as relentlessly dark and violent. 'I went on my ninth birthday into a weird Dickensian Victorian world with sub-corridors under sub-basements, one light bulb every 100 yards, and people coming down 'em beating wooden coat hangers on our heads,' he told the *NME*'s Lucy O'Brien in 1986. While still in the Clash, he had always cast himself in the role of the downtrodden, the victim, as had been appropriate to the band's view of themselves as representatives of the oppressed masses. Now, however, he was prepared to reveal the self-perpetuating nature of ritualistic bullying. 'It brutalised me. When I got to a position of power, *I* was a bad guy. I remember slapping a guy – he was only nine or ten – across the head – *ker-pow!* – and his National Health glasses falling off. Just 'cause he irritated me.'

For many years, it was impossible to judge the veracity of Joe's claims about his education, as he proved reluctant to volunteer the institution's name and location. In the November 1976 interview with Caroline he even tried to lay a false trail by claiming it was in Yorkshire; not until the 1980 *Rolling Stone* interview did he admit that it was near Epsom, Surrey; and it was October 1981 before he revealed its name to the *NME*'s Paul Rambali: the City of London Freemen's School (CLFS).

The CLFS was founded in central London in 1854 as a school for the orphan children of freemen of the City. In 1926, it moved out to its present location at Ashtead Park in Surrey, and the entrance requirements were modified accordingly. By September 1961, when the Mellor boys arrived, there were approximately 450 pupils, of which roughly 50 boys and 50 girls were boarders staying in two separate buildings, the boys' being known as Philp House. Contrary to Joe's dismissive comments about CLFS's academic record, the school currently boasts a success rate of over 85 per cent in GCSE and A level examinations, and current headmaster David Haywood doubts the standards would have been markedly worse in the Sixties.

Tom Critchley began to attend CLFS as a boarder in September 1966. Although he was five years younger than John Mellor, his stay at the school coincided with the latter's last four years there, and he remembers him well. In his recollection, aesthetically at least, CLFS was not quite the Dotheboys Hall Joe has made it sound. 'In actual fact, to be growing up in 50 acres of parkland, which is basically what it was, with an old manor house and all that kind of nonsense, was fantastic.' Psychologically, however, it was somewhat less ideal, and Tom finds it easy to empathise with what he describes as the 'semi-orphaning process' experienced by David and John.

In the Sixties, the function of public schools was still very much to lay foundations for the future pillars of the establishment: hence the emphasis on leadership qualities and team spirit, and the encouragement of ritualistic behaviour. CLFS was no different. 'It was the kind of school where you were either involved in everything or you weren't,' says Tom. 'I mean, you were either one of the people who played football, rugby, cricket and sang in the choir, and did the school plays, or you weren't. It was kind of participants or non-participants. And John was firmly *not* a participant in the regular kind of activities.' Outsiders were given short shrift. He missed John's early years, but Tom says, 'I wouldn't be surprised if he had been on the receiving end. His brother certainly had been, although by the time I got there, David was a bit too old to be bullied, if you know what I mean. But he was still regarded as being something a bit funny, a bit soft, because he was gentle. He was a loner.'

Having turned 16, David left CLFS in July 1967, at the end of Tom's first year, which meant the latter had less than 12 months in which to observe the Mellor brothers living under the same roof. Nevertheless Tom got the strong impression that they were not close. 'John definitely didn't go out of his way to spend time with his brother. It's a difficult thing to say, but I sort of felt John was a bit embarrassed about him. But maybe what I was seeing was that he was frightened that he too could turn out like that, and therefore made himself into this more entertaining loner. Because he was a loner too, but he was very, very funny, there's no doubt about that. Hysterically so. I remember him being in some particularly funny sketches at a DramSoc evening, which were quite *Monty Python*-esque. It's fair to say that his influences were generally more alternative than mainstream. For example, he wouldn't perform in "regular" drama.'

Thus, instead of using his wit as a means of buying his way into general popularity, John used it as a badge of rebellion. As with many defence mechanisms, it was at its most effective when employed as a means of attack.

'He used to hide behind his snarling lip and sharp, caustic humour,' remembers Tom. 'If you became the butt of it, he could be quite merciless, but never really to the point of viciousness. However, you certainly didn't feed him too many opportunities to take the piss out of you.' There were times, though, when John did push perilously close to being the 'bad guy' he described to Lucy O'Brien, especially in his last couple of years at the school, when he attained that 'position of power'. 'John was made dormitory prefect, and had to move out of the senior dorm to sleep in the same one as us,' says Tom. 'This obviously pissed him off somewhat, but he was determined to get some entertainment value out of the situation.' For the younger boys, lights-out was at nine o'clock. 'A boy a year younger than me, called Chris, would make an almost religious pilgrimage to the toilet at the stroke of 11. On several occasions, John would feel it necessary to prompt him into action by having someone dip his fingers into a mug of water while he was still asleep. Dazed, Chris would very formally get out of his bed, put on his glasses and slippers, and march to the exit, only to be intercepted by John and advised that he was in need of "bladder exercises". These could be anything from marching up and down the room to hanging from the fitted wardrobe doors and raising his legs to the horizontal. Although the onlookers found these routines amusing, Chris didn't, although John seemed careful not to take picking on someone for laughs to the point of sadism.'

Acerbic humour might have protected John from what he considered to be the harsh realities of his existence, but he had other avenues of escape. He read extensively and, perhaps understandably for a public schoolboy with a nomadic background, his favourite author was T. E. Lawrence. CLFS's remote location made keeping up with cinematic trends difficult, but the pupils got to watch older films on TV. In later interviews Joe recalled that both *Lawrence Of Arabia* – 'better than the book' – and *Viva Zapata!* had a particular impact, the musical score of the latter bringing back vague memories of his stay in Mexico City. Watching old Hollywood gangster and cowboy pictures certainly helped formulate his romantic vision of America and the wider world, and – as was also true for both Mick Jones and Paul Simonon – his ongoing interest in the cinematic arts would play no small part in shaping the development of the Clash.

It is rock'n'roll, though, that Joe – again like Mick - credits for rearranging his priorities in life. In his case, so he claimed in 1988 to the *NME*'s Sean O'Hagan, the transformation was due to one particular record: the third Rolling Stones single, released in February 1964. '"Not Fade Away" sounded like the road to freedom! *Seriously.* It said, "LIVE! ENJOY LIFE! FUCK CHARTERED ACCOUNTANCY!"' Joe might have felt obliged to deny the Stones a few more than three times while with the Clash, but once his own band had split, he was happy to set the record straight. 'They were definitely the first proto-punks. You can hear it all on those first few albums.'

Also in 1988, Joe made a *Desert Island Discs*-type contribution to Christine McKenna's show on KCRW, a college radio station in Santa Monica,

California. At that great distance from both London and the Clash he felt free to open up and enthuse about at least this one aspect of his time at CLFS. 'I'm going to try and spin records as they came to us in a small school 20 miles south of London in the late Sixties. This is my musical education,' he announced. 'I can even see at this moment the radio on its shelf on the wall of the Day Room. A nice big valve radio that boomed. We used to have it up loud.' First up, from 1964 (though he included it with a batch of records first heard in 1965), was the Beach Boys' 'I Get Around'. 'You've all heard the Beatles and the Stones already,' said Joe. 'Obviously, they were cracking our heads, but also I was into the Beach Boys alone of all my friends, and I suffered a lot of ridicule for it.' Other selections from 1965 were Them's 'Mystic Eyes' and Sam the Sham and the Pharaoh's number two US hit, 'Woolly Bully'.

'I had "Rock'n'Roll Music" by the Beatles, and then I came across a Chuck Berry EP in Tehran, where my father was stationed,' said Joe. 'And I remember putting on Chuck Berry's "Rock'n'Roll Music" and comparing it to the Beatles and being a bit surprised that they hadn't written it.' The enthusiastic EP sleevenotes were by none other than Guy Stevens and, after learning what he could from these, young John began to pay more attention when reading band interviews in the music press. He soon discovered that the Stones and the Beatles spoke openly of their R&B foundations. This PR encouraged further historical research, leading him on to more records by Chuck Berry and Bo Diddley, both of whom, despite a brief period of denial in 1976–8, were to remain lifelong favourites.

At this remove, it is perhaps difficult to imagine the impact the mid-Sixties music boom must have had on not just John, but all the pupils at CLFS. 'There was this aspect of being cut off from the outside world,' says Tom. 'Epsom was about the biggest fucking place you could go to, so it was quite strange. But people did go, and did get the records and all that.' Isolated communities are often so desperate for titbits from the outside world that their responses to new cultural phenomena are quicker and more intense than those of people whose readier access prompts them to take things for granted. CLFS was a classic hothouse environment: enthusiasm fed enthusiasm and competition fed competition. 'The release of new Beatles records, or whatever, was a really big thing,' says Tom. 'I think it was called the Hobbies Room, where the record player was, and everybody just flocked into there to hear new records.'

Joe's KCRW record selection went into 1967 with Jimi Hendrix's 'Manic Depression', followed by the Who's 'Mary Ann With The Shaky Hand' and Cream's 'Tales Of Brave Ulysses' (from the first album Mick Jones ever purchased, *Disraeli Gears*). The 1967–8 Blues Boom, coinciding as it did with the onset of John's adolescence proper, marked the peak of his infatuation with popular music. 'That's just a coincidence, that we had a Blues Boom in '68, and I was 16, and that's when music hits you real good,' he told Christine McKenna and her listeners. 'It's like now, when you're 16 and you don't know nothing about hip hop, you're not hip in the schoolyard. For me, when I was young, it was blues. You had to know your blues if you wanted to be part of the in-crowd at school.' As he was still largely a loner, the in-crowd as far as John was concerned consisted of a few equally rabid music fans who were trying to outdo each other with the extent of their forays down the Mississippi Delta. 'We were sending away for Sonny Terry and Brownie McGhee records,' recalled Joe, after playing Sonny Boy Williamson's 'Bring It On Home'. 'I was always glad later that I had that grounding, that I knew Bukka White.'

By now, John was spending most of his free time with his ear pressed up against a small transistor radio and his eyes glued to the music press. 'He used to avidly consume the *Melody Maker* and seemed to have an encyclopedic knowledge of contemporary music,' says Tom. It was something that would never desert Joe. In 1980, he inadvertently used it to humble *Sounds* journalist Robbi Millar, before telling him, 'You know, I listen to the radio and a record comes on and, click, I know *all* about that record. I think, "What's the use of knowing a million and one completely useless facts about rock'n'roll?" Most people forget them, but I seem to retain everything.'

After playing their 1968 hit 'Do It Again' on KCRW, Joe explained how that and other of the Beach Boys' mid to late period releases had vindicated his earlier championing of the band. 'When that strange sound at the beginning came on, it shut everybody up in the schoolyard. They all knew that it was really crucial. And then it shot to the top of the chart, so I was able to walk around the school going, "Yeah? *Yeah?*"' Although Joe's reminiscences would suggest otherwise, CLFS, being a mixed school, was not as exclusively trainspotterly in its approach to popular music as an all-male school might have been. 'You used to have these weird mixed Socials on Saturday nights where the two boarding houses would get together,' Tom recollects. 'The Beach Boys were certainly very big at those.' As they did for the other boarders, the Socials gave John his introduction to the world of romance. Discussing his professed cynicism about the concept of 'love' with Caroline Coon in 1977, Joe told her that the last time he had been in love was at the age of 16. But he didn't say who with . . .

Along with the conventional love song, punk also did its best to rid the world of muso snobbery, and in the process succeeded in inverting the standards of the previous generation of musicians: suddenly, it was the kiss of death to have been familiar with an instrument for more than a couple of years. In a 1980 interview for Radio Hallam Joe went out of his way to make it clear how unmusical he had been at school, saying he was thrown out of the choir. 'I couldn't even make it on a recorder when I was nine.' In numerous other interviews over the years he has claimed to have started playing guitar at 21; on more than one occasion, however, he has also contradicted himself (sometimes in the same interview) by saying he first came by a Spanish acoustic at 16. Which version is the true one depends on the rigidity of one's definition of 'playing guitar'.

'My cousin went to school with Pete Townshend,' Joe told Christine McKenna. 'And when "I Can't Explain" came out in '65, he was really proud that he knew someone who was in a group that was at number 14 in the charts, so he made sure I knew all about it. And a few years later, he presented me with an acoustic guitar that Pete Townshend had actually played. This is North Acton Grammar School we're talking about. He claimed Pete Townshend played guitar for a group called the Confederates, while he was in a group called the Union. And they were kind of rivals.' Elsewhere in the interview he said, 'Cream had a two-note song, an old blues "Spoonful" [written by Willie Dixon] and everybody learned to go, "duh *duh* / duh *duh* / duh *duh*", and then Clapton went off into incredible improvisation for 20 minutes. So I got as far as the first phrase, and then when I heard him go "*diddlyduhdeedahdooweeoowweee*", I just threw the thing down and said, "Forget it!"' In fact, he persevered long enough to learn a 'few blues tunes', as he admitted to the *NME*'s Paul Morley in 1979. 'Although he played guitar, he didn't seem particularly brilliant,' recalls Tom. 'I remember somebody called Paul Buck, who John was friendly with, made a bass guitar in woodwork – it didn't have the normal body, it just had a block of wood [Bo Diddley cigar-box style] – and they used to jam together.'

In their A level years John and Paul Buck shared a study room. By this time they had their own record player. 'My recollection is that there was normally music being played,' says Tom. 'They were as thick as thieves.' Preferred listening for 1969, when John commenced his final year at school, was represented on KCRW by a track from Captain Beefheart and his Magic Band's double album *Trout Mask Replica*. 'Out of nowhere, this dropped on our heads,' said Joe. 'That's when I became a weirdo.' Beefheart, real name Don Van Vliet, was a precocious artistic talent, having expressed himself as a sculptor and film-maker before making his first recordings in 1967. One of Frank Zappa's cohorts, he started off with a psychedelic variation on R&B before taking off into the musically avant-garde and the lyrically absurd on this, his third and most famous album. 'We sat in a dark room huddled over *Trout Mask Replica* for about eight or ten months. We were pretty fed up of being at school at that point. Swinging London was happening only 25 miles up the road, but we were locked in behind walls and gates. Maybe it was an expression that we wanted to bust out of there.'

Interviewing Joe for *New West* in September 1978, at a time when his adolescent listening habits were completely unknown, respected American rock writer Greil Marcus surprised and intrigued him by claiming to detect a Beefheart influence in the twists and turns of Clash songs like 'Complete Control'. Although the musical connection was something of a cul-de-sac, since Mick Jones had been responsible for nearly all the Clash's tunes up to that point, Marcus could possibly have made a better case by suggesting a lyrical debt: Beefheart's imaginative way with words and his skewed, humorously shaded world-view had caught Joe's attention at a most impressionable age.

Certainly, the Captain's love of bizarre pseudonyms – his fellow members of the Magic Band were rechristened Antennae Jimmy Semens, Zoot Horn

Rollo, Rockette Morton, Drumbo and the Mascara Snake – explains much about young John's subsequent fondness for bestowing unusual nicknames upon *his* friends and associates. It also explains why, when Paul Buck went out into the wider world, he did so as Pablo LaBritain, and why nobody other than representatives of officialdom would ever again know John Mellor by his given name.

In addition to Beefheart, Tom remembers, John was particularly fond of the Mamas and the Papas, which in retrospect, given the marked contrast between the vocal group's style and the aggressive all-out assault of the Clash's early music, he finds more than a little peculiar. It should be remembered that, concurrent with the Blues Boom, folk rock was very much in vogue in the late Sixties, as performed by the Byrds, the Lovin' Spoonful, the Flying Burrito Brothers and Buffalo Springfield, to name but a few. The Beach Boys had encouraged a fondness for harmony and melody, and the blues had given John a bias towards rootsy and folksy American music in general. Just as the Rolling Stones had motivated him to backtrack and investigate the blues, so, over his last couple of years at school, the somewhat twee ditties of the Mamas and the Papas pointed him in the far more rewarding direction of Bob Dylan, Phil Ochs and Woody Guthrie, whose protest and social commentary songs – lyrically, at least – have far more in common with the output of the Clash. However hard the lives and hard-hitting the lyrics of the originators of folk and blues, though, a series of filters represented by impassioned performance, immortalisation on vinyl, pop culture glamorisation, physical distance and personal imagination combined with his love of cinema to help John hold on to a highly romanticised view of America; or, as he described it on KCRW, 'a completely dazzling picture'.

'Yeah, you could call us a folk group,' he told Sean O'Hagan when discussing the Clash in 1988. 'I came out of Woody Guthrie, in a way.' Indeed, upon his arrival in London John went one step further than Bob Dylan, who had merely borrowed Guthrie's singing voice and identity, by adopting the folk singer's name: for the best part of six years from September 1970 onwards, everyone who met him knew him as Woody.

Joe's claim that he left CLFS at 17 was the truth, but misleading none the less. Young for his year, he had completed his A levels by the time of his departure in summer 1970. The CLFS records do not go back far enough to reveal all with regard to his qualifications, but he was accepted on to the Foundation course at the Central School of Art and Design, Southampton Row (now part of Central St Martin's School of Art), where the competition for places was hot: unless a would-be student's portfolio was of exceptionally high standard, the minimum academic requirement was five O levels and/or two A levels. So it would be reasonable to presume that John was not quite the hopeless educational case he would later feel punk required him to be.

Ronald and Anna Mellor returned to the UK for good in late 1969, whereupon Ronald was awarded the MBE. He continued as a Second Secretary at the Foreign Office in Whitehall until his retirement, aged 60, in

1977. The MBE is much valued by those who go in for that sort of thing, but it can be awarded for something as minor as helping to arrange a royal visit; thus, although they are hardly two a penny, it is not *that* rare a distinction for a long-serving FO official. Similarly, the rank of Second Secretary might sound rather grand to the uninitiated, but is in fact a middling sort of grade. Nevertheless, his father's honour and title threatened considerable embarrassment to the outspokenly egalitarian punk era Joe Strummer: he never so much as alluded to the MBE, and in *The Clash Songbook* he described Ronald as 'a white collar worker' in 'the Public Records Office'.

John spent the summer after he left school with Ronald and Anna in Warlingham, but this home life contact came too late to bind the family together. After eight years of regimented public school life, John was looking forward to freeing himself from his father's system of values. While he would return a few times over the next year or two, he would gradually cut off contact with his parents thereafter, only re-establishing it during the latter days of the Clash.

As it turned out, John's identity change was by no means pure affectation. Before he could take up his place at the Central School of Art in September, something happened which added a final, sour twist to the youth he subsequently professed to have hated so much, and quite understandably made him want to have as little as possible to do with any reminder of it. Since leaving CLFS three years earlier, his brother, David, had not had an easy time. He had become even more lonely and withdrawn, his morbid introspection shading his outlook on life increasingly black: he joined the National Front and became obsessive about the occult.

At 18, David had begun to study chiropody and taken a room in a hostel at 15 Fitzroy Square, just off Euston Road in central London. Unfortunately, student life failed to bring him out of his shell and his state of mind continued to deteriorate. On 31 July 1970, he crossed the road to Regent's Park, sat down under a bush and, according to Joe, 'took a hundred aspirins and some other tablets'. His body was found the following morning, the cause of death being registered as aspirin poisoning.

To his credit, the punk era Joe refused to exploit this tragedy in order to score credibility points in the teen *angst* department. The story first came out by accident in March 1977 when he was talking to Caroline Coon, and he only discussed it with one other journalist, the *NME*'s Chris Salewicz. He did not instigate the conversation on either occasion, and in both he gave much the same version of and unsentimental verdict on David's death. 'He was such a nervous guy that he couldn't bring himself to talk at all. Couldn't speak to anyone,' he told Chris. 'In fact, I think him committing suicide was a really brave thing to do. For him, certainly. Even though it was a total cop-out.'

Although Joe made the point that he and his brother were complete opposites, this would not have lessened the impact on him of the despair-induced death of the person who had provided his only day-to-day family contact from the age of nine to almost 15; especially as it occurred three weeks short of his 18th birthday, just as he too was about to go up to London, live in a hostel and try to strike out on his own. All the same, eight years later, the acknowledgement 'It happened at a pretty crucial stage in my life' was the extent to which Joe could be drawn on the subject of his own suffering.

Having arrived in London in September 1970, Woody was in a position to pursue further some of his hitherto constrained popular culture interests. In addition to attending gigs at the capital's music clubs, he bought the kind of underground comics and caught the sort of low-budget independent films to which Epsom and its environs had seldom afforded access. He developed a fondness for cartoonist Robert Crumb and a taste for trash movies, the virtues of which he was still extolling when interviewed for *Creem* by Susan Whitall in June 1980. London, however, had just about ceased to swing when Woody got there: it was going into its post-Sixties comedown, something that did little to brighten his own mood.

'Boy, that was the biggest rip-off I've ever seen' was how he described the Central School of Art to *Rolling Stone*'s James Henke in 1980. 'It was a load of horny guys, smoking Senior Service, wearing turtle-neck sweaters, trying to get off with all these doctors' daughters and dentists' daughters who'd got on mini-skirts and stuff.' After the rigorously structured nature of life at CLFS, the 18-year-old Woody was looking for some genuine freedom, not what he considered to be the stale bohemian-by-numbers poses of his fellow pupils. He did make friends, though. One of them, named Simon, shared a house at 18 Ash Grove in the far-flung northern London suburb of Palmers Green with some other Central students and assorted associates. Although not a student himself, Clive Timperley secured his room in Ash Grove early in 1971 through a contact at the college. When he moved in, he brought along a friend who had spent the previous two months sleeping on the floor at his former flat and who rejoiced in the unlikely sounding name Tymon Dogg. 'Right from when I first met Woody, I was slightly in awe of him,' says Clive. 'A lot of people were. "Ooh, *Woody's* coming up for the weekend!" He turns up, and he's just a quiet guy. "*Do something*, then! What's the deal?" And then he did say something, and it was just a crack up! He always had a direct way of talking: he wouldn't say much, but what he did say was shattering.'

After Simon left, Woody took over his old room. 'He used to play little jokes,' recalls Clive. 'It was a bit like *The Young Ones*, that type of house. We were all out of our heads all the time, and he put a sign above the front door saying "VOMIT HEIGHTS", all written out nicely. It was this real suburban street, so it was quite amusing at the time.' In addition to alcohol, the more readily available drugs in those days were marijuana and LSD; as a non-smoker, Woody only dabbled with the former, but he relished the opportunity to experiment with acid. 'I took it about 35 times over a period of a couple of years,' he told *Melody Maker*'s Paolo Hewitt in 1980. He eventually gave it up after witnessing one bad trip too many. Although he never suffered the down side of the acid experience himself, the drug played a part in his decision not to persevere with his studies at the Central. 'I was really shattered from this LSD pill, and I suddenly realised what a big joke it was,' he told James Henke. 'The professor was standing there telling everyone to make these little poofy marks, and they were all going, "Yeah", making the same little marks. And I just realised what a load of bollocks it was. It wasn't actually a drawing, but it looked like a drawing, and suddenly I could see the difference between those two things. After that, I began to drop right off.' Even in the period immediately following David's suicide, Woody did not discuss the subject freely, if at all: despite knowing him on and off for the five years after the tragedy, Clive remained unaware of it until interviewed for this book. It is tempting to see Woody's leaving art school after only one year as not just the result of an acid insight, but also a delayed and indirect reaction to his brother's death.

Both Clive and Tymon were proficient and experienced performing musicians, but during his time at Ash Grove, it seems that Woody was more inhibited than inspired by his housemates' endeavours: Clive has no recollection of him playing while there, either with others or on his own. Three years older than Woody and himself a guitarist, Clive had begun performing in bands in 1965 and, in keeping with the muso standards of the early Seventies, had developed a style that was more technically accomplished than passionate. Although this approach to music was not to Woody's personal taste, he did not feel self-assured enough to dismiss it outright, especially once he'd seen Clive on-stage at the famed Marquee club on Wardour Street, supporting Medicine Head in a progressive rock band called Foxton Flight. 'He couldn't get over the fact that somebody he knew was playing at the Marquee and had got him on the guest list,' says Clive. 'He thought that was really cool. I said, "It's only a gig!" He said, "But it's the *Marquee*!" "It's only a gig, and we're supporting." "But you're *up there* and *playing*! What's it like?" Not to sound conceited, but it did affect him.'

Tymon was an altogether more idiosyncratic musician. He wrote his own strange, folk-type songs and performed them on acoustic guitar, violin and harmonium. He could play the last two of these at the same time, holding the violin against his hip rather than his neck, and operating the harmonium with his feet. Deemed suitably eccentric, he had been signed up in the late Sixties by Apple, the Beatles' newly established label, and had subsequently suffered the same fate as most of the other artists involved with that disastrous undertaking. Plans for an album had failed to get off the ground. 'At home he's got half an acetate left, tracks recorded on one side and all shiny on the other,' Joe told *Record Mirror*'s Billy Sloan in 1981. 'They never really recorded the other side.' Unlike labelmate James Taylor, Tymon did not manage to overcome this setback. After an equally disappointing spell with the Moody Blues' label, Threshold, he gave up on the notion of mainstream success and began supporting himself by busking on the London Underground.

The Ash Grove household broke up in mid-1971, just about the time Woody decided to leave art school. That the following couple of years are the most shadowy and vague in the Joe Strummer story has a lot to do with what happened next. In 1980–81, following the release of *Sandinista!* and the Clash's support for the revolutionary cause in El Salvador, Joe came under particularly heavy fire for dabbling in political issues he supposedly knew nothing about. At this time, the Clash Myth was also subjected to some harsh scrutiny. In several interviews, reviews and asides it was suggested that Joe had been politically ignorant and uncaring until Bernie Rhodes had told him what to write in 1976; and that, four to five years later, he was merely going through the motions, churning out protest lyrics he had no real feeling for. Joe partly countered this by making the kind of claim he made in a 1981 interview with the *NME*'s Paul Rambali entitled 'The Clash Credibility Rule': that he had been politicised through 'experience *plus* Bernie Rhodes. See those guys [three tramps] down that alley? See the angle they see all this from? I saw it from that angle. I was 18 or 19 and I couldn't be fucked to play the game . . . And that's what politicised me, more than anything. Bernie Rhodes made me realise it could be sung about.'

'I've been fucked up the arse by the capitalist system. Me, personally,' he had told *Sounds'* Alan Lewis the previous year. 'I've had the police teaming up with landlords, beating me up, kicking me downstairs, all illegally, while I've been waving Section 22 of the Rent Act 1965 at them. I've watched 'em smash all my records up, just because there was a black man in the house. And that's your lovely capitalist way of life: "I own this, and you fuck off out of it!"' 'That was when he was living in Ridley Road in Harlesden,' confirms Clive. 'I think he moved there directly after Ash Grove. It was 1972. I wasn't living there, it was with some other people I didn't know, but they were evicted bodily. They sent the heavies round. All their goods, and all his records, were chucked out of an upstairs bedroom window into the garden. I lost touch with him for a brief period of time after that.'

Rather than transform him into an angry young activist, the eviction and loss of his beloved record collection encouraged Woody to complete the process of dropping out from mainstream society that had begun with his leaving the Central. Like his namesake, he became a drifter. 'I just went off and did absolutely nothing,' he told the *NME*'s Paul Morley in 1979. 'For at least two years, I was just bumming around. Everyone's got to bum around. I worked on a farm, but I stayed around London most of the time.'

He began to accompany Tymon on his busking expeditions, working as his 'bottler', or collector. 'It was like, I found out later, the apprenticeship of a blues musician. I got a real kick out of that,' Joe told Paul. 'All the great blues players started out collecting the money for some master, to learn the licks. The guy I bottled for would play the violin, and eventually, whenever there was a guitar lying around from another busker, I would borrow it and he would teach me how to accompany. Just simple little country and western and Chuck Berry.' He also learned the tricks of the trade. 'We used to go down the tube late at night, the 11 o'clock shift, when we judged everyone in town was drunk,' he said in a 1989 interview for Washington DC's WHFS radio. 'They'd always give more money when they were drunk.'

When it came time for Woody to buy his own instrument, believing four strings would be easier to master than six, he invested in a £2.99 ukulele from a music shop on Shaftesbury Avenue. One day Tymon left him on his own to work the pitch at Green Park while Tymon moved down to Oxford Circus. 'It was rush hour, and the train emptied at one end of the corridor. One second the corridor was empty, the next it was packed with people streaming through. It was like, now or never, playing to this full house. That was the first time I remember performing on my own.' Starting with 'Johnny B. Goode', Woody worked up a repertoire of uncomplicated blues, country and folk tunes, all of which he would bash out with considerably more verve than finesse. 'It's no use twittering away finger-picking some delicate ballad about roses when there's like 300 elephants charging along in an echoing passage,' he explained during another radio interview, this time in 1982 for San Jose's KSJO. 'They just want to go home, they're not interested in anything else. So from the very start, when I started playing music, I realised that you had to have a rousing, thumping type of tune. Which, in a crude way, was what punk was: it had to be simple, and it had to be loud.'

The next step was a joint European busking tour, which took in both France and Holland, and might have lasted longer and ventured even further afield had the two itinerants not been detained and deported back to England. It was just the latest episode in what was turning into a run of bad luck. Back in London, Woody continued to earn his living on the underground, until the day he underwent an unsettling Orwellian experience: he was busking at Oxford Circus when a loudspeaker above his head crackled into life and advised him to move on quickly because the Transport Police were on their way. 'This guy walked past,' he told Paul Morley, 'and I screamed at him, "Can you hear that? This is *1984*!" And he gave me a funny look, and rushed off. I thought, "Ah, fuck it", and packed it in.'

Although a portion of Woody's lost years was undoubtedly spent living out the down-and-out hobo part of the Guthrie legend, he returned to his parents' home in Warlingham for at least a few months. At a dead end, he began to bitterly resent not having persevered with the guitar from the age of 16. Cognisant of the limitations of the ukulele – an instrument which offered only Tiny Tim and George Formby as role models – and initially believing he had left it too late to master the complexities of guitar, he managed to swap an unwanted camera for a second-hand drum kit. 'I remember visiting him down in Surrey,' says Clive Timperley. 'He had the drums set up in a room, and he practised them. He was quite good.'

Woody had maintained some of the friendships he had made through the Central School, and one connection resulted in a relationship with a girl who went on to attend a course at Cardiff College of Art. Tired of roughing it in London and with no desire to retreat to Warlingham long-term, Woody followed her to Wales, and moved in with her, lock, stock and drum kit. Early in 1973, he paid a visit to neighbouring Newport with the intention of looking up another old Central friend called Forbes, at that time on the Fine Art course at Newport College of Art. 'There were various bands in the college,' recalls another student there, Alan Jones. 'I suppose the most notable one was this pure rock'n'roll band called the Rip Off Park Rock'n'Roll All Stars. I can remember being in a rehearsal in the Students' Union in Newport, and this bedraggled sort of character – which was Woody – coming in with his beaten-up black leather jacket, and sort of slinking to the floor with his eyes just shining. He was just electrified by what we were doing.'

It was the perfect introduction to what turned out to be Woody's spiritual home for much of the next year. 'He was so taken with this little Students' Union scene and our band,' says Alan. 'He was very affable in those days. People really took to him. He made about ten friends a minute, because he's very sharp, very intelligent. He could switch: he could be quite fearless, but he was very charming. His wit was quite astonishing.' In addition to Alan, Woody connected very quickly with a girl named Gillian Calvert – 'I can remember them being just buzz, buzz, buzz. Instant rapport,' says Alan – and through her with her somewhat less outgoing boyfriend, Micky Foote. Woody drifted in and out of Newport over the next few months, and when his relationship came to an end in mid-1973, it seemed only natural that he should base himself there for a while.

Alan Jones had begun to attend the college in September 1971, and had auditioned for the Rip Off Park All Stars that same month. By his own admission, he was not then a particularly good musician, but he was informed that, despite being up to jazz standard, his predecessor had been let go because he refused to move on-stage. Something of an introvert himself at that time, Alan had nevertheless taken the hint and essayed a sheepish version of the Shadows walk. 'I got the job on the basis of that and just about playing a bassline. I also got christened Jiving Al Jones, and it fucking stuck for years!'

One of the myths about the 1976 UK punk rock movement was that it came out of nowhere as an unprecedented reaction to progressive rock's delusions of grandeur and the stasis of the contemporary music scene in general. Mick Jones's musical history should be enough in itself to give the lie to that theory, but it tells only part of the tale. While glam rock might have been a cocktail of late Fifties rock'n'roll flash, early Sixties Teenage Idol posturing, mid-Sixties punk attitude and late Sixties heavy rock strut (with early Seventies decadence and drag queen camp thrown in for good measure), on single at least, it was based on the most simplistic of riffs and was consequently about as basic as you could get. Concurrent with the birth of the glam explosion was the more straightforwardly retro 1971–2 Rock'n'Roll Revival, which marked a renewal of interest in the high-energy performances of the original rockers, and also provided Malcolm McLaren with the bulk of the customers for Let It Rock.

The common ground represented by a raw and basic approach to music was enough to encourage a considerable amount of genre crossover: towards the end of their existence, the MC5, for example, headlined several Rock'n'Roll Revival festivals. The glam rock commercial mainstream was rapidly congested with born-again first-time rockers like Gary Glitter and Alvin Stardust, or would-be first-time rockers like Mud's Les Gray. Whereas Wizzard were probably the most bizarre synthesis of glam visuals and rock'n'roll-derived musical pastiches, Sha Na Na (in the US) and Showaddywaddy (in the UK) came closest to bringing rock'n'roll, albeit in a cabaret version, to the glam rock generation.

The more purist Rock'n'Roll Revival bands remained underground, appealing largely to local working class audiences who were more interested in a good fun time out than in contemplating their navels or posing in Bacofoil jumpsuits. Ironically, in spite of having a similar back-to-basics philosophy, this new generation of rock'n'roll fans were the same teds with whom punks would do battle in 1976–7. As for the bands that provided them with their entertainment: Wales produced its fair share, including Shakin' Stevens and the Sunsets and Crazy Cavan and the Rhythm Rockers, both of whose paths would later cross with that of the Clash.

The Rip Off Park All Stars were in at the beginning of this trend. They did their best to put on a good show and look the part, but they were not inclined to take themselves or the music too seriously. Their repertoire was all first generation rock'n'roll covers, but their approach to it was both over the top and tongue-in-cheek. 'It was well into leaping about performing. Not exactly Gary Glitter proportions, but very into caricaturing rock'n'roll,' says Jiving Al. Fittingly, all the others had 'wacky' pseudonyms too: Cool Hand Clive played guitar, Bob Jackson was the Wailing Saxman and Knock-Out Neil played drums. Almost everyone in the band had the unstyled long hair that was *de rigueur* at the turn of the decade, but they added leather jackets or, in Bob's case, 'a shiny, tight blue lurex suit which his girlfriend made him'.

Although the band was popular with both the students at Newport College and the regulars at local rugby clubs, it had pretty much run its course by mid-1972. Jiving Al believes the rehearsal Woody caught was for a one-off gig played early the following year, for which a new guitarist, Rob Haymer, had been added to the line-up. 'He'd just bought a guitar and taught himself to play in three to six months,' says Jiving Al. 'A really determined man.' Playing with Rip Off Park had changed Jiving Al's own approach to music. 'That band straightened me out no end, because before, I think, I was a very messy, confused bass player. I was also a very laid-back character, but it completely brought me out, and I saw rock'n'roll in a much more positive, exciting way afterwards.' Following the Rip Off Park All Stars' final gig, Rob and Jiving Al decided to form a similarly basic rock band of their own. They advertised for a drummer and received a reply from a slightly older non-student named Jeff Cooper, who dressed soberly in a tie and jacket, and worked in the local mortuary. 'His main job was cleaning up bodies, and he just used to talk about death all the time,' remembers Jiving Al. His age, attire and profession were not considered handicaps, a more immediate problem being that he did not own a drum kit.

'When I was a teenager, I thought musicians were a world apart,' Joe told Vic Garbarini for a feature published in the *Musician* magazine book *The Year In Rock 1981–82*. 'A secret society I could never join.' Rip Off Park's gung-ho approach to basic rock classics and self-deprecating, vaguely Beefheartian pseudonyms had gone a long way to altering that opinion. The newly relocated Woody saw his main chance, and volunteered himself as vocalist and second guitarist for Jiving Al and Rob's new band. The others had decidedly mixed feelings about the offer. 'At that particular time he hadn't mastered many skills, it has to be said,' laughs Jiving Al. 'It was like, "No, you can't join the band. You can't *do* anything!" He was such a bad guitarist that we wouldn't let him go near a guitar. He actually couldn't play barré chords, and you can't really play rock'n'roll if you can't. What he seemed to have accomplished was kind of Dylan tunes, really. He'd been busking folk tunes.' Nor did his singing voice offer any real compensation. 'Very nasal, very adenoidal, but deep. He's got something not naturally right about his nasal passages.'

As they were not overly hung up on technical perfection themselves, Rob and Jiving Al could see at least some merit to the idea of Woody as a frontman. 'The fucking charisma of this guy was just phenomenal. The atmosphere that came off him.' Legend has it that he finally secured his place in the band through a spot of good old-fashioned blackmail. 'That is true, actually,' concedes Jiving Al. 'He said, "Well, as I see it, it's like you've got a drummer with no drum kit, and I've got a drum kit. So you ain't really got a lot of choice, have you?" And everybody looked at one another and went, "He's got a point!"' The drum kit was duly loaned to Jeff Cooper, and Woody became lead vocalist and – very – occasional guitarist.

Jiving Al was living in a flat at 12 Pentonville, above a taxi rank behind the train station. Woody moved into the spare room for the remainder of his stay in Newport. 'This flat was very seedy, very basic. I remember the rent, actually: £15 a month. Always trouble with the landlord, all the usual stuff. Not to sound boring, but we were seriously poor. I can recall coming home one night after going to see my parents, and Woody said he'd had a whole weekend with no money, and there'd been great excitement because he'd found 50 pence down the back of a chair. I suppose we weren't very clean, and we weren't hygienic, and there were an awful lot of mice. Loads. Hundreds. Woody came up with this idea of making the mice walk the plank: putting bits of cheese around the kitchen surfaces, leading to a ruler – so that the ruler was like a plank off the surface – and then a bucket of water underneath. One night there was this plop and splash, and then I heard Woody shout, "Jiving!" "Yeah?" "There's a mouse in the bucket." "Yeah." And then there was this delay before, "It's terrible, innit?" "Look, I dunno, I'm *tired*." "Oh, I can't stand this!" So he actually gets up and gets this mouse out and – this is absolutely true – tries to give it the kiss of life! And then he took it outside and put it somewhere. About two or three days later he came in – he's one of those people with great energy: when he's excited, everyone's got to know about it - and he just runs up the stairs, and he's absolutely beaming, electric, and I'm going, "What? What?" He says, "I've seen the mouse in the subway: *it's alive!*" I mean . . . how could he know it was the same mouse?'

Little has been written about the band Woody joined in Newport, but it has been reported that the outfit was originally called Flaming Youth, before Woody took over and renamed it the Vultures. Although Jiving Al has no recollection of it, the former part of this claim may well be true. Rob was given to taking the stage in a grotesque face mask of the type Peter Gabriel was wont to sport while with Genesis; and Flaming Youth had been the name of Phil Collins's pre-Genesis band, which split up in 1970. The Vultures, however, was also Rob's choice of name. There is a strong possibility that it was inspired by a popular T-shirt of the time, depicting two such carrion-eating birds of prey sitting on a heat-frazzled tree branch, one addressing the other thus: 'Patience, my ass! I'm gonna *kill* something!' This was certainly in keeping with Rob's personality. 'I would say we were co-leaders, but Rob led more than me, if that makes any sense,' says Jiving Al. 'I do think he tried to manipulate me. He tried to . . . Well, he didn't just try, he succeeded in manipulating Woody too.'

Rob's control extended to the choice of material. 'Rob used to learn a song and say, "*We're fucking doing this!*" He was quite forceful.' In *The Clash Songbook* Joe stated that the Vultures 'played R&B when it wasn't fashionable', but their repertoire was more eclectic than this might suggest. No tape of the Vultures in rehearsal or at any of their six or so undocumented Students' Union gigs exists, but Jiving Al recollects that the band always opened with J. D. Loudermilk's 'Tobacco Road', a mid-Sixties hit for the UK's Nashville Teens. 'For a simple number, it's really beautifully aggressive.' A version of this song by the Blues Magoos appears on *Nuggets*, Lenny Kaye's famed 1972 compilation album of original Sixties punk rock classics, which lends the selection a certain retrospective cool. The same cannot be said for an only very vaguely remembered song from Jethro Tull's early blues period. 'Rob wanted to play it because it had a very biting wah-wah guitar solo.' The band's sole original composition was – perhaps unsurprisingly – a Rob Haymer song, entitled 'I'm Nuthin' But A Country Boy At Heart', which, as the title rather more than suggests, was in the then popular country rock tradition.

The only bona fide first generation R&B song in the set was 'Johnny B. Goode', and that was reserved for the encore. Woody's record collection in Newport consisted of one solitary Chuck Berry EP. Sounds familiar. 'I can't remember which one it was now,' says Jiving Al. 'He'd say, "It's the only fuckin' record worth fuckin' having!"' Despite coming on like an R&B purist, Woody made no real attempt to change the Vultures' repertoire. 'I remember him pulling faces, and he was very unhappy about a lot of it, but he still went along with it,' recalls Jiving Al. 'I don't remember any big fights.' This may have been because Woody was wary of tackling the dictatorial Rob, but Jiving Al believes that it was more a case of his being content to keep his head down while serving out his apprenticeship as vocalist and frontman.

There may be no aural record of the Vultures in action, but Jiving Al has kept a pictorial one, which includes some of his own shots of Woody and others of the band in action taken by various students on the college's Photography course. One of his photos depicts Woody in the Pentonville flat, his shoulder-length curly hair framing his serene, cherubic face. Wearing his habitual uniform of jeans, boots and checked shirt – an early Seventies update of the Woody Guthrie look – he is sitting with an electric guitar resting on his lap in front of a bank of amps and speakers, courtesy of Newport College. 'We set up a Music Society,' explains Jiving Al. 'Of course, the only reason we set it up was so we could then go out and buy a PA system, and then steal it. That should have been in the Students' Union. I mean, it's fucking massive, for God's sake, and it's in my flat! We did give it 'em back, though . . .'

The performance shots show Woody either clutching the mike and contorting his features like a young Joe Cocker or hanging off the mike stand and gazing at his fellow band members with an expression of childlike rapture on his face. His only concession to rock star glamour is the black varnish on his fingernails; otherwise, he's in his standard attire, complete with beat-up black leather jacket. The same is true of Jiving Al; but, amusingly enough, not of Rob, who is wearing his face mask, on this occasion with flasher's mac and empty Persil pack accessories.

'I can't imagine what that band sounded like,' says Jiving Al. 'I'd love to go back and be someone in the audience. Our intent was 100 per cent. Funnily enough, a bit like 1977 [and the punk rock movement]: people who really mean it, but can't play too good, and yet something comes out. I think it was tough, very hard, very basic.' Someone who was in the audience at almost every gig was another student who, confusingly, was only one 'l' away from having exactly the same given name as Jiving Al. Allan Jones began to write for *Melody Maker* shortly after leaving Newport and, in a July 1975 feature about the 101ers, he fondly recalled the Vultures thus: 'an erratic but occasionally stunning formation that played a handful of gigs before sinking without trace'.

Although not himself a student, Woody was benefiting from his close contact with people at Newport College and was living a life that was as full, stimulating and healthy as poverty would allow. 'He didn't drink or take drugs much at all: I remember him having two pints and falling over,' claims Jiving Al. 'He had a lot of friends. Women were quite fond of him. There were one or two I felt he knew really well, but I never really saw him having a relationship.' One of these women (who wishes to remain anonymous) was involved with the Communist Party, then the dominant force in the Newport Students' Union. Jiving Al suspects that Woody's brief flirtation with organised politics had more to do with his interest in her than any burning desire to overthrow capitalism. 'He never talked politics to me. I wouldn't have said he was unaware, but it wasn't something he talked about.' Even if his interest in communism was genuine, it was not particularly long-lived. 'Toeing any line is obviously a dodgy situation, because I'm just not into a policy or I'd have joined the Communist Party years ago,' Joe told Vic Garbarini in 1981. 'I've done my time selling the *Morning Star* at pit heads in Wales, and it's just not happening.'

Despite knowing a lot of people, Woody was not a great mixer, and much of his time was spent on his own, in his room, indulging in what Jiving Al refers to as his 'activities'. 'He was very well read. He'd go from reading to strumming his guitar, to writing, to painting.' Woody's environment was inevitably art-oriented: everyone painted or took photos of everyone and everything else. His own work conformed to a narrower brief. 'He always painted cowboys eating baked beans!' laughs Jiving Al. 'He always had this obsession with cowboys.' Partly, Woody was reflecting the Vultures' country rock leanings, but he was also betraying a fascination with pop iconography not dissimilar to that evident in Mick Jones's art school output. Whereas Mick's collages were Warholesque reflections of the superficial glamour and disposability of contemporary culture, however, Woody's paintings bought into the Hollywood version of American folk mythology. The cover art for the Clash's 1978 album *Give 'Em Enough Rope*, which depicts a couple of vultures feeding on the prone corpse of a cowboy, is more resonant for Jiving Al than for people who did not know the band's singer in 1973–4.

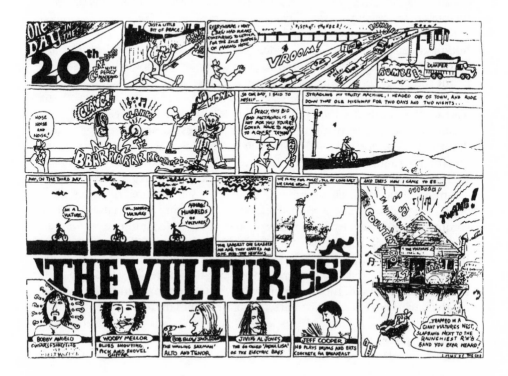

One result of the hours Woody spent writing and strumming was his first attempt at a song, a copy of which Jiving Al still owns. 'It's very telling. At the beginning of the tape, he says, "Really make it nasty and home-made, all right?"' It too shows the way its composer – already seeing himself as an outsider – both identified with and romanticised the outlaw figure. 'It's not "Bankrobber", but he does sing something about wanting to rob a bank.'

Woody's songwriting talents might have been overlooked in the Vultures, but his artistic endeavours were held in higher regard. In spite of the fact that Rob was on the college's Fine Art course, when the band decided to try its luck out of town towards the end of 1973, it was Woody who was commissioned to come up with a suitable promotional poster. 'I can remember Rob pointing his finger at Woody and saying, "I want that poster by tomorrow!"' says Jiving Al. 'And he went and did it, you know. He worked on it for 24 hours from start to finish.' The A3-sized result takes the form of a strip cartoon, very much in the style of Robert Crumb. In a doomed quest for some peace and quiet, Percy sets out on a bicycle ride, is plucked from the saddle by a giant vulture and is deposited in its mountaintop nest near a precariously positioned roadhouse, from which are emerging the strains of 'I'm Nuthin' But A Country Boy At Heart'. 'Trapped in a giant vultures' nest,' thinks Our Hero, 'slap bang next to the raunchiest R&B band you ever heard.' 'I just love this shit-kicking music,' comments the wildly frugging roadhouse cat.

Along the bottom of the strip are impressively accurate caricatures of the various band members, all of whom are given nicknames and/or brief character sketches in the tradition of the Magic Band and the Rip Off Park All Stars. The latter outfit's saxophonist had just been added to the Vultures' line-up, and he is listed as Bob 'Blow' Jackson, retaining his 'Wailing Saxman' tag; Rob becomes 'Bobby Angelo, guitars and singing, rumoured to be the illegitimate son of Bert Weedon' (Weedon being the author of the *Play In A Day* guitar book); long-haired pretty boy Jiving Al is 'the so-called Mona Lisa of the electric bass'; Jeff Cooper 'plays drums and eats concrete for breakfast'; and 'Woody Mellor' self-deprecatingly describes his own contribution as 'blues shouting and pick and shovel guitar'.

These posters were dispatched to various venues with a selection of performance photos, and almost immediately won the Vultures a gig at the Granary, a 500-capacity venue at 32 Welsh Back in nearby Bristol. 'Lots of good people played there, so you were supposed to have a high recommendation or to be someone,' says Jiving Al. The advance publicity was so successful that the venue was full, but the gig itself was a disaster. 'Something went wrong. Strings broke, equipment broke down, whatever. It was one of those moments where everything went quite surreal. The next thing I remember was some army guy on-stage who was threatening to take his trousers off. The music had completely collapsed. I remember Woody – I'd never seen him like this before – sort of egging on the audience to egg on this guy. He was just punching his fist in the air, like, "Off, off, off!" The whole audience was into it, thrusting its fists in the air and screaming, "*Off!*"

I was having flashbacks to Nuremberg! "What *is* going on, here?" But what I was watching was him controlling the audience in a big way. It was the first time it ever happened, and I think he learned something that night. Obviously, this is my interpretation, and I've thought about it a lot over the years, but something happened. He gained power that night.'

The Granary's promoters were not so impressed. 'They came up to us after and said, "You've got a fucking nerve!" They were really upset, because they thought they'd been totally conned. They did pay us, but reluctantly. We had to point out that the place was having a fucking good time, and it was packed out, whether they thought we were rubbish or not. I do remember bad vibes, and thinking, "We're not going to be booked here again!" And that was the big gig for us.' It was the Vultures' first out of town gig and their first paid gig in a proper venue. It was also their last ever. There was no immediate bust-up, but the experience left the band feeling deflated, and rehearsals gradually petered out. 'We were completely disorganised, basically,' says Jiving Al. 'We were the typical band who didn't know their arses from their elbows.'

Tired of having to turn the furniture inside out for loose change, Woody took a job tending the graves in the town cemetery. 'I wasn't strong enough to actually dig the graves, so I just used to wheel the barrow around and collect the broken jamjars,' Joe told the *NME* in 1988, referring to the receptacles provided for flowers. 'I spent a whole winter doing nothing but this in Newport.' As jobs go, there can be few worse: not only boring, repetitive and lonely, but also outdoors in the cold and surrounded by constant reminders of death. 'I remember him coming home from that and being really low,' says Jiving Al. '"What the fuck am I doing?"' Without the Vultures to keep his spirits up, even the usually buoyant Woody succumbed to depression. 'I didn't get much out of him for a while. He was just hidden in his room. I was invited in, but I wasn't wanted. He didn't speak.'

In spring 1974, Woody cut his woolly hair short and began to wear it combed back in the rocker style he has favoured – save for brief periods at the beginning and end of the Clash – ever since. Late one night, Jiving Al was invited to take a picture of the newly shorn Woody posing with artefacts pertaining to his 'activities': books, a typewriter, transistor radio, valve amplifier, several guitars (including a couple of Telecaster copies 'worth about a fiver each') and a cowboy painting. 'I think cutting the hair was quite symbolic,' says Jiving Al. As was the photograph. In the mid-Sixties, Bob Dylan was fond of staging similar pictures, posing with guitars, favourite records and 'meaningful' possessions; the best known of which is the one adorning the cover of the 1965 transitional folk to rock album *Bringing It All Back Home*. 'Woody was always very aware of that sort of thing.' Some of Woody's Newport friends had already completed their courses and moved on. Most of the remainder were due to leave in the summer of 1974. That May, he came to the conclusion it was time to take it all back to the closest place he had to a home: London.

5... ROUTE 101

When he arrived back in the capital in May 1974, Woody headed straight for the current home of his old busking partner Tymon Dogg, a squat at 23 Chippenham Road in Maida Hill. The other side of the Westway from Notting Hill, it was also just a couple of hundred yards from Mick Jones's high-rise. The other inhabitants of Tymon's squat were Dave and Gail Goodall, the proprietors of That Tea Room on Great Western Road. Since demolished, it was then the unofficial centre of the sizeable squatting community occupying Chippenham Road, Elgin Avenue and other smaller thoroughfares in Maida Hill. As a result, Dave and Gail were very well connected in the area, and were able to point Woody in the direction of a spare room in neighbouring Walterton Road. He moved in that same month.

Number 101 had been opened up a year earlier by Patrick Nother and Simon Cassell, who had previously shared a squat near Euston station before being put on to Walterton Road by Dave and Gail. Later in the summer of 1973, Pat's brother Richard, about to embark on the final year of his Zoology degree course at Chelsea College, had also moved in; at the beginning of 1974, though, he decided that living there was disrupting his studies and moved out again. In the interim period, the household had been swollen further by: a friend of Pat's from the Nothers' home town of Leek, Staffordshire, christened Julian Yewdall but usually known simply as Jules; a former Chilean squatmate of Simon's named Antonio Narvaez; and a friend and fellow-countryman of Antonio's, Alvaro Peña-Rojas. Around the time Woody moved into 101, Richard, having completed his exams, returned to the area. As 101 Walterton Road was now full, he took a room in the squat that backed on to it, 86 Chippenham Road.

The nature and implications of squatting have changed over the years: the increasing housing shortage has made it the only option for some, and it is therefore rarely condemned by those sympathetic to the plight of the poor and homeless. At the same time, laws have been tightened up to appease those who are not sympathetic, so squatting has grown progressively more difficult since the early Seventies. It was simple to gain access to empty property then – especially in those areas, like Maida Hill, awaiting redevelopment by the Greater London Council (GLC) - and if one knew the right people, making the place halfway habitable was no problem. 'At that time,' says Jules Yewdall, 'if you'd got the energy, you could see an empty house and just take it if you fancied it.' 'You had to rewire the whole house, because everything's been ripped out, pipes, everything,' Joe told *Rolling Stone*'s James Henke in 1980. 'We'd get a specialist who'd go down to this big box under the stairs and stand on this big rubber mat and make a direct connection to Battersea Power Station. *Bang! Bang!* I've seen some explosions down in these dark, dingy basements that would just light things up.'

Staying in was also nothing like as hard as it is today. If a few properties in a particular street were already squatted, the GLC would usually hold off from trying to have inhabitants evicted until they were ready to demolish and rebuild. At this point, they would attempt to have everyone moved on in one go. 'You knew that,' says Jules, 'so you could more or less say, "OK, we'll get in here now, and we're going to be all right for another year or two."' The only real risk was of being spotted by the police when first breaking in to a squat: Jules none too fondly remembers a later venture which resulted in his being taken to the police station and threatened with a charge of 'criminal damage to a piece of corrugated iron'. Of course, when the GLC did decide it was time to clear a street, the gloves came off altogether. For the Elgin Avenue–Chippenham Road area, the moment of truth came in late summer 1974. 'The GLC tried to get the LEB [London Electricity Board] to cut off our electricity,' says Richard. Court proceedings to evict the squatters were instigated on 1 September. In early November, the Maida Hill Squatters and Tenants Association organised a demonstration in Notting Hill, and 200 squatters objected loudly to the prospect of being made homeless *en masse*. 'It got quite heavy,' recalls Richard. 'The police charged us, the Special Patrol Group.' Nevertheless, the action won the squatters a brief reprieve.

In those days, the general public perceived squatting – a communal lifestyle involving youngish people with long hair - to be the preserve of hippies and alternative-type left-wing radicals, and events such as the November demonstration served only to reinforce this view. On the whole, however, it was a misleading one. True, there were many exiles from dictatorial regimes in the Maida Hill area – including representatives from almost every South American country – but many of them had left their homelands simply to be able to pursue a less restrictive lifestyle, rather than with the intention of grouping together to plot or campaign. There were one or two households intent on reforming British society, but there were also some that were downright antisocial: Richard's squat was dominated by a motorcycle gang who used to ride their machines into the front room. 'They were *crazy*,' he says. 'They'd destroy the house during the night, then spend the next day repairing it.' Maida Hill squats generally housed a cosmopolitan mix of all kinds of people with all kinds of beliefs and agendas.

Richard and Jules agree that squatting was political in itself, up to a point. 'If you hadn't got any money, it was a political act to take over an empty property and declare yourself as legally living there,' says Jules. In the final analysis, though, most people involved saw it as a simple trade-off: if one was prepared to cope with relative squalor, one did not have to pay any rent and, as a consequence, one was reasonably free to live the life one chose. 'It was basically, we were doing it ourselves,' says Richard. 'There were a lot of people doing their own project, whether it was art, photography, music – at least, in our houses – and it meant you could do it in your own way.' Aside from the unconventional nature of his lifestyle choice, then, there was little evidence at this time of the politicisation Joe claims was attributable to his experiences of the previous two years.

His return to musical performance was inspired by seeing a trio playing Irish folk music in the Elephant and Castle pub on Elgin Avenue. 'All these people were hanging around my squat just doing nothing, and I thought, "I'll just whip up a few of these guys, and we'll play in a few Irish pubs. I can do that!"' His original intention, he told Paul Morley in 1979, was just to make a bit of money over the summer. Pat Nother remembers it differently: 'It was two or three months after I met him that he said, "I've got a great idea: I'm going to be a pop star!" And he'd decided this, which I thought was quite funny. "What, you're just going to *be* one? You can't play anything!"' Indeed, Woody's guitar playing was still so rudimentary that Jules believed he had just picked up the instrument. Luckily, Woody was not the only one in the squat who refused to see this as an obstacle. 'I had an alto saxophone which I'd got in Portobello Market a year or so before,' Simon recollects. Between them, they managed to cajole a couple of the others into joining in with a jamming session in the basement of 101. Antonio, who had some experience as a drummer, borrowed a kit from someone in a nearby squat, and a bemused Pat did likewise with a bass, despite never having played the instrument before. Woody and Simon shared the vocals.

The results were not astounding, and it is doubtful whether anyone other than Woody and possibly Simon would have wanted to persevere had not Alvaro decided to co-opt the unlikely outfit for his own purposes. An experienced tenor saxophonist, he had enjoyed three hits in Chile with his bands the Boomerangs and the Challengers before moving to the UK in 1970. In September 1973, a military coup in Chile had overthrown the world's first ever democratically elected Marxist government, and the Chile Solidarity Campaign (CSC) had formed to co-ordinate support for the victims of the struggle. Alvaro took it upon himself to volunteer the services of the squat rehearsal group for the CSC's upcoming benefit concert, an Evening for the Chilean Resistance. The fact that Alvaro now describes it as 'some Mexican lost cause' suggests he was rather more interested in the opportunity to make music than in the reasons for the benefit itself.

It was already the middle of August 1974, and the gig, to be headlined by reggae band Matumbi, was scheduled to take place on 14 September at the Telegraph music pub at 228 Brixton Hill. Alvaro joined the rehearsals, and the band concentrated on working up a set of six songs. Out of necessity, these were the simplest of rock and R&B classics, something which suited Woody perfectly. They included Chuck Berry's 'No Particular Place To Go' and 'Roll Over Beethoven', Them's garage band staple 'Gloria' and Larry Williams's rock'n'roll evergreen 'Bony Maronie'. No sooner had these been knocked into some kind of recognisable shape than, just two weeks before the benefit was due to take place, Antonio suddenly left to go on holiday.

Desperate for a replacement, the band asked Pat's brother Richard to sit in on drums. 'I had a clarinet at the time, and a pair of bongos,' says Richard. 'Occasionally I used to bash about on the drums without actually playing with anyone. They asked me to see how it went with me sitting in with them.' Then the gig was brought forward a week. 'After a couple of days of frantic practice, I thought I could handle it,' he told Allan Jones for his July 1975 *Melody Maker* feature. 'It wasn't too difficult: I just bashed everything in sight.' On Friday 6 September (according to *Time Out*'s listings, not 7 September as is usually claimed) – just five days after Richard's first rehearsal and only two or three weeks after Woody had told a disbelieving Pat that he intended to become a pop star – all three turned up with Simon and Alvaro at the Telegraph to play their first gig. They were billed as El Huaso and the 101 All Stars, something which foreshadowed a future power struggle within the band: El Huaso was Alvaro, being Chilean Spanish for countryman; but the latter part of the name was a nod in the direction of Rip Off Park, the band Woody had really wanted to join in Newport.

As they had no serviceable equipment of their own, the band rather naïvely hoped they would be allowed to borrow that of the headliners. Matumbi were delayed when their van broke down, and arrived two hours later than scheduled. Almost unbelievably, in the circumstances, they acceded to the 101 All Stars' request. 'There was hardly time for them to do their set,' Joe told *Melody Maker*'s Paolo Hewitt for a 1981 101ers retrospective. 'But they still lent us their drum kit and their amps. I thought that was great.' Clive Timperley, who had connections with the Maida Hill squatters community, had heard that his old housemate Woody was in a band and had decided to go along and watch. 'They did their six songs and ran out of material, and that was it. They weren't very good, but they tried hard, and it was nice to see your mate on-stage. They were very nervous about it. To get a gig at a place with a stage where everyone can see you, supporting a fairly well-known reggae band, in Brixton, out of your home territory, must have been quite daunting for them. I remember thinking, "OK, you're fucking up, but at least you're keeping yourselves together on-stage."'

For the past month or two, Richard had been sharing his room at 86 Chippenham Road with a 17-year-old Spanish girl named Esperanza Romano. Within a day or two of the Telegraph benefit, they both departed for Spain. Rehearsals of a kind continued, but without any real sense of purpose. Always far more diffident about the band than the others, Pat's involvement was sporadic. He maintains that the line-up was fluid anyway. 'There were all sorts of other musicians around. We got through about two or three guitarists a week, who Woody was into attacking.' He also recalls at least two other bassists playing with the band before he was finally replaced for good. What made him more than happy to opt out was the battle that was going on for control of what he considered to be a fairly risible outfit. 'It was just fucking around on crap instruments with a bunch of crap musicians, you know,' he says. 'But there was some ego stuff went down. Rivalries, just silly boys' stuff, I can't remember exactly what.'

Woody, meanwhile, had taken a job as cleaner and maintenance man at the home of the newly formed English National Opera, the London Coliseum in St Martin's Lane. His sole intention was to save enough money to buy himself a decent guitar amplifier. His duties were no more arduous than carrying out the rubbish, cleaning the toilets and sweeping the pigeon droppings off the roof. 'A fucking great job,' he told Allan Jones in 1975. 'Only had to work two hours of the day. There was this hole in the basement where I'd creep off to play my guitar. Anyway, the manager found me and fired me.' Woody was hardly heartbroken. 'Gave me £120 to get out as soon as possible.' Before he obliged, he smuggled Pat in to watch a dress rehearsal of *Die Fledermaus*, due to begin its run on 31 September. Sitting up in the gods, the duo decided it was a good time to take a rest from the pressures of squat and band alike, and set off for a holiday in Wales.

Pat's motive was entirely recreational, but in addition to looking up a few old friends, Woody was intent on checking up on various bits and pieces of musical equipment in Newport. Pat stayed away for the best part of two months. Woody returned like Santa Claus after just a fortnight, not only full of *bonhomie* and enthusiasm, but also with the promise of rather more than a sackful of new gear. It was relatively easy for him to persuade Simon and his girlfriend to drive him back to Wales to pick it up. It included his collection of electric guitars, a custom-made semi-acoustic bass with violin holes and an AC30 amplifier, which he'd bought with his pay-off from the English National Opera. As for his drum kit, that had already made its way back to Surrey, on loan to old schoolmate Pablo LaBritain, who had expressed an interest in learning to play.

Not for the first time, Woody was able to use the possession of coveted musical equipment to improve his position within a band; besides, the other members of the 101 All Stars had missed the driving force of his personality. 'Most probably what happened was, by the time he'd got back to London, all the silly games that had been going on beforehand had sort of collapsed, along with the energy to get the band together,' says Pat. Nominally, at least, the band continued to be run as a democracy, but it was tacitly understood by most of the people involved that, without Woody, it would not be run at all. Nevertheless, Alvaro did not immediately back into the shadows.

The line-up was brought back up to full strength by Antonio, newly returned from his wanderings. The band managed to borrow two caseless Linear Concorde speakers, which Woody housed in a couple of knocked-together kitchen drawers; when combined with his amp, this represented the band's entire PA. 'We had a broomstick handle as a microphone stand,' Pat reveals. 'One microphone, you know.' Indeed, the 'twenty-two singers but one microphone . . . five guitar players but one guitar' coda to 'Garageland' has far more to do with the early days of Joe's second band than those of the decidedly better-equipped Clash. Perhaps unsurprisingly, the band – their name now officially truncated to the 101 All Stars – found that securing bookings was not easy for a ramshackle outfit with a six-song repertoire in the process of being gradually extended to nine or ten.

Pat remembers another three or four gigs taking place over the following two months. 'We did practise a lot, and we'd have these weird gigs where we used to turn up places and people let us play. I can remember playing in an abandoned cinema, I think it was in Lancaster Road, and there were puddles of water everywhere. I was terrified all through the gig that my lead might be running through them. "Surely, water and electricity don't go together?"' One of the more memorable of these sporadic early shows was another Chile-related event. Artists for Democracy arranged a two-week exhibition-cum-cabaret at the Royal College of Art under the title Arts Festival for the Chilean Resistance. It ran from 14 October to 1 November, and Alvaro volunteered the All Stars to play on one of those nights. We started playing "Bony Maronie", and they went, "Get this capitalist rock'n'roll out of here!" Really.' Joe told Paolo Hewitt, 'We got two numbers in and then we had to fucking clear out.' Pat confirms this story. 'They had a hall draped with revolutionary flags, Che Guevara, Allende, Marx and Lenin on massive banners everywhere. There was a lot of money's worth of art on display. It was a whole cultural convention thing, and then this bunch turn up and play "American imperialist jukebox music"! We were slung off.'

The impetus that brought about the next stage in the 101 All Stars' development came from a source outside the band. 'We never really got off the ground until this girl pushed us into renting that room above the Chip. Because we couldn't play, how could we get any gigs?' Joe said to Paolo Hewitt. 'The only thing we could do to learn to play was to start our own club up.' The girl in question was Liz Lewis; the Chip was the Chippenham public house, situated on the corner of Malvern and Shirland Roads (where they form a junction with both Chippenham and Walterton Roads), and the club was in the pub's small upstairs room. Liz hired it for the first time on Wednesday, 4 December 1974, and once again, having a deadline to meet helped galvanise the band into action. As if to pay testimony to this change of gears, the band name was truncated still further to the 101ers.

Everything appeared to be moving a little too fast for one of the band's two latest recruits, who – due partly to his physical appearance and partly to his nocturnal lifestyle - was known to everyone as Mole. 'I didn't think we were anywhere *near* ready to do a gig!' he says. Pat had finally left the band and given up the bass. 'He said to me in a pub, "I can't believe we're in a group,"' Joe told Paolo. 'And I said, "What do you mean?" He said, "I can't believe we're in a group. So I'm going to leave!"' Pat himself is vague about what happened. 'I think I was chucked out. I *think* so . . .' Simon had met Mole through a girl named Barbie, who was living with the latter at the time. 'I knew Simon Cassell,' says Mole. 'I remember, we were on Ladbroke Grove, and he asked me if I fancied coming along and playing bass with this band. I could play guitar, but I'd never played bass before. I said, "Yeah, why not?"' His first rehearsal, sometime in mid-November, left him in no doubt about the kind of band he was joining: the bass gave him an electric shock. When he ran a mains tester over the strings, it lit up, and he discovered that the 101ers had been rehearsing for over three months without any earth connections.

The other new recruit was more casual about the imminence of the gig, both because he was conversant with the 101ers' style and material and because, from a musical viewpoint, his role was a less demanding one: Jules Yewdall had been asked to take over as lead vocalist and occasional harmonica player. Although Woody, like Simon, still intended to sing some numbers, he wanted to be able to concentrate on his guitar playing. Also, he was beginning to have doubts about his voice. Besides being limited in range, it was now distorted by both his adenoidal problem and the appalling state of his teeth: they combined to dampen some of his consonants and sibilate others to such an extent that it was almost impossible to tell what he was singing. It has been suggested that his dental decay was due to unrestrained sulphate abuse, but, as he later admitted to Caroline Coon, it was a simple case of neglect: perhaps another rejection of the public school regime.

The new club was christened the Charlie Pigdog club in honour of Charlie, the squat mascot, a mongrel with a Heinz 57 pedigree. In fact, Charlie had two names, and at least as many personalities. 'If you knew him well, he was called Trouble,' says Jules. 'He used to get a bit schizophrenic, I think, because he didn't know who he belonged to. There were about eight or nine – 14, sometimes – people living in the house, and he was never quite sure who he was supposed to be following about.' On Wednesday, 4 December, and most subsequent Wednesdays for the next five months, Charlie had no problem working it out: everyone he knew was going to the same place.

As the Chip was 101's local and it was less than 50 yards door to door, the band's gear could be transported there relatively easily in an old pram. The initial audiences were made up almost entirely of the band's friends and members of the Maida Hill squatting community, so the atmosphere was both friendly and party-like. Woody took his portable Dansette record player along, and people brought records. Alvaro even made sandwiches. 'The room cost a pound,' recalls Liz Lewis. 'When I'd collected enough money at the door – 10p each – to pay for the room and a drink each for the band and me, I'd stop collecting. It was informal. If there was any money left over, it'd be a string fund. It was a good laugh. We'd all go down That Tea Room after.'

The casual approach spilled over on to the stage: friends who could find their way around an instrument were welcome to join the band for a number or two. Simon remembers that Mole's girlfriend Barbie sometimes played harmonica, and Clive Timperley – who, as well as knowing Woody, was also good friends with Liz – began to turn up with his guitar. 'I said, "Can I just sit in? Because you don't seem to have a lead guitar player."' Even Charlie was not averse to making the occasional guest appearance: according to Clive, when the sax players warmed up their horns prior to the gig, the dog would howl along with them. 'Used to crack us up. Hilarious.' In those early days at the Chip, the 101ers did not so much perform as provide the platform for an evening of audience participation.

Richard Nother and Esperanza returned from Spain just before Christmas 1974 and moved straight into 101 Walterton Road. Esperanza's sister Paloma came too, and she and her Bolivian boyfriend took over the squat's front room. It is Esperanza, then a relative newcomer to squat culture, who offers the most evocative portrait of life at number 101 at that time: 'The house was brilliant, I thought. It had a very nice feeling between the people who lived there. We were very good friends: it wasn't like other of the squats, where the people didn't have much to do with each other. We kittied together; or we used to have a bit of bread and butter always in the house, which was as far as it got! And we used to drink tea out of jam jars because we didn't have any cups. We didn't have any heating, so we used to just sit around a gas stove with the oven on and the four rings on top. There were broken panes in the windows, and it was pretty dirty, normally. So it was pretty shocking for a middle class 18-year-old from Spain. But that was the beauty of it. We loved it there. The mattresses used to set on fire every now and then, but we just used to throw buckets of water on them. We didn't have a bathroom, but we had a steam thing, a boiler, that you plugged in and it heated up a bit of water, and we bought between all of us a tin bath, and it was placed in the bike room. So, whenever you were having a bath, if someone came in from the street with a bike, they just wandered in, put the bike there and waved goodbye. When you finished, you just had to pick up this big steam bath full of soapy water and pour it out of the window into the garden below.'

Richard's return was perfectly timed. He was again asked to deputise on drums when Antonio once more decided to depart for foreign climes. Being fellow squatters, most of the neighbours had so far been reasonably tolerant about band practices, which were usually held in the basement and further soundproofed by carpets and mattresses fastened to the walls. The cold, however, encouraged the band to move rehearsals a little closer to the cooker. It was at this point the 101ers received their first bad review. 'We came under fire ... OK, it was from an air rifle, but it was quite a potent air rifle!' remembers Richard. 'Smashing windows, the lot. It was really like being pinned down: we couldn't come out because there was a guy in one of the houses in Chippenham Road just firing this gun into us!'

Someone who was rather more impressed by the 101ers, and especially by his old housemate, was Clive Timperley. Despite having relinquished some of his vocal duties, Woody's frenzied approach to stage performance made him the band's focal point. 'I thought, "Bloody hell, he's really come on!"' says Clive. 'A really enthusiastic frontman.' Eighteen months before he joined the Clash, all the elements of the Clash era Joe Strummer stage persona were already in place: the slack jaw, rolling eyes, the pumping left leg (or, as future Clash roadies would dub it, the 'electric leg') and the vicious, chopping, double-time rhythm guitar style that one journalist would later liken to a Veg-o-matic. 'I'm looking for the ultimate wipe-out, for the ultimate feeling of every song,' Joe told *Record*'s John Mendelssohn in 1984. 'It isn't something you can just do; you have to work yourself up to some elusive pitch.'

It was not a rare event for Woody to make a withdrawal from Liz Lewis's string fund; although he loved his guitars, particularly his cherry-red semi-acoustic Hofner, he took a perverse pride in the brutal punishment he meted out to them. 'He'd say, "I'll know I'm doing my job properly when I break the three top strings on the guitar,"' says Clive. 'And he did it once too, later. All three of the fat strings: not easily done. And he used to draw blood. That's how hard he played. Whatever he lacked in musical expertise, he made up for in pure energy, and that's always the way he would go.'

A sense of commitment to the cause was slowly beginning to filter through the band. January 1975 saw the end of the 101ers' 'open stage' policy. Seriousness of purpose was also evident in Woody's recognition that a more musical guitarist might add another dimension to the group's sound. On 15 January, Clive was officially invited to join. At the time, he was playing with 'a British Steely Dan-type band', which, while better suited to his own musical ambitions, involved more rehearsing than playing. He was attracted to the idea of a little light relief. 'I remember thinking it was quite funny, because Woody phoned me up one Sunday evening in Knightsbridge – where I was living at the time – and he says, "We've had a chat, and we'd like you to join the band." I thought, "This is all very professional!" and I said, "Yes, all right", thinking, "It's one gig a week at the Chippenham: you won't get any money out of it, but it's a laugh."'

It would appear there was another motive behind Woody's invitation. His love of rock'n'roll extended to not only the associated culture, but also the props, namely equipment and instruments. The collection of guitars he had begun in Newport was continuing to grow, and Clive was someone with whom he could talk guitar. 'He used to phone me up, about ten o'clock at night, and say, "What are you doing?" and I'd say, "Nothing much. I'm just going to go to bed in about an hour." He'd say, "I've just bought this guitar, and I want to see what you think about it." So he'd come down – walk through the park - and we'd be up till about one or two in the morning. It'd be like, Guitar Workshop: he'd learn a few licks while he was at it.' Thus, Woody would parlay each new acquisition into a free guitar lesson. 'We – me, Tymon, whoever – would just teach him to hold down the rhythm, to hold down the chord and strum. "That's all I wanna do," he'd say. "I don't wanna do anything flash."' It was a claim Joe was still making in 1988, when interviewed by Bill Flanagan for *Musician* magazine: '*Fuck the fiddly bits!* That's my motto.'

That same year, he revealed the reason for his distinctive style on KCRW. 'It's because I play the guitar the wrong way round. I'm left-handed, but I play strictly right-hand style, because I learned on other people's guitars. And I thought I was being clever, because my more agile hand was on the fret, which I figured would be the more difficult thing. It was only after I learned, and it was too late to change, that I realised I lost all subtlety that these lead guitarists have with *their* right hand: you've got to pick that string, then that string, and come back. I found I could either hit all six strings, or none.'

This was the source of his best-known and most enduring pseudonym. As soon as the Charlie Pigdog club got under way, Woody had begun handing out nicknames to his fellow musicians, in the style of Rip Off Park and the Magic Band. Jules and Alvaro escaped unscathed, and Mole was Mole before he joined; but the lanky Simon Cassell was rechristened Big John, Richard became Snakehips Dudanski, or Snakes for short (and calls himself Richard Dudanski to this day), and new recruit Clive Timperley became Evil C. Timperlee, usually known as Evil. 'Maybe I'm a bit boring, because all he did was reverse my first name,' says the decidedly mild-mannered Clive, still somewhat bemused. 'There was an element of irony about it,' mutters Mole, deadpan.

Woody's own stagename posed rather more of a problem. His first choice was Johnny Caramello, a fairly obvious corruption of his given name. In order to legitimise it, he told Clive that he had previously used it with the Vultures. In his July 1975 *Melody Maker* feature Allan Jones played along, referring to that band as 'Johnny and the Vultures'. Jiving Al denies that the band ever performed under that name, or that Woody was ever called anything but Woody while in Newport, and is supported in both claims by the Vultures poster. Woody had changed identity before, but this would appear to be the first time he attempted to rewrite history to suit the present, something that would become commonplace in the Clash.

His next choice was Joe Strummer. According to Joe, the surname was a reference to his limitations as a guitarist and the forename a more general acknowledgement of the fact that he was nothing special: just an 'ordinary Joe'. 'That's more defensive paranoia,' he told *Sounds'* Pete Silverton in June 1978. 'I could only play chords, and at the first two gigs I ever did [at the Charlie Pigdog club] there were like ten, 20 people in the room who could play better than me . . . I felt very inferior about it, playing music.' 'A kind of Trade Descriptions Act,' he told KCRW. 'So they wouldn't expect anything *but* strumming.'

Thus, the name Joe Strummer was self-deprecating, but humorously so. Hardly unintentionally, for one so well versed in the mythology of pop culture as its would-be new owner, it was also pretty rock'n'roll cool. Woody certainly liked it enough to insist that everyone, bandmates and other friends alike, address him in that manner from then on. The change from John to Woody had been relatively painless, effected between the worlds of public school and art college. The switch from Woody to Joe Strummer when residing in the middle of a close community, several of whose members had known him by the former name for over four years, proved somewhat more difficult. Having a nickname bestowed upon you is considered socially acceptable; bestowing one upon yourself is considered downright peculiar.

'There was this embarrassing period when you'd keep referring to him as Woody and he wouldn't respond,' says Jules. '"My name's Joe, man." "Oh, yeah. Sorry." But it stuck in the end.' Clive remembers it well. '"Call me Joe." "Do we have to?" "Well, in public." And you'd do whatever it was he asked you to, because you liked him.' Mole was less malleable. 'I always carried on calling him Woody, all the time I was in the 101ers.' Richard good-humouredly sidestepped the issue. 'I used to call him Luigi.' Although for the sake of convenience this narrative has Woody instantly becoming Joe Strummer in February 1975, it was not until he joined the Clash and – temporarily, at least – broke many of his ties with his former life that the long-drawn-out transformation was completed.

Most members of the 101ers agree that, by February, the band was beginning to shape up. Mole bought a bass amp and Clive brought along his own equipment, improving the sound and rendering the kitchen-drawer speakers obsolete. After Joe, Richard was probably the most enthusiastic participant in the band, so much so that he refused to surrender the drum stool to a returning Antonio and became an official member of the 101ers on 15 February. 'I was dead keen by then, definitely,' he says. 'The bug had bitten. I liked it, and they wanted me to continue, so I continued.' Antonio had his own lack of commitment to blame. 'I've been in loads of different bands, and the old joke is, you can't go on holiday,' notes Clive wryly. 'If you go away for a week or two, when you come back you're probably not going to be in the band any more. *That's rock'n'roll*, I'm afraid.'

Up to this point, the 101ers were still using the drum kit Antonio had borrowed back in August 1974, but, not surprisingly, the original owner now wanted it back. Richard recollects that when he called round for it, Joe and he pretended to be non-English-speaking Spaniards in order to hold on to it for a little longer. Aware that this ruse had a limited lifespan, they persuaded Clive – working as a van driver at the time – to take them down to Pablo LaBritain's house in Surrey in order to retrieve Joe's old kit. 'So we did that,' says Clive. 'Went down there, went to Pablo's house, and he's got the drums set up in the garage. I remember standing there, and Pablo says, "I'll just show you what I can do", and he played the drums, and he was *brilliant*. And me and Strummer are looking at each other, and Strummer's thinking, "I can't do it! I can't take the drums off him. It's cruel, because the guy's really worked hard and he's really good." So he didn't: he left them. And we spent the evening watching Pablo play drums!' A couple of weeks later, Richard bought his own Pearl kit on Portobello Market.

Towards the end of February, the 101ers made a joint investment. They had secured bookings at a long-forgotten venue in Brixton for 22 February, and at Chelsea College of Art for 1 March, supporting Ian Dury's pre-Blockheads band, Kilburn and the Highroads. Unfortunately, they lacked the transport to get them there. 'Simon came in one day and said he'd seen this great hearse,' recalls Jules. 'It was like, £50. Everyone chucked whatever they had in a hat, and he went and bought it. It was a great old thing.' It seemed intimations of mortality were destined to dog Joe throughout his musical career . . .

A photo-session was arranged on the day of the Brixton gig to capture the band at this key moment in its history and, as well as at the Chippenham and at 101, photographer Ray Eagle took several shots of them posing on the kerb next to their new purchase. One of these appears on the back cover of the 101ers' posthumous album, *Elgin Avenue Breakdown*, and another in Jules's 1992 photo-book *Joe Strummer With The 101ers And The Clash 1974–1976*. Alvaro donated a third picture from the session to this book, taken in the basement of 101. Most of the band are long-haired, idiosyncratically be-hatted and generally attired in the floppy and flared manner of late hippy; Joe is still favouring the leather jacket, straight jeans and boots, but his shortish, swept-back hair adds a touch of the Fifties rocker to his traditional Woody Guthrie ensemble.

Alvaro was decidedly less happy than the others about the way the band was progressing. 'We all thought that we were making shit music' is his recollection today. Pat's similar claim about the band *circa* autumn 1974 provokes little in the way of dissent, but Richard for one is keen to take issue with Alvaro about the 101ers' abilities by the spring of 1975. 'That's bollocks!' he states. '*He* might have thought that. We knew we were no great band, but we definitely thought it was something worth doing.' The selection and simplicity of the material and the generally limited standard of musicianship were two of the factors contributing to Alvaro's disgruntlement, but they were by no means the only ones. Nine years Joe's senior, a seasoned and (in his native country) successful musician and the person initially responsible for getting the band on-stage – to this day, he insists he and Joe were co-founders of the 101ers – it must have been galling for Alvaro to watch Joe assume leadership, something which Clive, Mole, Jules and Richard all concede had occurred by March 1975. Furthermore, the instrumental dominance of the horns and Alvaro's own role as musical arranger and featured soloist had been challenged by the arrival of the equally experienced and proficient Clive Timperley on lead guitar.

Alvaro left the band on 27 March to make his own music. Unless one counts the Mad Chilean, he was denied a nickname during his stay with the 101ers; thereafter, however, he dubbed himself Alvaro, the Chilean with the Singing Nose, and began to record and release his own undeniably eccentric compositions, commencing with the 1977 album *Drinkin' My Own Sperm* . . .

This, and all subsequent efforts, can be found on Squeaky Shoes records.

In his July 1975 *Melody Maker* 101ers feature Allan Jones described his first visit to the Charlie Pigdog club that February thus: 'It was the kind of place which held extraordinary promises of violence. You walked in, took one look around, and wished you were the hell out of there... After ten minutes glancing into secluded corners half-expecting to see someone having their face decorated with a razor, the paranoia count was soaring. The gig that particular night ended in a near massacre. As the 101ers screamed their way through a 20-minute interpretation of "Gloria", which sounded like the perfect soundtrack for the last apocalyptic days of the Third Reich, opposing factions of (I believe) Irish and gypsies attempted to carve each other out. Bottles were smashed over defenceless heads, blades flashed, and howling dogs tore at one another's throats, splattering the walls with blood. The band tore on, with Joe Strummer thrashing away at his guitar like there was no tomorrow, completely oblivious to the surrounding carnage. The police finally arrived, flashing blue lights, sirens, the whole works. Strummer battled on. He was finally confronted by the imposing figure of the law, stopped in mid-flight, staggered to a halt and looked up. "Evening, officer," he said.'

This is a million miles away from the cosy Dansette-and-sandwiches ambience of the club's early days, and it seems Allan approached his piece with the twin purposes of instantly mythologising his college buddy's band and indulging himself in a little bravura Gonzo-style journalism in order to shake up the staid and predictable pages of the 1975-vintage *Melody Maker*. Word of mouth had extended the 101ers' audience to include R&B enthusiasts from outside the squatting community, ensuring that the Charlie Pigdog club was invariably packed. The band's full-tilt approach to its material, highlighted by Joe's manic stage persona, tended to draw an excited reaction from the crowd. But there were no scenes of carnage. 'Downstairs, it was a violent pub,' says Mole, 'but it really didn't happen much upstairs, because it wasn't normal local punters, it was more hippies, younger types.'

The police were called out on a couple of occasions, but usually for reasons other than violence: 'When it had gone way beyond closing time, and the band was still going,' says Jules. 'Also, I think people were just coming in and stealing stuff, and dropping it out of the windows to people down below.' Joe and Richard both mentioned this outbreak of petty theft in Paolo Hewitt's 1981 101ers retrospective, and most people involved with the band now believe the resulting aggravation explains why the landlord shut down the Charlie Pigdog club following a gig on 24 April 1975. At the time, they were given no reason more convincing than a vague plan to redecorate. The club is now a snooker room.

The Chippenham residency lasted two days and one gig longer than Jules's performing membership of the band. Again, there was more than one reason for his departure. Firstly, Jules was planning a holiday. 'I had a Swiss girlfriend,' he says. 'Joe was into total commitment, and the idea of going on holiday with your girlfriend was, like, not serious.' In addition, his self-confidence much improved, Joe wished to reclaim the microphone for himself. Lastly, the 101ers wanted to pursue the possibility of playing more gigs further afield, and Clive and Joe in particular felt it would be practical to trim the band down to a more manageable size. 'I was sacked,' says Jules. 'It was OK. That's the way it was done. You were politely told, "You're out, man." It was democratically done, basically, by whoever was still in the band, and I can't think of a better way.' He bore no grudge, as he had been feeling vaguely embarrassed about his contribution for some time. 'A bit of singing and maracas. I couldn't really play anything. I didn't consider myself a musician at all.'

Jules continued to share accommodation with the band and, for a while, acted as a kind of unofficial manager, finding gigs and keeping any hustling would-be official managers at bay. 'No one was going to be told how to dress up or what to do,' he says. 'So it was easier to push all that away, and everyone did what they liked and organised it themselves.' Shortly afterwards, Jules began to study photography, film and television at the London College of Printing. He used the band, and especially Joe, as subjects to help hone his photographic talents, the results of which are preserved in his 1992 book; in turn, the band encouraged him to use his access to equipment and materials to produce promotional posters. (An early 1976 example boasted the slogan 'BEAT MUSIC DYNAMITE!', which came uncannily close to being ten years ahead of its time.)

Back in January 1975, Joe had replaced the Bolivian boyfriend in Paloma's affections, at which point – in an extension of the Beefheartian nickname fever surrounding the 101ers – she was rechristened Palmolive. It is Esperanza's opinion that the fact Joe and Richard found themselves dating sisters was responsible for strengthening the bond between them. That Easter, they commandeered the hearse and – somewhat ironically, given that short-notice trips away had been a factor in the dismissal from the 101ers of both Jules and Antonio – set off with their partners for a non-luxury holiday in Wales. 'It was a great adventure,' recalls Esperanza. 'The water pipe was broken and we had to fill it up every two miles.'

Within a month of returning to London, Joe got married; but not to Palmolive. As part of his preparation for the next stage of the 101ers' development, he had decided that it was time to get himself a decent guitar. Initially intending to earn the price of one with the sweat of his brow, he took a job with the council as a gardener in Hyde Park, 'cutting the verge that never ends'. As with the London Coliseum cleaning job, however, fate soon intervened to offer him some easy money that meant he could dispense with the need to work altogether. 'I met this South American chick who wanted to get married,' he told Allan Jones that July. 'To stay in the country, see? She paid me £100. So I quit the job and got a Telecaster to go with the AC30. I'll get the divorce through in about two years.'

The 'marriage of convenience' scam was fairly commonplace at the time, so many members of the Maida Hill squatting community being foreigners in the country on limited visitors' visas. It was considered such an everyday event and was over and done with so quickly that none of the 101ers, including Simon, who stood as one of the witnesses, can recollect anything about the wedding or Joe's bride. Even Joe had trouble remembering the girl's name and nationality, which caused problems for him when he eventually did get around to seeking a divorce: in September 1986, T-Zers, the *NME* gossip page, mentioned that he was trying to trace a 'South African' called 'Pam'. The marriage certificate states that John Graham Mellor, a 22-year-old musician of 101 Walterton Road (by this time no longer his real address), married Pamela Jill Moolman, a 25-year-old social worker of 51 Doynton Street in Archway, on 16 May 1975 at St Pancras Register Office, Euston Road. Only Esperanza seems able to provide further background and account for the apparent confusion over Pam's country of origin: 'She was a friend of somebody called Rose who also lived in 101. I think she was just travelling to South America after she married, or she'd just come back from South America and needed the visa to stay in England. But she was definitely South African.'

As it was just a paper relationship, the marriage did not upset Palmolive in any way at the time, but it did affect her indirectly. 'This was when Spain wasn't in the Common Market, so all our Spanish friends had trouble,' explains Richard. 'I married Esperanza, even though it wasn't *marriage* marriage, in August 1975. At least I didn't charge her! Joe was our witness. But Paloma did have problems. She couldn't marry Joe, who she was living with at the time, so she married my brother Patrick. People married anyone.' Clive, for one, is under no illusions about where Joe's affections really lay. 'Basically, Strummer married his Fender,' he says. 'It's true! I think that's a great image for him, because the Telecaster is definitely him, it's his prop.' Certainly, although the guitar-mad Joe had acquired and played many different styles and makes in the past and would experiment with others in future, the Fender Telecaster (and, later, the look-alike Esquire) was to be his instrument of choice from June 1975 onwards.

Early May of that year saw time finally run out for 101 Walterton Road. Anticipating eviction, the household relocated of its own accord when Richard and Simon picked the locks of another empty house at 36 St Luke's Road, just a few hundred yards to the south. They moved in with Joe, Esperanza, Palmolive and Joe's old Newport friend Micky Foote, who by this time was hanging around and showing an interest in the band. Number 36 became the new venue for rehearsals, but it never acquired anything like the atmosphere of 101. This was partly because St Luke's was not as squat-oriented as Walterton Road, and the new arrivals were to encounter more sustained hostility. 'We stayed throughout the summer,' says Richard, 'but we had some pretty heavy scenes with some of the local kids: nicking, breaking in, stuff like that.'

As a band, the 101ers' immediate priority following the closure of the

Charlie Pigdog club was to find a pub prepared to offer them a weekly residency, so that they could maintain the momentum they had already built up. That April, in the *Melody Maker*'s Hot Licks column, Allan Jones expressed his objection to the attention afforded New York bands like Television, while 'a really exciting band like the 101ers, with a stack of AC30s [are] playing gigs like the Charlie Pigdog club for a packet of peanuts and half a bitter'. Allan's appreciation of the 101ers was genuine enough, but it is hard not to see his championing of an old college friend's band as an act of nepotism. Nevertheless, in the 1981 101ers retrospective interview with *Melody Maker*'s Paolo Hewitt Joe was dismissive of this support. 'That was like the summit of a year's sweat. That was the ultimate, this little cutting. No-one was interested. *Nobody.*' His deprecatory remarks were questionably motivated, however, and history proves him wrong.

Micky and Jules took that cutting down to the Elgin pub, just south of the Westway on Ladbroke Grove, and parlayed it into a one-off gig for Thursday 12 May. This in turn proved successful enough for the band to be offered a weekly Thursday-night slot that began on 26 May and – it turned out - lasted the remainder of 1975. Like the Chippenham, the Elgin was chosen largely for convenience. 'It was just the next nearest place,' says Jules, who does not feel that the venue represented any kind of advancement for the 101ers. Richard disagrees. The band had found it necessary to set up the Charlie Pigdog club themselves in order to be able to play for their friends; by contrast, the Elgin was an established, if not particularly high-profile, music pub that booked the band on reputation and merit to play for an open audience; furthermore, the 101ers were the only band to be offered a residency there at that time.

Simon 'Big John' Cassell survived for just the first two gigs at the Elgin. With Alvaro no longer in the line-up, Simon was the sole horn player, but his musicianship was not strong enough to carry the burden alone. 'Sax is not an instrument that you can pick up and play very well from the word go,' says Richard, diplomatically. Again, the need to trim down the band was a factor, and again, there was some tension with Clive regarding musical dominance. 'I did have disagreements with Clive over different approaches to music,' acknowledges Simon. Clive went to work on Joe. 'I said, "You want to get this into a four-piece. Big John's a really great bloke, but, y'know ..."' Although getting rid of Simon would make Joe sole vocalist and leave him in near-total control of the band, he resisted the idea, partly because he considered Simon a good friend and partly because of the strong visual contrast he provided on-stage. In the event, his dissatisfaction with the change in musical style prompted Simon to leave the 101ers of his own accord following the 26 May Elgin gig. Soon afterwards, he moved to Germany, where he improved his skills playing sax in various jazz groups. After returning to the UK, he qualified as a barrister. He now concentrates on playing Middle Eastern music, his preferred instrument being the saz, a sort of long-necked lute. 'I'm not doing it full-time, but it takes up a lot of my life.'

Up to this point, the 101ers had always announced and advertised themselves as an 'R&B Orchestra'. Their horn-dominated line-up harked back to late Fifties urban R&B bands and even late Forties jump bands, but also reflected a by no means minor contemporary musical trend. There were the crossover glam rock'n'roll big bands, like Wizzard, ELO and Showaddywaddy; the Rolling Stones had featured a horn section on their 1972 album *Exile On Main Street* and their subsequent records of the early to mid Seventies; Van Morrison had captured his highly individual combination of Celtic muse, Stax soul and Chicago R&B on the 1974 double live album *It's Too Late To Stop Now*; the still largely unknown Bruce Springsteen was honing his particular take on the big-band sound on early albums like 1973's *The Wild, The Innocent And The E Street Shuffle*; and John Lennon was engaged in revisiting several original rock'n'roll and R&B classics in full-blown style for the album eventually released in 1975 under the hardly misleading title *Rock'n'Roll*.

Richard maintains that the live Van Morrison album was probably the biggest influence on the sound to which the Chippenham era 101ers aspired; if not necessarily the material played, which in turn evidences the sizeable input at that stage of the Morrison-loving Simon Cassell. Joe had listened to Them as a schoolboy, so it had not been too much of a leap for him to learn to appreciate the music of the post-Them Morrison. (In a July 1982 *Sounds* interview with Dave McCullough Joe admitted a respect for Van's early solo output, saying, 'I know a lot about him from my 101ers days.') His own preference, though, was for the more aggressive, basic and guitar-dominated R&B of the early Sixties Stones, and the late Fifties Chuck Berry and Bo Diddley. With the horns dismissed and Clive on hand to play the 'fiddly bits', Joe was now free to take his chosen musical direction.

Back in autumn 1974, expediency had been the dominant factor in the 101 All Stars' choice of material, but as 1975 progressed, changes in line-up and improving musicianship did not affect the band's repertoire in any way other than to expand it to fill a show of anything up to two and a half hours. 'Bony Maronie' and 'Gloria' remained the usual opening and closing numbers for the band's entire lifespan. Clive might have been partial to country and muso rock and Richard, whose tastes were eclectic, particularly fond of Sixties soul, but precious little proof of this made it to the live set. Similarly, Mole was a reggae enthusiast, but while he recalls playing a version of Desmond Dekker's 'Israelites' at the Charlie Pigdog club with himself on guitar and Joe on bass and, later in 1975, working up a 'more roots' reggae song in the Big Youth vein, such experimentation with Jamaican rhythms was confined to soundchecks only.

Having said that, no member of the band was deeply unhappy about the songs the 101ers performed, which were either vintage R&B and rock'n'roll or compositions in a closely related style by second generation bands born of those traditions. Unsurprisingly, Chuck Berry was the main source, providing 'No Particular Place To Go', 'Johnny B. Goode', 'Too Much Monkey Business', 'Maybellene', 'Roll Over Beethoven', 'Carol' and (though it was written in 1946 by Bobby Troup for the Nat Cole Trio) '(Get Your Kicks On) Route 66'. Bo Diddley furnished 'Who Do You Love', 'Don't Let Go' and 'Six Gun Blues', and Johnny Otis the Diddley-esque 1958-vintage 'Willie And The Hand Jive'. In addition to 'Bony Maronie', miscellaneous other classics from the rock'n'roll era included Gene Vincent's 'Be-Bop-A-Lula', Little Richard's 'Slippin' And Slidin'' (all of which, incidentally, were also covered on John Lennon's *Rock'n'Roll*), Elvis Presley's 'Heartbreak Hotel' and Eddie Cochran's 'Summertime Blues'.

The Rolling Stones were represented by the song they wrote for Chris Farlowe in 1966, 'Out Of Time', and by the Slim Harpo song they covered on *Exile On Main Street*, 'Shake Your Hips'. The Beatles bequeathed 'Day Tripper', 'I'm Down' and – perfect for Joe – the Chuck Berry meets the Beach Boys parody 'Back In The USSR'. Also from the mid-Sixties came the Small Faces' 'Sha La La Lee' and Roy C.'s 'Shotgun Wedding'. Van Morrison was responsible for not only 'Gloria', but also the 101ers' most up-to-date number, the 1970 composition 'Domino'. Some of the band's choices of cover version were a little less obvious: Louis Jordan and the Tympany Five's 1946 hit 'Choo Choo Ch' Boogie'; what Clive describes as 'an old cajun-type R&B number from the Fifties' called 'Hoy, Hoy, Hoy', lifted from an old compilation album; and an equally obscure song called 'Junco Partner', possibly from the same source. 'I learned it off this bargain record I bought,' Joe told *Record Mirror*'s Billy Sloan in 1981, shortly after he had recorded a reggae version with the Clash. 'Apparently, it's a 50-year-old New Orleans standard.'

By 1975, as far as London was concerned, the Rock'n'Roll Revival had been, if not superseded, then largely engulfed by yet another pre-punk back-to-basics movement. What has come to be known as pub rock was a direct result of record companies being more interested in the latest creatively bankrupt 'supergroup' than in searching out new talent. In fact, it was not a unified movement as such: most of the bands had little in common save the venues their lack of record company backing or commercial clout required them to play. Some of the outfits on the London pub circuit in the early to mid Seventies were just fairly ordinary country or progressive rock bands who had not yet managed to get a foot in the record companies' doors. Others were talented bands who were either too nonconformist to raise any interest or had already had their fingers burned by the music business.

A few had more in common with Joe's philosophy as expounded to Allan Jones in July 1975: 'I mean, if you go and see a rock group, you want to see someone tearing their soul apart at 36 bars a second, not listen to some instrumental slush. Since '67, music has been chasing itself up a blind alley with all that shit.' They were young, enthusiastic and wired, and they played a stripped-down, pugnacious rock music, drawing their core repertoires from the late Fifties or mid-Sixties golden ages before music – as they believed – chased itself up that blind alley. Eddie and the Hot Rods modelled themselves on a *Nuggets*-type Sixties US garage or punk band and covered Sixties rock classics like ? and the Mysterians' '96 Tears' and the Who's 'The Kids Are Alright'. Dr Feelgood adopted a sleazy and menacing East End gangster look to deliver viciously fast R&B, with a repertoire not a million miles away from that of the 101ers. 'The Feelgoods: we certainly admired them when we started playing,' says Richard. 'Late summer of '74 I think we saw them in the Windsor Castle. Wilko Johnson was great.' He was also, significantly enough, a manic guitarist who favoured the Telecaster.

In retrospect, it is clear that bands like Dr Feelgood did as much as the New York Dolls and Ramones to prepare the ground for the UK's 1976 punk rock movement. In the years immediately pre-punk, however, they had to be judged by their own achievements. Against the trend of the times, Dr Feelgood were signed by United Artists in late 1974, made the transition to the UK's larger venues and, in 1975, released two albums: *Down By The Jetty* and *Malpractice*. The decidedly Seventies edge the Feelgoods gave their R&B repertoire served, despite such idiosyncrasies as mono production, to make the band more than just a backwards-looking novelty act. In turn, the Feelgood Factor gave the 101ers commercial hope, a new-found credibility and, paradoxically, increased contemporary relevance.

Like the good Doctor, by mid-1975 the 101ers had another ace up their sleeve: the ability to compose their own genre-appropriate material. Joe had begun to write lyrics and vocal melody lines in Newport, and was now capable of working out rudimentary R&B chord progressions to fit. The finished version invariably required a little help from his friends. 'Strummer would say, "I've got an idea for a song,"' explains Clive, 'and he'd come and play it: Guitar Workshop. I'd say, "OK, let's work it out. If I just make that chord this chord . . ." Whatever, because I arrange things, I'm good at doing that in bands, get it into a viable thing without losing the raw integrity of the song.' Other band members would also add their ideas at rehearsals.

The first song written was 'Keys To Your Heart'. It was credited to Strummer, whereas most subsequent Joe-originated compositions were credited to Strummer–101ers in acknowledgement of the others' sizeable musical input. By June 1975, these included 'Motor Boys Motor' and 'Steamgauge 99'. As the year progressed, the band added 'Letsa-getabitarockin', 'Silent Telephone', 'Hideaway', 'Green Love' and a less typical Mole composition called 'Boo The Goose', which Clive describes as 'a funky soul number'. Musically, the 101ers proved they had a varied repertoire of tricks within the limits dictated by both line-up and genre. Joe's lyrics were rendered almost incomprehensible by his mangled delivery – even on later studio versions of the songs – but he revealed a distinctly Berry-esque style: verbose yet slick, with plenty of internal rhymes. The subject matter of his songs from this period is largely predictable. 'Motor Boys Motor' pays tribute to Chuck Berry's fascination with all things automotive and, in its title at least, 'Steamgauge 99' harks back to both 'Route 66' and Pete Johnson's late Forties boogie-woogie classic 'Rocket 88'. 'Letsagetabitarockin' promotes the idea of a rock gig as endurance test: 'I'm ready to drop / But I don't wanna stop.' 'Silent Telephone' concerns itself with that old staple, the girl who doesn't ring and who, in this case, is called Suzie, a name as generic in rock'n'roll as either Johnny or Joe. If it is a 'lost love' song, then 'Keys To Your Heart' is a song celebrating the redemptive power of love: 'I used to be a teenage drug-taker . . .'

Shortly after Simon Cassell's departure the 101ers were threatened with another defection from the ranks. In June, Clive Timperley was offered good money to join up with someone whom Joe described to Allan Jones as a 'lame-brained singer-songwriter'. Despite his active role in shaping the 101ers, Clive had found it hard to reconcile himself to having taken what he believed to be a backwards musical step: he had begun his musical career in a mid-Sixties R&B outfit, Captain Rougely's Blues Band, and had since moved on to work within more demanding musical structures. The issue lay dormant as long as the 101ers remained a once-a-week hobby band and he could continue to think of it as something to keep him occupied until one of his more serious projects took off. The approach from the singer-songwriter coincided with a demand from Joe for 100 per cent commitment, however, and Clive was torn between the two.

No longer so casual about the band that they were prepared to recruit amateurs from the local squatting community, the others placed an ad for a replacement guitarist. Meanwhile, Clive pondered the ultimatum. If not the most musically challenging of the bands he had been in, the 101ers were certainly the most fun; being involved in the writing and arranging of the band's own material at least gave him some opportunity to stretch himself creatively; he had seen little in the way of hard cash so far, but the 101ers were now beginning to play two or three times a week, and the prospects of some kind of breakthrough were definitely improving. After weighing up the pros and cons, Clive decided to stay. 'I had no time for the other bands, so I just let them fade away.'

Most of the 101ers' early ventures away from the Elgin were local: squatters' benefits and anniversary celebrations at Tolmer's Village in Euston and the Chippenham Factory in Maida Hill, a benefit for the Law Centre at Acklam Hall in Portobello Road and the first of several occasional gigs at the Windsor Castle pub on the Harrow Road. But in late June and July, Jules found the 101ers a couple of ostensibly prestige gigs in the heart of Soho, where the likes of the Rolling Stones had originally made their mark.

The first of these was at the St Moritz club, 159 Wardour Street. Unsurprisingly, given the club's name, the owner, a Mr Sweety, was Swiss. The gig came about because Jules's Swiss girlfriend was working as a waitress in the upstairs restaurant. The 101ers first played the club on 18 June 1975, and returned on 20 June, 2 July and 27 August. Whatever the repeat bookings might indicate to the contrary, these shows were not a success. 'It was just a dump,' says Mole. 'It was a really embarrassing place to play, really out of sync with us.' Jules elaborates: 'It was this tiny little basement, and it was full of students from the other side of the world who didn't really know what hit 'em when the 101ers cranked out this loud music. They did two sets, bashing out this R&B, and the people were all gawping at it because they couldn't respond to that kind of music. Then, as soon as the set was over, the jukebox came back on, all pop stuff, and everybody started dancing again. It was bizarre.' There were also difficulties with getting Mr Sweety to hand over the money. 'He did pay us, but he was busy running the restaurant upstairs, and he expected us to wait until he'd cleared it up.'

The most positive outcome of the experience was that it inspired the song 'Sweety Of The St Moritz'. Although the lyric of the recorded version is typically hard to decipher, Joe can be heard complaining at length about the 101ers' first experience of indifference, and making reference to the perceived shortcomings of venue, audience and owner as outlined above by Jules. A great driving rock song, it is notable for being the first Strummer composition to draw extensively on his own experiences, protest unfairness and spit vitriol. Admittedly, it gets its knickers in a knot about next to nothing at all, but it can be seen as a precursor of some of the first Clash album's protest songs, and of such later State of the Clash broadcasts as '(White Man) In Hammersmith Palais' and 'Safe European Home'.

Jules's second coup was a gig Upstairs at Ronnie Scott's, the small room at Frith Street's famous London jazz club. Clive explains the deal: '"We'll put your band on, we'll give you a listing on our little card and we'll give you 200 free tickets. Give them to all your mates, they come down, spend a fortune at the bar." We got paid £15. Not bad for 1975,' he concedes grudgingly. 'Meanwhile, the money Ronnie Scott's took over the bar would pay for the evening and probably the whole week. It's crap. *Downstairs* at Ronnie Scott's: *that's* a big deal.' Richard acknowledges that he has a point, but is less cynical than either Clive or Jules about the 101ers' first forays into Soho. 'It was great!' he enthuses. 'It was an incredible feeling of non-stop progression.'

If the St Moritz produced a song, then Ronnie Scott's led to the band's first (and only) radio broadcast, albeit on minor London pirate station Radio Concorde. The land-based station was forced to broadcast from a different location every night, and on an earlier occasion had set up at 101 Walterton Road. 'They used to put their aerials up, and the Post Office spotter vans would be coming around trying to get a line on them,' recalls Richard. 'It was real cops-and-robbers stuff. They'd just confiscate their gear if they found them actually doing it. I remember one of the Concorde guys escaping across the roof of our house.' In return, Concorde arranged to broadcast a tape of the Ronnie Scott's gig. Unfortunately, as part of its efforts to avoid being traced, the station also selected its frequency on a random basis. 'We didn't hear it,' says Clive, 'because we didn't know what to tune in to!' On the whole, though, the 101ers approved of the station, and on 13 February 1976, they would play a benefit for it at Hampstead Town Hall.

The summer of 1975 saw the 101ers venturing even further afield, usually thanks to the good offices of a friend of the band who owned a van and who luckily happened to be a 'manic dancer' and a fan. Dave McLardy, known as Dave the Van Driver (or D the VD for short), was happy to provide transport, up to a point. 'He would only take us within about 50 miles of London,' says Richard of his future brother-in-law. (Dave would ultimately marry Palmolive: *marriage* marriage.) 'If we went any further, we'd hire a van.'

Two of the furthest-flung gigs at this time were festivals in Wiltshire: the Stonehenge on 21 June and the Windsor at Watchfield on 24 August. The latter was memorable because the 101ers played different consecutive hour-long sets on each of the three separate stages, the former because, on the day of the event, Clive caught flu and refused to travel, leaving the others to muddle through without a lead instrument.

Almost as if to compensate for this, upon their return to London and Clive's return to good health the 101ers began occasionally to augment their line-up with a friend of Clive's named Dan Kelleher. At the time the bassist for another squat group named the Derelicts, Dan was frequently to be found in the audience at 101ers gigs. A musical all-rounder, he was sometimes invited to join the full-strength band on-stage for a couple of numbers as either slide or second lead guitarist. As an honorary member, he was awarded a nickname. 'Strummer would shout into the mike, "Is Desperate there?"' says Clive. 'And Dan would come on to the stage.'

On 26 July 1975, *Melody Maker* printed Allan Jones's enthusiastic full-length 101ers feature, which showcased the Strummer philosophy and made the band out to be the most exciting gritty lowlife band in town. In the wake of Dr Feelgood's move into the big league, Allan's decidedly slanted rave write-up was almost guaranteed to make something happen for the 101ers; and it did. The review was instrumental in establishing the 101ers as a name band on the London pub circuit, making it much easier for them to get regular gigs at a steadily increasing number of that circuit's more prestigious venues.

On 4 August, the band played the first of half a dozen occasional gigs at the Hope and Anchor, 207 Upper Street, Islington; on 30 August, they played their first at the Nashville Room, 171 North End Road, Kensington, which resulted in a weekly Tuesday night residency from 7 October to 4 November; on 4 October, the first of several occasional gigs at Dingwalls, Camden Town Lock; on 8 November, the first of an irregular series of gigs at the Red Cow, 157 Hammersmith Road; and on 20 November, the first of two gigs at the Speakeasy. By October and November 1975, the 101ers found themselves playing almost every other night; although their schedule subsequently settled down to a less exhausting pattern of a gig approximately every three nights, the band would never again be short of work. 'Allan Jones definitely helped' is Richard's verdict.

More press was to follow. Not wanting to lose out to *Melody Maker*, the

NME dispatched Chas De Whalley to witness the 101ers' first Hope and Anchor gig on what, as the writer subsequently explained at length, was an extremely hot night to be watching a sweaty R&B band in a cramped pub cellar. His review, published on 16 August, was a deliberately oddball one which indicated that he understood the spirit of the band, even if he was not prepared to spare some of its members' feelings: 'Only Clive Timperlee on lead guitar boasts any kind of real musical ability and, as for the others . . . they start out of time, finish out of time, and play out of tune. They also churn out some very fine rock'n'roll with no pretence at all towards music, let alone art . . . What separates them from some of the truly bad bands currently working in London is their honesty, and an intelligence which ensures that they attempt nothing they cannot handle . . . When they're good, they're very, very good . . . and their own compositions "Steamgauge 99" and "Motor Boys Motor" can stand unashamedly beside some of the rock'n'roll standards that make up the rest of their set. Now that . . . Dr Feelgood have left the pubs, the 101ers are definite contenders for London's rock'n'roll crown.'

For their own part, the 101ers did not feel they had succeeded in gatecrashing any pub rock 'scene'. 'I think we thought we were totally doing our own thing,' says Richard. 'It wasn't as if we were aspiring to become part of a thing that was there already. Obviously, objectively, we were, because we were playing these pubs, but we didn't *aspire* to being part of that group. And I think, increasingly through 1975 and the beginning of 1976, there was the notion that, "There should be something better!" Which didn't necessarily mean better groups or bigger gigs, but something more vibrant. Which is in fact what happened with the punk uprising of '76. In late '75, I remember *Time Out* once referring to us as a "punk" band.'

The demanding new schedule persuaded Clive to give up his van-driving job. 'It was getting really hard to get up in the morning.' Like the others, he signed on as unemployed, but he maintains there was no real element of fraud involved: at the time, the 101ers' gigs were generating just about enough income to keep the band functioning. In anticipation of things improving, though, the band borrowed the money to pay for a decent PA. Micky Foote, who was now working as roadie and occasional driver and had largely taken over from Jules as unofficial manager, also began to mix the 101ers' live sound.

As for the gigs themselves, the people involved with the band offer a mixed bag of memories and impressions. The October residency at the Nashville was where Dan's guest spot became a regular fixture; it was also where, both Richard and Clive claim, Eddie and the Hot Rods (with whom the 101ers were alternating as headliners) swiped the 101ers' extended version of 'Gloria'. The following year, the Rods' treatment made it to number 43 in the UK singles charts as part of their *Live At The Marquee* EP. 'We were really pissed off with them,' says Clive. 'But there's no licence, is there? It wasn't even our song.' It was at Dingwalls that Joe finally achieved his ambition, according to Clive, of breaking the top three strings on his guitar. As for having been intimidated by the prospect of playing the Speakeasy, that watering hole of rock gods, Richard reveals something of the 101ers' proto-punk attitude: 'No, we weren't at all impressed. Hopefully, we intimidated *them*.'

On 18 November, Joe went to see Bruce Springsteen's much-hyped appearance at the Hammersmith Odeon. With hindsight, Clive suspects Joe was very impressed by Bruce, another energetic, Fender-wielding fan of Chuck Berry and Bob Dylan who was similarly intent on using his own songs as an outlet for his obsession with rock'n'roll mythology. 'When Strummer saw Springsteen, I think he thought, "Hello, this is the kind of image I've already got, and *look* at this guy!"' Certainly, thereafter, elements of Joe's stagecraft began to develop along similar lines to Bruce's. He bought an especially long lead so he was free to move around more and indulge himself in some grandstanding showmanship. 'At one gig, there happened to be a mattress lying in one corner – I don't know what it was doing there – and he jumped on it and stayed on it for about ten minutes while we were doing "Gloria",' recalls Clive. 'He just kept looking at me while I was doing this solo, just blasting away, and I was thinking, "Come on, you've got to get back to the mike!" and he was just lying there. And then all of a sudden, he *rushed* back up on-stage and got to the mike just in time. Brilliant!'

As he became more at ease on-stage, Joe also developed an easy line in between-song patter. 'He always had something to say,' laughs Clive. Esperanza remembers an incident at the Red Cow that was more P. J. Proby than Bruce Springsteen: 'His trouser zip broke, and he just took his trousers off on-stage while talking into the microphone, and proceeded to change them for a pair from Micky Foote. The audience loved it!' When the occasion demanded, Joe was more than prepared to abandon on-stage wit in favour of off-stage confrontation. 'There was some bloke at the back who was shouting,' says Clive, 'and Joe just walked up to this bloke – long lead – and whispered something in his ear. There was not a peep out of him after that.' Richard recollectss another occasion when a front-row heckler was doused with a pint of beer.

By October, life at 36 St Luke's Road had become unbearable, so Micky and Jules went scouting for a new home and band HQ. Just over half a mile to the east they found an empty house at 42 Orsett Terrace. It too was awaiting redevelopment by the GLC, and it was relatively easy for them to break in through the corrugated iron covering the windows and doors. This act of forced entry was reported by the area caretaker, resulting in the arrest of both offenders. Charges were dropped for the usual reason: there were already several other squatters living in the street and it made more sense for the GLC to have them all cleared out together when it was time to proceed with its plans. Micky, Jules, Joe, Palmolive, Richard and Esperanza moved in and had the sizeable terrace house to themselves. There was room for a studio for the two sisters, both of whom made ceramics, and also a band rehearsal room in the basement. Micky even managed to get a payphone installed, which made it much easier to arrange bookings and practices. 'This terrace, there were all kinds of people living there. Some of them very good friends of ours. More Spanish people! The King of Spain used to call . . .' laughs Richard. Joe's exposure during his squatting days to most of the Spanish-speaking peoples of the world may offer one explanation as to why he would so readily lapse into cod Spanish when doing backing vocals with the Clash.

Not everyone was friendly. 'One night our friends heard something on their roof, and the next time it rained water poured in,' says Richard. 'These junkies from further up the road had come out over the roofs and nicked all their lead. So much for community spirit, eh? We thought, "We'll be the next ones, they'll nick ours." So I went to a carpenter's and bought a load of barbed wire to stop people coming on to our roof at night, and we nailed down their trapdoor from outside so they couldn't get out. That solved it.' On the whole, though, life at Orsett Terrace was far less problematic than at St Luke's Road.

On the subject of drugs: by mid-1975, while the popularity of marijuana remained constant, other late hippie favourites like acid and mandrax, (downers in tablet form), were being replaced in the drug-taking community's affections by amphetamine sulphate, an upper known for obvious reasons as speed and most commonly available in powder form. It was decidedly unhealthy – Joe was later to liken it to a well-known brand of household scouring powder – but relatively cheap, and easy both to find and to take (usually by being shaped into lines and snorted through a straw or rolled banknote, like the more upmarket cocaine). The Feelgoods' Wilko Johnson has since attributed much of his own mid-Seventies energetic stage persona to the effects of the drug. In his 1 November *NME* 'Pub Rock Report '75', journalist Geoff Hill dropped a sly hint to those in the know when referring to the 101ers, Eddie and the Hot Rods and other bands on the pub circuit 'whose virtue is their raw energy and whose vice generally tends to be their unoriginality of material or presentation and an over-reliance on speed'.

It was a suggestion that had been made before, and it was one that used to annoy Joe, as he explained to Paolo Hewitt in 1981: 'At the Western Counties [Praed Street, Paddington] one night we played this really blistering set, really firing on all cylinders. Then we went out into the bar to have a drink, and this bloke goes, "Not bad, that." And he's winking and nudging me, and I was going, "What's the matter with this geezer?" And he says, "How many lines did you snort before *that* set, then?" And we weren't into speed. We couldn't afford speed.' Clive confirms that Joe was remarkably health-conscious for a squat-dwelling rock'n'roller: a vegetarian, he looked after his voice with regular doses of honey and lemon, and although he liked a drink when money allowed, he did not smoke tobacco, and even insisted on rolling his occasional joints with an herbal substitute.

★

The next development for the 101ers was the opportunity to record. Since the Radio Concorde broadcast, there had been one other attempt to capture the band live. 'There was a guy called Gordon Tate, who now works for Steven Spielberg,' says Clive. 'He came along with a TEAC 4-track reel-to-reel recorder. I think it was to try out his machine! We set it up at the Elgin.' Nothing more was heard about it. In November 1975, however, the band was approached by Vic Maile, the man who had produced the first Dr Feelgood album and also recorded the two 1975 gigs that, the following year, would provide that band with a UK number one live album, *Stupidity*. 'Vic Maile was an ex-BBC sound engineer,' says Clive. 'He used to mix the sound of audiences at football matches!' Which might explain his preference for recording bands as 'live' as possible, either at gigs or in the studio. Maile was looking to follow up his success with the Feelgoods. 'He wanted to sign up bands, do recording and production deals with them and sell them off to the highest bidders,' recalls Clive. 'I don't know how he contacted us. I think he just got a tip-off and turned up one day at a gig.' Maile was also interested in Eddie and the Hot Rods, whom he subsequently recorded live on 4 December when they supported the 101ers at the Flamingo club in Hereford. He would later co-produce their *Live At The Marquee* EP. It may have been that he had taken a hint from Geoff Hill's 'Pub Rock Report', which described both bands as 'descending on your hitherto-quiet local in the wake of Dr Feelgood'.

On 28 November 1975, he took the 101ers into the studio where he worked, Jackson's in Rickmansworth, and recorded six songs. As if to disprove Geoff Hill's charges of 'unoriginality of material', they were all the band's own compositions: 'Letsagetabitarockin', 'Silent Telephone', 'Motor Boys Motor', 'Sweety Of The St Moritz', 'Hideaway' and 'Steamgauge 99'. 'We just went in and thrashed through a load of numbers,' says Mole. 'There were no retakes, or anything, just the vocals added later. The guy didn't want to listen to what anybody else wanted to do: not an amenable character. He just wanted to do it his way, and that was it. Nobody knew where he was at. It was horrible, nobody enjoyed it. We were all in really foul moods because this bloke was really miserable.' Clive puts it down to personality. 'Vic Maile was a little bald guy with a big nose, and he wasn't the highest key person I've ever met in my life.' Richard, as ever, is more positive about the experience. 'I don't remember that not being enjoyable. It was great! The first time we'd ever been in a studio . . .' Maile's empire-building came to naught, and at the time the band was not too distraught that Jackson's studio retained the copyright on the material.

Shortly after a two-week Christmas lay-off, on 15 January 1976, Mole was sacked from the 101ers. 'I certainly didn't leave of my own accord,' he says. 'I think I was an expedient sort of scapegoat. I think everyone was pissed off that we weren't getting anywhere, that there wasn't any success happening. This guy Dan was hanging around, and it was a case of, "We'll change something, and maybe then it'll happen." And the something they changed was me. I was very upset. That band was part of a whole network in the Chippenham Road, a whole café scene at That Tea Room, a little alternative family there. And it almost excluded you from the whole thing when you were thrown out of the band.'

The other 101ers, most of whom have since patched up their friendships with Mole, are reluctant to go on record about what is obviously still a sensitive subject. But the consensus seems to be that, whereas the other members of the band were basking in the attention they were receiving and becoming increasingly confident, Mole appeared to be growing less and less happy. Both the band's and Mole's explanations for the firing are perfectly credible. It may well have been his own self-doubt and a resulting general negativity that coloured Mole's reaction to the studio visit and convinced the band that he had an attitude problem. Alternatively, it might have been the failure of the Vic Maile session to further the band's career that made the others look around for someone to blame. If, as Chas De Whalley had claimed back in August, the problem lay in the band's lack of musicianship, then by a process of elimination – Clive being the most capable musician, Joe irreplaceable as frontman and songwriter and Richard a capable drummer and Joe's close friend – the fall guy had to be Mole.

As Mole suggests, it should not be overlooked that Clive's friend Dan Kelleher was waiting in the wings. Dan was keen to contribute more than just additional guitar embellishments to a couple of songs, and as a gifted bass player, guitarist, keyboard player and arranger he was the obvious candidate for Mole's job, perhaps even before the vacancy existed. According to Richard, Mole definitiely felt threatened by Dan during his final months with the band, and, as it turned out, not without reason. 'I remember me and Joe going around to see Mole to tell him we thought that was it,' says Richard. 'Looking back, I think it was probably a mistake: the relationship between Dan and Joe was ultimately one of the reasons the 101ers didn't continue.' Small consolation for Mole. He went to see the first gig without him, on 16 January at Queen Elizabeth College, Campden Hill Road, Kensington, and then had nothing more to do with the 101ers. He could not face playing with anyone else for the next two years, but went on to form his own late punk era band Pitiful, and shortly afterwards an outfit named the Vincent Units. Following another lengthy period of inactivity, he has recently taken up performing again.

The 101ers played their last gig at the Elgin on 8 January, and their residency there officially terminated on the day of Mole's departure because of complaints of noise pollution. Thereafter, the landlord was allowed to hire only unamplified musicians. The change in line-up and loss of their home base venue helped spur the 101ers into action, but they had already made the decision to concentrate on playing further afield. Relying on band associates to hustle gigs had largely limited the band to local venues, and so, towards the end of 1975, the 101ers had turned to a booking agency, Albion, to help them establish themselves on the national circuit: 'A guy called Derek Savage and a guy called Dai Davis,' says Clive. 'That's when we started doing things like [the 500-capacity] JB's in Dudley. Albion also had the Stranglers, so we did a couple of gigs with them.'

From January 1976 onwards, the 101ers began a punishing schedule of out of town dates. As the budget seldom ran to hotel accommodation, the gigs were either within easy access of London or else required hit-and-run ventures into the Midlands and the north with marathon overnight drives home. Between January and April 1976, as well as the gigs they played in and around London, the 101ers made a total of five trips up country to play the likes of Samantha's in Leek, Clarence's in Halifax, the Cocked Hat in Scunthorpe and the Black Swan in Sheffield, where the Clash would subsequently make their début. As it was too much to expect Micky Foote to organise band, transport and equipment under such circumstances, another member of the squatting community, John Tiberi, was taken on as roadie to help spread the load. Before long, he was given the obligatory nickname: Boogie.

A new spirit of professionalism was adopted. 'We used to be pissed a lot,' says Clive. 'But we cut that out. No smoking dope or getting rat-arsed before a gig.' Whereas the others continued to wear scruffy casual clothes, Joe decided it was time to give himself an image, and – possibly as another nod in the direction of the Rip Off Park All Stars – bought himself a stage suit. 'A kind of browny, sort of dirty colour,' recalls Clive, wrinkling his nose. Joe loved it, and was loath to take the stage in anything else, though he sometimes spoiled the effect by wearing it with sneakers. It became another of Micky's tasks to ensure that it was dry-cleaned between gigs, and the closest Joe came to throwing a rock'n'roll star-style temper-tantrum was if, for any reason, it could not be collected on time. The days of the Woody Guthrie look were over.

The 101ers had played occasional college gigs from their very early days. Most had been at London venues, like the South Bank Polytechnic, the London School of Economics or the University of London Union. Their frequency increased again when the band became associated with Albion, beginning with another clutch of London college dates in the Christmas party season that included, on 17 December, a return to Joe's Alma Mater, the Central School of Art. From January 1976 onwards, with Albion's help, further-flung student gigs became a regular feature on the 101ers' schedule, both around London, for example at Gypsy Hill College in Kingston and Essex University in Colchester, and in the north, at such institutions as Nottingham and Liverpool Universities.

There were disadvantages to college gigs. The audience were usually there to participate in the student social scene rather than specifically to watch the band. There was also a tendency to promote the 101ers as a kitsch nostalgia act. Sebastian Conran, Social Secretary at the Central (and, with Al McDowell, the man responsible for setting up the Sex Pistols' second gig, on

7 November 1975), designed a poster for the 101ers' December visit, using the famous 'Lolita with lollipop' photograph and bearing the legend 'Jitterbug Jive. Rock and Roll. Oo-Bop-She-Bam. In Fifties Dress Or Less.' On the positive side, the gigs were well paid, and the audiences large and invariably drunk enough to respond with enthusiasm. 'And it meant we were getting around,' says Richard. 'It was great to go to Liverpool, or whatever. In fact, I think I remember that gig [13 March 1976]: there were masses of people. We went down really well. We usually went down really well.'

Albion also arranged the 101ers' one and only European tour, consisting of four one-night stands over a long weekend: Boddy's Music Inn, Amsterdam, on 27 February, the Paradiso in the same town the following night, the Eksit club in Rotterdam on 28 February and Gringo's in Ghent on 1 March. 'We got the usual English band deal at Boddy's Music Inn,' says Clive. 'The guy who owned it would liaise with a British agency, and get an English band to come over. He also owned a hotel, which we could stay at, and he'd arrange two or three other gigs. It's basically a rip-off, but it gets you over there, and the guy who organises it gets an English band: the Dutch people love English bands.' The same is not necessarily true of the Belgian people. 'The place in Ghent was fucking horrible, awful. We tried to do [Hank Williams's cajun classic] "Jambalaya" is all I can remember about it. Real chickenwire stuff. We were at one end of the bar on a stage sweating, and there was people sitting there, no reaction. But we were having fun anyway. I mean, we were in another country.'

The 101ers did not need to travel abroad to experience that feeling. On 25 January, they played the Roundhouse in Camden Town for the first time as part of the traditional extended Sunday bill. Through the venue's promoter John Curd they learned that it was possible to play Sunday lunchtime gigs at Wandsworth Prison, and duly signed up for 15 February. 'You can imagine, our beaten-up old van turning up, and the screws dubiously letting us in,' says Richard. 'We walked into the sacristy, which was our dressing-room, because we were playing on a big stage which they'd mounted on top of the altar in the chapel. Which was a *big* chapel.' Taking up a position inviting sacrifice in front of 400 to 500 prisoners, many of them serious offenders, made the 101ers feel somewhat nervous; a feeling which intensified when there was no reaction at all during the first song. 'We were thinking, "This is going down like a concrete parachute,"' says Clive. 'But at the end of the number it was ... instant eruption! They were on orders: they weren't allowed to talk or shout or do anything while we were playing. We did "Out Of Time", [Leiber–Stoller's] "Riot In Cell Block No 9", "Jailhouse Rock" ...' 'It was just incredible seeing the bliss on their faces as we moved through these songs,' says Richard. 'For me, that was the best gig we ever did.' 'They loved us,' agrees Clive. 'Talk about a captive audience!' As a result, the 101ers were asked back for two more shows, on 21 March and 11 April.

Dan's arrival had a considerable impact on the band. In addition to playing bass, he added backing vocals to several songs and, being a confirmed Beatles fan, took over lead vocals on 'Back In The USSR'. It was behind the scenes, however, in the songwriting and arranging departments, that he made his most significant contributions. 'With a lot of Strummer's songs, he had the melody in his head, but he couldn't figure out the chords, so I sorted them out for him,' he told *Sounds*' Pete Silverton in 1979. The first three months of 1976 were therefore the 101ers' most prolific in terms of song composition. Perhaps influenced by his live vocal feature, Dan originated another cod surf song, 'Surf City'. He and Joe teamed up to write '5 Star Rock'n'Roll Petrol'. Joe came up with 'Sweet Revenge' ('I remember Clive having an input on that,' says Richard), 'Rabies (From The Dogs Of Love)' (credited to the 101ers when eventually released as a single B-side) and 'Jail Guitar Doors'. Richard offered 'Keep Taking The Tablets'. Only the last two failed to be recorded in the studio before the 101ers split, but in late 1977, with its verses completely rewritten by Mick Jones, 'Jail Guitar Doors' would become the only 101ers era Strummer composition to be tackled by the Clash.

The other songs are far more varied in subject and style than the band's earlier compositions, and in their new emphasis on musicianship indicate a deliberate move away from the aggressive, full-tilt approach of yore. At first, '5 Star Rock'n'Roll Petrol' would appear to be another Berry-inspired cruising anthem, but although the song is a straightforward rocker, the lyric is at the very least ambiguous. Either rock'n'roll itself is the superior energy-giving fuel in question or else the protagonist requires some other kind of fuel in order to pass some 'Letsagetabitarockin'-type endurance test. The idea of addiction to some sort of drug is certainly the song's central conceit: there are references to making connections and getting burned, and Joe declares, 'I need some more petrol / But I don't really want it', before the song ends with alternating whispered pleas and screamed demands for more 5 Star. This is pretty blatant hard-drug imagery for a band claiming to eschew such interests.

'Rabies (From The Dogs Of Love)' opens with a classic folk song greeting, 'Come now, all you gentlemen / Come now, all you ladies', and ends with a whistle recalling Rufus Thomas's 'Walking The Dog'. If '5 Star Rock'n'Roll Petrol' is concerned with drugs, then 'Rabies' is about sexual relations, rather than the 'madness of love' suggested by the title. Like the Rufus Thomas song, it sets itself up to be a novelty number, but the innuendo is altogether darker, and soon gives way to a blatant sleaziness unworthy even of the blues tradition. Initially, both sexes are addressed, but verse two tells of Crazy Daisy leaving something indecipherable in a plastic bag down on Shepherd's Bush Green and verse three of Jean, who passes on something that leads to the male victim spending the chorus down on his knees in the Praed Street Clinic. It almost goes without saying that the clinic in question is the part of St Mary's Hospital responsible for treating sexually transmitted diseases and that 'rabies' is a metaphor for such afflictions. As 'dog' is a derogatory term for a supposedly promiscuous female, it's hard not to see the song as the kind of nasty little male chauvinist sexual revenge number beloved of the Stranglers at this time.

In comparison with the others, the country rock-tinged 'Sweet Revenge' could almost qualify as a ballad. Again, the subject belies the title, but this time in a positive way: it's a song *opposing* the idea of self-perpetuating violence, an eye for an eye. One verse would appear to be directly autobiographical, referring to life 'back at school' where 'You hit him / He hits you back.' The conclusion is that blood is invariably spilled for nothing, bringing to mind a 1979 Clash song that would address itself to the same subject, 'Last Gang In Town'.

A surprise was in store in early March 1976. 'Ted Carroll and Roger Armstrong came up to us after a gig,' Joe told Paolo Hewitt in 1981, 'and said, "Do you want to make a record?" So we said, "Yeah!"' A year earlier, he told the same interviewer that he'd been 'flabbergasted' when the offer came. In 1972, Carroll had helped feed the Rock'n'Roll Revival by selling imported rock'n'roll and R&B records from his stall Rock On in a communal retail outlet in Golborne Road, at the north end of Portobello Road. Shortly afterwards, he had diversified into Sixties punk and garage music, and in 1974, had opened a second stall at a temporary market in Soho's Newport Court, managed by his friend Roger Armstrong. Their professional interest in related musical genres made the duo particularly receptive to both the harder-edged pub rock bands and the punk movement: they witnessed the Sex Pistols' fifth gig in December 1975. That same month, Ted and Roger formed an independent record label named Chiswick. Its first release was *Speedball*, an EP by the Count Bishops featuring a version of 'Route 66', which immediately prompted the 101ers to drop it from their own set. Since the Bishops were ploughing a not wholly dissimilar musical furrow, Ted and Roger were familiar faces on the scene and Joe was a regular customer at the Rock On stalls, it's hard to see why he should have been *that* flabbergasted when the approach came to make the record.

The 101ers selected three songs which showcased their versatility, 'Sweet Revenge', 'Surf City' and 'Keys To Your Heart', and recorded some rough guide demos in the basement at Orsett Terrace. The recording session proper took place on 4 March 1976, at Pathway studio, 2A Grosvenor Avenue in Canonbury, with Roger Armstrong producing. Two versions of 'Keys To Your Heart' were recorded, and also two of 'Sweet Revenge', the first of which featured Clive on acoustic guitar. A take of '5 Star Rock'n'Roll Petrol' was knocked off for a change of pace. The most problematic of the three serious contenders for the record was 'Surf City'. After an instrumental run-through, a version was attempted with Joe singing, which offers some idea as to why he did not attempt it again: the oft-repeated refrain 'Stuck in Surf City' brought on an unfortunate attack of the Daffy Ducks. After two or three further aborted takes, a version was recorded with a seemingly overawed Dan supplying almost inaudible lead vocals.

On 10 March, the 101ers returned to Pathway with Roger to re-record 'Surf City' and 'Keys To Your Heart', now with a phased effect on the guitar, and make a first attempt at 'Rabies (From The Dogs Of Love)'. Richard denies that this second session was organised because the results of the first were considered largely unusable. 'I think when you record, you often think, "God, we could do this one better", especially when you're doing it quite quickly. I don't think we thought the first session was below par, but the second was different, the sound.' Roger took the best take of 'Keys To Your Heart' from both the first and second sessions into Chalk Farm studios at 1A Belmont Street, Camden, and mixed them on 24 and 25 March, respectively.

The fact that no B-side was finished at this time suggests that the second session had also been deemed wanting, particularly as, on 28 March, the 101ers went into the BBC studios in Maida Vale – this time with house producer Simon Jeffes and house engineer Mike Robinson – to record '5 Star Rock'n'Roll Petrol' and yet another version of 'Surf City'. Again, Richard argues with this interpretation of events. 'I think we were thinking of an EP, actually. I think we had the idea of bringing something out ourselves, and with the BBC masters, the copyright belonged to us and not to someone else. That was a good enough reason to do it.'

This would make sense had the 101ers restricted themselves to previously unrecorded songs, but they returned to the BBC studios on 10 April to record backing tracks for a second version of 'Rabies' and yet another of 'Keys To Your Heart', the vocals for which were added on 13 April. Despite Richard's claims, it looks very much as though either Chiswick or the 101ers were unhappy with the bulk of the Pathway material. Alternatively – no contract having yet been signed – the band were not entirely convinced that Chiswick were going to put a record out. Whatever, when the single was finally released, the A-side, 'Keys To Your Heart', was taken from the first Pathway session and the B-side, '5 Star Rock'n'Roll Petrol', from the first BBC session. A convoluted history for what was supposed to be a quickly recorded, low-budget, independent-label single.

As if to cement the alliance between the band and Chiswick, Boogie helped arrange two gigs at the Nashville Room on 3 and 23 April 1976, with the 101ers headlining, the Rock On disco providing incidental music and the Sex Pistols appearing as the support band. The first of these nights looms large in the Annals of Punk: it was when Dave Goodman began mixing the Pistols' live sound, giving the band their own highly individual sonic identity; and it was when Joe Strummer claims to have undergone a conversion as dramatic as Saul's on the road to Damascus, Significant Event Two in the birth of the Clash.

In his review of the gig for *Melody Maker* Allan Jones was dismissive of the Pistols, 'a recently much-vaunted four-piece band of incompetents from West London', but predictably fulsome in his praise for the headliners: 'From the moment Joe Strummer – one of the most vivid and exciting figures currently treading the boards – took a flying, perfectly judged, leap on to Snakehips Dudanski's bass drum, to their third and final encore, the 101ers were a complete and utter joy.' The *NME*'s Geoff Hutt noted that the Pistols' attitude seemed forced, before going on to dispute their alleged lack of musical ability and generally damn them with faint praise. He too reserved his enthusiasm for the 101ers, who, he announced, were musically much improved and had 'finally made the transition from playing the tiny Elgin pub to successfully dominating larger halls'.

Clive's recollection of the Sex Pistols tallies with Geoff's. 'It was the first really important gig they did, and we had a ready-made audience who came to see us,' he says. 'People were all extremes in their reaction to them, appalled to very interested. A lot of the heckling was put up. It was very much a manipulative situation, I thought at the time. Not strictly my scene.' Richard did not think of the Pistols as being appreciably different to the 101ers in their early days. 'I saw them as doing, really, what we were doing, but they were younger. They'd started more recently. As I said, they'd called us a punk band the year before. I didn't like the emphasis on image.' For Joe, however, steeped in pop culture, the 101er with a suit, the image was a large part of the appeal. In Jon Savage's *England's Dreaming: Sex Pistols And Punk Rock*, published in 1991, he talked about overhearing Malcolm ask the Pistols what clothes they wanted to wear that night and being most impressed with this attention to detail. He went on to say that, rather than finding the on-stage affectations and poses offputting, he had been seduced by the intention behind them. Ten years earlier, in the *Melody Maker* 101ers retrospective, Joe explained to Paolo Hewitt the difference between his reaction and Richard's: 'You see, we're talking about a movement of ideas, and [Richard's] talking about a riff on a stage. See the difference? I saw it not only as a "good group", but as a new attitude.'

In the November of 1976, just over five months after he had left the 101ers for the Clash, Joe told Caroline Coon, 'As soon as I saw them [the Sex Pistols] . . . I just knew. It was something you just knew without bothering to think about.' The impact may have been immediate, but despite his melodramatic accounts in the *Melody Maker* and elsewhere over the years, his conversion to punk took place more gradually, over the best part of two months, and it involved a good deal of agonised deliberation. Although Joe has never credited it, Jonh Ingham's 24 April interview with the Pistols must have played some part in the band's effect upon him. In it Malcolm dismissed the pub scene because it required its bands to pander to expectations and lean too heavily upon the familiar. 'Basically,' summed up Jonh, 'what Malcolm wants is a rumbling, anarchic, noisy energetic rock scene, the likes of which haven't been seen in this country since the mid 1960's.' As well as making references to the Rolling Stones and echoing Joe's musical philosophy, the feature was also an open invitation to any rock'n'roll opportunist who wanted a fast lane to media attention: the Sex Pistols had only been gigging for six months, and here they were with a two-page spread in *Sounds*.

Significant Event Three in the birth of the Clash was a chance meeting in the street of Joe and a gang comprising Mick Jones, Paul Simonon and Glen Matlock. Glen, of course, had supported the 101ers at the Nashville; Mick and Paul, accompanied by Keith Levene and Bernie Rhodes, had been in the audience. The others approached Joe and told him that he was great, but that his band was 'shit'. This, legend has it, hardened Joe in his resolve to follow his instincts to leave the 101ers and go punk. The incident would be immortalised in the opening lines of the 1978 Clash song 'All The Young Punks (New Boots And Contracts)': 'I was hanging about down the market street . . . When I met some passing yobbos / And we did chance to speak . . .' A popular anecdote, it was told and retold for years by all three of the other Clash members involved. While the other details remained much the same, the location for this meeting tended to vary from account to account: Golborne Road, Portobello Road, Westbourne Grove, Ladbroke Grove, Lisson Grove or even somewhere in Shepherd's Bush. The reason for this uncertainty, and for the fact that Glen, supposedly present, has no recollection at all of the incident, was revealed by Joe once the Clash had split: Significant Event Three in the birth of the Clash – the most famous of all – never happened. It was a complete fabrication, probably inspired by Mick's original meeting with Brady. The intention was to make it seem the idea to get together had developed naturally from a mutual interest and respect, whereas it was really the result of premeditated and audacious head-hunting on the part of the management to be.

In a 1978 interview with the *NME* Mick Jones told Nick Kent, 'With Joe, I could see he was a great performer saddled with a duff band.' Eleven years later, Keith Levene told the same paper's Jane Garcia that he and Bernie had been the ones who had recognised the potential of the 101ers' leader – 'Joe used to wear zoot suits and just go fucking mad all over the place. He was always so great to watch' – and that they had approached Joe without consulting Mick, thus presenting the guitarist with a *fait accompli*.

In truth, the Davis Road contingent had *all* taken note of Joe's frenzied performance at the Nashville. They next encountered him not on Portobello Road (or any of the other 'street' options), but at the Employment Exchange in Lisson Grove. As it was during the Easter vacation, Mick - accompanied by Paul and Viv – was there to claim for the duration, and Joe was there to sign on as usual. No one told Joe that he was great, but his band was duff or shit; in fact, no words were exchanged. The others stared covertly at the singer and, vaguely aware of their shifty behaviour, Joe wondered if he was about to be attacked. That was the full extent of the encounter.

Some or all of the Davis Road bunch saw Joe once again on 23 April, at the second Nashville 101ers–Sex Pistols gig, which achieved notoriety for a fight precipitated by Vivienne Westwood during the Pistols' set. On 12 May, the 101ers played the Red Cow in Hammersmith. Clive Timperley's diary recorded that various members of the Stranglers, Eddie and the Hot Rods, the Count Bishops and the Sex Pistols were in attendance. The Sex Pistol was Glen Matlock, and he was again accompanied by Mick and Paul.

It may have been voiced as a fantasy option, but the idea of poaching Joe was not a concrete one at this stage. The inchoate Davis Road band were unaware that Joe was intrigued by Malcolm and the Pistols, and could not have held out much hope that a name performer (albeit on the pub circuit) would be prepared to quit an established band to join forces with them. It was Bernie who took control of the situation. On 11 May, the Sex Pistols had begun their ground-breaking – for the punk scene – weekly Tuesday night residency at the 100 Club on Oxford Street. Joe attended one or two of that month's gigs, where he was spotted by Bernie. Not given to feelings of awe, Bernie said he had a venture Joe might be interested in, and asked him for his phone number.

Meanwhile, things had not been running smoothly in the 101ers camp. 'In early '76, not long after I had joined the band, we were striving to develop a fuller range of musical capability,' Dan told Pete Frame for a Family Tree of the bands which developed out of the Maida Hill squatting community. 'And here were the Pistols playing with a rawness very reminiscent of the early 101ers!' Joe laid much of the blame at Dan's door for what he was increasingly coming to think of as the 101ers' recent musical wrong turn. 'This bloke was pushing his way in, this multi-instrumentalist,' he told Paolo Hewitt in 1981.

Joe's initial response to the Pistols was not to break up the 101ers, but to try to make them more of a punk-style band. 'I think there's no question that, before the 101ers split, Joe had a different, much more aggressive attitude while on-stage,' says Richard. To be maniacally thrashing away on guitar flanked by two men known as Evil and Desperate who hardly ever moved no longer seemed like such a good joke to Joe, and the discrepancy between levels of performance became another troublesome issue.

Meanwhile, in spite of Joe's subsequently voiced dissatisfaction about publicity and support, music press attention did continue to be afforded the 101ers. At the time, Pete Silverton was working as a London correspondent for *Trouser Press*, a semi-underground publication which, dubbing itself 'America's Only British Rock Magazine', was pretty much the US equivalent of the pre-punk *ZigZag*. Deciding he wanted to write 'a short piece on what it was really like for a struggling band in London, supposed Mecca of rock'n'roll', Pete had taken up the recommendation of an unnamed schoolfriend of Joe and gone to see the 101ers. He had accompanied the band to their 14 April gig at Rebecca's in Birmingham. 'I became so enamoured with the 101ers that what started out as a short article ended up as a veritable thesis,' he wrote in a 1978 article on the Clash for the same magazine. This thesis might well have made a significant difference to the 101ers' career, had not publication been prevented by one unfortunate detail: 'The day I mailed the piece, the band broke up.'

On 18 May, the 101ers finally signed a recording contract with Chiswick.

For Joe, being required to commit himself to a band he was no longer fully happy with proved difficult, and it was Clive who bore the initial brunt of his discontent. This might appear surprising, but Richard believes Dan's days were already numbered, whereas Joe still had hopes of bringing Clive round to his point of view. By this time, all pretence at democracy had been abandoned, and a one-to-one ultimatum was delivered on 21 May, after a gig at Camberwell Arts Centre. 'I felt pretty good, because I felt it had gone pretty well,' says Clive. 'Then Strummer said to me, "You'll have to buck your ideas up, mate, or you're out!" Something like that.' The idea of leaping around on the stage did not particularly appeal to the laid-back Clive. 'OK, I was brought up as a blues guitar player, but most of the time I'm a technical-type musician who plays things without showing much emotion about it,' he explains. 'I mean, what I feel is what I feel, but I don't show it. And he wanted the more brash element of it. I thought, "Well, I did that in my very first band, in '65", and I didn't want to go any further backwards than I had already.'

It seems likely that the initial approach to Joe from Bernie was made at the Pistols' 25 May 100 Club gig, because it was the very next day that Joe called round to see Clive for a serious discussion. 'We spent the whole day in my flat talking,' says Clive. 'He was smitten by the Maximum Impact - carefully chosen words, his words – of the Pistols. He wanted to go in that direction. Dan and I didn't, because we were musos: we were into Steely Dan and Little Feat. There was a long discussion, at the end of which I agreed to leave. I know why, it was perfectly correct, and I have no bad feeling. There was nothing wrong, or amiss, or unamicable about it at all. It was a perfectly logical evolution. I just didn't want to go with it . . .'

Looking back, he still bears no animosity. 'I did 160-odd gigs with the 101ers. It was a blast. It was one of the best times of my life from the point of view of gigging, and I got so much experience from that. I knew I wasn't going to stay in a band like that for the rest of my life, because I knew I had to progress musically, and I was on hold.' Although he still, albeit laughingly, refers to Joe's musical direction as 'misguided', Clive says he did take something other than fond memories away from the 101ers. 'I learned how to play less. I used to play an awful lot. Take [the Vic Maile-produced version of] "Letsagetabitarockin": there's not a second in that solo where there's not a note being heard, and when I hear it now I think, "*Shut up!* What are you trying to prove?"' A couple of years after leaving the 101ers, Clive hooked up with two former members of Dan's old band the Derelicts to form the Passions. 'Which was a huge step forward for me; maybe not musically, but creatively.' Coincidentally, their 1981 hit single, 'I'm In Love With A German Film Star', was a song about a former Clash roadie named Roadent. When the Passions came to an acrimonious end, Clive left the music business for a while to run a health food shop. Recently, he began playing the pub rock circuit again, first with the Boogie Brothers and currently with the Barflys.

Martin Stone – formerly of pub rock leading lights Chilli Willi and more recently of the Jive Bombers, who had supported the 101ers at Colchester University back on 17 March – was brought in at short notice for the 101ers gig on 28 May at Bromley College. 'He was another country-type lead guitar player,' says Clive. 'In other words, Joe got a replacement for me.' For this reason, Clive believes that Martin was always intended to be a temporary stand-in and that Joe was planning to fulfil existing commitments prior to breaking up the band. Richard agrees with the first part of this assessment, but not the second. 'I don't think Martin Stone was considered as full-time, no, but I don't think Joe was necessarily thinking of splitting it up. More a feeling that "This has got to change." Joe wasn't getting on with Dan, so it was just us two; myself and Joe had no problems. And for me, that was enough, to get in other people and carry on with the 101ers.'

The upset caused by Clive's departure was intensified when Bernie phoned to follow up his initial contact with Joe. Dan was at Orsett Terrace for rehearsals at the time, and it was he who answered the phone. Deeply suspicious of the evasive Rhodes, he pretended to be Joe in an unsuccessful attempt to find out what was going on. Now aware of the turmoil in the 101ers camp, Bernie decided it was time to make his move. Taking Keith Levene with him, he went along to the 101ers' next gig, on 30 May, at the Golden Lion pub in Fulham Road. After the show, a clandestine meeting took place outside, by the bus stop. This time, it was Joe's turn to be given an ultimatum. Bernie told him he was putting together a new band to rival the Pistols, and asked Joe if he wanted in. 'Joe was like, "Um, er, I don't know,"' says Keith. In the end, he was given 48 hours to make up his mind. Keith again insists that Mick knew nothing about the offer until after it had been made.

Joe spent the next 24 hours worrying over the decision. Then Bernie phoned him a day ahead of schedule, and demanded an answer there and then. 'When I was offered this job,' Joe told *Rolling Stone*'s James Henke in 1980, 'I recognised it was the chance I'd kinda been waiting for.' He said he was interested. Although Bernie had prepared the ground well, it was meeting Keith that had finally convinced Joe. 'In those days people looked really boring, and Keith looked really different,' he told Kosmo Vinyl for the *Clash On Broadway* booklet. Bernie and Keith picked up Joe and took him to 22 Davis Road, where Mick and Paul were waiting to meet their new bandmate. Still in awe of the relatively experienced Strummer, they covered it up with the usual show of casual gruffness. 'When I met Mick and Keith at the squat we went in and sat on the bed and looked at each other,' Joe told the *NME*'s Paul Morley in 1979. 'And Bernie said, "This is the guy you gotta write songs with", and Mick sort of scowled, and I thought, "Well, I haven't got any choice. This is what I've got to do."'

They then took it in turns to play selections from their existing repertoires. 'The first song we ever rehearsed was "1-2, Crush On You",' Joe told Pete Silverton for *Sounds* in 1980. When he discovered that Paul could not play and simply learned his bass parts parrot fashion, Joe had a twinge of doubt.

'In the 101ers, we taught ourselves to play, and I knew what a long process that was,' he said during a 1980 interview for Radio Hallam. 'I thought, "Oh-oh, I've been through this one before: it took us 18 months to learn how to play R&B numbers!" But then I thought, "Oh, hell!" and we just jumped in.' He took immediate solace from Paul's dynamic approach to the bass, noting that, despite the space restrictions, instruments were being slung around with abandon. 'He was like, "Wow, I really dig this, yeah, I'm gonna do it!"' says Keith.

'I remember Joe coming back one night when I was in bed,' says Richard. 'He came in and said, "Look, it's the end. The 101ers have finished." He'd met these blokes who I'd seen around. They used to come to our gigs, so I knew who he was talking about. "I wanna start a new band, and go with a new manager", and all this.' He also wanted Richard to become the new band's drummer. 'And I said, "Oh, God! Talk to you about it in the morning, Joe." And the following morning, the first bloke I bumped into in Orsett Terrace was Bernie, who spent a couple of hours trying to persuade me why I should go with the Clash, and telling me what the Clash were about. They weren't called the Clash then, but this new band, as it were. He turned me right off, really got up me nose. I didn't like the guy. I thought he was full of pseudo-political crap. "Words should be written about this kind of thing, we should wear this kind of clothing . . ." I certainly wasn't going to start wearing a uniform. I thought, "I'm not packing up *this* to go with that wanker!" So that was it, as far as I was concerned. I wouldn't have said no to going with younger people, but I wasn't going to go and be run by Bernie Rhodes, basically.'

Richard having stated his position, a band meeting followed at which Dan was informed of Joe's defection, and it was decided to split up the 101ers after one last gig – Martin Stone's third – on 5 June at the Clare Halls in Haywards Heath. Clive turned up for the show, and joined the others on-stage for the last few numbers. 'I happened to be in the area: I'd gone to an audition. I was on the way back, and I said, "Right, I'll play!"'

Some subsequent bookings were cancelled. One slot, as part of a Midsummer Music Festival Benefit on 17 June at Walthamstow Assembly Hall, with the Stranglers and the recently rechristened Ian Dury and the Kilburns, was taken over – appropriately enough – by the Sex Pistols. Richard kept his drum kit, Clive a Gibson SG guitar and Dan his bass amp, but Joe took the rest of the band gear, including the PA, on which money was still owed. Boogie went his own way, eventually becoming a roadie for the Sex Pistols at the beginning of 1977. Micky Foote decided to go with Joe and the gear.

It was Dan who felt most aggrieved by the split, as he intimated to Pete Silverton in 1979: 'I think Joe was really cuntish when the 101ers broke up.' 'I think Dan would say that what he hated, what he felt very resentful about, was that it was all behind our backs, the Clash thing,' says Clive. 'But that was Bernie, not Strummer.' Richard is less sympathetic to any dissatisfaction

Dan may have felt. 'He'd only been in the band six months, or something! I don't think the split was engineered. Dan could have carried on, if he'd wanted. *I* wasn't going to work with him.' What Dan did was to rejoin the Derelicts for six months. In 1978, he recorded a solo single for Chiswick, 'I Couldn't Help But Cry', on which he played every instrument. That same year, he formed a band called the Martian Schoolgirls in Dorset, where he now lives.

Richard decided to take a long holiday in Sicily with Esperanza, and they stayed there for three or four months. Upon their return, Richard teamed up with Tymon Dogg in a band called the Fools. Then, in 1978, he formed his own band, Bank of Dresden, before joining Public Image Ltd for a brief spell. He played for the Raincoats, followed by Basement 5, whom he left early in 1981 to go and spend a year in Brazil. He now lives in Spain, still with Esperanza, where he plays for a band called Por Si Las Moscas.

During his early years with the Clash, Joe did not have much contact with his former friends, but his relationship with Richard was re-established during the discussions that led to the release of the 101ers album, *Elgin Avenue Breakdown*. At the time, both were living in the Notting Hill area. On 31 December 1980, they arranged a one-off Sixties-style revue show, involving Mole and several other friends under the name the Soul Vendors, at the Tabernacle Community Centre in Powis Square. In 1983, Joe financed and helped out on the mixing of what was supposed to be a Tymon Dogg album with Richard on drums; unfortunately, it was never released. In 1994, Joe went over to Spain to help with the overdubs and final mixing of a Por Si Las Moscas album.

In the *Clash On Broadway* booklet Mick revealed that, when Joe turned up for the second rehearsal, 'he was in the gear and everything, he was already part of it, he was there'. But it transpired that making a commitment to his new band required more than a change of clothes. On a personal level, Joe severed many of his ties with the Maida Hill squatting community. Since much of the 101ers' career had taken place in the limelight, however, Joe was unable to pretend the band had never existed, as Mick Jones had done with the Delinquents and (albeit less successfully) the London SS. The only way he could prevent his very public defection from R&B to punk rock from appearing like an act of cynical opportunism was to exhibit the fanatical zeal of the convert and denigrate his former band and musical tastes at every turn.

The first opportunity presented itself in July 1976, when Chiswick posthumously released the 'Keys To Your Heart' single, and Caroline Coon invited Joe to comment on the 101ers split in her *Melody Maker* singles column of 24 July. 'It was very traumatic, yes,' he said. 'I formed the group with my sweat. I slogged at it. Then I met these others. Before, I used to think I was a crud. Now, I realise I'm the king, and I've decided to move into the future.' Within a couple of months, he was wearing a shirt bearing the legend 'CHUCK BERRY IS DEAD' and performing a song, '1977', with the chorus 'No Elvis, Beatles or the Rolling Stones / In 1977.' In November 1976, Joe told Caroline that he had realised R&B was dead the moment he saw the Sex Pistols. That December, something occurred that made it even easier for him to shake off his recent past. He was then squatting in the recently vacated premises of Robertino's Ice Cream Co., 7 Foscote Mews, just off the Harrow Road. 'I lost all my stuff at the ice cream factory, just under Mick's tower block where I lived,' Joe told Pete Silverton in June 1978. 'Some guy went and threw it on the skip. Everything, even my suit, still in its paper from the dry cleaners. I've got nothing left from the 101ers, not a tape, a poster, even a photograph.'

In March 1977, Joe told Caroline Coon that he had always felt inferior as a musician and singer before seeing the Pistols, but that their 'so what' attitude had inspired him to adopt the same approach. He even insinuated that the other 101ers had played upon his self-doubts to steer the band's musical direction. These remarks, it has to be remembered, came from the person who had been the single most dominant figure in the 101ers from February 1975 onwards. Having knocked two years off his own age upon joining the Clash, he added insult to injury by accusing the 101ers of having been 'just too old'! He reluctantly conceded that they had been a good band – 'In fact, as far as sound and excitement went, we were much better than Eddie and the Hot Rods' – but this interview was to be almost the last time he said anything remotely positive about them. His subsequent references to the 101ers amount to a long-running series of deprecatory remarks about both his own abilities and the unrealistic aspirations of the band as a whole.

'I certainly don't feel it now, but at the time I felt bitter that the 101ers were denied,' says Richard, whose commitment to the band had rivalled Joe's and ultimately outlived it. 'Not by Joe so much – although to an extent, to start with – but certainly by Bernie Rhodes. He didn't want any connections, any references from Joe to his past. I think he was a little bit embarrassed by the fact that Joe was involved with what he would consider a *hippy* band. We never considered ourselves hippies. It was all rather ironic to me, because the Clash's so-called political philosophy was for me trying to uphold a political reality that had actually existed in the 101ers. There was another ironic touch – I don't know who originated it – in saying that the 101ers' name came from the cell number of that bloke [he means the torture room] in *1984* by George Orwell. Not relating it to squatting, but relating it to some "political" thing. Which is totally ironic when you think that one of the themes behind Orwell's book was the rewriting of history.' This popular misconception about the origin of the 101ers' name was propagated in Tony Parsons and Julie Burchill's 1978 book, *The Boy Looked At Johnny*, and later repeated by several popular music encyclopedias. 'That's a load of bunk!' Joe admitted in 1989, when questioned about it on Washington DC's Radio WHFS. Who made it up, then? 'I probably did,' he chuckled.

Under the circumstances, the release in February 1978 of the Clash's version of the late period 101ers' song 'Jail Guitar Doors' as the B-side of

'Clash City Rockers', attributed as it was to Strummer–Jones, could not fail to rub salt into Richard's wounds. Determined to prove the 101ers' worth, Richard began assembling various studio and live recordings by the band with a view to releasing them as an album. First he had to approach Joe for permission. 'He's a fool,' Joe told Pete Silverton that June. 'If you do it as a proper album, you don't get any money out of it. If you do it as a bootleg, you're rolling in it.' It may have been the truth, but Joe's motive was probably to dissuade Richard from pursuing the idea of an official release, something that would stand as a record in both senses of the word. As it appeared to be the best option at the time, though, Richard did contemplate a bootleg. Bernie, however, objected to having 101ers material available in any shape or form, and made the mistake of trying to argue the toss with Richard, hardly his number one fan. 'He came down to my place and had the cheek to give me all these completely absurd reasons why I shouldn't be bringing out this album,' Richard told the *NME*'s Chris Salewicz in February 1981. 'I ended up having to literally get hold of him and throw him out of the door.'

By the end of 1978, Bernie was no longer manager of the Clash. The following year, Joe and his new musical colleagues began to move away from punk into more traditionally based music, some of which was not a million miles away from the spirit of the 101ers. In mid-1980, the band even recorded their version of the old 101ers' set staple 'Junco Partner' for the *Sandinista!* album. Keeping his former band's output a secret was no longer such a priority, and Joe agreed to team up with Richard to prepare an official 101ers compilation. Along with Clive, Dan, Mole and Micky Foote, they became co-directors of a specially established label, named Andalucía! in honour of Esperanza and Palmolive (and, it would appear, as a pun on the Clash's then current album venture). A distribution deal was set up with Virgin.

'I approached Jackson's studio, where we did the Vic Maile material, and we did a deal where they got paid a royalty for using their copyright material,' says Richard. Understandably, when they learned that the 101ers were about to be revived as a marketable commodity, Chiswick decided to exploit their copyright material themselves. This took the form of a second single, coupling 'Sweet Revenge' with 'Rabies (From The Dogs Of Love)'. Chiswick saw the wisdom in synchronised releases with some crossover of material: thus, Andalucía! were allowed to use the Pathway 'Sweet Revenge', but were not granted permission to use 'Rabies' or, for that matter, '5 Star Rock'n'Roll Petrol' and the original single version of 'Keys To Your Heart'. Luckily, the 101ers had the BBC studios material as back-up, the copyright in which had remained with the band. There was a problem, though. Oxide tape has a tendency to deteriorate, and this had begun to happen with the BBC recordings. 'Mike Robinson actually remastered them for us,' says Clive. 'He was always a big help with the 101ers.'

In order to make up an album's worth of material, Micky Foote supplied a cassette recording he had made of the 101ers supporting Van Der Graaf

Generator on 18 April 1976 at the Roundhouse in Chalk Farm Road, Camden. 'I'd been working the audience as hard as I could and I couldn't get nothing out of them,' Joe said, describing the gig in question to Pete Silverton in December 1980. 'And then Trouble, the dog, wandered onstage and they all went bananas. And I gave up. The tape's really good: fast number banging into another fast number. No messing about. No sloppiness. And we couldn't impress them. Mind you, I don't know what sort of music Van Der Graaf is. It's like Shakespeare crossed with Uriah Heep.' This makes the gig seem an unlikely choice for a permanent record of the live 101ers, but much of its appeal for Joe especially must have been that it came from that brief period between his first exposure to the Sex Pistols and the sacking of Clive Timperley.

Chiswick jumped the gun by releasing the 'Sweet Revenge' single in late January 1981, which effectively killed the cross-promotional idea stone dead. The album finally emerged towards the end of March that year as *Elgin Avenue Breakdown*. It was named after a jazz album entitled *Lennox Avenue Breakdown* Joe had seen in New York, but there were multiple puns at work: the first part of the title makes direct reference to one of the main routes through the old Maida Hill squatting community, but also suggests the 101ers' long-time home base pub on Ladbroke Grove; the second part both offers to provide all the facts and acknowledges the band's untidy demise. The specific sense of locale and resolutely downbeat feel are further reflected in the packaging, which makes a virtue of amateurish, sub-bootleg lettering and layout. The front cover features a picture of the Metal Man, a local hobo-type character who, during the 101ers' heyday, could be found festooned with metal objects, sitting on kerbs around the Ladbroke Grove area.

Both the *NME* and *Melody Maker* gave the project advance publicity. The former paper, having championed the Clash well beyond the point of hype for the first couple of years of the band's recording career, was now gleefully indulging itself in the inevitable backlash. In spite of this, unshakeable Clash aficionado Chris Salewicz wrote a half-page feature for the 14 February 1981 issue based on an interview with Richard and promoted the album without undue sarcasm. Allan Jones's continued association with the *Melody Maker* (by this time he was the assistant editor) assured a favourable reaction from that source. Paolo Hewitt's two-page retrospective in the 28 February issue brought Joe, Richard and Mole together to reminisce about the old days. Perhaps because fewer of his memories were good ones, Mole was largely silent throughout. Joe admitted to being worried that his taking part in the exercise might fuel speculation about a Clash split, and showed no inclination to revise his customarily dismissive appraisal of the 101ers. Nevertheless, he and Richard talked about their shared escapades with genuine affection.

Upon the album's release, Allan Jones himself waxed lyrical about the 101ers in *Melody Maker*'s review. Never having warmed to the punk rock movement, he made the claim that 'Strummer songs like "Motor Boys Motor" anticipated the frustrations of punk, but betray none of its empty rhetoric.' In his opinion, the 101ers' 'Junco Partner' 'makes the Clash version sound stilted', and, while he acknowledged the poor sound quality of the live material in general, he maintained that, on certain tracks, 'the ferocity cuts through'. In the *NME* Adrian Thrills – whose career as a music journalist had begun with self-produced punk era fanzine *48 Thrills*, named after a line in the Clash song '48 Hours' - took a different perspective. As far as he was concerned, the album had arrived too long after the event and was of interest only to hardcore Clash fans and collectors. 'This mixture of studio and abysmally-recorded live stuff is incredibly run-of-the-mill, and would be almost completely forgettable were it not for the unmistakable, unexpurgated dementia in Strummer's coarse vocalising.' On this latter point, at least, he was in complete accord with Allan Jones, who wrote: 'Strummer's coarse vocal still carries an enthralling potency, screaming through the crowded lyric [of "Letsagetabitarockin"] in an urgent blurred torrent.'

Elgin Avenue Breakdown is a perfectly fine rough-and-ready souvenir, but it does not show the 101ers in a particularly favourable light. Not being able to use the majority of the Pathway material was too great a blow for the album to ride. Ironically, the two Chiswick singles are still available as re-releases on the Rock On-associated Big Beat label, whereas the album is now long deleted. Although the limited use of studio material is annoying, it is understandable. More mystifying is the reason why the Roundhouse tape, the sound quality of which is indeed very poor, was used as the sole source of live material. During the lengthy period he worked as soundman, Micky Foote recorded almost every 101ers gig direct from the mixing desk. Even though he had what Richard describes as 'the horrible habit, if he didn't have a new cassette, of reusing one from two months before', that still left a wide selection. Clive and Richard both have stashes of tapes, the latter having recently unearthed a recording of one of his favourite Wandsworth Prison gigs. Mole also has tapes of early 101ers rehearsal sessions. 'I heard them a few months ago, and some of the songs blew my head off, because I'd forgotten all about them,' says Clive. '"Boo The Goose", "Hideaway" and "Green Love" are on there.'

In June 1993, former 101ers roadie Boogie compiled a CD of almost all the 101ers' studio recordings – including the Jackson's studios material in its entirety – under the title *Five Star Rock'n'Roll* for a Paris-based label named Made in Heaven. 'It's the usual stuff,' says Clive. 'It sounds fine, and it's got good packaging, but it went out without our permission. He was just after a few bucks out of us. We went apeshit, and the French record company that Boogie had arranged it through were really, really apologetic. It's been withdrawn. They destroyed the matrix, and returned all the CDs to us.' There were two results: firstly, as there are only a thousand in existence, the CD is now a collector's item. Secondly, at the time of writing, the 101ers and Joe's manager, Kosmo Vinyl, are negotiating for the release of an authorised

101ers CD that will, it is hoped, prove both definitive and a more fitting memorial to a much-maligned band.

The cumulative effect of what Mole refers to as 'Clash propaganda' has been to give the impression that Joe had the foresight to jump a doomed ship just before it broke up against the rocks. Whatever one's verdict on the worth of the 101ers based on the evidence offered by *Elgin Avenue Breakdown*, that was simply not the case. In the unlikely event that the Pistols and punk had not impinged upon the Strummer consciousness, the more musical Clive and Dan line-up of the 101ers could have continued using R&B as a sturdy foundation upon which to develop further their own individual sound, as the Rolling Stones, Van Morrison and Bruce Springsteen had before them. There is no reason to suppose that punk would have denied them success; it failed to hinder the career of the even more traditionally rooted band Dire Straits.

Alternatively – and more realistically – a revamped, back-to-basics 101ers could have benefited from a climate made receptive by punk to almost all aggressive uptempo music. Admittedly, Dr Feelgood and Eddie and the Hot Rods did not maintain their initial commercial impact, and it could be argued that this was because punk effectively served to render their more overtly retrogressive styles obsolete. Untimely line-up changes were also a factor in both bands' return to the shadows, however, and other pub rock acts succeeded in jumping on the punk bandwagon; one such were the Stranglers, who did so with not inconsiderable help from Albion, the booking agents they had shared with the 101ers.

Again, it could be pointed out that a contract with the minor and ultimately commercially unsuccessful label Chiswick offered little guarantee of a high-profile career. But, had their alliance continued, the 101ers might well have been the band to turn Chiswick's fortunes round, enabling it to emulate the triumphs of Stiff, a similarly tiny label formed in July 1976 by Jake Riviera and Dave Robinson, ex-landlord of the Hope and Anchor. Failing that, a move to a major record company could not have been ruled out. By the spring of 1977, most of them were desperate to sign any band that was even remotely 'new wave'.

When Joe made his decision, he was leaving a going concern playing a style of music he had always loved – if not quite in the style he wanted to play it – for an almost completely unknown and unproven entity. Getting in early for the Clash backlash, Tony Parsons and Julie Burchill's *The Boy Looked At Johnny* implied that to base such a major life choice on superficial things like clothes and attitude was indicative of a certain shallowness of character. For a start, Tony and Julie did not present quite the full picture: at least part of the motive behind Joe's decision was Bernie's forcefully expressed intention of creating something similar in spirit to the Sex Pistols. Even if clothes alone had been enough to persuade Joe to sign up, what of it? Popular culture and the mass media had developed hand in hand with rock'n'roll. As early as the late Fifties, it was almost impossible to experience contemporary music without it being placed in some kind of visual, social and cultural context, all of which were bound to have some kind of influence on the consumer. Some people profess – and a very few genuinely manage – to judge music on its own merits and ignore all the trappings. Fine. But however knowledgeable about music or musically gifted they may be, if they deny that – from Elvis Presley onwards – popular music has been at least as much about image, attitude and hype as 'the riff on-stage' (or on disc), they are not only kidding themselves, but also failing to understand a large part of its impact and appeal.

It was a gamble that involved considerable sacrifice and risk, but the only person who had to find his defection reasonable was Joe himself. As long ago as 1970, he had shown that he was prepared to change his clothes, name and even his identity to become the person he wanted to be. In the summer of 1974, when he was barely functional as a performing musician, he had told a friend and housemate that he intended to be a pop star. For all the self-doubt experienced since that day, he had not wavered in his determination to do anything necessary to make that ambition become a reality.

While he was busy divorcing himself from the 101ers, Joe's new manager was organising a new rehearsal room-cum-HQ. At the end of the first week of June 1976, Joe took his PA, his soundman, his new clothes and his new cropped hairstyle along there in search of the new attitude. 'And – *bang!* – that was it,' says Keith Levene. 'We had the band.'

PART 2...

PUNK MYTHS

6... GARAGELAND

Malcolm McLaren's April 1976 call for a London popular music scene reminiscent of the glory days of the early to mid Sixties struck a chord with a generation of music fans who, like Joe Strummer and his peer group at the City of London Freemen's School, had been unable by reason of youth or distance to participate last time round. 'That generation that came of age in the Seventies, we'd grown up in the Sixties, but we'd missed the Sixties,' says punk period *NME* journalist Tony Parsons. 'It was a party we'd been too young to be invited to. A party of fucking girls who looked like Julie Christie, and stopping the war in Vietnam, and the King's Road, and all that kind of thing. And by the time it got to the mid-Seventies, and we'd turned up with our bottle of cider and our peace badges, it was over, finished. Now, it's too far away: it's history to teenagers today. But we were close enough to it to want our turn.'

By the beginning of June 1976, Bernie Rhodes was the Davis Road band's manager in all but contract, and so took it upon himself to find a more suitable rehearsal space. Joe had just been recruited, and the musicians needed to pool their respective talents, work on a band identity and develop a live repertoire. Bernie found what he considered to be the ideal place right under his nose: not too far from his flat at 268 Camden Road, and next door but one to Harry's, the Renault garage in which he owned a share. Situated just inside the gates of the British Rail Yard, on Chalk Farm Road, halfway between Dingwalls and the Roundhouse – those two pillars of the Camden Town rock'n'roll music scene – it was a disused and dilapidated two-storey end-terrace railway storage shed.

The amps and other musical equipment were set up in the relatively large downstairs room. The two upstairs rooms were used to store pinball and fruit machines – one of Bernie's Arthur Daley-esque sidelines – but one of them also became an all-purpose band office and recreation area. Entertainment was provided by another of Bernie's acquisitions, a jukebox, which band members stocked with an eclectic selection of singles: as well as tracks by Jimi Hendrix and the Doors, there were some of Paul's reggae and ska favourites – including Desmond Dekker's 'Israelites' and the Rulers' 'Wrong 'Em Boyo' – and the song with which he had failed his audition for the London SS, Jonathan Richman's 'Roadrunner', since released as a single. Bernie dispelled any possible lingering doubts about the function of the premises when he christened them Rehearsal Rehearsals. When the novelty value of this mouthful wore off, unsurprisingly quickly, the band and their associates shortened it to just plain Rehearsals.

In Keith's mind, the band might have *felt* complete with the addition of Joe, but there was still one vital gap in the line-up to be filled: the drummer. Richard Dudanski having refused to join, Joe called in a drum kit and a favour from Pablo LaBritain, who sat in for the first couple of rehearsals while the band made up their mind about a full-time member. As a result, Pablo features in the first photographs of the band in their new habitat. Although an old schoolfriend of Joe, a proficient drummer (as Clive Timperley testifies) and visually more in keeping with the general band style than, say, Mick Jones (as the photos testify), Pablo did not stick around to fill the vacancy long-term. The fact that he went on to join the Clash-influenced punk band 999 suggests this decision was not entirely of his own making. Whatever, sometime in mid-June, Terry Chimes got another call from Bernie.

Born in 1956, in east London's Mile End, Terry had grown up in a stable, supportive and competitive environment. His two brothers were also musicians. The younger was a bass player, but, predictably, Terry took his lead from the elder. 'He plays timpani in orchestras. He's three years older than me, and when he was 18, he was going to the Royal College of Music. And so I thought, "If you're going to do that, I'm going to be a rock'n'roll star!"' An intelligent youth who had developed an early fascination for matters scientific – 'I was the kind of kid who would ask for a microscope at Christmas rather than a football' – Terry successfully juggled both interests while at school, playing drums in school bands and also passing the A levels he required to pursue a career in medicine. It was at this point that he felt pressured to make a choice; instead of abandoning one or other of his ambitions, however, he came up with a typically level-headed compromise. 'I figured that I could just be a rock star for a year or two, and then go and do medicine after that. Now, a year goes very quickly, and I thought that I'd better make a go of this, so I auditioned with every band I could find.' His account of his ensuing trawl through the *Melody Maker* classifieds echoes the experiences of Rat Scabies: 'It was an extremely exasperating process, because you'd go all the way miles down somewhere or other, carry all your drums, set them up and realise the other guys were just idiots. But you'd have to keep on relentlessly doing that if you were going to find the right band.'

Terry was as assertive as he was pragmatic. One of his auditions, in August 1975, was for Violent Luck, and Kelvin Blacklock recalls the drummer being mouthy and pushy to the point of obnoxiousness and refusing to leave until he was told whether or not he had the job. Three months later, Terry tried out for the London SS. Unimpressed by the likes of the New York Dolls and, despite being fond of Free and Led Zeppelin, having no unshakeable allegiance to any particular band or genre of music, he did not fare well in the interview part of the audition; nevertheless, he came away with the feeling that his loud, steady, precise drumming style had made a favourable impression. Which proved to be the case when he was called back to try out first for the Billy Watts line-up at Riverside studios, and then – following the Pablo LaBritain interlude – with the Joe Strummer line-up at Rehearsals.

Initially, Terry was bemused by the change in singers, which no one took the trouble to explain to him. 'Billy had seemed such an integral part of what was going on at the time. And, also, Joe seemed such a weird sort of guy. He's not the archetypal rock'n'roll singer, is he? They didn't say, "This is the new singer *because* . . ." they just said, "This is the new singer", and I looked at him and thought, "So what's so special about you that they booted the other guy out?" I got to know him quite quickly, and then it became evident why he was there.'

Nor was any special effort made to help him feel welcome. 'Mick was the most communicative one, and so we got on fine, because when you meet people, you naturally say a few things, and if you get a reply and you get some rapport, you feel comfortable with them. So I did that with Mick, and tried to do that with everyone, but he was the only one who responded.' Joe's initial remoteness can be partly attributed to the adjustments he himself was having to make. Terry soon came to understand that Paul's was due to shyness. 'Paul wasn't *un*friendly. He just spoke so little that you weren't sure what was going on in his head.' Although his relationships with Joe, Mick and Paul never became particularly close, they did become more open. The same was not true for the two remaining members of the team. 'Bernie irritated everyone intensely. One hundred per cent of the people he met, he irritated them intensely. That was a deliberate policy of his. He's a one-off, a strange guy. I've never met anyone like him, before or since.' If Terry found Bernie annoying, yet intriguing, he found Keith just plain annoying, and wondered why the others put up with him. 'I said to Joe that Keith was very hostile, and it was a pain that he was like that. Joe said that he'd agreed at first, but that he'd been at McDonald's with him, and they'd both ordered a milkshake. Joe had tasted his, and thought that it wasn't very good, but had decided just to carry on drinking it. But when Keith had taken a sip of *his*, he'd immediately started giving the staff there a hard time. And Joe thought this was the challenging sort of behaviour we should have in the band.'

Terry recalls that they began 'rehearsing frantically' straight away. 'After we'd done about three, at which time I felt I was still in the process of deciding whether they were any good, Keith announced to me that I was now a member of the band. Which offended Bernie, who jumped in, "You can't say that till I've given the go-ahead! I'm in charge here!" And then Keith and Bernie proceeded to argue about it, which was quite amusing to me. I was sitting there thinking, "Well, when you've finished, I'll tell you whether *I* want to join the band or not." Then we just carried on. Nothing more was said about it.'

This kind of despotic outburst was not untypical of Bernie, and it begs the question, why would a group of imaginative, intelligent and mostly articulate young men endure such behaviour? 'Bernie imagined the Clash, and he built it to fit the specifications of his vision,' said Joe on MTV's 1991 Clash *Rockumentary*. 'The Clash wouldn't exist without Bernie's imagination.' Whereas the latter part of this assertion is undeniable, the former part is overly generous, an instance of Joe's post-Clash policy of self-effacement. It would be wrong to assume, just because Bernie had taken a key role in assembling the group's personnel, that everyone was in agreement that it was his group operating under his instruction and had willingly placed their destinies in his hands. As with the Sex Pistols, although there were sizeable elements of opportunism and prefabrication involved, the band was not manufactured *wholly* at their manager's whim in order to embody his fantasy, test his theory or follow his game plan. Neither Bernie nor Malcolm had any real idea what was going to happen next.

Andy Czezowski first met Malcolm and Bernie in 1974, when he began doing the accounts for King's Road clothing emporiums Acme Attractions and Sex. In 1976, he briefly managed both the Damned and Generation X before going on to open the Roxy club. 'I don't believe anyone who ever says they actually *created* a scene,' he says. 'It's all accident, it's never design. The sort of people that get involved in band management, or clubs and promotions, are able to see and exploit something coming along. People like Malcolm, who people may now revere as being The Man Who Invented Punk. He was nothing of the sort: the man was nothing more than a T-shirt salesman. People came through the shop, ideas bounced off, and he was sufficiently aware and astute to realise that there might be an angle there somewhere. You roll with it. But believe me, if it hadn't have worked, it would have been on to the next thing.' While he did not go quite so far as to admit opportunism, in a 1980 *Melody Maker* interview with Paul Rambali Bernie acknowledged that the punk explosion was by no means as planned as it has since sometimes been made out to be: 'We didn't know it would spread so fast. We didn't have a manifesto. We didn't have a rule book.'

It would also be incorrect, however, to assume that the band were cynically using Bernie for his contacts, his rehearsal space and his creative energy, with the idea of dispensing with his niggling presence as soon as it was no longer required. Obviously, Bernie's proprietorship of Rehearsals encouraged them to indulge him to a certain extent. Equally obviously, Mick, Joe and Keith – Paul being content to follow their lead – held the belief that Bernie would be able to help them hitch a ride on Malcolm's Sex Pistols wagon.

What nobody knew was how far that wagon might take them. The band members' encyclopedic knowledge of rock'n'roll history included a sizeable entry under 'creative management'. It listed empire builders like Larry Parnes; seemingly avuncular hucksters like Elvis's manager Colonel Tom Parker; daredevil scammers like the Rolling Stones' Andrew Loog Oldham and the Who's Chris Stamp and Kit Lambert; intimidatory hard men like the Small Faces' Don Arden and Led Zeppelin's Peter Grant; bully-boy financial stroke-pullers like Allen Klein; and political activists like the MC5's John Sinclair. These were people who – whatever their individual personality traits – had made names for themselves by making things happen for their respective bands. In mid-1976, there was no reason to doubt that there was room at the bottom of the encyclopedia entry for the names of Malcolm McLaren and Bernie Rhodes; but both were yet to prove themselves.

Much of the time, the band were indeed responding to Bernie's ideas, but their relationship was a symbiotic one, and the venture they were embarking upon a joint one. Whatever other criticisms could be levelled at the Rehearsals set-up, everyone involved was hoping to contribute to something new and exciting within the rock'n'roll medium, and everyone who stuck with it did so because he had committed himself wholeheartedly to the project.

Bernie sometimes played the tyrant, but the band seldom allowed him to get away with such blatant attempts to establish his dominance. Paul, in particular, ran a non-stop one-man campaign of pranks and insults designed to undermine his attempts to assert his authority. What today makes it difficult to arrive at a true picture of what Bernie was doing are the discrepancies in his role as he perceived it, as the band saw it and as he portrayed it to people outside the band: it was important *at that time* to make it look as though the ideas were coming from the youngsters, rather than their not so young manager. 'I have no say about what goes musically,' he told *Melody Maker* in 1977. 'My job is to co-ordinate, understand and clarify exactly what the band are trying to express; if you like, the melting pot of all their talents. It works on a basis of respect and teamwork, although of course, we argue like fuck a lot of the time, almost to the point of fights.'

Fired up, the rest of the band quickly became as intense and serious about what they were doing as Mick had been during his abortive rehearsals with Alan Drake. 'It all seems a bit daft to have argued about, in retrospect,' says Terry. 'But however we managed it, we did get a lot of intensity going, and that was what we needed. But at the time, we weren't aware that the main function of all this marvellous arguing was just to get everyone wound up and get a performance.' Terry likens the process to the kind of brainwashing one might experience in religious cults, with defences being broken down to encourage openness, but also leaving the participants vulnerable to manipulation. 'What happened was, Bernie was quite clever, because he drew very definite lines, and said, "Everything this side of the line is your responsibility", and challenged people. So they didn't think he was controlling everything so much as he was doing his job and expecting them to do theirs. But he actually was controlling an awful lot.' Thus, Bernie was far more effective at getting his own way when he went by an indirect route.

Sebastian Conran, soon to be a band associate, believes this control was established by sheer verbosity: 'Paul Simonon used to laugh about "Bernie and his parables", because Bernie always talked in metaphors the whole time, all the time. He didn't actually ever stop talking. But he had some good ideas.'

Although they mocked Bernie's delivery, the band couldn't have blocked him out even if they'd wanted to. Joe began to display a tendency to talk in 'parables' himself - 'The Tale of Keith and the Milkshake' being an obvious example – and Bernie-speak began to sneak into the entire band's vocabularies, even Paul's; for example, 'that's his situation' became a catch-all phrase used when comparing and contrasting ideologies and circumstances. They might not have been fully aware of all its manifestations, but the band have always acknowledged Bernie's influence. 'He made us actually *think* about what we were doing,' Paul told *Melody Maker*'s Allan Jones in November 1978. 'Bernie was really responsible for a lot of the way we thought, and how we put ourselves across,' Mick told *That Was Then, This Is Now* in 1989. And Joe, of course, went even further on the Clash MTV *Rockumentary* in 1991, when he claimed that the band was put together to Bernie's specifications.

The band members' various friends and associates tend not to be quite so generous in their appraisals of the manager's talents. Alan Drake, Chrissie Hynde and Richard Dudanski were not alone in considering him a Malcolm McLaren wannabe, hoping to emulate his supposed mentor's successes with his band of Sex Pistols wannabes. Even Glen Matlock is wont to dismiss Bernie as a plagiarist: 'Everything Bernie did was the same thing Malcolm had done, but second-hand.' While it was certainly true that Bernie monitored Malcolm to the point of obsessiveness, it could be argued that this was only because Malcolm was further down the track with something that Bernie himself had set in motion in the first place.

In Stuart Bailie's 1990 *NME* retrospective of the Rhodes career – by which time there was no need for him to be modest – Bernie stated, '*I'm* the guy that created punk rock . . . If I told you that I wrote and produced the first Clash LP, you wouldn't believe me.' It was an overstated claim, but it contained a kernel of truth. Bernie had encouraged Glen Matlock to think about what he was doing, and had suggested Johnny Rotten as vocalist for the Sex Pistols; these were two vital factors in the creation of the band, which in turn did indeed spawn the UK Class of '76 punk scene. And although Bernie did not 'write' the Clash's first album, its lyrics certainly gave voice to many of his observations and beliefs. In the 1980 interview with Paul Rambali he explained his original inspiration and motivation thus: 'I was listening to the radio in '75, and there was some expert blabbing on about how if things go on as they are, there'll be 800,000 people unemployed by 1979. Another guy was saying if that happened there'd be chaos, there'd be actual . . . *anarchy in the streets. That's* what was the root of punk.'

Following along behind the Pistols put Bernie and his charges in a difficult position. In Jonh Ingham's April *Sounds* feature the Sex Pistols had stated their desire for a scene with 'more bands like us'. That the still unnamed Rehearsals band had been inspired by the Pistols was something which they did not try, and have never since tried, to deny; and they did very much want to be part of the Pistols' scene. On the other hand, the last thing they wanted was to be dismissed as second-rate copyists. It was a problem also being faced by the Damned, then in rehearsal at a gay club in a deconsecrated church hall off Lisson Grove. The trick was to be similar, yet different, something that, as Rat Scabies explains, required a mod's understanding of the importance of the telling detail: 'I certainly don't think that any of the bands who were there right at the start of punk dreamed of sounding or looking even vaguely like one of the other bands. In a lot of ways, it was a very mod mentality at that point. It was important to have your own identity, but to be cool with it. I remember, none of us would wear Malcolm's clothes, because that was the Pistols camp, and you had to have your own thing.'

'At this stage, we looked like the cat's whiskers, all this good gear from Malcolm's shop, and they used to look like a bunch of squatters' is how Glen sums up the gulf between the Pistols and the Rehearsals band. 'We had the style and they didn't.' They may not have had the advantage of being backed by the proprietor of Sex, but by this time Bernie's charges were not quite so desperately attired as Glen suggests. While the Damned made do with an image that, out of financial necessity, began with army surplus and then shifted quickly towards kitsch fancy dress, perfectly complementing music and presentation that was part stormtrooper assault and part theatrical high camp, the Rehearsals band were a little more literal in their response to the mod parallel.

The few photos that have since emerged of their June rehearsals show all the band except Mick looking like slightly scruffy Ivy League college boys, with hair short enough to recall early Sixties crew cuts, drainpipe jeans and trousers, sharp-looking small-collared shirts, skinny ties and narrow-lapelled jackets. Such details were rare in 1976, the era of unstyled shoulder-length hair, A-line jeans, jumbo collars, kipper ties and jacket lapels wider than the jackets themselves. Although the band's gear was mostly bought second-hand, considerable thought and taste had obviously gone into its selection, and the overall effect was not so much Squatter as Oxfam Mod: stripped down, with any suggestion of dandyism removed. Yet it had come to the Clash not direct from the Sixties, but via the Anglophile New York new wave bands: one cannot help but recognise the continuing influence of the *Horses* album cover, which depicts Patti Smith in her little black suit and loosened skinny black tie. Mick's version of the band look, with his leather trousers and hair still covering his ears, was pure Patti Smith. Whereas Patti was both paying tribute to the Sixties and subverting gender stereotypes, though, the signals given off by the Rehearsals band – again excepting Mick – were unequivocally macho. There was a hint of the skinhead in the stance, if not the hairstyle. 'I can remember having this conversation with Joe,' says Sebastian Conran, 'and him saying, basically, that what one did was, one dressed to intimidate other people. You would walk down the street, and people would have to get out of the way.' This was the effect Terry had noted prior to his Riverside studios audition, and it was largely attributable to Paul.

Bernie and the other members of the band had been quick to recognise that they had a trump card in Paul. The way he dressed, the way he looked and the way he carried himself were the epitome of cool. Mick was working class, from a broken home, and lived in a council high-rise, but he was grammar school educated, vaguely effete and had an embarrassing glam rock past. Joe signed on and lived in a squat, but he was a middle class, ex-public school ex-pub rocker. Paul, by contrast, *appeared* to have all the credentials of a bona fide punk: he was not only from a broken home, but he was also a former skinhead and football hooligan. He could get away with playing the Man With No Name because he brought next to no baggage with him to the band. Unlike Mick or Joe, he had no previous musical history, and none of his former school or college friends was inducted into the band's entourage.

Later, when the band began doing interviews, they were more than happy for Paul to be portrayed as a tough nut, hard man, bad lad or rude boy, because the resulting street credibility rubbed off on everyone else. Of course, the real Paul Simonon was a considerably more complex character than his media persona suggested. Most of those who knew him at 20 recognised – like Terry – that his self-contained manner was due to neither ignorance nor arrogance. 'He's really kind of shy,' confirms Rat Scabies. 'I think he's sure of himself as well, but he's not a way out front sort of chap. I think he is genuinely shy, and it can sometimes get misinterpreted.' This also partly explained Paul's lack of volubility. Although certainly no intellectual and no match for the verbal gymnastics of either Mick or Joe, when relaxed and in the right mood, he could reveal himself to be both eloquent and informed. The band member most given to laddish larking around, his humour did not begin and end with slapstick. A highly developed sense of the surreal manifested itself in monologues composed of goofball *non sequiturs* that kept his companions in stitches. Prepared, when he thought it necessary, to put the hard face to the rhetoric of the others, he was also the most consistently polite and charming member of the group.

As well as being responsible for the band's style, Paul ultimately provided its name. Various suggestions were in consideration from the moment the band first arrived at Rehearsals. The Phones and the Mirrors both had a shiny, modern feel to them and, with connotations of communication and image respectively, also brought to mind the contemporary New York new wave band Television. The Outsiders (whether inspired by the Albert Camus or the Colin Wilson book) suggested alienation and rebelliousness, in the tradition of Mick's original band, the Delinquents. The two names that came closest to sticking were even more interesting in view of subsequent developments in the band's identity. The first, the Psychotic (or Psycho) Negatives, recalled the Count Five's garage classic, 'Psychotic Reaction', and revealed the strong influence at the time of Johnny Rotten's nihilistic outlook. The Weak Heart Drops was taken from the 1975 track 'Lightning Flash (Weak Heart Drop)' by reggae toaster Big Youth, and in its shortened form of the Heartdrops it echoed – perhaps too closely – Johnny Thunder's Heartbreakers. Both names lasted about a week.

Then, flicking through London's *Evening Standard* newspaper one day, Paul noticed how often the word 'clash' recurred in titles and subtitles as shorthand not only for violent confrontation, but also disagreement and friction of any kind. The word seemed to sum up both the dynamic in the band camp and the impact they desired to make in performance. It also had a mod sharpness and directness to it, in the tradition of the Who. He suggested it to the others, and it struck an instant chord with everyone except – predictably - Keith. 'I wasn't too crazy about it, but there you go.' The guitarist was outvoted, and the band became the Clash.

Their slightly scruffy Sixties look was not inappropriate to the Clash's early material. Joe, having rejected the 101ers and R&B on the grounds that both were old hat, was loath to play songs he had written while with his former band, and so 'Jail Guitar Doors' and the others were quickly sidelined. Which left Mick's songs. Listening today to the stockpile Mick had amassed by the time of Joe's arrival, it comes as no surprise to learn that he had previously rehearsed with bands playing, at his instigation, songs by the likes of the Standells, MC5, Troggs and Flamin' Groovies: the influence of original punk rock is there in the riffs and the high harmonies of 'Ooh, Baby, Ooh (It's Not Over)', '1-2 Crush On You', 'Bored With You', 'Deny', 'Protex Blue', 'She's Sitting At My Party' and 'Mark Me Absent'. Lyrically, Mick's songs evince a ready wit, a neat turn of phrase and a suitably knowing mid-Seventies take on teenage life. This is demonstrated by 'Ooh, Baby, Ooh (It's Not Over)', a song based on the riff from Booker T. and the MGs' 'Time Is Tight': 'Now, I don't care how many of my good friends that you kiss / I'll just have another drink, it's better when I'm pissed / 'Cos if I start a fight, I'll lose / But if I'm drunk, then I won't feel the fists.' Nevertheless, the teenage life they depict – as defined by crushes, broken romances, school canteens, drunken parties and token rebellious gestures towards such everyday authority figures as teachers and parents – is highly stylised and a hangover from the mid-Sixties. Mick might have been updating, adding new twists and a veneer of dirty realism (with references to drugs and contraceptives), but, like his musical influence, his lyrical influence was coming second-hand from the original garage bands.

Although the Sex Pistols had started from similar roots - rehearsing the Count Five's 'Psychotic Reaction', the Who's 'Substitute', the Flamin' Groovies' 'Slow Death', Jonathan Richman's 'Roadrunner', the Kinks' 'I'm Not Like Everybody Else' and half the Small Faces' songbook – Johnny Rotten's unique delivery and original lyrical perspective had raised the band's own material to an entirely different level. Mick's were good songs of their type, but, understandably, Bernie did not think they had enough firepower to go up against the Pistols' canon. Both Keith and Joe agreed, the latter being aware of the irony of his having abandoned one retro-tendency in favour of another. The matter of song content was where Bernie's guidance was to prove most valuable. As both Mick and Joe have explained on numerous occasions, Bernie helped them to realise that songs about love were just a convention of safe, commercial pop, and that truly cutting-edge songwriters should be reflecting their own environment and experience. 'He said, "Don't write love songs,"' Joe told the *NME*'s Paul Du Noyer in 1981, '"write about something you care about, that's real."'

The problem for Mick was that so much of his experience - so much of what he cared about, of what affected him – was second-hand and unreal. 'He was a bedroom kid: one of those kids in the bedroom dreaming that someday he'll be as big as the guys on the posters, learning his chops in the bedroom,' Joe told *Creem*'s Bill Holdship in 1984. At the time he made this remark, Joe was intent on showing Mick in as poor a light as possible, yet his assessment was essentially correct. Shortly after rehearsals had got under way at Rehearsals, former bandmate Matt Dangerfield met Mick wandering apparently aimlessly around the streets near Warrington Crescent. Matt asked him what he was doing. 'Mick said, "Bernie says I've got to hang out." "Hang out?" "Yeah. He says I need to be *streetwise*,"' laughs Matt, who was so tickled by this exchange that he went home and wrote a song about it, though, perhaps fortunately for Mick, not one that he ever bothered to record.

In the event, the streets first conveyed their wisdom to Mick while he was riding the number 31 bus from Harrow Road to Chalk Farm Road for yet another rehearsal. The tune and chorus to what is arguably his first truly classic song, 'Janie Jones', came to him out of the blue. When completed, it told the story of someone working in a dull office job and resenting having to do so when he could be listening to music, getting stoned or driving over to see his girlfriend. Janie Jones was a real-life vice queen who had enjoyed a spell of tabloid notoriety before being given a seven-year jail sentence for controlling prostitutes and attempting to pervert the course of justice (by threatening witnesses); as a result, according to Joe, she 'seemed impossibly glamorous' to someone stuck in a tedious workaday routine. The song was originally sung in the first person and is obviously autobiographical, though Joe helped Mick complete the lyric. It is telling that Mick felt he had to go back to 1973, the year that Janie Jones was imprisoned and he himself last worked in an office, to find an experience that conformed even vaguely to the Rhodes brief. And even then, what he came up with was a love song . . .

In the *Clash On Broadway* booklet Joe said that most of the early songwriting consisted of 'revamping', for which one should read 'adapting Mick's existing songs'. Joe would take over most of the lyric-writing for new compositions, but it was some time before he felt comfortable enough with his position in the band to rewrite the words to Mick's already completed material. In the meantime, he and the others had to accept them as they were, with the exception of 'Ooh Baby Ooh (It's Not Over)', which was dropped. '1-2 Crush On You' remained in the band's set, unaltered, for the rest of the year, eventually becoming the light-relief encore in which Joe amused audiences by grimacing his way through the school romance lyric. It is not insignificant that, when it was eventually recorded in March 1978, it was sung by its composer.

Initially, then, most of the revamping consisted of arranging the music, and it is in this department that Keith maintains he took a leading role. 'There's a lot of me in the Clash. I was contributing to the helter-skelter factor, to the velocity of how the songs were played, making things go much faster,' he told the *NME*'s Jane Garcia in 1989. The key word here is 'contributing'. Mick was a fan of the high-energy MC5; Joe had been known as a frenetic live performer for well over a year; the whole group had been bowled over by the first Ramones album; and one of the few things there had been no arguments about was that the band should *move*. 'The idea of the band was to try to play it *maximum*,' Joe told Harold De Muir of the *East Coast Rocker* in 1988. 'That when we were onstage, there wouldn't be anybody standing around loafing.' Rob Harper – who joined the band as drummer for the December 1976 Anarchy Tour – recalls a conversation between Mick and Joe in which Mick said, 'Do you remember when this band started, and we said it was gonna be like an *explosion* coming off the stage?' Thus, although the band's uptempo policy was one of the ways in which they first distinguished themselves from the more mid-paced Sex Pistols, Keith was by no means its sole originator.

On the 1977 album *The Clash* Keith would receive a co-writing credit for 'What's My Name', the tune and chorus of which he and Mick wrote together at Riverside studios shortly before Joe's arrival. 'I wrote more than I got credited for on the record,' Keith now insists. 'Basically, I got credited for "What's My Name" because I wrote the whole fucking thing, really. Let's face it, all the other tunes I had a good fucking hand in. I mean, it was me and Mick that wrote those tunes. Mick is definitely more responsible for the inception of most of them than I am, but it was me who put any bollocks there were into them.' He becomes irritable when pressed to reveal for which other compositions in particular he feels he deserves part of the credit. Memory does not serve him well: he insists that all the songs written and performed during his time with the band appear on and make up the bulk of *The Clash*. In fact, apart from 'What's My Name' and the songs already in Mick's songbook by the time the band started, only four others dating from the Keith era made it on to either the band's first album or single: 'Janie Jones', 'London's Burning', '48 Hours' and '1977'. Mick and Joe have claimed co-authorship and detailed the circumstances of composition for all four.

It is understandable that lead instrumentalists should object to the way their contributions – which define so much of their bands' musical identities – are considered mere embellishments, when even the most familiar (even blatantly stolen) three-chord skeletons of tunes they work on are termed 'compositions' and later generate royalty payments for the person claiming authorship. In a 1980 *NME* interview with Chris Bohn Keith likened his role with the Clash to that of Brian Eno with the early Roxy Music, and when he speaks of 'putting bollocks' into the songs, he means not just mere speed, but also a weird spin, an attacking edge. 'I think the ideal band the Clash should have been, as far as Mick Jones was concerned, was Squeeze,' he says. 'That's what he was going after.' Bearing in mind the type of song Mick had been writing up to that point, it is not so wild a claim as it may first appear. The question is whether Keith was any more responsible for changing that than Bernie, Joe, Paul or the events of late summer 1976.

The only surviving tape of a gig involving Keith would be made at the Roundhouse on 5 September, which turned out to be his farewell performance. On that tape, the band sound nothing like Squeeze, but they also sound nothing like they do on *The Clash*, recorded five months later. It may be that they had to go through sound B to get from sound A to sound C, but it would be hard for anyone to make the case tight enough to squeeze composer credits out of it. Nevertheless, Keith's guitar style is revealed to be inventively harsh and metallic, working off Terry's thunderous drumming to create the kind of industrial noise that was to typify the experimentation of the period immediately post-punk, including that of Keith's own subsequent band, Public Image Ltd (PiL). If nothing else, it is quite clear that he did indeed play a large role in establishing an early Clash sound that was not retro, not remotely similar to that of the Pistols and – though ultimately not something with which the other band members wanted to persevere – quite possibly a couple of years ahead of its time.

Details of name, image, performance style, repertoire and sound had to be sorted out quickly (to at least temporary satisfaction) because the Clash's début appearance was scheduled for Sunday, 4 July 1976, supporting the Sex Pistols at the Black Swan (known as the Mucky Duck) in Sheffield. The headline band, time and place were not without significance. Obviously, it was Bernie's relationship with Malcolm that brought about the opportunity to play. From the point of view of Bernie and the Clash, supporting the Pistols was both an acknowledgement of influence and a chance to buy into the Pistols' scene. From Malcolm and the Pistols' point of view, it established the rightful pecking order.

The Clash had been rehearsing for less than a month, and this rush to get on-stage also demonstrated how fearful they were of being left behind. While their ages, choice of venues and length of time on the scene marked the Stranglers down as a pub rock band, they certainly had plenty of punk attitude, and were beginning to make all the right connections. Back on 16 and 17 May, their booking agents, Albion, had secured them the support slot for Patti Smith's UK début shows at the Roundhouse. On 4 July – the same day as the Sheffield gig – they were due to appear there again, this time supporting the Ramones and the Flamin' Groovies as part of the American Independence Day Bicentennial celebrations. Perhaps more importantly, the Damned were to make their début just two days later at the 100 Club, also supporting the Sex Pistols. Whereas the Damned were planning to walk straight into the lions' den, the Clash were choosing to take their first faltering steps in an altogether less perilous environment; but at least they were going to beat their rivals to the public stage. Suspicion that they were hardly ready at this time is reinforced by the fact it was to be another five weeks before the Clash performed live again.

The band set off for Sheffield at 5 a.m., in a lorry that was so large most of the equipment could be packed on to the ledge behind the cab while the band members stretched out on the floor and caught up on their sleep. That night was the first time Terry had ever seen the Pistols – 'an eye-opener' - and, possibly as a consequence, he can remember no details about the Clash's own performance. Interviewed in 1982 on San Jose's Radio KSJO, Joe was equally vague. 'I *think* it was good. I'm not sure . . .' The Pistols were a lot clearer about what they thought of their support band. 'I remember talking to John, and asking, "What do you think?"' says Glen. 'I really wanted it to work, because Mick was my mate, and I was keen for something to happen. And John went, "They're not very good, are they?"'

Some feedback from their peers was inevitable and, given Johnny Rotten's personality, almost inevitably negative, but the Clash might have expected such a low-key gig to avoid the attentions of the media. True, there were no representatives of the music press there, but an unsolicited review turned up on the *Sounds* letters page. The correspondent, 'An anonymous music lover, Sheffield', passed the following verdict: 'Clash were just a cacophonous barrage of noise. The bass guitarist had no idea how to play the instrument, and even had to get another member of the band to tune it for him. They tried to play early Sixties R&B, and failed dismally. Dr Feelgood are not one of my favourite bands, but I know they could have wiped the floor with Clash.' For a band doing their best *not* to play early Sixties R&B, that must have stung. In the interests of balance, though, it is worth noting that the Sex Pistols received a similar trashing. The general drift of the letter was established in the opening paragraph: 'Both bands were crap. It's enough to turn you on to Demis Roussos.'

Back in London the next night came the first example of the rivalry-induced squabbling that was to dog the punk scene and undermine any attempts to promote a spirit of unity among the bands involved. Following the success of the Ramones-headlined Roundhouse gig, a second show involving the same three bands had been hastily arranged down the road at Dingwalls. Offered an unexpected opportunity to catch one of the best bills London had seen that year, most members of the Pistols and Clash attended. After the gig, while Mick, Glen, Steve Jones and Viv Albertine were backstage chatting to the Flamin' Groovies, Joe approached Stranglers guitarist Hugh Cornwell in the adjoining restaurant, and said, 'I think your bass player's having a scuffle with my bass player: they've both been thrown out.'

According to Stranglers follower Gary Coward-Williams, interviewed for Chris Twomey's booklet *The Stranglers: The Men They Love To Hate*, everyone piled outside to find Paul Simonon and Jean Jacques Burnel squaring up to each other in the courtyard. The escalating tension was not relieved when another Stranglers fan, Dagenham Dave, punched Johnny Rotten for no apparent reason. It looked as though a full-scale brawl was about to break out between the Pistols and Clash on one side and the Stranglers and their followers on the other, but everyone was so confused about what was going on that the situation was gradually defused without further violence. Perhaps fortunately for Paul, as J. J. was a black-belt karate expert. Nevertheless, the Stranglers' bassist continued to bear a grudge for years, and the incident deepened the mistrust between the other bands and the Stranglers, who – at least as far as the Inner Circle punk bands were concerned – thereafter lived up to the title of Chris Twomey's booklet.

That week, the Clash resumed intensive rehearsals and also began working up the first fruits of the Strummer–Jones writing partnership. Over the next year, there was no set pattern for song construction: sometimes Joe wrote a lyric at home and brought it in for Mick to put a tune to it; sometimes Mick wrote the tune first, and suggested a chorus or rough lyrical theme for Joe to expand on; and sometimes both worked on the tune and lyric simultaneously in the upstairs office at Rehearsals, Mick with his guitar and Joe with a big pad of paper and, according to his own account, a crayon. (He soon progressed to a manual typewriter.) In the *Clash On Broadway* booklet Joe claimed that if a song took more than a day to write, it was invariably abandoned. Whereas this is undoubtedly true of the unsuccessful efforts, those with which the band chose to persevere continued to be refined - especially lyrically – until such a time as they were either dropped from the set or recorded.

'The thing was to be relevant, to have some kind of root in human existence,' Joe told the *East Coast Rocker*'s Harold De Muir in 1988. 'We wanted it to have something to do with the times we were living in. We wanted the songs to be about the everyday, and not about a romantic fantasyland, or whatever.' In *Diary Of A Rock'n'Roll Star*, after recalling a song he had co-written with Kim Fowley named after 'romantic' American location Hollywood and Vine, Ian Hunter wondered how British songwriters were supposed to write with a straight face 'about the corner of Wardour and Old Compton'. Mick and Joe had started groping their way towards answering this challenge even before joining the Clash, as is evidenced by their respective songs of sexual disgust, 'Protex Blue' and 'Rabies (From The Dogs Of Love)': the former makes reference to a West End bar and the Bakerloo tube line, and the latter to Shepherd's Bush and the Praed Street Clinic. The trick now, as Bernie continued to stress, was to capture a sense not only of the place, but also of the times.

Sneaking a reference to the 100 Club into 'Deny' was a start. As the Sex Pistols' home base for the summer of 1976, the venue was where the band's following had evolved into a recognisable punk scene. It was certainly the place of origin for most of UK punk's distinguishing features: the pogo (thanks to Sid Vicious), gobbing (thanks to Rat Scabies), the safety pin and razor blade craze and, by the time of September's punk festival, the bin-liner craze (all thanks to Johnny Rotten, according to Johnny Rotten).

Following the dissolution of the 101ers and Richard Dudanski's departure to Sicily, Paul, Keith and Sid Vicious had joined Joe and Palmolive in the Orsett Terrace squat. In the booklet accompanying the 1988 double compilation album *The Story Of The Clash, Volume 1* Joe's *alter ego,* 'band valet Albert Transom', described life there in lurid detail. In his version, the inhabitants picked up discarded vegetables from Portobello Road market stalls, preferring to spend their DHSS money at other stalls selling second-hand goods. These included clothes, at least one television (on which the sound did not work), a Dansette record player and batches of scratched bargain bin records by the Who, Bo Diddley, the early Rolling Stones, Woody Guthrie, Howlin' Wolf, Leadbelly and Big Youth, among others. The large communal basement room, where the food was eaten, the TV watched and the records played, was filthy, and in the relentless heat of that summer was also home to a dense cloud of flies. Reflecting his environment, Joe came up with a lyric which, when complemented by a tune based on a distinctive Terry Chimes drum pattern, produced one of the more disquieting songs in the Clash's early live repertoire: 'How Can I Understand The Flies?'

With the exception of Terry, the entire band were now living within a hundred yards of the Westway, and Mick, Paul and Joe had been based in and around the Notting Hill area for years. 'Four-square Portobello Road boys,' says Glen Matlock. 'Which was good, because it gave them a sense of identity. It gave them a base to work from, a foundation.' 'There wasn't a lot to do, so we'd just hang around,' said Joe, when interviewed for the Channel 4 TV programme *Wired* in 1988. 'We had to make it better. And glamorising it was part of it. We wanted to make ourselves feel good. Because the songs I was listening to were all about Mississippi or Alabama or Lafayette, all these exotic places, and what we had here was another world, so we wanted to bring some mythology to our world.'

His first fully-fledged attempt to rubbish Ian Hunter's dictum was written at Orsett Terrace after a visit to Wilmcote House. Although also a possible nod in the general direction of the MC5's 'Motor City Is Burning', a song inspired by the Detroit inner city riots of 1967, the title of 'London's Burning' makes more direct reference to the folk-cum-nursery rhyme celebrating the Great Fire of London of 1666. Joe adopts a singsong voice and childish language to tell of a different kind of conflagration: the lights of the Westway as seen from the balcony of Wilmcote House. The song rails against boredom and the apathy of television-watching zombies, and ends with a bleak expression of urban alienation, but the urgency of the chorus's repeated emergency call, the movement of the cars and the momentum generated by the band's performance serve to subvert its negativity: in the end, the song's very frustration generates a sense of excitement, of something about to happen.

It is no mean trick to celebrate and condemn your environment simultaneously without inducing head-scratching bewilderment in the listener. 'London's Burning' is informed by the same ambivalence that provokes street gangs to fight for territory one day and vandalise it the next: the kind of behavioural response to habitat explored by J. G. Ballard in *High-Rise*. 'Can you understand how much I hate this place?' a melodramatic Mick Jones demanded of the *NME*'s Tony Parsons at the end of March 1977. Just two weeks earlier, Joe had told *ZigZag*'s Kris Needs, 'We love the place. Blocks of flats, concrete', and Mick had chipped in with, 'I hate the country. The minute I see cows I feel sick.' What 'London's Burning' celebrates is urban adolescent confusion, something that Sixties punk rock (and even mainstream pop) had always toyed with, and Seventies punk rock was setting out to make its own.

As is true of most great rock'n'roll anthems, the song also documents a lifestyle. Like '5 Star Rock'n'Roll Petrol', it contains implicit drug references, but unlike the earlier song, these are not merely metaphorical devices. Joe might have eschewed amphetamines while with the 101ers, but most of his new squatmates were enthusiastic users, and time hung heavy between rehearsals. By the time of the song's composition, cars weren't the only things 'speeding around underneath the yellow lights'. 'All we'd do was take blues [pills] or snort loads of cheap sulphate and get out there and live all night,' Joe told the *NME*'s Sean O'Hagan in 1988. 'We'd take amphetamines and storm around the bleak streets where there was nothing to do but watch the traffic. That's what "London's Burning" is about.' (The melancholy final verse represents the comedown.) Joe might have had to spell it out 12 years after the event, but speed was the punk drug of choice, and in 1976, the original punk crowd had no trouble identifying with the song; just as, in 1965, any mod who had ever been pilled up knew why Roger Daltrey was stuttering his way through 'My Generation'. For such an ostensibly simple jingle, 'London's Burning' encodes a complex series of messages.

In the *Clash On Broadway* booklet Mick recalled '48 Hours' being written in a 96th of that time in the upstairs room at Rehearsals when the band required an additional song 'for some reason'. That reason was almost certainly to provide them with a full-length set in time for their second live performance. Perhaps predictably, under the circumstances, '48 Hours' breaks little new ground. Like 'Janie Jones', it concerns a working stiff feeling oppressed by the tediousness of his job, but it harks back even further to buy into the mid-Sixties mod-culture notion of living for the weekend, as exemplified by the Easybeats' 1966 hit 'Friday On My Mind'. What it adds is a whole new level of desperation: the working week is a 'jail on wheels' hurtling ever closer. The search for kicks is so panic-driven and couched in such violent language that any possibility of fun is denied, ensuring that the quest is unsuccessful. As in 'London's Burning', there is a definite sense of place (the protagonist 'takes the tube'), the influence of speed is blatant and the loser message is to some extent belied by the song's sheer kinetic energy.

Nevertheless, the Clash were still looking to mod culture to provide a blueprint for punk culture.

Between their first and second gigs, the Clash received their first bona fide music press coverage, courtesy of *Melody Maker*'s Caroline Coon. At 32, Caroline belonged to the previous generation. A former child ballet dancer and sociology student, she came from a wealthy background, but had done more than pay lip-service to the late Sixties counter-culture: in 1967, she had co-founded Release, the legal aid group that dealt with drugs cases, and had contributed to the underground magazine *It*. Along with several of her contemporaries, she had moved on to the mainstream music press in the early Seventies and was now responsible for the weekly singles column in *Melody Maker*. Her interest in clothes had led her to Sex, and her fascination with the sociological aspects of youth culture from there to the Sex Pistols' early gigs. Unfortunately, *Melody Maker* had so far lived up to its reputation as a bastion of musical snobbery and shown a marked unwillingness to let her report on the antics of these primitive row-makers.

Caroline had had to watch in frustration as the *NME*'s Neil Spencer wrote the first excitement-generating music press review of the Pistols at the Marquee. Then as a representative from her own paper – none other than Joe's old Newport friend Allan Jones – had rubbished the Pistols while praising the 101ers in a review of the same Nashville gig that had ultimately caused Joe to renounce R&B: 'They do as much for music as World War Two did for the cause of peace. I hope we shall hear no more of them.' Then as her gig-going partner Jonh Ingham – his imagination fired by Neil Spencer's write-up – had stolen a march on everyone by conducting the first full-length interview with the Pistols for *Sounds*.

Worldly-wise, from New Zealand via Los Angeles, where he had run his own science fiction magazine, Jonh Ingham later admitted to Jon Savage that he had been intent on mythologising the band as a means of establishing himself as one of the foremost rock journalists of a new generation. Andy Czezowski for one believes this kind of attitude was instrumental in breaking punk. 'When you consider the amount of journalists in the rock business at that time – I don't know how many, but assuming there were 50 to 100 – you had only really two or three rooting for punk: Jonh Ingham, Caroline Coon and Giovanni Dadomo,' he says. 'That's probably it. But it created enough of a stir to ensure the papers were taken over. Because those writers were the useful energy on the music paper scene. They would not have been *allowed* to interview Mick Jagger. They were nothing journalists. The bigger guys would have got that job. So who could they deal with? The people that were their peers, the new up-and-coming scene.'

To avoid being scooped entirely, Caroline resorted to subterfuge, using a review of the posthumous 101ers single 'Keys To Your Heart' as a transparent excuse to sneak the first brief interview with the Clash into her 24 July column. Under the memorable headline 'From a Crud to a King' Joe told of his conversion to punk and Caroline prompted Mick to reject her colleagues' dismissal of the new movement as (courtesy of Richard Hell) 'the Blank Generation': 'We don't see ourselves that way. We're showing you music that's great. We're challenging complacency, standing up for rock'n'roll. We want to get rid of rock'n'rollers like Rod Stewart, who kiss royalty after gigs.' Like many others, Mick had found it difficult to forgive Rod for disbanding the Faces and teaming up with Britt Ekland to join the jet set.

Editor Ray Coleman finally responded to the growing media buzz around punk rock. Competition amongst the three leading weekly music press inkies was intense. If punk was, after all, destined to be the next big thing, *Melody Maker*'s survival might depend on its coverage of the scene. He gave the go-ahead to Caroline for a positive-overview feature, but, just to hedge his bets, commissioned Allan Jones to offer the alternative opinion. Published side by side in the 7 August issue, Caroline's piece was headlined, 'Punk rock: rebels against the system?' – firmly establishing 'punk' as the title for the movement – and Allan's response, 'But does nihilism constitute revolt?'

Given that the movement was in its infancy – she had to include Manchester yob rockers Slaughter and the Dogs, Birmingham glam rockers the Suburban Studs and London pub rock stalwarts Eddie and the Hot Rods, the Stranglers and the Jam in order to even begin to make a case – Caroline showed a grasp of punk's antecedents, aims, affectations and rhetoric that would have been truly remarkable had she not spent much of the previous six months observing its development. And if she hadn't been given considerable uncredited help by supposed rival but in fact good friend Jonh Ingham, as was later acknowledged in the 1977 book compiling her punk writings, *1988: The New Wave Punk Rock Explosion*. Even so, this does not detract from what was an undeniably impressive feature.

Caroline drew parallels with the impact the Beatles, the Rolling Stones, the Who and the Kinks had made on the insipid British pop scene of the early Sixties. She made the point that those bands and their contemporaries were now part of the rock establishment, and that the subsequent generation of bands had abandoned the visceral and immediate in favour of the progressive and academic. She felt the State of Rock was symbolised by the stadium-type concerts given earlier that summer by the likes of the Who, the Stones and Elton John, causing her to opine, 'The time is right for an aggressive infusion of life blood.'

She also claimed the new London punk scene had not been inspired by the New York new wave, but was instead developing parallel to it. This was simply not the case, and was an example of Caroline toeing Malcolm's party line, as set out in Jonh Ingham's earlier feature. Although she acknowledged that, like the New York scene, the London one betrayed the influence of original Sixties punk, she stated that it was determined to develop its own identity: 'Nostalgia is a dirty word.' This much was true. She went on to explain that the music was performed with the minimal amount of equipment and the songs were short, basic and fast, with cynical lyrics and without solos or indulgent improvisations. Boredom was a pose, but it was a badge of punk in the same way as brooding cool had been the badge of the original Fifties rock'n'rollers and haughty detachment that of the Sixties rock aristocracy. The youth of its performers was a crucial issue: it was, after all, a youth culture.

A slick piece of propaganda, Caroline's feature was to remain the closest thing punk had to a manifesto for some months. In contrast, Allan Jones, weighing in with some perfectly valid points about punk's obvious debt to the likes of the New York Dolls, its violent overtones and depressing nihilism, nevertheless came over like an old fogey. He shot himself in the foot by signing off with yet another Second World War analogy: if Johnny Rotten and his ilk represented the future of rock'n'roll, then Allan was 'off with the old lady to the air raid shelter until it all blows over'.

The timing of the *Melody Maker* feature was perfect for the Clash, who were now ready to make their London début. Cannily, Bernie rejected the idea of a public show, where the band would be at the mercy of all kinds of variables – nerves, sabotage from headliners, indifferent or hostile crowd reaction – in favour of a controlled environment: Rehearsals, in front of a select, invited audience of potentially useful bookers and music journalists. No effort (but plenty of expense) was spared in transforming Rehearsals into a venue appropriate and sympathetic to such an event: the band and their friends were volunteered to redecorate it. 'We all did it up,' recalls Alan Drake. 'We all put a bit of work in.' The walls of the downstairs rehearsal room were painted shocking pink and black, those having been designated the band's colours, and so were the amps and speakers. Five old barber's chairs were lined up against the wall facing the equipment and pink drapes were hung at either side to make the performance area look even more like a stage. The finishing touch was added by Paul, who painted his mural behind the drum kit to provide the Clash with their first ever backdrop. The view from a window overlooking a car dump, tower blocks and the Westway, it was 'London's Burning' in oils.

But the band didn't stop at the walls and the amps. They also dripped, splashed and sprayed (courtesy of the nearby garage) bright colours over some of their Oxfam Mod clothes to provide eye-catching stage gear. Paul also custom-splattered his near-worthless bass, which provoked Joe into daubing black paint all over his Telecaster, making it appear near worthless. Over the years, the band have repeatedly claimed that what came to be known as their 'Pollock look' – after action painter Jackson Pollock, famous for his splash- and drip-painted abstracts – came about purely by chance. Decorating Rehearsals without benefit of overalls, they had inevitably got paint on their clothes, and had decided to add more in order to make a feature out of a flaw . . .

Glen Matlock takes exception to this version of events, believing he originated both the idea for the Pollock look and the Clash's 'accidental' explanation. 'They quite blatantly ripped it off me! When the Pistols got the

Denmark Street place, I was painting it up. In black drainpipe jeans, which were really hard to get hold of, and even though I could get 'em through Sex, they were still a lot of money. So, only one pair of trousers to wear, painting the ceiling white, get paint all over 'em. I remembered back – years – in *Emergency Ward 10*, one of the nurses got ink on her bra, couldn't get rid of it, so she dyed the whole thing dark blue instead, which kind of covered it up. So I thought, "More paint on 'em! Jackson Pollock!" So I really went to town, and everyone was like, "Wow, yeah, that's cool!"' Photographs show that he wore the jeans on-stage at the Nashville on 23 April 1976. 'Next thing, when the Clash started gigging, it was, "Do you like our stage gear, Glen? Good, eh?" And it was all paint-splattered stuff. I thought, "You bastards!"'

Whether or not it was originally inspired by Glen, with three art students and three students of rock'n'roll history in the band, and with a manager who claimed a previous association with the Who, it is difficult to believe that the Pollock look was not a premeditated punk adaptation of the Who's mid-Sixties Pop-Art look. Influenced by the likes of Jasper Johns and Robert Rauschenberg, the Who had covered their clothing in targets, flags, arrows and medals. The intention behind the adoption of these trappings was as ironic as that behind Pop-Art itself, but they were appropriate to both the Who's uptight sound and the rigidity of the mod culture's values. In contrast, Pollock conferred upon the Clash a visual expression of unfettered action, which implied both rage and violence and took them closer to their stated aim of exploding off the stage. Something that probably is coincidental, though tellingly so: J. G. Ballard intends his readers to pick up signals of adaptation to a brutal new environment when he observes that the inhabitants of his high-rise favour 'huge Pop-Art and abstract-expressionist paintings'.

Terry was not impressed. 'I quite liked the idea of outrageous clothes, but I didn't like all the paint splashing. It seemed a bit messy to me.' The others were far happier to have an image that was recognisably their own (even if it was stolen from a Sex Pistol, a mod culture update, or both), but did not initially take it as seriously as they would later. 'Me and Mick wrote this song in answer to Jonathan Richman's "Pablo Picasso",' remembers Glen, referring to the track on *The Modern Lovers* featuring the immortal line 'Pablo Picasso never got called an asshole'. 'It went, "I don't give a bollock about Jackson Pollock". We didn't get very far with it, but it was a giggle.'

As a suitably punkish defiant gesture, the showcase took place on Friday, 13 August. At first, it looked as though the fates were intent on wreaking immediate revenge, because, although a few bookers were present, only three of the numerous music journalists invited turned up. But, as Andy Czezowski has indicated, they were the right three to attract: Caroline Coon, Jonh Ingham and Giovanni Dadomo. Ultimately, by means direct and indirect, all of them would play a vital part in advancing the Clash cause. Bernie's plan was vindicated almost at once, when Giovanni reviewed the show for *Sounds* and his piece was illustrated with a photo taken by his wife, Eve. At nine o'clock, the band walked downstairs to where the small audience had been enjoying free drinks and listening to the jukebox, plugged in their guitars ... 'And for the next 40-odd minutes, it was like being hit by a runaway fire engine,' wrote Giovanni. 'Not once, but again and again and again.' Making allowances for one or two 'little cock-ups', he was quick to 'dispel any notion that the music is one relentless semi-cacophony, because in all that nuclear glare, there are incandescent gems of solos and references to everything from "You Really Got Me" to *you-name-it*. Also, Strummer seems to have finally found his niche, his always manic deliveries finally finding their place in a compelling tapestry of sound and colour.' He praised the band's image, 'as much the antithesis of the bearded bedenimed latterday hippy as the mods were the rockers. Clash have plenty of that old mod flash, too.' He signed off by declaring that he couldn't wait to see them again in a real venue, and, like Caroline and Jonh, he would indeed attend many of the band's gigs over the next few months. But the key sentence, part of which was blown up and used as the headline, was 'I think they're the first band to come along who'll really frighten the Sex Pistols shitless.'

Naturally, the Sex Pistols were among those who read the review. The Clash in a subservient, supporting role was one thing, but the Pistols were not so happy with the band striking out for glory on their own, or with how they had set about it. 'We persecuted them mercilessly about that showcase,' says Glen. 'We thought it was well out of order. Not because we didn't know about it – although, looking back, we were a bit peeved that we weren't in on it – but the fact that it was really pandering to the press.' Giovanni's challenge to the Pistols on behalf of the Clash had followed on from Caroline Coon's assertion that 'The atmosphere among the punky bands on the circuit at the moment is positively cut-throat. Not only are they vying with each other, but they all secretly aspire to take Johnny Rotten down a peg or two.'

Competition between bands on the scene was inevitable, and in his autobiography, *Rotten: No Irish, No Blacks, No Dogs* (1994), Johnny blamed the Clash for introducing 'the competitive element that dragged everything down a little. It was never about that for us.' In an interview he gave for the same book Paul Cook rather more astutely observed that the music press was largely to blame for stirring things up. Back in August 1976, however, the Pistols camp responded as though the gauntlet had been thrown down by the Clash themselves. Even today, Johnny and Glen evince an astounding capacity for double-think when it comes to the topic of competition: both are capable of adopting a self-righteous tone to blame others for the destruction of punk solidarity one minute, and of turning round to cackle about some wounding example of Sex Pistols one-upmanship the next. The Clash might have been in competition with the Pistols, but they remained deferential to them, and persevered longer than most with the idea of presenting a united punk front to the world. Malcolm and the Pistols gave almost all their attention to looking after their own interests; whatever was left, they devoted to sabotaging the interests of others.

Both bands had been approached to play the First European (in fact, first ever) Punk Festival on 21 August 1976, in Mont de Marsan, France. The Sex Pistols' connection with various destructive and violent incidents resulted in their being dropped from the line-up, and the Clash pulled out as a gesture of support. The Damned went, and what a long, strange trip it was for them. Along the way, Ray Burns became Captain Sensible; they fell out with manager Andy Czezowski; and they met their future record company boss and manager Jake Riviera. Their blatant 'betrayal' of punk unity also did little to endear them to the Pistols and Clash camps, who already believed that the Damned's unremitting hedonism devalued punk's seriousness of purpose.

This latter bone of contention would appear to be the source material for two of the songs the Clash added to their repertoire in late August. One, 'You Know What I Think About You', was based on a slowed-down version of the staccato riff from the Who's 'I Can't Explain'; the other, 'Deadly Serious', was based on a speeded-up version of the staccato riff from the Who's 'I Can't Explain'. Neither song was ever recorded in the studio (in this guise, at least), and any lyrical subtleties are trampled underfoot in the very few surviving live recordings. Given that early Clash interviews were mostly devoted to expanding or expounding on the band's lyrical themes, some hints about content may perhaps be gleaned from the interview Steve Walsh and Mark Perry conducted with the band for the October 1976 issue of *Sniffin' Glue*:

Mark: *What do you think of bands that just go out and enjoy themselves?*
Mick: *You know what I think, I think they're a bunch of ostriches, they're sticking their heads in the fucking sand! They're enjoying themselves at the audience's expense . . .*
Mark: *What if the audience say they're enjoying themselves?*
Joe: *Look, the situation is far too serious for enjoyment, man . . .*
Mick: *I think, if you wanna fuckin' enjoy yourselves, you sit in an armchair and watch TV, but if you wanna get actively involved, rock'n'roll's about rebellion. Look, I had this out with Brian James of the Damned and we were screaming at each other for about three hours, 'cause he stands for enjoying himself, and I stand for change and creativity.*

For the next few months, the Pistols contented themselves with keeping the Damned at arm's length, but an opportunity to show the Clash who was boss offered itself within a matter of days. As a result of the Pistols' bad reputation, Malcolm was finding it hard to find gigs at London venues other than the 100 Club. For the same reason, it was difficult to raise any firm record company interest in the band. Through his friend Roger Austin he arranged a concert for Sunday, 29 August, at the Screen on the Green cinema in Islington's Upper Street, and set about promoting it as an unmissable punk rock event: the Midnight Special. For all the scorn they had voiced about the Clash's showcase at Rehearsals, the Pistols' motive was the near-identical one of attracting music journalists and record company A&R men.

After a trip to London to see the Pistols Manchester-based Howard Devoto and Pete Shelley had set up a gig for their new heroes on 20 August in their home town's Lesser Free Trade Hall. The bill on that night had been completed by Slaughter and the Dogs, and, making their first ever appearance, Howard and Pete's own band, the Buzzcocks. Thus, when Malcolm included the Buzzcocks and the Clash on the bill at the Screen, it seemed he was reciprocating both bands' recent shows of support. By offering them this platform to make their respective live London débuts – an almost unprecedented opportunity to impress the music media and business alike at such early stages in their development – he appeared to be making an extremely magnanimous gesture of solidarity. If anything, the opposite was true.

'It didn't do us any harm to have other bands of our sort supporting us,' says Glen. 'Made it look as though there was a bit more of a movement, you know.' As Malcolm had suggested in the April 1976 *Sounds* interview, a group identified as being leaders of a movement would be a more exciting prospect for representatives of the music business. It was relatively easy to limit any danger of being upstaged by the hired help. One of the conditions of being allowed to play at the cinema was that the Pistols supply a stage, a problem which they instantly passed on to the Clash. 'Malcolm said they could support us as long as they built it. And Bernie said, "Yeah, we'll provide a stage", and Malcolm said, "No, no, you've got to *build* the stage!" I thought that was really out of order, you know,' sniggers Glen, none too convincingly. 'They had to put up the posters as well, which were basically Sex Pistols posters. That must have been very demeaning for them, having to build the stage *and* stick up posters of another band with "the Clash" in small writing at the bottom. So I went out and helped 'em stick up a few.'

For all the would-be originality of punk, the Midnight Special was an event styled on a late Sixties 'happening'. The bands' sets, which could not begin until after that evening's movie feature was completed, hence the event's title, were interspersed with a couple of Kenneth Anger's underground films and a disco dominated by Bowie and Roxy Music. This encouraged members of the Bromley Contingent to strut their stuff like so many extras from *The Rocky Horror Show*. The Clash had got up early on Sunday morning to build the stage, and did not get to take it until the small hours of Monday. Tired and nervous – Mick was aware that, as well as the media, most of Violent Luck were in the audience – the band were both mean-spirited towards opening act the Buzzcocks and under par in performance. Just to cap it all, both support groups were plagued by an appalling sound which, miraculously, improved as soon as the headline band plugged in. Glen admits that this was no accident. Again, here was punk rock resorting to the oldest of old rock'n'roll dirty tricks. 'Of course. Yes, indeed,' says Glen. 'But the band had no part of that. It's managers and roadies that do that, because they're there for one band and paid by one band.'

Apart from Bromley Contingent member Susan Ballion attracting a disproportionate amount of the photographers' and journalists' attention with her peek-a-boo plastic underwear, fishnets and swastika armband, things went much as Malcolm had hoped. Giovanni Dadomo and Charles Shaar Murray, reviewing the show for *Sounds* and the *NME* respectively, were less than complimentary about the general tone of the event and dismissed the twilight decadence of films and fans alike as inept, embarrassing and old hat. The Pistols themselves, however, went down extremely well. Giovanni countered any notion that they could not play with the repeated upper-case assertion that they were 'ONE DAMNED FINE ROCK'N'ROLL BAND'. CSM declared, 'The first 30 seconds of their set blew out all the boring, amateurish, artsy-fartsy, mock-decadence that preceded it purely by virtue of its tautness, directness and utter realism.'

By contrast, Giovanni described the Buzzcocks as 'boring and unimaginative' and 'rougher than a bear's arse'. Disappointed by the Clash's follow-up to the Rehearsals showcase, he astutely laid the blame on the equipment, which did them 'a grave disservice tonight, losing Joe Strummer's hard-to-mix vocals until they became an unintelligible mumble, and generally poleaxing the band's nuclear potential'. CSM made no mention of the Buzzcocks at all, and gave the Clash what was to become the most famous review of their career: 'They are the kind of garage band who should be speedily returned to their garage, preferably with the motor running, which would undoubtedly be more of a loss to their friends and families than to either rock or roll.' For the Sex Pistols, it was a giant step towards securing a recording contract; for both support bands, it was a case of one step forward to take a slap in the face that sent them reeling two steps back.

7... WHITE RIOT

O n Monday, 30 August 1976, the day after the Midnight Special (or, to be precise, later the same day), Joe, Paul and Bernie went along to the Notting Hill Carnival for a little light relief. An annual event which takes place over the Bank Holiday weekend, the carnival represents an opportunity for the local West Indian community to let its hair down in a manner associated more with the climate and culture of the Caribbean than inner city Britain. In 1976, the weather might have been more accommodating than usual, but the attitude of the host culture had grown admonitory and harsh: the police presence had increased eightfold from the previous year to well over 1,500. The atmosphere deteriorated steadily until, around teatime on Monday, there came the inevitable face-off between the police and disgruntled local black youth. An attempted arrest close to the Westway on Ladbroke Grove resulted in much jeering and the throwing of a few empty cans. Then the police lined up and charged, a few terrified middle-aged women started screaming and a full-scale riot ensued.

Caught in the first charge, the Clash representatives were scattered: Bernie lost his glasses and disappeared, Joe dived into his old stomping ground the Elgin for a couple of quick bracers and Paul wholeheartedly immersed himself in the action. Reunited, Joe and Paul spent the next couple of hours throwing bricks and traffic cones at the police. 'It was brilliant,' a still unrepentant 32-year-old Paul told the *Melody Maker* in 1988. 'The coppers were standing there and they couldn't do a thing. We could throw bricks right at 'em. It was great.'

With 60 arrests and over 450 injuries, it was the biggest, though not the only UK riot since Notting Hill had erupted in 1958 (as documented in Colin MacInnes's *Absolute Beginners*, later filmed by Julien Temple). It provided Paul with an obviously welcome opportunity to relive his not so distant violent past, and Joe with a slightly more romanticised vision of himself as a street fighting man at society's cutting edge. Any illusion that they were at one with the almost entirely black crowd was dispelled when they became the near-victims of a mugging attempt. 'We got searched by policemen looking for bricks, and later on we got searched by Rasta looking for pound notes in our pockets,' Joe told Janet Street-Porter that November on ITV's *London Weekend Show*. Paul came away just plain exhilarated. Joe was equally fired up, but found himself wrestling with the implications of the experience.

Sebastian Conran, who first drifted into the Clash orbit not long after the riot, says, 'Politics hadn't even been thought about. I think, when you look at the early stuff, the "Janie Jones"-es, it'd got nothing to do with politics. It was just rock'n'roll, really.' He believes that the subject only raised its head when the Clash first started talking to journalists who wanted a fresh angle for their coverage of the band. Terry insists Sebastian is mistaken – 'politics was always going to be there from the off' – and cites the continuing band debates as proof. Certainly, as early as May 1976, John Brown and Richard Dudanski had independently picked up a strong impression that the band was formed with the intention of following a political agenda. Bernie, like Malcolm, had been influenced by the Situationist/Class of '68 view that 'politics is how we live'. In their twice updated book, *Sex Pistols: The Inside Story*, Fred and Judy Vermorel quote him as saying, 'You can't live without politics. On the other hand, you don't need to display it every ten minutes. It's like the pair of shoes that you're wearing, right? They're there. You don't have to keep touching them to make sure.' The truth is that Sebastian simply wasn't around when the pre-riot shoe-touching was going on.

Nevertheless, his comments are not without relevance. The Notting Hill Riot was the catalyst that brought together and to the surface a lot of disparate elements already present in the Clash. Before meeting Bernie, Mick had been largely apolitical, but he was quick to learn and well-read, and had a good grounding in politically motivated and anti-authoritarian rock'n'roll. Joe was equally adept at taking in new information, had experience of living in society's underbelly and had a fondness for folk and protest singers intent on documenting its ills. Paul had been a football hooligan and part of the skinhead subculture, but was also creatively minded, and was just waiting to have his rebellious instincts channelled in a more positive direction. Bernie had come up through mod and the harder edge of the counter-culture, and was looking for a way to synthesise mod flair with late Sixties street politics. Suddenly Notting Hill was a flashpoint, just like Watts in '65, Detroit in '67, Paris in '68 and Ohio in '70 had been, only it was *now*, and right here on their doorstep: in their time and place.

The one snag was that, as the attempted mugging incident had illustrated so graphically, the Notting Hill Riot was not their fight. It was a spontaneous reaction to an apparently racially motivated – and certainly culturally ignorant – act of oppression by the host culture's forces of law and order; but it was also the expression of resentment generated by years of harassment and denied opportunity, an experience specific to the inner city black population. As Bernie was aware, though, the situation was deteriorating all across the board, and it was not unrealistic to construe Notting Hill as a taste of what was to come for the general population. The economy was in recession and unemployment was not only at its highest since the war, but increasing steadily, especially amongst the young. History shows that in such circumstances people look for scapegoats. Racial tension was rising, and the

National Front were finding it easier to recruit from the youngsters hanging around aimlessly on the estates and street corners, and to take advantage of the mob mentality already present on the terraces at football matches. In the excitement immediately following the Notting Hill Riot it looked to the Clash at least as though the whole country could go up at any moment.

The soundtrack to – and possibly even fuel for – the riot was the menacingly heavy beat and militant lyrics of that year's crop of reggae sounds, reflecting the even more unsettled political climate of Jamaica. In a year-long run-up to the country's elections on 15 December supporters of the rival Jamaican Labour Party (JLP) and People's National Party (PNP) had exchanged gunfire. Ostensibly to quell a situation bordering on civil war, but also as a means of exerting control, PNP premier Michael Manley had declared a State of Emergency. Jamaica, as he put it, was 'under heavy manners', and about to experience some 'heavy duty discipline'. To the Rastafarian religious cult – usually the first to be on the receiving end when such discipline was being meted out – it seemed like a reaffirmation of the apocalyptic visions encouraged by their literalist Old Testament theology. The political conflict was characterised as the 'Final Battle For Jamaica' and 1977 seen as the year when a new world order would come to pass.

In his 1994 autobiography Johnny Rotten claimed that reggae had not been played on the air in the UK before he made a guest appearance on Capital Radio's *Tommy Vance Show*. 'Then suddenly you'd get Joe Strummer and the Clash saying, "We always loved reggae." But those fucks never did.' The statement was as inaccurate as it was spiteful. While no one disputes his own long-standing fondness for the music, the Capital show on which Johnny played Dr Alimantado's 'Born For A Purpose' was not broadcast until July 1977, by which time the Clash had already recorded a reggae song. Nor was reggae quite such a well-kept secret in 1976–7 as Johnny would like the world to believe: Bob Marley was already a household name; a few singles by other artists had slipped into the mainstream and become hits; and there was regular coverage of the more hardcore releases in *Time Out, Sounds* and *Melody Maker*, Caroline Coon being just one of several music press enthusiasts.

To refute his particular allegation against the Clash: Paul had first begun listening to reggae's predecessor, ska, in the late Sixties; the 'likes' list on the 'What side of the bed' T-shirt Bernie had designed for Sex in 1974 includes 'Jamaican Rude Boys . . . Bob Marley . . . Dreadlocks . . . King Tubby's sound system'; and although Joe had shrugged off the influence of the reggae-loving Mole while with the 101ers, when Caroline Coon had asked him if he was into reggae, during her July 1976 singles column interview, he had replied, 'There's not much else around to listen to, is there?' By the late summer of 1976, most of the Clash had already recognised reggae to be some of the most vital music currently being made, and the entire band's interest increased dramatically once the riot gave a local context to its stirring militancy. That autumn and winter at Rehearsals, a turntable was linked up to a guitar amp. Between practices this rough-and-ready sound system blasted out, among others, Tapper Zukie's *Rockers*, Prince Far I's *Under Heavy Manners*, Joe Gibbs and the Professionals' *State Of Emergency* and Culture's *Two Sevens Clash*.

The Clash began to see reggae as a cultural blueprint for the development both of their own music and of punk in general. The punk scene, still largely an élite club for art school students and decadent poseurs, could be co-opted for the disaffected white equivalent of the rioting black youths; and could provide a more positive politicisation process than that offered by the National Front. 'We know the blacks've got their thing sewn up,' Mick told the *NME*'s Barry Miles that November. 'They got their own culture, but the young white kids don't have nothing. That's why so many of them are living in ignorance and they've just gotta wise up ... They used to blame everything on the jews, now they're saying it about the blacks and the Asians. Everybody's a scapegoat, right?' 'We're hoping to educate any kid who comes to listen to us, right?' said Joe. 'Just to keep 'em from joining the National Front when things get really tough in a couple of years.'

The Rasta was too laid-back and long-haired to provide a direct role model. Instead, the Clash version of the punk persona underwent a small, but significant, adjustment: the Paul Simonon-style skinhead overtones grew stronger, moving the band further towards the football terraces, and their updated take on mod culture gave ground to that of the rude boy outlaw figure mythologised in Paul's beloved ska and rocksteady records. The yob element of this new band character had already introduced itself into the Clash's music via the terrace 'harmonies' of 'What's My Name', but now repetitive chanted choruses became as prevalent as the previously dominant high-pitched 'oohs'. In 'You Know What I Think About You' Terry commandeered a break between verse and chorus and inserted the 'duh, duh / duh, duh, duh / duh, duh, duh, duh / duh, *duh*' tattoo familar to football fans, demonstrators and rioters alike.

To generalise a little, if Sixties punk rock was an American version of a British version of American R&B, then Seventies punk rock was a British version of *that*. Whatever the tangled web of its genealogy, in both its Sixties and Seventies guises punk was an almost exclusively white musical form, so far removed from its roots in the blues that nearly all the black influence had been lost: it was noisy, uptight and aggressive, the very antithesis of funky. In 1976, when the majority of mainstream British rock'n'roll bands emulated current American styles and their vocalists affected American accents, punk prided itself on its rejection of US cultural imperialism and trumpeted a return to Britishness. 'We sing in English' was a message that Joe – also keen to distance himself from his R&B years – proudly spelled out in the band's earliest interviews with *Sniffin' Glue* and *Melody Maker*. The fierceness of this parochial urge bordered on the xenophobic, and ran the risk of attracting racist thugs rather than achieving the stated aim of encouraging them to rethink their position. It was reggae that saved the Clash from the fate of later yob-punk bands like Sham 69, whose concerts were regularly ruined by their unsolicited and unwanted right-wing skinhead following. For the Clash, cultural enslavement to America might have been out, but reflecting and celebrating the multicultural nature of their own country and neighbourhood was most definitely in.

The reggae influence first revealed itself in the band's live variation on the 'drop-out' production technique. Drop-out was a feature of 'dub', or 'version', reggae; as its names suggest, this was a largely instrumental version of an existing song, stripped down to basics, heavily doctored with echo and reverb and imaginatively overdubbed with musical and lyrical snippets from the original. At first placed on single B-sides of the original song so that Jamaican sound system DJs could 'toast' – that is, chatter and rhyme – over the top, dub became a popular musical form in its own right. Before long, it was taking up entire albums and feeding its influence back into the parent genre. (It also contained the seeds of both sampling and rap.) In the context of a Clash gig drop-out meant that, instead of the entire band playing together all the time in ramalama Ramones style, at key points in certain songs one or more musicians would cease playing; this not only highlighted the efforts of those remaining, but also made a drama out of the absentees' eventual return to the fray. Although Jonh Ingham was the first to remark upon it as a 'Clash trademark' in his *Sounds* review of a 27 October gig at Barbarella's in Birmingham, the Clash were employing the technique as early as their 5 September Roundhouse appearance.

The first fully-fledged articulation of the new Clash outlook was '1977', introduced into the band's set within a week of the riot. If the Clash had not heard a Jamaican 'pre' (pre-release white label) of Culture's 'Two Sevens Clash' by this time, then the coincidence was uncanny. The reggae vocal trio's song evokes the prophecies of Rastafarian founder Marcus Garvey, and in the most apocalyptic of tones and terms warns of violent confrontation in the year 'when the two sevens clash'. Whether they knew it or not at the time, the destiny- and mythology-conscious Clash were reworking this message to reflect their own environment.

For reasons that had more to do with subsequent band posing and rhetoric than any shortcomings in its lyric, '1977' became one of the Clash's most misunderstood and maligned songs. Charges of casting the band as a highly romanticised cell of urban guerrillas were levelled at Joe for the lines in which he warns of 'knives in West 11' and 'Sten guns in Knightsbridge'. 'I imagined having a knife pointed at *me*, right?' a weary Joe explained, not for the first or last time, to *Melody Maker*'s Allan Jones in November 1978. 'I imagined Sten guns in Knightsbridge pointed at *me*. But people took it to mean that WE had them and we were pointing them at other people. That was a song written about the future. I thought the future was going to do us in. I really imagined it.' The chorus, 'No Elvis, Beatles or the Rolling Stones / In 1977', was considered a bit rich when the song's tune was a blatant lift of the Kinks' 'All Day And All Of The Night'. In 1979, the Clash's supposed transformation into a more traditional Rolling Stones-type rock'n'roll band – when they wrapped *London Calling* in a mock-up of an early Elvis Presley album sleeve – encouraged further retrospective sniping. In fact, the line has its origins in one of Joe's genuine enough reasons for leaving the 101ers and joining the Clash: the feeling that playing cover versions of songs made famous by those artists was no longer enough.

The song is devalued if the first person 'I' is too literally identified with its singer; better to see the protagonist as an Everyman suffering the slings and arrows of modern-day inner city life. With Joe himself removed from the picture, the first verse addresses rising unemployment; the second predicts a potential breakdown of the social fabric, as presaged by the Notting Hill Riot; and the third offers examples of the kind of apathy and denial that might let this come to pass. The chorus hints at racial tension or war ('you better paint your face'), and points out that the leading rock'n'roll icons are no longer relevant because, as Caroline Coon had suggested in her punk overview feature, they are out of touch with the people and no longer interested in or, for that matter, capable of reflecting the times.

Joe had flirted with apocalyptic imagery before, most notably in 'London's Burning', but '1977' lays it on especially thick, echoing the doom-laden prediction of 'Two Sevens Clash' and loading in a few extra non-Rasta cultural references to make sure. Year titles were nothing new in punk: the Stooges had bestowed the mark of the iguana on both 1969 - 'Another year with nothing to do' – and 1970, and '1977' could be seen as a continuance of this tradition. As Jon Savage pointed out in *England's Dreaming*, 1977 was already a year of prophecy in rock'n'roll mythology: in 1972, David Bowie had released *The Rise And Fall Of Ziggy Stardust And The Spiders From Mars*, the futuristic sci-fi concept album that had captured the imagination of a generation. Its opening track, 'Five Years', offers this prognosis for a dying world: 'Five years, that's all we've got . . .' Just to cap it all, after the Clash had been playing '1977' for a couple of months, Joe added a countdown coda, starting with 1977 and ending suddenly with the year 1984, thus also evoking George Orwell's futuristic nightmare world.

'White Riot', destined to become the Clash's theme song, came along in mid-September 1976. Riots were hardly virgin territory in rock'n'roll: Elvis Presley's 'Riot In Cell Block No 9', the Standells' 'Riot On Sunset Strip', the MC5's 'Motor City Is Burning' and the Rolling Stones' 'Street Fighting Man' had all been there and done that before. Only the last of these, however, relates to British culture – an anti-Vietnam War demonstration outside the American Embassy in Grosvenor Square – and it concludes that sleepy London town in 1968 is no place for a street fighting man. The Clash aimed to let Mick Jagger know that things had changed since then.

In a January 1980 edition of *Melody Maker* journalist and sociologist Simon Frith revealed that the Weathermen, a group of late Sixties American urban guerrillas named after a line in Bob Dylan's 'Subterranean Homesick Blues', had published a 'revolutionary songbook' including a number entitled

'White Riot' sung to the tune of 'White Christmas'. The title therefore almost certainly came from Bernie. The Clash's 'White Riot' attempts to make a much more straightforward and direct reference to the Notting Hill Riot and the black–white cultural divide than '1977'. Originally, it included lines about 'reading papers and wearing slippers' and, somewhat abstrusely, eating 'supermarket soul food', both of which were later replaced by 'And nobody wants to go to jail' in an effort to ensure there could be no confusion about the song's intended message. The effort failed.

In 1974, rock'n'roll had flirted with the trappings of fascism as part of a decadent pose; in autumn 1976, rock'n'roll luminaries Eric Clapton and David Bowie got themselves into hot water by making highly publicised racist and pro-fascist comments (albeit subsequently retracted). The National Front was steadily gaining support; the party polled nearly a fifth of the vote in that summer's Leicester by-election and its thuggish supporters were a threatening presence on street corners and the terraces. In this context, watching a band of short-haired, aggressive youths burst on stage to chant 'White Riot' was an alarming prospect. Why a *white* riot? Was the call separatist, or was it urging white-on-black violence? The confusion reached its apogee following a gig on 29 November 1976 at Lanchester Polytechnic in Coventry. 'They said we couldn't use the stage as a platform to spread racist propaganda,' recalls Terry. 'They needed to get their ears washed out!' All the same, as the Lanchester students' entertainments committee were plainly not the only ones with hearing difficulties, Joe took advantage of that November's *NME* interview with Barry Miles to explain, 'The only thing we're saying about blacks is that they've got their problems and they're prepared to deal with them. But white men, they just ain't prepared to deal with them. Everything's too cosy. They've got stereos, drugs, hi-fis, cars . . .' TVs, papers, slippers, supermarket soul food . . .

The only other misinterpretation of 'White Riot' was a wilful one, and it was made by the Clash themselves. By 1980, tired of being pilloried in the music press for failing to deliver on their rhetoric, they attempted a retrospective shift of meaning: apparently, the song had never been intended as a literal incitement to riot or revolution; rather, it was supposed to encourage listeners to take responsibility for shaping their own futures . . . It was a disingenuous claim. In the wake of Notting Hill, the word 'riot' was too specific and loaded to be interpreted as a metaphor for general pro-activism, as indeed was the taunt sung over the bridge in the single version: 'Are you taking over, or are you taking orders?' In an interview for BBC Radio One's *Rock On* programme which took place shortly after the May 1977 incident in which a Clash audience trashed a number of seats at the Rainbow Theatre, Joe, admittedly irritated by presenter John Tobler's condescending manner, nevertheless made it quite clear that the Clash meant it, man. Were the band trying to incite their audience to riot? ''Course. We try it every night. I want to hear the smashing of those seats, and the crumpling of the wood, the snapping of the iron.' Suppose the rioters tried to take your money away from you? 'I don't *care*. I don't care if the ceiling falls down and kills everyone in the theatre. Me included. I don't care what happens as long as it's out of hand, you know? As long as it's *out of control*.'

On 31 August 1976, the Tuesday immediately following the Notting Hill Riot, the Clash were again booked to support the Sex Pistols, this time at the 100 Club. The three-band bill was completed by Birmingham's increasingly confused glam rock band, the Suburban Studs. Once again, the Clash's set was marred by equipment problems, this time a broken guitar string. With no back-up instruments, they were forced to wait until the string in question could be replaced, an unenviable position for any performer on-stage in front of 200 people. Joe improvised with the aid of a recent Portobello purchase. 'I'd been lucky, and bought a cheap transistor radio in a junk shop for ten bob [50 pence] and it worked quite well,' he told the *Sniffin' Glue* team the following month. 'I'd been going around with it on my ear for a few days, just to see what it was like. When someone broke a string, I got it out, and it just happened to be something about Northern Ireland.' 'A State of Emergency,' added Mick, drawing a parallel between the Troubles in Ireland and those in Jamaica. Held up to a microphone, with delay added by Pistols' soundmixer Dave Goodman, the news report echoed around the 100 Club, and turned a potentially embarrassing hiatus into a Clash Statement. Inspired by this fortuitous occurrence, the band would continue experimenting with variants on the spoken-word address, both live and on record, for the remainder of their career; not least on 1977's 'Listen' and 1982's 'Know Your Rights'.

Five days after the 100 Club gig, on 5 September, the Clash made their first venture out into the wider world without the spurious patronage of the Sex Pistols. It only took them a matter of yards down Chalk Farm Road, but it also took them a long way outside the punk milieu: the Roundhouse's traditional Sunday band-fest, as attended by Little Mick while still at school and played by Joe Strummer when with the 101ers. The headliners were the Kursaal Flyers, an established pub rock band, and the main support were Welsh Rock'n'Roll Revivalists Crazy Cavan and the Rhythm Rockers. The Clash went on first, at six o'clock, before the bar had even opened and certainly before the typical Roundhouse audience of bedenimed latter-day hippies were in the mood to give their full attention to something so demandingly different.

Up to this point, the Clash had eschewed direct verbal communication with their audiences, preferring to hit them with song after song and, it was hoped, leave them as overawed as had been Giovanni Dadomo at the Rehearsals showcase. Suspecting this tactic would have next to no chance of achieving the same results at the Roundhouse, the band opted for confrontation. Five songs in, after 'Protex Blue', Joe began to deride the mostly seated audience for its apathy. After the next song, 'Janie Jones', he tried to goad them into some 'audience participation' by enquiring what they were doing there. There followed a painful four or five minutes of desultory heckling. Joe, who later explained he was unable to hear properly, found his famed 101ers era ability to manage such situations had deserted him, and resorted to the most stilted and embarrassing of put-downs. After general snide remarks about denims and mind-altering drugs, he berated one person for the sin of being overweight and dismissed another as a 'big twit'.

Following 'Mark Me Absent', he abandoned attempts at dialogue, and instead offered a sermon against boredom and the evils of television that culminated in a plea for anyone who wasn't 'past it' to get involved and make something happen. Quoted by Jon Savage in *England's Dreaming*, and included on the *Lipstick Traces* album issued by Rough Trade to complement Greil Marcus's book of the same title, this Stage Rap has latterly come to be portrayed as a punk landmark, the earliest recorded articulation of punk's DIY ethic: if you're bored, do something about it; if you don't like the way things are done, act to change them; be creative, be positive, anyone can do it. This kind of thinking and rhetoric would soon change the face of punk, but in its original, excruciating context, it's hard to believe the Stage Rap converted any of those present and persuaded them to shed their denims, cut their hair and form a punk band. Plus, if the truth be told, it was little more than a reiteration of a remark made by Johnny Rotten to Jonh Ingham during the Sex Pistols' April 1976 *Sounds* interview: 'I'm against people who just complain about *Top Of The Pops* and don't do anything. I want people to go out and start something, to see us and start something, or else I'm just wasting my time.'

Although the Clash played a varied and mostly proficient 14-song set, its pacing was ruined by these lengthy interruptions, which failed to generate any compensatory dramatic tension. The band left the stage to that most humiliating of noises, lukewarm applause. This had not been the object of the exercise, and Bernie was neither one to accept faint praise nor one to give it. 'I remember coming up to Bernard after the gig,' says Keith, 'and he was saying, "It was fucking shit! It was fucking *shit!*"' His language was more restrained, but Chas De Whalley intimated much the same in his *Sounds* review. In addition to dismissing the bulk of the songs – authorship of which he attributed solely to Joe - as being 'little more than rewrites of this year's punk classics', he compared the Clash unfavourably with the 101ers, whose 'love and warmth' he believed had given way to 'aggression and belligerence'.

Chas's review was filed quickly enough to make the 11 September edition and was printed on the page opposite Giovanni Dadomo's fair, but hardly uplifting, Screen on the Green review. After this damaging combination punch, the *coup de grâce* was provided by CSM's mauling of the latter performance in that week's *NME*. Sometime in the next few days, Keith Levene left the Clash. The first music press mention of his departure came during Caroline Coon's review of the 100 Club Punk Festival. She gave the official line that Keith had made the decision himself with the intention of forming his own band. The initial assumption, propagated by Pete Frame's punk Family Tree in September 1977's *ZigZag*, was that the *Sounds* and

NME reviews had rendered Keith too depressed to carry on.

Keith's subsequent spell with squat rehearsal band the Flowers of Romance came to an end when Sid Vicious left to join the Sex Pistols. Thereafter, the guitarist played with Cowboys International before teaming up with the former Johnny Rotten – now trading as John Lydon – in PiL. During PiL's May 1978 interview with the *NME*'s Neil Spencer, Keith gave his own reason for quitting the Clash: 'obvious . . . I wasn't into politics.' Neil offered an alternative reason of his own, voicing a rumour that, by then, had been floating around the music scene for 18 months: 'A flirtation with drugs is apparently another reason why Levene didn't stay the course; certainly, "Liar" [he meant 'Deny'] on the Clash's first album is widely reputed to refer to him at this time.' Tony Parsons and Julie Burchill went even further in *The Boy Looked At Johnny*, published in October 1978: 'Keith Levene was soon too involved with heroin to devote any time to playing guitar, and quit the Clash leaving behind him only one song . . .' In 'The Story Of The Clash', which Mick and Joe contributed to *The Armagideon Times*, a tour programme issued to tie in with the 16 Tons Tour of January 1980, they offered the following cryptic account of Keith's departure: 'he left the group early on, saying he had some urgent business to take care of in north London'.

In another *NME* interview, given to Julie Panebianco in November 1983, Keith came clean about his use of heroin. Admitting that he had indeed developed an addiction to the drug, he nevertheless insisted this had happened during his time with PiL; he had not even begun to dabble while still part of the Clash. In those days Keith's drug of choice had been speed. Joe confirmed as much in *England's Dreaming*, describing the former Clash guitarist to Jon Savage as something of a speed connoisseur who used it 'in a very pure form'. The confusion came about because, unlike the rest of the band, Keith was an intravenous user, and many people automatically equate syringes with heroin. As for 'Deny': it is about the denial that often accompanies serious drug addiction, and is addressed to someone with tell-tale trackmarks, but most of the lyric was in place before Keith left the band. The song may well have taken on a new relevance thereafter – rumours that it was about him were never denied and were quite possibly encouraged by his erstwhile colleagues – but this was largely serendipitous.

What he perceives as the hypocrisy of the Clash camp's suggestion that his friend was too drug-oriented to take an active interest in the band incenses Alan Drake. 'It's absolute bollocks! It wasn't that at all. I mean, *everybody* was doing drugs at that time. If it wasn't for speed, I don't think half the punk scene would have happened anyway. At that point it was speed, speed, speed.' 'They intimated that it was drugs, but it wasn't,' agrees Keith. 'Basically, I was very down; and when I was down, I was very quiet.' Even many of those who are liberal-minded on the issue of recreational drug use baulk at the idea of needles. The end result might be much the same, in that the substance enters the bloodstream, but intravenous administration suggests more commitment to a drug than eating, drinking or inhaling it.

There are more attendant risks, and it offers a more intense experience of both the drug's immediate effects and its after-effects. In a March 1988 *NME* interview with Sean O'Hagan Joe described his own experiences with speed thus: 'I'd have these comedowns where I'd want to bash my head in with a hammer. The up wasn't worth the down in the end. Like, what we were doing was next door to Vim: cheap and nasty.' If it was like that for Joe snorting, it must have been at least as bad for Keith injecting, for all the relative purity of his supply. Despite his and Alan's protestations to the contrary, it is almost certain that his drug use at least contributed to his mood swings from uptight hostility to non-communicative misery, and consequently to the on-off nature of his commitment to the Clash.

As Keith suggests, though, there were other reasons for his unhappiness. He may well not have been 'into politics', but as his interest was always more with the band's sound than the subject matter of its lyrics, it is hard to credit that the latter was a problem for him in itself. What did concern him was the extent to which the lyrical content was taking over in importance as the other band members seemingly pushed for increasingly direct and simplistic musical frameworks for the words: 'White Riot' was a prime example and, in fact, the final straw. Thus, although the lyrics were mostly Joe's and, as it turned out, it was Joe whose patience with Keith's irascibility was the first to snap, the single greatest reason for Keith's departure was the musical power struggle between himself and Mick.

Being a fan of the punk rock tradition and also devoted to the songwriter's craft, Mick was as uncomfortable with Keith's avant-garde reworkings of his songs as Keith was with the songs themselves. 'Mick was always Rock'n'Roll Mick,' Keith told Chris Bohn in 1980. 'I didn't realise then just how much I resented rock'n'roll. Any numbers I got together, they didn't really understand.' Alan agrees: 'I think, to be honest, Keith was just too radical for Mick.'

Also, replacing Billy Watts with Joe had created an imbalance in the group: three guitarists might have been justifiable had the intention been to indulge in endless Lynyrd Skynyrd-style boogie workouts, but in the strictly minimalist world of punk it was at least one guitarist too many. The vulnerability of his own position was not lost on Mick. Keith was the best guitarist, and played lead; Joe, though he was the worst guitarist, could generate a driving rhythm with his instrument, and was anyway firmly established as singer and frontman. As the band's other rhythm guitarist, Mick was therefore the one whose contribution was most likely to be deemed surplus to requirements. His songwriting skills might stand in his favour, but not everyone in the Clash appeared to admire them. They had not counted for much in Little Queenie/Violent Luck, his expulsion from which was still all too fresh in his mind. The best possible scenario for Mick was that Keith would leave and Mick would be promoted to lead guitarist and the band's sole musical director. (Paul was still learning his bass parts by heart. Joe, as he admitted to Caroline Coon the following year, was at this time no more capable of hearing arrangements in his head than he had been in the 101ers.) It was a situation of which Keith was well aware – or, at least, with the benefits of hindsight, it is a situation of which he is now well aware. 'It was quite possible for it to be Mick's *and* my band from my point of view, but it was not possible from Mick's point of view. So therefore, it had to be Mick or me, and I decided, let it be Mick.'

How much say Keith had in the making of that decision is open to debate. In various interviews given since the break-up of the Clash Joe has taken responsibility for instigating what he describes as Keith's sacking, and his 101ers track record certainly proves him capable of such ruthlessness. 'He rang up and said, "What you doin'?"' Joe told the *NME*'s Sean O'Hagan in 1988. 'I told him we were rehearsing "White Riot", and he goes, "Uh, it ain't worth me coming in then." So, basically, I told him to fuck off. Which he did. Me and Mick and Paul and Terry Chimes did it that afternoon.'

Terry remembers the lead up to the confrontation slightly differently. In his version, tellingly, it is Mick who first floats the idea of a showdown. 'To me it was a complete and utter shock, and very peculiar,' he says. 'I turned up one day, and Keith wasn't there. There were four of us sitting around waiting for him to arrive. I can't remember exactly who said what, but there was this conversation where Joe said he saw Keith as the Phantom Guitar Player: although he comes and goes, he's never really there. Paul said something vaguely agreeing with it, and then Mick said, to my astonishment, "Do you think he should leave, then?" And they all thought for a second, and then Joe and Paul nodded and said, "Yeah." I was just dumbfounded. I said, "What the hell's happening? First of all you're just talking about him being ten minutes late for rehearsals, then suddenly he's leaving the band! You're crazy! You can't just make decisions like that. You sit down and discuss the issues, and work it out. You can't just suddenly, on a whim, sack him!" Which is weird, because I'd found him harder to work with than anyone else, and now I found myself defending him. Anyway, by the time he arrived, I'd reluctantly given in and said, "OK, let's sack him", so he was sacked, and he was about as shocked as I was, I guess.'

Keith's version has the issue being being put to the vote in his presence. Although he could not have known it, this was a display of 101ers-style 'democracy': the outcome was already a foregone conclusion. 'The band got me upstairs and confronted me,' he says. 'Basically, they said, "Well, Keith, you're a miserable git. What's going on?" And I said, "I don't like what we're doing. It's not coming across like the thing I want it to be." What happened then was, there was this kind of vote, which I had the casting decision on. And I said to them, "Look, I'll fuck off, and if in two weeks you think it was a bad move, I'll still be open-minded. But after that, things have got to change or I'll be gone." But they never really changed their minds, and that was it.'

'I remember the first thing Mick said after Keith had left the room, slamming the door behind him,' says Terry. 'He looked around and said, "I'd better learn how to play the guitar, then, hadn't I?"' It seems not everyone in the Clash camp was as confident as Mick about his ability to do so. Bernie had not been party to the Keith-shedding exercise, and was initially as unhappy about the hole in the line-up as he was about its having been made without his knowledge. Shortly after the big upset, Mick's former bandmate Brady remembers Bernie turning up at a rehearsal room where he was going through his paces. Later, he heard through the grapevine that Bernie was considering him as a replacement for Keith. The compound irony of Brady's recruitment for the Clash can only be appreciated hypothetically, however, because when Bernie discovered the guitarist was 27, all other considerations became irrelevant. 'Apparently he said, "No, he's too old,"' laughs Brady. 'So I thought, "There goes my career . . ."'

The showdown having taken place over the weekend following the Roundhouse gig, the new four-piece Clash had just over a week to knock themselves into shape for their slot at the 100 Club Punk Festival, due to take place on Monday and Tuesday, 20 and 21 September. Terry does not recall it being a particularly arduous task. 'After Keith left, it seemed like it had been the right decision, just because of the mix of personalities,' he says. 'Mostly we were aware of fewer arguments, less tension in the band and everything being a bit simpler.' Having one guitar less to weave into the songs' structure helped, and Mick's necessarily economical lead guitar style also encouraged the Clash to experiment further with drop-out, heeding dub's lesson that musical dynamics are governed as much by what is not played as by what is.

'White Riot' was worked up in time to make its début at the gig as part of an 11-song set, three fewer than at the Roundhouse and seven fewer than the band's full repertoire. Terry has no recollection of songs being dropped specifically because of any close association with Keith or because their lead guitar parts posed Mick any problems, so it appears that the band simply took advantage of the situation to cut out a little dead wood. 'She's Sitting At My Party' was joined in the dumper by 'Mark Me Absent' and one other song that was included in the Roundhouse set but whose title has been forgotten. Also abandoned at this time was 'You Know What I Think About You', though the following year would see the tune cannibalised to form the basis of 'Clash City Rockers'.

The Screen on the Green gig having given the Pistols' career a considerable boost, Malcolm McLaren had devised the Punk Rock Festival on 20–21 September as another event intended to showcase the band as leaders of a movement. This time there would be no hippy trappings: the presentation would be as raw and basic as the music, and the venue would be the Sex Pistols' long-time favourite, the 100 Club. Less straightforward was the task of finding enough bands to fill two nights and justify the description 'festival'. As the Pistols were booked to appear in Cardiff on the Tuesday, they were forced to headline the Monday night. The ever-faithful Clash agreed to be main support. The scarcity of established punk bands meant that the Damned had to be included whether Malcolm liked it or not, but they were placed insultingly low on the second night's bill: the Buzzcocks headlined, and main support were the similarly named Vibrators, a pub rock band with an eye for the main chance and a guest spot reserved for former Sharks member Chris Spedding. In the event, they were also joined by a French punk band called Stinky Toys, held over from the Monday.

Eking out the first night's entertainment were two outfits making their début appearance. Festival openers Subway Sect were a bunch of teenage soul boys who had been inspired to form a band by the Sex Pistols' Marquee gig back in February, but whose music tended more towards the avant-garde. Malcolm paid for a week's solid rehearsal in Chelsea so the band could whip their five-song set into shape, and then Bernie offered them some time at Rehearsals over the weekend immediately prior to the festival. Siouxsie (billed as Suzie) and the Banshees formed specifically to fill the remaining slot, their members drawn from a cross-section of the Sex Pistols' more ardent followers: the Bromley Contingent's Susan Ballion (soon to become Siouxsie Sioux) and Steve Bailey (then calling himself Steve Havoc, soon to become Steve Severin) on vocals and bass respectively, Marco Pirroni on guitar and Sid Vicious on drums. Sid's friendship with the Clash enabled the Banshees to squeeze in a rehearsal at Rehearsals on the Sunday as well. Although neither he nor Steve had played their instruments before, Sid decided 20 minutes was more than enough: the idea of the band was to celebrate its own disposability, by making a God-awful racket for as long as the audience would tolerate it before splitting up for good.

Subway Sect's dress sense was as different from that of the Clash as possible – they habitually wore dull grey clothes resembling school uniforms, anticipating the look favoured by post-punk 'industrial' bands like Joy Division – but the band had a similar, if decidedly less macho, gang sensibility, and a kinship was recognised. Following the festival and the Pistols' success in finding a record contract, Malcolm's concern for Subway Sect's welfare suddenly disappeared. Planning some empire-building of his own, Bernie stepped in and effectively became their manager, though he continued to deny having an interest in anyone but the Clash for months afterwards. The Sect, accompanied by their friend, roadie and driver, Barry August, started rehearsing at Rehearsals full-time, alternating shifts with the Clash. In the interview the Clash gave to *Sniffin' Glue* later that month Mick talked up his stablemates as being one of the very few worthwhile punk bands (along with the Pistols, the Clash and 'maybe' the Buzzcocks). When Bernie's number one band began to headline their own gigs in late October, he would have a number two band conveniently on hand to offer regular support.

It would appear the Sect helped out the Clash in at least one other area. In the *Clash On Broadway* booklet Joe claimed that 'I'm So Bored With You' became 'I'm So Bored With The USA' when he misheard Mick's title during the very first band rehearsal at Davis Road. Subway Sect singer and lyricist Vic Godard begs to differ. In September 1977, he told Steve Walsh, by then contributing to *ZigZag*, 'We used to do political songs in the beginning, but we stopped doing them when the Clash started doing them. We had this song called "USA" that the Clash nicked and changed to "I'm So Bored With The USA".' It was a claim subsequently endorsed by Bernie during his period of estrangement from the Clash. It is true that the transformation of the Clash song's title and chorus occurred sometime between the Roundhouse and Punk Festival gigs, and so coincided with the band's first exposure to Subway Sect. While it is safe to assume the inspiration to give Mick's twisted love song yet another twist came from 'USA', however, Joe did not work up a coherent lyric for another four months, and *that* was extensively rewritten before recording for *The Clash*. Thus, accusations of extensive plagiarism are somewhat overstated.

Sounds' Jonh Ingham used the Punk Rock Festival as an excuse for a six-page overview of the scene, launching a belated and doomed attempt to rechristen punk '? rock'. The festival was given substantial coverage as a live event by both the *NME* and *Melody Maker*. Geoff Hill continued the former paper's unofficial policy of amused condescension, but Caroline Coon fulfilled Malcolm's wildest dreams. Through eavesdropping on audience members to complement her own enthusiastic response with a vox-pop perspective, she successfully conveyed the excitement of a scene on the cusp of becoming a movement. Indeed, both nights of the festival attracted full houses, and the recognised punk faces from the Pistols' earlier gigs were swamped by inquisitive newcomers. Again, just what Malcolm wanted.

Geoff Hill maintained he had been impressed by the Clash's potential, but contradicted this claim by putting all he had to say about them into three short sentences, one of which, in punk terms, bordered on the damning: 'they perform as if they actually *dig* rock music'. Caroline predicted they would be 'a cornerstone of the developing punk rock scene', listed some of their song titles and approached the group afterwards to enquire how they felt about their performance and playing together generally. Paul said he wanted to improve so that he could be more expressive. Joe told her he liked being on-stage with novices, where emotion counted for more than 'playing for playing's sake'.

Caroline's critical perspective was somewhat compromised by her determination to portray everyone and everything to do with the Punk Festival in as positive a light as possible. She neglected to mention the inter-band squabbling that marred the first night and, in woolly-minded liberal mode, shifted the blame for the kind of senseless violence that marred the second on to promoters who did not do enough to anticipate and prevent it. In fact, it was the absence of the very spirit of punk unity she was trying to capture that precipitated both.

The Clash had offered to allow the Banshees the use of their equipment, but Bernie withdrew that offer when he saw that Siouxsie intended to take the stage wearing her swastika armband. Instead, the Banshees borrowed the Pistols' gear, and Sid preceded their 20-minute version of 'The Lord's Prayer' with an announcement to the effect that Bernie was 'a fucking old jew'. The use of the swastika as a shock tactic was not only decidedly stale by 1976, but Bernie, understandably, believed it was inappropriate to flirt with fascist symbols in the current political climate. He later explained to Caroline, in an addendum to *1988*, that he did not want the Clash's distinctive pink equipment to be associated with such a 'loaded gun'. It was a brave stance to take, because it openly set him against Malcolm, who made frequent use of the Nazi symbol on his Sex shop clothes.

There was no antagonism between members of the Clash and the by now supposedly defunct Banshees when they returned as audience members for the second night. They even joined forces to heckle the Damned, who had annoyed the punk Inner Circle not only with their perceived betrayal in going to Mont de Marsan, but also with their claims to be 'better than the Pistols'. There was also a certain amount of jealousy towards the Damned, as they had become the first punk band to sign to a record label, even if it was the small independent Stiff. Part of the way through the much-reviled funsters' set a bottle was flung at the stage; shattering against a pillar, it sprayed the front of the audience with broken glass. It was subsequently reported that one girl suffered permanent damage to her sight, and while this may have been a case of hysterical exaggeration – the extent of the injury was never verified – Caroline herself stated that several people were cut, and Damned singer Dave Vanian's girlfriend was among those who required hospital treatment.

The police came to investigate, and arrested Sid Vicious. Although pointed out as the thrower of the glass, he was ultimately charged (after allegedly having been roughed up a little) with possession of an illegal weapon, namely a knife. Paul and Mick later testified that he had not thrown the glass. Caroline, who was taken into custody at the same time as Sid as a result of her Release-inspired objection to his arrest, did not think he was guilty then, and was still reluctant to believe it when interviewed for *England's Dreaming* and *Rotten*. After reading a letter written by Sid from Ashford Remand Centre expressing contrition, the author of the former book, Jon Savage, concluded that Sid had indeed thrown it. Eyewitnesses Marco Pirroni and Steve Severin confirmed as much in Johnny Rotten's autobiography. Thus, ironically, it was the Pistols' future bass player who had them banned, in their absence, from the 100 Club and who deprived the punk scene of a home base venue for the remainder of 1976.

Not that this mattered to the Pistols: the festival and its accompanying propaganda finally won them their coveted recording contract. Nick Mobbs turned up at the death to narrowly squeeze out scene regular Chris Parry, A&R representative for Polydor, and signed the band to EMI on 8 October.

By contrast, the fortnight immediately following the festival was relatively quiet for the Clash, enlivened only by their first full-length interview, which was conducted in the last week of September for the October issue of *Sniffin'*

Glue, the UK punk scene's original fanzine. Editor Mark Perry (then calling himself Mark P.) was a 19-year-old former Williams and Glyn's bank clerk. He had launched the magazine that July, having taken its title from the Ramones song 'now I Wanna Sniff Some Glue' and a Lenny Bruce routine with the same general theme. 'They call *Sniffin' Glue* the first ever fanzine, which is a load of crap, basically,' says Mark. 'There was a fanzine tradition in things like blues, country, jazz: non-mainstream musics that needed to be written about because *Melody Maker* and *Sounds* weren't doing it. I didn't suddenly invent the idea of fanzines, but I was lucky to be the first to do a fanzine within the English punk scene.' The original issue covered the Ramones, the Flamin' Groovies and even Blue Öyster Cult; by the second, Mark had seen the Pistols. 'A month later, it was *forget it*! We didn't even want to know about American bands.'

Mark had access to free photocopying, and *Sniffin' Glue* consisted of a few A4 sheets of paper covered in scrawled handwriting and hamfisted typing, with, by the third issue, occasional poorly reproduced photos. The results were sold for a nominal amount at punk gigs, or at record stores like Rough Trade. The minimalist presentation was not out of keeping with that of the Sex Pistols and was totally in sync with the Clash's Pollock look. Nevertheless, the two Inner Circle bands were not quick to extend the hand of friendship. Glen Matlock remembers being introduced to Mark by Caroline Coon and being horrified by the cheap'n'nasty production values of the fanzines he was holding in his hand. 'Some of the bands that didn't feel part of the Inner Circle welcomed us with open arms, but the Pistols and the Clash were initially a little bit hostile towards *Sniffin' Glue*,' recalls Mark. 'The Pistols and all their entourage were always very fashionable, going to clubs and all that. A big fashion thing involved in the Pistols. But the Clash became a little friendlier, particularly Mick Jones.' It took a while, but the penny finally dropped for the Clash that the fanzine offered them a platform from which they could communicate their ideas to their audience without worrying too much about any editorial tampering: *Sniffin' Glue* interviews were reproduced verbatim, a tradition begun by the late Sixties underground press.

'Where I was coming from was a totally naïve area,' says Mark. 'I wasn't a journalist, I wasn't interested in being cynical about it all. To hear a young band saying they were gonna do all *this*, and writing songs like "London's Burning", I loved all that. I wanted to believe in it. But then again, I wasn't a sycophant.' Steve Walsh was mainly responsible for conducting the interview with the Clash and asked some penetrating questions, but it was Mark, who had accompanied him to Rehearsals, who took issue with some of the band's more questionable statements. The band were intent on establishing themselves as Angry Young Men, so there was a good deal of attitude striking, and even some would-be intimidatory fooling around with an air pistol. Even so, because the encounter was more of a peer group conversation than a formal interview and because they were talking to a fanzine they believed had a small circulation and was ephemeral, the Clash gave a less studied performance than they would in later interviews with the more established media. While the first sketchy attempts to outline a Clash manifesto were being made, a few cats were let out of the bag. Mick confessed to being a Mott the Hoople fan, to having been naïve enough at one time to believe everything he read in the music press and to having a huge collection of embarrassingly uncool records that he was in the process of unloading for a fraction of their original cost. He also admitted to having had a previous musical life – 'I've played with so many arseholes, and my whole career has been one long audition' - in a way that he would not do again for many years.

Sniffin' Glue quickly achieved legendary status, which, despite Mark's own efforts to make it disposable, guaranteed it a longevity the Clash could not have anticipated. As a result, their more dogmatic pronouncements – the ones Mark argued with at the time – came back to haunt them over the years. Their insistence that punk should be taken deadly seriously characterised them as po-faced and dour, an impression that stuck, ensuring that the humour evident within the Clash camp and, more importantly, in Joe's lyrics was often overlooked. The immediate payback for this ill-advised preciousness was the mockery heaped upon a pronouncement Joe made elsewhere in the same interview. At the end of a discussion about the significance of clothing within rock'n'roll, during which Steve Walsh and Mark Perry took the position that such superficial details were irrelevant, and Mick and Joe argued that they were an important part of the subcultural package, Joe quipped, 'Like trousers, like brain!' Taken seriously and out of context, which, perhaps understandably, it invariably was, it is indeed a facile remark. It was obviously intended to be tongue-in-cheek, however, and followed on from Mick's perfectly valid point that the then ubiquitous flared denims and cowboy shirts were indications of the lack of individuality and imagination in contemporary mainstream rock.

The rest of the Clash manifesto-in-progress went as follows: they were hoping to shake up the music scene; they were 'definitely political'; they were against apathy, and 'into encouraging creativity'; although they would not accept that they were part of an American rock heritage, they would accept that they were part of an English one; in spite of their aggressive image, they were against violence; although they wanted change, they were not anarchists and not into chaos; they were against government secrecy; they wanted more punk bands, more venues and more events, and if they had the money, they would do their best to make these things happen. Over the years, the Clash would be brought to task about their failure to live up to many of these and other later claims, but at the time their chief intention was to communicate their enthusiasm and encourage others.

It worked. 'I think at first, if you look, earlier on, we're all sort of floundering around to try and find something to latch on to,' says Mark Perry. 'We're desperate, in a way.' Ideas were already circulating among the

bands, the involved journalists on the established music press and *Sniffin'*
Glue, soon to be joined by the numerous fanzines launched in its wake, so the
Clash were by no means solely responsible for making punk more than just
a cocked snook at establishment values. The UK scene's DIY ethic, for
example, was inherent in the determined amateurishness of both the musical
genre and the fanzines, and, as already mentioned, had first been voiced by
Johnny Rotten. What the Clash did was to bring a sense of focus, purpose
and righteousness to the movement.

At the beginning of December, via the *Today* television programme,
mainstream culture was to be fed an image of punk based on Sex Pistols-style
outrage and nihilism. By that time, as far as commentators within and around
the movement were concerned, punk had already been remade in the image
of the Clash. 'The Pistols: a lot of their songs were just nasty love songs,
except for "Anarchy In The UK",' says Mark. (Most were more like pure
hate songs.) 'But the Clash, you're listening to them, and they're saying
something. And they were saying things lyrically that became elements of the
punk thing, tackling the important issues like unemployment.'

Many of these commentators, awed by the Sex Pistols, but troubled, like
Allan Jones, by their determinedly irresponsible nihilism, found this new
positive version of punk ideology far more appealing. They continued to
cover the Sex Pistols with the appalled fascination of an audience at a freak
show, but they increasingly got behind the Clash as a force for Change,
Honour and Truth. The cliché describing the Clash as the new Rolling
Stones to the Sex Pistols' new Beatles got it nearly right: in fact, the roles were
reversed, with the Clash becoming the good guys to the Pistols' bad.
Inevitably, this meant that the Clash were loaded with the expectations of
others in a way that the Sex Pistols never were. It was something for which
they would ultimately pay dearly.

Mick and Joe rose to the challenge with their next song, 'Career
Opportunities', introduced to the band's set sometime in October 1976.
'Mick came up with the idea, because we were laughing about the careers
master at school,' Joe told *Melody Maker* in 1988. Joe wrote a lyric to order:
the chorus inverted the promise of long-running TV amateur variety show
Opportunity Knocks and the verses listed various unappetising job options,
some of which were imagined and some drawn from experience, like Mick's
stint with the Civil Service, when he was required to open the mail during the
IRA letter bomb campaign. The original version also contained a line about
pensions which Paul was supposed to sing, but he rejected the idea out of
hand. He could still be heard griping about it in the interview included on the
following year's *Capital Radio* EP.

When Mick added his tune, 'Career Opportunities' was revealed to be one
of the more powerful songs in the band's repertoire. In the wake of the
opening lines of '1977', about having been 'too long on the dole', it was
interpreted as a song about rising youth unemployment. Keeping one eye on

the street credmeter, the band felt compelled to discuss it in those terms. Mick had already told *Sniffin' Glue* that the band were 'all down the dole, coppin' our money off Rod Stewart's taxes'; the following March, Joe gave both Tony Parsons and Caroline Coon the impression that 'Career Opportunities' and the relevant part of '1977' had been written in response to a Department of Employment threat to send him to Birmingham for rehabilitation, as he had been unemployed for so long.

The threat was undoubtedly made, but Joe's case was by no means as desperate as was suggested. None of the band was among the long-term unemployed in the true sense of the phrase. 'Musicians live like that anyway,' says Sebastian Conran. 'The life of a musician on the dole, and the life of someone who's genuinely looking for a job and on the dole, well, you couldn't get further apart. Most of the people who used to talk about being on the dole would not have *dreamed* of getting a job. And times were nowhere near as hard then as they became later, in the Thatcher years, and recently.'

Although the Clash never claimed to be unemployable in their interviews, they did say the only options for them were late night washing-up marathons, menial warehouse stacking jobs or the factory production line. This was simply not true: had they so desired, any one of them could have walked into a white collar office job the next day, and could probably have found something more stimulating, even creative, within a few weeks. Joe had *chosen* to be a bum; Terry was taking time out between A levels and college; Paul had just dropped out of art school; Mick was still officially attending art school. In fact, Paul was so unaccustomed to signing on that he believed there was room in the process for pride and respect: 'I wasn't on anything for a whole year,' he told Mary Turner in 1982 for San Jose's Radio KSJO. 'You go down, stand in line and get insulted. I just got fed up with it after a while. I decided I'd much rather starve than have to deal with all that.'

If the notion of punk as 'tower block rock' derived from 'London's Burning', a song inspired by a high-rise flat that was not quite the long-time Mick Jones domicile the band made it sound, then the notion of punk as 'dole queue rock' derived from 'Career Opportunities', a song which came nowhere near to reflecting the realistic employment prospects of the band as a whole. The Clash were so obsessed with the concept of 'authenticity' that they put themselves in the confused position of misrepresenting the truth in order to suggest it.

Aware that the folk, R&B and rock'n'roll records they loved reflected the humble origins and necessarily marginal lifestyles of the songs' composers, Sixties musicians like Bob Dylan, Mick Jagger and John Lennon had played down *their* middle class origins and assembled their public personae out of working class and bohemian characteristics. This pose was quickly established as a rock tradition, and for all their punk era rejection of the past, the Clash were too steeped in such traditions to do anything but follow suit. As their notion of street credibility drew so heavily on the terrace yob mentality, their own public personae required even more artistic licence than those of the Sixties stars, and threw up even more contradictions. 'We urge people to learn fast,' Mick told Barry Miles in November. Three months earlier, at the Roundhouse gig, Joe had made a sneering remark about A levels being 'a trick'. 'Your drummer's got them,' piped up a girl in the front row who knew Terry from school. 'He confessed to me after the show that he'd been lost for words at that point,' laughs Terry. (Joe, of course, had at least one A level himself.) In *The Boy Looked At Johnny* Tony Parsons and Julie Burchill made a snide remark about Joe having taken 'de-elocution lessons'. Snide, but fair: in truth accentless and highly articulate, punk era Joe contrived a mangled Cockney speaking style, punctuating his affectedly impoverished vocabulary with many an assertive 'right?' and 'see?' There was considerable irony in his feeling obliged to sound inarticulate and unlearned while trying to fulfil the Clash's stated aims of communication and education.

Before the early to mid Seventies, pop and rock had always been a youth culture. Teenage subject matter had encouraged much celebration of 'the kids', a generic term for the young rock'n'roll audience that was regularly employed in the song lyrics of the Who, the Standells and the MC5, among many others. Generation gap-inspired ageism had been politicised in the late Sixties by the Woodstock generation's warning not to trust anyone over 30; but in the mid-Seventies, many of that same generation were still around, now over 30, and clogging up both the charts and the music business. Consequently, rock had attempted to aim itself at a more sophisticated and mature audience, a trend which explains the thinking behind a genre calling itself 'progressive'. As part of its campaign to shame the old guard into moving over, punk used their advanced age and self-consciousness about it as weapons against them: they were dismissed as 'boring old farts'. In her August 1976 punk overview piece, Caroline Coon had noted that Johnny Rotten's favourite insult was 'You're too old.' When the UK punk bands of 1976 talked about their followers, they too referred to them as 'the kids'.

Being young became increasingly important, as Brady had found to his cost. In keeping with this outlook, members of punk bands were supposed to be of the same generation as 'the kids' they thought of as their audience. In late 1976, the Pistols were all still safely between 20 and 21, as were all of the Clash except Joe, who was a comparatively ancient 24. As he had spent two years prior to joining the Clash in a pub band, some people on the punk scene thought of him as even older than that. 'When they got Joe, we was *really* surprised,' recalls Glen Matlock. 'Short on style there in a big way! I said that to Bernie Rhodes, and he said, "Give me a couple of weeks, and I'll have ten years off him." I don't think he ever did, really.' But he did have two years off him: in November 1976, Joe told Caroline Coon that he was 22, again in the name of authenticity. 'When you're 22, you're still a young man, you're practically a teenager,' he explained to Paul Morley of the *NME* when he finally came out of the age closet in October 1979. 'It's a great relief for me to be 27 in a way, 'cause I think the worst time of my life was when I was 24.

I used to lie about my age, make myself younger, say I was 22 or something. I was so paranoid about it. It was the early days of the Clash, like, "Fuck, if they find out how old I am, that's it! I'm in the bunker, the dumper . . .'"

All this fake authenticity did was invite accusations of phoniness when the truth was inevitably discovered. Lester Bangs, covering the Clash's late 1977 Get Out of Control Tour for the *NME*, dismissed such accusations as irrelevant. 'I surmise,' he wrote, 'that this is supposed to indicate that Joe isn't worth a shit, and that his songs are all fake street-graffiti.' He went on to state that the same could be said of Dylan, Jagger, Pete Townshend and Lou Reed, before asserting, 'all this blathering about authenticity is just a bunch of crap. The Clash are authentic because their music carries such brutal conviction, not because they're Noble Savages.' This was true, but the fault for not realising it lay not with their critics but with the Clash themselves. There was no need for the band to tell lies in order to validate their work, yet they chose to do so. And anyone who stands for office on a platform of truth, yet practises to deceive, is in danger of losing credibility, both on the street and elsewhere.

'Career Opportunities' is a case in point: it was not necessary for the band to embellish their own dole experiences and work histories to bolster the song. There is a distinction to be made between the issue of unemployment, that is, not being able to find a job at all, and the issue of limited career opportunities, that is, not being able to find a job that one *wants*. Like 'Janie Jones' and '48 Hours' before it, 'Career Opportunities' is perfectly effective as a straightforward rejection of the work ethic, an exercise in social observation. It is explained much better by Mick's November 1976 response to Caroline Coon's suggestion that *someone* has to do the dirty jobs like working in a factory. '*Why* have they?' he demanded. 'Don't you think technology is advanced enough to give all those jobs over to a few people and machines? They're just keeping people occupied by making them work. There's a social stigma attached to being unemployed. Like "Social Security Scroungers" every day in the *Sun*. I don't want to hear that. I cheer them. You go up North and the kids are *ashamed* that they can't get a job.' Or, as Joe would succinctly put it in another lyric that he wrote four years later, 'Who gives you work, and why should you do it?'

'The only thing I'm interested in is personal freedom,' he told Caroline in March 1977. But even by October 1976, punk in general and the Clash in particular were being infected with the kind of Orwellian revisionism and double-think that was guaranteed to deny personal freedom. Placed in this constantly shifting, paranoid context, a jocular remark such as 'Like trousers, like brain' could be strongly reminiscent of the *Animal Farm* dictum 'Four legs good, two legs bad.' 'Punk *was* very Stalinist in that respect,' agrees Tony Parsons. 'It was very much like that: "Denounce your parents! Turn them in to the Punk Police for having flared trousers!"' Like most subcultures, punk rejected the values of the parent culture, yet imposed its own set of rules upon its followers. There might have been some room for self-expression in the punk look, but a certain degree of conformity was insisted upon. Flared trousers were out, so it was conveniently forgotten that Mick had been photographed in a pair outside Davis Road just four months before the *Sniffin' Glue* denouncement. In autumn 1976, much to Mick's chagrin, it was also finally decreed, by Bernie, according to Glen, that long hair was unacceptable under any circumstances.

'We had to tie Mick down to cut his hair,' laughs Alan Drake. 'He liked it long, because he thought he looked a bit like Keith Richards, which he did. But we said, "Look, Mick, you've just got to fucking shut up and sit down!" And I cut his hair, and we dyed it black.' Although his new hairstyle was still markedly longer than those of his fellow band members, it was the first time the Jones ears had seen daylight since the mid-Sixties. 'I'll never forget the day he knocked on the door and I opened it,' says Honest John Plain, then still living at 47A Warrington Crescent. 'There he was in a ragged suit and really cropped hair, and I said, "What the fuck you *done*, Mick?" and he went, "It's punk rock, innit?" And it was! It freaked me out, anyway. One extreme to the other, overnight. It was funny, but he became very serious about it.'

The new overtly political direction and heavy duty seriousness greatly influenced the new Clash look, introduced during the course of October. This, for all Joe's claims that the lyric for '1977' was misinterpreted, most certainly cast the Clash in the role of urban guerrillas. The band had been without protection for their clothes when painting Rehearsals, or so their explanation for the Pollock look would have it, but they now miraculously found some boiler suits. Out of their intended work context, such all-in-one outfits remained functional and practical, but acquired other connotations. Used by criminals, revolutionaries and paramilitaries to protect their own identities, their very featurelessness encouraged prisons and oppressive regimes to employ them in order to *deny* identity. In Stanley Kubrick's 1971 film version of *A Clockwork Orange* Alex's ultra-violent gang habitually wore white boiler suits.

The four members of the Clash did not wear theirs all the time, but for the next couple of months there was usually at least one in evidence when photographs were being taken, and the band did their best to exploit and emphasise the suits' residual signals with accessories and slogans. Paul added some punk studs to the seams of his; Joe mocked up a fake ID from Sebastian Conran's Students' Union pass and attached it to his breast-pocket; Mick affected an armband bearing the legend 'RED GUARD' (taken, literally, from the military arm of communist China, it was a response to Siouxsie's swastika and, perhaps less intentionally, an indication of the distance he had travelled from his own flirtation with the decadent Nazi style). Boiler suits, shirts and T-shirts alike were daubed with patches of colour, some abstract, but some attempting rough approximations of recognisable shapes and images, such as the Union Jack. Jackson Pollock was giving way to Jasper Johns and Robert Rauschenberg, splatter painting slipping into Pop-Art via tachism.

The slogans themselves were initially crudely hand-painted, but before long were being applied with the aid of packing case stencils. This was partly because it increased the suggestion of institutionalisation, but also because Bernie recognised some connections – above and beyond those with Pop-Art and the Who – that were almost pleading to be made. Firstly, with the Lettrists, a Fifties Parisian avant-garde movement, who had also turned themselves into walking art statements by writing on their clothing. Secondly, with the similarly motivated late Fifties Situationists, who had brought art and politics together in their determination to stimulate a reaction, and whose witty and slightly skewed sloganeering had done so much to define the tone of 1968's Paris riots. Thirdly, with Malcolm McLaren, who had brought both influences together at Sex, decorating the shop's walls and clothing stock with provocative slogans.

The Boy Looked At Johnny's assertion that Bernie set about using the Clash as 'blank T-shirts on which to superimpose his own self-conscious political posturing', if taken literally, was not so far from the truth. Certainly, the Clash's flirtation with Lettrism was Bernie's idea: Joe admitted as much to Jon Savage, also claiming to have been totally ignorant about 'that Situationist stuff'. It might seem strange that Bernie should risk yet more accusations of plagiarising Malcolm, even if he could counter them by insisting that he had been part of the Sex creative team when those influences were first being explored, but this opportunity to bring his interests together was too great to resist. Also, the Clash approach differed from Sex's in two respects: Malcolm sold his clothes, but the Clash's were DIY, in keeping with the new punk ethic, a point they made repeatedly; and Malcolm's slogans tended to the glib or smutty, whereas the Clash's were *politically* provocative.

Crossover was limited to one slogan: 'PASSION IS A FASHION', which Joe stencilled on his boiler suit, had previously adorned the wall of Sex. Others were inspired by reggae records: 'UNDER HEAVY MANNERS' and 'HEAVY DUTY DISCIPLINE', for example, both came from Prince Far I's album and song of the former title. Phrases from the Clash's own songs turned up too: 'KNIVES IN W11', 'STEN GUNS IN KNIGHTSBRIDGE', 'WHITE RIOT' and 'JANIE JONES'. Social Security and other state registration and reference numbers were reproduced as comments on dehumanisation and governmental control. Individual band members pursued their own agendas: Mick challenged 'DON'T JUST TAKE PICTURES' while Paul advocated 'CREATIVE VIOLENCE' and Joe declared 'CHUCK BERRY IS DEAD' to distance himself from his R&B years. He also inverted the hippy slogan 'Love and Peace' to rub the previous generation's face in the new reality of 'HATE AND WAR'.

8... HATE AND WAR

October 1976 saw the real start of the Clash's live campaign. Although there had been nothing so confrontational as a row, the swastika issue had strained the relationship between Bernie and Malcolm McLaren. So had Malcolm's evident loss of interest, following the signing of his band to EMI, in promoting punk as a multi-band scene. The Sex Pistols devoted the next two months to recording their first single and playing numerous gigs around the national club circuit. The Clash were not invited; it was time to strike out on their own.

In addition to the Three Wise Journalists who were prepared to attend most gigs, the band had a small, but committed, following that could be relied upon to take the chill off any strange venue accessible by tube, even if the heat they generated was not always beneficial to the band's cause. Tony James, Alan Drake and Viv Albertine seldom turned up at Rehearsals, but they were still in Mick and Paul's social circle, and Sid, when not in the remand centre, was ubiquitous. 'He was around a lot. An awful lot,' says Terry. 'I remember him turning up at Rehearsals once with a suit on and a tie made from toilet paper. It looked quite neat, actually. Not that he'd say so, but I think he was trying his ideas out on us to see what we thought.' Through Glen, with whom he had attended St Martin's, the Clash also became friendly with Mark Helfont. He bore a marked resemblance to Eric Idle, but his facial expressions and vocal mannerisms were even more strongly reminiscent of Frankie Howerd, which prompted Steve Jones to dub him Frothler. Jane Crockford, her relationship with John Brown over, had drifted on to the punk scene and back into Mick Jones's orbit via a brief relationship with Sid. Something of an unstable character, she quickly earned the not particularly kind nickname Mad Jane. To greater and lesser extents, all the above were friends of the band; the absence of the Sex Pistols from the London live scene also swelled the Clash's audience with several other punk scene stalwarts, including Shane MacGowan.

Two newcomers were so taken with the band that they started to hang around on a regular basis, gradually joining Micky Foote as semi-official members of the Clash team: Sebastian Conran and Roadent. The first to arrive was Sebastian, son of millionaire designer Terence Conran (founder of the highly successful Habitat furniture business) and author Shirley

Conran (who wrote the highly successful book *Superwoman*). Sebastian had developed an acquaintance with Glen after booking the Sex Pistols for their gig at the Central School of Art back in November 1975. 'Sebastian said to me, "Do you want to come back to my place?" after we'd been somewhere, and it was this massive big house,' recalls Glen. 'I said, "Is it a squat?" And he said, "Well, sort of . . ." And it weren't, but it was unhip to say that.'

'I had got a lease on a house near Regent's Park, a huge squat, basically, is what it was,' says Sebastian, apparently still intent on propagating that myth despite all evidence, much of it provided by himself, to the contrary. '31 Albany Street. Well, the punks came in at 31 Albany Street, but when my brother [fashion designer] Jasper moved there, Bianca Jagger would come in at 9 St Andrew's Place, which was the other side. There was a smart side and a seedy side to the whole thing. I was renting it out to students. This was my dad's idea. Because I didn't get a grant at the Central, he thought it would be a good idea for me to earn the money, so he found the house and got me the lease, but I had to pay it all. It was gigantic, huge, 15 bedrooms, and the lease was £400 every six months.'

One of the students living there was the then-girlfriend of Micky Foote, which ensured that Micky was a regular visitor and that the entire household was aware of the Clash. Being an art student hang-out, 31 Albany Street was a hive of creativity, and had a darkroom set up in the basement. Another tenant, Rocco Macauley, subsequently took the live photos of the Clash that were used to illustrate the *Sniffin' Glue* interview. Yet another, Sebastian's best friend Henry Bowles, later did some voice-over radio commercials for Clash record releases because, according to Sebastian, he was possessed of 'a nice south London accent, and Joe thought he had a street cred voice'. He was impressed by the Clash live experience, but it was the overall atmosphere of creative energy surrounding the band that was the attraction for Sebastian. That, and the Joe Strummer punk persona. 'Joe was my absolute big hero. I used to dog him around, follow him everywhere. He seemed so clever and so glamorous. Micky Foote was a mate who I hung around with and saw a lot of, but it was a real privilege to go out for the night with Joe.' The rough-edged loner Joe and the naïvely enthusiastic Sebastian were an unlikely pairing, but it seems Joe initially found it easy to sympathise with another ex-public schoolboy attempting to shrug off a supposedly advantaged background. 'He's got a very high-class voice, but he means well,' he told the *Sunday Times Magazine*'s Gordon Burn in May 1977.

Paul and Terry were pleasant enough to Sebastian, being laid-back characters prepared to be open-minded about almost anyone they encountered. Also, both appreciated the fact that Sebastian was a kid with a lot of toys: the high-powered air pistol Paul wielded during the *Sniffin' Glue* interview (and which featured as a regular Clash prop over the following couple of years) was his; and Terry was so taken with Sebastian's Norton Commando motorbike that he eventually bought it from him. Mick – usually the most approachable member of the Clash – was the only one who was openly antagonistic. 'Mick Jones was just fucking rude, really.'

It was Bernie, with his keen eye for voluntary (that is, cost-free) assistance, who realised Sebastian's true potential. Like his father, he was not only a skilled and creative designer, but practically minded and industrious with it. As well as doing more mundane tasks like helping the band move equipment, Sebastian found himself increasingly being relied upon to realise Bernie's presentation ideas. Initially, he was entrusted with designing and printing (for free, at the Central) the flyers advertising the Clash's headlining gigs. Their cut-and-paste Xerox'n'scrawl style was partly derived from *Sniffin' Glue* and its disciples, but Sebastian had already been experimenting with a similar kind of minimalism at college: his entry for a January 1975 competition to design a poster for the Foundation Studies Exhibition had consisted of a crumpled copy of the competition brief, blown up to the specified size, with the prescribed text circled roughly in red. Under Bernie's direction, Sebastian would go on to design the band's early tour posters and single picture sleeves, manufacture their stage backdrops and produce and market T-shirts and other assorted items of clothing.

The Clash acquired their other helper in November 1976. Steve Connolly, who hailed from Coventry, caught the band's performance at the Institute of Contemporary Arts (ICA) at the end of October. During a conversation with Joe he mentioned that he had just come out of prison and had nowhere to sleep. Joe suggested he stay at Rehearsals for the night. Shortly beforehand, the squat at Orsett Terrace had been cleared and Joe had found himself alternative accommodation in the disused Robertino's ice cream factory in Foscote Mews, close to Wilmcote House. Rather than live by candlelight and without heat, Paul had instead elected to sleep at the only marginally more salubrious Rehearsals. Steve offered to work as the band's roadie if he could stay long-term, and, glad of the company, Paul made no objection. Steve got the (unpaid) job, and was promptly rechristened Roadent.

Within a few short months, Roadent was attracting almost as much media attention as the Clash themselves. This was partly due to his mischievous personality and considerable talent for self-promotion, but the version of his recent personal history that emerged also fitted in neatly with the yob-cum-rude boy image the Clash wished to promote – much more so than did, say, Sebastian's, whose very name was a dead giveaway - and Roadent's rapid promotion to centre-stage has sometimes been described as another Clash bid for credibility by association. 'He went along to see the Clash soon after his release from prison,' wrote Tony Parsons the following spring. 'At the time he was carrying a copy of *Mein Kampf* around with him. Prison can mess up your head. Strummer, in his usual manner of abusive honesty, straightened him out. Roadent's been with them ever since, and sleeps on the floor of their studio.' In those few short sentences Tony portrayed Roadent as a tough, simple, but basically decent working class lad who had been led astray, but had now seen the errors of his ways and thrown in his lot with his wise, compassionate saviours.

Roadent propagated this view of himself later in the year, when he told his interviewer for the German film *Punk In London '77* that he had been imprisoned 'for insurrectionary activities. Expropriation of substances from other, richer people: *stealing*. Political activities. That's what the Angry Brigade man said in court.' He sounded like a half-bright, uneducated petty thief who had just spent a year with a revolutionary left-wing cell learning their rhetoric by rote. The true picture was not quite so black and white. Roadent came from a working class background, but had won a scholarship to board at a public school. Then, after falling out with his father, he had left home and roughed it in Coventry in much the same way as Joe had in London, while running through a bizarre series of temporary jobs including selling bibles. His period of incarceration immediately prior to meeting the Clash had been for a mere two weeks, and not for theft, but for lapsed maintenance payments or non-payment of a previous fine (depending on whether one believes the version he gave *Melody Maker*'s Frances Lass in 1979 or *England's Dreaming* author Jon Savage 12 years later).

The restless curiosity that had led him to flirt with both religion and fascism by the autumn of 1976 was indeed quickly rechannelled by Clash-style punk rhetoric, but no one had to do Roadent's thinking for him. His interest in and grasp of leftist radical politics soon surpassed that of most of the band members. 'Roadent was intelligent,' says Sebastian. 'He probably had as much to do with the political background as anyone else.' In addition, he earned his favoured position with the band by being prepared to muck in and rough it, not by being an amusing tame thug. 'He was a good bloke, and he worked hard. He and Paul Simonon lived in the most disgusting manner. They used to smell dreadful. Personal freshness was not something they went in for.'

Bernie came up with a two-step plan to establish the Clash in their own right. The ultimate goal was to headline the kind of events at which they had previously supported the Pistols. Step one was the more traditional and decidedly less glamorous rock'n'roll process of hustling support slots wherever possible. Thanks to Sid and the Pistols, at this time punk was banned not only from the 100 Club, but also effectively banned from Dingwalls, the Nashville and the Marquee. In fact – as Mick and Joe revealed in *The Armagideon Times* tour programme (1980) – the Clash approached and were turned down by the last of these clubs. Some of the venues Bernie managed to line up had, like the Roundhouse, previously hosted gigs by the 101ers, which suggests there was a degree of trading on Joe's past reputation. Most of the places were low-key and obscure enough to qualify as anonymous and, although this was partly forced by punk's public image and the band's limited financial resources, it was not a problem. The primary aim was not so much to increase the band's exposure as to hone their live sound and stage presentation. As Glen Matlock so pithily puts it: 'You get a set together, but it doesn't mean jack shit until you've played it in front of a few people, regardless of the reaction.' 'In the early days, we had a little Ford

Transit, and we were going all over the place,' says Sebastian. 'The concerts out of town, the teeny-weeny ones, were all good fun. We'd all travel up there sitting on top of the gear in the back of the Transit. The group didn't have roadies: they did it all.' (Roadent was yet to arrive on the scene.)

The first of these gigs took place on Saturday, 9 October 1976, at Tiddenfoot Leisure Centre, Leighton Buzzard, about an hour's drive north-west of London. Along with local band the Aylesbury Bucks, the Clash were support to a pub rock outfit named the Rockets. The gig was attended by an old acquaintance of Mick from his Mott the Hoople gig-going days, Kris Needs, who lived nearby. Via Ian Hunter's friendship with Pete Frame, Kris had graduated from managing Mott's fan club to writing for *ZigZag*, the semi-underground music magazine of which Pete was the founder (in 1969) and proprietor. Responding with enthusiasm to punk, Kris would take over as editor early in 1977, when *ZigZag* decided to devote the bulk of its coverage to the new movement. In April that year, he looked back at his own first encounter with the Clash: 'The hall was like a large hotel lounge, which encouraged the crowd to drape itself over the seating. The Clash taking the stage was like an injection of electricity into the smoky air. They charged headlong into "White Riot" with shattering energy, strutting and leaping like clockwork robots out of control. They never let up for half an hour. Despite sound problems, they were astounding, almost overpowering in their attack and conviction.'

The band's second trip out on their own, not long afterwards on some forgotten date in October, was to a pub-cum-disco in Guildford, Surrey, run by Marmalade's former bass player. In February 1980, Joe informed *Sounds'* Robbi Millar that it was the smallest venue the band had ever played, and that the audience had consisted of 'one lone drunk refugee from the club/disco below, where the bouncers were having the shit kicked out of them by a bunch of squaddies'. Terry recalls that the Marmalade man came upstairs while this fracas was taking place and apologised to the band for the low turnout.

On Friday, 15 October, according to that week's *Time Out*, the Clash were scheduled to appear bottom of the bill to a couple of bands called Spartacus and Sukuya at the Acklam Hall, off Portobello Road in the shadow of the Westway. If this spiritual homecoming took place, it appears to have left no lasting impression on anyone involved.

The same cannot be said of the following night's show, at the University of London Union (ULU), on Malet Street in central London. Here the Clash were third on a bill of four, following Please Y'Self and preceding Brett Marvin and the Thunderbolts and headliners Shakin' Stevens and the Sunsets. Although the audience consisted mostly of mainstream student types, the Sunsets' substantial second generation teddy boy following was well represented, as indeed was that of the Clash. 'To the Social guy at the Union, it must have looked OK on paper,' reflected fictitious band valet 'Albert Transom' in 1988. 'A good rock'n'roll band from Wales and to warm up, this new London group. Well, he wasn't up on his street culture.' Subcultures are essentially large gangs, and there is invariably tension if two meet on the same turf. Punks and teddy boys were yet to repeat the mod–rocker conflict of the mid-Sixties, but such a conflict was inevitable; and if ever an event was liable to provide the spark, it was the ULU gig.

There was no friction between the groups themselves while setting up – 'We even lifted Shakin' Stevens's piano on to the stage,' laughs Terry – but the Clash had only played five numbers of their set when, according to 'Albert Transom', a ted approached the front of the stage, held up a five pence piece and said, 'Here's your bus fare home.' Further insults were exchanged and, upon leaving the stage, the band and their followers were forced to barricade themselves in the changing room to keep at bay a small, but rabid, mob. Grabbing a chair apiece, the Clash camp threw open the doors and prepared to meet their assailants. Only two rushed in, one of whom tried to throttle Sebastian with his own tie. Faced with the prospect of having half a dozen chairs broken over his head, however, he quickly decided discretion was the better part of valour, put Sebastian down, and retreated.

'I remember Bernie Rhodes came over to me, and he made a great statement,' says Polydor A&R man Chris Parry, who was there that night. 'There were these student girls in normal clothes, and he said, "In a very short period of time, they're going to have to decide which way to dress." And he was absolutely right.'

The Clash weren't the only punk, or would-be punk, band making waves that October, though not all of them were new, and, as far as the Inner Circle were concerned, most were trying to jump on the bandwagon. The Stranglers had been touting their Doors-style rock'n'roll around the London and Home Counties pub rock circuit for two years, but following their support slots with the visiting New York new wave bands and their inclusion in Caroline Coon's August punk feature, they had cut their hair short, abandoned flares and further toughened up their already menacing sound. October saw Patti Smith's second visit to the UK, and the Stranglers were again offered the support for her two London dates, on 22 and 23 October, this time at the 3,500-capacity Hammersmith Odeon. A recording contract looked inevitable.

The Jam had been playing the minor pub rock venues since 1974, wearing black mod suits to perform R&B material influenced by the Who and Dr Feelgood: Caroline had been stretching a point when she included them in her 'who's who in punk' round-up. Nevertheless, on 16 October, watched by the Clash, who were grabbing a pre-ULU gig snack at a nearby café, the band plugged in at Rock On records on Newport Court's Soho Market and played an open-air gig showcasing new, punk-tinged material like 'In The City'. The outcome was namechecks in both *Melody Maker* and *Sounds*.

October was also the month in which two further offshoots of the London SS chose to make their débuts. Matt Dangerfield and Casino Steel's Boys had originally dressed like a latter-day version of the Hollywood Brats to play their melodic high-energy rock'n'roll, but they cut their hair and adopted vaguely punk-style clothing in time for their first gig at the Hope and Anchor in Islington.

On 18 October, it was the turn of Tony James's new band, Chelsea, managed by Andy Czezowski and with Gene October on vocals, the Bromley Contingent's Billy Idol on guitar and John Towe on drums. In 1976, the ICA, at the other end of the Mall from Buckingham Palace, was intent on living up to its title. Ted White, the events organiser, Mike Laye, who ran the theatre side, and his assistant Keith Allen (future comedian and actor) were interested in the radical and provocative end of the arts spectrum. From 19 to 26 October 1976, a performance art group named COUM Transmissions were given free rein to hold a show-cum-exhibition entitled Prostitution, the general theme of which, according to group leader Genesis P-Orridge, was that art is prostitution. It included pages from pornographic magazines depicting COUM member Cosey Fanni Tutti, thus offering, as the show's flyer explained, 'Different ways of seeing and using Cosey with her consent, produced by people unaware of her reasons, as a woman and an artist, for participating.'

The flyer also made it clear that 'For us the party on the opening night is the key to our stance, the most important performance.' On that preview night, the 18th, COUM set out to be as anti-art as possible, hiring strippers and blue comedians, and launching their own avant-garde rock band, Throbbing Gristle. Being friendly with Acme Attractions' John Krivine, Genesis knew that Andy Czezowski was managing a new punk band, and invited Chelsea to provide musical support on one condition: that for this performance they call themselves LSD, a name deliberately chosen to counter the punk movement's prevailing anti-hippy sentiments. COUM invited as many way-out people as possible, and Chelsea brought along representatives from the punk scene – including the Bromley Contingent and Mick Jones – to mingle with the critics and other media representatives. Entering into the spirit of the evening, Mick tried to persuade some of the female punks in the audience to get up on-stage and disrupt the strippers.

That the mainstream press were more outraged by COUM's stunts was perhaps predictable, but not even Genesis expected to be physically attacked by the *Evening News* critic, who had to be forcibly subdued and ejected, and who still hadn't calmed down when he filed his vituperative review. The *Daily Mail* followed up with a photograph of the Bromley Contingent's Siouxsie, Steve Severin and Debbie Juvenile, captioned, 'This is the art connoisseur of today', and described the audience as comprising 'Hell's Angels, girls dressed as whores, and boys with dyed hair and nail varnish'. Tory MP Nicholas Fairbairn, also present at the show, but presumably failing to fall into any of the above categories, supplied the comment, 'These people are the wreckers of civilisation.' The press continued to exploit the Shock Horror Outrage value of the Prostitution exhibition until the Arts

Council joined in and denounced COUM. It was a foretaste of the media-manipulated fear and loathing that was soon to be directed at the punk movement itself.

The Chelsea connection and Bernie's own long-standing friendship with Mike Laye (who would go on to become a rock photographer and take the back cover picture of the Clash's 1985 album, *Cut The Crap*) resulted in the Clash securing their own ICA performance slot later in the week. Although Prostitution was still running, 23 October was individually billed as A Night of Pure Energy, and was the band's first headlining gig in the punk event style pioneered by Malcolm and the Pistols. The Subway Sect were given the support slot, and Sebastian and Bernie designed a flyer, which the Clash took out and pasted up around London. Upon returning from this mission, Paul heated up the remaining flour-and-water paste over Rehearsals' two-bar electric fire, and ate it. Never ones to let a useful anecdote go to waste, the Clash subsequently parlayed this isolated act of bravado into an illustration of the direness of their circumstances at that time. First recounted by Caroline Coon in her spring 1977 *Melody Maker* Clash feature, it was also dusted off years later for both the *That Was Then, This Is Now* TV programme and the *Clash On Broadway* booklet.

Barry Miles reviewed the ICA gig for the *NME*. At 33, Miles, as he preferred to be known, was another veteran of the late Sixties counter-culture. In 1966, he had co-founded underground magazine *It*, the launch party for which had simultaneously opened up the Roundhouse as a rock venue and introduced London to the kind of hippy happenings that the Midnight Special copied ten years later. Miles had done his homework, and read the *Sniffin' Glue* piece. Unlike his colleague Charles Shaar Murray, he was prepared to let the band push all his anti-establishment buttons, and announced that he had enjoyed them a lot more than Patti Smith the previous night. 'It was as if they had crystallised the dormant energy of all the hours of crushing boredom of being an unemployed school-leaver, living with your parents in a council flat, into a series of three-minute staccato blasts delivered like a whiplash at the audience, who were galvanised into frenzied dancing.' He went on to liken their 'musical intensity' to that of the Ramones, though he believed the Clash's lyrics to be far superior.

Miles also cast a sociological eye over the audience, noting the Sex-style clothes, the safety pins, the pogo dancing and various other bizarre rituals. His sensationalised report of one of these, illustrated by two Red Saunders photographs, ultimately overshadowed everything else about the gig, and gave one of the two people involved his first 15 minutes of fame: 'A young couple, somewhat out of it, had been nibbling and fondling each other amid the broken glass when she suddenly lunged forward and *bit his ear lobe off* [while the crowd] watched with cold, calculated hipitude.'

Like the COUM party, the Clash gig was a wild night fuelled by speed and alcohol. The bar staff entered into the spirit of the event to such an extent that, with Sebastian's assistance, they gave away a further £80 worth of booze, and the twosome Miles observed – Mad Jane and Shane MacGowan - were by no means content to loiter at the back of the queue. 'Me and this girl were having a bit of a laugh which involved biting each other's arms till they were completely covered in blood and then smashing up a couple of bottles and cutting each other up a bit,' Shane informed *ZigZag*'s Granuaille in 1986, setting the record straight on the occasion of punk's tenth anniversary and, in the process, offering another insight into the rock'n'roll myth-making process. 'That, in those days, was the sort of thing that people used to do. I haven't got a clue now why I did it or why anyone would want to do it, but that was how teenagers got their kicks in London *if* they were hip. Anyway, in the end she went a bit over the top and bottled me in the side of the head. *Gallons* of blood came out and someone took a photograph. I never got it bitten off – although we had bitten each other to bits – it was just a heavy cut.' As Shane noted, though, the anecdote was exaggerated with each retelling. 'It's like the old story about the bloke who catches the fish. He says that it weighs *this* much and it's *that* big, and within a couple of days it's a whale.' Over the years, few have been prepared to let the fact that his ear lobes are both quite evidently present and correct stand in the way of a good story.

Like Miles, members of the Clash had been to see Patti Smith the previous night. She took them up on their invitation to the ICA gig – thus becoming the Clash's first celebrity guest – and responded to the band's set with typical Smith reserve, leaping up on the stage to dance. 'I did it because I do it all the time,' she told Caroline Coon the following January. 'To me, that's what a fan does. I was really excited about the Clash. I thought they were great and I knew I wasn't going to be back in London for a long time and I thought they wanted a reaction.' They did, and were more than a little pleased with the one they got. Much later in his career, by which time he had met many of his former heroes, Mick would say that Patti Smith was one of the few that had lived up to his expectations. Paul's expectations must have been more than lived up to: Patti succumbed to the brooding Simonon charm, and invited him to accompany her to Birmingham, scene of her next scheduled gig, on 24 October. Coincidentally, it was also the scene of the Clash's next gig, which would at least save Paul the train fare home.

The list of provincial cities responding to punk did not begin and end with Manchester: back in early August, Birmingham's Suburban Studs had been included (albeit incorrectly named the Suburban Bolts) in Caroline Coon's punk overview feature. In fact, at that time, the band had been glam-rockers, and they still looked decidedly out of place when they supported the Sex Pistols and the Clash at the 100 Club on 31 August. Having seen them that night, Jonh Ingham was later moved to describe the Studs as 'a laughable mixture of tacky jumpsuits, tacky makeup, tacky props and tacky music'. It might have been bending the truth to include them on the punk rock roll-call, but for their part the Studs were intrigued and impressed by the London bands. Birmingham Barbarella's had hosted a Sex Pistols gig on 14 August, and the Studs contacted the club and persuaded the management to designate Wednesdays Punk Night. The Studs volunteered to get proceedings under way by headlining the first gig and bringing up a bona fide punk band from London for both moral and literal support. After catching the Clash again at the ICA, the Studs approached Bernie and explained their desire to ignite a Birmingham scene. Their missionary zeal thus appealed to, the Clash agreed to appear second on the bill to the local heroes that coming Wednesday, 27 October.

Upon arrival, the Clash found the Studs had undergone a miraculous change of image, starting, but not ending, with haircuts all round. 'When we played with them in London, they had satin flares on,' remembers Terry. 'When we went up to support them in Birmingham, they were in straight trousers like us, and Bernie was going, "Where's your flares, then? I want to buy 'em for my band."' Unfortunately, according to Jonh Ingham, who reviewed the gig for *Sounds*, the transformation in the band's material was neither extensive nor competent enough to allow the Studs to grab a place on the punk gravy train.

By contrast, Jonh believed the Clash's 45-minute set to have been their finest yet, despite the almost inevitable sound problems. This time a PA malfunction meant that only the vocals could be routed through the club system, with the band's own amplification equipment being required to project the sound of the guitars throughout the venue. Ironically, this made for one of the clearest vocal mixes they had ever experienced. When it came to stage presentation, the word 'relaxed' was not in the Clash lexicon, but away from the largely self-imposed restrictions of the London scene, they felt able to adopt a more populist, even humorous approach. The second number, 'London's Burning', became 'Birmingham's Burning', establishing something of a local-relevance tradition for the song, and the encore '1-2 Crush On You' involved some frantic self-deprecatory mugging from Joe. The crowd loved it. 'Every song is pared to the minimum required to get it across with maximum energy and zero flab,' concluded Jonh.

The band's next gig took place on 29 October back in London, at Fulham Old Town Hall on Fulham Broadway. The Clash appeared second on a three-band bill topped by Roogalator (whom the Sex Pistols had supported on their second ever gig) and tailed by the Vibrators. This show was also covered by *Sounds*, this time represented by Giovanni Dadomo. Giovanni was in a mood to be kind to all involved, even though Roogalator were about to slide down the slippery slope to unfashionability and the Vibrators were amongst the most blatantly cynical of punk bandwagon jumpers. He gave the Clash equal space with the headliners and, in spite of deriding the civic space's acoustics, played down the band's poor sound in favour of enthusing loud and long about their passion and commitment.

While he mentioned that there were 'a hundred or so' in the audience, Giovanni neglected to point out that the hall was only half full. That the Clash's friends in the music press were giving them an inordinately high ratio of reviews per number of gigs played was already plain, but only careful reading of their shameless propaganda revealed the supposed importance of the band to be out of all proportion to the size of the crowds they were able to draw. Nevertheless, Giovanni's enthusiastic hyperbole was far from being cynically motivated: he was genuinely entranced by the Clash experience, and he was by no means alone. Jon Savage, future author of *England's Dreaming*, saw his first punk concert that night and wrote in his diary of the Clash: 'Within ten seconds, I'm transfixed, within 30, changed forever.'

Another Clash-organised event was scheduled for Friday, 5 November, at the Royal College of Art (RCA). Called A Night of Treason in honour of Guy Fawkes, it featured the Clash, supported by the Rockets (whom the Clash had supported at Tiddenfoot Leisure Centre) and Subway Sect. Bernie had lined up press and record company interest, Pennie Smith was being sent along by the *NME* to take her first shots of the band and, just to make sure there was a record, Joe's friend and former 101er Jules Yewdall was also invited along with his camera.

On the night, however, as at the ULU, the RCA gig was marred by an ugly outbreak of violence. For years, no reason other than subcultural antipathy was given to explain why a contingent of long-haired types in the audience began hurling abuse and glasses at the stage during the Clash's set. Legend has it that Sid Vicious, determined to protect his friends, ran out from behind the stage and leaped, kamikaze style, into their midst. Whereupon, incensed by the bombardment and inspired by Sid's fearless display, Joe and Paul downed instruments and jumped in after him.

Truth to tell, the contingent was not particularly large, as Paul recalled in a 1991 interview with the *NME*'s Mary Ann Hobbs: 'Me and Joe checked these two blokes who was, like, chucking the stuff. We put our guitars down, jumped into the audience and gave 'em a kicking. I got back on stage and said to Mick, "Why wasn't you there?" And he goes, "Well, somebody's got to stay in tune."' Whatever his motivation, it would appear that Mick's refusal to get involved was the morally correct decision. The righteousness of his colleagues' position was put in some doubt in 1994, with the publication of Johnny Rotten's autobiography. Interviewed for the book, Marco Pirroni revealed that the glass-throwing long-hairs were actually intent on seeking revenge for an earlier incident in which Sid Vicious – newly released from Ashford Remand Centre after the 100 Club incident, but apparently loath to learn his lesson – had himself thrown bottles at the long-haired support band.

One of the enduring myths about the punk scene is that it only became violent when inundated with newcomers – labelled 'outside punks' by Caroline Coon – who had received all their information about punk behaviour from sensationalist reports in the tabloid press. While such coverage would certainly exacerbate the problem during late 1976 and early 1977, it was not responsible for starting it, and nor were the 'outside punks'. Violence had always been a part of the scene. Vivienne Westwood had provoked the fight at the Sex Pistols' show on 23 April at the Nashville, and

Mad Jane and Shane MacGowan had been responsible for the bloodshed at the Clash's ICA gig, but almost all the other more legendarily unpleasant incidents can be attributed to one person: Sid Vicious. It was he who had leaped in to the fray at the Nashville, famously chain-whipped Nick Kent at the 100 Club, thrown the glass at the Punk Festival and started the fight at the RCA. 'That can happen and *does* happen at many "hippy" rock concerts,' was temporary editor Steve Mick's spirited defence of such incidents in the October edition of *Sniffin' Glue*. 'It's just stupid, that's what it is, to blow up the violence in punk rock and so badly distort the truth!' Maybe, as he claimed, the violence was not widespread, but it has always been pervasive stuff: a little goes a long way.

Trouble was also being directed on to the scene from without before the media properly got to grips with punk. In an attempt to deflect blame from punks for instigating violence, Steve Mick's editorial also made vague references to street attacks on scene *habitués* by what he called 'discos' and 'footballs': that is, nightclub-goers and football hooligans. His admirable conclusion was 'It's all a bit silly, ain't it?' but the subheading he used for this part of his editorial sounded a tellingly defiant note: 'US AND THEM'.

The Clash's own reaction was at best ambivalent. On-stage at the ICA, responding to Jane and Shane's exhibition, Joe had sneered, 'All of you who think violence is tough: why don't you go home and collect stamps? That's much tougher.' Commenting on the same incident in Miles's November *NME* interview, Mick said, 'We definitely think it ain't hip. We think it's disgusting to be violent.' In the Clash *Sniffin' Glue* interview Steve Walsh had queried the band's image, wondering whether it was 'violent or suggestive of violence'. Mick had claimed that it reflected the band's 'no-nonsense' attitude. He believed violence on the punk scene was liable to escalate, but both he and Joe elected to take this as an indication that at least apathy was not holding sway. He hoped people would learn to 'channel their violence into music, or something creative'. This remark was the source of Paul's boiler suit slogan. When Miles attempted to quiz the band about it, Joe responded by waving a switch-blade under his nose and saying, 'Suppose I smash your face in and slit your nostrils with this, right? Well, if you don't learn anything from it, then it's not worth it, right? But suppose some guy comes up to me and tries to put one over on me, right? And I smash his face up and he learns something from it. Well, in a sense that's creative violence.' And in another sense, it's almost unbelievably stupid.

Bernie's contribution to the debate was a fragment of text lifted from Sixties pop-cultural document *Generation X*, which he had Sebastian incorporate in the flyer advertising the ICA show. Therein a mod recalled his part in seaside skirmishes with rockers: 'I'm not ashamed of it: I wasn't the only one. I joined in a few of the fights. I haven't enjoyed myself so much in a long time. It was great: the beach was like a battlefield. It was like we were taking over the country.' Paul was wont to boast in similar terms about his part in the Notting Hill Riot, not least in November's *London Weekend Show*

TV interview. During that same brief spot Mick facetiously, but irresponsibly, advocated beating up hippies: 'If there's any around, you should, like, jump into action immediately.' The following March, he defiantly informed the *NME*'s Tony Parsons, 'We ain't ashamed to fight', conveniently forgetting both his earlier rejections of violence and his preference for staying in tune at the moment of truth.

Intimidatory clothing, overly assertive speech (*right?*) and tendencies to make outlandish statements in interviews - waving guns and knives around the while – were by no means the only confused and confusing signals the Clash were giving off. The band's songs were characterised by aggressive delivery, mob-mentality terrace harmonies and brutal lyrical imagery; some of them included direct references to 'throwing a brick' or 'fighting in the road'. In late November, the Clash were to add two more songs to their repertoire. 'Hate and War' was partly inspired by the slogan on Joe's boiler suit, once more adapting the hippy salutation to state, 'And if I get aggression / I give it to them two time back.' 'Cheat' opens with the similarly uncompromising 'I get violent when I'm fucked up.'

The Clash may have claimed to be dealing in the currency of the day, reflecting the experiences of 'the kids' they were intending to address, but they often seemed to be justifying, even encouraging, violence as an expression of frustration and alienation. A reasonably well-centred individual like Paul Simonon might have been able to cope with the contradictions implicit in the glib slogan 'creative violence', but for unstable, high-velocity personalities like Mad Jane and Sid Vicious it was *carte blanche* to push the outside of the behavioural envelope. Instead of disowning Sid, or even remonstrating with him, Mick and Paul had covered for him following the Punk Festival incident, and Joe and Paul had backed him up in the RCA fight.

By the end of November 1976, the paranoiac siege mentality hinted at in Steve Mick's October *Sniffin' Glue* editorial was already well established on the punk scene, and the Clash had missed an opportunity to take a moral lead worthy of their rhetoric. Nobody in the band's camp had bothered to draw up the kind of pros and cons lists featured on Bernie's 1974 'What side of the bed' T-shirt, and nobody seemed to be thinking clearly enough to make the distinction between civil disobedience and mindless aggravation. As Bernie told Paul Rambali four years later, everything had happened so fast. A messy and unfocused battle was already under way, and it looked as though it might already be too late to define the exact identities of 'Us' and 'Them'.

The Clash's ambivalent attitude to violence rebounded on them almost immediately. The Damned had gone for the carrot and signed to the first label that showed an interest, Stiff. The Sex Pistols had played a waiting game, gigging for nearly a year before finally attracting the major-label deal Malcolm wanted. As the other well-known and acclaimed punk band, the Clash might have expected to be snapped up in the feeding frenzy following

EMI's netting of the scene leaders, but as October turned into November the band had to sit back and watch as two outer circle bands were signed instead: the Vibrators by RAK and the Stranglers by United Artists (UA). This despite the promotional efforts of the Clash's hardly unbiased friends in the music press not only in print, but also by word of mouth.

'I was friends with Jonh Ingham and Caroline Coon,' says Chris Parry. 'Neither of those two people had a car, but I had one.' Thus, Chris had chauffeured the other two to Sex Pistols gigs while himself intent on chasing that band for Polydor. When he lost out to EMI, Chris had been temporarily disconsolate. 'I remember Jonh saying, "Well, don't worry. You know the Clash are a great band, and you can get them, anyway."' He had accompanied the journalists to the ULU gig, and was impressed enough by what he saw to bring his director of A&R, Jim Crook, along to the RCA show. 'Somebody threw a bottle at Joe Strummer, almost took his fucking head off' is how Chris remembers it. 'He was really angry, and quite rightly so in my opinion. He came running down right by where Jim Crook was, and obviously thought he had thrown it . . . And it didn't do things a lot of good. Jim said, "If you think I'm signing *that* fucking band, you've got another think coming!" And he walked out.'

In spite of this not inconsiderable setback, Chris refused to give up. He had the authority to commission demos without higher approval and talked to Bernie about the possibility of doing so, in the hope that the results would persuade Jim Crook to think again. Wanting even the Clash's demos to be out of the ordinary, Bernie suggested bringing in a name producer acquaintance of his: Guy Stevens. Bernie had met Guy totally independently of Mick Jones. They just happened to live close to each other in Camden Town. Responding to another fast-talking ex-mod with more ideas than time to realise them, Bernie had cultivated the half-crazed producer as a potential ally in his planned assault on the fuddy-duddy record company establishment.

Bernie brought Guy along to Rehearsals to watch the band play, and Guy was immediately bowled over by the high energy and passion of the performance. 'They were doing "White Riot",' he told Charles Shaar Murray in 1979. 'And I just thought, "Right! RIOT! RIGHT! RIOT! Let's *goooooooh!*"' Things had not been going well for Guy since the break-up of his relationship with Violent Luck, and his stock had sunk even lower in music business circles. He saw the Clash as yet another chance to make a comeback. Paul and Terry were both impressed by his larger-than-life personality. Joe, remembering the sleevenotes to his Chuck Berry EP, was totally overawed. 'I used to listen to this EP a lot and stare at the sleeve,' he told *Mojo*'s Mark Hagen in 1994. 'So I knew his name from very early on.' Mick's feelings were, understandably, mixed. As he intimated in the *Clash On Broadway* booklet, although he had never lost his admiration for Guy's talents, he still carried some resentment about his sacking from the band that had become Violent Luck, and he also harboured fears that something similar might happen again.

While discussions were going on, the Clash continued with their eclectic approach to live work. On 11 November, a gig was arranged at the Lacy Lady, a soul boy haunt in Ilford, east London, with Subway Sect again providing support. Bearing in mind Steve Mick's comments about tension between punks and 'discos', the gig might well appear to have been asking for another ULU-style confrontation. Reviewing it for the first issue of his fanzine *48 Thrills*, Adrian Thrills mused on the possibility: 'the disco audience didn't know how to react. Would it be cool to dance? sit down? beat each other up?' In fact, the division between punks and soul boys was not quite so clean cut as that between punks and teds. For a start, soul boys were not exactly the same species as Steve Mick's 'discos', who were just your average nightclub-goers of the day. In effect, while punks were one type of latter-day mod, soul boys were another, and the difference between them was further blurred by the fact that their wardrobes were not dissimilar.

Pop sociologists have amused themselves for years by debating who took the role of the chicken and who the egg in the Soul Boy/Punk Style Crossover. Some commentators have maintained that the early punk look took a great deal from the soul boy styles of the 1975–6 period. Adrian Thrills made *his* position clear when, in his review, he described the Lacy Lady as 'one of those soul discos where kids are now starting to dress in the new trendy punk fashion'. In his autobiography Johnny Rotten rubbished the idea that punks stole clothing tips from soul boys, insisting that he and his similarly eccentrically dressed friends had started something of a punky trend when they visited the Lacy Lady one night earlier in 1976, and dominated the dancefloor with their wild cavortings.

His claim is both self-aggrandising and simplistic. There was, in truth, a two-way exchange of stylistic influence. As early as 1974, the soul boys' mod-like obsession with up-to-the-minute clothing had already led some of them to investigate the wares in Sex. In return, their own short hairstyles, mohair jumpers and plastic, or 'jelly', sandals did indeed become features of the nascent punk scene. Once that scene was established, there was also some social mixing: punks attended soul clubs like the Lacy Lady and Crackers on Wardour Street, and soul boys were interested enough to check out some of the early punk gigs. 'Suddenly punk was almost like a kitsch thing, in that it was totally the opposite of what the kids were listening to,' Gary Kemp, a former soul boy and regular at Crackers and Lacy Lady, told *The Face*'s Chris Salewicz in 1981.

Although David Bowie's then current plastic soul period offered some common ground, the distance between the dance music of the day and punk rock was considerably greater than the distance between R&B and Motown singles and the music of the Who and Small Faces had been in the early to mid Sixties. As Gary Kemp maintained, soul boy culture was oriented more towards records and clubs than bands and live gigs: 'I think the idea of going every night to see a band as a form of enjoyment never really appealed to a lot of those people. They *are* people who like being looked at: that's why dancing is so important, and why people try to beat each other at dancing. It's also why clothes are important. So punk soon lost that excitement, and those kids went back to the DJs, much to their delight.'

The initial *musical* crossover was both limited and short-lived, Subway Sect being quite possibly the only punk band to include former soul boys. The union bore its fruit a couple of years later. Late Seventies Bowie Nights in Soho and Covent Garden clubs attracted a clientele comprising both soul boys and former punks, and this cultural mix was responsible for hatching the New Romantic movement and producing some of the more successful UK pop groups of the early Eighties. Gary Kemp himself admits to having been inspired by punk's DIY ethic, if not the music, when he formed Spandau Ballet.

Even if there had been an outbreak of violence between the two tribes at the Lacy Lady on Thursday, 11 November 1976, there would have been little chance of it getting out of hand: only 20 people turned up. With low audience turnouts and less than keen record companies, the Clash hype needed to be stepped up a gear. On 22 October, Stiff had released the Damned's single 'New Rose', the first recording by a representative of the UK punk movement. Jonh Ingham had made it single of the week in *Sounds*. In the light of this development in the Damned's career, Caroline Coon was quite justified in interviewing them for *Melody Maker*. Instead of running the piece on its own, however, she twinned it with an interview she conducted on 5 November – the day of the RCA gig – with the Clash for no discernible record or tour related purpose, and rushed both into the 13 November issue under the joint headline 'NEW FACES: Caroline Coon introduces two hot punk rock bands'. Thus, ironically, the Clash got their first full-length interview in the mainstream music press by riding piggy-back on the achievements of the Damned. It is also worth noting that the Clash piece was accompanied by a large photograph singling out Paul Simonon on-stage at the 100 Club, and that by this point Caroline and Paul's relationship was no longer purely professional.

In the interview she gave for *Rotten* Caroline made several somewhat grandiose claims about her punk band interviewing technique. She said it was her university 'training' in sociology that had made her realise the importance of class as a key to understanding the movement, which in turn had prompted her to enquire about the bands' backgrounds. Whereas it is true that she was the first journalist to examine the Clash's upbringings in order to establish a context for their music and outlook, Steve Walsh had already taken a sociological approach in *Sniffin' Glue*. Nor was it as original as she seemed to think to reproduce excerpts from Joe's lyrics: again, Steve had beaten her to it. In *Rotten*, perhaps anticipating criticism, she claimed to have deliberately kept her own voice and opinions out of her punk pieces, despite reservations about certain aspects of the emerging punk manifesto, because she was 'not from the Tom Wolfe school of journalism that puts yourself at the centre of an article'.

In fact, Caroline did ask the Clash to defend their position. She took issue with their dismissal of hippies, questioned whether rock'n'roll had the power to change things, and wondered whether the band themselves would be as interested in upsetting the status quo once they achieved commercial success. All great stuff as far as it went; the problem was that it did not go far enough. Caroline neglected to pursue her arguments and to make the band justify their sometimes wild statements. Her emphasis on their individual backgrounds was inspired, if only because it forced them to tell all kinds of lies in the name of authenticity, but again, she missed the opportunity to expose those lies, preferring instead to take what the band said at face value. It may be that she was intentionally co-operating in the establishment of the Clash Myth, whether for the sake of her boyfriend or, like Jonh Ingham with his Sex Pistols piece, for the furtherance of her own career. Alternatively, she may have placed her trust in the band and been unknowingly duped.

Asked for their comments on contemporary society, the three Clash members present volunteered answers that, for all their passion, commitment and occasional exaggeration, sounded more rehearsed than heartfelt. Mick announced, 'It's alienating the individual.' Joe bemoaned the lack of leisure options, the state of radio and the paucity of affordable housing. Picking up the ball and running out of the stadium with it, Paul prophesied that this situation would precipitate more unrest from 'the kids', which would in turn encourage the government to bring back National Service, 'and we'll all be sent down to South Africa or Rhodesia to protect white capital's interests. And then we'll all be slaughtered . . .' But he maintained that rock'n'roll had the potential to change things. He promised that, if the band made any money, they wouldn't just take it for themselves, like the Stones or Led Zeppelin, but would reinvest it in getting 'something going'. Joe agreed. 'I'm not going to spend all my money on drugs. I'm going to start a radio station.'

Sounds had already gorged itself on punk coverage with its Punk Festival issue. Furthermore, both Giovanni and Jonh had recently filed partisan Clash live reviews, and any further ravings from them at this stage would be too transparently nepotistic to have the desired effect. Luckily, the Clash now had on their side another writer with access to the paper: Buckinghamshire stringer Kris Needs turned up to cover the band's next gig, on Thursday, 18 November, at the Nag's Head in High Wycombe. The support was Reading band Clayson and the Argonauts. Kris blamed another poor attendance – the small pub venue was only half full – on that night's televised Miss World contest, but brushed aside such trifling matters, instead employing the by then traditional combat metaphors to capture the band's impact: 'The Clash are now firing with more compressed energy than a flame-thrower at full blast. They play with almost frightening conviction and intensity, each number a rapid-fire statement delivered like a knock-out blow.'

He made no pretence at objectivity: Joe had recently dyed his hair blond, but only the truly besotted would have likened him, as Kris did, to a 'paint-spattered Greek god'. On 5 November the Vibrators had released their début single, 'We Vibrate', followed a week later by a single backing Chris Spedding, 'Pogo Dancing'. On the 26th, the Sex Pistols were due to release their first single, 'Anarchy In The UK'. The true purpose of Kris's review was revealed in its fourth paragraph: 'The Clash . . . seem forced to take a back seat on the new wave recording front while groups like the Damned, the Pistols and Vibrators shove singles out. Why is it that the hottest band this country has got hasn't yet had a chance to get themselves on vinyl? Dunno, but going on last Thursday's set, it won't be long before some record company wakes up.' Wishful thinking it might have been, but Kris's attempt to push the record companies' panic buttons was timely, if not exactly subtle.

By the time his review saw print, the Clash had already recorded demos for Polydor. Sometime in mid-November, the band spent two days in the record company's own studio at 17–19 Stratford Place, just off Oxford Street, and taped five songs: 'Career Opportunities', 'White Riot', 'Janie Jones', 'London's Burning' and '1977'. The sessions were by no means a success, and the fact that the demo versions of 'Career Opportunities' and 'Janie Jones' were included on the 1991 compilation *Clash On Broadway* had more to do with paying sentimental posthumous tribute to Guy Stevens than any belated recognition of their artistic merit. For similar reasons, in the booklet accompanying the CD boxed set, Mick put the problems at the sessions down to the differing objectives of Guy on the one hand and Chris Parry and Polydor staff engineer Vic Smith on the other: Guy, as ever, wanted to make an incendiary masterpiece; Chris and Vic wanted a simple, serviceable tape to sell the band to the higher-ups at Polydor. It was left to Roadent to suggest that, by November 1976, Guy's eccentricities and addictions were so far advanced that they were interfering with his judgement and skill.

Discounting the static electric shocks Terry kept getting from the studio's nylon carpet, recording the basic tracks went well enough, with, so Mick told Kris Needs, Guy 'really inciting' the band. It was these same crazed urgings, however, that troubled the Polydor representatives. 'We all had a lot of respect for Guy Stevens,' says Terry. 'It was evident that the A&R man paying for the sessions and the engineer didn't have the same regard for him, for whatever reason, and they weren't working in the most positive way with him, we felt. Joe actually said to me, "They've got him numbered." So the fact that he got drunk towards the end of it, and blew it, we felt was as a direct result of the lack of co-operation he was getting from those guys.' Although himself not present for the entire duration of recording, Chris Parry admits that Guy's reputation had preceded him, and that Vic Smith's chief function had been to keep an eye on the erratic producer. 'I was there for a while, and Guy was a bit all over the place.'

By no means all the tension was confined to the control room. Like many of those who appreciated the band and recognised that the subject matter of the songs was an important part of what the Clash were about, Guy was frustrated by his inability to make out the lyrics. When it came time to record the vocals, the producer insisted the singer make an effort to pronounce the words clearly. 'So I did it, and it sounded like Matt Monroe,' Joe told the *NME*'s Tony Parsons the following March. 'I thought, "I'm never doing *that* again." To me, our music is like Jamaican stuff: if they can't hear it, they're not supposed to hear it. It's not for them if they can't understand it.'

As a result of the compound tensions and his own method of taking refuge from them, when it came time to do the mixes, Guy was so tired and emotional he was unable to continue. It was left to Vic Smith to finish off and mix the demos, and the band were not happy with the results. Listening to the songs today and comparing them with the later album versions, it is not difficult to guess why: the musical fireworks Guy had supposedly ignited in the studio arrived on tape as damp squibs; and Joe's phrasing is so risibly hammy and precise it gives the strong impression that he deliberately set out to express his displeasure at receiving vocal instruction by sabotaging the recordings.

Although they would later take a more sympathetic view of his role in proceedings, the months immediately following the sessions found the Clash more than willing to point the finger of blame at the disgraced Guy. 'We picked Guy Stevens because we wanted a nut case to produce the band, because that's what our music is all about,' Bernie told *Melody Maker* in January 1977. 'But there are different kinds of nut case, and it didn't work out with him.' Two months later, when talking to Tony Parsons, Joe avoided mentioning Guy by name, but was even more scathing about the 'famous producers' the band had tried who were 'all too pissed to work'. There had been only the one.

While Polydor pondered the demos and the wider music business world digested the latest Clash propaganda, the band's campaign received yet another boost. The Sex Pistols were about to embark on a high-profile national tour, and the Clash were invited to occupy one of the support slots. Typically, Malcolm McLaren's motive was hardly altruistic. First announced in the 13 November 1976 issue of *Sounds*, the tour was originally intended to be a package showcasing both UK punk and US new wave, co-headlined by the Sex Pistols and the Ramones, and also featuring the Vibrators (with Chris Spedding) and Talking Heads. The selection of acts was influenced by business considerations: all were signed to record companies and had records out, and the idea was that some of the costs would therefore be covered by RAK for the Vibrators, and Phonogram – the UK distributor of US label Sire – for both American bands.

The following week, the music press announced that the American bands had pulled out. In her diary entry for 20 December 1976 (as quoted by Fred and Judy Vermorel in *Sex Pistols: The Inside Story*) Malcolm's secretary Sophie Richmond reported a convoluted chain of hearsay offering a reason why: Jonh Ingham had told her that Sire boss Seymour Stein had told Jonh that Phonogram had told Seymour that they were prepared to back a Ramones co-headlining tour as long as it did not involve the Pistols. In other words, it was a matter of record company politics. Having promised name acts (that is, name to the still relatively small circle of punk and new wave *cognoscenti*), Malcolm was put in the unenviable position of having little over two weeks in which to assemble an equally prestigious package. The Damned were brought in as second on the bill support because they were the only other established punk band with a current single and with a record label willing to meet their tour costs. Malcolm fell back on his old New York Dolls contacts to find a New York band of impressive enough status: he convinced Johnny Thunders that his still unsigned Heartbreakers would stand a better chance of making it via the UK scene. The Clash were asked along merely to shore up the bottom of the bill. When Chris Spedding and the Vibrators dropped out the following week, the poster Jamie Reid designed for what had by now been dubbed the Anarchy Tour left the Clash with no illusions about their poor-relation status among the remaining bands: there was their name, in insultingly small print yet again, crammed into the bottom left-hand corner like the afterthought it was.

At least the renewal of their association with the Sex Pistols brought the Clash an immediate reward: more media interest. London Weekend Television had filmed the 15 November 1976 Sex Pistols gig at Notre Dame Hall, off Leicester Square. This, plus brief interviews Janet Street-Porter conducted with the Pistols, various fans (including the Bromley Contingent) and the Clash, was used as the basis for the *London Weekend Show*, broadcast in the capital region only at 1.15 p.m. on Sunday, 28 November. The Pistols had already appeared playing 'Anarchy In The UK' on Manchester-based Granada TV's *So It Goes*, and as the focus of a brief run-down on the new punk movement on BBC1's national early evening magazine show, *Nationwide*. Nevertheless, the *London Weekend Show* – despite being a local programme broadcast in a relatively low-profile slot – was the first real attempt at a documentary about punk. Its bias was still towards the Sex Pistols, but it was also the first television programme to do anything more than namecheck the Clash.

The researchers had done their job well, plainly drawing heavily on existing music press coverage of the movement. Echoes of Caroline Coon's August punk feature could be heard throughout Janet Street-Porter's narration, which touched on established rock stars being out of touch, the DIY ethic and the difference between bands genuinely inspired by the Pistols and those jumping on the bandwagon. She even mentioned the Suburban Studs. But, like Allan Jones, she also questioned the negativity of the lyrics. Her interview with the Clash, conducted at Rehearsals, covered much the same ground: the stale soullessness of the current music scene; the topicality and social relevance of the Clash's lyrics; the lack of opportunities for young people. The soft target of the hippy generation received yet another broadside, with Mick making a remark that was destined to come back and haunt him: 'I suppose it ain't their fault. They've had too much dope.'

Far more impressive than the content of this somewhat stilted interview was its presentation. The band – minus Terry – were filmed in front of the pink drapes, next to the jukebox, dressed in their Pop-Art/Lettrist clothes, looking romantically pale and thin. Pushed up close together to fit into the frame, they appeared to be not so much sitting in a row as wrapped around each other. The few smiles and laughs were sly or knowing, and exchanged amongst themselves. Mick gave off a brooding intensity; Paul rocked backwards and forwards throughout like a traumatised child; Joe – smoking now – sat sideways on to the camera and, eyelids lowered disdainfully, sneered his deliberately inarticulate replies over his shoulder. There was – as Jon Savage suggested in *England's Dreaming* – a distinct whiff of amphetamine psychosis, whether real or affected, about the proceedings. Thus, whereas the band looked comfortable together and mutually reliant – in other words, exactly like a gang – the atmosphere between the Clash and the intruding camera crew crackled with barely suppressed hostility. They didn't get to play live, like the Pistols, but their body language was a performance in itself: pure Us and Them.

Barry Miles, genuinely enthused by the ICA gig, had turned up to interview the Clash for the *NME* not long after Caroline Coon had done likewise for *Melody Maker*. Scooped by Caroline's impressive feat of conducting her interview on the Friday and completing her feature in time for the following Monday evening deadline, editor Nick Logan – rather than take a lame second place – had chosen to sit on Miles's feature until the Clash's inclusion on the Anarchy Tour, and involvement by association in the attendant hoo-ha, provided justification for its belated inclusion in his paper's 11 December issue.

Miles's use of extensive song quotes betrayed his familiarity with the *Sniffin' Glue* interview and also suggested that it had by now become band policy to hand out lyric sheets to interviewers. The topics discussed confirmed the preparation undergone by both interviewer and interviewees, covering much the same ground as the band's two previous full-length excursions into print. On those occasions, however, the Clash had encountered people who were, if not exactly fellow members, then at least satellites of the punk scene; as an outsider, Miles had come in for much the same treatment as the television crew would, the intimidation climaxing with Joe's totally over-the-top flick-knife stunt. This lame-brained piece of shock theatre undermined an otherwise sound introduction to the Clash manifesto as it stood in early November, both by making Joe look foolish and by contradicting his slick opening announcement, 'I think people ought to know that we're anti-fascist, we're anti-violence, we're anti-racist and we're pro-creative.'

Unbelievably, Miles refused either to object to the knife-wielding incident at the time or to pour scorn on it afterwards from the safety of his desk. Instead, he chose to accept it as an indication of the band's authenticity. In retrospect, his swallowing of the Clash line – more completely than any previous interviewer – served to make him look foolish too; or, at least, gullible. The *NME*'s belated attempt to get in with punk's movers and shakers was further evidenced by the sub-editor's mythologising feature title, 'EIGHTEEN FLIGHT ROCK AND THE SOUND OF THE WESTWAY' (the first part a reference to Mick's tower block home), and by the selection and layout of Pennie Smith's backstage RCA photos: full-on and profile head and shoulders pictures of the individual band members were close-cropped to resemble police mug-shots, then arranged in a column and captioned with quotes as if illustrating a newspaper article on some bank robbery or gangland purge. Again, it didn't quite come off: a stray picture of Subway Sect's Vic Godard was identified as Paul Simonon, to whom was attributed a statement made by Joe Strummer; the picture of Paul was identified as Terry Chimes; there was no picture of Terry; and by the time the article was printed, Terry was no longer the Clash drummer anyway.

For many years, the Clash made out that the problem of violence – specifically the bombardment of the stage at the RCA – was chiefly responsible for Terry's decision to leave the band on the eve of the Anarchy Tour. Mick more than hinted at this in the stream of invective he poured on to the heads of Clash drummers past during the March 1977 Tony Parsons interview. In his contribution to 'The Story Of The Clash' in *The Armagideon Times* Joe spelled it out in no uncertain terms: 'One day during a particularly nasty gig when the bottles and cans were coming down like rain, Terry Chimes quit after watching a wine bottle come flying over and smash into a million pieces on his hi-hat.' Paul gave the same reason in 1991's *Clash On Broadway* booklet, wherein Terry was at least and at last offered the opportunity to deny his supposed cowardice: 'Nothing to do with bottles. I never minded that.'

In that same booklet Paul came closer to the truth when he offered the secondary explanation that Terry was not particularly enamoured of the Clash's leftist political direction. Joe went on to suggest that the drummer was more interested in personal gain. These points Terry does allow, up to a point. 'We used to argue about politics constantly. Well, not constantly: we took different positions, and argued periodically, never changing our stance. I always thought it was a mistake to overemphasise the politics, because implicit in that were the things like "We don't want to become pop stars, we don't want to make a lot of money." And I said, "Well, we *are* attempting to become famous and sell lots of records and become very important, and if we do that, then we'll come across as hypocrites", to which they never really had a proper answer. They would just say things like "Oh, you don't understand."'

Terry did understand; he just didn't agree. He lived in Hackney, ran a car (and wanted a better one), had his own social circle and was beginning to find the Clash regime both enervating and restricting. 'Rehearsing seven nights a week. No messing about. I had other friends and other things to do.

They were all just doing that and nothing else, really. It was part of the brainwashing thing that your priority must be the band, and therefore you never got involved with much else. I never really subscribed to that.'

After Keith Levene's departure, Terry had taken over as the band's token outsider. 'He didn't really fit in,' says Sebastian, 'because he wouldn't wear the gear.' 'Terry Chimes was a one,' laughs Glen Matlock. 'I remember coming out of Rehearsals and I saw this bird who I thought was gorgeous, and I said, "*Phwooar!* Look at that!" And he said, "Yeah, great, innit? The woodwork's in really good nick", and I said, "*What?*" And he was talking about this Morris Traveller that'd gone past. We'd say, "Are you gonna come out?" and he'd say, "Nah, I'm gonna go and put some shelves up." Which is where he was at, you know.' His refusal to be bullied or brainwashed into wholesale adoption of the macho gang mentality hardly marked Terry down as a weak link, but some people chose to construe his determined individualism that way. 'I don't remember any reason being given to us for him not being there,' says Mark Perry, recalling the *Sniffin' Glue* interview. 'But everyone seemed to know that he wasn't a proper member of the group. That he wasn't one of the people that was going to do interviews because he was "just the drummer" sortathing. That was the impression.' Tony Parsons got to know the Clash when they were officially a three-piece, which goes some way to explaining why, in *The Boy Looked At Johnny*, Terry was described as an 'unsatisfactory drummer' who had been 'fired and rehired constantly throughout 1976 and early 1977'.

No one involved with the Clash has ever suggested that Terry was fired. Mick's unhappiness with his decision to quit was recorded in the following spring's *NME* interview with Tony. In the *Clash On Broadway* booklet Paul remembered being aggrieved enough to threaten damage to Terry's car. 'I could have hit him with a spade,' Joe told the *NME*'s Paul Du Noyer in 1981. 'Joe was quite upset about it,' says Terry. 'Even when I rejoined in 1982, he kept talking about that one day when I came in and resigned. "The sun was shining, I went into Rehearsals, I felt good . . . and then you came in and said you wanted to leave." He never forgave me, in a way.' But the band members were too caught up in the punk image to allow themselves to appear hurt for long. 'It was anger for a day or so, and then, "OK, so we'll find someone else. That's no big deal."' Terry agreed to stay on until a replacement had been found.

If he had been as disposable as Mark Perry and Tony Parsons were given to believe, the band would not have been so annoyed by Terry's decision to leave. Admittedly, sentiment played only a part in the matter: things were beginning to happen for the Clash, and this was an irritating distraction. Also, auditioning is a dispiriting and time-consuming business for any band, let alone one with such a hard-line (if not particularly well-defined) agenda as the Clash. But if Terry had been truly unsatisfactory and not a valued band member, this would have been the ideal time to replace him for somebody more sympathetic to the cause, and the others would have leaped at the chance. On the cover of *The Clash* Terry is credited as Tory Crimes. This has always been taken as proof of the band's enduring spite, it being an apparently backstabbing reference to his materialist outlook. In fact, the nickname was a joke thought up by Roadent – the recently converted ex-fascist - while Terry was still with the group, and one which the drummer took in good part. 'There wasn't much of a reaction at the time. It didn't seem important either way. It's just that everyone's been asking me about it for umpteen years!'

According to Terry, he simply happened not to be around when the *Sniffin' Glue* interview took place. He was absent from all subsequent early interviews not because he was an embarrassment who would not dress correctly and could not be trusted to say the right thing; nor because he had never been considered a true member of the band; but because, from early November onwards, he was already an *ex*-member of the band. 'I actually said I wanted to leave quite early on, just after Keith, I think. So there was quite a long period when I was leaving, but still doing the gigs, and most of the interviews happened during that period.'

His bombshell left the rest of the band in a quandary. It would be difficult to impress the meaning of being part of the Clash upon a newcomer, someone who had not shared the formative experiences and discussions of the past months. Also, taking on an established musician from outside the punk scene would undermine both the DIY ethic and the band's street credibility. The most ideologically sound option would be to promote someone from within the Clash's immediate circle. Paul's brother Nick, who had begun playing the drums, was briefly considered, but even in a youth culture it is possible to be too young: he had only just turned 17. 'They wanted to teach *me* the drums at one point, but I was totally uncoordinated,' laughs Sebastian, also mindful of the strain his background would have placed on the Clash propaganda machine. Less testing, with the odd tweak here and there, might have been that of the recently arrived Roadent, who was also considered, at least by Joe. 'Joe wanted somebody who couldn't play fuck-all,' Roadent told *Melody Maker*'s Frances Lass in 1979. 'But Mick wasn't having any. Mick wanted to be a star.'

His romantic streak had encouraged Joe to embrace the DIY ethic completely. More musically minded, Mick was practical enough to realise that the Clash already had at least their fair share of eager amateurs, and he also knew from experience that, more so than any other component part, a poor drummer makes for a bad band. In the end, his argument prevailed and the Clash came up with a compromise that would sidestep charges of using their high-profile position to recruit an established musician: they placed an anonymous display ad in the *Melody Maker* classifieds of 20 November. It included Rehearsals' phone number and read: 'AMAZING YOUNG DRUMMER WANTED for inciting group with exciting prospects.' With just two weeks to go before the Anarchy Tour started, there followed a frenzy of auditions.

In September 1975, Rob Harper began to attend Sussex University in Brighton. He had been a drummer from the age of 15, but had switched to guitar a year or so previously, and when he met fellow student, guitarist and high-energy rock'n'roll enthusiast Bill Broad, the two decided to form a band together. The Rockettes (not to be confused with occasional Clash support band the Rockets) were a Sixties-style garage outfit whose repertoire included the Kingsmen's 'Louie Louie' and several Yardbirds songs. In spring 1976, via his home-town friends Siouxsie Sioux and Steve Severin, Bill heard all about a London band called the Sex Pistols with a not dissimilar musical bent. During the Easter break, on 4 April, he joined the Bromley Contingent to catch the Pistols at the El Paradise strip club in Soho's Brewer Street, and was immediately won over.

Back in Brighton, he told Rob about his discovery. When their third term (and first year) ended that June, Rob returned home to Loughton in Essex and Bill to Bromley, where he slotted into a more regular membership of the Bromley Contingent. Through attending the Sex Pistols gigs at the 100 Club over the summer Bill cultivated an acquaintance with both the band and their manager. He also introduced Rob to the Sex Pistols live experience, and the duo later took a tape of the Rockettes along to Sex. Malcolm, still interested at that time in promoting punk as a movement and looking to fill the bill for the Punk Festival, expressed interest in auditioning them. This trial duly took place at Rehearsals, but although Malcolm offered the opinion that their bassist was 'quite sexy', he was more scathing about Bill's talents and nothing came of it.

Rob maintains it was via an ad that he placed in *Melody Maker* that Tony James first met Bill. The former London SS bass player subsequently enticed the latter away to join Chelsea, whereupon he adopted the new identity of Billy Idol. Neither former Rockette returned to university, Billy because he had a new band and prospects and Rob because – having already completed one college course – he was sick of writing essays. His alliance with Mick Jones's best friend meant that Billy was kept up to date with new developments in the Clash camp. Sometime in the days immediately prior to 20 November 1976, possibly to make amends for having bailed out on him, Billy phoned Rob to tip him the wink about the ad. 'He said, "Look, the Clash are looking for a drummer,"' recalls Rob. '"The number's in *Melody Maker*. Why don't you ring it and see what you can do?" So that's what happened.'

Rob had already seen the Clash. He had been amongst the select crowd at Ilford's Lacy Lady on 11 November. 'I've got to say, it just totally knocked me out. I said at the time, it was like three Eddie Cochrans on-stage. The drummer played in a dry, clipped way and looked like a dry, clipped person, but the three frontmen were just the business. There was just so much force coming at you: it was so *alive* and colourful. I thought they were absolutely wonderful.'

When Rob arrived at Rehearsals, Rusty Egan had just finished trying out for the band. In October 1977, he told *ZigZag*'s Robin Banks that 'he used to play with the Clash'. Like a lot of other drummers who made this claim, the truth was that Rusty's audition was the full extent of his association with the band: for all his enthusiasm for punk and mouthy self-promotion, he was found wanting and turned down. A few months later, he would be more successful in talking himself into the drum seat with Glen Matlock's post-Pistols band the Rich Kids, and after that, via his involvement with the New Romantic club scene, he would go on to form Visage with Steve Strange. Back at the auditions, though, the Clash didn't always get to call the shots. Many of the drummers who had come along to try out for this anonymous band were either unfamiliar with their musical philosophy or familiar with it and deeply unimpressed. A significantly high proportion walked in, turned on their heels and walked out again.

Rob was far more empathetic. 'I didn't judge them on ability at all, because I've always been like an educated garage player. I've got the knowledge of a lot of good players, but I hate technical musicianship. I was sort of good enough to play in the Troggs. On the other hand, they were below even that! No, the musicianship was good, really. Paul's was fairly rudimentary, but that's what I like in a bassist. You're playing this stuff, you don't want some guy playing fluidly around an instrument, making it sing or whatever. It's more of an African drum thumping away, vaguely in tune. He was using this really cheap bass guitar. Mick was OK. Joe was a hard, scrubbing rhythm guitarist. Once he got on-stage, he was just flailing around breaking strings, but he was quite good.'

In addition to having caught the band live and having been primed by Billy about their outlook, Rob had also seen some of their media coverage. 'They'd had the press from Caroline Coon, and I sussed out when I got there that she was going out with Paul Simonon, so I knew there was a little insider dealing going on. I came to them knowing that they were going to be very big. I'd seen them, and they were marvellous. I knew that this was going to be something worth being in if you wanted a "career opportunity" in the music world.'

Like Caroline, Rob had taken Sociology at university, and also like her, he relates his grounding in that discipline to his fascination with the subcultural aspects of punk. At 27, his age was a problem, but he was fresh-faced enough to pass for several years younger. Digging deeper into his past would have revealed – yet again – middle class origins and a public school education, but at least he had been brought up in a council house and had a leftish political bent. As for musical compatibility, when his turn came to sit behind the drums, he made an instant impression. 'They definitely perked up as soon as I played, because I was very good in terms of what they were used to,' he says matter-of-factly. 'I'd been playing drums for 12 years at that point. There's a part of me that's a complete maniac, and I can really do that on drums, which is what they liked. I had some skill, but I was really violent.'

Rob might not have been 100 per cent ideal for the Clash in every department, but of the people they auditioned he came closest. After some deliberation, they offered him the job. Amazingly, he turned it down. As appears to be inevitable with those connected with the Clash – a circle in which everyone involved was encouraged to analyse every motive from every conceivable angle – Rob offers a complex of reasons for this decision.

His character assessments of the band members and their manager do not differ greatly from those made by other associates of the band around this time, but the same cannot always be said of his response to them. Of Bernie, he says, 'After you'd spoken to him for a bit, you found him kind of provocative and unpleasant. He'd use all this heavy duty psychology to goad you into realising something he wanted you to realise. He was quite a clever guy. Not likeable, but not *that* unlikeable. I always feel sorry for people who come in for a lot of stick from everybody else.' Although he recognised the poseur in Mick, he found him the easiest to get on with. 'Much more emotional on the surface than the others, obviously striking poses and throwing shapes, but so transparently so you found him quite charming. He was a pretty sincere guy.'

Interestingly, it was neither Bernie the tactician nor Mick the musician whom Rob identified as the group's 'leader' figure. As he had with the 101ers, Joe had by this time begun to assert a quiet authority within the Clash camp. Rob describes him as 'quite likeable, even though you knew he was manipulating you'. Paul was 'like a gentleman, a nice polite boy most of the time, always to the women, and usually to me and to other people'. Almost perversely, then, as Rob himself acknowledges, it was Paul who presented him with his first real obstacle to joining the Clash. 'Even before he said anything or even looked at me, I knew I wouldn't be able to get on with this guy. You meet people like that, occasionally, that you're just incompatible with. I took an active dislike to him within about five minutes of getting there, not through any fault of his.'

The second deterrent made itself evident shortly afterwards. Whatever his personal feelings about them, Rob quickly came to the conclusion that Mick and especially Joe were so charismatic that it would be close to impossible for him to assert himself. 'I'm a leadership type of person. Everything I'd been involved in up to that point I'd either been running, organising the whole thing or had an equal say in. I've got quite a few ideas and things to say, and when you're around Joe Strummer, you're never going to be at the apex of the pyramid.' He also deduced that a fourth strong-willed member was not even desired. 'There was this assumption that they would be telling people who came to them what they would be doing. They had this thing going, and what they wanted was a really good drummer, kicking shit at the back and minding his business the rest of the time. Just hanging around, second only to the backline in lack of importance. And there's no way I could do that.'

These reservations were compounded by something that had been niggling away in the recesses of his mind ever since he'd agreed to follow

Billy's advice and respond to the ad. It was his not insignificant ego that had prompted Rob to switch from drums to guitar in the first place, 'because I felt it wasn't much good being at the back'. Hence the explanation he gave the band for not taking them up on their offer. 'I said to them, "I can't do this because I'm trying to be a guitarist now", but what I meant was, "I can't do this because you are powerful characters and you're in charge here, and there's no room left for me to express the kind of things I'd want to express. I'm more than just a drummer; or I'd like to be."'

Panic by now having begun to set in among members of the Clash camp, Terry Chimes suddenly found he was no longer being given the cold shoulder. 'After they auditioned 50 or so, and couldn't find anyone they liked, they changed to a reconciliatory mood,' he laughs. 'Bernie in particular kept on and on and on telling me I was making a mistake. He couldn't understand how anyone could walk out on what he saw as his masterplan taking shape.' Nevertheless, Terry remained adamant that he was going to quit.

So Rob was persuaded back for a second audition, and Mick Jones's charm was turned full on. 'I said, "I can't do it, I'd be wasting your time." And Mick said, "But look, this is going to be a classic rock'n'roll tour. Why don't you come on it and see what you think? We need you. After we've done the tour, we'll all sit down and talk about it." And that was the final arrangement. That was how it stood.' He might have let himself be talked round, but Rob was under no illusions about the situation. 'You mustn't think that Mick was mad keen that I was the drummer for them: it was more a matter of expediency, because they had to have *somebody*.'

Rehearsals began immediately. 'Very thorough. Turn up every day at 11 or 12 and run through the set a couple of times.' He never got to play 'How Can I Understand The Flies', abandoned at this point either because it no longer fit in with the rest of the material or because its drum pattern was dependent on Terry's style. Also dropped was 'Deadly Serious', probably because it was not a particularly remarkable song, though a similar riff resurfaced the following year in 'Capital Radio'. The repertoire for the tour initially numbered 11 songs, which Rob listed – along with self-addressed tips and reminders – in the front of the diary he kept for the duration of his time with the Clash: '1977', 'Protex Blue', '48 Hours', 'What's My Name', 'Janie Jones', 'I'm So Bored With The USA', 'White Riot', 'London's Burning', 'Career Opportunities', 'Deny' and encore '1-2 Crush On You'.

'Mick Jones thought he knew – and did, in most cases - how Terry played the drums on all these songs, and he was telling me what to play, which is fair enough,' says Rob. 'I made the mistake of asking him, "Does Terry do the hi-hats four to the bar, or eight?" And he said, "Oh, eight." So there we were doing, say, 'White Riot' at a hundred miles an hour, and me going, "tsch-tsch-tsch-tsch-*tschhhhhhhhh* . . ." Subsequently, listening to Terry on the album, I found he was just doing four. So my skills were strained!' In order to help him learn his parts, Rob asked if he could record one of the early rehearsals. Already concerned with maintaining as tight a grip on their public image as possible, the Clash initially refused permission, but in view of the limited number of rehearsal opportunities remaining, they reluctantly gave way.

The tape is fascinating not only because it appears to be the only surviving record of Rob's stint with the band, but also because it captures the rest of the Clash with their guard down at this, the most self-conscious and studied period of their career. Rob says they were 'just slopping through the material', explaining why there is only occasional evidence of his characteristically fluid, vigorous style. 'Janie Jones' misses Terry's crisp staccato, and '1977' sounds lifeless and mid-paced.

Joe's guitar was down to two strings on this particular day, and funds did not appear to be available for replacements, so he concentrated on singing. Or, rather, he just sang: the evidence suggests that his concentration was somewhat lacking. Most of the time, Joe cannot remember all the words, and in the case of 'Protex Blue', usually sung by Mick, he cannot remember any of them. Conversely, 'I'm So Bored With The USA' and 'What's My Name' are indecipherable because Joe had not yet written proper lyrics for the songs. Although the tape catches him in loose rehearsal mode, his tendency to mess up the words during bona fide performances was to remain a feature of Clash gigs, despite the supposed importance of the band's message.

Paul's 'African drum' bass plods along, between the songs as well as during them; in fact, so loudly and relentlessly that Mick and Joe – trying to explain the finer points of drumming Clash-style to the new recruit – are moved to express their irritation by alternately screaming at him and pleading with him to stop. Mick attempts to add some colour to this undeniably basic musical palette by breaking into quite frankly appalling solos at every opportunity. An early effort in '1977' is so bad it sounds like someone systematically de-tuning a guitar. Joe cracks up laughing, prompting Mick to explore new extremes of atonality, which in turn causes greater and more general hilarity. There is little evidence here of the 'deadly serious' face the Clash insisted on showing to the media. The punk code was already so rigid that it forbade anything other than the most brief and infrequent of solos in more public performances. 'There's no room for instrumental excess,' Mick announced on Radio One's *Rock On* programme the following May. Interviewer John Tobler enquired whether this was because he didn't want to play like that or because he couldn't. 'I can't at the moment,' admitted Mick, mock-sobbing while Joe chuckled.

Once Rob had mastered the established set, the band decided to work up two new Strummer–Jones compositions. These came too late to be included on the tape, but Rob duly added them to the list in his diary. 'Hate And War' betrays distinct signs of being written to back up some of the band's media pronouncements: it appears to attempt justification of the anti-hippy stance, Us and Them paranoia, punk movement violence and the band's love–hate relationship with their harsh urban environment. Joe's defiant, ugly lyric refuses to have any truck with 'right on' attitudes of any kind, making disparaging references to both 'wops' and 'kebab Greeks'. Even taken in context, these risk crossing the border into xenophobia; taken out of context, they could have caused just as many problems for the band as did the misinterpretation of 'White Riot', but, strangely, no one picked up on them either then or later.

Joe came up with the lyric for 'Cheat' at much the same time, and, indeed, in terms of subject matter, it appears to be an offspring of 'Hate And War'. The lines beginning the latter song's second verse, 'I have the will to survive / I cheat if I can't win', provide a précis of 'Cheat' in its entirety and also give away Joe's source material. A flyer for latter-day Situationist publication *King Mob Echo* features the following slogan: 'In order to survive, we steal, cheat, lie, forge, deal, hide and kill.' This was revolutionary rhetoric and, as Joe claims no knowledge of Situationism, almost certainly came to him via Bernie. Like 'White Riot', the new brace of songs pitched the band directly against the forces of law and order, forcefully making the point that only a fool obeys rules made by an oppressor with the express intention of keeping the oppressed in their place. All heady, confrontational stuff, and the Clash's later backtracking about the 'political' content of their songs suggests that, yet again, not enough thought had gone into the possible repercussions.

In the *Clash On Broadway* booklet Joe said he wrote the lyric for 'Hate And War' by candlelight at Foscote Mews and took it in to Rehearsals the following day, whereupon Mick immediately knocked up a tune. The fact that it was written in this fashion at such a rushed and stressful time goes some way to explaining why Mick's musical contribution fails to live up to the anger of Joe's words. The quality control was beginning to slip. Compared with the band's other material, the backing for 'Hate And War' verges on the insipid, so it is perhaps surprising that it was chosen for inclusion in the set for the tour, while the slightly more musically assertive 'Cheat' would never be performed publicly prior to being recorded for *The Clash*.

Rob was the first person to drum on these songs, and also the following month's 'Remote Control'. Later, he would discover that he had inadvertently made a contribution to their recorded incarnations. 'What happened was, I applied my slightly more exuberant techniques, battering my kit and smashing cymbals, whatever,' he says. 'And when Terry Chimes played on the album, I could hear him being forced to play by Mick Jones what Mick thought I'd been doing, and it came out all wrong. It wasn't a bad job, but whereas I was doing very free Keith Moon-type things, with Terry's very clipped approach, it came out as a tattoo. I chuckled, because I thought, "That's what happened to me, only the other way around." But they weren't the greatest of songs, those.'

On Monday, 29 November, the Clash supported the Sex Pistols at Lanchester Polytechnic in Coventry. To all intents and purposes, the bands were using it as a warm-up gig for the Anarchy Tour, due to open that

Friday, 3 December. Instead of taking this opportunity to let Rob break himself in for live work, however, the Clash asked Terry to play what was supposed to be one last farewell gig. Rob went along to watch, travelling with friends. Roadent and the bulk of the band travelled up with the gear in the van. Joe decided it would be more of an adventure to ride pillion on Sebastian's motorbike. 'It started snowing, and it's really boring going on the back of a little 400cc thing, especially that far,' laughs Sebastian. 'He was saying, "Sebastian, I can't stand this! Just drive into the next lorry, please, *please!*" It was like a real test of virility, and we arrived *so* cold.'

Nor was the reception significantly warmer at the gig. Both the Clash's 'White Riot' and the Sex Pistols' new song 'No Future' (later to be retitled 'God Save The Queen') were misinterpreted: an emergency committee meeting of students decided both were fascist. 'They didn't want to pay us,' says Terry. Thus, he left in the middle of a fraught situation that was, if nothing else, at least typical of his time with the Clash, and therefore somehow appropriate. For the remaining members of the two bands, notice had been served that the images, meanings and signals of punk were not only ambiguous to outsiders, but also no longer within the control of the scene-leaders and their supporters.

9... ANARCHY IN THE UK

The Anarchy Tour had been set up, not without considerable difficulty, by the inexperienced Sophie Richmond, Malcolm's secretary. By the end of November 1976, at which time she also began the diary that was subsequently used as the basis for Fred and Judy Vermorel's *Sex Pistols: The Inside Story*, she had confirmed a total of 19 gigs all over England, Scotland and Wales, running from 3 to 26 December. Although there were occasional relative tiddlers like the 550-capacity Torquay 400 Ballroom, most venues held around 2,000, while the Glasgow Apollo stretched to 3,000: the largest audiences any of the bands had faced thus far. The tour was due to end on Boxing Day with a triumphant homecoming gig at the Roxy Theatre, a former cinema in Harlesden, north-west London.

It was here that the bands – including the Heartbreakers, who had flown in that same day – were supposed to spend 1 December running through a final stage rehearsal, timing sets and change-overs. In the event, the Sex Pistols were unable to take their turn. Labelmates Queen had been forced to drop out of a brief interview on *Today*, Thames TV's London-region early evening magazine show, and the Pistols were suggested as a last-minute substitute. Feeling the publicity potential was too great to miss, Malcolm agreed to the band's being ferried back from Harlesden in an EMI limo. They were joined in the studio by several 'typical punks' in the shape of Siouxsie, Steve and a couple of other members of the Bromley Contingent. After this programme was broadcast, the punk scene would never be the same again.

The story of the band's fateful encounter with 52-year-old presenter Bill Grundy has been told and retold countless times. The cause of all the fuss, essentially, was that Bill was either annoyed at having to interview the band without adequate preparation or drunk, or both. Consequently, instead of carefully manoeuvring the Pistols through a few token rebellious utterances suitable for the teatime viewing slot, he openly sneered at them, made Johnny repeat a rude word and leered at Siouxsie, and when Steve Jones, justifiably, called him a 'dirty old man', Grundy goaded him into adding, 'You dirty fucker!' and 'You fucking rotter!'

Such public misbehaviour was meat and drink to the UK's tabloid press. Were it not for the fact that little has changed during the intervening years, the exaggeration and hypocrisy evident in the following day's headlines and accompanying articles would be hard to believe. 'ROCK GROUP START A 4-LETTER TV STORM,' bellowed the *Sun*; 'Four letter Punk Rock group in TV storm,' seconded the *Daily Mail*. 'THE FILTH AND THE FURY!' howled the *Daily Mirror*; 'Fury at filthy TV chat,' agreed the *Daily Express*. All the papers responded to the viewers' reactions as much as the incident itself, reporting the flood of calls to Thames and, in the case of the *Mirror*, to the paper from its readers. After admitting he had been so overcome by the band swearing in front of his eight-year-old son that he had kicked in his TV screen, lorry driver James Holmes found himself on the front page of his favourite daily read. 'I can swear as well as anyone, but I don't want this sort of muck coming into my home at tea-time,' he announced, doing his best to keep the double standard flying high.

The *Mail*, attempting to lay some of the blame at Bill Grundy's door, discovered from his wife, Nicky, that a similar capacity for hypocrisy existed in the presenter's household: 'I know that with the boys in the pub after a few drinks he uses some pretty strong language, but he's never allowed swearing in his own home because he hated it, and the family were never allowed to indulge.' Later that day, London's *Evening Standard* gave its front page to Bill's point of view, its headline targeting 'THE FOUL MOUTHED YOBS'. After attending a hastily convened press conference at EMI HQ, its competitor, the *Evening News*, chose instead to go with 'GRUNDY GOADED PUNK BOYS SAYS RECORD CHIEF'. On 3 December, the *Sun* reported that the TV presenter had been suspended for two weeks.

This tacit admission of culpability on behalf of *Today* came too late to save the Sex Pistols in particular and punk in general from trial by tabloid. According to Glen, Johnny and Sophie, Malcolm spent the day and a half between the TV appearance and coach departure time for the Anarchy Tour in a state of total panic, wondering whether the band had gone too far. Only when he recognised like minds at work amongst the cynical hustlers of the popular press did he realise he was on familiar ground and start to exploit the situation: a businessman hates a spanner in the works, but an opportunist loves to run with a scam.

That same day, the *Mail*'s editorial decided to place the blame for the Grundy Incident on the music business's backroom boys – the people who 'manipulate for money' – under the title 'Never Mind Morals or Standards, the only Notes that Matter Come in Wads'. Malcolm turned the attack round by admitting it was true, and facing it out. From now on, he had *carte blanche* to play Fagin to the Pistols' street urchins. Ultimately, the editorial headline would be the source not only for the version of the Pistols Myth propagated by the film *The Great Rock'n'Roll Swindle*, but also the mocking album title *Never Mind The Bollocks, Here's The Sex Pistols*.

The music press was wrongfooted by the timing of the incident: that week's papers had already gone to press. It was not until the issues dated 11 December that they could offer more sympathetic coverage from a pop

1. The Delinquents, September 1974. *Left to right:* Mike Dowling, John Brown, Mick Jones, Paul Wayman.

2. Sister Ray, formerly Violent Luck, formerly Little Queenie, summer 1976. *Left to right:* one-time London SS member Matt Dangerfield (making up numbers), Brady, Kelvin Blacklock, John Brown.

3. The Damned, 1976, with former London SS member Brian James (*right*) and rejected candidate Rat Scabies (*second left*).

4. Former London SS member Tony James with Generation X, 1976.

5. Bernie Rhodes, 1977.

6. The Young Colts, 22 Davis Road, May 1976. *Left to right:* Alan Drake (making up numbers), Mick Jones, Paul Simonon, Billy Watts. Keith Levene not shown.

7. Mick Jones's high-rise: Wilmcote House, Harrow Road.

8. Joe Strummer's Alma Mater: the City of London Freemen's School, Ashtead Park, Surrey.

9. Woody Mellor, 12 Pentonville, Newport, 1973.

10. The Vultures, Newport, late 1973. Woody and Alan 'Jiving Al' Jones.

11. The 101ers in the murk of the Walterton Road basement, February 1975. *Left to right:* Clive 'Evil C.' Timperley, Simon 'Big John' Cassell, Alvaro Peña-Rojas, Richard 'Snakehips Dudanski' Nother, Jules Yewdall, Joe Strummer.

12. The 101ers, early 1976. Joe Strummer (with suit and Telecaster) and Richard Dudanski.

13. A Night of Treason: the Clash at the RCA, 5 November 1976. *Left to right:* Mick Jones, Joe Strummer, Terry Chimes, Paul Simonon. The Pollock look gives way to Pop-Art/Lettrism.

14. The Anarchy Tour, December 1976. With Rob Harper on drums.

15. The Roxy, 1977. Johnny Rotten and Mark Perry.

16. Pop Star Army Fatigues, spring 1977.

17. Creative violence?

18. With Nick 'Topper' Headon.

19. The White Riot Tour at the Rainbow, 9 May 1977.

20. Gates of the West, 1979. The Hollywood rock'n'roll look.

21–3. On-stage during the Bonds Casino residency, New York, June 1981.

24. The first of the mohicans and the return of both Terry Chimes and
the Pop Star Army Fatigues, June 1982.

25–6. The new Clash on the May 1985 busking tour. *Left to right, top:* Vince White, Paul Simonon, Pete Howard, Nick Sheppard, Joe Strummer.

culture perspective, and by then the Grundy Incident was old hat. There is a certain symbolic resonance to this fact: the music papers and the fanzines would go on commenting about punk, examining its ideas and refining its rhetoric, but punk was now out in the public domain, and as it developed into a mass movement, it would move further and further away from their influence.

The tabloids had taken punk national, emphasising its more negative and lurid aspects for the sake of outrage and titillation. From now on, Caroline Coon's comment about 'outside punks' bringing the movement into disrepute would hold sway. By taking a stuffy, pompous, establishment stance, the predominately right-wing UK tabloids had unwittingly created the ultimate Us and Them situation: any teenager who did not hold with the repressive dark age values and blatant hypocrisy those newspapers represented was now going to call him- or herself a punk. And the hints they picked up on typical punk behaviour would come from those same tabloid punk exposés: wearing bin-liners, swastikas and safety pins through their cheeks and trying to look as ugly as possible while spitting, swearing, jeering and generally being obnoxious.

It would be several months before these new punks would be able to buy albums and so pick up from the bands' lyrics a first-hand idea of what punk was about. Even then, it would be all too easy to find reaffirmations of their negative stance in the nihilistic posturing that had so troubled Allan Jones back in August. There was a comic mania about the Damned's presentation, but their more wantonly destructive and self-destructive side was echoed in Brian James's proto-goth songs of drugs and pain. The Stranglers, marketed as punks, and the first to score big with the new following, wallowed in sleaze and violent misogyny. The Sex Pistols introduced themselves with 'Anarchy In The UK', the initial impact of which owed much to Johnny Rotten's drawled 'dee-stroyyyy'. The negativity manifested in his habit of stubbing cigarette ends out on his arm was echoed by much of the Pistols' remaining repertoire, which, as Glen Matlock pointed out in *I Was A Teenage Sex Pistol*, included songs whose very titles offered a succinct impression of the band's outlook: 'No Lip', 'No Feelings', 'No Fun', 'No Future'. The Heartbreakers were responsible for introducing the relatively naïve UK punk scene to heroin, as well as promoting the fatalistic junkie loser ethos in their anthems 'Chinese Rock' and 'Born Too Loose'.

Not surprisingly, the Clash's would-be pro-creative message was initially swamped by the output of their contemporaries. The new punks were encouraged to be anti-everything: anti-establishment, anti-authority, anti-parents, anti-work, anti-education, anti-morals, anti-hope, anti-life. This attitude fed into such post-punk musical developments as goth (part punk, part *Sticky Fingers* era Rolling Stones *fleurs du mal*) and 'industrial' music (part punk, part Velvet Underground, part Bowie's *Low*). Goths dressed in black and came on like the undead. The most influential band in the industrial genre were Joy Division, whose lead singer, Ian Curtis, would help keep negativity alive for a new generation when he hanged himself in 1980. By that time, the loser-punk image itself would have been reinforced by the death of Sid Vicious, helped on his way to oblivion by both heroin and an introduction to heroin-addicted Heartbreakers groupie Nancy Spungeon. Like him, his senseless sensibility crossed the Atlantic. There it would gradually sink into the USA's mainstream rock consciousness along with punk itself, cross-breeding with the more morbid strains of heavy metal to produce grunge and, in the end, another nihilistic martyr in the shape of Kurt Cobain.

There were problems that threatened to have a more immediately damaging effect on the Sex Pistols and the punk movement as represented by the bands on the Anarchy Tour. Concerts were being cancelled even before it began. At that stage, however, the scale of the eventual devastation to the schedule could not have been guessed at and preparations for departure went ahead as planned. At manager Jake Riviera's behest, the Damned were to travel in their own van and stay separately from the others in bed and breakfast accommodation, as befitting both Stiff's limited funds and the band's outsider status. Neither the Heartbreakers nor the Clash had any record company support, but their travel and board were to be taken care of by EMI, while their share of the receipts from the gigs would cover other expenses. Thus, they, along with their managers, were to travel in a coach with the Pistols, and stay with them in upmarket hotels. Accompanying them would be a couple of people Malcolm had enlisted to make a record of the 'classic rock'n'roll tour': photographer Ray Stevenson (brother of Pistols' roadie Nils) and student film-maker Julien Temple.

When the tour party set off on 3 December, its initial destination had already been altered: despite the objections of the Students' Union social committee, the Vice-Chancellor of Norwich University had refused permission for them to use the hall on the night in question. Thus, the coach went straight to Derby for the following night's concert at the King's Hall. By the time it arrived, all the hoo-ha had resulted in a total of five concerts being cancelled or banned. Any thoughts the bands might have had of escaping the media and allowing the uproar to die down were dashed as soon as they checked into the Derby Crest Hotel. 'Cannot go to bar,' Rob Harper wrote in his diary. 'National press there.' Included among their number was a reporter from the muck-raking Sunday paper the *News Of The World* who offered Malcolm £500 for an interview and followed the tour for the next four days. 'We thought, "Shall we go out there with syringes stuck in our arms just to get 'em going?"' Mick told Tony Parsons the following March. 'Yeah, and the furniture seemed to have labels saying, "Please smash me", or "Out the window, please."'

On the following day, the 4th, the local council tried to arrange a private afternoon viewing of the Sex Pistols in performance for its Leisure Committee before granting permission to play. Most accounts have it that Malcolm refused outright. Thereafter, the Pistols were denied permission to play, but the other bands were offered the chance to go on without them; and whereas the Clash and the Heartbreakers closed ranks and refused, representatives from the Damned made statements indicating that they would be prepared to do so. This latest failure to show solidarity would be given as one of the reasons for the Damned's eventual ejection from the tour. In truth, Malcolm's own stand was not quite so firm. At first, he agreed to the councillors' demands, and the 15-strong delegation duly turned up at the venue. A police escort was sent to accompany the Pistols there, and it seems that it was the prospect of having the sizeable press contingent photograph and report on this far more visual symbol of the band's taming that prompted Malcolm to refuse to let his charges leave the hotel. It was only after being kept waiting for over an hour that the council representatives withheld their permission and made the alternative offer. In the light of this information, it is difficult to see why the Damned – physically isolated from the other bands, and therefore not in regular contact – should have been castigated for what amounted to the sin of failing to keep pace with the change of policy from compliance to defiance.

The next day's concert at Newcastle City Hall had already been banned by that city's councillors 'in the interests of protecting the children'. Instead, the coach made straight for Leeds, where the bands were due to play the polytechnic the following night. The tour party booked into the Dragonara Hotel. Once again, the press were in attendance. Catching Steve Jones and Paul Cook on their own, a photographer urged them to do some damage, so they uprooted one of the potted plants in the foyer for the benefit of his camera. Afterwards, as previously agreed, the hotel was paid £25 to replace it. The front page of the following day's *Daily Mirror* announced: 'The four-man Punk Rock group wrecked the lobby of a luxury hotel, uprooting ornamental plants, hurling plant pots around the room, and scattering soil over the carpets . . . A *Mirror* man who watched the group go wild at the Leeds hotel said, "As they walked away they shouted, 'Don't blame us. That's what you wanted.'"' Well, quite.

By 6 December, the rest of the tour was already in a shambles. It being a Monday, the music press were putting the following week's issues to bed, and were finally able to provide a different perspective on the drama. All three major inkies reported in some detail both on the immediate problems facing the bands on the tour and on the other repercussions and implications of the Grundy Incident. *Melody Maker* proved particularly good at ferreting out the reasons given for the numerous cancellations, now standing at 13 of the original 19 dates. The final tally would be 16.

There was no longer much point in treading softly. 'This is pure censorship and a complete denial of the principle of free speech,' Malcolm told *Melody Maker*. 'I don't see why councillors should dictate to people what kids go out and listen to any night,' added Johnny Rotten. 'It's ludicrous that people who are 102 years old should be passing judgement,' Bernie Rhodes chipped in over at *Sounds*. Malcolm took it to the masses – or, at least, the local masses – that same day when he told a Yorkshire TV news team, 'People are sick and tired of people telling them what to do.'

That night, the gig went ahead as planned. Both the national and the music press were heavily represented. Caroline Coon, of course, was there on behalf of *Melody Maker*. *National Rock Star* had recently been set up as a would-be rival to the three established papers, and although destined to be short-lived, it was doing its best to be where the action was, sending along a certain John Shearlaw. Back in July, realising that his paper could use an injection of new blood, *NME* editor Nick Logan had run an ad for a couple of 'Hip Young Gunslingers' to join the staff. The successful applicants had been 17-year-old Julie Burchill and 21-year-old Tony Parsons, both working class, both punky of dress and attitude. In addition to helping out on the paper's media section, the idea was that the two would provide more youthful, street cred coverage of punk. Thus, it was Tony who turned up to cover the Leeds gig.

'I've been going around for two days thinking Big Brother is really here' was how Joe opened proceedings when the Clash took the stage at 8 p.m., but his remark failed to ignite the crowd of poly students. It quickly became apparent that most of the audience had come along in a spirit of curiosity rather than enthusiasm: they stood still, hardly applauded and occasionally indulged themselves in some token punky act, like gobbing, or the throwing of slightly larger missiles. It was not a reaction peculiar to the Clash's set: Johnny Rotten was moved to comment, 'You're not wrecking the place. The *News Of The World* will be *really* disappointed.' The music press reviewers remarked on the apathy of the crowd, which turned what could and should have been a defiant celebration into an anticlimax with, as Johnny so rightly said, not even the tabloid press getting anything much out of it. All three music journalists gave perhaps predictably good reviews to all four bands, but their disappointment at the lack of atmosphere inevitably came through in their less than scintillating reports.

The gig originally scheduled for 7 December had been at Bournemouth Village Bowl. Rank Leisure Services, the owners, had pulled out because 'We were concerned about the security aspect of it all. We were certainly not keen to be associated with a band of this sort.' Instead, the tour party set off for Sheffield, where a last-minute replacement gig had been arranged at the university. Whether or not it would have been allowed to go ahead is debatable, but, upon arrival, the bands discovered that the PA was in Berkshire anyway. Thereafter, they spent a frustrating two hours in the union bar before making for Manchester, where the tour's next scheduled gig was due to be held at the Electric Circus in two days' time. The bands booked into what Rob described in his diary as an 'expensive, claustrophobic, poor quality' hotel.

Before leaving Sheffield, with nothing more constructive to do to occupy his time, Malcolm threw the Damned off the tour. Malcolm had never forgiven the band for their attempts to steal a march by playing the First

European Punk Festival back in August, and every subsequent ground-breaking move of theirs had rankled. 'We'd already started touring and built up quite a hefty following,' says Rat Scabies. 'We were filling clubs on our own. We were kind of beating them to it: we'd done it with the single, we were gonna do it with the album. We were ahead of the game. The story I got from Carol Clerk [author of the Damned's biography, *The Light At The End Of The Tunnel*] was that McLaren said he felt we were the only real threat to the Pistols.' There was also the fact that Malcolm couldn't cope with any punk-related band or project not being under his control. He hated Jake Riviera for setting himself up in competition as a manager, and for having gone one step further by establishing his own record label. There was also a clash of styles and backgrounds, as Glen explains: 'Jake thought Malcolm was a fucking prat, and Malcolm thought Jake was like Bill Brown from the public bar.'

Inviting the Damned on to the tour had caused Malcolm discomfort in the first place, and he had only done so because he believed the package needed their added pull. 'But once Malcolm got the infamy with the Grundy show, he felt he could call all the shots,' says Brian James. 'Really, he just figured we weren't needed any more,' agrees Rat. In *England's Dreaming* Malcolm gave three reasons for his decision. One was that the Damned 'were no fucking good'. Neither Glen nor Rob is prepared to go that far, though they do say they thought the band didn't really fit the bill and that they personally found their theatrical presentation 'a bit old-fashioned'. 'I remember watching them in Leeds before we went on,' says Glen, 'and Malcolm – real devil's advocacy in the air – saying, "Don't you think they bring down the pacing of the show?"' The second reason Malcolm offered Jon Savage was that he was being put under pressure by Bernie Rhodes, who objected to his band having to open for the Damned. 'Malcolm suddenly shoved us down the bottom of the bill,' confirms Brian, 'and it was because Bernie was in cahoots with him.' Malcolm never did anything for Bernie unless it suited his own purposes, and his juggling with the running order was intended solely to humiliate the Damned and provoke a confrontation, which it did. Malcolm's third reason was the one he announced to the music press when the Damned were sacked: that their supposed treachery in Derby had rendered them untrustworthy. 'At the time, it served the political purpose of stuffing the Damned and making us look unreasonably unhip,' says Rat. 'Which wasn't that difficult.'

It was not just the tour that was being affected by the aftermath of the Grundy Incident. Workers at EMI's pressing plant had staged a lightning strike in protest at having to handle 'Anarchy In The UK', which had resulted in the interruption of supplies to some of the country's smaller retail outlets. One of the bigger outlets, Boots, had made public its lack of enthusiasm for continuing to stock the single. With the exception of John Peel, Radio One DJs were not playing the record, and this unofficial ban also extended to Capital Radio in London, Piccadilly in Manchester and BRMB in Birmingham. Sheffield's Radio Hallam played it once and asked its listeners to vote whether or not it should be banned. They said yes. Radio Luxembourg DJ Tony Prince was suspended for one night for sending out an on-air invitation for the Pistols to appear live on his show.

This was the background to EMI's Annual General Meeting, held on 7 December. Chairman Sir John Read had already begun huffing and puffing about the Pistols, and despite the efforts of the staff who knew something about pop culture to play down the situation, he and his fellow pillars of the establishment carried the day. After the meeting Read made the following statement to the press: 'Whether EMI release any more of their records will have to be very carefully considered.' This information slowly percolated through to the tour party during the next day, 8 December. It had originally been designated a rest day, but as the bands had already had more than enough of these, some attempts were made to schedule a second date at Leeds Poly for that evening. They failed, and the day was taken up by moving to another hotel in Manchester, the Midland. Rob's diary entry read: 'During afternoon learned that EMI have withdrawn money for rest of tour and want Pistols back in London to "cool out". What will happen now?'

What happened then was that Malcolm refused to heed EMI's advice, correctly deducing that the ongoing publicity of the tour would at least keep the Pistols' chance of a future career alive, even if that future might ultimately be with a slightly more daring and supportive record company than EMI. The other bands agreed to continue as well, but more as a gesture of unity than in the expectation of playing anything like the number of dates originally scheduled. It certainly wasn't because they were having a good time. Rob's diary recorded a few examples of high jinks in the early days of the tour which, had they heard about them, would have given the tabloids a little more to work with. A huge communal meal at the Dragonara on the 5th only just stopped short of degenerating into a full-scale foodfight. Following the Leeds gig, Jerry Nolan was so keen to join in an attempt to drown Johnny Rotten in the bath that he kicked a hole in Mick Jones's door. On another occasion, members of the road crew defecated in Bernie's bed. (Road humour: you have to be there.) But the dominant strain in the diary and in Rob's and Glen's recollections is the sheer, unmitigated *boredom* of being stuck in hotel rooms and on the coach day after day, besieged by the press, with all prospects of release through performance frustrated and with nothing to do but drink. As Johnny Rotten told *Melody Maker*, 'We feel like a bunch of prisoners.'

On the morning of the 9th, the management of the Midland asked the tour party to leave, making it necessary for them to look for their third base in the Manchester area in as many days. This task was accomplished not without some difficulty. The Belgrade Hotel in Stockport was among those who refused entry – 'I don't want this sort of rubbish in my place when there are so many nice people in the world' – before a booking was finally arranged at the 'decidedly downmarket' Arosa Hotel in Withington.

The gig at the Electric Circus took place as planned, and was reviewed by Pete Silverton for *Sounds*. Although he opined that the tour was 'shaping up to be an all-time rock'n'roll classic', his examination of the component parts did not quite add up to justify this statement. The Sex Pistols were 'visibly tired and disoriented by the happenings of the past week' and 'lacked a degree of certainty and concentration'. The Buzzcocks, who had been added to the bill in place of the Damned for this home-town gig, were dismissed as 'a second-rate provincial Pistols copy'. The Heartbreakers were praised but deemed to be 'in need of match practice' and to have 'only cut loose three quarters of the way through their set'. Pete also commented on how the audience reacted to the media representation of punk and, indeed, the presence of the media themselves. Predictably, there was some half-hearted pogoing and, despite the bands' objections, a lot of gobbing. There seemed to be pockets of more genuine, deep-rooted response, however: Pete talked to a group of young lads present who were already planning on forming a band called the Stiff Kittens. Two of their number, Hooky and Bernard, would follow through: the Stiff Kittens would beget Warsaw, who would beget Joy Division, who would beget New Order.

Rob's diary entry described the Clash's soundcheck earlier in the day as 'Really shitty and depressing. Quote from EMI press rep: "You really must get in tune and balance it properly. It sounded terrible."' On the night, according to Pete Silverton, the Clash were 'probably the best-received band'. After requesting that the psychedelic lightshow be turned off, they stormed through their full set, a flurry of furious sound and vision. 'The gig was *amazing!*' wrote an incredulous Rob. 'Encore, second encore.' 'Shitty soundcheck, brilliant gig,' he says now. 'Sometimes, the Clash took over. Other times they were just OK.' Pete took the trouble to give Rob the only full namecheck he received all tour, noting that he 'beat hell out of his kit and had lots of fun'. His greatest compliments were reserved for Joe, whom he had met previously when covering the 101ers for *Trouser Press*: likening his appearance at the microphone to the image of Che Guevara on the popular early Seventies bedsit poster, he also stated, 'I still reckon he's currently *the* quintessential English rhythm guitarist.'

This was pretty decent of him considering Joe tried to get him ejected from the coach on the way back to the hotel. Pete knew too much about Joe's pre-punk past for comfort, his introduction to the 101ers eight months previously having come about at the instigation of one of Joe's former co-pupils at the City of London Freemen's School. The journalist could not resist mentioning the singer's 'fit of child-like pique' in his review, and nor could he resist describing Joe as an 'ex-public schoolboy'. The fact that Pete went on to ghost Glen's autobiography explains why the coach incident - described as involving a 'particular journalist' – reappeared there. More relevant to the greater scheme of things, as *Sounds* reported on its news pages the following week, was that the police forced the coach to park a mile away from the hotel to avoid trouble. Yet more police had been stationed at the Arosa, just in case that trouble arrived. Some tabloid journalists had also been stirring it up with the management, and so, once again, the tour party were asked to leave.

The next week of the tour calendar looked particularly bare. On 10 December, the bands had originally been scheduled to play Lancaster University. The gig had been cancelled, but at least this time not for the usual reasons. According to Lancaster student and future Clash associate Johnny Green, a group of feminists had called a special meeting of the union because they believed punk bands to be not racist, as the students at Lanchester Polytechnic had, but *sexist*. An attempt to reschedule the earlier cancellation at Norwich University failed, as did last-minute talks with the Preston Charter. The gig on the 11th at Liverpool Stadium had fallen foul of the local council, who had also put a block on what was to become the leading punk venue in that city, Eric's. The 12th had been a day off anyway. The original booking on the 13th had been at Bristol Colston Hall, but council opposition had seen it switched to the city's university, where it had again been cancelled. Rank Leisure Services had pulled out of another gig originally lined up for the 14th at Cardiff Top Rank – 'we had signed no contracts' – but a substitute venue had been found in the shape of the Caerphilly Castle Cinema.

With no hope of playing until that date at the earliest, Malcolm decided it was pointless running up any more hotel bills. The coach drove back to London through the night, setting off at 3 a.m. on the morning of Friday, the 10th, and arriving six hours later. The pressure was not lifted even then. Sophie Richmond's diary entry for the following Monday recorded arguments about money and an attempt on Malcolm's part to prise more from EMI. The record company was playing it cool. Also in progress were attempts to patch up the remnants of the tour schedule. The previous week, the manager of the Roxy in Harlesden had jumped aboard the bandwagon, informing first the *Evening Standard* and then the music press that 'The date has been pulled out because of the group's behaviour and what they represent. They have rehearsed here and it has been brought to my attention that they have written all over the gentlemen's toilet walls.' Efforts were still being made to line up a replacement London venue for the tour's finale; the Rainbow in Finsbury Park was among those approached, unsuccessfully.

Inevitably, attempts were made by local councillors to ban the Caerphilly Castle Cinema gig on the 14th, but it was still going ahead when the Anarchy Tour party set off that morning. It was a long way to go to play a one-off show in a seated venue holding 110 people – especially with losses on the tour already estimated at £9,000 – but it was now a matter of principle. 'It's a piss-off, but we're not going to give up,' Johnny Rotten told Brian Case. 'We're now bankrupt. But if we give up, no new band will get a chance to play again. Ever.' Brian – a sometime *NME* contributor – was covering the gig as the basis of a four-page spread on the Grundy aftermath in the *Observer*

Magazine, whose parent newspaper was considerably more intelligent and balanced in its outlook than those the bands had encountered thus far. Brian's insider knowledge of musical movements ensured the feature, published on 30 January 1977, was the best and most reasonable in a national paper to date.

The bands arrived in Caerphilly to find that, although their attempts to have the gig cancelled had failed, two Labour councillors had refused to give up without a fight. Joining forces with members of the town's Pentecostal Chapel, they had arranged a carol concert in the car park outside the cinema. 'That was insane!' says Rob. 'All these idiots denouncing us in religious terms.' There was indeed a distinct odour of witch-hunt about the proceedings. 'Are children's minds to be vandalised and prostituted?' frothed Councillor Ray Davies. 'This group not only come out with obscenities in their programme, but they also bring all the dope pedlars and filth pedlars in their wake.' As with most witch-hunts, it seems there may have been an ulterior motive. A prospective Conservative candidate voiced his own suspicions to Brian Case about the opposition's recently discovered determination to maintain high moral standards: 'They are trying to make political capital because there are elections next May.'

Again, the pillars of the local establishment were not the only ones to have been affected by what they had read. Brian noticed that the seated audience seemed subdued and self-conscious, before finally responding with 'an unconvincing spit fight and some desultory pogo dancing in the aisle'. Talking to some of the members of the audience, he found their thoughts on the 'meaning of punk' consisted of phrases regurgitated from newspaper articles. The more clued-up could offer some music press propaganda about dole queues and Rod Stewart being out of touch. Song lyrics remained largely unknown or only vaguely understood. More worrying still were some of the accessories: bandaged wrists were the latest thing in faked self-mutilation, and the swastika was by now ubiquitous. 'I've got pictures of Hitler in my bedroom,' announced Josie Rafferty. 'It's not that I admire him. I just like the way he shows all his wickedness and that.'

Attempting to put the music in context, Brian made reference to the MC5, the Who, the Small Faces, Lou Reed, the Stooges and the Ramones, also noting some hangovers from David Bowie's past incarnations in the preponderance of red spiky hairstyles. He traced the idea of the street gang as musical outfit all the way back to Bronx doo-woppers Dion and the Belmonts. This tied in neatly with Malcolm's almost Clash-like line about the bands on the tour playing music as an alternative to the dole, factory or prison. There was little discussion of the Sex Pistols' musical performance - and the other bands hardly received a mention throughout – but Brian surpassed himself in his description of Johnny's stage presence. Trussed at the knees by Malcolm and Vivienne's latest Sex line, bondage trousers, the singer apparently resembled 'a cross between [Shakespeare's] Richard III and Pinkie in Graham Greene's *Brighton Rock*'. Eighteen years later, Johnny would surprise some reviewers of *Rotten* with his erudition when he cited both characters as influences. Strange coincidence.

Following the show, it was back to London once more. The gig scheduled for 15 December at Glasgow Apollo had been cancelled by the local council – 'we have got enough problems in Glasgow without importing yobbos' – who had revoked the venue's licence for one night only. An alternative gig had been lined up for Lafayette's in Wolverhampton, and also scuppered. Although it had survived longer than most, the gig on the 16th at Dundee Caird Hall had been cancelled. Sheffield Council had taken the 'unprecedented' step of banning the Pistols from the City Hall on the 17th; the replacement show arranged at Carlisle's Market Hall had met a similar fate. Southend Kursaal had been cancelled for the 18th, likewise a replacement gig at Maidenhead Skindles. Guildford Civic Hall had pulled out of the show scheduled for the 19th, but at least this had been replaced by a fairly safe bet in the shape of a second night at Manchester's Electric Circus.

In the interim, the situation on the home front did not improve dramatically. According to Sophie's diary, influential American syndicated music columnist Lisa Robinson made derogatory noises about the Pistols, as did Capital Radio DJ Roger Scott. Tension in the band's office resulted in outbursts and a (temporary) walk-out by Sophie herself. The Sex Pistols might have been saving on hotel bills, but the PA and lighting crews still insisted on being paid. Billeted in Earls Court with very little money, the Heartbreakers were making mutinous noises. Nor were things appreciably better in the Clash camp. It was at this time that Joe returned to Foscote Mews to find renovators had taken over the ice cream factory and thrown all his possessions on to a skip. So he too moved into Rehearsals to share one room, a couple of blankets, one couch and the tiny electric fire with Paul and Roadent, which did nothing to alleviate the place's overpowering smell of old socks. On the 18th, members of all three bands, plus members of the Damned, attended the *NME*'s Christmas party at Dingwalls, where the main attraction was as much the free food and drink as the entertainment courtesy of the Flamin' Groovies. At least there were no fights in the courtyard.

The next day, the coach set off once more for Manchester. There were no choirs and councillors lying in wait outside the Electric Circus, but the audience had to run another type of gauntlet: the venue was surrounded by old Thirties council blocks, about a third of which were boarded up, and some local hooligans climbed on to the roofs to rain bottles down upon the heads of the punks below. The gig was covered for the *NME* by local stringer Paul Morley, who had been offered freelance work following his response to the Hip Young Gunslingers ad. Over the coming years, Paul's tendency to sacrifice straightforward communication to structural experimentation would earn him well-deserved accusations of pretentious élitism, but although his approach to the second Manchester gig was irritating, his review was not without insight.

He attempted to describe the three bands on the Anarchy Tour bill as representatives of three separate strands of the rock tradition. His distinction between the Clash and the Heartbreakers was forced, blurred and unconvincing, but that between the Clash and the Sex Pistols contained more than a kernel of truth. For all Joe's attempts to distance himself from 'nostalgia bores' the 101ers, Paul saw the Clash as a hard rock'n'roll band, with echoes of Eddie Cochran as well as the Ramones, and (perhaps less persuasively) 'only a few steps removed from Showaddywaddy'. At the time, this did not sit well with punk's stated desire to forge something new, but in retrospect, it reveals that the musical and stylistic change of direction the band would take in 1979 was not totally unsignalled.

Paul saw the Pistols as more of a pop group. It was tantamount to heresy to make this claim for such a determinedly left-field act; again, however, at today's distance from the initial shock of the band's image and presentation, the pop sensibility in Glen Matlock's tunes is more than evident. Not only that, but – while Paul did not comment on it and, indeed, could not have known it – from the Grundy Incident onwards, the Pistols' career would be led and defined by the media as much as those of the Bay City Rollers and the Monkees had been. Paul's other comments were more down to earth: he echoed Pete Silverton's appraisal of the previous Manchester gig, contrasting the Clash's energy and total commitment with the Pistols' apparent weariness and resultant sloppiness.

On 20 December, the tour had been due to visit Birmingham, but the local council had banned the bands from playing the Town Hall, and a subsequent arrangement with the city's Bingley Hall had also fallen through. Instead, a gig was quickly arranged, and played, at the Winter Gardens in the Humberside seaside town of Cleethorpes. The following day, after an exhausting coach journey almost the length and breadth of England, the party turned up at Plymouth Woods Centre to play only the third date of the Anarchy Tour's original schedule. According to Glen, it was a great show, with all three of the bands going over well to a packed and enthusiastic audience.

The next night had been scheduled for the 400 Ballroom in Torquay. It had subsequently been replaced by Penelope's Ballroom in nearby Paignton, and a second show at Plymouth Woods Centre had been belatedly tacked on to the end of the tour, on the 23rd. The Paignton date fell through at the last minute, and to save unnecessary hanging around, the second Plymouth show was brought forward a day.

Unfortunately, it was too late to advertise it properly, and hardly anyone turned up. In her diary Sophie Richmond, who travelled down from London specially for the show, estimated the audience at 'about ten'; in his autobiography Glen reckoned 'six Hell's Angels'. Each band took it in turn to get up on to the stage and play their set while the others watched. According to Sophie, the Clash and the Heartbreakers played 'brilliant', but, although the Sex Pistols did their best to compete, they were bedevilled by sound problems: ironically, their mix was inadvertently sabotaged by their own soundman Dave Goodman, 'out of his head on pills'.

Thus, after playing only three times in the first two weeks of the tour, the bands had managed to string together four consecutive shows at its close, but had still been unable to end on a high note. It was all something of an anticlimax. Even the after-tour party back at the hotel, which involved some more damage to property, failed to attract any attention from the national press, though it did result in the Sex Pistols being banned from the premises for life.

Also, while the final gig was played in a spirit of mutual support, the punk solidarity it represented had long since evaporated. During the tour the hothouse atmosphere had made it all too easy for personality conflicts to come to a head. According to Glen, Malcolm and the rest of the Pistols had never been too happy about his friendship with Mick; Malcolm and Johnny in particular believed that the Pistols should hold themselves aloof from the competition. Glen and Mick roomed together for much of the Anarchy Tour, which invited comment. 'As they went up the stairs one night, I think it was Johnny Rotten turned to Strummer and said, "Good boys in together, eh?"' recalls Rob. 'That kind of attitude that Glen describes, that was just one example of it.' Glen himself perhaps took the significance of this a little far in *I Was A Teenage Sex Pistol*, where he mused on the possibility that his friendship with Mick had caused the deterioration of his relationship with the rest of the Pistols, ultimately leading to his departure from the band. As Malcolm, Steve and Johnny have all been more than happy to point out on numerous occasions over the years, the reasons were entirely personal.

Glen repeats another claim he made in his autobiography, that 'the Clash's drummer' – namely Rob – was ostracised by the other members of *his* band. Rob concedes that no one in the Clash made much of an effort to bring him into the fold, but counters that he himself, not being especially gregarious, didn't go out of his way to mix either. To alleviate the boredom, he slipped out from the hotels whenever he could to go for solitary walks around the various towns the tour visited. As much of an individual as his predecessor, he did not attempt to ingratiate himself by toeing the punk party line: he even listened to Bob Dylan tapes on the coach.

A hyperactive person, he tired easily. He found the long days with nothing to do enervating. And as for those relatively few nights when the band did get to play . . . In *Rotten* Johnny backed up his claim never to have liked the Clash as a band by criticising their live pacing, stating that the band would go so crazy at the beginning of their set that they would run out of steam by the end. This charge has some basis in fact. For the first couple of years of the Clash's career, Joe seldom made it to the end of a show without being reduced to a hoarse, sweat-sodden wreck incapable of playing guitar and desperately hanging on to the microphone for support. Rob was not only responsible for detonating the Clash's on-stage explosion, but also, unlike Joe, was required to maintain momentum throughout. While playing double time on the cymbals, even the relatively short half-hour Anarchy Tour sets were shattering. 'It was really loud and fast,' he says. 'I could play loud, and I could play fast, but up to that point I'd never been required to do both at the same time. Sometimes I didn't sound quite as good as I wanted to. I was always in time, but I frequently felt I wasn't on top of it.' The upshot of this was that Rob did not join in with the after-gig revelry, drank little and tended to go to bed earlier than everybody else.

Although, in retrospect, he can believe that adverse comments were made about him, he was not aware of them at the time. 'As the tour went on, perhaps the only way their sort of gang mentality could deal with it was to typecast me as a one-dimensional nerdy sort of character,' he concedes. 'But they never said anything to me about it. Maybe Glen's hit on a truth, but if he has, he's exaggerated it hugely, particularly about people not talking to me. I had no problem speaking to anyone. They were all quite civilised, really.' Perhaps surprisingly, he cites supposed junkie bad-asses Jerry Nolan and Johnny Thunders as being among the most open and friendly, offering advice and retelling amusing road anecdotes. Johnny Rotten also made an effort to be sociable: after the first Plymouth gig, Rob recollects him admitting that the Pistols sometimes found it difficult to follow the Clash on-stage, something which no bona fide member of the latter band – or, indeed, any member of the general public – has ever heard him say.

The tour was the first opportunity for Mick Jones to meet Johnny Thunders, one of his idols. Glen does not remember his room-mate being noticeably star-struck, and wonders whether this was because the Heartbreakers had all had their hair cut to conform more closely to the UK scene's idea of acceptable punk *coiffure*. 'He might have been disappointed. If you were a Johnny Thunders fan and you'd had long hair, and really wanted it like that, and you'd been ordered to have your hair cut by Bernie Rhodes, and your hero comes over and he's got shorter hair than you, you'd feel let down, I suppose.'

Tony Parsons, another fan of the New York Dolls, recalls Mick commandeering Johnny backstage after Anarchy's Leeds gig, but on the whole a distance was maintained between the two guitarists, as indeed it was between their respective bands. Age difference, road experience and heroin all contributed to the gap. Jerry Nolan spent the tour trying to kick his habit, so he tended to be wrapped up in his own worries; Rob, who shared a room with him one night, remembers him crying out in his sleep. Johnny, a more determined adherent to the junkie lifestyle, was not above playing streetwise one-upmanship. 'Johnny Thunders . . . would wave a syringe in the face of some uninitiated, impressionable shill,' wrote Nick Kent in a 1986 feature about Sid Vicious, printed in *The Face*. '"Are you a boy or a man?" he would tease, turning the issue into a matter of puerile machismo.' That such behaviour rankled with the Clash is more than suggested by the lyric for 'City Of The Dead', a song they would add to their repertoire the following summer: 'New York Johnny', on finding that the Clash cannot tell him where to 'cop' heroin, sneers, "'You should get to know your town / The way that I know mine.'"

Money was also a significant issue on the tour. Since most gigs were cancelled, some of the rescheduled venues had much smaller capacities than the originals and there was a poor turnout on the last night, the bands made next to nothing from door receipts. The Heartbreakers survived December on about £20 a week, and had to borrow £5 off Sophie Richmond while billeted in Earls Court for the few days immediately prior to the tour's final leg. Joe had taken the stage in Leeds wearing a green shirt stencilled with the legend, 'SOCIAL SECURITY £9.70', his weekly income, and Bernie told the *NME* that other Clash expenses were coming out of his own pocket. EMI had initially footed travel and accommodation costs for all three bands, but when they withdrew support, that burden fell on to the Pistols' shoulders, and such bills came straight out of the band's EMI advance. Before, as Glen noted in his autobiography, it had seemed unimportant when the Heartbreakers made lengthy transatlantic calls to their girlfriends and charged them to their rooms; it had even been amusing when they and the other bands had made room service orders for food and drink and had signed the bills Donald Duck. Suddenly, as far as the headliners were concerned, such behaviour was no longer quite so funny.

As the tour went on, the atmosphere between the haves and the have-nots became increasingly sour. By the time it ended, the financial drain on the Pistols had levelled both camps out somewhat, but no one was prepared to be particularly gracious about it. The Heartbreakers found themselves stuck in London, practically destitute. 'I bumped into them in the Ship on Wardour Street,' says Andy Czezowski, referring to the pub closest to the Pistols' office in Dryden Chambers, which for that reason was something of an Inner Circle punk haunt. 'They were moaning and groaning about how they'd been fucked over by Malcolm, how he hadn't paid them all the money he'd promised, how they'd got nothing and they were hanging out in people's flats, sleeping on the floor, couldn't eat, and all the rest of it.'

The Clash came out of it equally poorly, as Joe told Caroline Coon the following March: 'When I got off the coach, we had no money and it was just as awful. I felt twice as hungry as I ever had before.' Despite the superior reviews the Clash had received – and, in the main, from non-partisan journalists – their dominant post-Anarchy Tour feeling was one of inferiority. 'I *hated* it!' said Joe. 'It was the Pistols' time. We were in the shadows in the background.' Five years later, reminiscing about the Pistols and the Anarchy Tour in an interview with Phil Gifford of the *New Zealand Listener*, Mick would be considerably more cheerful when acknowledging the headliners' superior status: 'They were just great. The best. Better than us. What they did to an audience never really came through on record, and the papers never wrote about it fairly, but the energy they put into an audience was amazing.'

Immediately following the Anarchy Tour, however, such generosity was conspicuous by its absence. At a Christmas Day party at Jonh Ingham's Notting Hill home (according to Jon Savage's diary account) there was little festive spirit evident among the gathering that comprised members of the Pistols, Clash, Damned and Heartbreakers. With what seemed like the entire rest of the world against them, they still preferred to keep to their own tight little groups and seethe at each other for the duration.

The sincerity of Malcolm and the Pistols' desire to promote the punk movement as anything other than a platform for their own career had always been questionable, but at least some of the other people who had become involved, whether as followers or bands, had believed in it wholeheartedly.

The Anarchy Tour bands had not been alone in their suffering during the aftermath of the Grundy Incident: other punk and would-be punk bands soon found themselves deemed guilty by association. After withdrawing from the tour, the Vibrators set up a series of dates of their own. Three of them were subsequently cancelled by promoters, which, after it had been reported in the music press, at least earned them some *credibility* by association.

In early December, trying to find gigs for the totally unknown Chelsea proved even more difficult for band manager Andy Czezowski. While still managing the Damned, he had told *Sniffin' Glue* of his desire to set up a club for the London scene that would play a similar role to CBGB's for the New York scene. It was now more a matter of necessity than of vague ambition. Luckily, Chelsea vocalist Gene October had a friend who owned a club in Covent Garden, and he took Andy along to see him. His name was Rene Albert, and the club he co-owned with a sleeping partner – apparently a barrister - was at 41–43 Neal Street and had formerly been known as Chaguaramas. 'It was all 40- to 50-year-old faggots who were into Gene, who used to hang around this place,' announces Andy, breezily. 'It was, I think, the first openly gay bar run as such in London, but it had failed, and they had changed the name to the Roxy literally that month. It was not my name at all: we didn't like it, and it was hardly original, but they'd done it and it didn't seem to make much difference anyway. They didn't know a thing about punk rock. They didn't care either. They didn't care what was on at the Roxy as long as the money was paid, because they knew they were going to lose their licences imminently anyway.'

The Roxy was not particularly well suited to live rock music, being tiny, laid out on two levels and consisting of little more than an upstairs bar area, a downstairs dancefloor and an office. Nevertheless, Gene was given the go-ahead to set it up. Again while still managing the Damned, Andy had accompanied that band to 47A Warrington Crescent, where they recorded their first demos on the 4-track studio belonging to Matt Dangerfield and Barry Jones. Thereafter, Andy had developed a friendship with Barry, which now came in useful. Andy had found a venue, but he didn't have the £50 required for a deposit. 'Barry became a partner because he had a guitar, which he managed to hock in order to get the money to get the first night going.' As a third partner, Barry brought in his friend and fellow Warrington Crescent resident Ralph Jedascheck. Although Andy maintains that he shouldered the bulk of the work involved in running the Roxy, Barry also employed his artistic talents to design the flyer for the first gig, due to take place on 14 December. He continued to take responsibility for publicity when the club's life as a punk venue was extended. 'He was quite talented, but totally messed up, always out of his head. Ralph was pretty useless all round.' For more practical help, Barry's ex-girlfriend Celia Perry was brought in to run the office, and Acme Attractions shop manager Don Letts as DJ. In his turn, Don volunteered his brother Des and his good friend Leo Williams to man the bar.

This Rasta contingent was initially suspicious and contemptuous of the punks, but when some of the regulars showed an interest in the reggae he was playing – there being precious little recorded punk material available at that time – Don responded in kind. Having just bought a Super 8 camera, he was eventually inspired enough by the DIY ethic to film events at the club. He and his friends also made a more immediate connection with the punks when they realised they represented a hitherto untapped market for ganja, and began selling Jamaican cone-style joints over the bar.

In the time between Gene arranging the first gig and Andy paying for it and commissioning the publicity, Chelsea underwent a change of personnel. Tony James had written most of the band's lyrics and Billy Idol most of the music. The two of them had begun to feel increasingly uncomfortable that such songs as 'Youth, Youth, Youth' were being sung by someone in his late twenties. Andy insists that it was he who decided Gene had to go. Billy became the singer, and the band quickly found a new guitarist. 'The songs didn't change, it was just that Billy learned the words,' says Andy. The name did change, to Generation X, after the Sixties book that had provided the quote for the Clash's ICA flyer back in October (not to be confused with Douglas Coupland's 1991 novel of the same title reflecting the *Zeitgeist* 30 years on).

Before the band played the Roxy gig – actually their second under the new name, following their 10 December début at the Central School of Art – Andy arranged a second Roxy show. This time it was a lifeline for the Heartbreakers, still penniless in London after the Anarchy Tour. 'I wanted to put Generation X on again, but I didn't want to put them on two weeks running,' he explains. 'So I said, "Why don't you come in after Generation X, then I can put them on after you again?"' For their first show Generation X and support band Siouxsie and the Banshees (re-formed around the nucleus of Siouxsie and Steve Severin) drew about 120 people, who were given flyers advertising the Heartbreakers' appearance. This number was close to being the venue's full capacity by any reasonable standards, but the Heartbreakers, being better known than Generation X, pulled in 300. 'Which was brilliant, of course, and that rolled on to Generation X again. It was like a three-week promotional plan.'

It was already more than that: an application form for membership of the club had been included in the November–December issue of *Sniffin' Glue*. Andy was hoping to open the Roxy as a regular venue with a New Year's Day show featuring the Sex Pistols and the Damned. He had suggested the idea to Malcolm following the cancellation of the Anarchy Tour's Boxing Day gig at the other, larger Roxy in Harlesden, and before he learned of the Damned's disgrace. Even so, it looked for a while as though the Pistols at least would be playing the gig. 'We were talking and talking, and then, at the last minute, he changed his mind, which was typical of Malcolm.'

One of the reasons Glen Matlock gives for the decision not to play was the size of the venue, but the audience would have been larger than it had been at the Caerphilly Castle Cinema. Anyway, the idea behind the gig had less to do with attracting a big crowd than with defying the powers that be. 'All the papers were saying how they'd been banned, that the GLC was going to stop them playing anywhere,' says Andy. Rumours of a more general GLC blacklist had begun to spread at this time. They were given some credence when the GLC forced the plug to be pulled on the Stranglers at the Rainbow on 30 January 1977 after Hugh Cornwell defied a contract restriction at the Rainbow forbidding him to swear on-stage or wear his beloved 'Fuck' T-shirt. The rumours were duly investigated by the music press. Questioned, the GLC denied the existence of a ban relating to either punk or the Pistols in particular. After the evidence was weighed, the Stranglers incident was generally deemed to have been an isolated one caused almost entirely by their own wilful behaviour; and although it was true that fewer and fewer London venues were willing to book the Pistols, that was attributable to their management. No blacklist existed. As both Glen and Andy soon came to realise, Malcolm had decided to play up the idea of a ban for promotional purposes. 'It was a complete hype and a complete lie,' says Andy. 'The GLC didn't have those sort of powers.'

With the benefit of hindsight, Andy offers what he believes to be the real reasons for the Pistols' withdrawal: 'Malcolm couldn't commit himself for two reasons. One, it would blow the whole myth of the band being banned from playing anywhere; and two, it would give me and the club too much credibility. Malcolm never did come down. He felt, "This is punk: *I* should be doing this nightclub." I have heard since that he had always wanted to run his own club. He felt it didn't deserve his presence, which would have made it legitimate, as it were.' Echoes here of Malcolm's feud with Jake Riviera, and the ongoing one-upmanship tussle with Bernie Rhodes.

Shortly after Generation X's arrival on the London scene, it was Andy's turn to find his services no longer required by the band. Jonh Ingham had been included on the press list for the first Roxy show. Liking what he saw and, now that it had established itself in the national consciousness, ambitious to do more than comment on punk, he seized his chance to sweet-talk the highly ambitious Billy Idol and Tony James. Before they played their second Roxy gig, the band told Andy of their plans to defect and join forces with Jonh and his managerial partner, Stewart Joseph from the Rough Trade record shop. After his experiences with the Damned and Generation X, Andy was beginning to think that groups were more trouble than they were worth. He decided to put his full energies into running the Roxy. 'By then I'd been having discussions with the owners of the place, and I said, "Look, I could fill up more nights." So I came up with a deal to rent it off them. Quite a lot of money.' The contract was for three months, at £350 a week. In order to get the club off the ground, he still needed a guaranteed crowd-pulling band, so he approached the Clash to play the New Year's Day slot abandoned by the Pistols.

According to Andy, Bernie was just as hung up on the idea of a punk Inner Circle as Malcolm. 'It was, "Me and Malcolm, we set this scene up, we're into the politics, the anarchy, we were at the revolution in Paris. Where were you?" I got this sort of vibe off them because I wasn't into this deep philosophy that they had about punk, which they made up as they went along. I couldn't speak to them about those things, because I thought, "This is all absolute shit!" It sold papers, it got bums on seats, but I think they tried to believe it.' Nevertheless, having none of Malcolm's advantages – neither nationwide publicity, however negative it might have been, nor record company funding, however short-lived it might prove to be – Bernie could not afford to be too standoffish. The Clash agreed to headline the official 1 January 1977 Roxy opening night, thus beginning the new year with a highly symbolic act: stepping into the Sex Pistols' shoes.

10... CAREER OPPORTUNITIES

Rob Harper had not exactly bonded with the Clash during the December 1976 Anarchy Tour, and once it finished he headed home without anything further being said about his continuing to work with the band. After Christmas, however, he received a call asking him to play the Roxy gig, and duly turned up for rehearsals. Like the others, he found he had a new song to learn. 'Mick said, "I've been working over Christmas while you lot've been lazing around."' 'Remote Control' is, in part, a direct response to the experiences of the Anarchy Tour: the lyric opens with an attack on 'remote control from the civic hall', and it is likely the 'meeting in Mayfair' is an allusion to the EMI shareholders' AGM in nearby Manchester Square. But it widens its brief to cover other examples of perceived oppression, recalling both 'Janie Jones' and '48 Hours' in its references to dead-end jobs, the lack of leisure facilities and the restrictions placed on those staples of adolescent life, noise and drugs.

The *1984* references Joe had already made in the coda to '1977' and on-stage during the Clash's Leeds Anarchy Tour set are again present in the song's overwhelming sense of paranoia; or what might have seemed more like paranoia had the establishment's attack on punk not been so blatant. The evocation of Orwell is fully intentional too: in *The Clash Songbook* (1978) the illustration accompanying the lyric was a poster reading: 'BIG BROTHER IS WATCHING YOU.' The protagonist sees no means of escape and, like Winston Smith, reconciles himself to unquestioning obedience. What saves 'Remote Control' from sliding totally into negativity and despair is the angry finger it points at the oppressors and their agents: not just local government, but also national politicians, the business community and the police. At last, it seemed, 'They' were becoming more clearly defined.

Sadly, the rush to introduce this topical material into the band's set made for another weak tune which detracts considerably from the song's impact. 'Round about that time, Bernie said to Joe, "Some of these songs are getting a bit soft, Joe. Can't you come up with something a bit tougher?"' remembers Rob. 'And he said, "Yeah, don't worry about it. I've got some tough ones in the pipeline."' This vote of no confidence in his recent efforts may go some way to explaining why Mick got to sing both 'Hate And War' and 'Remote Control' on the album. Thereafter, even he quickly came to recognise the

weakness of the latter composition, and it was to be the band's desire for quality control – as much as their objection to CBS meddling – that was at the root of the squabble about its subsequent release as a single.

Joe's Telecaster being in for repairs, when he took the stage at the Roxy shortly after 9.30 p.m., he did so with a large white Gretsch-type semi-acoustic hanging round his neck. Even that could not hide the huge slogan daubed across the front of his shirt which read, simply and appropriately: '1977'. In the packed, sweaty, low-ceilinged club, the Clash thrashed their way through a frantic set. 'I had to have bandages on my fingers,' recalls Rob. 'I did myself in, and at the end I thought, "That's over, thank God."' But he hadn't read the small print on Sebastian's poster, and nobody had bothered to tell him what was due to happen at 12.30. 'I found out there was a second set, and I had to do it all again!' At least the punters got their £1.25's worth. 'Mega-gig, sold out, so great: that paid the first week's rent,' says Andy Czezowski. The Roxy was under way.

Soon afterwards, Andy received a phone call from Jake Riviera sounding out the venue for the Damned. After Andy had reminded their new manager that the band still owed him money, an arrangement was worked out whereby they would play the club for free on Monday, 17 January, if Andy would give them a month-long Monday-night residency. It proved to be a lucrative deal for both parties, word of mouth about the Roxy ensuring audiences of close to 400. The Heartbreakers drew similar crowds for their return appearances. As a venue for established punk bands, however, the Roxy's size would have limited its lifespan. Fortunately, one of the more positive aspects of the publicity following the Grundy Incident was a deluge of new groups, and as the Roxy was the only bona fide punk club in town, the spring of 1977 saw it playing host to punk's second wave.

'The time was right and everything was right,' says Andy. 'I filled it up with other acts that were coming through, from Penetration to Slaughter and the Dogs, X Ray Spex, the Slits, Johnny Moped …' He could also have mentioned the Adverts, the Cortinas, Eater, the Lurkers, Squeeze and Wire, among others. Most of them were from out of town; some, like Wayne County and the Electric Chairs, followed the Heartbreakers over from New York. The Roxy became not just a venue, but also the base of what now passed for the punk scene. 'We were the Cavern of the day. It was the core, the centre of the whole scene. Even though it lasted just a short space of time, it really did open up all these doors. I really do believe without a major club – even though we were tiny, we gave out the right vibe – the whole thing could have imploded. I think the Pistols and the Clash could have remained a left-field area of the pop-rock business, whereas, by having a central point, it actually became a movement and developed the whole thing. Unconscious, once again. It was genuinely *the* band hang-out. Everybody played and everybody checked out everybody else. The Clash were always there, the Pistols. The Clash were friends of Don Letts. They would come down to listen to the reggae and just hang out and drink until the club closed at one o'clock. Some nights we were open but nothing was happening. There might be a couple of bands just drinking beers in the upstairs bar, maybe 20 or 30 people. But you just came because, as a punk, where else would you go?'

Exactly. Although members of the Inner Circle bands turned up at the club, that didn't necessarily mean they liked what they saw there. Glen Matlock's prime reason for attending was Celia Perry, now his girlfriend, and still by day a student at Ravensbourne College of Art. 'There'd be all this punk mayhem going on, and all these rude boys hustling dope and stuff, and Celia'd be in the office doing her knitting homework, and I'd be having a cup of tea with her. It wasn't that I thought the Roxy was so great.' Even while the club was still in operation, the Clash were prepared to articulate their doubts about the bands that played there. 'What's great about this scene is the way kids are starting up bands,' Paul told *ZigZag*'s Kris Needs that March. 'The only thing is, they have to do something original, and that's really hard.' 'All the new groups sound like drones, and I ain't seen a good new group for six months,' Mick told Tony Parsons a few days later. 'Their sound just ain't exciting. They need two years.' In that same interview Joe opined that things were just too easy for the new bands. Talking to Caroline Coon not long afterwards, he was totally dismissive of both the current punk scene and the Roxy, which he described as a 'dormitory'. The last time he had been in the club, he had been so offended by the lack of energy that he had squirted tomato ketchup over the mirrored walls before storming out. 'The sooner it closes the better.'

Harsh words indeed, and ones betraying complicated and even contradictory feelings. Like the Sex Pistols before them, the Clash had pushed for new bands and a new surge of energy, but when they got what they asked for, they were no longer quite so sure they wanted it. Admittedly, some of the new groups were and would remain talentless bandwagon jumpers, but by no means all of them were as one-dimensional as the Clash members suggested. Rough-and-ready as performers and musicians these bands may have been, but the Clash, who had been together for little over nine months when they made their comments, were not much more advanced. And wasn't the whole *point* of the DIY ethic that such things didn't matter? The new bands might well have needed to gain some experience, and that was exactly what they were setting out to do through playing the Roxy.

Similarly, the Clash, like the Pistols, had always said they wanted the punk movement to grow, yet now it was beginning to do so, they were unhappy with the people it was attracting. True, they had not anticipated the influence of the tabloids' twisted version of what punk was all about, but one cannot but suspect an element of élitism in their attitude to what Glen Matlock also dismisses as 'the safety pin and bin-liner brigade'. Following the ICA ear-lobe incident, Shane MacGowan had started to run Sid Vicious a close second as Most Famous Punk Scenester, even appearing on the front cover of *Sounds*. In his 1986 *ZigZag* interview he summed up the general feeling among his contemporaries about the post-Grundy Incident days: 'One thing that's got to be pointed out about the original punk scene is that it was extremely élitist, like the mod scene in the early Sixties. The whole thing was basically created by the beginning of 1977, and anyone who got into it after that was just a pile of shit, in terms of the way people thought.'

Many of the original punk followers were themselves established in bands by the turn of the year. The mass-media interest saw off the remaining soul boy followers, and also the style-obsessed art school types like Alan Drake. 'We'd been at the centre of something that we could feel was really exciting, but we never called it "punk" or anything. I always dressed weird, we all did. And suddenly, one day, after all that business on the telly with the Pistols and Grundy, people would point to me in the street and say, "Oh, look! There's a *punk!*"' he says, with considerable distaste. Some old faces continued to hang around, but, as far as hard-line Sex-clothed poseurs like Marco Pirroni were concerned, even the presence of a drunken slob like Shane MacGowan was a symbol of the original scene's decline.

Joe's passionate denunciation of the Roxy also smacks of a snobbish reluctance to accept anything as bona fide punk that was not conceived or controlled by a member of the Inner Circle. The Clash might have opened the club, but they never played there again. Initially, there was a practical reason for this – the lack of a committed drummer – but that obstacle did not last for the duration of the Roxy's existence. Until they filled the gap, however, former movers and shakers the Clash were forced to be mere spectators at somebody else's show, and they evidently found it hard to take. Yet another reason for disliking the Roxy: it was such an obvious focus for the London punk scene that all a record company looking to snap up a punk band had to do was turn up with a contract. The publicity generated by the Grundy Incident and its aftermath meant more record companies were sniffing around for their own pet punks. Thus, the Clash felt a mixture of envy and irritation about the lack of dues-paying involved, just as the Pistols had with the Clash.

That the Clash were still suffering for their art was supposedly evidenced by their paleness, skinniness, grubbiness and general aspect of extreme poverty. In his review of the Leeds Anarchy Tour gig *National Rock Star*'s John Shearlaw had described them as 'looking and playing as if they'd been starving for days'. The subtitle for Caroline Coon's November interview had been 'Clash: down and out and proud'. Talking to her again in March 1977, Joe looked back and said, 'A lot of the time me and Paul did nothing else but wonder where our next meal was coming from. We were hungry all the time.' The impression given by such remarks and backed up by the anecdote about Paul's flour-and-water paste snack was that these dole queue boys were living only one step up from rough in their decrepit rehearsal room, soldiering bravely on despite being snubbed by an unheeding music business.

Predictably, things were not quite so hopeless. The band's preferred drug explains both the weight loss and pallor: speed burns up calories, which is why amphetamines were prescribed as a slimming aid in the early Sixties, and it keeps users awake, promoting a nocturnal lifestyle. Hence these lines from the summer 1977 song '(White Man) In Hammersmith Palais': 'I'm the all night drug-prowling wolf / Who looks so sick in the sun.' Joe still chose to think of his Social Security giro cheque as a 'prescription' for drugs (as in 'Career Opportunities') rather than money to spend on food or, apparently, soap. It would be unfair to pass knee-jerk judgement on this supposed abuse of benefit payments: people caught in the poverty trap are, if anything, more in need of escapism than the better-off and fully occupied.

But were the members of the Clash caught in such a trap? Mick, for one, was still living at home with his nan, and at least being fed and getting his washing done. As for the others, Sebastian Conran is right when he says there was more than an element of choice in their lifestyle. Paul had two parents living within daily travelling distance of Rehearsals. He was too proud to sign on, but he was more than happy to be helped out by his girlfriend, Caroline Coon – a telling scene shot for the film *Rude Boy* a year later had him, the Bit of Rough, sneaking money from her purse – and she had her own flat. Likewise, Joe, who insisted he didn't believe in love in Caroline's March 1977 interview, was still (apparently not so) romantically involved with Palmolive. Had he not been so determined to portray himself as a lone wolf with no life away from the band, he presumably could have squatted somewhere slightly more salubrious with her; or, indeed, with any of his erstwhile friends from the Maida Hill squatting community.

Whether self-imposed or not, the lifestyle Paul and Joe felt they needed to live in order to be part of the Clash was a hard one, and not all its privations were physical. The lie detector works on the principle that it is more taxing to fabricate a story than to tell the truth. However much the Clash genuinely wanted to embody the myth that was being constructed around them, to do so essentially involved living a lie. Of all the band members, Joe was the one who had made the most effort to reinvent himself, not only adopting his punk persona, but also keeping his previous life at arm's length. And that was not all. 'He had to get himself into a miserable state to be able to write,' says Sebastian. 'Happy people don't create anything,' Joe himself confirmed when talking to *Musician*'s Vic Garbarini in 1981. 'I find creation hinges on being well fucked-up.' All in all, it was a tough discipline, making for a lonely, stressful existence.

By the early part of 1977, it was beginning to take its toll. In addition to using speed, Joe was drinking copious amounts of Special Brew and, as a consequence, behaving erratically. His ketchup-flinging flare-up at the Roxy was by no means an isolated incident. In a July 1978 *NME* feature Chris Salewicz referred back to 'the days when those close to the band would tell you that "the real problem in the Clash is Joe Strummer", the days when Joe would be found lying drunk in the gutter outside Dingwalls with rain water washing into his mouth'. Some of his antics verged on the kamikaze, as his *alter ego* 'Albert Transom' recalled in the booklet accompanying *The Story Of*

The Clash, Volume 1. Already the ted–punk violence augured by the ULU gig had flowered into full-scale running battles on Saturday afternoons down the King's Road, as well as more random assaults by representatives of one subculture upon the other whenever their paths should happen to cross. Against this background, Joe chose to grease his hair back, dress up in ted gear and take a besotted and similarly-attired Sebastian along with him on visits to known ted pubs and haunts. Sebastian recollects these trips all too well. 'I remember going with Joe to a teddy boy gig, dressed up and hoping we wouldn't get rumbled. And then someone said to Joe, "Oi, I recognise you! You're Woody from the 101ers. Bloody great band! What you doing now, then?" We were *shitting* ourselves!' After that narrow escape, still dressed up, the duo went for a late drink at the Roxy, an act of bravado which was also akin to walking into the lions' den with dead lambs strapped to their backs. 'Really, we were *asking* to get beaten up,' says a retrospectively appalled Sebastian.

If that were the case, Joe got his wish in February. While the rock stars' haunt was supposedly against everything punk stood for, some of the more recognisable punk faces had taken to going along to the Speakeasy after the Roxy shut. Johnny, so he claimed in *Rotten*, had befriended a ted who was also 'a Millwall football hooligan', 'a big fat motherfuck' and 'real hard'. In Johnny's typically gloating version the ted took against Joe for being a working class fake, got him in the toilet at the Speakeasy and 'absolutely pummelled' him. 'Soon after Joe was going on about being beaten up by gangs of teds.' It is true that Joe mythologised the incident. The following month, he told Tony Parsons, 'I had a knife with me, and I shoulda stuck it in him, right? But when it came to it, I remember vaguely thinking that it wasn't really worth it, 'cause although he was battering me about the floor I was too drunk for it to hurt that much, and if I stuck my knife in him I'd probably have to do a few years.' Nauseating macho posturing it might have been, but there was no mention of 'gangs of teds', just one 'giant, psychotic teddy boy', which tallies with Johnny's own description. Among considerable other minor injuries, Joe lost part of a front tooth, which didn't do much for his already sibilant vocal delivery.

Even accepting for a moment the myth that Joe and the rest of the Clash had no choice about living such a basic, desperate, hand-to-mouth existence, it was not as though there were no escape in sight, the true definition of a trap, poverty or otherwise. They had prospects: 'I continued to pursue them, irrespective of what Jim Crook said to me,' says Chris Parry. 'As far as Bernie Rhodes and the band were concerned, when they went on the Anarchy Tour, they were going to be signed to Polydor. We were sending telegrams to the Clash wishing 'em luck, and we had a deal in place. I just needed to get Jim Crook to sign it off, and he wouldn't.'

Since their return from the Anarchy Tour, Bernie and the band had been doing their best to help matters along. Being in such close contact with

Malcolm over the preceding month had provided Bernie with the chance to exploit the latter's contacts, one of whom was Julien Temple. At Malcolm's behest, Julien had filmed on- and off-stage highlights of the Anarchy Tour. Some of this footage was ultimately incorporated in 1979's posthumously released Sex Pistols movie, *The Great Rock'n'Roll Swindle*, which was directed by Julien and told Malcolm's version of the band's story.

Julien had been brought up on a council estate in St John's Wood, a fairly salubrious part of north London. After being educated at grammar school, he had gone on to attend King's College, Cambridge. In 1975, his degree completed, he had enrolled at the National Film and Television School in Beaconsfield, 25 miles north-west of London. Happening upon the punk scene at a relatively early stage, he had decided to abandon his other projects in favour of unofficially documenting the phenomenon using the school's equipment.

Always vigilant when it came to the possibility of free and freely rendered assistance with furthering the Clash's career, Bernie learned that the Film School not only had a film studio in Beaconsfield's Station Road, but also a separate 8-track sound studio. For students, access was easy and supervision non-existent. Unfortunately, the Clash still had no drummer. For the same reasons he gave prior to being persuaded to play the Anarchy Tour, Rob had left immediately after the Roxy gig. Bernie phoned Terry Chimes, and the ever-amenable drummer agreed to sit in as a one-off favour. He and the rest of the Clash duly made their way to Beaconsfield. The recording session was filmed by Julien and stills were also taken, but, as between-song conversational snippets captured on a bootleg tape of proceedings reveal, far more attention was paid to sound than vision. Although Bernie, again competing with Malcolm, was not averse to getting some potential promotional footage of the band in the can, the filming was little more than a smokescreen for the covert recording, a second attempt at capturing the True Spirit of the Clash for the benefit of Polydor and whoever else might be interested.

After the bad experience with Guy Stevens, it was decided to attempt something closer to the band's live sound. The Pistols had done the bulk of their recording to date with live soundman Dave Goodman. Taking a leaf out of their book, and also living up to the DIY ethic, the Clash installed Micky Foote in the control room. Or someone did: the between-take chatter has Mick Jones loudly expressing both surprise and dismay at this turn of events, and not once, but twice, just in case Micky missed it the first time.

In fact, the dialogue as a whole could give the infamous Troggs Tapes a run for their money. Mick whines about everything else too, including his new, enforced short haircut (this time genuinely close-cropped), being hungry, being broke and being told by Joe to shut his face for complaining. His one halfway constructive comment is a suggestion to lose part of a Paul Simonon bassline. Joe, meanwhile, snarls at Mick and threatens to 'smash' a foreign-sounding female onlooker – probably Palmolive – if she follows up her offer to give the guitarist money for food. In full Luddite mode, he objects at length to being asked by Micky to do a second take, before almost immediately doing a 360-degree turn and demanding better and more frequent instruction from the unfortunate soundman. After some terrible boogie-woogie piano playing courtesy of Joe, everyone takes it in turns to rubbish the in-studio sound quality.

Partly because they were consciously trying to better their previous recordings and partly because Terry was unfamiliar with the more recent songs, the band recorded the same selections as they had with Guy Stevens: 'London's Burning', 'White Riot', 'Career Opportunities', '1977' and an instrumental version of 'Janie Jones'. The one addition was old standby 'I'm So Bored With The USA', for which Joe had finally got round to writing a full lyric, albeit an inchoate version of that which would grace the band's début album. This early effort begins with the line about Yankee detectives always being on the TV, but offers a far less witty reason: 'because there's a murder in America about every ten seconds'. It goes on to work up a head of steam about tasteless baseball shirts and sleep-inducing West Coast music, in which context the lines 'I'll salute the new wave / And I hope nobody escapes' make more immediate sense. The band would defend the revised version of the song as being not anti-American, but anti-American imperialism, both literal and cultural; this version is just plain anti-American, its targets petty and obvious. For Joe, this was just so much punk method acting: he was in fact besotted with both America and American culture.

Overall, despite the band's expressions of dissatisfaction during recording, the Beaconsfield demos were far more aggressive and impressive than Guy Stevens's efforts. Although Chris Parry didn't have the authority to sign the Clash himself, he kept pushing, and the new recordings may well have helped sway opinion: by mid-January he had won approval and was in a position to formalise a Polydor deal. But now it was Bernie's turn to delay. 'I'd say something to him, and it was always, "I've got to think about that." And I'd say, "Bernie, you're thinking too much! It's pretty straightforward." And he'd say, "Oh, you can never think *too* much."'

Bernie had a reason for stalling. On 4 January, one of the Sex Pistols had been sick at Heathrow Airport, resulting in another flurry of tabloid activity. Two days later, EMI had finally terminated their contract with the band; shortly afterwards they handed over £30,000, the balance of the recording and publishing advances, making the total paid to the Pistols since 8 October 1976 £50,000. Almost immediately, Malcolm began talks with various other record companies, including A&M, CBS and Warner Bros. The bands involved might not have found the Anarchy Tour conducive to ongoing friendships, but it had finally shown Malcolm that Bernie could be a useful ally. As ever, when not 100 per cent sure of himself, he began to think there might be safety in numbers. Discussions were held about the possibility of keeping the Anarchy Tour bands together under some kind of joint management and recording deal.

The two managers brought out the more machiavellian aspects of each other's characters. They decided that their first priority should be to exert more control over their respective bands, certain members of which were deemed to be getting ideas above their station. For Malcolm, Johnny Rotten would always be a handful. Glen Matlock, meanwhile, was not only loathed by the vocalist and unpopular with the rest of the band, but was also beginning to express his resentment at being treated like a pariah. When it came to a stand-off between the bassist and the singer, even though he had written almost all the band's tunes, it was Glen who was the expendable one.

Bernie had varying degrees of trouble with all three of *his* charges. When they had moved into the band's circle at around the same time late the previous year, neither Rob Harper nor Tony Parsons had picked up the impression gained by some earlier *habitués* of the Clash scene, namely that Bernie was the one in charge. Instead, Mick was growing more and more assertive in the musical department; Joe's charisma was such that he seemed to be the band's leader in all other areas; while Paul's endless mockery and pranks made the manager out to be little more than a figure of fun. In an attempt to assert himself, Bernie held a meeting in the Ship during which he told the Clash he wanted 'complete control'. Joe's and Paul's immediate response was to burst into hysterical laughter.

The direct method having failed, both managers fell back on sneakier moves. Almost unbelievably egotistical though it may sound, they came to the conclusion – without bothering to consult their respective bands – that a mutually beneficial solution would be a straight swap of bass players. Whether this would have come about had Malcolm and Bernie's alliance continued is debatable, but that Paul's move to the Pistols was at least discussed was subsequently confirmed in Nick Kent's December 1978 *NME* interview with the Clash. It was finally decided that Glen should leave the Pistols early in February, whereupon Johnny Rotten insisted the replacement should be his old friend Sid Vicious. Sid had been singing and playing rudimentary bass with the loose rehearsal band called the Flowers of Romance, whose personnel at various times also included Palmolive on drums and Keith Levene, Viv Albertine and *Sniffin' Glue*'s Steve Walsh on guitar. Interestingly, Sid's method of learning his instrument was identical to Paul's: playing along to Ramones records. He never did master it.

As for the other part of the exchange, Glen believes he was sounded out about it shortly before he officially left the Pistols on 24 February. The approach came not from Bernie, but from Mick and Joe, though it is anybody's guess whether they were aware of their manager's schemes by this time or theirs was an independent and coincidental approach. 'Mick called me up and said, "Hey, what's up? They going to have a leaving party for you?"' says Glen. 'And I said, "I dunno." So I went and met him and Joe down the Marquee, and we had a drink, and they was like, "What are you going to do, then?" And without actually saying, "Will you join the Clash?" that was what they were saying.'

While the band personnel questions were still being mulled over, the managers did some market research about the possibility of setting up a recording equivalent of the Anarchy Tour package, only without the complications offered by the increasingly bothersome Heartbreakers. 'At one point Malcolm and Bernie both came up to me and said, "Well, what we think might be the best thing to do is, maybe we should both go to the same record company,"' says Chris Parry. '"That way we might get understood."' Since they had already messed them about once, however, the Sex Pistols' stock at Polydor was too low to make the suggestion a goer there. According to Glen – who, like the other members of both bands, remained unaware of this at the time, and was let in on the secret by Bernie only when he worked with him briefly in the late Eighties – Maurice Oberstein, head of CBS UK, was also approached with a similar proposition. 'Bernie said to him, "What we want to do is start a label", and Oberstein said, "That's interesting." And he went away and thought about it, and phoned Bernie up and said, "Right you are: I'm going to give you £100,000 to do it."'

Bernie and Malcolm held a last meeting about the planned joint venture on 18 January, but, as had happened on all previous occasions, when it came to the crunch, Malcolm just could not bring himself to accept anything less than total control. 'Malcolm wouldn't do it,' says Glen, reporting what Bernie told him over ten years after the event. 'He didn't want to be one of the pack, he wanted to be ahead of the pack. So that went down the dumper.' With most record companies concerned less with the tabloids' condemnation of punk than with the publicity value it gave the movement, it now seemed likely that Malcolm would be able to pick and choose his own deal for the Pistols. Most of the other first wave bands had already signed contracts and released singles. A&R men were already sniffing around the second wave bands at the Roxy. If the Clash were not to be left out in the cold, it was time for Bernie to make his move.

And, although the band had laughed at the idea of his taking complete control in other areas, it was entirely Bernie's move. 'To be honest, I'm a total idiot in business affairs, more so then, and I'm really dumb and naïve now. I'd freely admit I didn't know what the fuck was going on,' Joe, in confessional mode, told the *NME*'s Paul Morley in 1979. 'When Bernie said we were going to sign to Polydor, I just left it all to him, and I just thought, "Fucking great, we can put out a record."' In her diary entry for 26 January Sophie Richmond noted that there had been a change of plan: 'Bernie has signed with CBS. Poor old Polydor – again.' As Mick revealed in the *Clash On Broadway* booklet, the band themselves didn't find out until it was time for them to append their signatures the following day. They expected to be signing with Polydor until Bernie phoned up and told them to be over at CBS's Soho Square offices in half an hour. 'It was January 27, 1977: that was the day we signed to CBS,' Joe told *Melody Maker*'s Ted Mico ten years later. 'I forget my birthday, but I never forget that date.'

Poor old Polydor, indeed. And, especially, poor old Chris Parry. Having pursued first the Pistols and then the Clash for the best part of six months, he was left with nothing. Once again, he was urged to pick himself up and move on to the next most likely band. 'It was Shane MacGowan who came to me and said, "Don't worry about it, Chris. There's a great fuckin' band playing at the Marquee you should see." So I went to see the Jam playing, and we took it from there.' This time, Chris impressed the need for rapid action upon his colleagues at Polydor – Chiswick were in the process of negotiating a deal - and the Jam were snapped up immediately for a mere £6,000. While the contract was later renegotiated, it still turned out to be one of the best bargains Polydor ever got.

Initially inspired by the Who and Dr Feelgood, Paul Weller's songwriting had already taken on a Clash-influenced angry political edge, though at first, and briefly, he adopted an oppositional pro-Conservative stance. 'I sort of meddled in politics,' Paul told Paolo Hewitt for his Jam biography, *A Beat Concerto*. 'Like I really just followed the Clash and I didn't really know what the fuck I was on about.' The Jam's singles would fare much better than those of the Clash in the domestic market, and as Paul Weller's writing matured, the Jam would take over from the Clash as the darlings of the UK music press and, if polls are any indication, their readership. All this helped to fuel the rivalry between the two bands.

The Jam's first few records were produced by the Polydor house team of Chris Parry and Vic Smith, the engineer who had worked on the Clash demos. After elongating his name to Vic Coppersmith-Heaven, the latter took over as the band's sole producer in late 1978 when Chris Parry went off to found his own label, Fiction, from where he launched the immensely successful career of the Cure. In 1985, the Cure headlined the last ever gig played by the Clash, and Chris was present. 'It's funny that, isn't it?' he says, with no trace of malice in his voice, and no cause for regrets.

In a report accompanied by a still from the Beaconsfield session the 22 January issue of *Melody Maker* had announced an imminent Clash deal, and had suggested it would be with Polydor. Thus, unaware that there had been earlier contact between Bernie and Maurice Oberstein, *everyone* was caught out by the last-minute switch to CBS. Subsequently, there was much speculation about the details of the contract. In November 1978, the *NME*'s Steve Clarke disclosed that Polydor had offered the band an advance of £25,000, plus free recording costs. Chris Parry confirms that the January 1977 offer was much the same as the one that had been made to the Sex Pistols four months earlier. A lot had changed since then, however, with the publicity value of the Grundy Incident having upped the ante considerably. Bernie and the Clash were initially loath to admit the size of the successful CBS bid - nearly two years later, Steve Clarke was still tentatively guestimating that 'it was in the region of at least £50,000' – but rumours of a six-figure sum continued to circulate until the band finally admitted to £100,000.

It seemed, and seems, an unbelievable leap. True, again according to

Glen, the sum had already been tabled by CBS, but that had been for a joint Pistols–Clash label. Bernie had the advantage of knowing, roughly, what Malcolm was asking for the Pistols – when they finally signed with A&M on 9 March, the overall deal was for £150,000 – but it was still an astounding piece of hustling on behalf of a seven-month-old band which had played fewer than 30 gigs, most of them as a support act. Especially as CBS were still independently chasing the Pistols at the time, bumping up the potential pay-out faced by the record company to over twice their original offer for the two-band package. At 50-plus years old and after an adult lifetime in the music business, Maurice Oberstein was no mean operator, a master of unsettling and intimidatory negotiating techniques. The question has to be asked: why was he prepared to throw so much money at what had every appearance of being a short-lived style-led fad, without any hint of the musicianship and stability that might promise a long, productive career?

'They signed us up for that much money because they wanna try and keep us quiet,' insisted Joe that May on Radio One's *Rock On* programme. 'You watch: they're gonna attempt to muffle us up in the next six months so they can get on with their lovely little Johnny Mathis and Vibrators and Abba records. [After failing to sign the Pistols, CBS picked up the Vibrators in March.] I reckon they paid a lot of money just to silence us.' Understandably sceptical, presenter John Tobler asked Joe to confirm that he suspected industry intrigue. 'What do they need us for?' demanded Joe. 'I think they see us as a threat to their already fantastic rivers of money, you know? They see us as something to block it up, right? So if they own us, and we haven't got any money . . .' At which point John interrupted to suggest that, if the Clash had already spent £100,000, then that was their problem. 'Exactly,' said Joe. 'They're training us to take a helicopter to the supermarket.'

It sounded like total paranoid fantasy, but part of it was true, as the Clash were due to find out: an advance is a loan, and once it has been spent, a band is in debt to the record company until it has been repaid. Nevertheless, Maurice Oberstein did not sign the Clash because he saw punk as a threat to CBS and its established artists, but because he saw no difference between the band and any other potential money-maker. Like any businessman, when market forces denied him a bargain, he was prepared to pay the going rate.

But that was not the whole story. Maurice took his job as head of the UK division seriously, and objected to its poor-relation status in the eyes of the parent company across the Atlantic. His personal agenda was to sign British and European acts and rub CBS America's faces in it by making them huge international successes. As he told the *Guardian*'s Adam Sweeting in 1993, 'It became my great joy to attend a CBS-Columbia convention in America, and have the presidents of Epic and Columbia [CBS's US labels] asking for my acts.' Sure, punk bands were a risky investment, but what could be more British than a street-level London rock'n'roll movement?

At the time, Clash observers were more concerned about the *band*'s motives for signing to a major record company for so much money. Having not even been party to the deal, the members found themselves forced to justify it both to the music press and to fans who picked up on the critics' muttered asides about the Clash having 'sold out' to the establishment. They had two lines of argument, both of which Mick tried out on Kris Needs in March. The first was, 'You've got to make records. You can do your own label, and not many people will hear it. This way more people will hear our record.' The second was that the band had retained 'complete control' over artistic matters.

Mick would quickly come to rue the latter boast, but the former claim – that the band needed financial backing and an efficient publicity machine in order to get their message across to as many people as possible – was to be given regular outings over the next couple of years. 'If we hadn't signed to CBS, none of you lot would have heard of us. So stuff that down your gizzard!' Joe admonished a heckling audience on the May 1977 White Riot Tour. Two years later, he gave a more reasoned version to Paul Morley. His argument was that both Malcolm and Bernie were concerned that, without the involvement of major record companies, the UK punk scene might have become as ghetto-ised as had been the US new wave scene before UK punk's success gave it a new lease of life. 'CBGB's on the Bowery was how it stayed for five years. It never came out of there,' he said. 'Our stuff and the Pistols' stuff was great. I don't want to brag, but it didn't deserve to stay in a hole in Covent Garden for five years.' Bernie confirmed his position in 1980 when talking to the *NME*'s Paul Rambali about the only other option open to the Clash: 'An independent [label]: you mean a small business. If you don't have access to gain the means of production, whatever you do is peripheral.'

By June 1977, Mark Perry had handed over the running of *Sniffin' Glue* to his friend Danny Baker, whose editorial in that month's issue came to the Clash's defence: 'There's no point screamin' to the converted on privately owned/distributed labels that could sell about two hundred, is there? We wanna be heard, fuck being a cult.' It should be pointed out that the fanzine had itself recently moved up in the world and was sharing offices with Miles Copeland (manager of his brother's would-be punk band, the Police, and boss to be of successful independent record company IRS), who, in March 1977, had launched his independent punk label, Step Forward, with Mark Perry as A&R man.

It was Mark who, famously, was the most vocal in his condemnation of the Clash's move. 'I was insisting it was up to bands like the Clash – that were very popular and were courting a lot of record company interest – to say, "No! We're not going to become part of the establishment, we're gonna do it ourselves." I knew it could be done. The Buzzcocks did their first EP themselves. [In late January 1977, the Buzzcocks released their début record, *Spiral Scratch*, on the self-financed label New Hormones.] We did the *Glue* without being part of a big publisher like IPC. I think the last *Glue* sold about 20,000 copies.

'Even if we take the Clash's arguments about wanting a bigger audience, distribution problems and whatever, it's still possible. The Pistols had stirred this thing up. *They'd* made this thing interesting to a big audience, *they'd* made everyone look at us to see what was going to happen next. There was a massive audience for something you could have done on your own. I mean, UB40 proved that later with their own label. And yet the Clash go and sign to CBS. If you talk about just music, it doesn't matter – I've got loads of CBS albums - but if you talk about what the Clash talked about in their songs, then they completely sold out. If the Clash didn't believe – and didn't want to stick with – the ideas they were trying to put over, then they were the biggest bullshitters around. Eric Clapton wasn't, because Eric Clapton just wanted to play music, so let him sign up to whoever he wants and make loads of money out of it. But the Clash: it disappointed me immensely, and I said so. My big quote was "Punk died the day the Clash signed to CBS." CBS were one of the biggest weapons and communications systems manufacturers in the world! This massive conglomerate. Basically, it's why the world's dying, because of industries like that. If you look at it in those terms – and I'm no longer that serious that I want to, but if you do follow my argument – they *completely sold out.*'

Joe's response to Mark's 'big quote', given to *Melody Maker*'s Allan Jones in November 1978, was 'The dirty fucking rat!' 'The strange thing is that *he* becomes a director of a record company,' added Paul Simonon. 'He was just blaming us for his own cop-outs,' continued Joe. 'Any time that I've copped out I've never blamed anyone but myself. When I heard that he'd said that, I was so annoyed, you know. It was like him saying, "It's all their fault. They let us down." Why should he hang on to us? Where's his own two feet?' Mark's own two feet had by then taken him from editing the fanzine he founded to talent-scouting for a small independent record label to forming his own avant-punk band Alternative TV. All were sound DIY or near-DIY ventures: even bearing in mind Miles Copeland's involvement, Step Forward was hardly in the same category as CBS, being pitched somewhere between New Hormones and Chiswick. As a counter-attack on Mark's own integrity, then, Joe's and Paul's efforts were somewhat lame.

As Mark says, the Grundy Incident had already brought punk enough publicity to guarantee the Clash respectable sales on a self-financed or independent label. So it was not just for him but for many other thinking punk scene observers that the band's argument about needing CBS-style backing failed to stand up. Those who believed the band were responsible for, or at least participated in, their own business decisions could not help but suspect that the Clash were suddenly placing old-fashioned rock ambitions ahead of their much-trumpeted political agenda. Of course, in reality, it was Bernie alone who was making those decisions, and for all his radical claims, Bernie was as much concerned with keeping up with Malcolm and the Sex Pistols as with knocking down the pillars of the existing music business establishment.

Also, having reluctantly and somewhat stingily bankrolled the Clash's efforts thus far, he was not uninterested in the financial rewards of signing to a major for as high an advance as possible. Whether this was in the band's best interests is arguable. As so much upfront money was involved, the CBS contract had few of the safety and support clauses the band might have enjoyed with a smaller advance, like guaranteed tour support, say, or – as with the Polydor contract offered by Chris Parry – free recording. Everything the Clash did would have to be paid for by the Clash themselves; meanwhile, Bernie was entitled to his 20 per cent managerial cut straight off the top of the advance.

Nevertheless, it is all too easy to use the benefit of hindsight to point out supposedly suspect business practices. It should be noted that, whatever their hopes for punk or their own individual futures, neither Bernie nor the others had any reason to think of the Clash as a long-term career option; the Sex Pistols' experience with EMI did not bode well for CBS's commitment. 'Signing that contract did bother me a lot,' Joe admitted to Caroline Coon in March 1977. 'But now I've come to terms with it. I've realised that all it boils down to is perhaps two years' security. We might have an argument with CBS and get thrown off!' In this context, it made perfect sense for Bernie to take as much money as possible, with a view to cutting and running with it like Malcolm and the Pistols had whenever it might prove necessary or advantageous.

The intention with Polydor had been to go into the studio as soon as possible, and the band carried this sense of urgency with them when they switched to CBS. It was born of the competitive drive and a need for topical relevance, two concepts that a big business like a major record company could readily understand. The Damned had already recorded their album, which was due for release in February, the Stranglers were recording their first album for UA and the Sex Pistols were still working on studio material with Dave Goodman, ready for when Malcolm secured them a deal. Not only that, but a song like 'White Riot', with its references to the previous summer's Notting Hill Riot, was in danger of passing its sell-by date.

As the need to record was so pressing, the Clash had spent the latter half of January doing their best to fill the gap in their line-up. A certain weariness of tone is detectable in the display ad carried in the classifieds section of the 15 January issue of *Melody Maker*: 'DYNAMIC DRUMMER WANTED for young professional Rock Group. Must look great, play great.' Once again, the anonymous band had been deluged with applicants, and had spent much of the following week auditioning all those drummers who turned up and stuck around long enough to try out. Unfortunately, nobody had proved suitable, and another ad was placed in time to be included in the issue of *Melody Maker* dated 29 January. Decidedly more buoyant, it read: 'POWERFUL YOUNG DRUMMER WANTED FOR NAME BAND. No jazz, no funk, no laid back.' The three negative criteria ran the risk of sounding narrow-minded, but were a convenient shorthand for 'punk', and as such set something of a trend over subsequent weeks among other advertisers hoping to catch hold of punk's coat-tails.

The second of these ads hit the streets only the day before Bernie secured the deal with CBS, meaning that the band signed to the record company as a three-piece. 'Robin Blanchflower, the A&R man at the time, was the guy that phoned me up,' says Simon Humphrey, then a staff engineer at CBS Studios (now the Hit Factory) on Whitfield Street in central London. 'He said to me, "There's a new band we've just signed. We're sending them over because we want to stick 'em in the studio straight away." I basically got the nod as the youngest engineer: he probably thought I was more suitable to do the punk stuff. I can't remember who came over. Joe, I think, and Bernie Rhodes, and they were kind of grumpy and not very communicative, but anyway, they booked in for the next day.' That was Friday, 28 January, just one day after the contract was signed. The idea was to record 'White Riot' and '1977' over a three-day weekend session for the band's first single release, with an album to follow almost immediately afterwards.

The drummer problem was now critical. When he turned up for an audition in response to the second of the January *Melody Maker* ads, Jon Moss was initially put off by the dirtiness and scruffiness of his potential colleagues to be. Then realisation dawned, as he explained six years later to *Smash Hits'* Dave Rimmer: 'I said, "You're the Clash, aren't you?" and Joe Strummer went, "How do *you* know?" And I said, "Well, it's written on the back of your jacket . . ."' Aside from illustrating the difficulties faced by the would-be anonymous Lettrist, this gave the Clash fair warning of Jon's far from retiring personality. Although asked back for further rehearsals, he was by no means the only candidate, and it was anyway too late to integrate a new drummer in time to record.

Both Terry Chimes and Rob Harper were approached to help out. The plan – hinted at in the news pages of the following week's *National Rock Star* – was to use Terry on those tracks with which he was familiar, namely the single and the bulk of the album material, and Rob on those songs written since the original drummer's departure. 'Bernie phoned me up, and it was like, "Come up for a meeting, and we'll all put our cards on the table and see who is in the group and who isn't,"' says Rob, 'And I said, "No, I've fucking had enough. Bye-bye." That was it, really.'

That wasn't quite it for Rob, though. The care he takes to give as balanced an account as possible of his time with the Clash stems from his irritation at the revisionism to which it has since been subjected. Upon Glen Matlock's departure from the Pistols, the bassist found his decision to leave portrayed as a sacking, and thereafter he was vilified at every opportunity by his former group and manager. At first, the circumstances of Rob's departure were similarly altered, but before long, instead of being mocked or scorned, he found he had been written out of the Clash's history altogether. He had already fallen out with Billy Idol when the former co-Rockette got in touch a few days after Rob had quit the Clash for good. 'Billy rang me and said, "You must have had a terrible shock when they sacked you." Gloatingly, you know. "No, they didn't sack me. I went as planned."' It turned out not to be mere Idol spite, but the Clash's managerial line. 'I ran into the Clash once or twice at clubs and things, and Mick said, "Oh, Bernie told me he'd sacked you."' Apparently, as with Terry, Bernie could not believe that Rob would walk out on him voluntarily. In this case he altered reality to fit his idea of how things ought to have been.

Later still, Rob had a conversation with a couple of people who had got to know the band since his departure, and mentioned having taken part in the Anarchy Tour. Next time he saw them, they said they'd checked his story with the Clash and been told, 'Oh, *him. He* was never really with the group.' Despite having been involved in one of the most celebrated rock events of all time – more than just 'a classic rock'n'roll tour' – Rob was not mentioned in any further interviews, family trees, encyclopedia entries or band histories, whether official or otherwise. Even Glen Matlock's 1990 autobiography made reference to him without providing his name. Only in 1991's *Clash On Broadway* booklet was he finally credited as being the drummer for the Anarchy Tour. Until then, had it not been for one or two Ray Stevenson photos taken during the tour and at the 1 January Roxy gig, as far as the Clash and their followers were concerned he might never have existed.

'The definite offer to join them wasn't there, but the possibility was there,' concludes Rob. 'That may purely have been bait to get me to do the tour and whatever; it may have been genuine; who can say? But I actually said to myself at the time, "One day you'll regret that you left so abruptly, threw up this opportunity, and didn't just knuckle down and do what they wanted, walk how they wanted, play how they wanted, dress how they wanted and behave how they wanted, because then you could have gone around the world. And you've got to remember, years later, when you think those things, that there was no way that it was going to work, and that's why you didn't do it." You know that [1979] Clash song, "Four Horsemen"? "When they picked up the hiker he didn't want the lift"? Well, that's probably not about me, but it could have described me, and maybe some other people. That sums it up quite well . . . I guess I *was* a bit cavalier with my opportunities back in those days.'

Back in 1974, Rob had been playing guitar in a college band when another guitarist approached him and asked to join. Quickly realising that the newcomer was more talented, Rob switched to bass, and the band changed its name to the Café Racers. Rob quit when he went to Sussex University. During the holidays, the guitarist contacted him, said he was forming a new band to play his own material and asked Rob to be the bassist. He declined. The guitarist was Mark Knopfler, and the band was Dire Straits. Between 1974 and 1977, Rob was also involved with New Hearts, playing bass on the demos that won them their CBS contract. Later the band adopted a mod image, and became Secret Affair. Following his inadvertent contribution to the formation of Generation X and his stint with the Clash, Rob played guitar, then drums, then guitar again for the UK Subs, before deciding that he'd already gone down that route once with a better band. Also in 1977, he spent two weeks as guitarist for a new band being put together by a singer named Stuart Goddard. When asked to suggest a band name, Rob came up with two before he left: the Humans and the Ants. Stuart picked the latter, and then changed his name to Adam. 'I've had so much of this, it means nothing to me,' laughs Rob. 'It's all just like fate, you know.' He still plays a variety of instruments in a variety of bands. 'The Clash were bloody good. Best band I've ever been with.'

As a result of Rob's refusal to co-operate, the Clash had to rely wholly on the goodwill of Terry Chimes once more. It was he who accompanied the others to the CBS studios to record the first single. 'Studios were a hangover from the Sixties, even in the mid-Seventies,' says Simon Humphrey. 'We all had long hair – or aspired to have long hair, in my case – and we all wore cowboy boots and stuff like that. The British studio scene was a very cosy, insulated one that was full of old-time producers and techniques. We were all in love with the Beatles, and I'd grown up with progressive rock, Yes and Led Zeppelin. In the studio, we'd only heard the rumours about what was going on in the street, as it were. We weren't prepared for punk, and we didn't particularly fancy having it thrust at us head on. I must admit, I was viewing it all with a fair amount of trepidation. I mean, the girls at the head office were terrified every time the band went in. They thought there was going to be a riot every time they walked through the door. None of us knew what to expect, whether they were going to burn the place down . . .'

By the time the band arrived at the studios, someone had beaten them to it. 'The second floor was gutted because there'd been a fire,' recalls Beryl Ritchie, then as now responsible for disc mastering. 'It was funny because we had a receptionist downstairs, an Irish guy, and when they came in in all their tatty gear, he thought they were workmen. He said, "The fire's on the second floor", and they said, "Nah, we're 'ere to record." They were only in with me for an hour and a half when I was doing the cut for the album, but they were actually very nice.' Simon Humphrey isn't prepared to go that far. 'There was no smashing up of equipment, and they were reasonably civilised. But there was a vaguely unpleasant side to them. Personal hygiene wasn't of the greatest order. By today's standards it was all fairly tame stuff: a bit of swearing, a bit of rough and tumble. Nothing outrageous, really.'

The wariness cut both ways. 'They were suspicious of studios generally. They hadn't been in too many, and you've got to understand they were trying to knock down all the doors of accepted behaviour, which is why they didn't particularly want any old-school producers sorting them out, and they didn't want to do anything that was considered to be "what had gone before".' For this reason, Micky Foote was once more appointed producer. In view of later difficulties between CBS and the Clash over their conflicting interpretations of the phrase 'complete control', it might seem odd that the record company should allow their new £100,000 investment to go into the studio with someone who was totally unknown and inexperienced. In fact, representatives from the record company's A&R department were familiar with the Beaconsfield demos, which had informed them of two things: firstly, that Micky was evidently capable of getting the band the raw, basic sound the Clash defined as 'punk'; and secondly, that, as the A&R men themselves could not understand this sound, it was unlikely that any 'old-school' producers would be able to either.

'Robin Blanchflower said to me, "We don't know what the hell it's all about, but they've got this *presence*,"' says Simon. 'The record company never showed their faces at all during the recording of the single or the album. They kept well away. I was given *carte blanche* to let them go in and do what they wanted.' Two months later, Micky Foote explained to Tony Parsons why he had taken on the job: 'You do it yourself because nobody else *cares* that much.' In 1990, Bernie Rhodes informed the *NME*'s Stuart Bailie that it was he, Bernie, who had produced (as well as written) the band's first album. During research for this book, more than one of Simon's former colleagues intimated that *he* had been the 'real' producer.

'Bernie didn't really have anything to do with the recording process, to be honest with you,' says Simon. 'He used to say things to Mick, or Joe, but he never addressed me. And they would tell him to piss off anyway. They were always screaming and shouting at him. And Micky: well, he was *there*. I mean, he was just the bloke on the other side of the control room glass. He was credited with the production, but you can't really say he contributed to it. He had the odd idea, I suppose.' Not that Simon is prepared to take the credit for himself. 'The role of an engineer before punk was that we weren't expected to chip in ideas, or anything like that. Our job was to make sure it was recorded technically correctly.' In other words, the engineer's role then was very much what most people outside the music business believed and, for the most part, still believe the producer's role to be: having the know-how to realise the ideas of others.

Simon's and Terry's accounts of the band's initial approach to studio work suggest it was amazing anything was produced at all: the spirit of Beaconsfield certainly lived on. The band went into Studio 3 (which, Mick was ecstatic to learn, was where Iggy and the Stooges had recorded *Raw Power*) and set up as though for a live performance. This was not particularly rare in those days, even in a 16-track facility. 'But the idea was that you separated stuff off because, although it was recorded live, you still wanted some control over different things,' explains Simon. 'Then if the bass was no good, or something, you could at least have the opportunity to redo it. They didn't grasp that.

'The first time they came in – the first time I'd met them all – Joe put his amp right next to the drum kit, and when he played it was like, full-blast guitar. You don't do that in a studio. You have it at the other side of the room, behind a screen, so you've got some kind of separation. So he was playing, and it was no good, because the sound was going right across the drums. I explained it to Joe, and he looked at me and said, "I don't know what separation is, *and I don't like it*." That was his opening shot.' Terry remembers another early hiccup in proceedings: 'We were going great guns with the drums, got the sound we wanted, no problem. Turned to the bass, and had an immediate difference of opinion about how it should sound. I don't think Joe or I really cared much about which way the argument went, but Paul and Mick were not going to budge, either of 'em. We spent hours, completely unproductively, arguing. I just thought, "This is an incredible waste of studio time." And the engineer suddenly said, "Why don't we do *both* sounds and decide later on, at our leisure, which one to use?" So that was unanimously voted on immediately, and we carried on.'

Which is not to say that all Simon's suggestions or opinions were so keenly received. It remained an uphill struggle. 'You had to be very careful about what you said. They'd be doing something, and you'd think, "Well, that doesn't sound very good", and they'd say, "How was that?" So you'd say, "Mmm, well, I dunno. I'm not sure it's right", and they'd say, "Oh, well, we'll keep it then!" Deliberately being provocative in a silly way. They just wanted to be in and out pretty quick, and they were hostile to anything that had been employed as a technique pre-punk. So, if there was like a harmony part, or a double-tracked guitar, or even dropping-in – you know, doing a little bit again because it didn't sound good enough – they'd think you were trying to polish them up or break down the whole punk ethic.'

Mick was more amenable than the others, being the band member not only the most interested in the studio's potential, but also with the most emotional investment in the tunes. 'They were Mick's songs. Well, Mick's music, and Mick was the musical one. Terry, the drummer, was basically told what to do. I think it's pretty well known that Paul didn't really play. There were quite a few bass parts where, I'm not saying Mick actually played the bass, but he showed them note for note to Paul, and Paul learned them parrot fashion. Paul definitely played his own parts, and I would say that, by the time it came to doing the album, he was beginning to show his own personality, but . . . he just did his bit, and that was it.'

It was Joe who continued to be the most troublesome. 'He was an incredible performer,' says Simon. 'It wasn't like he was in the studio doing it, he really was giving it 110 per cent at all times.' Unfortunately, out of his depth and resentful of Mick's relative capacity to adapt, he retreated further behind the gruff Joe Strummer punk persona. 'Joe's guitar sound was just *horrible*, it really was. Even Mick would say, "That is *terrible*, that sound!"' Knowing that Joe was still without a functioning guitar of his own, CBS sent over a brand new Telecaster from the shop underneath their offices in Soho Square. 'He just took the piss out of it. He certainly never used it. Anything that smacked of the Establishment.'

Nor were things any easier when it came to doing Joe's vocals. Having finally been convinced they would be better recorded separately, he was nevertheless extremely jittery about singing unaccompanied. 'He actually had to play the guitar at the same time as sing. We tried to get him to do it without, and he just couldn't do it. So all his lead vocals have got this unplugged guitar bashing away underneath. He also used to sing in a corner, facing away from us, but a lot of singers are like that. His vocals would be a one-off thing, like a straight-through performance. Joe wasn't really a singer in the accepted sense of the word: he just did his vocal, and that was it. There was no camouflaging or processing. He didn't take an interest in that.'

Although loath to heed their engineer, the band proved suggestible when it came to advice offered by the friends and followers who accompanied them to the single session, including Sebastian, Roadent, Frothler and Mad Jane. 'The Clash seemed to have this small group of middle class fans who followed them around,' recalls Simon. 'They were almost like rich kids who were hanging on to them. They liked the anarchic side to it. They would wander into the studio, and they'd be listening to the music, and they'd say, "I think it'd be really good if we had a gun firing here." And you'd think to yourself, "Christ, here we go . . ." And one of them would produce this gun. And I seem to remember him shooting it into the wall, and we recorded it. Of course, it didn't sound very good. And another day, they'd bring up a whole pile of corrugated sheeting from some building site. "What about if we belt this with a hammer?" This kind of stuff. So there was a bit of indulgence there.'

This was the origin of the sound effects included on the single version of 'White Riot': the siren at the beginning, the alarm bell at the end, the breaking glass and what Simon refers to as 'the famous stomping overdub' in the middle. Sebastian's air pistol might not have made it on to record, but his feet did. Reflecting on the earlier suggestion that he might take over as band drummer, he says, 'My sole contribution to the rhythm section was, you can hear my feet stamping on "White Riot". We were all jumping around the microphone.' 'I remember him being very keen to get on that,' laughs Terry. The single proved acceptable to CBS, though the band themselves were not overly impressed with 'White Riot', believing the Beaconsfield demo version to be braver.

According to Simon, the record company was running on a minimum four- to six-week turnaround at that time, so the single was scheduled for the earliest possible release date in mid-March. Under Bernie's direction, Sebastian was given the job of designing a picture sleeve, something which was already *de rigueur* for punk singles. For the front cover he used a Caroline Coon photograph taken the previous November, showing Joe, Mick and Paul with their backs to the camera, adopting a hands against the wall pose borrowed from the cover of Joe Gibbs and the Professionals' *State Of Emergency* album. The connection with repression in Jamaica was reinforced by the slogans 'HEAVY MANNERS' and 'HEAVY DUTY DISCIPLINE' along the seams of Joe's boiler suit. The back of Paul's boiler suit read 'WHITE RIOT' and the back of Mick's shirt 'STEN GUNS IN KNIGHTSBRIDGE', both of which slogans related to the two songs packaged within. Less directly relevant was the large 'HATE AND WAR' adorning Joe's back, but Sebastian got round that problem by blanking it out and superimposing '1977' instead. The overall effect was as clear an illustration as possible of Joe's oft-repeated claim that, rather than identifying *with* terrorists, the Clash envisaged the Sten guns in Knightsbridge to be implements of state control pointing *at* the band.

In view of the escalating violence between punks, other youth cults and 'straights', it was even less clever of Bernie to have Sebastian reproduce on the back of the sleeve the *Generation X* mods and rockers quote previously used on the ICA flyer. It was balanced to some degree by another excerpt from the book: 'Youth, after all, is not a permanent condition, and a clash of generations is not so fundamentally dangerous to the art of government as would be a clash between rulers and ruled.' It was more than just a clever way to amplify the signals given off by the band's name. The Grundy Incident had swollen the punk movement considerably, but it lacked positive direction, as had been testified by the confused behaviour of the audiences on the Anarchy Tour. Local government interference with the tour had likewise made Bernie and the band realise there was a real enemy to face, and it was no longer enough just to stir things up for the sake of it. The Clash were campaigning to win over a new constituency, hoping to persuade the nascent nationwide punk movement to escalate from token teen rebellion to a rebellion that offered a more genuine threat to the status quo. Or, at least, they were hoping to persuade them to buy records by a band making those kinds of noises.

The Clash booked back in at CBS Studio 3 to record the album over three consecutive Thursday-to-Sunday sessions, beginning on 10 February 1977. Joe spent what little spare time he had in the two weeks between the single sessions and the first album sessions refining his lyrics. Most of the songs were tweaked slightly: 'London's Burning' no longer burned with boredom 'babe', but with boredom 'now', as Joe was trying to exclude as many clichéd Americanisms as possible. The otherwise trite griping of 'I'm So Bored With The USA' was stiffened by some judicious pruning and the addition of a new first verse. The USA was now guilty of military and monetary, as well as cultural, imperialism.

It made for a much stronger song, even if it still carried a whiff of knee-jerk punk xenophobia. Ultimately, this was how most people chose to interpret it, which would bring accusations of hypocrisy down upon the Clash's heads when they began to turn their attentions to the American market in 1979. All three long-serving members of the band were called upon to defend themselves time and time again over the following years. 'That song is about the Americanisation of Europe,' Mick insisted when talking to *Rip It Up*'s Duncan Campbell in 1982. 'It's about the McDonalds and Burger Kings that we've got. It's about the American deployment of nuclear missiles on our island. All these things that we don't want. It's about the way America pushes around small countries, like ours, or any Central American country. It's *not* about being bored with the USA, because America is a very exciting place to be. We weren't saying, "We're not going to go", we were talking about the American imperialist attitude.'

The other lyric to undergo a substantial make-over was that for 'What's My Name'. While one or two lines that had been just about decipherable in earlier live versions made it on to the album, Joe earned his songwriting credit by blending them in with other scattered excerpts from the mental diary of an alienated urban teen. The protagonist fails to measure up to social standards, suffers rejection, expresses his frustration through violence and is punished by authority and abused at home. This serves to confirm his outsider status - specifically, as a criminal intent on revenge against mainstream society – and his loss of true individual identity, as expressed in the title chorus and the terrace-chant method of its delivery. All in all, the overhauled song is a concise sociology lecture from the point of view of the subject under examination. Although perhaps a little overblown, it is also chilling. It would have been even more so in both departments had Joe, as originally planned, placed the juvenile offender 'round the back' with a 'flick-knife' rather than a 'celluloid strip': the threat of burglary thus replaced the threat of something unspecified but potentially much nastier.

During rehearsals for the album the band took to fooling around with a punked-up version of Bob Marley's early reggae single 'Dancing Shoes'. This was partly for their own amusement, but it was also an attempt to go one step further than the use of drop-out in exploring the reggae influence. It didn't quite click, and Joe was further put off the idea by Johnny Rotten, who had declared that white people playing reggae was a form of cultural exploitation. When it came time to return to CBS Studio 3, the band set up with relatively little fuss and began playing through their repertoire while Simon adjusted the levels in the control room. Soon bored of playing familiar songs, they started to mess around with another reggae song.

Junior Murvin's 'Police And Thieves', co-written by producer Lee Perry, had been one of the previous year's more popular reggae singles; Murvin's high, pure voice made his despairing depiction of gangsters and policemen apparently determined to turn Jamaica into a war zone all the more poignant. 'My conception of it was, "Great, a reggae tune. Let's do it like Hawkwind!"' Joe told *Melody Maker* in 1988. 'But Mick was more intelligent.' Through the latter part of 1976, and into 1977, reggae had developed yet another sub-genre called 'rockers', which was characterised by a slow, heavy rhythm and had a ska-derived single *chocka* of wah-wah or heavily echoed guitar accentuating the off-beat. Mick got Terry to play drums rock'n'roll style, in 4/4 time, while he added greatly exaggerated rockers-style guitar and sang Murvin-style back-up to Joe's gruff, yet impassioned, reading of the lead vocal. 'We played it through while trying to get the right sound,' says Terry, 'and really started to groove on it.'

The more serious business of recording the remaining original compositions in the band's repertoire began shortly afterwards. The *Clash On Broadway* booklet claimed that the recording was a smooth and painless operation. It was, relatively. 'Sometimes they didn't really talk to me, but sometimes they didn't really talk to each other, either,' says Simon. 'Quite often, Joe would turn up and he'd go, "Is anyone else here?" And I'd go, "No, you're the first one here, Joe", and he'd go, "Oh well, bugger that then!" and he'd leave. Then Mick'd turn up and repeat the whole process. So, occasionally, you'd have days when no one would turn up because no one wanted to be the first to arrive.'

Mick made the most effort to break the ice. The fascination with the workings of a studio that Brady had found so embarrassing during Little Queenie's Pye demo session had not been without purpose. When Mick told Tony Parsons, 'There ain't no young producers in tune with what's going on. The only way to do it is to learn how to do it yourself', he did so not in support of Micky Foote, but to promote his own ambitions. On a couple of the occasions when none of the other band members was around, he invited Simon over to the nearby Spaghetti House for something to eat. As recording progressed, he took to staying on later at the studio.

'Mick got into the techniques of guitar solo double-tracking,' says Simon. Joe remained uninterested and made little effort to improve the sound of his rhythm playing, with a predictable, but previously undocumented, result: 'There's hardly any of his guitar on the album.' On one particular night there was hardly any of Mick's either. He left his Les Paul Junior propped up against the wall while he popped into the control room to hear a playback. As everyone watched helplessly through the glass, it slowly toppled over. 'The head cracked, just broke,' says Simon. 'Mick was devastated. He was actually pretty close to tears. I've got a feeling that he went home because he was so upset.'

All things considered, though, the recording went as well as the band have since suggested. 'I think, once the initial suspicion had been got out of the way and they realised I wasn't going to be a pain in the arse, they saw they could make the album without too much trouble, learn a lot in a brief period of time and stamp their own mark on it,' says Simon. 'So I'd like to think they were fairly grateful that it wasn't too painful for them. Our brief was, if they were happy, we were happy, and even if they didn't know the difference between an E major and an E minor, and wouldn't know if something was out of tune, and didn't want to do something again when you knew damn well they could do it better, you would always respect their ideas.'

One of punk's great concerns was the principle of Value for Money (VFM), a reaction to the inflated ticket prices charged by the rock'n'roll stars of the day. Just as entrance to gigs should be affordable, so singles should not have throwaway B-sides and albums should not contain tracks previously issued as singles. In keeping with this philosophy, the Clash had earmarked two of their most memorable rabble-rousers for their first single. Unfortunately, this threatened to diminish the impact of the album somewhat. They sidestepped this problem by deciding to include a *different* version of 'White Riot' on *The Clash*. As Simon confirms, it was not another new recording, but a remix of the earlier 8-track Beaconsfield demo version.

The band's canon was further expanded in one of the midweek gaps between recording stints. Joe presented Mick with a new lyric and Mick, back on form, came up with the music for the anthem-like 'Garageland'. The lyric is Joe's reflection on the implications of punk's move from the clubs to the record companies. By the end of February, the Jam had signed to Polydor, the Heartbreakers to Track and the Boys to NEMS. Dismissing any suggestion that the Clash's own signing represents a sell-out, he rubbishes the supposed attractions of upward mobility and declares the band's intention of remaining true to its heritage (conveniently forgetting the visits to the Speakeasy). The song's point of departure is Charles Shaar Murray's comment (made in his 29 August 1976 Screen on the Green review) that the Clash were a garage band who should be quickly returned to the garage, preferably with the motor running. The reference is an ambiguous one: even as it acknowledges the band's humble beginnings, it is also a defiant retort to CSM, and a proud boast about how far the Clash had progressed in the intervening months.

In March, Mick told Kris Needs that 'Garageland' was to be placed last on the album, being the band's most recent composition and 'where we're moving on next'. Although in itself a powerful song, both in the light of Mick's comment and in retrospect 'Garageland' can be seen to augur ill for the future. CSM's review had been thoughtlessly flippant and unduly harsh for a band playing its second public gig – he was later to acknowledge as much and retract his criticisms – but almost all the reviews the Clash had received since then had been positive to the point of sycophancy. Being mollycoddled by their friends in the music press had led the Clash to *expect* good reviews as their due. To be smarting at one of their very few bad ones six months after publication did not say much for the Clash's ability to accept criticism.

Simply by existing 'Garageland' flirts with self-contradiction: for a band even to consider writing that kind of self-referential song implies they have an inflated idea of their own importance, something hardly concomitant with the garage band spirit. A Clash song about the problems of being in the Clash was a move away from the Everyman perspective of their earlier material in favour of a viewpoint that was specific and exclusive to the four – or three – band members. Joe has since defended the likes of 'Clash City Rockers' as being tongue-in-cheek celebrations of self in the tradition of Bo Diddley, a performer famous for singing songs about Bo Diddley in a proto-rap bragging style as ironically humorous as it is self-mythologising. This may be true of that particular Clash song and several others, including 'Four Horsemen', and there was certainly room for intervals of light relief between the band's more demanding communiqués. 'Garageland', however, cleaves more to the Mott the Hoople tradition of songs about the trials and tribulations of Mott the Hoople: sentimental self-aggrandisement with next to no irony or humour to render it more palatable. At least Mott had been together and suffered hardships for three or four years before Ian Hunter set off down this path; at the time they wrote 'Garageland', the Clash had been together for less than nine months. By anybody's standards, this was far too early for Mott the Hoople Syndrome to be setting in. The song was little more than food for the Clash Myth and, as Mick suggested to fellow Mott fan Kris Needs, there would be plenty more to follow.

When Mick also told Kris, 'We had lots of our own material, but we wanted to do one song by someone else', he was being somewhat disingenuous. With the inclusion of 'Garageland', the yet to be performed 'Cheat', and the Beaconsfield 'White Riot', the band had a total of 13 self-penned tracks for the album without having to resort to novelty numbers like '1-2 Crush On You' or any of the material discarded as substandard during the previous few months. That number of songs would usually be considered generous, but, as most Clash compositions lasted closer to two minutes than three, the total running time was just under 29 minutes. Brevity was a virtue for individual tracks, but not for an album, where it would undermine the VFM principle. Someone proposed rectifying the situation by including the band's warm-up arrangement of 'Police And Thieves'. 'I think there was some laughter at the suggestion,' recalls Terry, 'but then we realised it did sound good, and we did it.'

This agreement was not arrived at quite so quickly as Terry suggests. Joe agonised a while about the cultural exploitation issue, before eventually coming to the conclusion that the Clash's version was an honest attempt to meet an inspirational musical genre and its attendant culture halfway. For Simon Humphrey, the band's decision to record it was something of a relief: if the law of punk decreed that next to no studio effects should be used, then the law of reggae and dub decreed that everything plus the kitchen sink should be thrown on. The same double standard applied to the length of the song. 'That was the one that was produced, in that it had dub effects and tape phasing at the end, which was a fairly sophisticated thing to do on the album. It's the one track where everyone got into the techniques.'

Accidental though its inclusion may have been, 'Police And Thieves' proved to be more than just a six-minute filler track. The song provided an almost uncanny counterpoint to 'White Riot', its lyric echoing Paul and Joe's encounters with both police and would-be thieves at the Notting Hill Riot. As well as spelling out the band's empathy with black Jamaican and inner city British youth, it made it clear that 'White Riot' was not racist or separatist, but envious. Musically, it added immeasurably to the dynamic and the texture of the album. It also accentuated *The Clash*'s other, less immediately obvious reggae influences: the use of drop-out throughout; the heavily echoed 'Oi!' on 'Career Opportunities'; the staccato rhythm guitar cutting across the dominant pumping bass on 'Janie Jones'; the phased guitar on 'Cheat'; and the harmonica on 'Garageland', floating in the mix like the melodica on one of Augustus Pablo's dub recordings.

The album was all wrapped up and mixed by the end of the band's third long weekend in the studio. It all happened so quickly that they later got confused about the duration of recording, variously boasting to have completed it, as well as the preceding single, in two straight weeks or even two weekends. In 1978, Mick told the *NME*'s Nick Kent, 'I was so into speed, I mean I don't even recall making the first album.' Instead of offering an explanation for the confusion, however, Mick was indulging in some punk posturing. 'That was just one of those things I said,' he admitted to the same paper's James Brown 13 years later. 'I don't recall any sort of drug-taking, and none of us was naïve: the studio was a haven for drugs and rock'n'roll behaviour,' says Simon. 'We'd had Stephen Stills in! It wouldn't have shocked me to have seen anything, but I didn't.'

The finished album was mastered and delivered to CBS by 3 March. 'Everyone knew it was punk and a New Thing, and nothing would have been rejected by the company,' says Simon. 'They just bunged 'em in the studio, let 'em do their own thing, let 'em put the album out with minimal artwork and non-existent A&R control over recordings. Not that the band would have let them have it anyway, but they certainly didn't try. And it simply went out.'

While the artwork may have been minimal, its impact was anything but. Since they wanted to rush the album through for as early a release date as possible, the Clash allowed CBS's in-house team, rather than Sebastian, to design the packaging, though Bernie directed operations as usual. Kate Simon, one of the regular punk scene photographers, took the front cover picture, which captures the three-piece Clash posing like street fighting men in the little alleyway opposite the front door of Rehearsals. Sebastian's housemate Rocco Macauley had also been present at the Notting Hill Riot, and his back cover photograph depicts a police charge in the lee of the Westway.

Paying lip-service to the fanzine aesthetic, the photographs have roughly torn edges and are reproduced in black and white half-tone against a background of military green. The limited sleeve information is reproduced in Xerox-decayed typeface. The typography is all in lurid red, as is the razor-slashed band name-cum-album title on the front. These details, and the splurges of red and pink aerosol paint across Rocco's photo, recall the band's own customised clothes, suggest the neon and graffiti of the urban environment and evoke the fire and blood of riot. As a visual introduction to everything the punk era Clash stood for, the sleeve is near perfect, and the charging policemen photograph quickly gained the status of rock'n'roll icon. The nearest thing to a Clash logo, it would be reproduced first as the band's White Riot Tour stage backdrop and then as a semi-abstract design on T-shirts and all manner of clothing.

Having been out of the public eye since 1 January, the Clash themselves had gradually toned down the more garish excesses of their Pollock and Pop-

Art/Lettrist phases. Increasingly, they were tending back towards their original basic Oxfam Mod look, with the other influences reduced to details: a paint-splashed tie, say, or an armband, a shirt with a Union Jack panel, a relatively discreetly stencilled slogan. It was in this mode, complete with mod-style white socks, that they posed for the cover of *The Clash*. Even while the album was being readied for release, though, Bernie was taking advantage of the recent cash injection from CBS to provide the band with a new image. He hired the Clash's first outside helper, a machinist named Alex Michon, who duly moved her sewing machine into the noisome upstairs room at Rehearsals.

The Sex Pistols had made a big splash with Malcolm and Vivienne's bondage suit line, based, as ever, on sexual fetishist gear. The Clash's area of provocation was entirely different, so Bernie took the idea of conflict as his basic theme. With input from Paul and practical help from Sebastian, he and Alex came up with a style that was a logical development from previous Clash looks, but moved away from the urban guerrilla boiler suits immortalised on the picture cover of 'White Riot' towards something more reminiscent of army battle fatigues. In addition to the obligatory stencils, detail was provided by numerous pockets and zip fastenings, and instead of military green, the colours mixed sombre black, white and grey with more vivid blue and red.

When these new outfits were given their first public outing on 11 March, Vivien Goldman described them as 'couture bezippered ensembles' and Nick Kent as 'extravagant space cadet uniforms . . . with big lapels and all manner of seamstress embellishments' and, more succinctly, 'pop star army fatigues'. Ironically, in the interview he gave Kris Needs that same day for *ZigZag* Mick was still promoting the DIY ethic: 'We encourage the kids to paint their clothes. That way they get involved, feel part of it. Now they come along and show us ideas we like.' Bernie, for one, had noted how the Pistols' post-Grundy Incident notoriety had boosted sales of Malcolm and Vivienne's various clothing lines: if the new punks were wearing their clothes, then that made them Sex Pistols punks. In direct competition, as always, Bernie came to the conclusion that in order to convert them into Clash punks, he would have to sell them *his* designs. The chief problem was that, unlike Malcolm, whose Sex shop had recently been redecorated and renamed Seditionaries, he didn't have his own outlet.

During the spring of 1977, Sebastian, Frothler, Celia Perry and Sebastian's former co-Social Secretary at the Central School of Art, Al McDowell, opened a shop at 271 Brixton Road. It was an independent venture, but owed a considerable amount to the Clash, as its name – Pollocks – and its wares – 'art clothing' decorated with Jackson Pollock paint splashes or Piet Mondrian colour squares – suggested. Although not involved, Bernie was not one to stand back and be exploited when he could be doing the exploiting. Pollocks was never a particularly committed project and ran down over the summer. Before it closed, Bernie had already harnessed

Sebastian's entrepreneurial spirit for his own devices, using more of the CBS money to form a company with him named Upstarts. 'Upstarts was purely there to provide the Clash with their outfits and their backdrops,' says Sebastian. 'The work I did for the Clash, I did through Upstarts: it was a design arm for the Clash.'

It was conceived as slightly more than that: it was also intended to mass-produce and market Clash-style clothes to the general public. Bernie availed himself of an 'office' at Sebastian's house at 31 Albany Street. Sebastian screen-printed the T-shirts at his home base, and helped Alex design the trousers and jackets. 'We had a little pattern-cutting shop in south London,' says Sebastian, 'and we used to take the stuff to the East End to get it made up.' One plan was to sell the clothes by mail order, and ads were placed in the back pages of the music press. Another was to open up a shop, but this failed to materialise. Instead, some of the designs made it to the former Acme Attractions – renamed Boy in March 1977 – and the similar punk-type outlets that were emerging in London.

Bernie was less keen on spending money in other areas. Both Joe and Mick had recently found themselves in difficulties when the one halfway decent guitar each of them owned suffered damage, and Paul's bass was a total piece of trash. Although Mick had a decent Marshall stack, the rest of the pink PA, as donated by the 101ers, had seen some hard use and was barely functional; it had been largely responsible for the sound problems that had plagued the Clash throughout their live career to date. Not surprisingly, the band members wanted to invest some of their advance in upgrading their equipment. 'We'd had enough of crappy amps and shitty equipment. At first we were using terrible equipment and we sounded awful,' Joe told *Melody Maker*'s Allan Jones in 1978. 'But Bernie thought that us getting decent amps was contradicting the original aims of being a punk band . . . When we went out in front of an audience, we wanted to sound as good as possible. They've paid to see us, right? They want to be able to *hear* us, too.'

The band won that battle. As well as the new PA, Mick bought a tasteless Plexiglas guitar (Keith Richards used to own one) and Paul a brand new Rickenbacker bass, which he promptly customised Pollock-style. The band also managed to squeeze some money out of the fund for a few minor luxuries. For his part, Mick bought a new stereo and paid for his nan to go and visit his mother, Renee, in America. That aside, though, Bernie insisted on putting his charges on a wage of £25 per week. It was a considerable boost from Joe's Social Security payment of £9.70, but, as he told Caroline Coon, it hardly meant he would be abandoning his regular order of beans on toast at George's Café on Camden High Street for more exotic fare elsewhere. By this time, Paul had moved in with Caroline, Mick was still at Wilmcote House, having moved Tony James in to keep him company while Stella was away, and Joe and Roadent had taken over a squat in Canonbury, north London. Thus, accommodation expenses were not an immediate problem. Over the next year or so, the band members would find their own homes and succeed in persuading Bernie to hand over additional money for rent. Nevertheless, as long as he managed the Clash, the weekly wage stayed the same, and the issue consequently became a source of considerable bitterness.

If squeezing money out of their manager for their own needs proved difficult, it was almost impossible to get it on behalf of the band's helpers, some of whom, it seemed, Bernie expected to continue working for free. 'I remember when Mick Jones was going to leave because Bernie wouldn't buy Roadent a pair of socks,' says Tony Parsons with a chuckle. 'Great moments in rock'n'roll history! Roadent didn't have any socks, and Mick thought this was morally reprehensible, and that Roadent should be bought some out of band funds. Bernie was equivocating. "Keep 'em hungry and sockless" – I suppose – being the motive.'

By early March, the band had not played live for over two months. Not only was their perceived laziness provoking occasional sniping from *Sniffin' Glue*, but they were in danger of losing ground to the groups who had either remained active or else had appeared on the scene since the Roxy opened. The Pistols had also been in mothballs while breaking in Sid and recording, and it was an ideal opportunity for Bernie and the band to make their move and usurp the position of Malcolm and his band as the Kings of Punk. The Clash now had sufficient financial clout to ignore Andy Czezowski's club and to follow up on their earlier promises to finance their own events as soon as they were able. The Colosseum in Harlesden's Manor Park Road was a cinema specialising in trashy porn and kung fu films. Kris Needs was told that the band had first considered this 'classic definition of a flea pit, all peeling paint and stained seats' as a potential venue when practising change-overs for the Anarchy Tour at the nearby Harlesden Roxy. If it was indeed a mere matter of chance, the choice was serendipitous: in organising gigs as near as possible to the intended location of the Anarchy Tour's finale, it was as though the Clash were announcing their intention of delivering, both literally and symbolically, where the Sex Pistols had failed.

In fact, Bernie's plans were even more ambitious. The *NME* reported that the venue was to host 'occasional gigs by upcoming bands', while *Melody Maker* went further with 'the Clash open London's latest new wave club this week'. The cinema venue may have been redolent of the Screen on the Green and the nature of the event as planned may have recalled both the Midnight Special and the 100 Club Punk Festival, but it would appear that Bernie's long-term aim was to set the venue up as a rival to the Covent Garden Roxy. To begin with, Sebastian's poster promised Two Nights of Action on Friday, 11, and Saturday, 12 March, both headlined by the Clash, supported on the first night by the Buzzcocks and Subway Sect and on the second by Generation X and the Slits.

Previously, the Clash had been the number two band in an Inner Circle dominated by the Sex Pistols. Bernie was now intent on building a new Inner Circle around the Clash: the kind of Larry Parnes-like stable of artistes Malcolm had first dabbled with in late 1975 and finally abandoned in January

1977 when he passed up on the chance of a joint Clash–Pistols label. Due to drummer problems, Subway Sect had been dormant for several months, but they were already established as Bernie's second band. Although they were pursuing their own path to success, Generation X recognised that associating with the already signed and critically lauded Clash would do them no harm at this early stage of their career.

The rehearsal band the Flowers of Romance had disintegrated following the departure of Sid Vicious, and Keith Levene was temporarily unoccupied. At the end of February, Buzzcocks vocalist Howard Devoto announced his departure from that band. For Bernie, it was a situation ripe for exploitation: he made several calls to Buzzcocks guitarist Pete Shelley, in the hope of luring him down to London to form a new outfit with Keith. Having already decided to persevere with the Buzzcocks and take care of the lead vocals himself, Pete declined. As the Buzzcocks were practically having to relaunch themselves from scratch, however, they were more than happy to accept the platform offered by Bernie and the Clash.

Following the demise of the Flowers of Romance, Palmolive had teamed up with Boogie's girlfriend, Kate Corris, who had taken up guitar and changed her surname to Korus. Along with 14-year-old singer Ari Up and, eventually, bassist Tessa Pollitt, they had formed a band appropriately (if indecorously) named the Slits. The Colosseum gig was to be their public début. In a 1990 interview with her former paper's Stephen Dalton Julie Burchill declared, 'What annoys me is feminist revisionists now saying punk was a wonderful time for women because we all started expressing ourselves more. That's a load of bollocks because bands like the Slits actually got their gigs supporting the Clash because they were fucking the Clash! The whole casting couch routine was still going on.'

Obviously, the fact that Palmolive and Kate knew the Clash and Bernie through Joe was a considerable factor in the Slits being offered the gig, but no more so than Tony James's friendship with Mick had been for Generation X. Bernie was simply interested in collecting Clash associate bands, full stop. Novelty value, like stimulating ideas, might have counted for something, but keeping girlfriends happy, like musical ability, did not.

The inextricably linked issues of punk sexuality and punk sexual politics are worth a brief detour. As Julie Burchill said, prior to dismissing it, one of the givens about punk is that it was somehow pro-feminist in providing an opportunity for self-expression for so many women. Caroline Coon is one of those who believe this to be true. When interviewed for *Rotten*, she claimed the punk movement was the first rock'n'roll-related subculture that allowed women to play an equal role. Elsewhere in her *NME* interview Julie chose to propagate, rather than explode, another punk myth, that punk was basically asexual: 'Everybody was taking so much speed there was very little sex around.' Over the years, in various interviews and books, both this opinion and the reasoning behind it have been echoed time and time again by other *habitués* of the punk scene.

Although it undoubtedly played a part, speed was by no means the only influence on punk sexuality. That punks attended lesbian clubs like Louise's on Soho's Poland Street and hung around in mixed groups, or in couples without necessarily being sexual partners, has coloured observers' and, seemingly, participants' perspectives. It is true to say that establishing relationships and making sexual connections were not always the highest priorities for *everyone* on the punk scene. Johnny Rotten made his famous remark about sex being 'two minutes of squelching noises' because, at that time, he'd had little experience of anything but the most casual of sexual encounters, and none at all of romance. The concept behind Johnny's phrase 'the Flowers of Romance', which began life as a Sex Pistols song title before Johnny donated it to Sid's rehearsal band and ultimately reclaimed it for a PiL album title, was that love is just lies.

It was a mentality that pervaded punk, and not wholly in emulation of the admittedly trendsetting Johnny. All the new bands were bored with the previously dominant cloying, banal and stylised tradition of romantic songwriting, which had so little to do with the reality of their lives. There was also a hangover from the decadence and ennui of the era of the Rolling Stones, Bowie, Roxy Music and *Cabaret*, when pleasure was inextricably linked with excess and sleaze, and it was decidedly unhip to be seen to care. In the late Sixties, supposedly, love had been free; by the mid-Seventies, sex was cheap. Again, what began as a reaction to the morality of the parent culture quickly became the new code. In the *NME* interview Julie talked of the boys not being interested in the girls, but much of this was show: when it came to male sexuality, behind the blank expressions there lurked some pretty basic feelings of lust. Even 18 years after the event, several of the interviewees for this book were more than keen to hint at or openly volunteer unsolicited accounts of their own and other key figures' various liaisons.

Caroline was right to say there had been no female equivalents to previous male subcultural types. There had been female camp followers, true, but they had always been dominated by the males and treated as support systems or glamorous accessories. The studied lack of interest built into punk, however artificial and superficial it might have been, freed the females from their previous subcultural roles because it empowered them to behave in the same way as the males: to do whatever they felt like doing, including sexually, without worrying too much about verbal or physical repercussions. (Not that they didn't sometimes get them.)

The truth is that the people on the punk scene, being for the most part young and, often with chemical assistance, both adventurous and uninhibited, had sex with each other all the time with relatively little discrimination. What they *didn't* do was bother overmuch about such concepts as fidelity, monogamy or romance. This apparent equality in the area of sexual activity, however, was not necessarily indicative of underlying attitudes. Caroline Coon has tried to make out that safety-pinned clothing was significant because it signalled that no little woman was sitting subserviently at home with sewing kit in hand, this, apparently, being the opposite of the message given out by the hippies in their patched jeans. Julie Burchill noted that male punks 'were not oppressive generally. They didn't expect you to go and make the tea.' Maybe not, but that didn't make them New Men. It was quite possibly the strain of keeping hidden their true, confused feelings about sexual roles in punk that made for the sexism, chauvinism, sexual disgust and misogyny that was so prevalent on the scene.

Caroline accused both Bernie and Malcolm of being bad influences because they were 'basically disappointed chauvinist pigs'. Sexually motivated fear and loathing drive Johnny Rotten's lyrics for 'Satellite', nastily directed at early fan Shanne Hasler, and 'Bodies', even more nastily directed at a disturbed fan named Pauline. Steve Jones was, by his own admission, 'a sex addict' who barely registered his conquests were human. Members of the Damned took laddishness to new extremes: Rat Scabies famously boasted to the *NME* about a sexual encounter with Runaway Joan Jett that had never even occurred, and after their first trip to the States in mid-April 1977, the band as a whole regaled *ZigZag* with tales of degrading acts involving groupies and, amongst other things, a bass guitar. On occasion, Mark Perry's editorials in *Sniffin' Glue* took an anti-'girl' stance that smacked of the school playground. To list all the Stranglers' crimes against womankind would take at least another two pages, but their obnoxious 'London Lady' is allegedly addressed to Caroline Coon. Similarly, following a liaison with Sue Catwoman, the Jam's Paul Weller put her down as a deluded, talentless groupie in 'The Butterfly Collector'.

For all their supposed ideological rigour in other areas, the Clash were a long way from coming to terms with feminism. Reminiscing with Ian McCann for the 40th-birthday issue of the *NME* in 1992, Tony Parsons said, 'I can remember going down the Speakeasy with the Clash to look for models to give us cocaine and blow jobs.' It was one of those *serious* jokes. When Joe was asked about his personal morality in a stilted would-be promo interview filmed round a pool table in April 1977, he replied, 'I wouldn't steal money off a friend. But I'd steal his girlfriend.' Love might have been unfashionable at the time, but the way he discussed Palmolive with Caroline the previous month also showed scant respect for his female partner of two years' standing. Three years later, talking to *Creem*'s Susan Whitall, Joe was still struggling to get a grip on the concept of sexism. After saying such tendencies had to be watched because they were 'inbred', he lambasted heavy metal groups for their macho cockstrutting routines, then attempted to show the Clash in a more positive light. 'We'd be standing in the warehouse in Camden Town and these kind of surveyors were coming in off the pavement, and they'd go, "Oh – blah, blah, blah – these *chicks*, man!" And I remember we'd get up and say, "You can call them *girls*, or *birds*, or *women*, but you can't call them *chicks!*" I remember sometimes they could really get my goat. And then, the other day, I found myself saying it.'

The Clash's apparently unconscious sexism was evident in everything they wore, did, said and sang. Their paramilitary clothing styles, their gang mentality and their aggressive stance were just as unequivocally macho, albeit in a different way, as the posturing and bragging of the heavy metal cockstrutters Joe claimed to despise. In their interviews, when the Clash spoke to or of 'the kids', those kids were always male. No hint of the female urban experience emerged in their early songs, where the protagonists were also exclusively male and invariably sexist themselves (see 'Janie Jones', 'Protex Blue' and '48 Hours'). In neglecting to incorporate the female perspective, the band not only restricted themselves to painting 50 per cent of the picture, they also drastically reduced their potential appeal and market. For the duration of the Clash's existence most thinking women – and not a few thinking men – sneeringly dismissed the band's combative pose as trite laddish wish-fulfilment and their recorded output as *boys' music*.

Despite all this, Julie Burchill was wrong to conclude that it was a 'load of bollocks' to consider punk a 'wonderful time for women because we all started expressing ourselves more'. Some male punk scensters, often the same ones who appeared so offensive or unheeding elsewhere, did encourage rather than belittle the creative efforts of the female punk scensters, but that is beside the point. The punk era was a wonderful time for women because they didn't wait or ask to be allowed to express themselves by men; they did it anyway. Patti Smith, Vivienne Westwood, Chrissie Hynde, Siouxsie Sioux, Viv Albertine, Poly Styrene of X Ray Spex, Gaye Advert of the Adverts and Pauline Murray of Penetration and writers like Caroline Coon, Julie Burchill, and *Sounds'* own punk *enfant terrible* Jane Suck all did their bit to open up the doors for women in punk and, subsequently, strong, independent women in rock generally. The Slits were especially important because they were the first all-female non-puppet punk band (the Runaways having been put together for exploitative reasons by male rock'n'roll hustler Kim Fowley) and arguably the first all-female non-puppet *rock* band. That all-female bands, and bands including women who are either in charge or considered equal partners, are now commonplace in rock music is not something that should be taken for granted: they owe much to punk's female pioneers.

Back in early March 1977, the prospect of putting the Slits on-stage for the first time was not particularly high on Bernie's list of worries. The Harlesden Colosseum gigs represented a bold takeover bid, and as such a considerable risk. It was important for reasons of status and reputation that nothing went wrong. Unfortunately, several things did.

Jon Moss had long hair, was not particularly impressed with the Clash philosophy and was not shy to say so. Nevertheless, as well as being a good drummer, he was a handsome 19-year-old, and so had been hired on the condition that he agreed to get a haircut. Now, after five or six weeks of hanging around waiting for the Clash to finish in the studio and get active again, Jon's disillusionment was about to peak. Like Rob Harper, he felt the Clash had no room for his input. 'I had a personality and ideas, and they didn't want that,' he told Dave Rimmer. His own politics tended to the right and, as Terry Chimes had done, he argued with both Mick and Bernie about what he saw as the Clash's hypocrisy. 'They were always promising things, but nothing ever happened.' Shortly before the Colosseum gigs, he phoned Bernie and said, 'Look, it's not me. I don't believe all this political shit, and I don't believe you believe it.'

Although the band may have been partly to blame since they had failed to learn from their experience with Rob that it was important to make a new recruit feel welcome, it was understandable that they were furious at being let down at the last minute in this manner. Less excusable was the way in which they expressed that fury. In the tirade against drummers Mick Jones let loose in front of Tony Parsons later that month, Jon – though unnamed – was the one threatened with having his legs broken: the band's anti-violence stance contradicted once again. Almost immediately upon resigning, Jon formed a punk band named London which toured with the Stranglers that summer. From October 1977 to February 1978, he replaced Rat Scabies in the Damned. He left following a car crash, then formed the Edge, which became Jane Aire's backing band, the Belvederes. After briefly supplying Burundi-type drums to the remodelled 1980 version of Adam and the Ants, Jon finally experienced success on his own terms when he teamed up with Boy George in Culture Club.

The timing of his departure threw the Harlesden gigs into disarray. Terry agreed to sit in on drums, but it was decided to turn Two Nights of Action into one, and the Saturday gig was cancelled. Generation X were already committed to play an Easter Ball at Leicester University on Friday, and had to be dropped from the bill. The Slits were brought forward to join the remaining bands on the Friday night, which made for an earlier start time than the advertised 10.45 p.m. It was too late to circulate the change of plan, and the news pages of *Sounds* reported 'confusion . . . disappointing many fans'.

Kris Needs turned up early to cover the gig and interview Mick for *ZigZag*. He commented on the efforts made to ensure swift change-overs between the bands who would play on a stage specially built (though this time not by the Clash themselves) in front of the red cinema curtains. 'I'm really excited,' Mick told him. 'This is more than a gig, it's an important event!' It was an impression also picked up by *Sounds* reviewer Vivien Goldman: 'Everyone knew it was An Event.' The *NME*'s Nick Kent was less open-minded: after having had his head split open by Sid Vicious the previous July, he had approached the punk scene with caution for the remainder of the year. Then, following Glen Matlock's departure from the Sex Pistols, Malcolm McLaren had sent telegrams to the music press announcing Sid Vicious's appointment: 'HIS BEST CREDENTIAL WAS HE GAVE NICK KENT WHAT HE DESERVED MANY MONTHS AGO AT THE 100 CLUB.' Although Nick made fun of this unpleasantness in his review, it was decidedly bitter fun. He pretended to be attending the Colosseum in order to offer himself as a sacrifice for the furtherance of other punk careers; in fact, he had gone to seek revenge by proving that the pen was mightier than the bike chain. All the same, his full-page write-up of the gig, with its mock-heroic *High Noon*-style introduction, did nothing to diminish the sense of occasion.

The usual posse of off-duty music journalists was there, including Giovanni Dadomo; Rough Trade's Geoff Travis, the DJ, was playing mostly reggae; Shane MacGowan, likened by Nick Kent to 'a vole sniffing glue', was messing around in the audience as usual, encouraging others to pogo; Jules Yewdall was one of many who took photographs (his later turned up in his 101ers–Clash book, incorrectly ascribed to the Screen on the Green gig); Don Letts filmed in Super 8, and some of the footage later appeared in *The Punk Rock Movie*; and Julien Temple made another visual record of the event for the band.

Because of the unexpectedly early start, Vivien arrived partway through the Slits' set. Nick, busy fortifying himself in the pub, missed them altogether. Both Kris and Vivien were more impressed by extrovert performers Ari and Palmolive than the other two members of the band, and both concluded that the Slits were worth seeing again. They were less enthusiastic about Subway Sect, who remained static on-stage and whose largely new material the band themselves said was 'anti-rock'. Kris described it as 'complicated and a bit weird' and Vivien as 'Can-type monotones'. These two writers tried their best not to be overly negative, Kris saying little and Vivien concluding: 'though I can't say I *enjoy* 'em, I'm told it's music that grows on you. (If it grew on me I'd cut it off . . .)' It was left to Nick to really stick the boot in: 'Such planned obsolescence, so resolute a "blankness" of attitude . . . such crappy instruments . . . and such a determined inability to finger even the most mundane chord shapes imaginable.' The remodelled Buzzcocks, wearing Mondrian-patterned shirts in a not wholly original image revamp, were seen by Kris to have a 'lot of potential', while Vivien praised their 'authentically MEMORABLE tunes' and declared 'they have to go far'. Nick mocked them for being northerners, wearing tasteless clothes and for sounding dreadful.

By the time the Clash hit the stage, Joe Strummer was so fired up that, so Giovanni told Vivien, he was literally frothing at the mouth. The tension did not diminish. Mick was incensed when the new amps initially failed to function properly, and Joe screamed abuse when one of the long-hairs manning the mixing desk accidentally pulled the plugs on the band. There were also a few sporadic taunts about the CBS contract from the otherwise partisan audience. Rather than succumbing to the pressure, the band fed on it. Making reference to one of the Colosseum's more traditional attractions, Joe announced, 'I'm Bruce Lee's son. What are you gonna do about it?' before thrashing into another song. During 'White Riot' the strap on Mick's new Plexiglas guitar broke. Instead of grinding to a halt, he held it up by the neck and repeatedly slashed across the strings, before, as Kris reported, 'holding up the guitar like a machine gun to finish the number'.

It was a powerful, charged, exciting performance. Vivien admitted to being equally awestruck by the band's new image: she was so impressed by Paul's new blond hair-dye job that she became the second journalist to liken a Clash member to a Greek god. Almost against his will, even Nick Kent 'suddenly felt involved in this music' and, ironically, in praising the Clash found the ideal way of getting his own back on Malcolm and the Pistols: 'it's all to do with real "punk" credentials: a Billy the Kid sense of tough tempered with an innate sense of humanity which involves possessing a morality totally absent in the childish nihilism flaunted by Johnny Rotten and his clownish co-conspirators'. Interestingly, he also stated that 'the Clash took up exactly where Ian Hunter's Mott the Hoople left off'.

The Colosseum gig may have been a triumph, but despite the music press speculation that had heralded it, it was not repeated. Things had hardly gone smoothly either beforehand or on the day, and Kris's *ZigZag* feature suggested that the venue's owners had been somewhat taken aback by the audience. It seems likely that the culture shock proved too much for them and they deemed the experiment with hosting live gigs a failure. Bernie and the Clash put plans for any similar ventures on hold while they awaited the release of their records, prepared themselves for promotional duties and contemplated a satisfactory long-term solution to their drummer problem.

Following the abandonment of the idea of a joint label, the relationship between Malcolm and Bernie had soured once again. In spite of the EMI pay-off, the Anarchy Tour had left a huge hole in the Sex Pistols' pockets and, after the CBS signing, Bernie had been prevailed upon to help out with the bills. As Sophie Richmond's diary entries for 4 and 17 February testified, he had done so, but 'not very willingly'. On the latter date, he had also offered her a lecture, intended for Malcolm, about how mercenary, hypocritical and bitchy the Pistols camp and, by extension, the punk scene were becoming.

Apart from demonstrating Bernie's capacity for double-think – he despaired at the steps Malcolm was taking, but followed in them anyway – what he had to say represented an astute summary of the situation. By March 1977, Malcolm was far more interested in manipulating record companies and the media than he was in looking after the career or well-being of his band. On 9 March, the Pistols signed to A&M; on the 10th, they turned up at the record company headquarters drunk and disorderly; on the 12th, they had a violent tussle in the Speakeasy with *Old Grey Whistle Test* presenter Bob Harris; and late on the 16th, A&M terminated the contract, and the Pistols walked away with a total of £75,000 severance pay. The following day's *Evening Standard* quoted a blasé Malcolm as saying, 'I keep walking in and out of offices being given cheques.' The 'White Riot' single was due for release on 18 March, and by this stage Bernie was so paranoid about Malcolm's stroke-pulling that, convinced the A&M sacking was a publicity stunt designed to upstage the Clash, he phoned Sophie at the Pistols' office to complain.

As it turned out, the Clash record got its own fair share of attention. In conversation with Kris Needs both Paul and Mick had expressed a vague disappointment in the single version of 'White Riot'. Having heard an advance copy prior to attending the Night of Action, Nick Kent had also confessed to being unimpressed by its lack of impact at first, before further listens had revealed that 'the chorus had been made insidiously catchy enough to become a sort of football chant'. Pete Silverton's review for *Sounds* echoed these sentiments, saying that it took 'three days and maybe 25 plays' – 24 and a half more than most new singles would have been afforded – to make its mark. But make its mark it did, achieving single of the week status. Even if the production could have been a little tougher, 'for sheer power and resolute nowness it makes everything else here look a bit sick'. Unsurprisingly, Caroline Coon chose the single to lead off her *Melody Maker* singles column. The 400 words she devoted to 'White Riot' functioned as both an open fan-letter to the band and a potted biography of their career to date: all valuable publicity. Even she managed to temper her swooning adulation long enough to comment that 'the overall sound is a little safe and the lyrics between verses are sadly unintelligible', faults she fully expected to be rectified on the – plug ahoy! – 'forthcoming album'.

Guest singles reviewer at the *NME* was Tom Robinson, a former member of acoustic trio Café Society. Although two years older than even Joe Strummer, as a committed gay activist Tom had responded strongly to the political potential of punk and was in the process of writing new material and forming a new group to play it, the Tom Robinson Band (TRB). If anything, his 250-word appraisal was more biased than Caroline's, but his perspective was fresh and uncannily in sync with the band's. 'It's pointless to categorise this with the other records: "White Riot" isn't a poxy single of the week, it's the first meaningful event all year' was his opening shot.

After noting the crafty and unintentionally ironic cop from 'All Day And All Of The Night' in '1977', he went on to list other criticisms the Clash had attracted, many of them valid: 'Go on, say they sold out to the enemy at CBS, say it's another idle London fad irrelevant to the lives of working people, say it's all a clever hype that's conned everyone, say it's just the Sixties rehashed and you can't make out the words. Say what you like, you still can't discount it 'cause Clash aren't just a band, and this is more than a single . . . Whatever your standpoint, everyone basically agrees there are two sides. You know it's coming, we know it's coming, and *they* know it's coming.' The importance of establishing the identities of the real Us and Them was something Tom knew all about. In his own 'Up Against The Wall', a song he had already written, but which could almost have been inspired by the 'White Riot' picture cover and was effectively a lyrical distillation of the Clash's entire repertoire to date, he asked, 'Just whose side are you on?' This was the Clash's kind of propaganda.

More was to follow. Kris Needs's interview-cum-Harlesden review, published in the April issue of *ZigZag*, was another extended fan-letter. A

Record Mirror interview, published on 9 April, was more ambivalent, as well as being too garbled to make much overall sense, but it gave both Mick and Joe the opportunity to restate the band's position for the benefit of the more pop-oriented market. On 26 March, Joe met Caroline Coon in Red Lion Square for a lengthy solo interview, which was published in the 23 April issue of *Melody Maker*. Again, she was probing in her questioning, but ended up with a feature that seemed more revealing than it was. Joe treated it as an exercise in damage limitation. Rumours about his schooling and so-called privileged past had been spreading around the punk and music press communities, as had some sniping about his opportunistic abandoning of the 101ers. Because of this he was, as Caroline claimed, prepared to be 'more forthcoming than ever before', but with slanted information and partial truths.

This personal strand was interwoven with more up-to-date material. Joe gave his thoughts about the current punk scene, explaining how the Clash had felt after the Anarchy Tour and dismissing the new punk bands and the Roxy. He responded to criticisms directed at the Clash regarding the CBS deal and the band's supposed manipulation by Bernie. He threw in the by now almost obligatory rant about state oppression, and was contemptuous of politicians. His humble appraisal of his musical talents was nothing new, but something that was totally unprecedented was his admission that rock'n'roll was 'completely useless' when it came to effecting political change. 'I'm just saying that because I want you to know that I haven't got any illusions about anything, right? Having said that I still want to *try* to change things.'

Realistic maybe, but the Clash had stood for office on the positive, pro-active hopeful ticket, and for that to give way to what amounted to an acknowledgement of the futility of such gestures was not a little sad. In fact, although Joe's manner was relaxed and easy-going for the duration of the interview, to read it today is to pick up a strong sense of depression, of someone who is finding it difficult to cope. During the inevitable discussion on violence he said, 'Being honest with yourself: that's much tougher than beating someone up.' Resolving that struggle was something that being part of the Clash denied him and would continue to deny him for years, at no small cost to his personal well-being.

Perhaps unsurprisingly, in view of its raw sound and incendiary content, 'White Riot' did not immediately establish a niche for itself on the nation's playlists. Radio One's John Peel played it on his late night show, but by the time Joe was interviewed by Caroline nearly a week after the single's release, he still hadn't heard it anywhere else. He railed against Radio One's national monopoly, the enforced death of the pirate radio stations and, especially, London's independent station, Capital Radio. Capital had been founded in October 1973 with the slogan 'In tune with London'. 'What they could have done compared to what they have done is abhorrent,' said Joe. 'They could have made the whole capital buzz. Instead Capital Radio has just turned their back on the whole youth of the city.'

The night of the interview, Joe went out, accompanied by Roadent, and sprayed 'WHITE RIOT' across the glass-fronted street-level reception area of Capital Radio on Euston Road and on the entrance of the BBC Radio building in Portland Place. Neither Joe's diatribe to Caroline nor the graffiti campaign was particularly spontaneous: the Clash had decided to launch an attack on UK radio before the single was even released. At the soundcheck for the Harlesden Colosseum gig they had worked on a version of Jonathan Richman's 'Roadrunner'; where Richman's version celebrated the medium of radio, the Clash's was more deprecatory, changing the chorus of 'radio on' to 'Radio One'. There had been talk of performing it as an encore, but it didn't quite come together, and Paul had hated the song ever since his London SS audition.

Instead, in the week following the gig, Mick and Joe had turned their attention to the other key offender in a song of their own based on another uptempo reading of the Who's stop-start 'I Can't Explain' riff. 'Capital Radio' is an all-out assault on the station and its programme controller, Aiden Day. Joe was reading *The Rise And Fall Of The Third Reich* at the time, which explains his opening evocation of the Nazi minister of propaganda, Joseph Goebbels. Adopting a line of attack similar to the one 'London's Burning' and 'I'm So Bored With The USA' had directed at television, 'Capital Radio' accuses radio of being a mind-numbing opiate of the masses, 'To keep you in your place, OK.' The morning after the graffiti raid, Sebastian Conran was dispatched to Capital Radio with his camera to record it for posterity.

With next to no radio play, 'White Riot' made it only as high as number 38 in the charts. It might have been helped on its way by being heard on *Top Of The Pops*, but the Clash refused to appear on the show: it required bands to mime along to a pre-recorded backing track and was therefore deemed unauthentic.

Tony Parsons might have arrived relatively late on the punk scene, but he had quickly immersed himself in it and his response was more that of willing participant than objective observer. A working class and extremely class-conscious Londoner, he had worked in a gin distillery prior to securing his job at the *NME*, and it required no great leap of faith for him to connect with the Clash's songs and rhetoric. He became particularly close to the band during the first few months of 1977, when he accompanied them to the Roxy and on their not always successful attempts to gain entry to the Speakeasy. Whereas Bernie was loath to let writers who were uncommitted to the cause get too close – 'Bernie used to say, "I don't want the boys to talk to that journalist, because that journalist's a *careerist*,"' laughs Tony – he and the band were well aware of how valuable it was to have wholehearted Clash champions in the music press. The likes of Caroline Coon, Jonh Ingham and Giovanni Dadomo had all done their bit, but Tony was of the right sex, the right age and the right background to fit right in. It was a fortuitous relationship that Bernie, the Clash, CBS, Tony, the *NME* and the paper's publisher, IPC, all came to recognise and exploit. The advantages for the Clash camp were obvious; for the *NME*, their writer's connection with the Clash represented a belated opportunity to grab a sizeable chunk of the growing market for punk coverage.

On 21 March, the day of the Sex Pistols' first gig with Sid Vicious at the Notre Dame Hall, Joe, Mick and Paul met Tony to record an interview. 'I had to be at a certain tube station at a certain time, and a couple of trains went past, and then it was like *Help!* or *A Hard Day's Night*: suddenly these heads popped out of the door and I jumped on, and we just went round and round on the Circle Line – as you know, you can ride the Circle Line until hell freezes over – shovelling amphetamine sulphate up our noses and just talking, talking, talking.'

The resulting feature was very different from Caroline Coon's in both approach and tone. Her championing of the band had at least been balanced by some would-be probing questioning, and she had, perhaps without fully realising it at the time, caught a real sense of Joe's inner turmoil. Tony's fanzine-derived gung-ho writing style whipped up the intensity and excitement levels, coming on like a literary equivalent of a Clash gig. There was no room for doubt or lack of conviction. The stance was macho-militant: the feature focused on Paul's football hooligan past, Joe's recent fight with the giant ted, the ted–punk battles, Mick's threats to ex-Clash drummers, the band's sense of honour, their refusal to compromise, their gang-style reliance on each other and Mick's repeated declaration, 'I ain't ashamed to fight.' Tony accepted their version of their backgrounds: the lack of career opportunities, long periods on the dole, life in high-rises and squats.

Tony's interview took place just two days before Caroline's, but this time the *NME* beat *Melody Maker* into print by no less than three weeks. A stark Chalkie Davis photo of the three band members' heads, with Mick and Joe facing each other in profile, appeared on the cover of the 2 April 1977 issue, captioned 'Thinking Man's Yobs'. The combination of this memorable icon, the whizz-bang Parsons–Clash rhetoric inside and the pre-emption of the *Melody Maker* piece served to make this the key feature in establishing the Clash Myth. It has been suggested that Tony Parsons, like other journalists before and since, was duped by the Clash. Conversely, in *England's Dreaming*, Jon Savage deemed the article a 'brilliant fixing', implying intent on the part of the writer. 'It wasn't objective journalism,' says Tony. 'It was very much a collaborative piece. They did it with me. It wasn't like we sat down and spoke for an hour and I went away and coolly wrote it. Savage got it about right. It was a "fixing", but that makes it sound like it was just me projecting my fantasies, my visions. It wasn't like that either. I felt very much a part of it all, emotionally. I know that was a big piece for a lot of people. It got a lot of people into the Clash and defined what it should be for them. It was a wonderful piece of myth-making, but myth is a very important element in any type of rock music.'

A mutually advantageous deal was arranged whereby CBS would insert stickers in the first 10,000 copies of *The Clash*; if one of these stickers was affixed to a coupon included in the *NME* and sent to the address supplied, the sender would receive a free Clash EP. For the Harlesden gig Terry Chimes had taken the stage in a T-shirt bearing the legend 'GOOD-BYE', as definitive a statement of intent as he could make, but he was called upon to sit in with the band yet again when, accompanied by Tony Parsons, they returned to CBS Studios on Sunday, 3 April. First 'Capital Radio' was recorded, then a new instrumental entitled 'Listen'. One track was to be included on each side of the EP, along with excerpts from the cassette of the Parsons–Clash tube interview. The spoken material was spliced into 'Listen', an unusual example of early Clash studio experimentation: both a logical progression from Joe's 100 Club IRA radio broadcast and an exercise in dialogue-sampling that predated hip hop's (and Big Audio Dynamite's) use of soundtrack samples by several years. For all that, it only just qualified as a song, and calling the *NME* freebie an EP flirted with contravening the Trade Descriptions Act.

Sebastian Conran designed the sleeve, which used a photo taken during the tube train interview on the front cover. The 'picture withdrawn' space on the other side had originally been intended for Sebastian's own photograph of the graffiti-covered Capital Radio offices, but that would have been a taunt too far for the station's legal department to resist. The *NME* ran the coupons from 9 April onwards, the demand was considerable and the 'EP' has been an expensive collector's item ever since. As part of a June 1994 retrospective of the band included in the *Record Hunter* supplement of *Vox*, Barry Lazell valued it at £40.

Terry Chimes finally managed to leave the Clash following the recording session. He formed his own band, Jem, briefly replaced Jerry Nolan in the Heartbreakers, teamed up again with Keith Levene in Cowboys International, then joined Generation X in 1981. 'I thought it was stupid to do just one musical style. The mistake I made was in thinking it could all happen again the next time, with the next band.'

The Clash was released on 8 April 1977 to mixed reviews that sometimes – and sometimes literally – said more about the reviewer than the album or the band. The Boring Old Fart stereotype, as personified by Michael Oldfield, was alive but mellow at *Melody Maker*. The salvaged pre-recording contract Beatles album *Live At The Star Club In Germany, 1962* had just been released. Michael conceded the point that the Fab Four had been equally musically limited when they first started out, relying on energy, enthusiasm and imagination to override this consideration. Nevertheless, he thought punk was 'an experience to be savoured in small doses ... closer examination, I find, leads to headaches, due to the tuneless repetition of chords at a breakneck pace'. He commended bands like the Clash for moving away from 'moon in June' lyrics, but objected to not being able to make them out. The album, he concluded, 'should go down a treat with the Blank Generation. Thank God I'm "too old" to have to enjoy it.'

At *ZigZag*, the album also arrived on the desk of one of the old guard, John Tobler. He opened with his most enthusiastic comment of the review, 'It's all right', before going on to echo Michael's complaints about the lack of tunes and decipherable lyrics: 'It seems more likely to alienate than inform.' John had not changed his position about the paucity of hummable melodies by the time he interviewed the band for Radio One's *Rock On* programme that May. 'I think you'd better go back and have another listen,' muttered an understandably peeved Mick Jones.

Elsewhere, fortunately for the Clash, the album fell on less stony ground. At *ZigZag*, Kris Needs had already pre-empted his colleague's appraisal by previewing it in the most gushing of terms: 'I can't think about it for a moment without feeling like I'm going to explode (let alone write about it!). You can hear all the words, there's the hardest guitar/drum sound ever ... but most of all, it's captured the essence of the Clash. Their intense conviction is here in all its blazing glory ... Even if you don't buy it, at least HEAR it. It's one of the most important records ever made.'

At the *NME*, safe bet Tony Parsons turned in a near full-page review in very much the same tone as his interview feature. As far as Tony was concerned, the Clash were Telling It Like It Is: 'Jones and Strummer write with graphic perception about contemporary Great British urban reality as though it's suffocating them ... The songs don't lie ... They chronicle our lives and what it's like to be young in the Stinking Seventies better than any other band, and they do it with style, flash and excitement. The Clash have got it all. I urge you to get a copy of this album. The strength of a nation lies in its youth.'

Yet to make his famed announcement blaming the Clash for the Death of Punk, Mark Perry might also have been expected to react positively to the album in *Sniffin' Glue*, and he did not disappoint. His identification with the world portrayed therein was even more total than Tony's. So much so that his review began with a brief autobiography, then opened out to consider the quality of life for the average urban teen, before shifting into upper case for its impassioned conclusion: 'THE CLASH ALBUM IS LIKE A MIRROR. IT REFLECTS ALL THE SHIT. IT TELLS US THE TRUTH. TO ME, IT IS THE MOST IMPORTANT ALBUM EVER RELEASED. IT'S AS IF I'M LOOKING AT MY LIFE IN A FILM.'

At *Sounds*, *The Clash* landed on the desk of Pete Silverton, someone who knew too much about Joe's past to swallow the Clash Myth whole. But that did not make him dismiss it out of hand. 'In their interviews ... they give the impression that they're poor white trash, straight out of the tower block on to the dole queue. In Joe Strummer's case, at least, nothing could be further from the truth but, given his lack of experience of being born (as opposed to living) at the bottom of the heap, the fact that he can so eloquently express the frustrations and obsessions of society's overlooked is nothing short of an outrageous indication of his talent.' In Pete's eyes, the Clash were setting the pace for their era in the same way as Elvis, the Beatles and the Rolling Stones had for theirs. He awarded the album a maximum five stars, and signed off with the assertion 'If you don't like *The Clash*, you don't like rock'n'roll. It really is as simple as that. Period.'

Anticipation, curiosity, word of mouth and such rave reviews helped the album make it to number 12 in the UK album charts. 'I remember everyone at the record company saying, "Well, *we* don't know why!"' says Simon Humphrey. 'It was beyond their understanding that they could release an album and people would simply go out and buy it because they knew about the band. Obviously, they'd signed the band on the basis that there was a groundswell of people interested, but there was no one at CBS who could understand what was going on musically.' Being a record company employee, Simon was by definition a representative of the establishment. For this reason he was not credited on the album, but his contribution was not completely overlooked. 'They sent me a silver disc, a proper silver disc, which was a very nice gesture. Very few bands take the trouble to do that, and it was them that did it, not the record company. One of the things you'd expect them not to do, on principle. Every now and again, you work with an act that you're proud to tell people about, and I'll tell anyone that I worked with the Clash. The first Clash album is a real landmark album. I mean, I can barely bear to *listen* to it, because sonically it's rough, but . . .'

It's a big but. In his *Melody Maker* review Michael Oldfield held that punk was best experienced in small doses, and it is true that the best punk songs were short sharp shocks better suited to singles than albums. Few punk bands managed to sustain momentum and hold the interest over the long distance of a long player. The Damned's *Damned Damned Damned*, released in February, lacks variety, texture and, for the most part, tunes. The Stranglers' *Rattus Norvegicus*, released in April, is confident and varied, but the tracks are a little too long and musically ornate to pose convincingly as punk rock, and it is difficult to get past the hateful lyrics. The Jam's *In The City*, released in May, shows promise, but is as monochromatic as the Damned album and contains too much filler. By the time the Sex Pistols finally put out *Never Mind The Bollocks* on Virgin in October, four of the tracks had already been released as singles, most of the songs were old and stale and Steve Jones had buried everything under countless layers of guitar sludge.

The Clash is far and away the best album to emerge from the UK punk scene. As Rob Harper says, 'It has such a rich sort of texture. It sounds like a silly thing to say about a punk record, but the more you looked into it, the more there was there. They just had that knack.' In the tradition of all the best albums, the weaker songs grow in stature next to the stronger, and the whole is made better than the sum of its parts. This is also the case with the lyrics. Sections are rendered indecipherable by Joe's idiosyncratic delivery, but the gist is evident almost immediately, and finer points of detail gradually fill themselves in over repeated playings: an incremental initiation to Clash culture, where the song's overlapping themes make for a unified world-view.

Caught up in the impassioned rhetoric and paranoid mood of the times,

Tony Parsons and Mark Perry saw *The Clash* as a straightforward journal of the here and now, and even the Clash themselves had fallen into the trap of discussing their work in those terms. Although this did not detract from its initial impact, it pointed to built-in obsolescence and fails to explain why the Clash's début album still sounds vital, relevant and, references to Janie Jones and the odd Ford Cortina apart, contemporary today, while so many other punk records sound dated, hackneyed and contrived. Pete Silverton came closest to touching on the reason when he talked about the 'SF/Fantasy phraseology' of 'Remote Control'. *The Clash* might have more than a hint of dirty realism in its language and situations, but it is as much a work of the imagination as David Bowie's *The Rise And Fall Of Ziggy Stardust And The Spiders From Mars* and *Diamond Dogs*. The futurist branch of science fiction takes the events, moods, trends and political, technological and cultural developments of the present, and from these extrapolates a possible outcome. Invariably, these future worlds are bleak dystopias, and the implied moral is that humankind should mend its ways before it is too late. Like Bowie before them, the Clash were walking ground already trodden by such literary luminaries as George Orwell, J. G. Ballard and Anthony Burgess: *The Clash* is *1984* meets *High-Rise* meets *A Clockwork Orange*, with tunes.

Since mid-March, the music press had been carrying news reports about the possibility of the Clash supporting former Velvet Underground member John Cale on his UK tour, or at least taking part in his Roundhouse gigs on 10 and 11 April. Much confusion resulted, with more than a few disappointed fans turning up only to find Generation X in the support slot. The Clash denied they had ever agreed to appear – following Terry's departure, they were hardly in a position to do so – but it would seem Bernie was guilty of not making that clear to the promoter at the time. The band did have plans to play a few dates in France in late April, however, in preparation for their own Anarchy-style UK package tour in May, and finding that elusive fourth member again became the burning issue. Although no new ads had been placed, auditions for a replacement drummer had been continuing on a word-of-mouth basis throughout late March and early April 1977. On 24 March, the band had gone along to see the Kinks at the Rainbow in Finsbury Park. There Mick had bumped into Nick Headon, one of the few successful applicants for the London SS's drummer vacancy, and invited him along to audition for the Clash.

Nicholas Bowen Headon was born in Bromley on 30 May 1955. When he was around secondary school age, his schoolteacher parents – both of whom went on to become head teachers – moved to the Kentish coastal town of Dover. Although not particularly academically gifted, Nick began to attend Dover Grammar School for Boys: like the Strand School, it had managed to sidestep the educational reforms going on elsewhere in the country. Nick ended up with three O level passes, in Geography, History and English Literature, and dropped out of school before completing his A levels.

The loves of his life were football and music, the latter taking over when, at 14, he broke his leg so badly playing soccer that he was confined to bed for weeks, which ultimately required him to resit a year at school. A fan of the Beatles, the Blues Boom and its spin-off sub-genre of 12-bar boogie bands like Canned Heat, he was already able to find his way around an acoustic guitar. He was an active – even hyperactive – youth, and his father bought him a drum kit, partly as a form of physiotherapy, partly to keep him occupied and partly to allow him to burn off some of his excess energy. He quickly became an accomplished drummer, learning all he could from heroes like Terry Williams of Man (later to join Dire Straits) and jazz drummers Buddy Rich, Elvin Jones and Billy Cobham. 'I wanted to be the best drummer in the world. That was it. And I wanted to be in *Melody Maker*. Serious!' he told that paper's Mick Mercer in 1985. 'I thought if you got your picture in *Melody Maker*, you didn't have no problems in your life at all.'

He would later boast that he had begun to sit in with local jazz outfits at 14, but his first band, formed with schoolfriend and novice bassist Steve Barnacle, was called Crystal Carcass, and played extended 12-bar boogie instrumentals. Always ambitious, Nick thereafter enjoyed overlapping spells with several other local bands: the similarly influenced Back to Sanity; established progressive band Mirkwood, featuring Wishbone Ash-style twin guitars, 7/4 rhythms, three-part harmonies and Tolkien-influenced lyrics; a hard rock outfit named Expedition; and their spin-off fun band Dead Dogs Don't Lie. As he claimed, while he was still in his mid-teens, he was also occasionally called upon to man the traps at local pub the Louis Armstrong for landlord Bod Bowles's trad jazz band.

Nick was always a little wilder than his secure middle class background might suggest or warrant. Steve Barnacle and his brother Gary, a session saxophonist who would later play on several Clash records, both suspect that it was because his upbringing was a little *too* secure. 'I used to steal a lot and run with a gang,' Nick told *Time* magazine's Jay Cocks in 1979. What he didn't say was that the gang comprised fellow Dover Grammar School boys, and the stealing consisted of shoplifting sweets on the way home. Small beer it might have been, but Nick always had to push his luck that little bit further than anyone else. 'We'd ask for something on the top shelf, and sort of cover him, but he'd always start giggling,' says Steve Barnacle. 'Almost wanting to get caught. I think it's significant, later on. He told me as much.'

Steve is referring to Nick's interest in drugs, which he had certainly developed before he left Dover. 'At school, I was told that if you have a puff on a joint, you're a junkie, right?' he told *Melody Maker*'s Will Smith in 1986. 'So, at 17 years old I had my first puff, and I thought, "Bullshit!" So you do a bit of speed, and you can handle that, and do a few downers, and you just think you can handle anything. It progresses and progresses, and if you're in a band you can get easy access to all these things.' There is no proof that this sort of progression is inevitable for *everyone* who dabbles with recreational drugs, but, given his character, it was almost inevitable for Nick.

Having moved up to London for the first time after leaving school in 1974, he attended and failed the same auditions for Sparks as Geir Waade. When he returned to the capital for good, in summer 1975, he did so with his new wife, Wendy: they were married on 24 May that year. Shortly afterwards, Nick passed an audition with Pat Travers, who had recently arrived from Canada, and suggested Steve Barnacle as a bassist for a proposed hard rock trio. Unfortunately, Steve was already committed to another venture, and Nick's second choice messed up an important audition so badly that Pat's management insisted he replace both sidemen with name musicians. Nick returned to the auditioning circuit. One of his many outings resulted in his being offered (and briefly taking) the drum seat with the London SS. Immediately afterwards, however, he was also offered a gig that paid: a tour of American military bases in Germany with a soul band called the GIs. (The band's vocalist, J. D. Nicholas, would go on to form Heatwave and replace Lionel Richie in the Commodores.) Although unknown at the time, the GIs made good money; the wages offered Nick were £50 a week plus expenses. He accepted.

Following the completion of the tour, Pat Travers, now with a record deal, put him in touch with two Canadian friends who had also come to the UK to try their luck. Nick brought in Steve Barnacle, and the resulting Travers-influenced hard rock band, Fury, began gigging on the London pub scene. A regular venue was the same Golden Lion from where the Clash poached the 101ers' Joe Strummer. Fury came close to being signed by CBS at much the same time as the Clash, but even though the band had been given the firm impression that it was all in the bag, the deal fell through. One of the excuses made to Fury was that their drummer's wristy, jazz-derived style lacked sufficient power. When he met Mick Jones at the Kinks gig, Nick was still part of the band and still earning £50 a week, but his long-term prospects did not look good.

He had a typical long-haired muso's contempt for punk rock, but the tenuousness of his position encouraged Nick to accept Mick's invitation, and he turned up at Rehearsals in the first week of April. Ironically, the recently voiced criticisms of his style were instrumental in securing him the job: he hit the drums as hard as he could, and the deafening barrage deeply impressed the Clash. The band had been considering hiring Mark Laff, who had tried out earlier that same day, but Nick got the job and Mark was given the consolation prize of the drum seat with Subway Sect.

Nick – or Nicky, as he now styled himself – was introduced to the general public via the 30 April 1977 issue of *Melody Maker*, courtesy of Caroline Coon. The photograph showed him after an image make-over, wearing Pop Star Army Fatigues and with dyed spiky hair. His past had also been rewritten to suit: he was described as an 'ex-office clerk' and claimed never to have played live before. Although from out of town, it was important that he was not perceived to be too utterly devoid of street credibility. In 1978's *Clash Songbook*, Wendy was described as his 'girlfriend': shades of John and

Cynthia Lennon. Most of the bands on Nick's résumé would never be acknowledged in interview, even after he left the Clash in 1982; and somewhere along the line the GIs would be miraculously transformed into the Temptations.

Nick's fondness for fooling around made him good company for Paul Simonon and Robin Crocker, also taken on at this time as Mick's guitar roadie. More importantly, he was content just to go along for the ride, creating none of the ideological friction of a Terry Chimes, a Rob Harper or a Jon Moss. He was quickly given a nickname, a sign of his acceptance by the band which also said much about his character: Topper, after a supposed resemblance to the character Micky the Monkey in the comic of that name, his preferred reading matter at the time. Following the tour, he would be asked to stay on full-time – on £25 a week – without officially being made a member of the band. 'I remember, quite a long time after I left, Bernie saying, "It's too late to come back now. We've got Topper, and we're happy with him." Almost gloatingly,' says Terry Chimes. 'He was dying for me to say this upset me, but I said, "Well, it's good that you've found a drummer you like. I'm pleased." He was a bit puzzled by that.'

A drummer was needed for reasons other than live work. At the end of March, Malcolm had got Boogie – the former 101ers roadie, by then working for the Pistols – to collect together various bits of footage pertaining to the Anarchy Tour, and Julien Temple had intercut them with his own footage to make a 25-minute propaganda short in the style of a Pathé newsreel. Entitled *Sex Pistols Number One*, its public première was at the Screen on the Green, immediately prior to a Pistols performance there on 3 April. The video age had yet to dawn, and promo films were something of a rarity for any but the most established of bands. But since *Top Of The Pops* was a no-go area, other means of conveying the visual element of the punk experience were required, and if Malcolm's band had a promo film, Bernie's band had to have one too. The Beaconsfield footage had been shot before the Clash's image make-over and Topper's arrival, and so was outmoded. It was decided to take advantage of CBS's promotional budget and have another go at capturing the band in all their glory.

The shoot took place on 26 April 1977. The idea was to film the band performing live, and also in a casual interview with Tony Parsons. 'By that time, CBS thought that I would maybe be the Clash's representative on earth,' he laughs. 'Y'know, kind of like the Pope, bringing their Word to the People.' The gear was set up as though for a gig, in front of Sebastian Conran's giant blow-up of Rocco Macauley's charging policemen photo, which subsequently accompanied the Clash on the White Riot Tour and became known as the Groovy Backdrop. The Clash performed both sides of the 'White Riot' single and 'London's Burning'. 'They were fucking *blistering*,' says Tony, and the film evidence proves him right. 'There was nobody there, other than me and a camera crew, so it was for an audience of one. The great thing about the Clash was, you didn't actually need a headful of sulphate and a sweaty little club and five pints of lager and a packet of pork scratchings: they were great anyway. They were an incredibly exciting live band.' The interview segment was less successful. A pool table was set up in a corner of the studio, with the intention of capturing the band relaxing in a supposedly natural environment. 'We didn't really understand how TV worked then,' says Tony. 'It was kind of embarrassing to play pool, and talk, and have these cameras pointing at you at the same time.' Again, the film evidence proves him right, and in *The Boy Looked At Johnny* he and Julie vilified the band for going along with this 'contrived spontaneity'.

Excerpts from the live performance received some exposure at the time, but only at the Virgin record shop near Marble Arch. Another segment was included in BBC2's Mick Jones career retrospective *That Was Then, This Is Now* (1989), and another in MTV's Clash *Rockumentary* (1991). The latter also showed a brief clip from the interview, which, until that time, had been allowed to gather dust. Tony is unsure where the filming took place, but says, 'I think it was done out of town. I seem to remember travelling.' The live version of 'London's Burning' was later remixed from the soundtrack and issued as the B-side of the 'Remote Control' single; the label claims it was recorded in the Bedfordshire town of Dunstable.

For all the critical praise and domestic commercial success afforded the album, it is difficult to see how the Clash thought they might sustain their position. They had ostensibly signed to CBS to be heard and to enjoy the benefits of a major record company's promotional machine, but the live promo film was little more than a token gesture towards mass exposure. They had rejected *Top Of The Pops*, which, in those days before MTV and *The Chart Show*, was the single most powerful promotional tool for a recording act, and alienated the radio stations, thus closing off all audiovisual channels of communication save for live shows. Far more people bought records than attended gigs. Instead, the Clash had thrown in their lot with the music press. Although the inkies had a relatively high circulation – the best-selling *NME* got up to 250,000 during the heyday of punk, no small thanks to its 'close relationship' with the Clash – they were still specialist titles read by a narrow section of the populace. Far more people bought records than read the music papers.

Nor was there any logic or consistency in an attitude which took moral exception to mainstream outlets like radio and television, but made excuses for teaming up with a multinational record company and positively relished getting into bed with the music press: the inkies might have affected to give off a certain anti-establishment, underground-press vibe, but they were all commercial, capitalist concerns. Those two great supposed rivals, *Melody Maker* and the *NME*, were and are both owned by magazine publishing giant IPC and kept afloat by advertisements bought and paid for by the major record companies. 'I can see now that there were masses of contradictions in punk,' says Tony Parsons. 'We were all part of the music business. They were on CBS, and I was writing for an IPC magazine. It was all mixed up:

the idea of making the world a better place, and suddenly having a career, and having excitement, sleeping with lots of girls, taking lots of drugs, fighting fascism. All that. It was all that. So that's where all the contradictions came in.' It was those contradictions that would ultimately see the end of both punk as a viable movement for change and the Clash as a functioning creative unit.

PART 3...

STAR TURNS

11... GIVE 'EM ENOUGH ROPE

The May 1977 White Riot Tour echoed the previous December's Anarchy Tour in its package format – 'It was a good idea that we'd had in the first place,' grumbles Glen Matlock – and in several other areas, to both positive and negative effect. It was the first high-profile, big-name punk tour to hit the road since the tabloid uproar surrounding the Pistols' outing, which guaranteed a large turnout and an enthusiastic reaction from many people who hadn't even heard of punk five months previously. The support acts were, for the most part, predictable: the Buzzcocks, Subway Sect and the Slits, in which band Viv Albertine had just replaced Kate Korus on guitar. Generation X were unable to take part as they had just said goodbye to drummer John Towe, and were yet to poach Mark Laff from Subway Sect. The only band on the bill that was not already part of the Inner Circle was the Jam, brought along for much the same reasons as Malcolm had included the Damned on the Anarchy Tour. The Sex Pistols being out of the picture, Bernie had gathered together some of the best and best-known bands on the punk scene, so that the White Riot Tour could establish a new pecking order, with the Clash indisputably first in line. 'I kinda liked the Clash, and I thought they had some good songs,' says Glen. 'But I just thought they wore the crown by default, really.'

The band certainly treated the tour like a lap of honour. In addition to Roadent, Sebastian and Robin Crocker, they took on Subway Sect roadie Barry August – known as the Baker – to look after Topper's drums. Friends and acquaintances, including Chrissie Hynde, were invited along to share the experience. Bernie tried to persuade the Jam to cover some of the cost of supporting such a huge retinue on the road, but as they were second on the bill, they thought it enough that they should be required to finance themselves. As a result, there were many hotel rooms and much in the way of expensive high jinks for which the Clash had to foot the bill.

On an episode of the Channel 4 programme *Wired* in 1988, Joe was asked what single moment he held most dear from his time with the Clash. He chose the 9 May White Riot show at the Rainbow in Finsbury Park: 'That was the first night that punk really broke out of the clubs. The Rainbow at that time was a big venue; it was kinda, "Supergroups go there!" We played there with the Jam, Subway Sect and the Slits, and the audience came and filled it. Trashed the place as well, but it really felt like – through a combination of luck and effort - we were in the right place doing the right thing at the right time. And that kind of night happens once or twice in a lifetime.' It also put a further strain on the tour budget. Despite the Clash's best efforts, the management refused to remove the seats. During the course of the gig the audience took matters into their own hands, smashed the seats up and deposited them in a pile at the front of the stage: as Joe said, they trashed the place.

In another echo of the Anarchy Tour, this 'riot' garnered the Clash extensive tabloid coverage – 'PUNK WRECK' declared the *Sun* on 11 May – but much of the witch-hunting zeal that had characterised press reports of that earlier tour was missing. Unlike the Pistols, the Clash got to be rebels without having the moral wrath of the multitudes whipped up against them. Part of the reason for this was that Rainbow manager Allan Schaverian refused to curse and condemn the perpetrators. Secure in the knowledge that someone else was going to have to pay for the mess – 'We expected some damage, and arrangements were made to cover the cost of it' – he was aware that punk was now, as the *Sun* stated, 'big business'. He was happy to attract the publicity. 'It was not malicious damage, just natural exuberance,' he said. 'We shall have more punk concerts soon.' One or two other venue managers were less pragmatic, and cited the bad reputation of the band and its following as a reason for pulling out. But most of the extensive rescheduling that plagued the tour could be attributed to the last-minute organisation of the original dates, which left all the kinks to be ironed out while it was in progress. Nevertheless, it all added to the size of the bill. The disastrous Anarchy outing had lost the Pistols over £10,000; in March 1978, Joe revealed to *Melody Maker*'s Simon Kinnersley that the ostensibly triumphant White Riot Tour lost £28,000. 'None of us had any wages for eight weeks.'

Joe might have been able to look back at the Rainbow gig as a career highpoint, but it also marked the beginning of the end of Bernie's Inner Circle. Just as the Pistols had fallen out with the Damned on the Anarchy Tour, so the Clash fell out with the Jam. Disagreements over financial contributions were followed by accusations of sound-mix sabotage at the Rainbow by representatives of the headliners: shades of the August 1976 Screen on the Green gig. There was an attempt to follow up the White Riot Tour with a Clash-headlined punk festival in Birmingham on 17 July – 'the last big event before we all go to jail' – but it was cancelled when local magistrates refused to grant a music licence. Thereafter, the bands involved concentrated on furthering their individual careers. Although Bernie and the Clash did their best to keep the tradition of the varied package tour alive – even bringing over Richard Hell and the Voidoids from New York for the October–November 1977 Get Out of Control Tour – it was more about offering 'the kids' VFM than presenting a united punk front.

Things were not going any better for the second wave punk bands back in London. The Roxy had set itself up as a base from which these bands could project a collective identity. It was also an environment in which a peer group made and controlled its own entertainment without undue interference or exploitation from outside agencies. All that came to an end in April 1977. A friend of club owner Rene Albert saw the money-making potential of the venue and paid to take it over, placing himself in charge. His idea was to operate the club seven nights a week and book bands through established agencies, rather than follow Andy Czezowski's policy of making direct contact with the bands themselves. He would take the profits while Andy and his staff received token wages. Unsurprisingly, Andy refused to co-operate. When he turned up for a Siouxsie and the Banshees gig on 23 April, he was denied entry by representatives of the new owner.

The rest of the Roxy staff left with Andy. Don Letts and Leo Williams roadied for the Slits on the White Riot Tour and for a while afterwards. A live album had been planned and recorded at the club while it was still under Andy's guardianship. Released in June 1977 on EMI's Harvest label, *Live At The Roxy, London WC2* contained tracks by the likes of the Buzzcocks, Slaughter and the Dogs, X Ray Spex, the Adverts, Eater, Wire and Johnny Moped, interspersed with snippets of dialogue recorded in the club toilets. Other performances are preserved on Don Letts's *Punk Rock Movie*. These are usually thought of as posthumous souvenirs of the club, though the new owner did try to keep it going under the same name. 'He booked in people like the Boomtown Rats and Tubeway Army,' says Andy. 'But people realised it had nothing to do with me. The attitude had changed.'

Andy fully intended to bounce back with a new, larger club run on much the same lines. He leased Crackers, the former soul boy haunt at 201 Wardour Street, renamed it the Vortex, booked in two weeks' worth of acts, organised the flyers and notified the music press. The Heartbreakers were scheduled to open the new venue on 4 July 1977, supported by a trio of Manchester acts: the Buzzcocks, the recently formed Fall and punk poet John Cooper Clarke. Exactly a week later, Siouxsie and the Banshees were to be supported by the Slits and the newly formed Adam and the Ants. Unfortunately, Andy did not get to savour his comeback. When he turned up for the club's first night, it was to go through a depressingly familiar experience. 'I was messed about by the people who *said* they owned the place. They wouldn't let me into the club! They just used me to set it up, and then they continued to book any old bands for as little as possible.' The next time Andy opened a club, he made sure no one was in a position to take it away from him: the Fridge in Brixton has been one of London's leading dance clubs since 1983 and was instrumental in launching the career of Soul II Soul, among others.

For a while, being new and being in a position to book the likes of Sham 69 and Glen Matlock's new post-Pistols band the Rich Kids, the Vortex became by default the centre of the punk scene. Never a comfortable place, it was staffed by intimidating bouncer-types – style writer Peter York described them as '*Sweeney* extras' – who were openly antagonistic to the clientele. This did nothing to dispel the undercurrents of violence and paranoia in punk, but it showed that the rump of the punk scene was at heart timid when confronted with displays of superior force from representatives of the establishment (albeit in a somewhat shady guise). Paul Weller was so affected by the oppressive atmosphere that he was inspired to write 'A-Bomb In Wardour Street'.

The post-Grundy scares having died down a little by the summer of 1977, the more traditional pub and club venues, including the Nashville, the Marquee, Dingwalls and even the 100 Club, started allowing punk bands to play again. Instead of representing a triumph, this was another indication of punk's toothlessness: whatever threat it had once represented was clearly no longer perceived to exist. In Manchester punk was still based at the Electric Circus and in Liverpool at Eric's, but in London, lacking the tight focus and a separate identity offered by a single high-profile club, punk slipped from being a scene into being just another sub-genre of rock.

The music business establishment may have been able to overlook punk's violent image, but that image was not in any hurry to go away. On 18 June 1977, Johnny Rotten was attacked by a razor-wielding gang not far from Wessex studios. Luckily, he needed only two stitches in his arm. The following night, Paul Cook was assaulted by five men armed with knives and a metal bar at Shepherd's Bush tube station. He required 15 stitches in the back of his head. The phlegmatic Paul managed to shrug off the incident, but the far more visible Johnny began to feel like a marked man.

Joe's earlier beating at the hands of the 'giant, psychotic teddy boy' aside, the Clash managed to avoid too much in the way of payback for their ambivalence on the subject of violence, just as they had failed to suffer the same pressures from local councils and the media on the White Riot Tour. The police did their best to compensate.

The band would later claim that the almost continual police presence during the tour, at venues, hotels and even during transit, amounted to harassment. One cannot help but wonder what they expected: they had appeared on television boasting about open conflict with the police at the Notting Hill Riot; they had released records inciting their followers to riot; and they had just presided over a mini-riot at the Rainbow. On 21 May, the Clash were stopped by police outside St Albans (though not strip-searched, as their contemporary version of events would have it). Eleven pillows and a room key from the Newcastle Holiday Inn were discovered on the tour coach – some of the pillows are evident in the *Punk Rock Movie* – and Topper and Joe were subsequently charged for the theft of these items. Back in London, on 2 June, Joe was arrested again for spraying 'The Clash' on a wall near Dingwalls. After that, brushes with the law became commonplace for the band. Over the next few years, various members were arrested and charged with everything from smashing a bottle of lemonade to possession of drugs. The pettiness of most of the offences resulted in a certain amount of mockery from the music press, but the frequency of arrests supported the band's contention that the police had it in for them.

So did the following year's infamous Pigeon Shooting Incident: on 30 March 1978, Paul and Topper, accompanied by Robin Crocker and two of Topper's friends from Dover, Steve and Pete Barnacle, went up on the roof of Rehearsals to try out an air rifle Pete was hoping to sell to Topper. In so doing, they shot and killed what they thought were three ordinary pigeons, but were in fact expensive racing birds. The police duly arrived and arrested them. Music press reports made considerable fun out of this somewhat childish comedy of errors, and when the song 'Guns On The Roof' turned up on the Clash's second album, even more scorn was heaped upon the band for blowing up such a trivial incident into a melodramatic rant about international arms dealing and terrorism. The band's critics were unaware that the police had arrived not in answer to the pigeon owner's summons, but following a tip-off from the British Rail Transport Police, whose office was within sight of Rehearsals. Knowing that 'anti-establishment band' the Clash were based there, they presumed they had come out on the roof to indulge in terrorist activities: namely shooting at the trains. Thus, the incident was taken extremely seriously, and a police helicopter and armed CID officers were involved in the arrest. Bail was set at £1,500 per person, and Thursday night in the police station cells was followed by a trip to Brixton Prison before Mick Jones and Caroline Coon arrived to bail everyone (except the Barnacles) out. Thereafter, all five defendants were required to sign on daily at the local police station. The original charges – later thrown out of court – related not only to pigeon-slaughter, but also to possession of a supposedly illegal weapon and attempted manslaughter.

The May 1977 White Riot Tour was also the first time that, from the Clash's perspective, CBS tried to get away with murder. While the band were out on the road, their record company, which had recovered from the shock of having a hit with a cheaply made practically unproduced album by a band whose musical approach and general philosophy they couldn't begin to understand, decided it was time to start making good on their promising new investment. On 13 May, without bothering to consult either Bernie or the Clash, they released 'Remote Control' as the band's second single in a picture sleeve, designed in-house, that merely echoed *The Clash* album cover. Having insisted that signing to a major record company did not mean they were abandoning control over their output, the band understandably felt humiliated by this turn of events. It was the chief source of inspiration for the song 'Complete Control', which was composed solely by Mick Jones and for many remains the Clash's greatest musical achievement. In some quarters the fuss the band made was attributed to their horror at CBS's undermining of the VFM principle in releasing a second single from the début album, whereas in truth the band were simply annoyed by the choice of track: back on 30 April, *Melody Maker* had announced that the new single was to be 'Janie Jones', the band's selection.

The Clash's insistence that 'Complete Control' should be their third single was considered a bold move on the part of artists prepared to put their entire futures at risk on a point of principle. The release of the song on 23 September 1977 was construed to be a tit-for-tat public humiliation of the record company by the band, a sign that the Clash had re-established in no uncertain terms the control about which they sang. It might just be, however, that Bernie and the band were hoping for quite the opposite outcome: a bad-tempered Mexican stand-off precipitating the cancellation of the contract altogether, in the lucrative tradition of the Pistols with EMI and A&M. Whatever, CBS were far too wily to fall for that one and were prepared to take all kinds of flak as long as the money kept coming in. There was no sign, either then or later, that the record company had meekly backed down with a promise to leave well alone henceforth. The skirmish over the band's second single was just the first of many that would dog the band throughout their career; and CBS increasingly got the upper hand as the Clash's finances were depleted and, as a consequence, their negotiating position weakened.

These external pressures from record company and police did nothing to diminish the Clash's highly romanticised view of themselves as outlaws. This in turn, did nothing to discourage their tendency to succumb to Mott the Hoople Syndrome: it was evident in most of the songs they wrote or revised in the summer of 1977 and released over the following year as the A- and B-sides of their inter-album (and non-album) singles. 'City Of The Dead' revisits tired old alienation themes and includes a cringe-inducing verse about the band's 'dangerous' Pop Star Army Fatigues. 'The Prisoner' takes its title from the enigmatic and elliptical television series, but is saturated with outlaw and outsider imagery and somewhat bleakly concludes that the only freedom possible is becoming a 'star': not very punk at all.

The old 101ers' song 'Jail Guitar Doors' was revived chiefly for its title. Its verses, rewritten by Mick, allow him to indulge himself by namechecking other rock'n'roll guitarists who had suffered persecution from the authorities: the MC5's Wayne Kramer, Peter Green of blues period Fleetwood Mac and Keith Richards. (More romanticism: all three were victims, true, but primarily of their own drug habits.) 'Complete Control', although about the recent trials and tribulations of being in the Clash, is saved by its relative musical complexity and sense of defiance. The self-celebration of 'Clash City Rockers', a rewrite of 'You Know What I Think About You', is mitigated by its tongue-in-cheek imagery and pro-creative message: 'You won't succeed unless you try.'

The band had worked up a version of the Maytals' 'Pressure Drop' for the White Riot Tour, and their own post-début album songwriting also showed their ongoing fascination with reggae culture. 'The Prisoner' makes reference to the Slickers' 'Johnny Too Bad' and rude boys, and 'Jail Guitar Doors' to the Maytals' '54-46 That's My Number', inspired by Toots Hibbert's 1966–8 incarceration for marijuana possession. Musically, 'Clash City Rockers' is another attempt at reggae–punk fusion, as advertised by its title:

literally, how we play rockers-style reggae in these here parts.

By far the boldest songwriting move was '(White Man) In Hammersmith Palais'. Not only was it the band's first attempt to slow down the tempo (still an act of heresy in punk circles) and play the bona fide reggae beat, but its complex lyric addresses the poor prospects for unity between such widely different cultures when even their respective followers seemed unwilling to live up to their ideals. Although not released as a single until June 1978, it was written almost exactly a year earlier and inspired by two separate – but, to Joe, not unconnected – incidents.

The song begins by describing events at a 5 June reggae allnighter at the Palais, as attended by Joe and Roadent. Hoping to hear some radical reggae from Dillinger and the other artists namechecked in the lyric, they were disappointed to be offered the equivalent of a chicken-in-a-basket soul revue: very slick, but no soul. Meanwhile, there were some ugly scenes on the dancefloor. 'A lot of the black sticksmen were running around trying to snatch these white girls' handbags, and I intervened,' Joe told the *NME*'s Sean O'Hagan in 1988. It was strongly reminiscent of the attempted mugging at the previous year's Notting Hill Riot. 'I was trying to talk about revolution, and how we weren't ever going to have one, because who had an answer to the British Army?' he explained in a *Melody Maker* retrospective, also in 1988. 'I was really getting at the division between the black rebels and the white rebels, and the fact that we gotta have some unity or we're just going to get stomped on.'

From musing on black and white solidarity, the song moves on to consider the State of Punk, and the movement's apparent lack of commitment to change. In May, following his departure from the White Riot Tour, the Jam's Paul Weller had gone public with what he subsequently admitted were his confused political views, telling the *NME*, 'All this change the world thing is becoming a bit too trendy . . . We'll be voting Conservative at the next election.' At least part of his motive was to rile the Clash, in which he was successful. The band's response came in two parts. Firstly, a telegram reading: 'MAGGIE WILL BE PROUD OF YOU. SEE YOU IN SOUTH AFRICA FOR GUN PRACTICE.' Secondly, verses seven and eight of '(White Man) In Hammersmith Palais', which make digs at 'the new groups' refusing to learn anything, 'changing their votes', wearing 'Burton suits' and 'turning rebellion into money'. Overall, the song is stirring enough emotionally to transcend its ostensibly defeatist conclusion: the same difficult trick the band had pulled off on several of the tracks on the first album.

By the time '(White Man) In Hammersmith Palais' was released, the sincerity of the Clash's own rebel stance had already been called into question. On 23 August 1977, the National Front were granted the right to march through the multicultural south-east London borough of Lewisham, and a thousand of their supporters turned up. So did 5,000 protesters and 4,000 policemen. At the previous year's Notting Hill Carnival the police had been there in force to intimidate the largely black crowd; at Lewisham, they were there to protect the fascists; as a result, it was hard not to infer a political and racial bias. Feelings ran predictably high, and before long another riot erupted. Tony Parsons, an ardent anti-fascist, was present. In the light of 'White Riot' and the band's outspoken stance on the NF, he quite understandably presumed the Clash would want to be there too. He knew they were in the studio that day, and so phoned up to pass on the urgent message. 'Bernie Rhodes said . . . Well, he didn't actually say, "The band are having their hair done", but that's my memory of it,' he laughs. 'And I thought that was kind of pathetic. Just their presence there would have been good, and they didn't have to do anything, really, apart from turn up, but that wasn't to be. And I thought, "Jesus, what is this? The *Monkees*?"'

The Clash had been the Great Hope for political punk, and the realisation that their supposed militancy and commitment were nothing more than another variant on the tired old rebel rock pose irretrievably soured the whole movement for Tony. Over the next few months, he watched in increasing disgust as the band posed for photographs in front of the barricades in Belfast at the start of the Get Out of Control Tour, and then as Joe took the stage at the Anti-Nazi League rally in Hackney on 29 April 1978 in a T-shirt romanticising the Brigade Rosse terrorist movement. Nor was he impressed by the way the Clash's involvement with anti-fascist and anti-racist political causes tailed off following that particular high-profile concert. That spring, he and Julie Burchill were already at work on *The Boy Looked At Johnny*, which was published in October 1978. An extraordinary cocktail of disillusion, vitriol and amphetamine that veers from spot-on criticism to wild accusation, from eyewitness anecdotes to unproven hearsay, it offered no quarter to any of their former friends as it ripped into punk's pretensions and hypocrisies.

'What disappointed me most was that it was boring to read,' Joe told *Melody Maker*'s Allan Jones shortly after publication. 'And also the fact that they'd invented so many lies. They needn't have. They could've put that kind of cynical slant on the facts.' To which Tony's riposte is 'Jon Savage's *England's Dreaming* is a brilliant book, but it's a book *about* punk. *The Boy Looked At Johnny* is a punk book. It's "Ah, bollocks to the lot of you!"' But time has mellowed the Parsons perspective somewhat. 'I was disappointed with the Clash on a personal level, because I thought they would be more involved in trying to effect change. Essentially, they were a band, and I can now see that it's ridiculous to expect a band to behave like a political party, but I think a lot of people did then.'

In the autumn of 1977, it looked, briefly, as though Joe's prognosis for punk and reggae unity had been unduly pessimistic when two leading artists representing the latter culture made an effort to meet the Clash halfway. Bob Marley and his old producer Lee 'Scratch' Perry had teamed up in London for a recording session. Island press officer and *Sounds'* resident reggae aficionado Vivien Goldman popped into the studio for a visit, taking with her a copy of *The Clash*. She was curious to see how the famously eccentric Lee would react to the band's version of the song he had co-written with and produced for Junior Murvin. 'They [Lee and Bob] said, "What are these people with funny hair?"' she recalled in 1981. 'And I explained what I thought they were trying to do. A week later, I went round and they said, "Listen to this!"' 'This' was 'Punky Reggae Party', a song the duo had written together and recorded as a response in kind to the Clash's gesture of solidarity. Consisting chiefly of a list of reggae and punk bands invited to attend the mythical party, it relates what they have in common: 'Rejected by society / Treated with impunity / Protected by their dignity.' Released that December as a double A-side with Bob's 'Jamming', it was inevitably overshadowed by the stronger song and failed to set the world alight.

Intrigued by this very different, but politically and spiritually aligned, music, Lee Perry was prepared to take the matter further. It was arranged that he should produce a session with the Clash at Sarm East studios, 9–13 Osborn Street, Whitechapel. The band chose to record 'Pressure Drop' and 'Complete Control', one example each from the reggae and punk genres, in the hope that the master reggae producer would help them perfect the hybrid. Sadly, once again the project failed to live up to its potential. While the band enjoyed the experience, the result fell between two stools. 'Pressure Drop' was shelved. (The band recorded their own version the following spring, and it was eventually released in February 1979 on the B-side of 'English Civil War'.) After Lee had gone, Mick took 'Complete Control' back into the studio and remixed it with louder guitars. 'Which is fair enough, because it didn't sound so good with a reggae mix on it,' Joe told *Melody Maker* in 1988.

Those record companies which had signed punk bands at the start of 1977 and rushed out their first albums in the spring, pushed them into recording follow-ups just six months later in order to cash in on the Christmas market. The results were uniformly underwhelming. The Jam simply didn't have the songs, and consequently *This Is The Modern World* consists of some embarrassing teenage poetry and a lot of filler. The Stranglers had plenty of material, but little that was new: in fact, *No More Heroes* had been recorded at the same time as their début, of which it is a pale imitation. Despite the addition of second guitarist Lu, the Damned were nearly as stretched as the Jam when recording the inaptly titled *Music For Pleasure*. In October, the Heartbreakers finally got round to releasing their début album, *LAMF* (Like A Mother Fucker). Poorly mixed, it was more a case of LADS (Like A Damp Squib).

At the end of 1977, the Clash were also put under pressure to record *their* second album. Mick and Joe were in an even worse position than their peers, having very few unused songs at their disposal. Encouraged to go away together on holiday to write some new material, they suggested Jamaica, and were astounded when Bernie not only agreed, but also came up with the money. In Kingston, the duo hoped to make a first-hand connection with the culture they had been singing and talking about for the past year. 'We came out of the Pegasus Hotel all togged up in our punk threads,' Joe told Sean O'Hagan just over ten years later. 'I tell you, we was like two punk tourists on a package tour. Completely naïve. We knew Lee Perry, sort of, but we couldn't find him, so we were on our own.' While walking down to the docks to score some ganja, they were openly called 'white pigs' on the street. 'The only reason they didn't kill us was that they thought we were merchant seamen off the ships.' Drug supply secured, they promptly retired to their hotel room where they remained for the next fortnight.

One of the songs that came out of this experience was 'Safe European Home', another punk–reggae hybrid song whose theme picks up where '(White Man) In Hammersmith Palais' left off. A bluntly honest account of culture shock, naïvety, rejection and fear – 'Where every white face is an invitation to robbery . . . I'd stay and be a tourist, but I can't take the gunplay' – it would be the standout track on the much-delayed album *Give 'Em Enough Rope*. But to hear Joe tell it to the *Melody Maker*'s Simon Kinnersley in March 1978, this latest bad experience marked the end of the band's experimentation in that direction: 'We got swept up in that crossover reggae, but I've got over it: it's nothing more than trash reggae. I'm getting into early skanga [another name for ska] and rocksteady now. That's far stronger.'

Several other bands took up the gauntlet and built their careers on punk–reggae crossover variations. The Police were ageing musos masquerading as punks; by the time they made the singles charts in October 1978 with Sting's composition 'Can't Stand Losing You', it was hard to identify any trace of punk. In spite of that, the band's polished pop struck a chord and, by dint of some committed punk-type low-budget tours of the US, they managed to establish themselves as one of the most successful international acts of the period. The Ruts started out as a fun side project for some members of a funk band and a couple of their road crew. Influenced strongly by the Clash, their reggae-tinged rock gave them a run of four hit singles, beginning with 'Babylon's Burning' in June 1979. Their October 1979 album, *The Crack*, suggested a bright future, but the band's career suffered an insurmountable setback when singer Malcolm Owen died from a heroin overdose the following July.

By 1979, Joe was not the only one believing that ska was 'far stronger' than contemporary reggae: the Ska Revival drew its musical inspiration from Jamaican music of the mid to late Sixties, but filtered it through skinhead style and, especially in the case of the Specials and the Beat, Clash-style social commentary.

The beginning of 1978 brought a new set of pressures and problems for punk in general and the Clash in particular. From a chart-watcher's perspective, 1977–9 might seem to have been a golden age for bands associated with the movement, but it is telling that this period saw the very term 'punk' replaced by the catch-all term 'new wave': although previously used to describe bands from the New York scene, the latter had fewer negative connotations and was less specific to any one style of music than 'punk'.

Several of the second wave punk bands from the London scene, many of them products of the 100 Days of the Roxy, went on to make the charts, but they lacked much of the first wave's venom. Despite being wonderful, witty and tasteless, the Adverts' 'Gary Gilmore's Eyes' was essentially a novelty song, as was X Ray Spex's 'Germ Free Adolescents' and also the Tom Robinson Band's biggest hit, '2-4-6-8 Motorway'. Squeeze were never anything but a classic pop band.

Siouxsie and the Banshees drew more from the decadent glam period immediately preceding punk, and their cold, disengaged music set something of a mini-trend soon followed by the likes of Joy Division, the Cure and Howard Devoto's new outfit, Magazine. These bands pioneered an arty, cerebral, borderline pretentious sub-genre usually referred to as 'post-punk', some of whose subsequent exponents would be difficult to differentiate from the pompous dinosaur acts and self-indulgent progressive rockers they were supposedly replacing.

Many of the third wave of UK bands were no more genuine punks than the Police were. Mostly from provincial towns, they were inspired by punk records and media reports either to form from scratch or to change their existing musical style. Dublin's Boomtown Rats, Londonderry's Undertones, Dunfermline's Skids and Swindon's XTC all went on to enjoy varying degrees of chart success, but only Belfast's Stiff Little Fingers and Hersham's Sham 69 attempted to express anything other than cartoon anger, and both quickly lost the plot.

The water was muddied even further when the early chart successes of the London punk scene bands effectively opened the floodgates that had previously kept back both New York's new wave bands and London's pub rock artists. Of the former, it was those with the most evident pop sensibility, such as Blondie and Talking Heads, who went on to bona fide superstar status. Meanwhile pub rockers like Ian Dury, Graham Parker, Elvis Costello, Nick Lowe and the Motors were smart enough to recognise an opportunity, cut their hair and shed their flares.

It is a typical pattern for anything perceived as new and challenging that the pioneers make the breakthrough and take the flak, and those who come behind reap the benefit of awakened interest. Running directly counter to punk's anyone-can-do-it amateur-hour ethic though it might have been, most of the bands who 'made it' via the new wave were experienced and/or musically competent enough to sweeten the punk staples of basic production, speed and attitude with melodies and hooks.

Certainly, by no means all the original first wave punk bands were able to establish lengthy and successful careers. Following the débâcle of the Damned's second album, Rat Scabies walked out in disgust. The others struggled on until February 1978 with Jon Moss, and then went their separate ways. Jerry Nolan was so offended by the quality of the

Heartbreakers' album that he quit the band immediately before the tour arranged to promote it. The Pistols' Paul Cook sat in for a while, and Rat Scabies tried out as a permanent replacement, but it was Terry Chimes who got the job on 21 November. On the 23rd, after two gigs at the Vortex, the band split.

Although they had been hero-worshipped by more than a few punk scenesters, that the Heartbreakers were older, American and relative latecomers to the UK scene prevented the band's disintegration from causing too much anguish. Similarly, while the Damned's slapstick approach had been a welcome antidote to the deadly seriousness of so many of the other punk bands, it somehow made their passing equally difficult to take seriously. (Whatever sting it had was soothed when they re-formed, initially as the Doomed, in September 1978, with Rat but without main songwriter Brian James.) Nor did much wailing and rending of garments result when the Vibrators began to break up following the release of their second, inferior, pop-punk album, *V2*, in April 1978.

More epoch-making, if inevitable, was the demise of the band that had started it all. Playing up to the myth of a Sex Pistols ban, Malcolm distanced the band from its close supporters during 1977: only a couple of semi-secret gigs and the aborted Jubilee Boat Party were held in the capital. The Pistols played brief low-key tours of Scandinavia and Holland, and another of small UK clubs under a variety of pseudonyms (including the Spots), but they never regained the momentum lost during the Anarchy Tour. Their development was further retarded by the replacement of Glen Matlock with the multi-untalented Sid. By the end of the year, the various band members were barely communicating, let alone writing new material. Following a 14 January 1978 show at San Francisco's Winterland Ballroom, the last date of their short, but hardly uneventful, début US tour, the band split with considerable acrimony.

The break-ups of the Heartbreakers, the Damned (for much of that year, at least) and the Sex Pistols left the Clash feeling isolated. The Pistols in particular had always been the Clash's pace-setters, the band against whose achievements they measured their own. 'It made us feel a bit lonely, somehow,' Paul told *Melody Maker*'s Allan Jones later that year. 'There was nothing to chase.' 'We'd never have beaten them anyway,' added Joe, and Paul agreed. Their humility was touching, but ignored the fact the Pistols had long since ceased to progress creatively.

Although the Stranglers and the Jam were both still going strong, the Clash felt no great affinity with either group, and relations were strained. Also, like the Buzzcocks and Generation X, both of whom also continued to make regular chart appearances, the Stranglers and the Jam were developing a more pronounced pop sensibility. Of the old guard, other than the Clash, only the Jam persevered with lyrics that offered anything in the way of social comment. Aside from Sham 69, whose singer Jimmy Pursey took to joining them on-stage during this period for encore versions of 'White Riot', the

Clash felt no kinship with any of the bands that broke through with the new wave, and even Sham rapidly lost their charm when they began churning out sub-Chas-and-Dave Cockney knees-ups. As far as the Clash were concerned, by spring 1978, they really were the Last Gang In Town.

Their sense of isolation was exacerbated by the disintegration of the original punk community and their own support network of followers and friends. Whatever the Clash might have thought of the Roxy, it was hard for them to deny that the capital's punk scene had fragmented following its demise. Tony Parsons had given up on the Clash before the end of the year. Viv Albertine was concentrating on the Slits. Chrissie Hynde had embarked on the long road that would result in the formation of the Pretenders. Shane MacGowan had formed the Nipple Erectors, and would go on to form Pogue Mahone, later the Pogues. Even Mad Jane was in the process of forming a band, teaming up with former Slit Kate Korus in the Mo-dettes. Sid Vicious was on his way to a significantly less happy ending, immersed in the mutually destructive relationship with Nancy Spungeon that would come to an end on 12 October 1978; another pointless, drug-related fight in their room at New York's Chelsea Hotel resulted in Sid pushing a knife into Nancy's stomach, for which act he was later arrested and charged with murder.

Instead of a smart, angry, dynamic London scene defined as much by its landscape and architecture – the Westway, high-rise blocks, Soho clubs – as by its fans, most of whom were known faces, the Clash's audience was now a more shadowy national one, its members, 'the kids', products of largely unfamiliar provincial cities and towns. Their information about punk came partly from record covers and the music press, but was still polluted by a kind of folk memory of Anarchy Tour tabloid coverage. They dressed poorly in shabby copies of 'punk' clothes and betrayed the sheep-like mentality of young rock'n'roll fans the world over; they expressed their adoration with sneers and unrelenting hails of gob because they believed that was what punks were supposed to do.

The Clash had also begun to lose even the closest of their helpers. First to leave was Roadent. The position of a roadie working for one band in particular is a peculiar one: since he spends so much time with the band, he is encouraged to think of himself as their friend; in addition, some of their glory reflects on him, which inevitably inflates his ego; but when it comes to the crunch, he is an employee, expected to do as he is instructed. The relationship is closer to master–servant than equal to equal, and is open to all the abuses, humiliations and resentments that might suggest. Including having to make do without socks. Before they had a record contract, it was relatively easy for the Clash to maintain the illusion of equality befitting a punk band opposed to the notion of rock stardom. Once they had the contract, were making records, appearing regularly in the music press and attracting adoring young fans, it was not quite so simple. The determinedly egalitarian Joe did his best not to let things change; Paul continued to deal with people one to one, taking them as he found them; new boy Topper was not yet confident enough of his own status to play power games; but Mick had always been a bit of a spoiled brat, and all the attention did nothing to encourage more equable behaviour.

In the second half of July 1977, Roadent disappeared without leave to roadie for the Sex Pistols on their Scandinavian tour, quickly clicking into another roadie–star friendship with Johnny Rotten. 'Rotten treated me just great,' he told *ZigZag*'s Robin Banks (né Crocker) in 1980. 'He'd get on the blower in hotels and go, "No I don't want two beers: I want two fuckin' *crates*!" We had some real fun.' Back in London, Roadent temporarily patched things up with the Clash, but began to feel he was being taken for granted. Following a flaming row, he left in the middle of the October–November 1977 Get Out of Control Tour. 'Bernie was a real cunt,' he told Robin. 'He didn't pay me proper, and I was forking out for the gear from that! Also, I felt that some members of the band needed a personal valet instead of a roadie.' That remark, as Robin well knew from his own experience, was aimed at Mick.

Roadent's replacement was Johnny Green, recently graduated in Arabic and Islamic Studies from Lancaster University, who arrived in much the same fashion as had his predecessor: a casual roadie on the tour, he asked if he could stay on full-time and promptly moved into Rehearsals. Roadent went to work for the Pistols, who unfortunately split up shortly afterwards. Luckily for him, back in September 1977, Bernie had insisted that a German film crew making a documentary on punk rock should film Roadent rather than the Clash. His mischievous performance in the resulting *Punk In London '77* went down so well that he was invited to Munich to appear in a TV film entitled *Brenende Langweile*. Somewhat ironically, having just changed professions, he made his bid for stardom acting as a roadie to a band played by the Adverts. Thereafter, he took a succession of other roles, which, at least partly, explains why he was immortalised in the Passions' single 'I'm In Love With A German Film Star'. He went on to run his own PA hire company.

Next to go was Micky Foote. 'Clash City Rockers' had been recorded prior to Mick and Joe's departure for Jamaica, to be released on 17 February 1978. In their absence, Bernie deemed the recording to be 'too flat', and Micky suggested varispeeding the master to perk it up a little. Not only were such production tricks considered contrary to the punk ethic (though there is a persistent rumour that the entire first Damned album was varispeeded up), but the band had also made a public stand on creative control with their record company, and having that undermined by their own support team was too much to take. When Mick and Joe returned and heard the results, Micky was sacked. In many ways, it was a godsend for Mick, who had designs on the producer's chair; he was chiefly responsible for any subsequent production work credited to the Clash. The original mix of 'Clash City Rockers' was reinstated for the US version of *The Clash* and used on all later compilations. Micky did some more production work after that, notably for Tymon Dogg, but his experience with the Clash put him off seriously pursuing a career in the music business.

Sebastian Conran's departure was more gradual, but no less fraught. Robin's arrival on the scene for the White Riot Tour marked the beginning of the end: the two took an instant dislike to each other. 'He'd got a loud voice, and he was a bully,' says Sebastian of Robin. 'Mick felt sorry for him, but he was a complete berk. All he did was get into trouble. Basically, he was Mick's gopher. It was nice for Mick to have a little slave, so we all had to put up with him.' As far as Robin was concerned, Sebastian's accent and slight lisp were a red rag to a bully, and he did his best to make his life miserable from then on. He was not the only one. When Gordon Burn made his revelations about Sebastian's background in the 17 July 1977 issue of the *Sunday Times Magazine*, it was as if open season had been declared. Tony Parsons began to take cheap shots at him in the *NME*'s gossip page. As late as the December 1978 issue of *ZigZag*, Robin used a PiL interview as an excuse to humiliate 'the ghastly Habitat heir', recounting tales of Johnny Rotten's friend and PiL bass player Jah Wobble being sick all over Sebastian's house, and then beating him up in Dingwalls. 'Sebastian was always a loser.'

Following Roadent's departure, Joe moved out of the squat they had shared in Canonbury and into a spare room in Sebastian's house at 31 Albany Street. Although this made perfect sense, it being the nerve centre for the Clash's 'design arm', Upstarts, and also reasonably close to Rehearsals, it was not a wise move as far as street credibility was concerned. Joe treated his new home much like a squat – 'I gave him this nice room,' says Sebastian, 'and the first thing he did was aerosol all over the walls' – but more jibes began to appear in the music press gossip pages about Strummer having sold out by moving into the 'White Mansion' of a millionaire's son. These were picked up by hecklers in the band's audiences. For someone who had roughed it for the past seven years and was more conscious than any other member of the band of the importance of being seen to live up to the Clash's ideals, it was too much for Joe to bear. In the spring of 1978, he moved out again to share a genuine squat near Marble Arch with Boogie, Kate Korus and various other associates of the Mo-dettes. After making a point of inviting *Sounds*' Pete Silverton round there for an interview that June, he demanded, 'You're gonna write where I live, aren't you? I've had enough of this White Mansion rubbish.'

When it came to Sebastian, Joe showed no more loyalty than he had to Micky Foote, and joined the rest of the band in trying to maintain as much distance as possible. 'It all got a bit acrimonious. "What's *Sebastian* doing here?" when I'd been around for ages.' Before long, he found he was being accused of exploiting his association with the band for personal gain, via Upstarts' plans for Clash-related merchandising. Once again, he believes he was a convenient scapegoat. 'It was a very uncomfortable political situation for them,' he acknowledges. 'But the whole thing did start off as a commercial venture, and frankly, *Bernie* started it up, and he started it up with the purpose that it should be like that.'

Squeezed out, Sebastian ran down Upstarts and, from the summer of 1978 onwards, concentrated more on helping Bernie operate his various sidelines. He designed posters and helped organise gigs for Subway Sect and the other artists the Clash manager had started to promote around town under the banner Club Left. On 5 November, Sebastian and his friend Henry Bowles (sometime narrator of Clash radio advertisements) were sitting having a drink at a Subway Sect gig when some bouncers took exception to the way Henry was laughing and beat him to death. The folly of his excursions into ted territory with Joe suddenly dawned on Sebastian: this was no longer a joke. The Clash would subsequently dedicate *London Calling* to Henry, but by the end of 1978, a grief-stricken Sebastian had already concluded that anything and anyone was expendable and incidental when it came to the Clash Myth and the band's continuing success. He split with Bernie and thereafter pursued a successful career in industrial design. It took him a long while to develop a perspective on his association with the band that wasn't tainted by resentment and self-doubt. 'For years I regretted it all, because I came out of it feeling very, very depressed. I feel much more positive now,' he laughs. 'Basically, they were being a bunch of fucking hypocrites. The whole thing was completely hypocritical.'

Glen Matlock describes Malcolm McLaren's management style as 'divide and conquer'. By 1978, it was debatable whether the bickering Bernie encouraged was intended to keep the Clash motivated or to subdue them. Team talk brainwashing and constant arguments might have got the Clash as far as making their first album, but it had left them with next to no means for coping with the pressures of fame and the contradictions inherent in their own ideology.

Up until mid-1977, Joe had represented the band's biggest problem in terms of the moodiness engendered by his self-denial and alcohol and speed intake, but that had changed towards the end of the year. During the October–November Get Out of Control Tour an abscessed tooth had resulted in glandular fever. By February 1978, he had contracted hepatitis. Although in rock'n'roll circles hepatitis is usually associated with careless intravenous drug abuse, this was certainly not the cause in Joe's case. He himself believed he had caught it through involuntarily swallowing audience spit during the tour. The resulting spell in hospital persuaded Joe to take more care of his health. He decided to give up speed altogether, and he cut out drinking for several months.

By the time he became ill, Joe's role as the Clash's biggest problem had already been usurped by Mick. Bernie announced as much to Lester Bangs in November 1977, for public consumption via the pages of the *NME*. The reason wasn't given at the time, but it was generally presumed to be his move away from toeing the punk line in terms of visual style, stage craft, lifestyle and behaviour, all of which suggested he had succumbed to what, by punk standards, was the ultimate evil of 'playing the rock star'. The crop Mick had in January 1977 was the last time his hair saw the barber's scissors until the end of 1978; for 18 months of that period, he wore it in his favoured style of old. Or, rather, Keith Richards's favoured style of old. Mick's clothing also began to drift back to the flamboyance of the pre-punk era. In concert, his stage moves became less about communicating energy and more about preening in the spotlight. Early in 1978, he and Tony James moved into an upmarket flat in Pembridge Villas, just off Portobello Road. He made no attempt to hide his new abode from representatives of the music press and – unlike Joe, who had been needled by the White Mansion jibes – positively revelled in their descriptions of it as a 'flash Jason King-style pad', complete with blonde model-type accessories. A few months ago, he had been jeering at the Rod'n'Britt lifestyle; now he was emulating it. His attitude to the other members of the Clash grew increasingly inconsiderate and high-handed, yet he appeared completely oblivious to this. Sebastian was not the only person who knew him at this time to describe him as a prima donna: the nickname the rest of the band conferred upon him, Poodle, was by no means solely inspired by his hairstyle.

While speed had always been accepted on the punk scene as a cheap street drug, cocaine was considered the province of the champagne jet set and frowned upon as an indulgence. Mick's use of it was made known to the general public following a police bust in summer 1978. More music press sneers ensued. What was not revealed was that Mick's dabblings had by then escalated into a fully-fledged drug problem, which did nothing to help keep him on an even keel. In July that year, Joe told the *NME*'s Chris Salewicz, 'If you snort coke, you're in on your own. You don't *want* anybody, and you don't *need* anybody. Which is a *horrible* place to be.' 'He was getting at me, and he was right,' Mick admitted to *Sounds*' Garry Bushell in November, by which time he was working on cleaning up his act. 'That sort of drug is really soul-destroying.' 'On Janet Street-Porter's *London Weekend Programme*, me being all young and naïve, I blamed drugs for the great mid-Seventies drought in rock. I recall saying it really well,' he told Nick Kent the following month. 'And a year or so later, I found myself doing just as many drugs as them! Y'know, taking drugs as a way of life, to feel good in the morning, to get through the day. And it's still something I'm getting over right now.'

Thus, while Joe felt he had to be seen to be living in a manner that was true to the spirit of punk and deny himself the trappings of the rock'n'roll fame and success he had always craved, Mick was openly living out his adolescent fantasies with no regard for his own integrity and well-being or, indeed, the maintenance of the Clash Myth. It naturally led to considerable tension between the two, and to related divisions within the band and their associates. Joe was certainly more popular than Mick in the Clash camp. In fact, on more than one occasion both Joe and Paul became so irritated by the guitarist they resorted to expressing their frustrations with their fists: yet more blows struck for the cause of anti-violence.

Contact between band members was limited more and more to rehearsals, recording and playing live, and as a consequence being part of the Clash became like having a job. Paul spent much of his free time with Caroline, Joe – while he still considered himself a loner – with his squatmates and Mick with the new aristocracy of the new wave, most of whom Joe despised. When members of Tony James's Generation X wandered into the café where Joe was being interviewed by *Melody Maker*'s Simon Kinnersley in May 1978, he sneered, 'Bands like that make me sick. They don't stand for anything, they don't mean anything: they're just a pathetic collection of wimps.'

In the emotionally charged March 1977 interview with Tony Parsons Mick had declared, 'The people involved with the Clash *are my family*.' This view of the Clash as a tightly-knit group of people who might sometimes disagree about matters creative yet were steadfastly loyal to one another would be propagated in interviews and in touchy-feely group photographs until the divorces began in mid-1982. In 1991, Mick told the *NME*'s James Brown that the band had never been that close. This was true, but Mick's realisation was entirely retrospective; because being in a group meant so much to him, as long as he remained with the Clash, he shut his eyes to the not inconsiderable evidence that the other members did not necessarily believe that a passionate professional relationship had to be founded on deeply felt personal ties.

Strangely enough, one of the few people who managed to bridge the gaps in the Clash camp and who therefore made a substantial contribution to holding the whole mess together was Robin Crocker. Although his original links were with Mick and he still socialised with him, he acted as a court jester for the rest of the band, keeping everyone amused with his slapstick routines, sly wit and outrageously yobbish behaviour. As at school, he usually went that bit further than anyone else, but Paul and especially Topper's acceptance of the challenges he threw down gave them much-needed, if usually irresponsible and antisocial, opportunities to let off steam. Fortunately, as the media considered Mick and Joe to be the band's moral core, the transgressions of the others were made light of, when reported at all, and seldom criticised with any seriousness for being contrary to the Clash's high-minded ideals.

Another unifying factor was Bernie, though in a different way: the entire band had become unhappy with their manager. For the latter half of 1977 and most of 1978, he had very little personal contact with the Clash, relying increasingly on overlapping combinations of Roadent, Micky Foote and Johnny Green to oversee the day-to-day running of the band. The Clash accepted that dealing with the record company, booking agents and the like took up a good deal of Bernie's time, but they were also aware of his experiments with promotion through Club Left and his continuing fascination with empire-building, as indicated by his involvement in the early careers of the Specials and Dexys Midnight Runners, among others.

Bernie was primarily an ideas man: he was far more interested in possibilities and potentials, scams and confrontations, than in maintenance work. It might have been hard for the Clash to adjust to a world where there was nobody to compete with following the break-up of the Pistols, but it was almost impossible for Bernie. During the lull between the respective demises of the Pistols and Sid Vicious, when not working with Julien Temple on *The Great Rock'n'Roll Swindle*, Malcolm McLaren found himself at something of a loose end. He amused himself by sitting on Bernie's shoulder wearing little horns and a pointed tail. He told his friend that the Clash were betraying him with their decadent behaviour. Bernie agreed. 'He didn't want us to become what we'd started out against. All credit to him,' Joe told Allan Jones in November 1978. 'But his method of preventing this was to come and attack us, to come in with *scorn.*'

With the benefit of hindsight, the squeezing out of both Micky Foote and Sebastian Conran may be seen as exploratory attacks on – and therefore warnings to – Bernie, whose pawns they were by then perceived to be. A case can also be made for Mick's rock star behaviour being the equivalent of a teenager's rebellion against an overly strict or absentee parent. Mick and Bernie's relationship had provided the foundation upon which the Clash was built. Mick had been the first to be seduced by Bernie's vision, but was now rejecting his mentor in the most demonstrative of ways. He became evasive when the subject of 'political punk' was brought up in interviews and regularly refused to play 'White Riot' in concert, which on several occasions precipitated another outbreak of fisticuffs.

Towards the end of the Clash's June–July 1978 Out on Parole Tour, former Sex Pistol Steve Jones began to present himself at gigs and join the band on-stage for the encores. As Steve was by now a notorious ligger and jammer-about-town, the first time it happened Mick thought nothing of it. After a few repeat performances, however, it dawned on him that it was a little odd that Steve should just keep happening to turn up with his guitar under his arm. A confrontation resulted in Steve blithely admitting that, as far as he was concerned, he was there by invitation to audition as Mick's replacement. It turned out to be another of Bernie and Malcolm's little plots. 'Of course, I wasn't going to have any of *that*,' Mick informed Nick Kent that December. 'And, more to the point, neither were the rest of the group.' Bernie had hoped that Mick's unpopularity with the others would make it a relatively simple matter to get rid of him; what he hadn't anticipated was that his own standing was even lower. The scare was the main motivation behind Mick's decision to get on top of his drug problem. It also made him Bernie's enemy for life.

The first Clash album had done surprisingly well in the UK, but the production was deemed too raw for it to be given an official release by either of CBS's US labels, Epic and Columbia. Culture shock was an undeniable factor in this spurning, but Maurice Oberstein was not too far wide of the mark with his suspicion that inter-label rivalry was at its root. Certainly, there would have been a healthy market for the album: it would go on to sell over

100,000 copies as an expensive import before Epic finally got round to releasing a revised version of it in 1979. In the mean time, CBS UK did their best to help this capitulation along. Their determination to court the US market began with paying for celebrated American rock writer Lester Bangs to fly over especially to cover the October–November 1977 Get Out of Control tour for the *NME*. Lester came with no guarantees attached, but it was a fairly safe bet that such a garage punk aficionado would respond favourably to the band. In fact, he responded so favourably that the paper had to run his epic screed over nine A3 pages in three consecutive issues, an instance of hype so blatant, even by the notoriously Clash-friendly *NME*'s standards, that their letters page received several scornful blasts from outraged readers.

American tastemakers thus alerted, CBS wanted to be sure that any future albums at least got a chance at reviews and radio plays in that country, and so urged the Clash to pick a proven US-radio-friendly rock producer for their second album. The rumour was that the band were handed a short list of approved candidates and ordered to pick one. Unsurprisingly, they hotly denied this whenever a music journalist brought it up. The producer they ended up with, Sandy Pearlman, best known for his work with heavy metal band Blue Öyster Cult, was hardly somebody any member of the Clash would have picked entirely of his own volition. Undoubtedly, CBS put great pressure on the band, but the truth is, despite their protestations to the contrary, the Clash made creative concessions in order to gain the access to the American market they craved.

The original sessions had to be cancelled when Joe contracted hepatitis in February 1978. In March, the band went into the Marquee studios to record assorted demos and B-sides. Between April and May, they worked with Sandy on further demos and then backing tracks for the album proper at Basing Street studios, and also visited CBS studios and Utopia studios for further recording in May. Sandy was a more exacting taskmaster than Micky and made the band record numerous retakes. Paul got so bored that he asked for war films to be projected on to the wall between takes: the origin of the bomber plane backdrop that would be a feature of Clash live performances for the remainder of the year. Sandy and CBS were still not satisfied with the mixes when the Clash had to leave the studio for that summer's Out on Parole Tour. In August, Sandy insisted Mick and Joe join him in San Francisco's Automatt studio for guitar and vocal overdubs, and these sessions were followed by a visit to the Record Plant, New York, in September for last-minute additions and mixing.

It was a fiendishly long-drawn-out and expensive process, and it brought pressure from all sides. Firstly, the UK music press sniped about the delays, the expense and the American jaunt, all of which were perceived to be redolent of the excesses of the pre-punk era. Secondly, the band were unhappy with Sandy's techniques, and continually pushed for something less polished. Thirdly, CBS kept interfering; panicked by the massive upfront investment they had made in the venture, they wanted something *more* polished. The Clash then discovered that, unbeknownst to both Sandy and themselves, CBS men Muff Winwood, whom they had not so affectionately rechristened Duff Windbag, and Jeremy Ensall had been sneaking off with the tapes and attempting some alternative mixes of their own.

The extremely fraught situation was not helped when Bernie made an announcement, in Mick and Joe's absence, that the band would be playing a gig at the Harlesden Roxy (now under new management) on 9 September 1978. As there was no way the duo could make it back from the States in time, the Clash saw it as an attempt at emotional blackmail by Bernie, who was worried at not being close enough to have any control over proceedings and determined to bring the band back into his sphere of influence. Bernie was right to worry, but he picked a bad time to make his point and a worse way to do it. The *NME* news pages of 30 September reported that, after their first few attempts to deal with him regarding the possibility of releasing the Clash's records in the US, Epic were 'anxious for a management change' and had even nominated their preferred successor. Following the announcement of the Roxy date, an 'untypically humourless' Paul rang the *NME* to declare, 'Bernie Rhodes makes us look daft, and it gets our fuckin' backs up the way he assumes he can just speak away for the four of us. He can't, right?' Bernie was officially sacked on 21 October 1978; the management contract was to expire on 1 December.

Bernie's statement in *Melody Maker* opened with the unintentionally hilarious cliché 'I took them off the street and made them what they are!' Thereafter, however, he went on to score more telling hits by enumerating his soon to be erstwhile charges' rock'n'roll star self-indulgences, not least of which were 'recording in big New York studios and staying in top New York hotels'. He also complained that his association with the Clash had 'ended with the group owing me money'. Financial issues – everything from the meagreness of the band's £25-a-week wages to the extent of their debt to CBS – might not have provoked the split directly, but it quickly became apparent they were significant contributory factors. In the interview conducted by Allan Jones the next month Joe countered Bernie's statement by saying, 'The reason we had to part company is that Bernie – although he's like some kinda genius, a great *ideas* man – he can't, you know, *do sums*.' Speaking to *Sounds*' Jane Simon in 1985, Topper put a figure on the band's financial problems of seven years earlier: 'Bernie Rhodes managed the group, and after a couple of years we found out we were £250,000 in debt to the record company. He had more money than the rest of us put together and it went on and on, and it cost us £25,000 to get rid of him.' Intentionally or not, Joe's and Topper's remarks imply that Bernie had been lining his pockets at their expense, and more than one interviewee for this book has suggested that *someone* involved with the band must have been guilty of financial impropriety.

Even a cursory glance at the figures exonerates Bernie. The first £100,000 of the debt was accounted for by the Clash's initial advance. Whether or not it seems fair (and whether or not he actually took it), by the terms of the CBS contract Bernie was entitled to 20 per cent of the band's gross income: that is, he was perfectly within his rights to skim off £20,000 for himself before any other deductions were made. A further £28,000 was lost on the White Riot Tour and, despite stricter control, £10,000 each on the two subsequent UK tours. European dates over the period in question probably accounted for at least another £10,000. Recording costs for the first album came to £4,000, a figure more than equalled by the cost of miscellaneous other recording sessions for singles. The Clash had also contributed retrospectively towards the Anarchy Tour. One can only make guesses at the spring 1977 outlay for the new PA and instruments and, via Upstarts, the Groovy Backdrop, clothes and record cover designs – not forgetting the Colosseum gig, Dunstable film and the late 1977 Jamaican trip – but even a conservative estimate would push the total over the £100,000 mark. Bernie might have been notoriously stingy with the wages he was prepared to pay the band and their permanent employees, but over the period preceding his dismissal the total must have amounted to another £15,000 to £20,000, before the rent and bills for Rehearsals were taken into consideration. As for the remaining portion of the £250,000 debt: £150,000 was spent on recording the second album, and that was the fault of the Clash, their producer and CBS. For his part, Bernie believed the album should have been recorded as quickly and cheaply as the band's début.

To sum up, then: Bernie had put the Clash into what he believed was manageable and recoupable debt in order to establish them as the foremost band of the punk rock movement; unfortunately, that debt had given CBS a lever to encourage the band to do things their way; in allowing themselves to be pushed further down this road than was absolutely necessary, the band had put themselves even further into debt and even further into the record company's power; and upon realising this, they blamed Bernie for allowing the situation to develop in the first place. The first thing the band did following Bernie's dismissal was give themselves a wage rise.

Towards the end of 1978, Bernie was not alone in finding the Clash's rock star pretensions increasingly irritating. The Clash were soon to wonder whether it had been quite so wise to tie their fortunes so closely to those of the weekly music papers, the inkies. In 1976, the circulation of all three papers together came to over half a million, but these were not the working class Thinking Man's Yobs of the Clash's original target market. The statistical breakdown of the readership was similar for all three, and revealed that the archetypal inky reader was male, in his late teens or early twenties and in a white collar job or attending some institute of further education. In *Style Wars* Peter York dubbed him a 'student manqué' and quoted an *NME* representative's description of 'a 19-year-old clerk in Middlesbrough who wants to be one-up on his mates with his inside knowledge of the rock world'.

It is true that punk changed the papers, but only *Sounds* became an out-

and-out punk fanzine, albeit better written and better designed. Although early Clash champion Jonh Ingham had soon departed and Giovanni Dadomo had faded away shortly afterwards, Pete Silverton had been converted to the cause, and new recruits Garry Bushell and Dave McCullough joined the paper as ardent fans of punk and, particularly, the Clash. Unfortunately, *Sounds*' attempt to orient its coverage towards the Thinking Man's Yob came just as the Clash started to rethink their own objectives.

Following Caroline Coon's departure, *Melody Maker* resumed its more ambivalent approach to punk: writing about it in some detail, but objectively, while also maintaining its traditional eclectic coverage of other, less fashionable genres. The Clash were perceived to be an important rock band, and the likes of Allan Jones afforded them considered appraisals worthy of their status; no more, no less. Of the three, the inky the Clash had most closely aligned themselves with was the *NME*. There too the Clash had lost their original champion, but Tony Parsons's role as resident Clash fan was quickly filled by Chris Salewicz, who would occupy it until he left to join *The Face* in 1980. As befitted its special relationship with the band, in addition to detailing hard Clash news on its news pages and reviewing records as and when released, the paper ran lengthy interviews several times a year, reviewed live gigs as often as possible, covered any slightly unusual Clash event in its Thrills pages and included even the most inconsequential pieces of Clash gossip in T-Zers.

There might have been a lot of coverage, but it wasn't all positive. Like *Sounds*, the *NME* had committed itself to punk, but it approached the movement from a more serious, intellectually and ideologically rigorous angle: hard more often than kind. Chris might have been on the Clash's side, but other writers, including Charles Shaar Murray and Nick Kent, were determined to call it how they saw it, and some of the paper's newer recruits were actively looking to explode the Clash Myth. The old music press cliché of 'building 'em up to knock 'em back down again' has always had an element of truth in it, whatever the papers themselves might say to the contrary: they are, after all, dependent on the turnover of product and therefore susceptible to changing trends. Just as the established bands of the pre-punk era had been vilified by the Clash, so, now that they themselves were one of the established bands of the post-punk era, they in their turn were fair game for the latest Hip Young Gunslingers in town. *Melody Maker*'s balance was integral to nearly all parts of its coverage, but the *NME* preferred to encourage opinionated writers and allow balance to emerge as, when and if it chose from the resulting contrasting viewpoints. For every record or gig given to a recognised Clash aficionado to review, another would be handed out to someone known to be either indifferent or antagonistic. The dominant tone of interviews was still pro-Clash, but this in turn was offset by the barrage of bitchy gossip items in T-Zers.

What soon became painfully obvious was that the Clash could give it out, but they couldn't take it. Their time with Bernie had encouraged them to think of the inkies as organs of propaganda, and the feeling persisted that any press that wasn't wholly for them was wholly against them. The band seemed to believe that the kind of sycophantic coverage still offered by Mick's mates at the relatively low-circulation *ZigZag*, and to some extent by *Sounds* (up to spring 1979), was their due. The constant probing, questioning of motives, criticising of wrong moves, attacks on perceived hypocrisies and mockery of pretensions to which they were subjected by the *NME* and, to a lesser degree, *Melody Maker* fed their paranoia. Joe, more than anyone, found it difficult to take negative feedback in his stride: for every claim he made not to be affected by it, there was a rabid counter-attack or an interlude of depressed soul-searching.

On the other hand, Mick's and Joe's egos were flattered by the seriousness and depth of the two inkies' questioning and analysis and, possibly unconsciously, they rose to the challenge: their public personae – again, especially Joe's – altered noticeably between 1977 and 1979 as the gruff, snarling semi-articulate yobs turned into thoughtful (if sometimes confused) and humorous left-field artists. But they never relaxed enough to be wholly unguarded and wholly honest. In September 1977, Joe remonstrated with Mick, in front of Chris Salewicz, for being so open with the press. Mick countered that Joe was overly concerned with maintaining his mystique. Joe responded by snarling, 'All journalists are swine!' That October, Giovanni Dadomo asked the band if they manipulated the press. 'No, we're not that clever,' retorted Mick. Whether or not that was true, it didn't prevent them from trying. The band had not lost their punk era penchant for rewriting the band's history to suit the present, and would continue to do so following each new musical direction or change of personnel. As time went on and the various papers built up large archives of proof of this tendency, they, hardly surprisingly, became distrustful of the Clash's rhetoric and increasingly loath to take them seriously.

It was not that the band held the music press in contempt. In fact, the opposite was true: the inkies' role in the punk propaganda campaign, and the avid perusals to which Mick, Joe and Topper had subjected the papers in their respective adolescences, had combined to give the band members a totally distorted impression of the power of the music press. Thus, if the Clash received a bad review, they took it as a sign that they were losing their grip. Also, the band presumed that the inkies accurately reflected the feelings of 'the kids'.

The Clash were forced by last-minute GLC seating restrictions to play the postponed Harlesden Roxy concert, originally arranged by Bernie, over two nights, on 25 and 26 October 1978. Ever in search of a fresh perspective, the *NME* sent along post-punk recruit Ian Penman to review one of the shows. This is what he saw: 'A joyless, emotionless, directionless, self-important music, something like a shambolic HM quartet converted to Mao minutes before a show, but still retaining the original ego-pushy set, swaggers and all . . . The Clash don't know what to do with themselves, don't know what to do with rock music, but I and you know what it's doing to them. The Clash is a dying myth.' It hurt because much of it was true, as the album that hit the shops shortly afterwards served to testify.

Even by the beginning of 1978, the *Zeitgeist* that had inspired both *The Clash* and the rhetoric that had preceded and accompanied the album's release was no more, and the new situation in which the band found themselves was depressing and disorienting. They were beset by problems both internal and external, and the punk movement of which they had assumed leadership was no longer something they could recognise or identify with. 'I remember what a fuck up it was after the first record,' Joe told the *NME*'s Paul Morley in 1979. 'We kind of turned around and said, "*Now* what are we going to do?" We just couldn't think of anything to follow it with, really.' This was evidenced by the lyrics Joe came up with for the songs written in Jamaica before Christmas and during the first few months of 1978 at Rehearsals, which were released that November on the band's second album, *Give 'Em Enough Rope*. Its half-petulant, half-defiant title alone points to the unenviable nature of the Clash's position.

'Guns On The Roof' and 'Last Gang In Town' might use Clash experiences as points of departure for other lyrical explorations, but 'Cheapskates', 'All The Young Punks (New Boots And Contracts)' and Mick's 'Stay Free' are all inexcusably self-indulgent examples of Mott the Hoople Syndrome. 'Stay Free' even sounds like an Ian Hunter ballad, while the title of 'All The Young Punks' acknowledges Mott's generational anthem, 'All The Young Dudes'. Unlike earlier Clash songs, the latter approaches bleak subject matter with a decided weariness of tone to ultimately dispiriting effect. The verses tell a potted version of the Clash story to date: the fictitious meeting on Portobello Road, the gigs supporting the Pistols, the management problems, the realisation that the future looks grim. The pay-off line – that however bad being in a rock band can get, it beats working in a factory – fails to uplift. So does the chorus. Previously, Joe had addressed his audience as equals, but now he adopts an avuncular role to advise 'the kids' to 'Laugh your life, 'cause there ain't much to cry for . . . Live it now, 'cause there ain't much to die for.'

'Cheapskates' makes no attempt to compare the Clash's experiences with those of their audience. Instead, it unnecessarily repeats the assertion, already made in and by 'Garageland', that the band has no intention of selling out. Instantly working itself into a lather, Joe's lyric attempts to reinforce the band's street credibility with its opening catalogue of the dead-end jobs and demeaning effects of poverty they have experienced, even throwing in the alleged near-illiteracy of one member as another point in their favour. It then complains at length – and with no little venom – about criticisms received from both the music press and 'the kids'. In the light of Mick's documented dalliance with cocaine and penchant for blonde trophy girlfriends the final verse's repudiation of suggestions that the band are rich, sleep with models and hoover up copious amounts of charlie on a regular basis pushes its luck somewhat. In fact, the words 'rank' and 'hypocrisy' spring all too readily to mind. 'The lyrics are meant as a satire on the situation,' Mick explained to *Sounds'* Garry Bushell in November 1978. 'That last bit was me and Joe writing together and coming to a conclusion instead of talking it out.' Unfortunately, the *angst*-ridden delivery of both this and the preceding verses disabuses the listener of any notion that the Clash are consciously trying to amuse. Within a year of the album's release, Paul would be living with a model and by Joe's admission all four band members would have 'experimented' with cocaine.

A satirical edge was also intended on the album's two other drug songs, 'Drug Stabbing Time' and 'Julie's In The Drug Squad'. The latter was inspired by Operation Julie, during which an undercover policewoman of that name helped infiltrate an LSD manufacturing and distribution network, thus earning the perpetrators hefty prison sentences. Both songs suffer from the reverse problem of 'Cheapskates': they are supposedly humorous ditties given a playful delivery, but merely end up seeming ambiguous and, in the context of the rest of the album, lightweight.

Joe's attempt to stretch himself with the social commentary songs 'Last Gang In Town' and 'English Civil War' also got him into trouble. The former was meant to articulate the stupidity of gang, subcultural and race-related violence: 'it's all young blood flowing down the drain'. Unfortunately, Joe's depiction of these different gangs emerging from their lairs is so heavily romanticised that the song has the exact opposite effect to the one intended. Furthermore, in the company of so many other Mott the Hoople Syndrome tracks, it is all too easy to make the assumption that the 'Last Gang In Town' is meant to be the Clash, rather than the 'zydeco kids from the high-rise' who earn the title because they have no distinguishing characteristics and therefore cannot be located and beaten up by other gangs. 'English Civil War' suffered from the same misinterpretation as '1977'. Joe borrowed the tune to the traditional 'When Johnny Comes Marching Home' and tried to graft on to it a futuristic vision of what might happen were the National Front allowed to get out of control. At the time of release, it was construed as a completely hysterical reaction to the then current situation.

Like Mick, Joe began playing down the political side of the Clash early in 1978. Whereas Mick seemed to be merely refusing to continue to play a role with which he had grown bored, however, Joe recognised that the band had talked themselves into a corner, both in terms of the expectations engendered by their rhetoric and in terms of the limitations placed on their lyrical scope. Almost perversely, then, he proceeded to exacerbate the situation by using the band as a platform to voice his obsession with international terrorism and bona fide urban guerrillas.

Having raised the issue of direct political action on *The Clash* and having been required to expound upon its possibilities ever since, Joe had given the matter much thought. Sometime prior to his illness in early 1978, he had recorded two versions of 'Heartbreak Hotel' – one cajun and one 'terrorist' – for the soundtrack of a film directed by Diego Cotez and released that May under the title *Grutzi Elvis*. 'It's about Elvis and the Baader–Meinhof gang,' Joe told the *NME*'s Jack Basher in February. The charges of terrorism following on from the Pigeon Shooting Incident and freewheeling late night conversations with Roadent about political extremist groups had further fired his imagination. He took to wearing T-shirts on-stage proclaiming 'BRIGADE ROSSE' and 'H BLOCK', and began exploring his new interest in song and, subsequently, in interview. 'Guns On The Roof', a group jam on the by now decidedly overused 'I Can't Explain' riff, asserts that assassins are an inevitable consequence of corrupt societies. 'Tommy Gun' illustrates how media coverage turns the terrorist into a celebrity: 'I'm cutting out your picture from page one.' Another contemporary, unreleased track named 'RAF [Red Army Faction] 1810' concerns the supposed, but highly dubious, suicide of a terrorist cell while being held in custody.

It was not only the moral of the songs that was ambiguous: so was Joe's own position on the terrorists. 'The bad thing is that they go around murdering bodyguards and innocent people,' he blithely told *Melody Maker*'s Chris Brazier in July. 'But you've got to hand it to them for laying their lives on the line for the rest of the human race. They're doing it for everybody, trying to smash the system that has broken everybody.' Called to account for this statement later in the year by the same paper's Allan Jones, he stated, 'I *am* ambiguous. 'Cause at once I'm impressed with what they're doing, and at the same time I'm really frightened by what they're doing. It's not an easy subject.'

In attempting to broaden their canvas to reflect their new national – and, they hoped, international – audience *Give 'Em Enough Rope* sees the Clash sever the direct connection to their material that gave *The Clash* its emotional power and unified vision. When Joe sings in the first person on that album, he is either Joe Strummer or Everyman; on the follow-up he plays ill-defined, confusing roles. Sandy Pearlman's stodgy, sterile AOR production serves only to play up the bombast, sentimentality and melodrama.

For this last reason, at least, the album's initial impact was not inconsiderable. *Sounds*' Dave McCullough succumbed totally, and gave it a five-star review. While the *NME*'s Nick Kent was similarly impressed by the sound, he was at least perceptive enough to take issue with Joe's unfocused lyrics and histrionic vocals: 'one is never entirely sure just which side Strummer and company are supposed to be taking . . . What it all adds up to, I fear, is Strummer's totally facile concept of shock-politics.'

The best appraisal came from Jon Savage in *Melody Maker*. He deemed the production to be 'an unsatisfactory compromise'. After astutely placing the album in historical and cultural context – that is, amongst the ruins of punk – he noted the weight of expectation the Clash had to shoulder: 'It's hard when you define a period so accurately.' Nevertheless, he was disappointed by the lack of direction, the mood of defeatism: 'The Clash's view of the human condition, while imprecisely expressed, isn't very sanguine this time out. The sharp, direct attack of the first album, itself holding out hope by the accuracy of targets selected and hit, has been replaced by a confused lashing-out and a muddy attempt to come to terms with the violence of the outside world, which the Clash plainly see as hostile through and through ... Flicking through the titles, you catch the words repeated – Drugs, Guns – and the general themes of gangs and fights, all too rarely enlivened with the humour that marked the first album. They sound as though they're writing about what they think is expected of them, rather than what they want to write about, or need to. It's as though they see their function in terms of "the modern outlaw" – obligatory "rock'n'roll" rebellion similar to the Stones – and conservationists of the punk ethos they so singularly helped to create.' He concluded: 'So do they squander their greatness.'

The band's core following, who had waited a long time for the album's release in November 1978, rushed out to buy it *en masse*, and pushed it up to the number two position in the album charts by the end of the month. Despite its relative commercial success, however, within a few weeks of its release, it became evident to almost all that *Give 'Em Enough Rope* had none of its predecessor's stature. They did their best to enthuse about it while it was still their current album, but the Clash came to recognise it as one of their artistic low-points.

Another artistic low-point, though supposedly contemporaneous, eventually followed on some way behind. Malcolm McLaren's plans to make a Sex Pistols movie had, unsurprisingly, motivated Bernie to think along the same lines. Unfortunately, Julien Temple's commitment to Malcolm's project not only ruled him out of the picture, but also tied up his Clash material. There was talk of Julien's 50-plus hours of band footage being edited into a movie in time for the August 1977 Summer in the City film festival hosted by the Other Cinema in Tottenham Court Road, but nothing came of it. The footage is still in the director's possession, and remains mostly unedited and unseen.

Meanwhile, in 1977, the experimental film partnership of Dave Mingay and Jack Hazan had decided to use the Queen's Jubilee celebrations and the birth of Thatcherism as background to an as yet vaguely defined film about racial and political tensions in the UK. The emergence of punk was a gift to their project. In search of a band they could build the film around, they met Ray Gange, a Clash fan on reasonably friendly terms with Joe Strummer, at a punk club. Ray suggested that Dave and Jack approach the band. Bernie in particular was impressed by the duo's radical approach to film-making, and it was agreed that the Clash and their roadies would co-operate with the venture.

The original intention was to introduce Ray Gange as a new Clash roadie in the style of Roadent or Robin Crocker, and document the developing relationship between himself and the band over the course of a few months.

The Clash were also to be filmed live, in rehearsal and in the studio, beginning with the Anti-Nazi League rally in April 1978. The film crew couldn't hope to be present for every key event, so as time went on, members of the group were also required to re-enact certain scenes and improvise others to help give the film some shape. Although initially happy to go along with this, the Clash became more and more confused about the project's direction. 'The ultimate structure was not known to us until very late in the movie,' Jack Hazan told the *NME*'s Neil Norman in 1980. 'The Clash always used to ask us, "What's the film about, then?" as though we had something over them.'

In October 1978, just before Bernie's split with the band, he put the previously verbal contract with Dave and Jack in writing, giving their company, Buzzy, full copyright. That the Clash themselves did not sign this document goes some way supporting their later insistence that they knew nothing of its existence at that time. Towards the end of the year, it was discovered that the relatively limited and primitive sound equipment Buzzy had been using had not adequately captured the band in performance. The Clash agreed to two separate salvage operations. The first was to use more sophisticated equipment, including a mobile studio, to film and record one of the band's post-Christmas Lyceum dates. The Clash dressed all in black for the gig and, on request, played 'I Fought The Law', which at that stage was being considered as the film's title song. The second was to set up as if for a live show in Wessex studios, 106A Highbury New Park, Highbury, and, with the earlier live footage running on large TV screens in front of them, play and sing along in sync while engineer Bill Price and tape operator Jerry Green re-recorded the soundtrack. The crowd noise was then dubbed back on.

Editing the film took the best part of 1979, and had relatively little input from the Clash. That November, they donated the studio songs 'Rudie Can't Fail' and 'Revolution Rock' to the project, by then going under the title *Rude Boy*. After viewing a cut of the film, though, the band disowned it, objecting in particular to what they perceived to be unrelated footage of black pickpockets being arrested by police. 'They were showing them dipping into pockets and then they were shown being done for something, and that was their only role in the film. And that's a one-way view,' Joe told *Melody Maker*'s Paolo Hewitt in December 1980. 'That's what the right wing use: all blacks are muggers, which is a load of rubbish.'

Joe's objection sounded like an excuse. In the name of realism, the film is full of unpleasant, casual right-wing remarks from Ray Gange and friends, many of which go unchecked by the Clash members and associates who overhear them. Also, the pickpocket footage was among the first shot for the film, predating the Clash's involvement, so it is hard to see how its inclusion could have come as such a last-minute surprise to them. The existence and contents of the contract were also questioned by the band, who claimed they had not been properly consulted. By the start of 1980, however, the Clash

had already been given £2,550 of the £4,000 the document had guaranteed them (along with a promise of 10 per cent of net profits over £25,000), which suggests a degree of acceptance of terms.

It is quite possible that the Clash, with good reason, were embarrassed by the poor quality of their 'acting'. Almost certainly, they were keen to distance themselves from any reminder of the Bernie era, especially the fraught and confused final year. But the chief reason for their hostility towards the project in its latter stages, unbelievable though it may seem, was that they had spent much of 1979 trying to play down their past life as a 'political band' and were therefore unhappy to be so closely associated with the debate that provides the film's central theme.

Despite the Clash's threat of legal action, *Rude Boy* was made an official British entry for the Berlin Film Festival in February 1980 and released in the UK the following month. The *Daily Mail*'s film critic, Margaret Hinxman, asked, 'MUST WE SHOW OFF THIS FOUL VIEW OF BRITAIN?' Tom Davies, the *Observer*'s gossip columnist, was so incensed at the preview that he punched Dave Mingay in the mouth. The *NME*'s Neil Norman described the film as 'an innovative piece of cinematic art . . . a genuine cri de cœur for a generation already on the retreat'. Although he was not prepared to go that far, *Sounds*' Phil Sutcliffe believed there was 'obviously a clear plan behind it'. *Melody Maker*'s Paolo Hewitt was less convinced that was the case and, like Phil, found it highly ironic that the Clash, of all bands, should have distanced themselves from the film's politics.

The musical content failed to make much of an impression on most of the older reviewers of the national press. An exception was the *Guardian*'s Derek Malcolm who, in spite of referring to the band as the Slash – one can only assume unintentionally – declared that 'musically, at least, the film is extraordinary . . . there could not be a better advertisement for them or their records'. Almost everyone in the music press agreed with him that, if nothing else, the film was a fine document of the Clash as a performing band.

True, it captures the moves and the passion, and so provides an exciting *visual* record, but the effect is spoiled somewhat when one knows, as relatively few people do, even today, that most of the supposedly live soundtrack is as fake as, apparently, the band's political commitment.

Give 'Em Enough Rope and *Rude Boy* are records of a time of great confusion. At the end of 1978, the Clash responded by calling the tour they arranged to follow Bernie's departure and the album's release the Clash Sort It Out Tour. They might have dared to hope that the recent shake-ups had helped them achieve that aim already, but the real work was yet to be done.

12... GATES OF THE WEST

By the start of 1979, the Clash camp had been whittled down to a core group of trusted associates. Closest to the band were roadies Johnny Green and the Baker, who had played sizeable roles both in the film *Rude Boy* and in attempting to smooth the relationship between band and directors. Leery of going outside their immediate circle to replace Bernie with an established manager, the Clash had asked Caroline Coon to take over on a semi-official basis. For such a distinctly macho band to take on a female manager might have seemed like an unusual move, but her relationship with Paul made her trustworthy, and she had already proved herself useful as a PR agent while with *Melody Maker* and as a legal adviser during the aftermath of the Pigeon Shooting Incident.

Don Letts had worked as the band's occasional tour DJ up until mid-1978, since when he had been concentrating on video work for the Clash and others. His former function had been taken over by Barry Myers, previously the resident DJ at Dingwalls. In August 1978, Barry had handed in a review of one of the band's Music Machine gigs to *Sounds* that was firmly in the Friends of the Clash tradition: 'It was a privilege to spend four nights with the greatest band in Britain, nay, at this moment in time, the greatest band in the world.' Alex Michon continued to make the clothes. When not writing for *ZigZag*, Robin Crocker carried on as court jester. Terry McQuade, seen in *Rude Boy* as Ray Gange's obnoxious skinhead companion, had a similarly vague role as a kind of supplementary roadie.

The *Rude Boy* soundtrack re-recording sessions were neither the first nor the last on which the Clash collaborated with engineer Bill Price and tape operator – later engineer - Jerry Green. The duo had previously worked on the Sex Pistols' *Never Mind The Bollocks* at Wessex with Chris Thomas producing. Jerry for one believes that the Clash were hoping to link up with Chris, having determined from his Pistols work that he might prove to be the missing link they were searching for: sympathetic to the spirit of their music and yet record company friendly, having previously worked on the Beatles' *White Album* and with Roxy Music, among other notables. If so, the Clash's latest and final attempt to follow in the Pistols' footsteps was thwarted: Chris was unavailable, and the band's first recordings at Wessex were made early in January 1979 with Bill Price doubling as engineer and, along with the band (namely Mick), co-producer.

The Clash's original plan was to rush-release a single of non-album material, and to this end they had Bill record their version of Sonny Curtis's 'I Fought The Law', re-record a new version of 'Capital Radio' – the intention being to kill off the inflated prices being charged on the collectors' market for copies of the original *NME* EP – and rework a couple of songs that had been recorded the previous year. 'Groovy Times' had been written in early 1978; Joe's lyric had been inspired partly by sundry examples of heavy manners UK-style, but chiefly by the fencing in of the nation's football grounds that would ultimately contribute to the Hillsborough disaster. First recorded in a rough electric version at CBS and Utopia studios during the May sessions for *Give 'Em Enough Rope*, it was reworked at Wessex as an acoustic number, with some bravura guitar and harmonica work from Mick. 'Gates Of The West' had an even more convoluted history. Originally Mick's pre-Clash song 'Ooh, Baby, Ooh (It's Not Over)', it had been recorded in that guise at Basing Street in April 1978, along with a tell-tale version of Booker T. and the MGs's decidedly similar 'Time is Tight'. To celebrate Mick and Joe's arrival in New York in September, the lyric had been rewritten first as 'Rusted Chrome' and then as 'Gates Of The West'. The new vocal was dubbed on to the original backing track at the Record Plant, with engineer Dennis Ferranti providing the high backing vocal. Only the final mix was done at Wessex.

Back in November 1978, CBS had incurred the group's wrath by trying (unsuccessfully) to sneak a copy of Don Letts's video for 'Tommy Gun' on to *Top Of The Pops*. Now, following the Wessex recording session, another falling out ensued when the Clash's proposed new single, a coupling of 'I Fought The Law' with 'Capital Radio Two', was blocked by the record company's insistence on the 23 February 1979 release of a second track from *Give 'Em Enough Rope*, 'English Civil War'. The Wessex material was held over, and eventually released in its entirety on 11 May as *The Cost Of Living* EP. Ironically, considering that all four of the tracks were old, the record represented something of a statement of intent, an indication of the Clash's proposed new direction.

Although two of the songs date back to the Sandy Pearlman era, they retain none of the album's HM bluster. *Give 'Em Enough Rope* had featured several experiments with musical genres that were new to the Clash. It had also broadened the palette of instrumentation by adding horns and piano courtesy of session musicians, but the overall overbearing density of sound detracted considerably from any sense of variety. On the EP, by comparison, the acoustic backing for 'Groovy Times', the soul strut of 'Gates Of The West' and the cod-disco coda of 'Capital Radio Two' provide a more successful showcase for the Clash's efforts to stretch themselves, allowing them to bask in their new-found freedom and space.

Being a cover of an American oldie, 'I Fought The Law' is '1977' rescinded: a repudiation of the punk notion – as propagated by the Clash themselves in their first year of existence – that modern British music should look neither to the past nor to America for its inspiration. 'Gates Of The West' goes even further in turning that edict round: it namechecks rock'n'roll original Little Richard, and revels in the romance of America from the perspective of people brought up on and in love with its mythology. 'I first landed in San Francisco, and I thought it was tremendous,' Mick told Duncan Campbell of New Zealand's *Rip It Up* magazine in 1982. 'It just opened my head up totally.' In between the Automatt and Record Plant sessions, Joe had realised a long-cherished dream by driving cross-country in a Cadillac, from San Francisco to New York via New Orleans. Their sense of awe seeps into the song, but it is not quite such a gung-ho celebration that it makes a complete lie of the title (if not the disputed sentiment) of 'I'm So Bored With The USA'. It is underscored with threatening intimations of loss, which might have been inspired by simple homesickness, the Sid'n'Nancy drama, the break-up of Joe's relationship with Palmolive (recently departed for India, 'the Gates of the East') or something on an altogether grander scale, like the East–West showdown depicted on the *Give 'Em Enough Rope* album sleeve. This is an instance of ambiguity working in a song's favour. That said, the chorus makes it perfectly clear what overriding message the Clash picked up from America, and more than hints at their intention to answer Eastside Jimmy and Southside Sue's call for 'something new'.

In March 1978, Joe had memorably described the Clash's live sound to Simon Kinnersley as 'like a mad seal barking over a mass of pneumatic drills'. The definition of punk as three-chord guitar music with lots of shouting over the top had been questioned by the band the previous year, when Mick's post-début album compositions had all pushed against the restrictions of the form. Following the abandonment of 'trash reggae' in mid-1978, however, the Clash had – as Ian Penman suggested – found themselves at a loss, directed by Sandy Pearlman into a bombastic HM mire. The largely negative reaction to this development had left them feeling rejected and confused. By the beginning of 1979, it seemed as though CBS were determined to be uncooperative, the police were determined to harass them, the music press had turned against them and their own following had abandoned them: this last impression despite the evidence to the contrary offered by a number two album and their position at the top of numerous categories in the end-of-year music press readers' polls. The upshot of it all was the decision that, instead of trying to please by living up to the Punk Myth, they might as well pursue the Rock Dream. In 1979, both literally and musically, the Clash went to America.

Give 'Em Enough Rope had become the band's first US record release, through Epic, and had received favourable reviews from doyens of rock criticism Lester Bangs, writing for New York's *Village Voice*, and Greil Marcus, for *Rolling Stone*. The latter noted that the production was not all it could have been, yet had nothing but praise for the band and the songs. 'Imagine the Who's "I Can't Explain" as a statement about a world in flames, not a lover's daze, and you've got the idea,' he wrote, before going on to condemn 'the snivelling backlash' against the band in the UK music press. It was something he was going to have no part in: 'The Clash are now so good they will be changing the face of rock'n'roll simply by addressing themselves to the form.'

In February 1979, the Clash undertook their first brief (eight-date) tour of America, supposedly to promote the album. The break with their past life was both symbolised and sealed by the death of Sid Vicious, the news of which reached the band shortly after they had entered the States from Vancouver, Canada, *en route* to San Francisco by coach. The Clash had been loyal to Sid to the end. After being approached by his mother, they had played a benefit concert for his legal fees on 19 December 1978 at the Music Machine in Camden. Early in the new year, they had played a gig at the Lyceum that was both filmed and recorded for *Rude Boy*. That night, Joe had changed a line in the band's recently learned cover of 'I Fought The Law' from 'I left my baby' to 'I *killed* my baby . . . I guess my race is run.' That was for Sid, and it proved prophetic when, out on bail but contemplating a lengthy prison sentence for killing Nancy, he took his fatal heroin overdose on 2 February 1979. In 1991, the live Lyceum version of 'I Fought The Law' would be used to round off the first CD in the *Clash On Broadway* boxed set: the Clash's farewell to Sid and punk both.

Back in February 1979, if the US thought it was about to witness a display along the lines of the previous year's Sex Pistols tour – a sort of Second Coming of Punk – then it was sadly mistaken. The Clash were intent on following their own new two-part agenda: firstly, to reclaim the US airwaves from the likes of Aerosmith, Kansas, Styx, Foreigner and Boston rather than persist with *Give 'Em Enough Rope*'s efforts to sound more like those groups; and secondly, to remind America of its own musical roots, to which end they had hired Joe's great hero Bo Diddley as support act. In the Clash camp, these two related ambitions soon became known as The Quest.

Not that the band were prepared to give any ground in order to fulfil it. There was plenty of punk attitude to be found in their approach: the tour was given the hardly tactful title of Pearl Harbour '79, and every show opened with 'I'm So Bored With The USA'. There were run-ins with hotel managers and gruff interviews with ill-informed radio DJs and journalists. The Clash played one gig in San Francisco that had been booked by the powerful Billy Graham; and then agreed to play a hastily arranged benefit the following night for a collective of promoters attempting to break his near-monopoly on rock promotion in the city.

By far the biggest ruck was with Epic. When the band first attempted to arrange the tour, their American record company tried to persuade them there was no point as the album was not selling: it failed even to reach the Top 100. There then followed a period of haggling about how much Epic would be prepared to advance to cover costs; the record company grumbled about the size of the Clash's entourage before finally settling on a budget of

$30,000. They then objected to having Bo Diddley as support considering his genre of music inappropriate and wanting the Clash to tour with another Epic 'new wave' band instead. When the band arrived in the States, they found that next to no attempt had been made to publicise the jaunt, and that the record company had taken it upon themselves to bill it as the Give 'Em Enough Rope Tour on the few posters that could be found. Everything came to a head backstage after the band's gig at the Santa Monica Civic Auditorium. According to Joe's estimate, 40 to 50 Epic area representatives had been flown in from all over the country for a meet'n'greet session with the band. 'I was disgusted that they were there,' he told Allan Jones not long after. 'They've done nothing for us, and they were there poncing around backstage with their slimy handshakes and big smiles.' The Clash ignored them prior to the gig, and afterwards, when an attempt was made to arrange a huge group photograph, simply walked out of the room. Exit representatives, humiliated and fuming. The short-term pleasure of expressing their distaste for smarmy corporate behaviour had encouraged the Clash to score a spectacular own goal: there might not have been much record company effort put into breaking the band in the States before that incident, but following it there would be even less.

There were some positive signs: most of the gigs sold out, and most of the audience reactions were wildly enthusiastic. Bruce Springsteen, the New York Dolls' David JoHansen, Andy Warhol, Nico, John Cale and Robert De Niro were among the star liggers who turned up to see the band at the New York Palladium, which did nothing to hurt their credibility. The prestigious *Time* magazine ran an admiring feature on the band by Jay Cocks, which concluded: 'Out of the pieces of a shared precarious existence, the Clash has fashioned music of restless anger and hangman's wit, rediscovered and redirected the danger at the heart of all great rock.'

Initially, the band attempted to give the impression – and may well have believed – that their American campaign was just part of a wider bid for global contact and recognition. The Clash stage backdrop for 1979 certainly did its best to send that signal, being a giant patchwork quilt made up of the flags of all nations. Joe wrote up an account of Pearl Harbour '79 for the *NME* (using the upper-case letters on the typewriter, as was now his wont when composing lyrics) which ended with the declaration 'WE ARE GOING TO GO BACK AND PLAY THE US AGAIN BUT WE MUST ALSO PLAY BRITAIN, JAPAN, EUROPE, AUSTRALIA, AND IT'S FAIR SHARES ALL ROUND. HEY! I HEAR THEY'RE REALLY ROCKING IN RUSSIA . . .' Whether or not it was indeed fair shares all round would become a bone of contention over the next two years.

The US tour proved to be a unifying experience for the band members, something that was reflected in their dress: they started to look like a gang again. In honour of the Clash's romance with America, hair (even Mick's) was cut short and slicked back and the band began to run through the classic monochrome Hollywood and rock'n'roll outlaw looks – Forties gangsters, Fifties rockers and bikers, modern-day cowboys (in Topper's case, complete with spurs) – that would both keep them amused and define their public image for the next couple of years.

Back home, in spite of being aware that their stock with the record company was now so low that they were in danger of being shut down at any moment, the band decided to forget such worries for the time being and concentrate instead on writing, rehearsing and recording their third album. 'I don't know why, but the problem seemed to relax us,' Joe told *Melody Maker*'s Chris Bohn in December 1979. 'The feeling that nothing really mattered any more, that it was make or break time.'

Since splitting with Bernie and losing access to Rehearsals, they had been hiring various rooms around London when necessary and where possible. They now sent Johnny Green and the Baker out in search of somewhere a little more permanent. The duo came up with Vanilla studios, a dingy low-key rehearsal room in Causton Street, Pimlico. In March 1979, the Clash moved in with their instruments, equipment and a portable TEAC 4-track studio. Determined to maintain the team spirit encouraged by the US tour, they approached the songwriting, arranging and rehearsal sessions as though they were in training camp preparing for a major sporting event. This theme was picked up by the daily two-hour football matches played on a nearby school playground, for which the band were joined by the crew and whoever else happened to be around.

They had hoped to be returning to the States in June 1979 for a second, lengthier tour. Caroline Coon had even got as far as booking dates before debt, the outstanding legal problems with Bernie, and Epic's intransigence got in the way. It was Caroline's turn to be the scapegoat. On 16 May, while she was in New York attempting to explain to the band's New York booking agent why the Clash were going to have to pull out of two gigs at the city's Palladium for which tickets had already gone on sale, she was informed by the band that her services were no longer required. Her tenure as Paul's girlfriend had also come to an end. She was not immediately replaced (in the former capacity at least). After flying on to Los Angeles, she signed up as adviser on *DOA*, a documentary on punk which took as its point of departure the Sex Pistols' first and final American tour. The Clash, meanwhile, continued to write and rehearse at Vanilla.

At the end of June that year, Joe told the *NME*'s Charles Shaar Murray that the band were considering recording the album on the TEAC in order to cut out expensive studio costs. In 1982, he told the same paper's Roz Reines that *London Calling* had been 'recorded . . . in a garage in Pimlico'. In the early Nineties, *Q* magazine briefly ran a feature called Sleevenotes, for which they asked music journalists to pen CD-sized booklets offering background information on selected classic albums. Robert Sandall's *London Calling* booklet took Joe's remark literally, but in fact, the album was only written, rehearsed and demoed at Vanilla. A few of these rough, basic versions might possibly have made it to the record had not, as he shamefacedly admits, Johnny Green lost the only copies of the tapes on the London Underground. The entire album had to be recorded from scratch at Wessex.

When it came time to go into the studio, the band were once again put under pressure by CBS and Epic to do so with a name producer. They chose Guy Stevens, whom Joe promptly tracked down in an Oxford Street pub. If anything, Guy's condition had deteriorated since the last time he had crossed paths with the band, and the decision to work with him was considered by some commentators to be an act of near-suicidal daring. In some ways it was: at least part of the motivation was a massive 'fuck you' to the record company, mavericks siding with maverick. But Guy also offered a direct connection to the musical roots the Clash wanted to investigate, being steeped in US blues, soul and rock'n'roll, and on first-name terms with many of those genres' greats. He believed in inspiration, and valued feel over painstaking multi-tracked perfectionism, a welcome prospect after the Sandy Pearlman experience. Also, although Guy was an aficionado of American music, he was quintessentially British, with roughly the same background and reference points as the band. 'We've done it the American way, and it don't work. It's a load of shit,' as Mick diplomatically informed *Creem* magazine's Dave DiMartino that autumn. Another not insignificant factor was that Bill Price had worked with Guy before, including on the Violent Luck material, and was therefore, in theory, more likely to humour him and less likely to depress or offend him.

The Wessex sessions took place over six weeks in August and early September 1979. On 4 August, recording was interrupted while the Clash flew to Finland to play the Rusrock Festival. They insisted on being paid their substantial fee in cash, part of which they put towards recording costs. The *NME*'s Roy Carr spoke to Guy while they were away and was informed that, after just three days in the studio, the band had already recorded 12 tracks. These included – at the producer's instigation – Bob Dylan's 'Billy The Kid' and 'Brand New Cadillac' by early British rocker Vince Taylor.

Guy's antics during the album sessions have gone down in rock'n'roll legend. In addition to the usual chair-throwing during recording takes, he swung a ladder at Mick Jones, fought over the faders with Bill Price, blew up the studio TV by pouring beer into it and – to prevent him from leaving one day – lay down in front of Maurice Oberstein's Rolls-Royce. He insisted on being taken to the studio via Arsenal's football ground so that he could pay homage to Liam Brady. He phoned up Ian Hunter in the States for interminable pep talks. On one occasion, he arrived with someone he introduced as his minder, who duly sat around the studio for 18 hours; it subsequently transpired that the man was a taxi driver, and his cab was outside with the meter running. The band had to foot all the bills.

But the mayhem appeared to pay dividends. Upon the album's release, reviewers singled out Guy's production for praise, and Charles Shaar Murray conducted a lengthy interview with him for an *NME* career retrospective. Drunk and raving for his first meeting with the journalist, Guy was nevertheless portrayed as an amusing raconteur; he turned up for the second meeting sober and buoyed by the critical reaction to the album. The Clash contributed kind words and recommendations to CSM's feature, and it seemed as though Guy's rehabilitation was well under way. Not long afterwards, he began taking a drug prescribed by his doctor to help him reduce his alcohol dependency. On 29 August 1981, he would overdose on it, and die.

Thus, *London Calling* has come to be seen as the final testimonial to Guy's talents, the last flourish of a career otherwise on the skids. It is a view the Clash have been happy to propagate. Less than three weeks after Guy's death, they recorded a tribute song, 'Midnight To Stevens', and Guy was also credited with 'inspiration' on *Combat Rock*. When it came time to compile the *Clash On Broadway* retrospective in 1991, the Guy Stevens association was highlighted by the inclusion of two of the original Polydor demos and the previously unreleased tribute song, as well as a number of Guy-related anecdotes in the accompanying booklet. Their motives were undoubtedly pure, but the result was that the Clash effectively annexed the Guy Stevens Myth to feed the Clash Myth. *Mojo* magazine took the cue in its 27-page August 1994 Clash retrospective, eight pages of which were devoted to Mark Hagen's version of the Guy Stevens story.

Their liking and respect for Guy has prompted most of the parties who have gone on record about the *London Calling* sessions to make light of his transgressions and play up the extent of his contribution to proceedings. Although they also take care to express their affection for Guy, between them Johnny Green and Jerry Green paint a somewhat different picture. In their versions, Guy appeared only for the first two weeks of recording. His attendance at the studio was irregular even during that time, and when there he invariably got so drunk that he had to be sent home or encouraged to sleep it off in the tape cupboard. His wild cavortings before passing out were not quite as amusing at the time as they would be made to sound later. Jerry remembers the Night of the Taxi Driver-Minder all too well: he was the last one in the studio when Guy demanded £55 to pay the bill. Jerry didn't have any money, but Guy refused to believe him and poured a two-litre bottle of red wine into the studio's newly acquired and extremely expensive grand piano. Jerry, responsible for the studio equipment, was furious. So were the Clash, and Guy was seldom encouraged to turn up thereafter.

'The band basically took over, and most of the stuff was produced by them and Bill Price,' says Jerry. 'As soon as Guy was out of the way, we got on with the serious work. Before that, it was pretty much playtime and trying it Guy's way.' Most of the dozen tracks Guy boasted about recording in the first three days were oldie cover versions, and of these only 'Brand New Cadillac' made it to the record. Otherwise, he was nominally in control for the recording of some of the backing tracks, and he gave Joe the inspiration for 'The Right Profile' by lending him a Montgomery Clift biography. His main contributions to the sessions were the creation of a charged atmosphere and what Mick described to CSM as his almost supernatural ability to act as a purgative: 'All the mess goes into him like Dorian Gray's portrait, or whatever. All the messy sound goes and it *becomes* him, and what's left on the tape is clarity.'

In early September, the Clash left Bill Price to mix the album and returned to America for a longer tour under the banner the Clash Take the Fifth (as in Amendment). On 26 July, Epic had finally bowed to the pressure of the US market and released a modified version of *The Clash*: minus 'Deny', 'Cheat', '48 Hours' and 'Protex Blue', plus all the single A-sides to date. To make the package even more desirable, 'Groovy Times' and 'Gates Of The West' were added on a free 7-inch disc. 'I Fought The Law' had been released simultaneously as the band's first US single. With no promotion from Epic, the single flopped, but, thanks partly to the original import's ground breaking efforts, the album fared considerably better.

'Like Francis Coppola's camera journeying upriver in *Apocalypse Now*, this LP roves over scenes of a struggle that seems as endless as it is brutal,' wrote *Rolling Stone*'s Tom Carson. (It was a review ahead of its time: 1982's *Combat Rock* would take his analogy a little more literally.) He went on to make the point that the chopping and changing of material had altered the original album's meaning, even destroyed its unified vision, but maintained that the result still made for compelling listening: 'Despite the trimming and the compromises, their music remains a crackling live wire that can't be silenced. What it has to say is part of our currency, too. And anyone in America who still cares about rock'n'roll must listen.' In the *Village Voice* Robert Christgau opined that it might just be the most important album ever released in America.

Belatedly aware that they could have a potential money-spinner on their hands, Epic began to come round to the idea of a tour, which would raise the profile of the band's début album and prepare the ground for the release of their third. Still, relations remained strained. The band insisted on bringing along an even larger entourage than previously. In addition to the usual suspects and technical crew, it included support band the Undertones and photographer Pennie Smith and cartoonist Ray Lowry (both of whom were there partly to document the tour for the *NME* and partly to come up with the cover illustrations and design for *London Calling*), as well as most of the band's girlfriends. Earlier in the year, Joe had begun a relationship with Gabrielle Salter, known as Gaby, who had only recently left school; Topper's marriage to Wendy had foundered, thanks largely to his ever more committed rock'n'roll lifestyle, and he was now seeing a girl called Dee; Paul's new girlfriend was a model called Debbie who, as he cheerfully admitted to Chris Salewicz later that year, was effectively keeping him; only Mick travelled alone.

The Vanilla rehearsal sessions had seen the Clash camp swollen by a slow influx of new personnel. Kosmo Vinyl had first encountered the Clash in the late spring of 1977, when Mick Jones had approached him at his Portobello Market record stall and somewhat peremptorily requested him not to sell the sole copy of the 'Remote Control' single he had in stock. Over the next two years, Kosmo had involved himself with Stiff records, becoming the independent label's PR agent and package tour MC. During this period, he had developed a special relationship with Stiff artists Ian Dury and the Blockheads, and through them had re-established contact with the Clash. Kosmo had taken to hanging around at Vanilla, gradually taking over the role of the Clash camp's court jester. This connection led to Mickey Gallagher, the Blockheads keyboard player, being invited to guest on the Wessex album sessions. It also led to an association with Blackhill, the management company run by Peter Jenner and Andrew King. Blackhill had promoted the very first concerts Mick Jones attended in Hyde Park and had managed the Syd Barrett era Pink Floyd. Since then, they had gone on to manage several other artists, and Peter Jenner had even branched out into production work, one of his credits being the 1973 Sharks album *Jab It In Yore Eye* so beloved of Mick when he was in the Delinquents. More recently, Blackhill had involved themselves with Stiff and the Blockheads. It seemed a natural progression for the Clash to invite them to fill their management vacancy, though Johnny Green for one has his suspicions that Kosmo's arrival at Vanilla was no accident, rather the first stage in an elaborate courtship ritual intended to convince the Clash of Blackhill's charms. Whatever, when the Clash departed for America, they did so with Mickey Gallagher augmenting the line-up on keyboards, Kosmo doing the band's PR and Peter Jenner and Andrew King fulfilling the role of management 'on a trial basis'.

Epic quibbled about the budget required to keep the seemingly ever-expanding Clash camp on the road, and the arguments went on for the tour's duration. Hotels could be booked only two days in advance, and on several occasions it looked as though the Clash would have to exchange taking the Fifth for taking the next plane home. On one night, *Sounds* journalist Pete Silverton had his credit card pressed into service to put up 30 people for three nights at the Chicago Holiday Inn. Taking advantage of the situation, CBS UK suggested they be allowed to release the US version of *The Clash* in Britain, in return for forwarding the band some of the money they could expect to realise from sales. 'Typical of them to try and trick us while we're away,' Mick muttered to the *NME*'s Paul Morley. 'They always do that.' 'We just said we'd come back home if they did,' added Joe.

Nothing to do with the tour ran smoothly. There were more squabbles with DJs and journalists. Joe in particular did little for the Clash cause when he directed a pre-show temper-tantrum at Dave DiMartino, there to interview him for *Creem* magazine. After the Boston show, the entire band plus Kosmo took part in an extraordinarily obnoxious and foul-mouthed phone-in interview on the local WBCN radio station. Nor were the Clash any more accommodating during the gigs themselves. Audiences were still sometimes slapped in the face with the opening 'I'm So Bored With The

USA', after which the set would be liberally sprinkled with new, unfamiliar and decidedly un-punky material, leaving many unsure how to react. Some were overly quiet, some clapped anything, good or bad, and some gobbed because . . . they'd read that was what punks were supposed to do.

Mick's mother, Renee – looking, according to Johnny Green, just like Elizabeth Taylor – came to the show in Minneapolis, which put the guitarist in something of a panic. Wayne Kramer and Rob Tyner of the MC5 came to the show in Detroit; Wayne was agreeable and enthusiastic, Rob was the exact opposite. The ups, downs and uncertainties seemed to get to Paul at the New York Palladium gig: he started to smash his bass against the stage, providing Pennie Smith with an irresistible photo-opportunity that produced the front cover picture for *London Calling*, one of the most recognisable and enduring of rock'n'roll icons.

The tour lasted for just over a month, coming to an end on 16 October 1979. Thereafter, the Clash returned to the UK and went straight back into Wessex to finish the mix of the album and record Willie Williams's contemporary reggae song 'Armagideon Time', which had started life as a soundcheck jam and progressed to an encore feature. Now it was to become a high-profile B-side for the similarly apocalyptic 'London Calling', the album's lead single. Even forgetting this new song and its dub versions, 'Justice Tonight / Kick It Over', planned as Jamaican-style extras for the 12-inch version of the single, the band still had 18 tracks in the can, too many to fit comfortably on to a single disc.

Annoyed with CBS for having charged £1.49 for *The Cost Of Living* when they had wanted to ask the standard single price of £1, something which had both gone against the band's VFM policy and given the EP title an unintentionally ironic note, the Clash floated the possibility of including a freebie single with the album, in the style of the US version of *The Clash*; but this one would be a 12-inch. CBS agreed, and only then did the Clash reveal that they intended the 12-inch to play at 33 r.p.m. and contain eight tracks, and the entire package to retail for the lowest possible single album price of £5. Kosmo had been having talks with the *NME* about releasing another freebie record in the style of the *Capital Radio* EP, this time a flexi-disc to be attached to the paper. He asked the band if they could come up with something appropriate. Mick wrote 'Train In Vain' that night, and it was recorded and mixed at Wessex the following day. Unfortunately, the *NME* arrangement fell through, so, although it was too late to list it on the sleeve or label, the track was tacked on to the end of *London Calling*. The total playing time for the resulting record comes to little over 60 minutes and the entire album today fits comfortably on to a single CD, but it has always been regarded as a conventional double. It was certainly a triumph for the Clash's VFM policy, and Joe believed it was more than that. 'I'd say it was our first real victory over CBS,' he gloated to *Sounds*' Chris Bohn that December. If so, it was a pyrrhic one: CBS felt justified in counting it as a single album, meaning that the Clash still owed them two more albums under the terms of the original contract.

In the UK, *London Calling* was released on 14 December 1979. On first hearing, the production and experimentation with different musical styles give the impression that the Clash have made a complete break with the past as represented by their previous two albums. Closer examination reveals this not to be entirely the case. It could be argued that the somewhat melodramatically apocalyptic four-square rockers 'London Calling', 'Clampdown', 'Death Or Glory' and 'Four Horsemen' signal another misguided scaling up of subject matter: from urban rucking on the first album to global terrorism on the second, to the end of the world on the third. Yet the recent threat of meltdown at the Three Mile Island nuclear plant near Harrisburg, Pennsylvania, lend Joe's musings some weight. Also, the production is far less bombastic than on *Give 'Em Enough Rope*, which removes part of the sting.

'Four Horsemen' exudes Mott the Hoople Syndrome to the extreme, but its braggadocio is so over the top that it qualifies as self-mockery. It is a celebration of the Clash, true, but at the same time an acknowledgement of earlier transgressions like 'Cheapskates'. 'Death Or Glory', on the other hand, is evidently serious and therefore a worse offender. It revisits a character from 'Last Gang In Town' in later life and observes him attempting to deal with the frustration of settling down and, to an extent, selling out. As with the older song, Mott the Hoople Syndrome may not be intended, but it is difficult not to infer it, especially from the infamous and apparently confessional line 'He who fucks nuns will later join the church' and the defiant rallying coda, in which Joe steels himself for the struggles ahead.

The theme of growing up, calming down and relaxing one's principles is picked up in 'Clampdown', which, like 'All The Young Punks' before it, urges 'the kids' not to waste their lives in factories propagating a system apparently hell-bent on self-destruction. It seems torn between a fatalistic belief that ageing automatically equates with becoming part of the machinery of repression and a determination to encourage organised resistance, insisting that 'anger can be power'. Against the same background of imminent global catastrophe, the album's title track and lead single restates punk's DIY ethic in not dissimilar terms, advising 'the kids' not to follow leaders, the Clash included: 'phoney Beatlemania has bitten the dust'.

'Spanish Bombs' continues Joe's interest in terrorism, having been inspired by Basque bombings of tourist hotels on the Costa Brava and making reference to the IRA. It contrasts the modern-day tourist experience with the noble cause of the Spanish Civil War, however, courtesy of George Orwell's *Homage To Catalonia* and the poems of Federico García Lorca. There is also an autobiographical element: Joe's ex-girlfriend, Palmolive, hailed from Andalucia. The historical perspective and acoustic pop context combine to make it a sort of latter-day folk song, and folk songs have always been heavy on romanticism; the overall effect is genuinely stirring, rather than misguided and offensive in the manner of a 'BRIGADE ROSSE' T-shirt.

As with *Give 'Em Enough Rope*, there are two out-and-out drug songs, but here there can be no charges of ambiguity. 'Hateful' deals with the vicious circle of addiction. 'Koka Kola' steals a march on Jay McInerney's *Bright Lights, Big City* by satirising American Yuppie cocaine culture. 'London Calling' itself also contains negative allusions to drug dependency with its talk of 'nodding out' and hepatitis-induced 'yellowy eyes'.

Direct links with the subject matter of the first album are rarer. Mick's 'I'm Not Down' restates the 'kick my way back in' theme of 'Hate And War', but is more vulnerable and less violent in its determination. The lyric of 'Lost In The Supermarket' touches on the sense of urban alienation expressed throughout *The Clash*, and again reveals a sensitivity one might not previously have expected from Joe, who wrote it (and then promptly hid behind Mick, whom he persuaded to sing it).

Although Joe had turned his back on the punk–reggae hybrids – or, in his words, 'trash reggae' – of the band's early career, reggae still had a strong hold on the Clash. Partly as a result of Paul's influence and partly because Don Letts had given him a Trojan compilation album, Joe's ska craze is evident in his musical compositions of the period, 'Rudie Can't Fail' and the yet to be recorded prototype of 'Bankrobber'. It also explains the presence on *London Calling* of the cover versions of the Edwards–Ray song 'Revolution Rock' and the Rulers' 'Wrong 'Em, Boyo'. In 1979, Paul had started to come up with his own basslines. The other group members helped him to work up one of these into his first song, 'Guns Of Brixton'. 'Trash reggae' might have been out of favour, but the band's ongoing interest in contemporary bona fide reggae is further evidenced by their 'Lovers Rock' spoof and the reworking of Willie Williams's 'Armagideon Time' they had set aside for the single.

When later criticised for soaking the album in Americana, the Clash responded by citing the Jamaican influence in the record's five reggae songs and the Englishness of the London-specific references, not least in the title track and Paul's 'Guns Of Brixton'. That spring, Joe and Gaby had started living together in her mother's high-rise flat on Chelsea's World's End estate, where the King's Road runs closest to the Thames. Hence 'London is drowning and I live by the river', 'On the route of the 19 bus' (from the World's End to Wessex studios) and the experience of high-rise life recounted in 'Lost In The Supermarket'. The supermarket in question is located beneath the flats, next to the car park.

'I never thought about beefburgers once, or Mickey Mouse, or the Statue of Liberty,' Joe declared to Roz Reines three years later, refuting *London Calling*'s supposedly strong American influence. He was being not a little disingenuous. Much of the album does indeed follow 'Brand New Cadillac' and the Clash's own wardrobe into a mythological American fantasy land, the details and parameters of which are informed by rock'n'roll and Hollywood myths. Even the ska song 'Wrong 'Em, Boyo' is based on the old R&B legend of Staggerlee, and the Clash do their best to create similar characters with the eponymous heroes of their own 'Jimmy Jazz' and 'The Card Cheat', while American method actor Montgomery Clift stars in 'The Right Profile'.

Admittedly, it could be argued that the AOR HM of Sandy Pearlman's *Give 'Em Enough Rope* was closer to the sound of then contemporary America than that of *London Calling*, and, as the band claim, there is a sizeable reggae quotient. But the other sounds and songs have their origins in vintage US musical genres: the rockabilly of 'Brand New Cadillac', the Bo Diddley beat of 'Hateful', the Phil Spector Wall of Sound of 'The Card Cheat', the Motown syncopation and corny C&W lyric of 'Train In Vain'. The overall impression is reinforced by Ray Lowry's cover graphics, inspired by an early Elvis Presley album, and Pennie Smith's photos, all of which are from the Take the Fifth Tour and feature the band in their American outlaw togs.

Having exhausted the possibilities of punk, the Clash were now collectively making music that accurately represented their individual interests and influences. Reviewing the album for the *NME*, Charles Shaar Murray was predisposed to be sympathetic, sharing much the same tastes in roots rock musics. 'The Clash have been criticised for becoming a "straight-ahead rock band", which is specious in the extreme,' he declared. 'The Clash love rock'n'roll, which is why they play it, but they want it to live up to its promises, which is why they play it the way they do. With groups like the Clash on the case, rock ain't in the cultural dumper: *London Calling* makes up for all the bad rock'n'roll played over the last decade.'

CSM had a couple of reservations, notably with the macho stance of 'Guns Of Brixton' and the hamfisted sexual politics of 'Lovers Rock'. (Joe was still finding it hard to win his PC certificate on this issue, even with his tongue in his cheek.) Those aside, his endorsement was wholehearted. For *Melody Maker*, James Truman expressed much the same feelings, albeit in a more understated sort of way: 'the Clash have discovered America and, by the same process, themselves'. Both believed the band had come back from the disaster that had been *Give 'Em Enough Rope* with their finest album to date.

Over at *Sounds*, Garry Bushell took the opposite view. Back on 6 July 1979, he and colleague Dave McCullough had attended a secret Clash show at Notre Dame Hall in Leicester Square, at which the band had previewed much of their new material. The duo had not been impressed, and an interview confrontation had done little to set their minds at rest. Having arrived eager but late for the punk scene, they were extremely unhappy to see indications of its demise. (Their questionable taste would be exposed by their role in their paper's championing of Oi! and the New Wave of British Heavy Metal, and Garry's subsequent decision to ply his trade as knee-jerk reactionary TV critic for a tabloid newspaper.) In his album review Garry gave the game away rather by looking back on the turgid *Give 'Em Enough Rope* as 'a magnificent fiery rock album, brimming with metal attack and renewed purpose'. Wrong!

Nevertheless, his sneering, condemnatory two-star review of *London Calling* expressed opinions that were shared by writers at other inkies who were less punk-obsessed than Garry or rock'n'roll-oriented than CSM. That November, John Lydon's post-punk outfit PiL (with former 101er Richard Dudanski briefly occupying the drum seat) had released *Metal Box*, a collection of avant-garde dub–disco anti-rock tracks spread over three 45 r.p.m. 12-inch discs packaged in a circular tin. As its playing length was much the same as that of *London Calling* – the PiL album's second pressing would be packaged as a standard double – comparisons were inevitable, and the Clash's more traditional work was found wanting in terms of artistic progression.

Garry Bushell's points were, firstly, that there was little genuinely new about the band's supposed new direction: 'Unable to go forward, they've clutched at straws, ending up retrogressing via Strummer's R&B past and Jones' Keith Richards fixation to the outlaw imagery of the Stones and tired old rock clichés.' Secondly, that there was something disquieting about their '"guns and gangs" outlaw vision-lumpen lyrical fantasy world populated by druggies, crooks, gambling dens, dingy basements and gun-toting niggers' (as, indeed, there was about some of the words Garry used to make his point). Thirdly, that the band had failed to live up to many of the promises they had made three years earlier: 'one of the Clash's biggest failings has been their inability to link their righteous sentiments with the power struggle in the real world. Like, shouting "Long live the revolution" don't make it come, y'know.'

Aside from a few, mostly low-key and semi-secret London gigs, including a couple of Christmas shows at the Acklam Hall under the Westway and their late addition to the bill of a benefit concert for Kampuchea headlined by the Blockheads, the Clash had not played in the UK for over a year. This seemed to be yet more proof that they had deserted their original following for the sake of breaking America, and was consequently cause for further rumbles of annoyance. Dissatisfaction also seemed to be reflected in the end-of-year music press readers' polls, votes for which had been cast before *London Calling* had a chance to make an impact; they showed the revitalised Jam taking over the Clash's crown as the erstwhile punk constituency's favourite band.

The truth is that the Clash's principles had created a catch-22. As long as they continued to insist on low record prices, they were going to remain in debt to CBS, who were therefore unlikely to come up with tour support. Without it, the penniless Clash could not tour the UK, unless they went against their VFM policy with ticket prices. Co-manager Peter Jenner explained the situation to *Q* magazine's Paul Du Noyer in 1989: 'The refusal to face dilemmas was the essence of the Clash. I'd cost out a tour for them, and say, "With the ticket price you want, and the scale of equipment you want, even if we sell out every show, you'll still lose money. It won't add up." But they'd go, "We can't rip off the kids!" "All right, keep the ticket price down, but scale down the stage show." "But we're a big rock'n'roll band, we've got to have all the stuff!" So they'd go to CBS for extra money, and end up further in hock. CBS always had them by the short'n'curlies.'

That was only half of it. With the positive influence of the music press having already peaked, the Clash's one remaining chance of extending their fan base in the UK was via hit singles, which would help to sell albums and subsidise tours. Unfortunately, to be successful, singles usually need airplay, and radio was still loath to broadcast records by bands which refused to play the game the way radio thought it should be played. The coda to 'Capital Radio Two' makes this point in no uncertain terms: Joe complains to the others that they will never get on the radio playing punk rock; whereupon the band adjust the rhythm and tempo until they are aping John Travolta and Olivia Newton John's execrable number one hit of 1978, 'You're The One That I Want'.

The only other way to force a record into the upper reaches of the charts and on to the nation's playlists was through TV exposure. In March 1978, the Clash had performed 'Tommy Gun' live on BBC2's *Something Else*. A programme which lived up to the DIY ethic, in that it was devised and presented by teenagers for teenagers, it featured a mixture of music and discussion about contemporary issues. More recently, in April 1979, the band had played 'English Civil War' and 'Hate And War' live on ITV's pop magazine programme *Alright Now*.

Neither show lasted long (though the Tyne-Tees team responsible for *Alright Now* would go on to make *The Tube*), and tired old *Top Of The Pops* maintained its position as the only mass-audience pop programme, boasting viewing figures of around eight million. All the other contemporary punk bands – the Jam, the Buzzcocks, the Stranglers, uncle Tom Robinson and all – had given in to commercial pressure to appear on the show. It had been the Sex Pistols rather than the Clash who had instigated the boycott in the first place (Johnny Rotten had first denigrated the programme in Jonh Ingham's April 1976 *Sounds* interview), and even they had allowed a film of themselves performing 'Pretty Vacant' to be broadcast on 14 July 1977. But the Clash had remained adamant they would neither appear in person nor permit their videos to be shown. Thus, their singles tended to stall somewhere between number 30 and number 20, and it seemed that things could only get worse.

To their credit, the Clash came up with an imaginative solution to their between-record slumps in visibility and popularity, something that would counter the impression that they were devoting too much time and attention to America. They decided to launch a non-stop UK singles campaign, releasing a new record each time the last one dropped out of the charts: 'A Clash Singles Bonanza', as Joe described it to the *NME*'s Paul Du Noyer at the end of 1980. 'Fire them off like rockets all through the year.' The novelty aspect, word of mouth and the cumulative impact of the songs themselves would surely overcome all obstacles. Over a decade later, a similar scam would get the decidedly less commercially-obvious Wedding Present into the *Guinness Book Of Records* with 12 hits in as many months.

But that was a medium- to long-term campaign, and the Clash believed they had a lot of ground to make up in the short term. Their only option was to take – or, rather, beg for – the CBS shilling, and tour after all. A lengthy schedule was arranged, occupying most of January and February 1980. The tour's title, 16 Tons, was a wry acknowledgement of the band's situation. In 1956, Tennessee Ernie Ford had enjoyed a UK number one single with a song whose chorus was based on a saying of writer Merle Travis's father, a Kentucky coal miner: '16 tons, and what do I get? / Another day older and deeper in debt.'

The tour began well. The first gig, on 5 January at Aylesbury Friars, not only sold out, but was the venue's fastest selling of all time. The Blockheads returned a favour from the Kampuchea benefit and provided one-off support. The Who's Pete Townshend turned up at the Brighton gig and joined the Clash on-stage for the encore. *Nationwide* considered the tour enough of an event to send a crew to the Dundee show to film the band and their fans. The tour and related exposure helped the 'London Calling' single climb as high as number 11, a good foundation for the Clash Singles Bonanza.

The support act was reggae toaster Mikey Dread, a DJ and producer whose real name was Michael Campbell. Back home in Jamaica, Mikey had hosted his own radio show on which, as well as playing other artists' discs, he had accompanied his own toasts with backing tracks comprising humming and rhythmic sound effects created by an oddball selection of found objects. He and the Clash got on so well together that on 1 February, they booked into Pluto studios, Granby Row, Manchester, for two days in order to record 'Bankrobber' as the first instalment of the Singles Bonanza. Mikey produced, and Bill Price and Jerry Green came up from London to assist. Although Joe had originally written the song in the ska style, Mikey was contemptuous of such retrogressive tendencies and persuaded the band to push the song in the direction of a slow, heavy dub reggae. The backing track for the A-side begat two potential B-side versions: one instrumental entitled 'Robber Dub' and one with Mikey toasting his impressions of the 16 Tons experience over the top known as 'Rockers Galore ... UK Tour'. The band also worked with him on a reggae 'instrumental' for squeaky toy and matchbox entitled 'Shepherds Delight'.

After the hiatus, the formerly positive vibe of the tour evaporated. Topper cracked his pelvis while messing around, which limited his mobility and affected his drumming. Joe was busted for possession of marijuana following Kosmo's birthday party at a hotel in Southsea. The *NME*'s Gavin Martin attended the 15 February gig at the ill-ventilated Electric Ballroom in

Camden and caught the Clash on a particularly bad night. According to his review, Joe was an over-emotional wreck and Mick was once again displaying 'the complacent detachment of a guitar hero'. 'They need a rest,' concluded Gavin. 'The tour has fatigued them and sapped them of willpower and cohesion.' A couple of days later, Topper tore a ligament in his hand, forcing the band to take a rest whether they wanted one or not: the last six dates of the tour were postponed until June.

Topper had not just suddenly become accident prone. Upon joining the band, he had not anticipated a lengthy tenure and so, unlike Rob Harper and Jon Moss, had not worried overmuch about the nature of his role. Having always been something of an extrovert, he had contented himself with fooling around and having a good time. Before long, however, his proclivity for self-destructive excess had transformed him into the classic Crazy Drummer stereotype: what he himself later described as a 'poor man's Keith Moon'. 'Joe was the Spokesman, Paul was the Good-Looking Moody One, and Mick was the Sensitive Songwriter,' he told *Record Mirror*'s Lesley O'Toole in 1985. 'The only role left over was the Wild One, and I found myself creating an image I had to live up to. I always had to be first at the party and last to leave.' And parties inevitably meant drugs. From marijuana, mandrax and speed he had quickly moved on to cocaine and, by mid-1979, speedballs (a cocktail of cocaine and heroin). By the time of the 16 Tons Tour, his behaviour had become decidedly erratic.

Topper recovered from his injuries in time to play a gig in Paris on 27 February and to fly out to the States for the band's third American tour. This visit, running from 2 to 10 March, was no longer than the band's first; it was so short that it was not deemed worthy of its own title, instead using the same one as the British dates. Nevertheless, it saw a new addition to the Clash camp: Ray Jordan was hired to take charge of security, and thereafter stayed on to become part of the permanent team.

In the US, *London Calling* had been released in early January 1980. *Creem* had been lukewarm in its review: Billy Altman found the apocalyptic language of the title track so explosive and challenging 'that the rest of the album's lyrics just seem to be a weak addendum to a case already stated as well as it can be ... the absence of relief is wearisome'. But when Susan Whitall filed her interview with the band for the magazine, she more than compensated: 'What other band has so successfully absorbed the music of so many cultures, digested it, and emerged with a startling, evocative language of their own?' *Rolling Stone*'s Tom Carson had been far more enthusiastic in his appraisal of the album, apparently able to recognise both the sense of light and shade and the humour that passed Billy Altman by. He had positively revelled in the album's variety and romanticism, his review straying into the realms of hyperbole in the first two sentences: 'By now, our expectations of the Clash might seem to have become inflated beyond any possibility of fulfilment. It's not simply that they're the greatest rock & roll band in the world ...' The band's return to the US was greeted with the accolade of a front cover feature entitled 'Rebels With A Cause And A Hit Album'.

London Calling made only number 27 in the US chart, but went on to sell 625,000 copies there; in the smaller UK market the album reached number nine, stayed in the charts for 20 weeks, the band's best stretch to date (beating the début's 16 and the follow-up's 14) and sold just 180,000. On 12 February 1980, Epic had released 'Train In Vain' as a single in the US, without significant objection from the Clash, and, somewhat ironically for such an atypical, throwaway song, it became the band's first American hit, making number 23 in late April.

The Clash were now considered popular enough on that side of the Atlantic to be asked to do a commercial for the soft drink Dr Pepper, a request they turned down. Of more appeal to them was an approach that followed on from director Martin Scorsese's attendance at their New York Palladium gig. One of Martin's pet projects was a film about 1850's New York gangland with the appropriate, if unimaginative, title *The Gangs Of New York*. He asked the band if they would like to contribute to the soundtrack and, possibly, as actors. Given their shared interest in cinema, they were predictably enthusiastic, but the project was still at an early stage of development and everything was left hanging for the time being. Part of the reason the American tour had been so short and the postponed UK dates put back so far was that Paul had already been offered a role in a film. *Ladies and Gentlemen, The Fabulous Stains* was to be the story of an all-female American Slits-type band of that name. Paul's part was none too demanding – he was to play a member of a male English rock'n'roll band, alongside ex-Pistols Steve Jones and Paul Cook – but his presence was required on set in Vancouver for six weeks from 11 March.

Johnny Green also departed at this time to work with Joe Ely, occasional Clash support act and friend; he never came back to the fold. He went on to work with Wreckless Eric and Mick's former bandmate John Brown, among others, but eventually retired from the music business and settled down in Kent.

At a loose end, the rest of the Clash established themselves in New York's Iroquois Hotel, having heard that James Dean used to stay there, and took advantage of their recent rise in status to prise some money out of their record company in order to book into the Power Station studio for a couple of days. The idea was to record some cover versions for fun, and maybe sketch out a couple of songs from scratch with Bill Price and Mikey Dread for possible release as future instalments in the Singles Bonanza. After recording a version of the Equals' 'Police On My Back', though, they began to get into the swing. The Power Station was fully booked for the next few days, but they phoned around and were offered a three-week block of sessions at Jimi Hendrix's old studio, Electric Lady. Mickey Gallagher was asked to fly over from the UK and bring Blockheads bassist Norman Watt-Roy with him. Norman stayed for five days, after which the three remaining Clash members took it in turns to play bass on new material. 'We'd always make up lines in Paul's style,' Joe told the *New York Rocker*'s Richard Grabel at the end of recording.

Mick bumped into Joe's old busking partner Tymon Dogg on a Manhattan street corner, and invited him along to the first session, where the Clash–Blockheads aggregate backed him on his eccentric composition 'Lose This Skin'. Tymon released it as a single that June on the Ghost Dance label. Following his departure, the others warmed up on the Spencer Davis Group's 'Every Little Bit Hurts', as played by Mick and Chrissie Hynde at Wilmcote House four years previously, before settling into the more experimental part of the sessions. Almost certainly as a direct response to criticisms of the retrogressive tendencies of their recent recordings, they now started to go in every direction imaginable.

Much of the material recorded over the next few weeks derived from studio jams, something which is perhaps most evident in the loose skiffle sound of 'Junkie Slip' and the mellow jazzy reggae of 'Broadway'. In keeping with the spirit of the proceedings, Joe improvised lyrics for both tunes on the spot. The former perhaps indicates how much Topper's drug problem was playing on his mind while the latter free-associates about the past life of a Manhattan down-and-out. Enthused by this spontaneous approach, Joe had the engineers wipe the squeaky toy background to Mikey's Pluto-recorded 'Shepherds Delight' and replaced it with a double-tracked rambling stream-of-consciousness about New York and Electric Lady which he gave the new title 'If Music Could Talk'. The song also alludes to a 'bunker'. Rather than sit with the others in the sometimes overcrowded control room between takes, Joe built his own private room in the main studio out of flight cases. He would retire there to work on lyrical ideas and, as he freely admits in 'If Music Could Talk', smoke spliffs. The Clash's in-studio intake of marijuana had always been considerable, but since Mikey's arrival on the scene it had reached a level that could only be described as prodigious.

While in New York, Mick started picking up on the relatively new hip hop scene. Joe was equally enthused by its music. It was then still at the fairly basic funk with rap stage, which, he recognised, owed an obvious debt to dub reggae with toast. Also, rap was not a million miles away from the extemporised vocals with which he was already experimenting. Built on a tape loop of a funky riff that takes full advantage of Norman Watt-Roy's fluid style, 'The Magnificent Seven' (originally entitled 'Magnificent Seven Rappo-Clappers') is the band's tribute to the Sugarhill Gang. Joe improvises a humorous rap juxtaposing the fates of the world's great free thinkers with his own experiences of the capitalist system's daily grind. Everyone enjoyed it so much that they did more or less the same again with 'Lightning Strikes (Not Once But Twice)'. Only this time the music is a kind of dub–funk hybrid, and Joe's rap is another self-indulgent ad lib romanticising multicultural New York at length before guiltily squeezing in a mention of the Westway at the end. Joe would later claim that the New York influence was inevitable: there was a transit strike while the band were in the city, which meant they had to walk many blocks to and from the studio each day, forcing them to soak up the atmosphere whether they liked it or not.

Mikey Dread was not as impressed with the Sugarhill Gang as Mick or Joe. As a response to the group's 'Rapper's Delight', he wrote 'Rockers Delight', which puts them down in no uncertain terms – 'strictly chatting and tripe' – and extols the primacy of reggae. Mikey was not particularly impressed with the UK Ska Revival either. As well as affecting Joe's own attitude, this prompted another Clash–Dread collaboration, 'Living In Fame', the general gist of which is that bands should make more of an effort to live up to their names. According to the lyric, the Specials are not that special, the Selecter do not put enough thought into selecting their material and Madness are not wild enough. Running out of ska groups, Mikey goes on to remark that Shane MacGowan's Nipple Erectors also fail to do much for him, before (diplomatically) proclaiming that at least the Clash get it right.

Mikey's influence is also evident on the Clash's own reggae track 'One More Time', whose lyric depicts the cycle of poverty and violence to which the mostly black inhabitants of America's inner city ghettos are condemned. Relatively Mikey-free, 'The Call Up' bookends a reggae tune with the Marines' marching song, while the lyric finds Joe in 'Spanish Bombs' mode, using the slightly archaic, romantic imagery of period folk songs to address contemporary issues; in this case the senselessness of young people wasting their lives at war (and, indeed, work) at the behest of uncaring and manipulative political leaders. Romantic it may be, but it is not without a grounding in reality: after the March tour's San Francisco gig the Clash had talked a fan named Freddie out of joining the Marines, and taken him on as a roadie instead; as Mick recalled in the *Clash On Broadway* booklet, registration for the draft was still 'a big deal' in the States, where it had become an issue in that year's presidential campaign.

Some of the material recorded conforms to more recognisable song structures, even if it is by no means four-square rock'n'roll. Joe's love affair with American folk culture finds perhaps its ultimate voice in 'Version City', a funky R&B paean to US roots music and the mythical train that features in so many of its lyrics and rhythms. The subjects of sin and temptation drive the gospel number 'The Sounds Of The Sinners', which affectionately lampoons its religious subject matter and yet puts some real conviction into its evocation of forthcoming Armageddon. Some reviewers and interviewers were prompted to wonder whether Joe had got religion. 'I was just thinking that a spiritual solution is just as important as a social solution,' Joe told Paolo Hewitt. 'Just solely talking about economics like, say, Marx did, I don't think it's enough.'

Whether or not he took his cue from *Rolling Stone* writer Tom Carson's review of the American version of *The Clash*, Joe had become a fan of Francis Ford Coppola's 1979 film *Apocalypse Now*. In February 1980, he told *Sounds*' Robbi Millar, 'You know, it doesn't leave you, it's like a dream.' It is also the inspiration for the song 'Charlie Don't Surf': the synthesizer drone re-creates the sound of whirring chopper blades, and the title, chorus and tone of the lyric are drawn from a remark made by Robert Duvall's battle-crazed officer. (Charlie is, of course, US military slang for Viet Cong.) Like 'The Call Up', the song is anti-war and takes a global perspective; but the ironic approach gives more punch to its attack on those who impose their religious and political beliefs on other people, especially superpowers whose machinations run the risk of bringing about apocalypse very soon.

Following Paul's return, the Clash made their first US television appearance on the ABC show *Fridays*, performing 'Train In Vain', 'London Calling', 'Guns Of Brixton' and 'Clampdown'. Things looked less positive on the home front. The intention had been to get the Clash Singles Bonanza under way in late February or early March, but it had hit an instant snag: CBS head Maurice Oberstein didn't like 'Bankrobber' – either the song or the production – and refused to put it out. Arguments had been going on all through March and April, and the Clash were fuming at this latest show of contempt for their artistic freedom clause. Partly as a way of hitting back at the record company, they started talking about using the Electric Lady material to form the basis of another cut-price double album.

Resolved to record even more songs and determined to stick by their choice of producer, the Clash flew with Mikey Dread to Kingston, Jamaica, for further sessions at Channel One studios. These were quickly and forcibly abandoned following demands for money, with menaces, from representatives of the local music business scene who believed a big name rock'n'roll band should be able to afford a little baksheesh. This was particularly ironic as by this time the band were penniless and living on the credit card of Paul's girlfriend, Debbie. Much to their annoyance, CBS had to wire them enough money to make good their escape.

All the Clash had to show for the visit were two incomplete tracks. The first was a reggae-style version of the old 101ers R&B standard 'Junco Partner', in which Joe namechecks his 'sweet Gabriella', yet another hint that the former confirmed loner was getting soft in his late twenties. The other was a backing track for 'Kingston Advice', a heavy rock–funk–dub crossover documenting the further escalation of poverty and violence in the city since the visit that had inspired 'Safe European Home'.

That European home proved to be no longer quite as safe when the band visited the Continent in mid-May 1980 for more live dates. Punk had finally caught on in a big way, as Joe told the *NME*'s Roy Carr later that year. 'It's nothing but a complete 1976 Revival . . . just another fashion. It's become everything it wasn't supposed to be. And what we were confronted with was junior punks in their expensive designer uniforms with concrete heads and no ears.' Tensions in the Clash camp were, understandably, running high over the 'Bankrobber' issue, and having to deal with yet another flood of criticism for betraying their original punk style proved too much for Joe. At the Hamburg gig, on 20 May, he became so incensed by the antics of one particularly aggressive audience member, who was 'using the guy in front of him as a punch bag', that he leaned out and swiped him across the head with his Telecaster. After the gig Joe was arrested, and only freed when a Breathalyser test proved negative. He was stricken with remorse. 'I nearly murdered somebody, and it made me realise that you can't face violence with violence. It doesn't work.' It seems somehow fitting that it should take a tussle with an over-excited punk rocker to teach him that.

The European tour finished early in June 1980, and was immediately followed by the UK dates that had been postponed when Topper damaged his hand. Mikey Dread had been pencilled in as a support act, but now he wanted more money; or, to be precise, for the Clash to pay for him to bring a backing band over from Jamaica, something they simply could not afford to do. A falling out ensued, and Mikey was replaced by rockabilly band Whirlwind. The situation was a sticky one, and not only because Mikey had played a part in the production of so much of the Clash's recent work. Ebullient self-starter Kosmo Vinyl had just set up his own independent label, Dread at the Controls. Although he had scored a personal coup by securing the UK rights to release the soundtrack to Martin Scorsese's *Mean Streets*, the label's main function, as its name suggests, was to release material either recorded by Mikey (like that month's single release of 'Rappers Delight') or leased with his aid from Jamaican labels.

The UK dates took the band up to the end of June. By then, 'Bankrobber' still had not been released in the UK. The Clash had managed to sneak it out earlier that month as the B-side of the Dutch release of 'Train In Vain', and import copies were making their way into the country. The band derived a certain amount of pleasure from this scam, but it was to be short-lived. For at least the past year, they had kept their spirits up by telling themselves they had only two more albums to deliver before they were rid of CBS for good – a tally mark taunt to this effect had been included in the liner notes for *London Calling* – but now CBS dropped another bombshell. Lurking previously undetected in the Clash's contract as approved by Bernie Rhodes was an obscure sub-clause allowing the record company an option on a further five albums, which option they now elected to take up.

Exhausted after months of non-stop touring and studio work, the band had intended to take July off anyway, but they gave the impression they were downing tools as a protest about the 'Bankrobber' situation, that is, effectively offering CBS an ultimatum. Within a few weeks, Joe was brushing off music press rumours that the band had considered splitting, but it was certainly a particularly low point in what had always been a fraught career. To cheer himself up, Joe produced an album for London R&B band the Little Roosters. Mick went to New York to be with his girlfriend, Ellen Foley, formerly Meatloaf's backing singer. She was also signed to CBS–Epic, and had recorded a solo album produced by Ian Hunter and Mick Ronson. It was decided that her new boyfriend should perform that function on the follow-up, and Ellen returned to London with him at the end of the month.

CBS finally agreed to an official UK release for 'Bankrobber', backed with 'Rockers Galore . . . UK Tour', on 8 August 1980. The single was given no promotion, and yet made it to number 12 on notoriety alone. The Clash chose to see it as a victory, but the reason for CBS's capitulation soon became evident. Following the success of the band's albums in the US, Epic had taken note of the demand for Clash import material and were keen to exploit it. The project they mooted was a 10-inch compilation album of odds and sods previously unavailable on that side of the Atlantic, to go by the apposite title *Black Market Clash*. On this the UK album version of 'Cheat' was to be joined by the original 'Capital Radio' from the *NME* EP and early single B-sides 'City Of The Dead', 'The Prisoner' and 'Pressure Drop'. 'Armagideon Time' and its twin dubs, 'Justice Tonight / Kick It Over', were also to be included, along with 'Bankrobber', unreleased in the US, and 'Robber Dub', unreleased in the UK. 'Rockers Galore . . . UK Tour' was left off, probably because it was by now out of date. To add extra spice and make up the numbers, that August found Bill Price remixing the band's previously unreleased March 1978 version of Booker T. and the MGs' 'Time Is Tight'.

That project sorted out, the band recommenced work at Wessex on material for their fourth album proper. Establishing exactly what was recorded during these sessions and when is close to impossible. Recording segued straight in from work on the compilation and straight out into work on Ellen Foley's album, which used much the same personnel. Mikey Dread was present in the studio at this time, but engineer Jerry Green recalls working with him only on material for Dread at the Controls. He believes that, although given a 'version mix' credit on the Clash album, Mikey performed this function on just the tracks recorded *before* the band moved to Wessex, and did not contribute any further following the row about the postponed UK tour dates.

The evidence offered by the finished album suggests Jerry is mistaken. Mikey may be conspicuous by his absence on several of the album's reggae and dub tracks, but he is equally conspicuous by his presence on others, including one or two that were unquestionably recorded at Wessex. He had definitely made up with the band by then, having joined them on-stage for the encore at the 17 June Hammersmith Palais gig; he and Paul went on to work together on a Dread single, and Stiff records subsequently offered to pay for them to depart to Jamaica that winter for more recording. To confuse matters further, during the album sessions at Wessex the Clash continued to work on the 30 or so tracks – some nearly complete, some the most basic of backing track sketches – recorded at Pluto, the Record Plant, Channel One and especially Electric Lady, several of which had involved Mikey's participation.

Even the wholly new songs were not recorded systematically. The Clash were still experimenting, recording as they wrote. Jerry remembers that a fresh batch of backing tracks would be taped, then the band's attention would turn to older material, before returning to the overdubbing of the recent backing tracks, or even moving on again to the recording of yet another fresh batch. Bill Price tended to take charge of the backing tracks and Jerry of overdubs. Blurring the picture still further was the non-stop intensity Mick and Joe in particular brought to the sessions. Initially, these began at 2 p.m. and ended around 4 or 5 a.m., but they soon began to lose shape, and Jerry estimates he and the others went round the clock several times during August and September.

Nor, it must be said, did the band members' substantial drug intake encourage a more regular working pattern. Whereas the others were content to escalate their marijuana consumption to the point of stupefaction, Topper's heroin problem was starting to spiral out of control. Off the road, and bored, he had fallen in with some dealers who lived in the vicinity of the flat he rented at the bottom end of Fulham Road.

The recording process involved Mick at every stage: he co-wrote the songs, arranged them, played on the backing tracks, taped numerous guitar and piano overdubs, sang vocals and backing vocals and worked with Bill and Jerry on the production. Joe was involved at slightly fewer stages, but could always occupy himself writing lyrics for the growing backlog of new material. Paul and Topper, though, found their services were mostly required only at a relatively early point in the development of each song, and the lack of a coherent overall work plan made for lengthy periods spent just hanging around. For Paul, it was always easy to relax – in fact, his ability to sleep anywhere at any time was a visual joke running through Pennie Smith's photo-book *Before And After*, published later that year – but for the hyperactive Topper it was torture. At Wessex, he too built himself a bunker out of flight cases, but while Joe spent most of his time in his with pen and paper, Topper, according to Jerry, 'would be out the back with tubes and pipes and goodness knows what, doing what he was doing'.

What he was doing was getting himself in such a state that he could barely sit upright behind his drums. 'Before, he'd had that natural ability to make his drums talk, almost,' says Jerry. 'Come certain things during those sessions, it was down to the bass drum, snare and hi-hat; y'know, nice and safe. He could keep time in that, didn't have to get out of pattern, get out of tempo, wouldn't have to think.' Inevitably, this caused some recording setbacks and raised concern. 'I tried to get the band to do something about Topper,' Peter Jenner revealed to the *NME*'s Len Brown in 1989, 'and I was told to fuck off and mind my own business.' Despite this response to what they perceived to be managerial interference, the other members of the Clash were just as worried, but they also recognised that it would be hypocritical to deliver ultimatums: it was not as though they themselves were practising abstinence. Towards the end of September, Joe was busted near King's Cross station by the Special Patrol Group. They made him take them back to his flat, where they discovered three ounces of home-grown marijuana. He was duly fined £100.

The messiness of the album's making is masked to some extent by the abandonment of the traditional Strummer–Jones composer credit in favour of attributing all original material to the entire band. 'They said, "What we'll do is make the credit the Clash, and we'll split all the money four ways", so I thought, "OK, fair enough,"' Topper told *Melody Maker*'s Mick Mercer in 1985. But the democratic gesture extended only as far as the album's liner notes and label. 'When it came to the next business meeting, it was decided the money should be shared out among the people who wrote the songs, so it meant people never realised that I wrote songs for the Clash.' What the credit also obscured was that, although Topper had been heavily involved with Mick in working out most of the music for the Electric Lady sessions – playing piano, guitar and bass, as well as drums – his input tailed off at Wessex. That said, he is the sole musical composer of the disco-funk 'Ivan Meets GI Joe', which he also sings. Joe's lyric works off both the musical genre and the electronic Space Invader bleeps that power the song, casting the personified superpowers as contestants in a dance competition and complementing 'Charlie Don't Surf' with another droll metaphorical exploration of mutually assured destruction.

Several interviewees for this book have alleged – either claiming direct knowledge or quoting supposedly impeccable sources – that Paul's bass technique was so poor that he played on very few of the Clash's records. This is denied by both Simon Humphrey, who engineered *The Clash* and various singles sessions throughout 1978, and Jerry Green, who worked as a tape operator or engineer on nearly all the band's sessions for the next three years. True, prior to 1979, most of Paul's basslines were devised by Mick, and Jerry concedes there may have been a few occasions when Mick even recorded a guide bassline for Paul to play along with, but that was as far as it went.

The 1980 sessions found the extent of Paul's contribution going to opposite extremes. Not having been present at the time, he had not assisted with the composition of any of the Electric Lady tracks. Although Norman Watt-Roy's bass was for the most part retained, Paul subsequently overdubbed some – but by no means all – of the other basslines laid down in his absence by Topper, Mick and Joe. When it came to the new material, however, he was actively involved in much of the writing, and the bias of the unseen composer credits shifted from Strummer–Jones–Headon to Strummer–Jones–Simonon. The song he both originated and sings, 'The Crooked Beat', is his follow-up to 'Guns Of Brixton' in more ways than one, revisiting its location, macho stance and musical genre. The last of these was not his fault, or so he claimed to *Melody Maker* in 1988: 'I was heavily into reggae, and whenever I had an idea for a song and played it to the others, they'd immediately start playing it reggae, which wasn't always what I intended.'

Paul was not the only reggae enthusiast in the band at this time. Contact with Mikey Dread had set Joe off on another of his periodical musical crazes, this time for dub, and his brief exposure to Jamaican radio earlier in the year had done nothing to dampen his enthusiasm. 'I heard some incredible rhythms,' he enthused to *Trouser Press* in 1981. 'Stunningly inventive. A couple of years ago, I started to think that reggae had had it, but I've since found I was a bit hasty: that music is growing all the time. I like listening to dub a lot; not a lot of people do. I'd like to hear it on the radio all night long, instead of the soothing dribble of the big band sounds.' As 'The Magnificent Seven' indicates, he had also had his enthusiasm for the writings of Karl Marx rekindled, and both interests find expression on the heavy dub reggae-stylings of 'The Equaliser'.

Upon hearing some rough mixes of the Electric Lady sessions, the *New York Rocker*'s Richard Grabel had asked what had already been the band's least favourite question for the best part of a year: did the American influence evident in their new material represent a betrayal of their original vision? To which Joe replied, 'Who gives a shit whether a donkey fucked a rabbit and produced a kangaroo? At least it hops and you can dance to it.' Which might not have made much sense in itself, but certainly sets the scene for 'Rebel Waltz', possibly the strangest of the band's attempts at reggae fusion. Joe had a dream one night which inspired another of his romantic folk lyrics about battles of long ago. His idea for a musical setting for it was to marry the whitest musical form he could think of, the waltz, to the blackest, reggae.

Whether or not Joe was in any way influenced by Richard Grabel's question, some of his Wessex lyrics turn their attention to subjects closer to home. Another folk ballad, 'Something About England', allows an English counterpart of the tramp in 'Broadway' to testify, and throws in a few First World War singalongs and a 'brass band' for good measure. Gary Barnacle, Topper's schoolfriend, had been invited along to play saxophone on a few tracks. Asked to recommend an appropriate brass section, he contacted his father, Bill, who played jazz trumpet and taught at a military college in Dover. Bill duly turned up with military bandsman David Yates to record the track. Mick's vocal leads off the song, and everything about it suggests it will be one of the band's more sentimental indulgences until Joe, in the role of the tramp, kicks in with a venomous, heartfelt (and historically accurate) diatribe about the failure of two world wars and the technological revolution to break down the British class system.

While on home turf, the Clash also addressed some familiar topics. Following a burglary at his Pembridge Villas pad while he was in America, Mick had returned briefly to stay with Stella in Wilmcote House. Taking up the baton from the previous album's Strummer composition 'Lost In The Supermarket', he launched his own attack on 'the towers of London, these crumbling blocks' with 'Up In Heaven (Not Only Here)'. Joe, meanwhile, was not finding Chelsea any more salubrious. 'Somebody Got Murdered' was commissioned as 'a heavy rock number' by Jack Nitzsche for the Al Pacino movie *Cruising* (1980). 'We wrote the song, but we never heard from Jack again,' Joe told *Melody Maker* in 1988. The film is set in New York's gay S&M scene, but Joe drew direct inspiration from an incident that occurred in an another underworld entirely: 'It's about the car park attendant in the

World's End Flats that was stabbed to death for £5 while I was living there.'

That August Bank Holiday saw the Clash returning, both literally and inspirationally, to the Notting Hill Carnival. The 1976-vintage Rocco Macauley photo depicting a lone Rasta walking towards a line of policemen that had been chosen to adorn the front sleeve of the *Black Market Clash* compilation had been intended partly to identify it as a companion volume to the US version of *The Clash* and partly to invite comparisons and suggest connections between the Clash music of 1976–7 and now. Although there was no riot in 1980, there were tensions, not least for the band members, who found it difficult to forget former associations when listening to some of the more militant sounds. Drawn there principally by the reggae sound systems, the band responded strongly to the other strains of Caribbean music on offer: calypso and its soul-crossover offshoot, soca, as performed by the Trinidadian steel bands.

Steel drum players became the latest in a long line of guest artists to grace the Wessex sessions. Three of the tracks to which they contribute find Joe turning his lyrical focus to the carnival. On both 'Corner Soul' and 'Let's Go Crazy' he adopts the perspective of the local black community coming to the carnival carrying the baggage of a year of oppression and the folk memory of 400 more. The brooding reggae of the former track asks, 'Is the music calling for a river of blood?'; the boisterous calypso of the latter seems to be losing itself in celebration, but is in fact answering in the affirmative. The haunting and less genre-specific 'Street Parade' has touches of steel drum and dub-effect guitar, and a more personal lyric which contemplates disappearing into the crowd.

Thoughts of oppression and the Caribbean also encouraged the making of other connections. The Trinidadian steel drums become similar-sounding Central American marimbas for 'Washington Bullets', a folk-style lament about US attempts to undermine leftist governments in the lands south of its borders. As with 'Somebody Got Murdered', the lyric takes its cue from a real-life experience, so Joe informed *Trouser Press* the following year, this time in the run-up to the 1980 elections in Kingston, Jamaica (Jamdown town): 'A youth of 14 was shot dead on Hope Road just ten minutes after we'd gone past.' On the American leg of the 16 Tons Tour a San Franciscan radical named Armstrong had made contact with the band, and helped furnish them with information about the victory in Nicaragua of the left-wing Sandinista rebels over military dictator General Somoza in 1979.

In the lyric for 'Washington Bullets' Joe considers some local background – 1973's US-backed overthrow of democratically elected Marxist president Salvador Allende in Chile and 1961's US-backed attempted invasion of communist Cuba – before celebrating the Sandinistas' victory as a triumph over US imperialism. In the interests of balance, he also points the finger at the USSR's invasion of Afghanistan, China's of Tibet and the activities of British mercenaries and arms dealers the world over. His spontaneous closing shout of 'Sandinista!' was to give the album both its title and catalogue number (FSLN stands for Fronte Sandinista Liberación Nacional).

Disarmament on a larger scale is the subject of 'Stop The World'. At Wessex a lyric on the post-nuclear holocaust nightmare was added to a Strummer–Headon jam held over from the Electric Lady sessions: Joe had tried to play Booker T. and the MGs' 'Green Onions' on the organ and, although he kept getting it wrong, had asked Topper to play along anyway. A more successful attempt at creating a Sixties soul groove is Mick and Ellen's duet 'Hitsville UK', whose backing track is strongly reminiscent of the Supremes' 'You Can't Hurry Love'. The band had visited the original Motown studios while in Detroit, and been amazed by the primitive facilities with which Berry Gordy's independent label had made all those classic singles. The Clash had already adapted one of the label's slogans – 'The Sound Of The Westway' derives from 'The Sound Of Young America' – and the title and chorus of Joe's lyric to this song borrow another, 'Hitsville USA'. Partly a celebration of the British independent label scene for picking up the Motown torch, it is also intended as a slightly less direct attack on CBS than 'Complete Control', a belated acknowledgement that taking the big advance from a major record company had been a bad idea after all.

Joe provided another break from the dominant reggae focus of the album when he brought in a cassette of Mose Allison's 'Look Here' and the band tried to capture its jazzy R&B feel. His long-time interest in rockabilly – now also shared by Paul – led to the group compositions 'Midnight Log' and 'The Leader'. The former is a wry, yet spooky, meditation on the spiritual cost of crime and corruption, and the latter an exposé of government vice, as inspired by the Sunday papers and *The Denning Report* on the Profumo scandal. 'The hypocrisy of it all is what I'm trying to get at,' Joe told *Melody Maker*'s Paolo Hewitt that December. 'The way that people are jailed for this and that, and yet up on the Top Floor they're setting no example at all. So how can they dish it out to us?'

By the end of September, the Clash already had too many tracks for a double album. Rather than hold any over, Mick suggested releasing a triple set. Such epics had previously been the preserve of self-indulgent pseudo-classical progressive rock bands and represented the direct antithesis of everything the Clash and punk had supposedly stood for, so Joe was understandably taken aback. But he responded to both the challenge and the perversity of the gesture, and the others agreed to go along. There was also, of course, the joy of presenting CBS with an unwieldy triple after they had expressed so much unhappiness at being given a double last time.

Back in July 1979, while being accused of being a punk traitor by Garry Bushell, Joe had informed him, 'Don't misinterpret what I'm saying; I'm saying that THERE WILL BE NO SIX QUID CLASH LP EVER. It's a fact. Why don't ya ring up the other bands and get them to say that?' Determined to maintain their VFM policy, the band insisted that CBS put out *Sandinista!* in the UK for the price of a single album, £5. The record company refused, but, after negotiation, agreed to a cover price of £5.99 . . . providing that it again only counted as one album as far as the Clash's obligation to CBS was concerned and the band renounced all claim to royalties on the first 200,000 copies. To put this in perspective: *London Calling* had so far sold 20,000 less than that total in the UK. It was amazing – not least to CBS – that the Clash accepted these terms. 'The thing I like about making a stand on prices is that it's *here and now*, and not just a promise,' Joe told *Musician*'s Vic Garbarini the following year. 'It's dealing with reality: how many bucks you're going to have to part with at the counter to get it. It's one of the few opportunities we have to manifest our ideals, to make them exist in a real plane. To do it in Thatcher's Britain during a recession was kind of a flamboyant gesture.' Asked how CBS had responded by Duncan Campbell of *Rip It Up*, Mick replied, 'Let's put it this way: if it had happened in Japan, all the record company executives would have killed themselves.'

The problem now was that the Clash didn't have quite enough for a triple album. Jerry Green recalls them scrabbling around for material. 'Stop The World' was earmarked for the non-album B-side of the first single, 'The Call Up', and 'Every Little Bit Hurts' was dropped as one oldie cover version too many. (It would eventually be included on *Clash On Broadway*.) Even though it had already been released as a single under his own name, it was decided to include Tymon Dogg's 'Lose This Skin' to give him some exposure. Recordings of Mickey Gallagher's young children singing karaoke versions of 'Career Opportunities' and 'Guns Of Brixton' made the cut. So did Mikey Dread's 'Living In Fame'. 'If Music Could Talk' was included, despite having exactly the same backing track as 'Shepherds Delight', the Mikey-dominated instrumental from the Pluto sessions chosen to end the album because of its suitably apocalyptic closing explosion (hence its title, from 'red sky at night').

The band had already worked with Mikey on dub versions of 'Out Of Time' and 'The Crooked Beat', both of which were sequenced on the album to run straight on from their parent songs. They now began mixing versions of other tracks: 'Version Partner' was spawned by 'Junco Partner', and Joe's talkover track 'Sapphire and Steel' comes directly from 'Washington Bullets'. Both are placed on the final side, making them seem like the afterthoughts they were. Even more desperate is 'Mensforth Hill', a noise collage strongly reminiscent of the Beatles' unlistenable *White Album* track, 'Revolution Number 9', and described in the liner notes as the 'title theme from a forthcoming serial'. In fact, it is 'Something About England' played backwards. As well as wanting to sequence the tracks so that they linked together – sometimes with the aid of 'found' snippets of dialogue, or Mikey Dread exhortations – the band developed an obsession with having six tracks a side. Among other oddities, this explains why 'One More Dub' is credited as a separate track, while 'The Crooked Dub' is not. Mick, who had been largely responsible for production throughout, oversaw the final mix.

Joe's massive sheaf of lyrics was handed over to political cartoonist Steve Bell to illustrate. Don Letts filmed a video for 'The Call Up' at the somewhat worrying militaria collection-cum-warehouse of former Sixties pop star Chris Farlowe, where the band performed while attired in a selection of uniforms. A hasty cover photo-session was arranged with Pennie Smith behind King's Cross station; the band lined up against a wall, Mick still wearing a GI helmet from the video shoot. The various packaging elements were given to the album cover design specialist Jules Baulm, the start of a lengthy relationship.

Then it was straight back to Wessex to begin work on Ellen Foley's album. In addition to producing what became *Spirit Of St Louis*, Mick prevailed upon Joe to help him write six songs for the project. Having met Tymon Dogg during the Electric Lady sessions, Ellen raided his repertoire for a further three songs. Tymon played on the sessions, along with all four members of the Clash plus Norman Watt-Roy, Mickey Gallagher and Davey Payne from the Blockheads. The album was recorded and mixed by Bill Price and Jerry Green. Perhaps surprisingly, then, it sounds nothing like *Sandinista!* Ellen wanted her approach to be that of an Edith Piaf-style chanteuse and, for their part, Mick and Joe welcomed the challenge to venture into one of the very few areas they had not already visited with their own record. 'It gave us a chance to do stuff we don't regularly do for the Clash,' Mick told *Musician*'s Clint Roswell in 1981. 'It worked out well all around, letting us expand our range a little.'

Gradually, throughout the year, the UK music papers' dissatisfaction with the Clash had continued to build. The positive US reviews and the New York recording sessions had combined to convince them that the Clash were intent on breaking America at all costs. They certainly felt the band had abandoned their original principles and their UK following, even though the 16 Tons Tour had lasted for a total of two months in the UK and just eight days in the US. Increasingly, the worries Garry Bushell had expressed in his *London Calling* review – about how tired old R&B and rock clichés, outlaw imagery and lyrical fantasy worlds were in danger of replacing the carefully honed vision and direct communication of yore – were becoming the general consensus. Chris Bohn's *NME* review of the rescheduled 17 June 1980 Hammersmith Palais gig summed it up: 'At times the Clash appear so immersed in their own myth it's difficult for them and us to see each other straight. Ever conscious of their future position in the history books, they've fashioned their collective rock'n'roll persona to fit it even more perfectly since their American tour, where their less threatening traditional approach has now won them lots of new friends ... While their music has been enriched by the assimilation of their roots, it does make them more conservative.'

Reviewing 'Bankrobber' for the same paper, even the previously pro-Clash Paul Morley objected to the record's sentiments, and concluded: 'I just wish the Clash would go wild, and smash out of those strenuous traditionalist restrictions.' In *Sounds* the single was dismissed as deathly slow, dreary stuff, and Joe's claim that his daddy was a bank robber held up for ridicule: 'Actually, John Mellor's daddy was a Second Secretary of Information at the Foreign Office. One of my mates' daddies was a bank robber, and he ended up in little pieces after a gangland feud.'

The *NME*'s gossip pages had also started making snide digs about Topper's drug problem. The 12 July issue claimed that he was 'sickly, his continued bad health being the cause of some band friction'. The following week's paper 'retracted' the statement by saying 'it was apparently news to both Topper and his mum, who rang up concerned after reading T-Zers, as is her habit'. Accent on the final word. In September, the paper recounted the story of a prank staged by the Blockheads: after appearing on *Top Of The Pops* dressed as policemen, they had driven directly up to Wessex, stormed in the back door and besieged the control booth. Topper, it was reported, panicked and ran, and 'was last seen wearing a hopelessly false beard and reading a paper upside down in the Gatwick departure lounge, sweating profusely'. (In fact, Jerry Green recalls that it was Mick who came closest to having a heart attack . . .)

That October's two Clash-related releases did not improve their relationship with the music press. The cut-price US-only *Black Market Clash* did nothing to dispel the notion that the band were favouring America. The band's position on a UK release for the record was the same as it had been for the revised version of *The Clash*. Nevertheless, the album's inclusion of the original 'Capital Radio', which was hard to find, and the otherwise unavailable 'Time Is Tight' made it a desirable object for UK fans and collectors, and its ready availability as an expensive import gave some the feeling they were being exploited.

At much the same time, Pete Townshend's Eel Pie imprint published Pennie Smith's book of Clash photos, *Before And After*. Although it included photos taken from 1977 to 1980 and in the UK as well as the US, the book seemed to be dominated by the American pictures. Pennie acknowledges that the band's latter-day outlaw images were almost designed to be shot in black and white against classic American backdrops, and that as a result those photographs were bound to have more impact. Some of the shots captured the Clash members in a less than flattering light and Mick and Joe's captions were mostly wittily self-deprecating, yet the book was seen by some as another of the Clash's efforts to reinforce their mythic status. During his year-end *Melody Maker* interview with Joe Paolo Hewitt gave it the unofficial subtitle 'A Book Of Clash Poses', and asked him to defend it. Joe made the point that it was Pennie's project – 'she's an artist herself, and that's one of her testaments' – but did address the myth-making issue: 'That's part of the lure of hoisting yourself out of a duff environment. You can't take the glamour out of this scene, no matter how hard you try.'

It did not pass unnoticed that the Clash's early promises to put something back into the culture that spawned them had gone largely unfulfilled. In the far-off days of 1976 and 1977, the band had promised to start up a club, an alternative radio station and a live music TV programme to replace the despised *Top Of The Pops*. Those plans had even been restated more recently: in June 1979, Joe had told the *NME*'s Charles Shaar Murray that he was attempting to set up a musicians' collective in order to establish a musician-owned London venue, and was also trying to persuade a London TV company to create a real rock'n'roll show. That December, the same paper's Adrian Thrills had learned that the venue was to be the Lucky Seven, 'a disused West London theatre' from where Joe also hoped to broadcast the TV programme. Unfortunately, representatives of local ITV companies who had been approached about the latter development had failed to act. 'What I need is a maverick, left-field, renegade, rebel TV producer. The aim, hopefully, is to get past the blinkered, half-dead nitwits who control the media.'

A year later, there had been no further developments. Grilled in December 1980 about the band's failure to deliver, Joe explained that the plan to take over the Lucky Seven - located on Ladbroke Grove – had fallen through when the landlord decided to turn it into a snooker hall. And a maverick, left-field (etc.) TV producer had failed to materialise. The main problem was, inevitably, finance, as he explained to Paolo Hewitt: 'We came flooding out with these ideas, and everybody wrote them down and said, "Well, this is all really good stuff. Right on!" Then we realised we weren't getting any money . . . It took a couple of years for that to sink in, whilst in the meantime all these people were saying, "Where's all these radio stations? Where's all these wonderful things?" . . . But I haven't dropped any project at all.'

As well as having antagonism directed towards them for their own perceived failings, the Clash were also beginning to find themselves out of step with prevailing musical and pop-cultural trends. The New Romantic movement shared the same Bowie and Roxy foundations as punk's art school followers, and provided a new home for many of them. Culture Club's Jon Moss, Visage's Steve Strange, Rusty Egan and Midge Ure and the Ants' Marco Pirroni had all been associated with punk in some way. Adam had formed the original Ants as a dark punk band in the mould of Siouxsie and the Banshees, before turning his attention first to Burundi drumming and then to pantomime kitsch. Despite having many of the same origins, the New Romantic movement's flamboyant, decadent image was the diametric opposite of punk. Its practitioners were self-absorbed, clothes-obsessed, hedonistic and (in song, at least) apolitical. 'The new dandyism is in,' Joe announced to Kosmo on the promotional Clash interview album *If Music Could Talk*. 'Dressing up like Robin Hood and Friar Tuck, Napoleon and Billy Bunter.' Which was amusing, but would have packed more punch had not the Clash spent most of the past four years at a slightly more butch fancy dress party of their own. The bands at which Joe scoffed opened the floodgates for what became known as the New Pop of the early Eighties:

music without a care in the world, whose practitioners ran the gamut from sophisticated ennui to screaming camp to arch naïvety. Not for nothing did Dave Rimmer entitle his 1985 Culture Club biography *Like Punk Never Happened.*

Some of 'the kids' this music appealed to were very young indeed, and their interests were catered for by *Smash Hits,* a spectacularly successful colour magazine which combined the innocence of Sixties pop journalism – songwords and questionnaires – with a cheekier, Eighties irreverence. Unlike the inkies, it did not expect its interviewees to be committed, responsible or opinionated, but nor did it pander to their egos. Early in 1980, former *NME* editor Nick Logan founded another publishing success story, glossy pop culture and lifestyle magazine *The Face,* which although eclectic in approach, tended to cover the adult end of the New Pop spectrum.

Meanwhile, the more serious world of the 'post-punk' bands was mutating into what would henceforth be known as 'indie', after the independent labels on which, confusingly enough, by no means all of its exponents released their recordings. New influences and technologies were being adopted to forge new directions and sub-genres. Thus, there was a stripped-down funk element to the Gang of Four and the Au Pairs; a psychedelic edge to Echo and the Bunnymen and the Teardrop Explodes; a futuristic slant to the synthesizer music of the Human League, Ultravox and Depeche Mode.

Concerned about diminishing sales and mindful of the new trends indicated by the success of *arriviste* publications *Smash Hits* and *The Face,* the inky old *NME* tried to adapt, a move that was as expedient as any change of policy ever adopted by the Clash. The paper wanted to continue covering the serious indie sector, but also wanted to reflect the carefree nature of the New Pop and the studied élitism of London's new club-culture. Its two most willing boys about town were Paul Morley and Ian Penman. They patented an affected decadent intellectual style which initially succeeded in covering all the bases and in making some telling points about the inherent conservatism of the rock'n'roll scene. Before long, they would start to wear out readers' patience with some of the most impenetrably pretentious copy ever published in the *NME*; in the short term, however, they had sufficient clout to ensure that any kind of rock music that was deemed too traditional or earnest was sneered at; the expression 'rockist' became a commonplace term of abuse. On the whole, this was no time for the Clash to be releasing a triple album full of brooding dub, political harangues and intimations of apocalypse.

A chance for the paper to sharpen its teeth was offered by 'The Call Up'. T-Zers anticipated the single's 28 November release thus: 'It was inspired by the group's current bid for US citizenship.' Paul Morley used the singles review column as an opportunity to hand in his resignation from the Clash fan club: 'With the general shifts in moods and desires that are going on, the Clash are already old fashioned. Too sternly stuck inside a political phase, too wrapped up in those used-up myths. A set of passions I can't get to grips with . . . "The Call Up" sounds like a lost album track, proud and bravely cheerless, but lost in the murk . . . It doesn't seem right for the times. They care so much but seem so lost.'

In the UK *Sandinista!* was released on 12 December 1980. The task of reviewing it for the *NME* fell to Nick Kent, hardly one of the paper's new dilettantes, but, as someone who had responded favourably to *Give 'Em Enough Rope*'s pedestrian rock sound, if not subject matter, no more likely to appreciate the band's new direction. He dismissed the three-album set as 'ridiculously self-indulgent', and ran through the list of the band's genre experimentations – for which he blamed Mick - with scorn. The Clash had made a mistake in trying to be musically professional, believed Nick, who went on to attack Joe's and Mick's limited vocal ranges and poor pitching and Mick's lack of projection for not being professional enough. Ditto the production, 'too grandly embellished by (particularly) Mickey Gallagher's keyboard work' and 'riddled side after side with a wafer-thin, soft-focus mixing down of instruments that divides everything off instead of building up textures. This mix problem is such a crippling flaw that song after song fails because its clout is dismembered . . . A producer would be advisable as the band have no real perspective on their work in the studio.'

Nor did Joe's lyrics get off lightly. He was criticised for failing to address the current British malaise, instead resorting to cliché, turning to freedom fighters abroad or hiding in fantasy land. To Nick, the songs were either 'another set of neatly-glib black and white snapshots of "the good fight" be it in Nicaragua or in a pub down Shepherd's Bush Junction (after all, when you've seen one ghetto, you've seen 'em all, eh lads?)' or just plain 'blinkered romanticism'. He seemed particularly offended by the band's critical reception in America: *Rolling Stone*'s Greil Marcus had accused Nick of starting a 'snivelling backlash' against the Clash with his *Give 'Em Enough Rope* review; he now responded with a jibe at the 'absurdly sycophantic' reviews the band had been receiving 'across the Atlantic'. Eventually finding it in his heart to praise a select handful of tracks, he concluded: 'The Clash will survive. Why they bother to is the really painful question that *Sandinista!* forces me to ask.'

Melody Maker's Patrick Humphries continued the paper's tradition of taking the balanced approach. Three albums for the price of one was generous, he conceded, but quantity did not always compensate for quality: '*Sandinista!* is a floundering mutant of an album. The odd highlights are lost in a welter of reggae/dub overkill.' He believed it managed to suffer from both lack of direction and similarity of sound. Although he found the album to be lyrically 'interesting', he agreed with Nick Kent about 'the black and white way' the band equated rebellion with just causes; he even objected to the choice of title, which 'reeks of the political "awareness" which many find so glibly unattractive'. Unlike Nick, however, he believed 'the Clash really do still care, and remain a radical committed band'. In summary, the record set was a disappointment to him after 'the consistent excellence of last year's offering', but he was rather more hopeful about the future than the *NME* reviewer: 'That aside, I can't wait for the next Clash album.'

Perhaps surprisingly, given that a representative of the paper had been so scathing about the Clash's retreat from punk with *London Calling*, the most positive of the inky reviews came from *Sounds'* Robbi Millar. Like the other two, he worried that the band's 'busy body interference is too eager to glorify war, in Nicaragua or Brixton', though he cited 'Corner Stone' as proof that they could 'stick the dagger in just where it's needed . . . the selfishness of violence is once again exposed'. He was more open to Joe's romantic streak – 'the romantic aspects of the album are some of its strongest points whether they're social or personal' – but he too found the American references on the album to be 'a bore', and maintained that its best music 'involves Britain, whether it be a black, white or two-tone Britain'.

His principal differences with the other two reviewers concerned what he perceived to be 'the fine production', 'the band's increase in technical competence' and the pleasing variety of musical genres attempted. He also noted that 'rhythm is the key throughout *Sandinista!*' Robbi closed by asserting that too much of the band's punk spirit was in evidence for them to be dismissed as would-be Rolling Stones, but he had already summed up his overall opinion earlier in the review: 'The fourth Clash album is an adventure of diversity and wit, of struggle and freedom, of excellence and dross. When it is good, it is very good. When it is bad . . . maybe aiming to provide us with three albums' worth of value was aiming too high.' He gave it four out of a possible five stars.

To greater and lesser extents, prejudice lurked behind all three inky reviews. The accusations of an American bias on *Sandinista!* are unfounded. Aside from the fact that the bulk of the album's music is reggae-derived – reggae being a non-US genre with no commercial track record there whatsoever – only eight of the lyrics refer directly to the States; while a couple of these indulge in the cosy Americana-mythologising of *London Calling*, most actively criticise the country's government. If that were not enough, the band were only able to make the gesture of selling the album for £5.99 in the UK because they were charging a relatively hefty $14.98 in the US: in effect, US fans were being required to subsidise British fans, which, if anything, was an indication of bias the other way.

The suggestion that the band should stick to British subject matter in their lyrics was evidence of a blinkered and parochial mentality – which, ironically, had quite possibly been inspired by the punk era Clash – and just as limiting as it would have been to insist the band arrest their musical development at the sound of barking seals and pneumatic drills. The Clash had improved as musicians since the first album, and had also been out into the wider world; to pretend otherwise would have been a lie. 'Really to see where you've come from, you have to go someplace else', as Mick explained to *Rip It Up*'s Duncan Campbell early in 1982. 'Otherwise you wouldn't understand that the world didn't finish at the end of your street.' Eight of the lyrics refer to specifically British locations and experiences, but attempt to put them in a wider context.

The reviewers were all lazy in assuming that 'Washington Bullets' is solely 'about' Nicaragua, when it is 'about' covert armed interference worldwide. A song clearly denouncing such activity is, surely, far preferable to the only semi-ironic celebration of terrorism that was 'Tommy Gun'. Political upheavals anywhere in the world affect us all, either directly or indirectly, which gives everyone the right to comment on them. That said, having spent several years in the early to mid Seventies sharing squats with refugees from various South American regimes, having formed the 101ers with two Chileans and having played his first gig with that band on behalf of the Chile Solidarity Campaign, Joe could lay claim to feeling more genuine empathy with the Nicaraguan rebels' cause than most white middle class Britons.

As for adopting *Sandinista!* as the album title, the motive was not to bestow radical chic upon the Clash, but to focus on the overthrowing of a despot by his own people, an event most people in their right minds would choose to celebrate had they only been aware of it. 'There was a media blanket covering the whole bloody thing, and people didn't even know there was a revolution there,' Mick told Duncan Campbell. 'We really wanted to have a title that was useful for once. It was something that would draw people's attention to something that was going on at the time.'

Less easy to defend was and is the band's continuing *stylistic* fascination with rebel chic. Patrick Humphries remarked upon the GI helmet Mick sports on the cover of the album, and the other two reviewers also evidently allowed it and the band's appearance in military uniforms in 'The Call Up' video to colour their response to the lyrics within. When tackled about Mick's helmet by *Sounds'* Pete Silverton, Joe rather lamely replied, 'He's wearing that helmet for the reason that we're all going to be wearing them soon. We spent a lot of time making this album wearing helmets . . . Admittedly, there's nobody strafing us and napalming the neighbourhood, but it seems like war to me out there.' Those songs on the album that touch on the subject are for once unambiguously anti-war and anti-violence, but the Clash's knee-jerk costume-donning inevitably served to undermine both the message and their own credibility.

Sandinista! is indeed deeply flawed. Firstly, as the reviewers all agreed, there is far too much of it. 'It's pretty much designed to last for six months to a year of listening,' Mick explained to Kosmo on the *If Music Could Talk* promotional interview disc. 'People don't have to listen to it all at once. They can listen to it a bit at a time. However much they can take.' The band, and especially Mick, showed considerable naïvety in believing that the Clash could rewrite the rules of popular music consumption overnight. Most of 'the kids' who buy a new rock album do so with a sense of urgent anticipation. Even the most ardent fans were always going to have problems familiarising themselves with a triple album of often demanding new material, and newcomers or browsers were always going to be put off by the level of commitment demanded. Furthermore, and not unimportantly, since they were forced to assimilate the record quickly in order to make deadlines, reviewers were always going to feel overwhelmed, disoriented and, frankly, resentful.

Patrick Humphries was right when he said that the band's experiments with other genres were overshadowed by the number of reggae and dub tracks. Some, like 'One More Time' and 'One More Dub' are excellent, standout tracks. Others, like 'The Crooked Beat', 'The Equaliser' and the last-minute padding dubs on side six, are simply boring. The charge of self-indulgence also applies to some of the Electric Lady jams, 'Junkie Slip' in particular being a complete waste of space. 'Mensforth Hill' is just plain unforgivable. Nick Kent's comments about the mix apply in some, if not all, instances, simply because there was too much material for every song to be given due attention. One of the victims is 'The Call Up', which in the form of a single does, as Paul Morley suggested, sound like an album track: an instrumental remix made the following March and released on the US 12-inch of 'The Magnificent Seven' under the title 'The Cool Out' indicates just how powerful the parent song could have been.

Nick Kent saw the album's diversity of musical genres as a 'blight'. In drawing together influences and styles old and new from all over Britain, Europe, Jamaica, Trinidad, New York, New Orleans, Memphis, Detroit, Central America and – indirectly, via several of the above – Africa, the Clash were making a point about the connections that exist between them all. Nor were they content to leave it there. Their attempts at often complex fusions and crossovers made them more than just tourists or archivists. At the end of the previous year, they had been found wanting for exhibiting retrogressive tendencies and compared unfavourably to the supposedly avant-garde PiL. Now they were being criticised for experimenting with form. It was more than a little unjust. While it could be argued that the Rolling Stones and the Beatles had both attempted similar projects in the past, *Sandinista!* was a bold exploration of world music long before such a category existed in the record racks or Paul Simon went in search of *Graceland*.

At the time, the received wisdom about the triple set was that it was the product of too much dope: Mick's November 1976 *London Weekend Show* remark about the problem with hippies had come back to haunt him. In a way, this is true: it is a stoner album, just like the slow dub reggae of the mid to late Seventies is stoner music and punk is speed-freak music. Perhaps more tellingly, much of *Sandinista!* is groove-oriented, and rock fans and a few of the more traditional rock critics of the period were notoriously uptight about post-Motown dance music, 'disco sucks' being the general drift of their thinking.

Only Robbi Millar found anything praiseworthy to say about the band's foray into funk, and only he correctly identified the Sugarhill Gang as the chief source of inspiration. Patrick Humphries avoided mention of the new departure altogether, and Nick Kent gave it one of his typically florid muggings: 'the "disco" pulsebeat – usually a surly repetitious bass figure punctuated by an ethnic piano chord – is featured twice on side one alone'. The musical branch of hip hop culture of which he was being so dismissive – a.k.a. rap – would go on to be the most innovative, influential and commercially successful force in the popular music of the Eighties and early Nineties, its crossover with rock injecting essential new lifeblood into the form. The Clash were the first non-New York rock band to get on the case.

Reggae and its various sub-genres and offshoots have gone in and out of fashion with the rock audience over the years, but, as Joe remarked to *Trouser Press* in 1981, heavy dub has always been a minority taste; thus, the UK music critics' unanimous thumbs down for its dominance on the album is perhaps understandable. Yet by choosing to carp on about *Sandinista!* being 'too grandly embellished' by keyboard work and 'psychedelic' sound effects rather than acknowledging these features as conventions and techniques of dub production, Nick Kent seemed to be flaunting his own lack of knowledge about – or, at least interest in – the genre.

Lyrically, the album succeeds in bringing together all the Clash's previous concerns. The Ladbroke Grove area, tower blocks, oppression and urban alienation all feature. Political machinations in the wider world are also addressed without resorting to the histrionics of *Give 'Em Enough Rope*. Myths and romantic legends have a place, but they are rooted in historical fact or balanced by more realistic or satirical neighbouring songs. The sense of coming Armageddon is not mere empty stadium rock bombast, but a genuine expression of empathy with the fears and woes of Third World peoples condemned to eke out a living against a background of disease, famine and war, and of supposedly First World peoples living in poverty in ghettos riddled with drugs and guns. The overall impression is of a document of 1980, made up not only of first-hand experience and news, but also historical and political texts, memories, stories and dreams, captured in a variety of folk-ballad and oral tale-telling forms. 'Up In Heaven (Not Only Here)' quotes from a song by Phil Ochs, a Greenwich Village contemporary of Bob Dylan who, like Joe Strummer, was 'from the school of Woody Guthrie'. The title of Phil's 1965 début album was an adaptation of the tagline of the *New York Times*: *All The News That's Fit To Sing*; the liner notes and lyric sheets to *Sandinista!* are presented as another edition of *The Armagideon Times*.

The much-maligned *Sandinista!*'s groove-oriented stoner music would have a significant impact on the UK music scene. With the addition of a little late Sixties psychedelia and James Brown's 'Funky Drummer', it would help shape the sound of the late Eighties: the Farm and Happy Mondays have both acknowledged an influence, and the Stone Roses would find it difficult to deny one. Mick Jones himself would pursue the line of enquiry instigated by 'The Magnificent Seven' with his post-Clash band Big Audio Dynamite, which in turn would beget a posse of followers and wannabes. In the years immediately after the album's release, however, it became something of a standing joke that one would be hard put to compile a worthwhile single album from the triple set's material. In fact, with the benefit of hindsight and a couple of judicious remixes, one could put together a double that might have been praised as a worthy follow-up to *London Calling* . . . in almost any year other than 1980.

But 1980 it was, and the Clash had to come out and face a pugnacious music press. Or, rather, Joe did. Following completion of Ellen's album, Mick had returned with her to New York. Topper did one or two phone interviews, and Paul talked at length to Chris Salewicz for *The Face*, but it was Joe who was left to handle the bulk of the promotional interviews. Which meant that he spent much of December on the defensive, justifying both the album and the Clash against accusations of self-indulgence, toadying to Uncle Sam and other hypocrisies and failings many and various. He started off in reasonable form, polite, witty and informative, but the cumulative effect of his interviewers' negativity and the poor reviews afforded *Sandinista!*, coming as they did on top of the latest in a succession of difficult, demanding years, finally proved too much. Having helped steer the Clash from the Gates of the West towards what he thought would be the Gates of the World, Joe had somehow found himself staring down through scorched portals into an altogether more hostile environment.

Still susceptible to inky opinion, he privately began to blame Mick, as had Nick Kent, for forcing the band down an unpopular musical path. True, Mick had been responsible for suggesting the triple album and for the production; but Joe conveniently forgot that he had been the one who had wanted to rap, that he had been the one who had fallen in love with dub and that he had been the one who had wanted to scat and ad lib over band jams. These niggles would come to a head during the course of the next year, but they were by no means the most damaging influence on Joe's future relationship with Mick.

By the end of 1980, the Clash were close to half a million pounds in debt to CBS, a situation that sales of *Sandinista!* seemed hardly likely to rectify. The feeling that everything was turning to ashes was exacerbated by developments on the domestic front. At the age of 28, and in a stable relationship with Gaby Salter, Joe was growing tired of squats and borrowed flats. He had recently applied for a mortgage to buy his own home and been refused. The couple were now living just off Ladbroke Grove in a tiny, short-let rented flat. After nearly five years of going without material comforts in order to live up to the Clash's ideals, all Joe had received in return was critical scorn for supposedly failing to do so. A brief period of despondency was followed by a determination to get back on the right track. And that, as far as Joe was concerned, whether Mick liked it or not – and when he heard about it, Mick most certainly did not – meant bringing back Bernie Rhodes.

13... SHOULD I STAY OR SHOULD I GO?

The arguments over ticket prices and Topper's health that had already strained the relationship between the Clash – especially Joe – and Andrew King and Peter Jenner came to a head during the Wessex recording sessions for *Sandinista!* Blackhill's services were dispensed with before the album made it to the shops, and they are 'thanked' on the lyric sheet under the guise of 'the two ogres'. 'What offended Joe most was that I seemed schoolmasterly, and the very type of authority figure he was kicking against,' Peter Jenner told the *NME*'s Len Brown in 1989. 'He seemed to think it was uncool to be efficient. The relationship was never easy.' The band kept Kosmo on as PR man and, briefly, looked after their own affairs.

The second single from the album to be released in the UK, on 16 January 1981, was 'Hitsville UK', backed with Mikey Dread's 'Radio One', yet another of his critiques of the contemporary music scene. The A-side was joined by 'Police On My Back' when released on 17 February as the first single in the US. As far as the American market was concerned, 'Hitsville UK' was the track closest in sound to the band's only hit to date, 'Train In Vain'. For the domestic market, it was most likely selected to balance the supposedly American bias of 'The Call Up'. The *NME*'s Ian Penman was not impressed, describing it as the band's creative nadir. After damning the lyrics for their romanticism, patronising tone and hypocrisy, he set about the tune in similar vein, before sticking the knife into the Clash themselves: 'What do they see when they look in the mirror? Third world guerrillas with *quiffs?*'

The slide in popularity with the general public the band had feared before devising the aborted UK Clash Singles Bonanza seemed to be under way: 'The Call Up' had climbed no higher than number 40; 'Hitsville UK' peaked at number 56. Although they featured in the *NME* end-of-year readers' polls and still commanded enough loyalty to hold on to third best group, most other categories for which they qualified found them lurking mid-table. Meanwhile, the Jam once again lifted every trophy. 'If you're a musician, and you listen to the Jam, all you hear is lock, stock and barrel lifts,' Joe grumbled ungraciously to *Trouser Press*.

At the end of November 1980, the music press had reported that plans were being laid for an 'extensive' Clash UK tour early in the new year. At the end of January, this was amended to 'selected' dates, and during an interview for Wolverhampton's Beacon Radio an untypically petulant Joe explained why: 'I'm not going to pretend that we're going to do a great big tour. There's a lot of things putting us off. Like, a group tends to believe what it reads in the press as reflecting the true mood of the country. And this past year, reading the English press has been pretty depressing for me, because every time they mention the Clash it's been a dig, or to say we're irrelevant. After a while, you start to accept that, and you think, "Obviously everybody's got a big downer on us." So we aren't too keen to come rushing out every-bloody-place and play and get gobbed on in the face by 30 people while 3,000 stand by passively watching. They can just stuff it.' Once upon a time, Us and Them had meant punk bands, the music media and the punk audience against all agents of oppression; now it appeared to be the Clash against their one-time supporters.

The 7 February edition of the *NME* announced that the tour had been called off altogether. Kosmo's lame excuse was 'We cannot find enough alternative venues to play.' Rumours of a split began to circulate once more, and again, they were not without foundation. Joe had been pushing for Bernie's return for some weeks, having bumped into him in a café and invited him along to a band meeting. He encountered considerable resistance from the other members of the band, but, just as the tour dates were about to go to press, he played his trump card: he announced he was leaving the band, and would only return if Bernie were reinstated as manager. Faced with such an ultimatum, the others were left with no option but to capitulate. It was especially tough on Mick, who had pressed hardest for Bernie's dismissal just over two years earlier and was now put in the humiliating position of being deputised to approach him with the proposition.

Bernie did not make it easy for anyone. During the hiatus he had involved himself in the careers of the Specials and Dexys Midnight Runners – two of the foremost UK bands of the early Eighties, critically and commercially – and had delivered where the Clash had failed in establishing a club of his own in London: the once occasional and peripatetic Club Left had become a regular Boho joint based in the former Whisky-A-Go-Go club in Wardour Street (later the Wag), with former Subway Sect vocalist Vic Godard as resident house crooner. As far as Bernie was concerned, he had no reason to show any humility upon accepting his old job back. Nobody was doing *him* any favours now – 'I certainly don't see it as a permanent position,' he airily informed Chris Salewicz for the August 1981 issue of *The Face*; 'Malcolm McLaren and I have plans for something quite big that we'll probably get under way in about a year or so' – and nor did he believe he had been at fault before: 'Every situation needs a scapegoat, and I became it.'

Joe's demand cannot be dismissed merely as evidence of nostalgia for the good old days or as an example of a rebellious son finding himself in a jam and running for help to a previously spurned father-figure. These were factors, yes, but there was also a more practical consideration: the Clash's finances were still tied up in the legal wranglings Bernie had instigated upon his dismissal. Bringing him back would give the band – crippled by massive debts – at least some freedom to operate. This time, Bernie agreed to take his managerial percentage out of the band's net profits, rather than the gross.

Even so, only Joe thought it was an exchange worth making, and the manner in which he went about getting his own way caused irrevocable damage to the band. As with the 101ers, when it came to the crunch, Joe had proved he was prepared to abandon his, and the Clash's, supposedly democratic principles in order to achieve what he wanted. In so doing, he effectively announced that he was taking control, which was bound to have long-term repercussions on his relationship with the others, and especially with Mick. 'I could quite easily have walked out then,' Mick told Paolo Hewitt in 1986 (by which time the former was with Big Audio Dynamite and the latter was writing for the *NME*). 'But it's like a marriage, or the people you love: you cling on hoping it's going to work out.'

Although the band had pulled closer together in 1979, Mick had continued to be the one most prone to displays of rock star airs and graces. Reminiscing about the Take the Fifth Tour in a 1994 *Mojo* retrospective, cartoonist Ray Lowry wrote: 'Oh, but Mick, you were a perfect spoiled brat at times!' Now, plunged against his will into an ego battle with Joe, Mick's faults were magnified as he began to erect his defences. Understandably, it was the other members of the Clash camp who got the worst of it. Mick kept to himself while on tour, usually staying in his room, and was truculent and unresponsive in rehearsals and high-handed in the studio, which he considered his domain. His difficult behaviour was not reserved exclusively for his bandmates and manager, however. Mick could still turn on the charm for press interviewers when he wished, but did not always make the effort: 'Consciously or unconsciously, Mick Jones always seems to be taking the piss,' wrote *Rip It Up*'s Duncan Campbell early the following year. 'His cockiness borders on arrogance, but it's an integral part of his personality.'

Even long-standing friends were not guaranteed an easy ride. Making use of the hiatus in Clash activities enforced by the tour's cancellation, while Joe got involved with the 101ers' *Elgin Avenue Breakdown* project, Mick produced a single for new band Theatre of Hate, then accepted an opportunity to co-produce, with one of his teen heroes, Mick Ronson, an album for his greatest teen hero, Ian Hunter, subsequently released as *Short Back'n'Sides*. At much the same time, hoping to put a band together for Ellen, he contacted John Brown, whom he had not seen for several years, to see if he would be interested in playing bass. As John had been a fellow Mott the Hoople fan, Mick invited him along to the Wessex sessions, telling him Robin Crocker was also going to be present. It would appear he was gathering friends around him for moral support; but if so, he was too proud to voice his troubles, and he made no effort to break the ice with John. He picked him up on the way to the studio. 'My wife had just had a baby girl, who was about three months old, and I was full of it, you know,' says John.

'Mick came in, and I said, "Look, here's my daughter!" He walked straight past, walked around the room once and said, "Come on, let's go!" I thought, "Fuck me! You've never even *met* my wife before!" He was *not* interested, really distant.

'We went to Wessex. Mick had a huge lump of dope, which he would roll a jay from, and smoke it all to himself. And then he'd walk away, roll another one, and smoke *that* all to himself. He was very withdrawn. He'd come into the control room, say a few things, then disappear again. I didn't understand what I'd walked into. I couldn't feel at home, even though I'd known Ian Hunter for years. This was when I suddenly thought, "I don't know Mick at the moment." I don't think I've ever known him since.' Nothing more was said about John joining Ellen's band, but that could have been due to the damning with faint praise *The Spirit Of St Louis* suffered upon its release in late March: according to the *NME*'s Adrian Thrills, it was 'an intermittently worthwhile indulgence'. This, in turn, did nothing to improve Mick's mood.

Nor did CBS's and Epic's grumbles about the Clash's proposed next single, 'The Magnificent Seven'. At the end of the original six-minute version Joe mutters, 'Fucking long, innit?' with which appraisal both record companies agreed. (The swearing didn't exactly endear it to them either.) The Clash came up with a compromise solution. One of the spin-offs from the rap and dance scene in New York was the idea of bringing in an outside DJ to produce a 12-inch extended dance remix for the clubs: a sort of funk equivalent of a reggae version. The band agreed to supply a straightforward, edited version of 'The Magnificent Seven', along with a longer more experimental instrumental version, 'The Magnificent Dance'. In the UK these tracks appeared on both 7- and 12-inch versions of the single, released early in April. In the US, they were joined by 'The Call Up' and a new instrumental version of that track entitled 'The Cool Out' on a 12-inch-only EP released at the end of March. Credit was given to 'Puerto Rican producer Pepe Unidos'. In fact, this was a pseudonym for Mick, who remixed the tracks at Wessex in early March; an in-joke nod in the direction of dance culture, but also an attempt to sidestep prejudice against Clash production work.

Dance music aficionado Paolo Hewitt reviewed the UK release for *Melody Maker* and described it as 'a great record . . . it features a superb bassline, an intelligent lyric, and succeeds beautifully because Joe Strummer understands that the rhythm of his words are just as important as Mick Jones' careful funk guitar'. For the *NME*, 'Rockin' Sydney' was contemptuously dismissive. The single failed to climb higher than number 36 in the charts.

Part of Joe's determination to take control of his life manifested itself as body-consciousness. During the Clash's time out of the public eye, he finally got his teeth fixed and capped, and, at the end of March, he entered the London Marathon. It was an indication of his willpower that he completed the course despite having done no prior training whatsoever. In early April, the band returned to Vanilla once more to recommence rehearsals, and, in an attempt to recapture the vibe of the preparations for *London Calling*, daily football matches were once again built into their schedule. Little of the former camaraderie was regained, however, and during the course of one game Mickey Gallagher broke his arm, which put him out of action as guest musician for the Clash's forthcoming dates.

Instead of immediately reorganising the UK tour that was cancelled when Joe delivered his ultimatum, the band elected to launch a huge 60-date US tour as a bid to break through into the mainstream in that market. The reasoning was simple: neither its various singles nor *Sandinista!* itself had made any real impression in Britain, and the band were no longer prepared to throw money away wooing an apparently uninterested public. In the States the album's January release had not exactly met with unanimous approval. *Creem*'s Jeff Nesin had shown himself to be in accord with his UK counterparts by opining, 'Generally, the further the Clash stray from their great theme, The Dying of England, the more specious and patronising their songs become.' In the more mainstream *Rolling Stone*, though, John Piccarella had given it a five-star review: '*Sandinista!* is an everywhere-you-turn guerrilla raid of vision and virtuosity.' The album would go on to sell around 800,000 copies worldwide, well over half of them in the States. Later in the year, in separate interviews, both Mick and Joe would talk about being prophets without honour in their own land, and both would say they now felt more comfortable in New York than London. Although it pained them, it seemed the Clash were about to give up on the UK. Some dates were pencilled in there for October, but it was evident that their home country was now pretty low down on their list of priorities.

Which made it all the more surprising when the nationwide American tour was abandoned at the last minute. Making the best of a bad job, Bernie came up with a promotional wheeze that was thematically appropriate to their current record release: a residency of a magnificent seven dates to be played in late May and the first week of June 1981 at Bonds Casino in New York's Times Square. Clever though it was, it was still a massive comedown from the original plan. That August, the band told *The Face*'s Chris Salewicz that their hand had been forced when Epic had refused to help finance the jaunt. 'The Epic decision was an odd one,' commented Chris. 'A series of 60 gigs would have cemented the already colossal Stateside Clash popularity once and for all.' He wondered whether objections from Epic regarding Bernie's return might have had something to do with it.

There were other factors behind the scenes to take into account. Mick's interest in studio recording and dance music had eclipsed his interest in touring as part of a rock band. 'Mick doesn't like being on the road at all,' Joe had told *Trouser Press* at the beginning of the year, even before Bernie's return had become a factor in the guitarist's intransigence. 'So there was a conflict there in that the rest of us really enjoy touring, and Mick thinks it's a trial and tribulation. So something or somebody has to suffer.' If Mick was reluctant, then Topper was unreliable. By the spring of 1981, he was in a terrible state, the cost of his habit, as he himself admitted the following year, running at approximately £100 a day 'just to feel normal'. He had been busted during the band's lay-off period, and appeared in court in early April charged with possession of 'illegal powders'. While he was conditionally discharged for a year, it meant that his habit was now common knowledge and that any future busts might well lead to incarceration. Aside from doubts about his ability to function for the duration of a 60-date tour, there was also the logistical problem of keeping him supplied with the massive amounts of heroin he needed while travelling across the US by coach and plane.

Nevertheless, what the Clash came up with as an alternative to the aborted American tour gave the lie to any idea that they might have cancelled it of their own volition. A European tour was arranged instead: not the Clash's usual token Continental jaunt, but one that ran for a full month from the end of April. After years of dividing their attentions between the US and the UK, the Clash, at Bernie's instigation, had decided to live up to the more globally conscious bent of their recent music. It was not so much an extension of The Quest as a recognition that there were other markets out there besides America that could help put the Clash finances back in order. The European tour was to begin in Spain, the economy of which was enjoying a post-Franco boom, and take in France, Holland, Denmark, Sweden, Germany and Italy. The band would play to crowds of between 8,000 and 15,000: a considerable escalation from the 2,000- to 3,000-seater venues they usually played in the UK. For the first time, they were intending to make a profit. In the words of Mikey Dread's 'Radio One': 'Airplay might be vital / But right now it is insignificant / Because I man going international.'

Before they departed for Europe, the Clash went back into the studio to record material for their next single, this time choosing Marcus Music in Kensington Gardens. Shortly after Bernie's return to the fold, he and Kosmo had cemented their new partnership by hatching the concept of Radio Clash, which, in the absence of a Clash-operated alternative radio station, would be more a radio station of the imagination, a symbolic rallying point for a new scene or culture, where exciting, relevant music of all genres would be played and encouraged to cross over. Likewise ideas. 'Information comes to youth through the mass organisations like record companies and TV,' Bernie told the *NME*'s Paul Rambali that October. 'In order to create an ethnic scene that these kids feel part of, they have to have their own sources of information.'

The musical vehicle for the song 'This Is Radio Clash' is more New York-influenced rap–funk, only this time coming via an unusual source: 'That's ripped straight off Queen's "Another One Bites The Dust",' Joe admitted to *Melody Maker* in 1988. Queen, in turn, had ripped it off Chic's 'Good Times'. Mick just altered the riff slightly. Its lyric – the information – is an echo of the days of '76, in that it equates lack of leisure time opportunities – specifically, the non-existence in reality of the kind of radio station Bernie and Kosmo envisaged – with more blatant means of oppression.

Apocalypse Now's effect on Joe had not stopped with 'Charlie Don't Surf'. The film takes Joseph Conrad's *Heart Of Darkness*, a book which employs a journey into the interior of Africa as an allegory for facing the darkness in one's own soul, and transplants it to the near-contemporary nightmare of Vietnam. Enthused, Joe was receptive to the wave of Vietnam-related films of which it was just part; each of them explored different aspects of America's involvement and multiple losses (of lives, face, innocence, righteousness and confidence) during the course of that unwinnable war. Michael Cimino's *The Deer Hunter*, Hal Ashby's *Coming Home* and Martin Scorsese's slightly earlier *Taxi Driver* are all concerned with traumatised veterans' struggles to come to terms with their experiences and readapt to life at home. The last of these films, especially, makes its point by relocating Travis Bickle from the jungles of Vietnam to the urban jungle that is New York's Times Square region at night. There were multiple connections for film buffs and 'Third World guerrillas with quiffs' like the Clash to make: this was a world where rap met their upcoming Bonds residency met their acquaintances Robert De Niro and Martin Scorsese met *Apocalypse Now* met the Sandinistas.

Jerry Green recalls that Michael Herr's Vietnam memoir, *Dispatches*, was being passed around the Clash camp at this time. Along with the above-mentioned films, that book is the direct inspiration for such lines in 'This Is Radio Clash' as 'Them that see ghettology as an urban Vietnam'. It also inspired the music, title and lyric of the other song recorded by the Clash at Marcus, the film soundtrack-like moodpiece 'Sean Flynn'. Son of Errol (namechecked in the previous album's 'If Music Could Talk') and a friend of Michael Herr, Sean had gone missing, presumed killed, while covering the war as a member of the press corps. In the song, Joe imagines Sean approaching his personal heart of darkness: 'Each man knows what he's looking for.'

Topper's own twilight wanderings could no longer be ignored. Gary Barnacle attended the Marcus sessions, and the eerie melancholy of the original seven-minute version of 'Sean Flynn' owes much to his multi-tracked and treated saxophone contribution. Aware that Gary had known Topper since they were both young boys, the rest of the Clash asked if he could do anything to help get the drummer back on course. Being tied up with work commitments, Gary passed on the request to his brother Steve, the member of the Barnacle family who had always been closest to Topper. Steve was willing to help, but was unable to take any action while the Clash were away on the road.

Roadent briefly returned to the fold at the end of April, supplying the PA for the European tour beginning on the 27th in Barcelona. *Record Mirror*'s Mike Nicholls was in attendance and filed a revealing report. The Clash were experimenting with visuals: their backdrop was now a sheet of urban wasteland-type corrugated iron, upon which were affixed posters promoting selected causes and on to which were projected slides of Right to Work marchers in Detroit, UK dole queues, devastation in Cambodia and numerous other flashpoint images. Topper collapsed immediately after the band's set that night, which did not augur well for the rest of the dates. Clash camp humour was bearing up, but not without underlying barbs. Everyone had been put in charge of a fictitious Department: Bernie got Ideas, Kosmo got Information, Paul got Insults and Mick, tellingly, got Complaints.

Although Mike Nicholls believed the band's manic behaviour to be celebratory, with the benefit of hindsight his account of the two-day drinking session and compulsive wisecracking is more suggestive of desperation. But *Melody Maker*'s Paolo Hewitt caught up with the tour nearly a month later in Milan, and wrote: 'Now the Clash have never seemed more buoyant. Both on and off stage.' Drumming nearly every night for two hours – the Clash had added extended dub and funk codas to many of their songs – was always going to kill Topper or force him to channel his attention away from drugs, and so far he appeared to be holding together. Either that, or the band were putting a little more effort into controlling their press relations.

The band had recently become prophets *with* honour in their own land: the previously slightly ludicrous lyric of 'Guns Of Brixton' had become both topical and realistic when the ever-touchy relationship between police and locals in that area erupted into riots early in April 1981. While they were no longer focusing on the UK, the band were not indifferent to such events, and Paul's vocal feature was turned into a big production number. 'It was about the poor being up to their necks in shit,' said Mick, offering his interpretation of the upheavals to New Zealander Duncan Campbell the following year. 'It was beginning to come out of their mouths, they were about to drown in it. And it wasn't just the black people who were rioting. The media have tried to make it into a racist thing, because the English media is basically racist, the Tory press incredibly so.' The Clash seemed to be on a roll: even the *NME* T-Zers page admitted that the European tour was a success, reporting on crowds in Lyons and Paris going 'apeshit, monkeypoo and orangutangdung'. All the signs indicated that the New York Bonds Casino residency would bring more of the same: the tickets for all seven shows sold out on the day they became available.

The gig at Bonds on Thursday, 27 May 1981, went ahead as planned, but the band came off-stage to find firemen storming through the club. The next day, the Fire Department announced that Bonds' supposed 4,000 capacity represented a fire risk, and insisted that no more than 1,750 should be allowed into any future gig. Unbeknownst to the Clash, they had arrived in New York just as it was entering into one of its periodic club wars: there were simply too many live attractions in the city to keep every venue in business, and the band and Bonds were victims of a resultant dirty tricks campaign.

Following a meeting with the club management, it was agreed that Bonds would cancel its forthcoming bookings (Gary Glitter and the Stranglers) and the band would extend their residency to a total of 16 days, including some

★ EXTRA ★

FOR INFORMATION:
(212) 944-6075

BOND INTERNATIONAL CASINO
NEW YORK CITY, MON. JUNE 1, 1981

45TH STREET
AT
BROADWAY

The CLASH

WILL PLAY!

BOND SETS NEW DATES
FOR INCONVENIENCED CLASH FANS

TICKETRON TICKET HOLDERS

ALL TICKETRON TICKETS WILL BE HONORED ON ORIGINAL DATES EXCEPT:

ORIGINAL DATE	REVISED DATE:
THOSE TURNED AWAY MAY 28th	EVE. JUNE 4 (THURS.)
MAT. MAY 30	MAT. JUNE 6 (SAT.)
EVE. MAY 30	EVE. JUNE 6

BOND TICKET HOLDERS

ORIGINAL DATE	REVISED DATE
THOSE TURNED AWAY MAY 28th	EVE. JUNE 4 (THURS.)
MAT. MAY 30	MAT. JUNE 13
EVE. MAY 30	EVE. JUNE 13
EVE. MAY 31	EVE. JUNE 12 (FRI.)
JUNE 1	EVE. JUNE 8 (MON.)
JUNE 2	EVE. JUNE 9 (TUES.)
JUNE 3	EVE. JUNE 10 (WED.)
JUNE 5	EVE. JUNE 11 (THURS.)

BOND WILL EXCHANGE ALL TICKETS FOR THOSE FANS WHO CANNOT ATTEND NEW DATES. THANK YOU.

extra matinée shows. The Clash decided it was worth absorbing the cost of extra accommodation, equipment and crew wages in order to allow everyone who had bought a ticket to see them, if not quite on the date they had originally planned. Friday night saw a bit of bad feeling in the Square from those who were turned away, but Bonds had time to warn future audiences in advance, thus avoiding further last-minute disappointments. Or so they thought: on Saturday morning, the city's Building Department declared Bonds a potential fire trap and used a court order to close the club indefinitely. The fans who turned up for that afternoon's performance blocked the Square and caused a mini-riot, requiring the area to be cleared by mounted police.

Although this situation was not of the band's own making, it was a PR man's dream come true, and Kosmo immediately started wheeling and dealing with the media. Promising each of them an exclusive, he managed to get all seven of New York's major TV channels to carry a news item on the 'riot'. A special edition of the *New York Post* ran the front cover headline '"CLASH" IN TIMES SQUARE'; the band were so excited they quickly had the cover reproduced on T-shirts. The media were fascinated not only by the riots, but also by the fact that the band had chosen to play Bonds in the first place, rather than the 16,000-capacity Madison Square Garden.

On Sunday, having been badgered ceaselessly by his Clash-loving daughters, the New York Building Commissioner stepped in. He decreed that, providing Bonds reworked their fire escape system, improved security and stuck rigidly to the limit imposed by the Fire Department, they could continue with the shows. It felt like a triumph. Back in town with BAD II almost exactly ten years later, Mick told the *NME*'s James Brown, 'We ran this town. We took Broadway. De Niro was bringing his kids to see us, and the city stopped. The Clash were in town.' This highly romanticised view of the fiasco preceding the Bonds residency is made more understandable when one considers that the publicity it engendered played no small part in establishing the band in the States. As former White Panther Mick Farren, who was there to interview the Clash on behalf of the *NME*, remarked at the time, 'America seems to need a big, bold bad-ass rock'n'roll band. For some reason they're unable to produce one for themselves. [This was many years pre-Guns'N'Roses.] Basically, the Rolling Stones' old slot is going begging . . . and, if not the whole of America, at least New York seems anxious to shoehorn the Clash into it.'

It was an exciting period for the Clash. Don Letts accompanied them, with the intention of shooting a video for 'This Is Radio Clash' as well as a longer documentary feature entitled *Clash On Broadway*, capturing both the band's performances and all elements – rap, graffiti, breakdancing – of New York's emergent hip hop culture. The scenes outside Bonds provided him with dream footage, excerpts from which were projected on to the backdrop during the shows. Don introduced the band to graffiti artist Futura 2,000, whom they persuaded to spray backdrops while they played and also to take the microphone while they backed him on his own rap, 'The Escapades Of Futura 2,000'. Cutting-edge rap group Grandmaster Flash and the Furious Five, soon to push the idiom to a whole new level with 'The Message', were hired as one of the supports.

The Clash were ecstatic to tune into black New York radio station WBLS and find that the DJs were not only playing 'The Magnificent Dance' up to five times a day, but also doing their own remixes of it, dubbing on samples from the soundtrack of *Dirty Harry*. 'That bit where Harry goes, "To tell the truth, in all this excitement I kinda forgot myself . . ."' burbled Joe to a visiting Alan Lewis from *Sounds*. 'Why isn't radio that good in Britain?' Picking up on the cue, the Clash started using Ennio Morricone's theme '60 Seconds To Watch' from another Clint Eastwood movie, *For A Few Dollars More*, as their play-on music.

Martin Scorsese came along to the second night's show and, although his proposed movie *The Gangs Of New York* was no nearer production and never did get there, he invited the band to appear, fleetingly, as street hoodlum extras in *King Of Comedy*, the film he was currently shooting with favourite leading man Robert De Niro. It was an offer they could not refuse. Joe and Kosmo lived out a movie of their own, spending most nights after the gig drinking and playing pool in sleazy dive bars until the early hours of the morning.

The Clash's much-publicised interest in Nicaragua encouraged representatives of the Democratic Revolutionary Front of neighbouring El Salvador to approach them. Flattered, and happy to help the cause, the band agreed to allow them to man a stall at the venue, but baulked at the request that they be allowed to take the stage to make speeches. Instead, Joe said he would shout 'El Salvador!' towards the end of 'Washington Bullets', and they could take it in turns to declaim over the music while information leaflets were dropped from the ceiling. Alan Lewis challenged Joe about trendy cause-hopping, suggesting that the political situation was less clear-cut in El Salvador than it had been in Nicaragua. 'They haven't been given the chance to self-determine,' Joe replied. 'You ask me how deeply I've gone into the situation, and I'd have to say not deeply at all. Where can I get my information? There's an absolute restriction on accurate information . . . But I've talked to a few people from El Salvador, and I know the number of people dead or missing is running at about 60 a day at this moment.' Then, tellingly, he began to relate US intervention in that country to the situation in Vietnam in the early Sixties. 'Now today, the US is limbering up for *another* Vietnam. It's only films like *Apocalypse Now* that are gonna save El Salvador.' Alan Lewis expressed his discomfort that the Clash were in New York 'getting the kudos while other people are shedding blood'. 'I have no confusion about this,' said Joe. 'I know what I'm here to do, and I'm doing it.'

Yet another stage guest to be presented himself at the 12 June show. Poet Allen Ginsberg was one of the leading lights of the American Beat literary movement, and therefore a figure held in some regard by Mick and, especially, Joe, who greeted him by asking when he was going to run for president. Allen was invited to read a couple of poems preceding the band's encores, but instead suggested the band accompany him on a 'poem with chord changes' called 'Capital Air'. Everyone enjoyed the collaboration (except, possibly, Paul, who later admitted to Chris Salewicz that Allen, a hippy before hippies existed, was not exactly his 'cup of tea'). Allen told Barry Miles, author of the 1989 biography *Ginsberg* (and the same Barry Miles who, while interviewing the Clash back in 1976, had had a flick-knife stuck up his nose by Joe), 'They're all good musicians, Mick Jones especially, and they're very sensitive and very literate underneath all the album cover roughneck appearance. I don't know of any other band that would, in the middle of a big heavy concert, be willing to go onstage with a middle-aged goose like me.'

All this action apart, the Bonds residency was something of an anticlimax after the news hype, and even a little unpleasant. Pearl Harbour (formerly singer with the Explosions, until recently Kosmo's girlfriend and now Paul's) was along as the DJ, but one night someone spiked her drink with acid and she began to trip so badly that she had to be taken to hospital. The marathon stint at Bonds, coming directly on top of the European tour, finally proved too much for Topper. Perhaps Mick Farren caught him on a good, early night when he described him as 'rock steady . . . he lays down the foundation rhythm for the Clash with a dependability that can't be beat', or perhaps he was just trying to offer encouragement. In March 1982, Topper himself admitted to Roz Reines that his drumming had been below par for the past two years. Louise Bolloton, who had won a trip to see the band in New York in an *NME* competition (which had required readers to come up with a magnificent seven insults for the Clash), begged to differ about his state of health: 'Topper spoke to us a couple of times, but he seemed to be out of his brain most of the time.' She also described Bernie as obnoxious, astutely noting, 'It seems the only people who like him are Strummer and his girlfriend, Gaby.'

The predominately white American audience proved resistant to anything that challenged their preconceptions of a rock'n'roll gig. Most of the support bands were given a rough ride, particularly Grandmaster Flash and the Furious Five, who had rubbish thrown at them. Mick made it a furious six. 'It's disgusting,' he fumed to Mick Farren. 'I mean, it's an insult to us when you look at it. We picked the bands that opened for us. We wanted to turn the crowd on to something. They're too narrow-minded to open up to something new.' The reality of the multicultural Radio Clash appeared to be a long way off.

Even Don Letts's *Clash On Broadway* film came to nothing in the end. He had started work on the project before the band arrived in town and continued after they left, spending nearly 18 months in all travelling back and forwards between London and New York. Paul Tickell interviewed him for the *NME* the following June and was most impressed with the rough-cut he was shown, reporting that it 'runs on ideas and kaleidoscopic editing. It avoids not only clichés in its portrait of a band, but also works as a fresh depiction of New York.' In the previous month's issue of the *Face* Chris Salewicz had reported that Don was still in New York, pressing on with the 'rigorously tight editing and assembling' of the film's 'dense information content', and that 'Letts and Bernie Rhodes are currently negotiating with major distributors for an autumn release'. Subsequent upheavals in the Clash camp led to the project being shelved. 'As far as I know, the reels were stored in a rental place in New York,' Joe told Chris in 1994 for *Mojo*. 'Bernie forgot to pay the rent, and the footage was destroyed. The only surviving bit was ten minutes that Don found at the bottom of his wardrobe. Part of a cutting copy, but only ten minutes of it.' That and the footage used in the video for 'This Is Radio Clash' are all that remain of yet another ill-fated Clash movie attempt.

June and early July 1981 saw further insurrectionary activity in the UK, with London, Liverpool, Birmingham, Wolverhampton, Reading, Luton, Chester, Hull and Preston among the cities and towns wanting a riot of their own. Some of the band's critics started to get a little tetchy – much as Tony Parsons had done four years earlier – about the irony of the former White Rioters playing 'Guns Of Brixton' on Broadway while genuine expressions of frustration and dissent were taking place in their home country. That October, it was Mick's turn to put the case for the defence to the *NME*'s Paul Rambali. 'I don't think I'd make such a good rioter. I don't think I even agree with them,' said the man who, in fairness, had tried to have 'White Riot' dropped from the Clash's set as early as 1978. 'Destroying your own places, especially when the government ain't gonna give you another one, it seems really *double* dumb. I do my thing and it's a creative thing, that's how I feel I contribute. And if my absence is conspicuous on these occasions, then I say, "Don't look to me in the first place." I'm not a street fighting man. I still got a belief in the power of reason. I think I'd be really *stupid* to go out and think I could lead the people.'

Even Bernie took a measured approach: 'I don't know whether the riots were that major in terms of people being clear about what was going on. It was just a fracas. The Clash are interested in politics rather than revolution. Revolution sets a country back a hundred years. Revolution is very, very dangerous. I don't think we were ever revolutionary, I think we were always interested in the politics of the situation. And I think we still are. But I think that England's less interested.' A year earlier, he had told the same writer, 'I think you could have a cultural revolution, but not an actual revolution. The culture side of it is the interesting thing. That's possible. The other one isn't.' Bernie's argument was specific to the UK, and therefore did not necessarily contradict the band's stance on Central America. That said, both he and Mick were adopting positions that were a long way from the Clash rhetoric of 1976, without making any attempt to acknowledge or explain the change.

And Mick's and Joe's insistence that they were just artists and observers was also somewhat removed from the first-person authenticity of yesteryear.

Upon returning to London, Topper went back to his flat in Fulham where, it had been arranged, Steve Barnacle was going to move in to keep an eye on his drug intake and help him get back in shape. Unfortunately, like Gary, he was a working musician and couldn't be there all the time. For his part, Topper was both inactive and surrounded by temptation in the shape of aggressive dealers whose profits depended on keeping him hooked. 'He was telling me he didn't want to do drugs any more, he wanted to get fit and healthy,' says Steve. 'I'd come back in of a night, and there'd be this big party going on, and it was just drugs à go go. It was almost like a schoolmaster finding the pupil doing wrong. He'd be all embarrassed, but I'd say, "If you're going to do it, you're going to do it." I lived there for a couple of months, but I had to leave because I had a couple of run-ins with these dealers.'

In August 1981, the band went into Air studios, off Oxford Circus, to work on alternative DJ mixes of 'This Is Radio Clash'. With Jerry Green engineering, and fired up by their recent exposure to New York's radio and (particularly in Mick's case) clubs, the band made a pretty fair stab at getting a radio programme's worth of material out of the one song. The first remix, simply entitled 'Radio Clash', features alternative, semi-improvised lyrics from Joe. A second, entitled 'Outside Broadcast', is an interminable wig-out with female backing vocals, the main riff played on sampled car horns, and Joe's nonsense lead vocal varispeeded as low as it can go. A third, 'Radio Five', features dub effects like backwards taping and heavy echo, but is chiefly a showcase for Mick's adventures on the wheels of steel, attempting to get to grips with another of New York DJ culture's innovations, scratching.

After the expense and time devoted to recording *Sandinista!* and the accusations of self-indulgence it brought down upon the band's heads, Bernie and Joe wanted the follow-up album to be recorded quickly and cheaply in the UK. Joe was doubly determined to do so following Guy Stevens's death at the end of August. Rehearsals for the Clash's next string of dates commenced at the beginning of September, at Ear studios rehearsal room, in the Peoples' Hall, Freston Road, in the shadow of the Westway. It was suggested that the Clash should combine these rehearsals with songwriting sessions in an attempt to recapture the spirit of *London Calling*. Joe was also harking back to his 1979-vintage idea of making an album on a TEAC portable studio. His interest in production values had never been marked, as he told the *NME*'s Richard Cook in 1984: 'The greatest records on my shelf are the ones made with a couple of microphones.' Paul was in accord, his passion for obscure and primitive rockabilly having increased during the course of the year.

Mick's interests had, of course, taken him in almost completely the opposite direction in both musical and technological terms. To him, Joe's suggestion seemed to be – and perhaps was – another attempt to undermine his own position in the band. A compromise of sorts was agreed. The Clash hired the Rolling Stones' mobile studio – several steps up from a portable – and linked it up to the rehearsal room. Jerry Green was once again brought in to act as engineer. Joe was still standing up for funk and reggae in the interviews he gave at the end of the year, telling Keri Phillips of Australian magazine *RAM*, 'When I put on a rap 12-inch or a Jamaican reggae record, I know that the singers are gonna hit me with something I'm not gonna expect in a million years.' But this was so much lip-service. The critics had shaken Joe, and his commitment to the Clash's recent musical direction was already in doubt: several of the songs recorded on the mobile evidence a bias away from the funky groove music that was Mick's preference at the time towards the retro musics favoured by Joe and Paul.

Even Mick's solo composition 'Should I Stay Or Should I Go' is old-fashioned. It owes something to the Sharks' 'Sophistication', but is more strongly reminiscent of Mitch Ryder and the Detroit Wheels' 1966 US hit 'Little Latin Lupe Lu' (a long-time favourite of Chrissie Hynde). Its lyric was made to seem prophetic by future events. 'Midnight To Stevens' is the band's tribute to Guy. Credited to Strummer–Jones, it is a sentimental ballad, part Ian Hunter, part Sixties girl group, with a lyric alluding to the producer's achievements as well as failings. Paul, Mick and Joe co-wrote 'Long Time Jerk', harmonica-driven cajun skiffle with a lyric on a vaguely romantic theme. Also 'First Night Back In London', a sort of club-footed rockabilly funk soundtracking the spooky account of a drug bust. Either the lyric was added later or else it too was to prove uncannily prophetic. Although Topper's lifestyle would seem to be the source of inspiration for the song, it had also reduced him to the status of 'just the drummer': he did not contribute as composer to any of the above material. Whether or not he had any say in other songs written and recorded at this time was subsequently obscured by the band's decision to persevere with the collective Clash songwriting credit for their fifth album.

Political subject matter had so far been off the agenda, but Joe set this straight with the sardonic 'Know Your Rights'. A souped-up hard rockabilly number with rolling guitar in the style of the Ramrods' 'Ghost Riders In The Sky', it can think of only three basic human rights to list, all subject to provisos which ultimately render them worthless; it closes by suggesting the only rights most people are likely to experience are the ones the police read while making an arrest. 'Inoculated City' adapts a military march for another anti-war song, this time attacking the unquestioning chain of command from president to private. Some of these songs were worked up for the tour, the imminence of which meant further recording had to be suspended until late November.

At the end of September 1981, the Clash revived the magnificent seven residency concept at the Mogador in Paris, before commencing their long-delayed UK tour in October: a mere six provincial dates followed by another magnificent seven residency at the Lyceum in London. Robin Crocker attended the Mogador residency. The account he filed for *ZigZag* was predictably enthusiastic, and included one revealing vignette: a dressing-room discussion instigated by Bernie that developed into a row about Topper's condition. Robin dismissed this as 'completely unnecessary paranoia', citing Topper's ability to count off 50 press-ups before taking the stage as proof that he was in the best of health. Always physically fit, Topper's physique was just about coping; the problems were with his co-ordination, erratic behaviour and unreliability. Robin was himself a heavy drinker and gung-ho hedonist, which goes some way to explaining his refusal to recognise the damage Topper was doing to himself.

The *NME*'s Paul Rambali also caught up with the Clash in Paris, but his access was limited to Joe and Mick. He asked the usual spiky questions and was met with defiant retorts. Mick objected to being called a remote rock star. Joe objected to what he perceived to be the paper's obsession with the band's credibility and its relentless negativity. 'If they're teaching their readers to hate us, then I'd like to ask the *NME* who they're teaching their readers to trust? Which groups? Which ideas? I'm looking hard, and I can't see anybody.'

As ever, the Clash had allowed themselves to be conditioned by the music press to expect hostility from the audiences on the UK tour. They were consequently taken aback by the positive reception and the accompanying belated revelation that most fans were unlikely to have their opinions swayed by a little negative criticism. 'They were so keen to see us, and I can't say there was any resentment, or anything like that,' Mick told Duncan Campbell the following year. 'It touched us all.' 'That's another bum steer that the *NME* gave me,' Joe grumbled to that paper's Roz Reines in March 1982. 'I believed them when they said we weren't liked there [in the UK]. In fact, the guy on the street was digging us. But I believed them, and they lied to me. I assumed that they would accurately reflect the mood of the country.'

The response they received from their UK fans confirmed the band in a belief that both Mick and Joe had been voicing since early that summer, when a roadie named Jerry had told them that British rock fans were becoming dispirited by the Clash's failure to make it big. 'If I don't make it, then all the kids who are watching can say to themselves, "Well, shit, they didn't make it, they didn't get out, what hope is there for us to make it?"' Joe had later told Mick Farren in New York. 'If we make it, then those kids know that *they* got a chance, too.' Now enshrined as Clash policy, this theme was taken as a mandate to relax more and more of their punk era principles as they went in search of success: not to line their own pockets, *heaven forfend*, but as a symbolic gesture on behalf of the downtrodden masses. It was conveniently forgotten that the Clash had never previously thought of 'making it' in commercial terms as a goal in itself. Nor was it acknowledged that the idea of 'the kids' living vicariously through rock'n'roll heroes was the very antithesis of punk's DIY spirit. The bottom line was that the band wanted to make a lot of money because they were sick of being in debt, but, being the Clash, they couldn't just admit that to journalists; nor, it would appear, could they admit it to themselves.

The desire to make an 'urban Vietnam' come to life on-stage had encouraged the Clash to bring over graffiti backdrop artist Futura 2,000, adorn the stage with tiger-striped checkpoint barriers and open the show with an air raid siren. They also wore Alex Michon-designed updates of 1977's Pop Star Army Fatigues, which were just as colourful as the earlier versions, but had sawn-off sleeves and a more American military feel; adverse reaction to the *Sandinista!* sleeve and 'The Call Up' video had obviously affected the band not one whit. Barney Hoskyns attended the first of the Lyceum gigs on behalf of the *NME* and gave the Clash the traditional good kicking. According to Barney, their material consisted of 'wavering, sanctimonious pseudo-songs' and 'decisively *unloose* funk-rock'; Joe kept 'emitting that absurd screech about five times during the course of every song'; Mick played 'some of the worst guitar the Lyceum has probably ever witnessed'; and 'the Clash aren't terribly exciting on stage – had you ever noticed?'

Melody Maker's Adam Sweeting was more reserved, though he agreed with Barney about Mick's guitar playing that particular night. He began his review, 'Who'd be the Clash? Not me, squire. They can't win', and ended it, 'They've had the sense to move on and diversify, and in many cases they've done it well ... Whose fault is it that, however well the Clash play, their fiercest finest hour has passed?' After attending two more shows during the course of the residency, he wrote a second, longer piece acknowledging that he had warmed to the band more on each occasion and wondering why it was they were now so out of favour with the music press. Under the heading 'The Clash And Cocktail Culture' he likened the New Pop *Zeitgeist* to that of the flappers in the Twenties. 'This new attitude seems to me like an abject admission of defeat ... Instead of determination we have submission. Instead of heart, we prefer plastic soul ... Maybe everything's too serious and depressing for music to be serious anymore ... After the challenges of punk and the earthy dynamics of its aftermath, I think we're back to worse than square one. I think we're working for the clampdown.' Over the next year, Joe would be increasingly drawn to this line of thinking.

The debate on the Clash's relevance was continued by Gavin Martin in his *NME* review of 'This Is Radio Clash', released as a 7-inch single on 11 November 1981 and a 12-inch on 4 December (the staggered release of different formats is a typical record company marketing ploy intended to attract repeat buyers): 'Another rag bag of musical clichés and political simplifications ... a sprawling, splintered fantasy which presents the zombified vision of would-be media guerrillas with rampant hysteria. "This Is Radio Clash" is a four part epic: scrubbed up, dubbed down and sellotaped together ... More than any group I can think of – and that's not to say their intentions aren't sincere – the Clash highlight the age-old inadequacy of the white musician as culture vulture.' The single stalled at number 47 in the UK charts and failed to show at all in the US.

Satisfied with the way recording had progressed using the mobile at Ear studios, Joe suggested continuing in similar vein once the tour was over. Mick, however, decided the shift away from what he wanted to do had gone far enough. It was his turn to offer an ultimatum. 'He said, "Good luck to you then, because I'm not coming to the sessions,"' Joe told Richard Cook in 1984. '"If you do it in New York, I'll turn up." So we got a studio there, so the Emperor could attend.' The studio was Electric Lady: familiar, but ruinously expensive. Not only did the band have to pay for the recording facilities, but – not having just completed a US tour this time, and therefore without their own equipment – they also had to hire just about everything else. Jerry Green, by now their engineer of choice, had just become a father. Whereas he would have been available for recording in London, he made it clear that he had no intention of leaving his family in order to come to New York. Which meant the Clash also had to work with unfamiliar personnel.

Joe, Paul and the management team shared similar feelings about the Clash's future development. Mick was out of favour partly because of his refusal to acknowledge budget restrictions and partly because of his errant behaviour over the last six months. Topper was simply becoming a liability. Although not necessarily of like mind, the two outcasts teamed up for mutual support, and the band thus split into two factions. Mick and Topper were still by far the most musically gifted members of the Clash and, as songwriters, Joe and Paul had previously relied heavily upon the creative input and arrangement skills of the other two; with Topper's capabilities limited and Mick's co-operation withdrawn, the singer and bassist now found themselves musically marginalised. Joe was still in charge of the lyrical content, but much of the music recorded at the Electric Lady sessions shows a shift towards Mick's preferences. His insistence on taking charge of production – more assertively so than on previous occasions – also gave him control over the sound of both the new material and that recorded earlier at Ear studios. To put it mildly, this did not go down too well with Joe and Paul.

The unsteady boat was rocked even further when, upon returning to the UK for Christmas, Topper was arrested – on what was indeed his first night back in London – for smuggling heroin into Heathrow Airport. Prison was a real possibility, but when Topper appeared at Uxbridge Magistrates Court on 17 December, his defence counsel pleaded that he was a valuable member of the band – 'recently voted one of the world's top five drummers' – and was needed at the recording sessions; it was also admitted that he was an addict, but one who was now determined to mend his ways. He was fined £500 and told, 'Unless you accept treatment, you will be the best drummer in the graveyard.' Realising he had pushed his luck about as far as it would go, Topper began the long struggle to kick his habit.

It had been decided to make the record a single album. Joe believed that

Epic had deliberately failed to promote *Sandinista!* because it was in danger of setting a precedent for economically unsound multi-disc releases. Labelmate Bruce Springsteen had followed up *London Calling* with *The River*, and Epic, according to Joe, were determined to stop the rot. This was another possible explanation for the cancellation of the 60-date US tour earlier in the year. 'Even here in New York,' Joe told *RAM*'s Keri Phillips during the album sessions, 'if my tape-operator wants to buy a copy of *Sandinista!*, which is supposedly my current LP – and remember we're not in Peru or Baghdad or Bombay or even Alice Springs, we're here in New York, supposedly the centre of the Western World – he can't even buy it. *That's* why it's gonna be one record.' Whether or not his conspiracy theory was grounded in fact, this was a rationalisation of an expedient move: the Clash wanted to make money from their fifth album, and would not be able to do so if they continued the trend established by their last two VFM releases.

With some material already in the can and far fewer songs required than for the last two albums, recording should have been completed relatively quickly, but the unsettled atmosphere was not conducive to productivity. 'I had a stand-up argument for two hours with Mick when we were making [the album],' Paul told Richard Cook in 1984. 'We weren't solving anything. There was just no compromise. With Mick, it was do it his way or sulk.'

Futura 2,000 was on hand, and the band helped him record 'The Escapades Of Futura 2,000', eventually released on Celluloid records in May 1983. They also roped him in to rap on their own 'Overpowered By Funk'. Other songs continued the fusion trend of *Sandinista!*, but, instead of globe-hopping, used the exotic ingredients to create a more individual sound. 'We're just trying to boil it down to one music,' Joe told Roz Reines early in 1982. 'Not trying to ignore anything that we've heard before, but we want to make it our own, and all at once in every track.' In 'Car Jamming' Joe sings of a 'funky multinational anthem', which seems to have been the general idea.

'Car Jamming' is a melodic funk groove with a half-sung, half-rapped lead vocal and backing vocals from Ellen Foley. 'Cool Confusion' is sort of semi-electro dub–funk. Both 'Ghetto Defendant' and Paul's 'Red Angel Dragnet' have reggae lurking somewhere in their rock grooves. 'Atom Tan' has a soul strut riding behind its call-and-response vocals. 'Kill Time' and 'The Beautiful People' are variants on calypso–funk. Topper gave some indication of working methods in the *Clash On Broadway* booklet when he revealed that 'Straight To Hell' began as a Mick Jones guitar doodle that would not work with a rock'n'roll beat; so Topper grafted on a bossa nova drum pattern, itself drawn from a Brazilian hybrid of samba, baiao and jazz.

It would be a mistake to take this, and the fact that Topper single-handedly wrote the music for 'Rock The Casbah', as an indication of his creative resurgence. The piano riff for the latter song was one that he had been toying with for years. Nevertheless, finding himself the only member of the band in the studio one morning, Topper was sufficiently industrious to record the piano, the drums and the bass (though Jerry Green maintains one of the American engineers was responsible for the last of these) for what was supposed to be a rough demo. In the event, the band just looped the tape to double its length and used it as a backing track. Mick added guitar and Joe the lyric he had written to suit, inspired by the floggings meted out to anyone owning a disco album in Iran.

The inspiration for Joe's other lyrics was as varied as usual, while touching on several familiar themes. The New York street vibe – specifically rush-hour gridlock – is largely responsible for 'Car Jamming'. The New Year's Day shooting of Frankie Melvin, a member of subway vigilante group the Red Angels, resulted in 'Red Angel Dragnet'. The inner city drug crisis informs 'Ghetto Defendant', in which heroin-induced despondency is blamed for lack of positive communal action, and part of 'Straight To Hell'. This song also offers 'Washington Bullets'-style vignettes about the rejections by their parent culture experienced by unemployed English northerners, mixed-race children of Vietnamese women and American GIs, and immigrants in general. 'The Beautiful People' and 'Cool Confusion' are both vicious critiques of those who live on the other side of the social divide. 'The beautiful people are ugly, too' insists the former, while the latter takes its inspiration from a first-hand observation made in New York's clubland: the in-crowd's tendency to sweep into a place, make a show of looking around with disdain, then sweep out again. Both 'Ghetto Defendant' and 'Atom Tan' allude to the bigger picture, ending on decidedly Strummeresque apocalyptic notes.

Like the music, however, the lyrics seem more unified than those for the Clash's previous album. Joe's vision of an 'urban Vietnam' is pervasive: an inner city ghetto overrun by drugs and guns is the scene for 'Ghetto Defendant', 'Overpowered By Funk', 'Car Jamming', 'Red Angel Dragnet' and much of 'Straight To Hell'. Not only that, but some tracks make a direct connection between this scenario and the real Vietnam: 'Straight To Hell' juxtaposes verses dealing with both environments; 'Red Angel Dragnet' depicts the Red Angels as taxi driver Travis Bickle's heirs; napalm is mentioned in 'Overpowered By Funk' and a crippled veteran and Agent Orange in 'Car Jamming'.

Because Joe's central conceit requires him to adopt a specifically American perspective, the lyrics have little to do with London or even UK life. The steel mills in 'Straight To Hell' and Jack the Ripper in 'Red Angel Dragnet' are the sum total of references to the culture that bore the Clash. But nor are the songs located in a 'real' New York, or any other American city. 'What is the dream? I'll tell it / To live like they do in the movies,' states 'Red Angel Dragnet', and that applies to more than just the vigilante squad of the song's title; Joe's 'urban Vietnam' imagery owes much to the movies, and movie references abound. 'Death Is A Star', like 'Sean Flynn', could almost be an atmospheric soundtrack piece, piano courtesy of Tymon Dogg. 'It's about the way we all queue up at the cinema to see someone get killed,' Joe told Roz

Reines early the following year. 'These days, the public execution is the celluloid execution. I was examining why I want to go and see these movies, because deep in my heart I want to see a man pull out a machine gun and go *blam, blam, blam* into somebody's body.' Similarly, the protagonist of 'Atom Tan' whiles away the four-minute nuclear warning watching the skies for the Lone Ranger or some other comforting celluloid or comic superhero.

The album as eventually released bears the catalogue number FMLN 2, a gesture of support for El Salvador's rebel forces (FMLN stands for Farabundo Marti Liberación Nacional). Yet the lyrics do not go out into the world as did those on *Sandinista!* Instead, they are set in Clashworld, a movie-like Joe Strummer-created fantasy land where the Vietnam jungle abuts the urban slum. Appropriately enough, when the sessions were coming to a close, the album was going by the working title *Rat Patrol From Fort Bragg.*

Everything was supposed to be wrapped up by the end of December, and at the end of January 1982 the Clash were due to resume the tour aimed at breaking into new markets, which would take them to Japan, New Zealand, Australia and South-east Asia. But between Christmas and New Year the band were still recording backing tracks for new numbers. The project was growing and growing, and beginning to get as far out of hand as the last one had. Not only did they finish up with far too many songs – 17, counting unused material brought over from the Marcus and Ear studios sessions – but the tracks themselves were lengthy, more in the tradition of extended 12-inch rap and funk mixes than the short sharp shocks of punk singles and album tracks. Bernie Rhodes was heard to grumble, 'Does everything have to be as long as a raga?' It gave Joe the opening line for 'Rock The Casbah', but was intended as a real criticism of the Clash's, and particularly Mick's, self-indulgence: experiments with Indian ragas in the mid to late Sixties had precipitated the progressive rock so loathed by Class of '76 punks. More importantly, as the tussle over 'The Magnificent Seven' had proved, both the record company and mainstream radio were antagonistic towards extended singles.

As recording went over schedule and way over budget, tempers became even more frayed. During one memorable argument Joe accused Mick of beginning all the rot by insisting the album be recorded in New York. 'He turned around and said, "I was only joking,"' Joe told Richard Cook, still aghast over two years after the event. In early January, Mick and Joe, by this time barely talking, started working separate shifts, the former recording guitar overdubs by day and the latter vocals by night. Unhappy with how things were going under Mick's overall direction and finding it difficult to communicate with the American engineers, Joe made a desperate phone call to Jerry Green, begging him to come out and help for just a little while. Against his better judgement, Jerry heeded the call on 5 January, and ended up being away from his partner and new-born child for a total of three weeks. 'At the end, we had two studios going simultaneously,' he says.

It was during one of Joe's vocal overdub sessions that Allen Ginsberg turned up to visit the band. Joe, who was working on 'Ghetto Defendant' at the time, invited him to supply 'the Voice of God' for the track. Allen asked for the name of some typical punk dances (the Worm being a favourite in San Francisco), and improvised a poem around Joe's lyric, to which he also contributed. 'He said, "You're the greatest poet in America; what can *you* do with this?"' Allen told *Rolling Stone*, modestly. 'So I made some suggestions, and he was real smart and open, not resentful or begrudging.' Barry Miles's *Ginsberg* revealed that the poet attended a total of seven night-long sessions and worked on 'three or four' lyrics altogether. Worried that Allen's contribution had been blown up out of proportion, thereby robbing him of due credit for developing his own lyric-writing skills, Joe tried to play it down in the *Clash On Broadway* booklet: 'I asked Ginsberg for a word once, but it was just one word.' In fact, it was slightly more than that, but not all the tracks Allen worked on made it to the finished album, and the verse he helped most with on 'Ghetto Defendant' was subsequently excised from the song.

On another occasion, Joe decided that he and a visiting Joe Ely should record the backing vocals for 'Should I Stay Or Should I Go' in Spanish. It was such a spur of the moment thing that they had to get tape operator Eddie Garcia to phone his mother to translate. 'I've had some Spanish people tell me it's rubbish,' Joe told *Melody Maker* in 1988. 'But I've explained that it's Ecuadorian Spanish and got off the hook.' Another late item was the toilet cleaner commercial '2,000 Flushes' that was added to the fade of 'Inoculated City', evidence of Mick's continued enthusiasm for unusual dance mix samples. It was a joke that was to rebound on the Clash. The next time they were in the US, following the record's release, they had to sneak around like wanted men in order to avoid being served with papers pertaining to a multi-million dollar lawsuit launched by Flushco Inc., the manufacturers of the product in question. Perseverance from the company's lawyers led to a temporary injunction against further production of the album, prefiguring the sampling and copyright debate of the mid to late Eighties.

Shortly before the band was due to leave for Japan, Mick presented the rest of the Clash with what he considered to be a final mix for a 15-track 65-minute double album including everything in the can except 'Overpowered By Funk' and 'Long Time Jerk'. The others rejected it out of hand. Joe later referred to it as a 'home movie mix'. There was also too much of it. 'I don't believe anyone is that great that they don't write crap sometimes,' Joe told *Creem*'s Bill Holdship in 1984. 'Mick wouldn't have that. In his mind, he was a great artist, and great artists don't write crap. It was dangerous. I think Mick's got a tendency to bring yes-men close to him, and shut out people who will tell him the damn truth. Remember, I'm supposed to be his buddy and partner, and I said to him, "Mick, I don't think you can produce." What I meant was that you can't just sit in the chair, move some faders, and claim to be the producer. And it was, "You bastard! I thought you were my friend!"'

Some efforts were made to repair what the other members of the band considered to be the damage, but work had to be abandoned when the Clash made a last-minute dash for the plane to take them to Japan. As the album was now long overdue and CBS–Epic were piling on the pressure, it was decided to continue working on it in Australia, the only place where the band could book studio space and still hope for an April release.

The live shows were to feature a career-summarising 'best of' set in acknowledgement of the virgin territories the Clash were visiting. The Japanese dates, beginning on 24 January 1982 at Tokyo's Shibuya Kohkaida, generated mixed feelings among the Clash: if anything, the audiences were a little too eager, and the band were somewhat disconcerted to be treated like 'part-time Western Gods'. Joe grumbled that the Japanese should look to themselves and their own culture. As the band had gone to Japan in the first place because its young people's enthusiasm for western rock music made it the second largest single-nation record market in the world (after the US), this was a little rich, but Joe was not being wholly hypocritical. 'If we'd wanted to make money in Japan, we would've played Budokan like Bob Dylan,' he announced at a Sydney press conference that February. 'Thirty thousand Nips jumping in the air, throw yer money on the plane and – *bingo!* – *that's rock'n'roll.* We played nine times in as many days, and never to more than 3,000 people. And that's nine days' worth of expenses, and all.'

The Sydney press conference was set up at short notice, in the mammals section of the Museum of Applied Arts and Sciences, to boost flagging ticket sales of the magnificent seven dates scheduled at the city's Capitol Theatre as part of the Australian leg of the tour. It required the band to make a stop-over on the flight from Japan to New Zealand. In fully-fledged ranter mode, Joe allowed no other member of the Clash – or, indeed, the assembled press – to get a word in edgeways for the half-hour of the conference's duration. Standing while the rest of the band sat by his side and nodded, he held forth on any subject that entered his head, but did not forget that the point of the venture was to hard sell the Clash as a live attraction: 'We're here because we're exciting. We jump about, wiggle our bums, and there's nothing wrong with that!'

Under the headline 'MAMMALS BABBLE: the Flying Sydney Press Conference' Bruce Elder and Ed St John, there on behalf of the New Zealand edition of *Rolling Stone*, described it thus: 'Joe Strummer's performance is an immensely amusing one. This wasn't the usual deadly serious affair as uninformed journalists ask the subjects inane questions, but a holy rollin' one-man stand up, political flag-waving harangue by a man who – if he delivers one tenth as good live on stage – must be a performer to leave others flatfooted. The Clash's Sydney press conference was a real occasion.'

Topper's reputation had preceded him, and before being allowed into Auckland, New Zealand, the band were subjected to a four-hour customs examination that added further to their jet lag. The impression that Joe was the band's leader was one that was picked up by nearly all Antipodean media representatives. Back in late 1976, both Rob Harper and Tony Parsons had found him to be the most striking member of the Clash, but somehow the band had managed to maintain the impression they were a team. Now Joe seemed to be pushing himself forward. Having declared 1982 the Year of the Body, he was physically and verbally active at all times to the point of mania. In the New Zealand edition of *Rolling Stone* Malcolm McSporran recounted how Joe had been up at 7 a.m. the morning after his arrival, asking questions about local culture and politics and busking in the town's main street with a ukulele bought specially for the purpose. Shades of 1972.

Won over – despite Joe's initial reluctance to grant him an interview – Malcolm went on to describe him as both enigmatic and charismatic and backed up his own impressions with those of New Zealand tour manager Graeme Nesbitt: 'Joe calls all the shots. After a show, everyone goes out and rages. Sometimes he goes too, but invariably he's up at six o'clock or even five the next morning wandering the streets writing notes. He's always writing notes. Everybody wakes up to find notes from Joe under their doors bearing legends like, "The order of the songs tonight is . . ." or "I don't like that lighting bit . . ." or "Raymond, you're fucking up the backstage passes. Don't do it again!" His overview is complete, right down to the last detail.' Having had limited contact with the Clash Myth, let alone the band themselves, Malcolm and Graeme had no idea that this autocratic behaviour was a departure from the Clash's formerly – nominally, at least – democratic set-up. Nor could they imagine how difficult it was for Mick to take. Feeling isolated within the Clash camp and therefore unable to compete, when not playing live, he stayed in his room and brooded.

Mid-February's return to Sydney for the magnificent seven residency allowed Roz Reines to catch up with the band for an *NME* interview. There were a few words from Mick and a message from Topper regarding the evils of heroin, but Joe once again dominated the resulting feature. Still manic – lifting the hotel room television in the absence of weights – he advised, at some considerable length, mass emigration from England to New Zealand. After attacking the *NME*, he gave yet another indication that the Clash were no longer overly concerned with the UK: 'I'd rather they hated us in Britain as long as they hear what we have to say in America. I don't think that the English need the Clash too much because they're too smart.' Again, this was a convenient view to hold, and not a little glib. He sidestepped questions about any contradictions inherent in the new Clash approach by hiding behind the word 'paradox': 'don't be afraid of the word paradox'.

The band enjoyed the heat and the sunshine of New Zealand, but even when advising emigration from dull grey England, Joe admitted that he was talking of Australia and New Zealand purely as *scenic* paradises. An acknowledgement that all was not rosy beneath the surface came during the Sydney Capitol residency, when Aboriginal Land Rights Campaigner Gary Foley was invited on-stage to speak over the end of 'Armagideon Time'. The band did not find their reception in the two former British colonies any less unnerving than it had been in Japan. 'Every time we come to a town, they go, "Oh, we've been waiting for five years for you,"' Joe told Roz. 'I'd rather come as an extra, a bonus to the local scene, not like the staple diet was in town for 20 minutes and then left.'

In New Zealand Joe placed the audience at 'around 1978'. One of them even spat at him . . . because he thought that was what punks were supposed to do. 'The message of punk was Do It Yourself,' Joe told Roz. 'The bands were home-made, the fanzines were home-made, and sometimes the guitars and instruments. Somehow it's been distorted along the line. Now you just get carbon copies of skinheads and punks in far-flung corners of the globe. They're not dealing with their own town, they're just wishing they could be somewhere else.' Yet another 'paradox': how did this fit in with resorting to emigration as an escape route?

The lengthy shows were rendered even more arduous by the intense heat and humidity, and the Clash started to push themselves during the Sydney residency, when they would head for the recording studio straight after the gig and work through the night. Before going in, Joe admitted to Roz that he had been trying not to think about the album since leaving New York, and that he was 'semi-scared'. She met Mick a couple of days later, and he told her that band relations had been further strained by a 4 a.m. disagreement which had forced the most recent session to be abandoned. Not only were the arguments continuing – with all the rest of the band contributing their two penn'orth to the attempts to correct Mick's original mix – but, as Topper recalled for the *Clash On Broadway* booklet, it was not easy to make the fine sonic judgements required when everyone had been half deafened by a lengthy rock'n'roll gig. The album remained unfinished. An indication that Joe, in particular, had been driving himself too hard was given when he collapsed from heat exhaustion and dehydration during the Perth show.

At the end of the month, the band made their début in Hong Kong, then went on to Bangkok. In his liner notes for 1988's *The Story Of The Clash, Volume 1* 'band valet Albert Transom' described the gig at Thamasat University thus: 'when people ask me what it was like, all I can remember is I spent the gig doubled up behind the back curtain with my hand over my mouth 'cause of the sight of all these blokes with turbans doing the pogo. Then some of the turbans began unravelling and it all began to get into a big orange tangle while they kept thrashing about.'

The motive for the Thailand jaunt, unlike the other legs of the tour, was not to open up a new market. 'We were number one there, but I think everybody who visits there is automatically number one for the time they're there,' Mick told the *NME*'s James Brown in 1991. 'I think it's quite corrupt, like the police chief and the guy in charge of the music industry are the same man. They don't have real records, just bootleg tapes.' Not that this meant that the band were playing there for altruistic reasons: they were in search of something as close as possible to the Vietnam vibe, partly to live out their own fantasies and partly to enable Pennie Smith to take some suitable photographs for the album cover and forthcoming *NME* feature.

'We went mad in Thailand,' Mick told James Brown. 'It was like *Apocalypse Now*. When you go that far away, it takes a long time to get back ... One great thing that happened was we were out in the bars, dressed like *The Deer Hunter*, and they have these girls in the really heavy places dancing on the bar. Joe and Kosmo got up and did the frug on the bar with these girls. When you come back from that, it's hard to get back into normal life. It was a fantastic adventure.' The Vietnam veteran fantasy was given an unwelcome shot of realism when first the band's money was stolen, marooning them in their hotel until more could be wired over, and then Paul got sick. 'He'd jumped into what looked like a black puddle, and thousands of flies flew up at him,' Mick told James. 'Then a couple of days after, he had some dodgy food and he got seriously ill.' The rest of the band elected to stay on and keep him company, and the supposedly brief visit was extended to three weeks. According to Pennie Smith, the local hospital diagnosed a twisted colon, and at one point were proposing removing a section of his bowel. Unconvinced, Paul postponed a decision until he was able to make it home, where doctors revealed he was suffering from a bug that, though severe, neither required nor justified such drastic surgery.

Band unity was rent asunder again in mid-March 1982 when the Clash turned their attention once more to the vexatious topic of the new album. The mixes were still unsatisfactory, and there seemed no way of selecting a balanced single album from the raga-length tracks as they now stood. Having failed to reach any kind of compromise with Mick, the others agreed to override him completely and bring in an experienced producer-engineer to oversee a substantial remix. Drawing up a short list, Bernie astounded everyone by suggesting Gus Dudgeon, Elton John's producer; then it became apparent that he meant Glyn Johns. Glyn was an inspired suggestion. Not only had he worked with the Rolling Stones, the Beatles and the Faces, but he had developed something of a speciality in salvage operations. While he had been commissioned to put together a warts'n'all Beatles album from songs recorded in 1969 during the making of the *Let It Be* film, his *Get Back* was ultimately deemed to have a few warts too many. The source material was subsequently reworked by Phil Spector to form the frankly syrupy *Let It Be* album, released in 1970. The following year, though, Glyn got a chance to prove his mettle when Pete Townshend, on the point of a nervous breakdown, brought him in to put together a single album from the over-ambitious, aborted double *Lifehouse* project. The resulting *Who's Next* was arguably the Who's last great album.

Rat Patrol From Fort Bragg had originally been pencilled in for release at the end of April 1982, to coincide with the beginning of a UK tour. With no time to spare, Glyn and Joe booked straight into Wessex and got to work. During the Sydney press conference Joe had set out his agenda: 'We're going to deliver an album that those suckers down at CBS [including Epic] won't even suss, so they'll just serve it up with their Boston and Foreigner. Then we're going to get out there and fight for it, because it's no use being priests. It's all very well getting heard by cult freaks, but I want to get through to the creep who's filling his head with "Stuff 'er on the bed and shove it to her, yeah, yeah, yeah!" That's the person I want to reach. All eight million of him.' This had not been merely a statement to the effect that The Quest was ongoing, but also a first-time acknowledgement that, at least as far as Joe was concerned, the band were prepared to compromise musically in order to achieve success.

The album Joe had described in Sydney bore little relation to the album the Clash had recorded in New York. Glyn's job, as Joe saw it, was to do as much as possible to eradicate that discrepancy. Much of the more left-field material was dropped altogether. 'The Beautiful People' and 'Kill Time' remain unreleased to this day; 'Cool Confusion' and 'First Night Back In London' joined 'Long Term Jerk' on the future single B-sides list; 'Overpowered By Funk' was reinstated, bringing the total number of tracks to be included on the album to a manageable dozen.

These then underwent a substantial overhaul. The drums and guitars were pushed up in the mix, and the former dosed with echo to give the album the big sound beloved of American AOR radio. The tracks were edited, often severely, to fit the space available. 'Straight To Hell' lost a verse from the middle, 'Red Angel Dragnet' and 'Ghetto Defendant' their final verses and 'Car Jamming' and 'Inoculated City' their codas; the longest raga of all, 'Sean Flynn', was cut from its original seven minutes to four and a half. Two of the three more blatant 'rock' songs on the album were also designated single material and were afforded even more attention. Joe improved the lyric for 'Know Your Rights' and re-recorded the vocal. The Spanish backing vocals were dropped from the first verse of 'Should I Stay Or Should I Go'. Mick was prevailed upon to re-record the lead vocal, omitting the jocular phrasing of the line 'Should I cool it or should I blow?' and substituting 'If you want me off your back' for the smuttier original, 'On your front or round the back?', which was distinctly less suitable for mainstream radio.

Futura 2,000 had already designed a lyric sheet and, although the myriad changes rendered it obsolete, it was too late (and too expensive) to have him redo it from scratch. Thus, some lyrics appear on the inner sleeve in their original form and some have been sloppily altered. Joe also decided to stream-line the album title to the less quirky but decidedly vulgar and unimaginative *Combat Rock*. Everything about the salvaged album was ostensibly Joe's show: Paul and Topper were not consulted over the remodelling, and Mick was so devastated that, aside from re-recording his vocal, he seldom attended the Wessex sessions. 'Mick's attitude was that I ruined his music,' Joe told *Creem*'s Bill Holdship in 1984, before going on to make it clear that, had he had enough alternative material to hand, he himself would have gone even further with the changes: '50 per cent of *Combat Rock* was great rock, but the other 50 per cent was what Phil Spector would call *wiggy*.'

When reading that appraisal, one has to bear in mind that, during 1983, Joe disowned the belief he had so frequently laid claim to between 1980 and 1982: that rap–funk and reggae were the cutting-edge musics of the day. Joe and Glyn's final version of the album is by no means a desecration, but it goes far enough – perhaps too far – in its pursuit of the mainstream; and, while it could have used some editing, even Mick's original double was not a disaster. More than anything, the salvage operation proved that effective compromise within the band was now totally beyond the Clash.

After taking delivery of the tapes at the beginning of April 1982, CBS set about a rush-release schedule that would put the album into the shops by 14 May, preceded on 23 April by a single coupling 'Know Your Rights' with 'First Night Back In London'. Meanwhile, the band went straight into rehearsals for a 19-date tour of the UK, which would go under the banner of the Know Your Rights Tour, and open on Monday, 26 April, in Aberdeen. Or that was the plan. The 1 May issue of the *NME*, the news pages of which went to press on Tuesday, 27 April, reported that Joe had gone missing. He had disappeared on the 21st and, as a result, the first two dates of the tour had been postponed.

'Joe's personal conflict is: where does the socially concerned rock artist stand in the bubblegum environment of today?' pontificated Bernie. 'I feel he's probably gone away for a serious rethink.' The manager went on to make digs at both the general public – following the previous year's poor singles and album performance, the Clash had slumped to a new low in the 1981 end-of-year *NME* readers' poll while the Jam still held sway at the top – and the UK music press itself: 'I think he feels some resentment about the fact that he was about to go slogging his guts out just for people to slag him off, saying he's wearing the wrong trousers. A lot of people want to destroy the group, but we won't let that happen because we're an international group. But they could still destroy the Clash in this country.' After which exhibition of rampant paranoia, he appealed to everyone for help in finding Joe, pointing out that the situation was costing the band a small fortune.

A stop-press addendum in the same issue of the paper reported that Steve Taylor, a journalist for *The Face*, claimed to have shared a compartment with Joe and his girlfriend on a boat-train to Paris on Thursday, 22 April. The following week's *NME* revealed there was still no sign of the Clash singer, and that the first half of the tour had now been rescheduled for July. The Paris lead seemed to have been a false trail. As Charles Shaar Murray later reported, rumours circulated that Joe was living in Amsterdam, working as a navvy in Marseilles or had been fished out of the river in Glasgow, among several other options. The third week's *NME*, dated 15 May, stated that he was still missing and another five dates had been postponed. The next week's paper announced that all the remaining dates had been blown out, but that at least Joe had been found: on Monday, 17 May, Kosmo had set off to some unspecified location in Europe to fetch him back. The news pages of the 29

May issue dropped another bombshell. Joe had rejoined the band in time to play the Lochem Festival in Holland on Thursday, the 20th, but, upon the Clash's return to London the following day, Topper had quit the band. His reason, according to Kosmo, was 'a difference of opinion over the political direction the band will be taking'.

That Saturday, Charles Shaar Murray arranged a summit with the remainder of the band to find out just what was going on. Everyone met in a café on the Portobello Road. The Clash camp made a show of displaying a united front, with both Paul and Mick sticking to the party line on Topper's departure and being vocal in their support for Joe. Joe explained his disappearance thus: 'It was something I wanted to prove to myself: that I was alive. It's very much like being a robot, being in a group. You keep coming along and keep delivering and keep being an entertainer and keep showing up and keep the whole thing going. Rather than go barmy and go mad, I think it's better to do what I did, even for a month. I just got up and went to Paris without even thinking about it. I might have gone a *bit* barmy, you know? I knew a lot of people were going to be disappointed, but I had to go. I only intended to stay a few days, but the more days I stayed, the harder it was to come back because of the more aggro I was causing that I'd have to face.'

One of the other rumours that circulated during Joe's absence was that it was all a publicity stunt. This idea was offset to some extent by the symptoms of stress that had been evident in Joe's behaviour before he went and by Topper's departure upon his return, both of which combined to suggest that something altogether more serious had been taking place. It was to be years before anything approximating the full story emerged, and then it would do so in sometimes contradictory dribs and drabs.

In an apparently frank interview he gave to Channel 4's *Wired* programme in 1988 Joe maintained that his disappearance had indeed begun as a publicity stunt dreamed up by management: 'It was the eve of a tour, and the tickets weren't selling. So Bernie Rhodes – who, like Malcolm McLaren, used to like the odd scam – came to me one night and said, "Look, you've got to disappear." I said, "Well, Bernie, if you really think I should, I will. Where do you want me to disappear to?" And he said, "Well, I don't know . . . Go to Austin, Texas. You know Joe Ely, go and stay with him. But ring me every morning at 10 a.m." I said, "OK, Bernie. I'll be seeing you." But I took the boat-train to Paris instead. Then I thought it'd be a good joke if I never phoned Bernie at all. So he was going to be *thinking* he was acting, "Oh, where's Joe gone?" and after a few weeks he would be going, "Where *has* Joe gone?" I stayed with a bloke I knew in Paris, and I ran the Paris marathon, too. Eventually, they hired a private detective to find me, because they didn't know what continent I was on or anything. But he never found me. It was Kosmo Vinyl who eventually tracked me down.' Joe had contacted his mother to reassure her that he was well, and Kosmo managed to prise the information from her. 'One day, there was a knock on the door, and I opened it, and there was Kosmo dressed head to foot like Rambo, for some reason.' (The *Combat Rock*-appropriate fancy dress had been inspired by the recently released original Rambo movie, *First Blood*, starring Sylvester Stallone as yet another traumatised Vietnam veteran.)

Thus, Bernie's remarks accompanying the *NME*'s original report that Joe had gone missing were insincere and manipulative, the first couple of dates of the tour having been deliberately sacrificed in order to boost ticket sales for the remainder. But this did not explain Joe's reasons for staying away so long. Back in early 1978, he had told *Melody Maker*'s Simon Kinnersley, 'I haven't got any sense of responsibility . . . I'm capable of disappearing right off the face of the earth.' That simply wasn't true. Joe had always had a highly developed sense of commitment to both the band and 'the kids', as he impressed upon CSM following his return from Paris. For him to stay away for a month meant either that his joke had spun wildly out of control and he had indeed gone 'a bit barmy', or that he had some other ulterior motive: one that he was unhappy to dredge up for TV consumption even in 1988.

The 1982 year-plan Joe had outlined at the Sydney press conference had two parts. Firstly, to deliver an AOR radio-friendly album, which had been duly accomplished at the expense of Mick's finer feelings. Secondly, to go out on the road and tour hard behind the album – in Joe's words, 'fight for it' – in order to break the band into the big time internationally. Immediately before his disappearance, that part of the plan had come under threat from two quarters: from Mick, because he no longer enjoyed touring, and from Topper, because he had once again succumbed to temptation and was consequently both unreliable and legally vulnerable.

The fact that the 'political differences' given as the reason for his departure were just an excuse to cover for Topper's heroin problems was an open secret, but it was only officially acknowledged later in the summer of 1982. Talking to *Sounds*' Dave McCullough at that time, Joe took full responsibility for the dirty deed. In 1985, Topper told *Sounds*' Jane Simon that he believed Joe's Parisian holiday had been deliberately conceived as a reprise of the underhand tactics used to reinstate Bernie early in 1981: a control-asserting gesture preceding a pre-planned ultimatum. 'They knew that if they'd said, "Get rid of Topper", Paul and Mick would have said no. But Joe proved that we couldn't go on tour without him, so I had to go.' Topper recalled that, whereas Paul had ultimately just gone along with whatever was easiest, Mick had spoken up in his defence – as he had done for Geir Waade in a similar situation seven years previously – but to no avail. Isolated by the loss of his one ally, Mick was cowed into going along with Joe's game plan. 'Well, I felt that anything he does is all right,' Mick told CSM, who, perhaps sensing that all was not as it seemed, made a point of describing the fixed stare on Mick's face while he was saying his piece.

Meanwhile, the UK single 'Know Your Rights' had been greeted with some enthusiasm by the music press. For the *NME*, Paul Du Noyer wrote: 'Orator Joe storms back with a bitter-edged pep-talk for the troops, and the

Clash make their best single in a long time . . . Hard and economic, instead of laid-back-flat and sprawling, tough and direct and properly thought-out instead of indulgent, sloppy and confused.' It's hard to see this as anything more than an expression of relief and encouragement: the song is tunelessly one-dimensional, and failed to climb any higher than number 43 in the charts.

Released during Joe's absence on 14 May, *Combat Rock* also fared well at the hands of the critics. Since it was the Clash's most American-oriented and non-British album to date – in terms of both subject matter and slick sound – and further distanced itself from life's realities with its use of cinematic imagery, a savaging might have been more predictable. As it was, scorn was reserved for the album title, while the contents were judged to represent a renaissance. Instead of complaining about the lack of punk ramalama, *Sounds'* Dave McCullough praised the album's wordiness, AOR production and strange musical landscapes, and awarded it the maximum five stars. 'The Clash . . . aren't static anymore, but sailing down into their own Heart of Darkness, trying to settle those wild contradictions they seemed doomed by.'

Melody Maker's Adam Sweeting was similarly disparaging about the title, but again refused to allow initial prejudice against the record to colour his reaction (though he was dismissive of the opening track, 'Know Your Rights': 'the worst first'). He was unhappy with what he called 'the hard, dry mix', but found 'the music increasingly effective the more you listen to it'. The Vietnam imagery was impossible to miss, but unlike Dave McCullough, Adam also picked up on the cinematic feel. 'There's a darkness here, yes, but it's distanced, a zoom shot from a low-flying helicopter,' he wrote. 'Like editors of old documentary film, the Clash re-process imagery through the shifting lenses of their music. "Red Angel Dragnet" . . . isn't *really* about the people's fight against street violence, it's about a Martin Scorsese movie. With "Sean Flynn", same again . . . doubtless the Clash have nicked the idea from Michael Herr's *Dispatches* or *Apocalypse Now*.' His appreciation was a little more qualified than Dave's: 'I have doubts about the more exploitative aspects of the Clash, and the way they milk death and repression until they become meaningless, but I'll be listening to *Combat Rock* for a while yet.'

Over at the *NME*, usually their toughest taskmasters, the Clash benefited from a publicity stunt that was not of their own making. Early in April, the leader of Argentina's ruling junta, General Galtieri, had ordered the invasion of what Argentina calls the Islas Malvinas and Britain, which claims sovereignty despite being a world away, calls the Falkland Islands. Her popularity slumping in the polls, Margaret Thatcher seized the chance to be seen to act decisively and dispatched a Navy Task Force to deal with the problem. In early May 1982 a series of sea and land skirmishes took place, to which the UK tabloid newspapers responded with some of their most memorably rabid headlines since the heyday of punk. Hundreds of young men, most of them teenage Argentinian conscripts, lost their lives for the sake of a few sheep and a Tory election victory.

Such goings-on had more to do with the reportage of *Sandinista!* than the stylised dramatics of *Combat Rock*, as Adam Sweeting noted in the opening paragraph of his review, but the *NME*'s recently recruited skinhead politico, X. Moore, a.k.a. Chris Dean of Clash-influenced band the Redskins, believed the album 'has inadvertently become the best counterblast on the Falklands'. Whereas its predecessor had been released into a hostile environment, *Combat Rock*'s timing could not have been better. 'Listen, I'll tell you where the "socially concerned rock artist" stands in the bubblegum environment of today: s/he stands HERE!' wrote Chris. '*Combat Rock* is too important to be snidely lumped with all the other dross, and this band are too important to tear themselves apart.' (This was before Joe's return and Topper's sacking.)

Combat Rock took only a week to make number two in the UK album charts. Although this position equalled the feat of *Give 'Em Enough Rope* back in 1978, the new album eventually stayed on the charts nine weeks longer – 23 in all – making it the band's most successful in the UK to date. Even before its release, the band found themselves out of the red for the first time since signing to CBS in January 1977. The money they had made on the road over the past year had paid for their keep, while between them *London Calling* and *Sandinista!* had chalked up enough sales to repay their debt to the record company and even to cover the exorbitant costs of recording their latest album. A four and a half week US tour was due to start on 29 May, and for the first time, the Clash were facing the prospect of going on the road to make money for themselves.

There was only one problem: Topper had quit on the 21st, and therefore they didn't have a drummer. So they did what they had always done in the same situation: they phoned Terry Chimes. Having worked as a session musician since the dissolution of Generation X the previous year, Terry pronounced himself available. The arrangement was temporary – to see the Clash through the gigs they had booked up until the end of the year – and also canny; firing one of their members had undermined the band's gang image, but bringing back a former member in his stead immediately repaired much of the damage. Terry had just five days to work up the set before opening night. 'What made it really difficult was their policy of having a pool of 40 or so songs, and selecting a different permutation every night,' says Terry. 'But I'm used to that: I learn fast.' Nevertheless, although he had to familiarise himself with the key *Combat Rock* songs in a hurry – that being the album the band was promoting – for a long time, the set was biased towards the early Clash material with which Terry was familiar. This expedient move would have a significant influence on the band's future.

The US release of the album was delayed slightly when the Clash insisted Epic remove the 'Home Taping Is Killing Music' message they were including on all album packaging at that time. The band had heard that it was common for US college bulletin boards to carry notices offering to tape an hour's worth of the customer's choice of *Sandinista!* tracks for $3, something that was at least in keeping with the original 'consume it any way you want to' thinking behind the album. 'We don't care *how* many people tape our records,' Kosmo announced to CSM.

Either as a consolation prize or as an attempt to mollify him following Joe's hijacking of the album production, Mick was given the opportunity to remix 'Rock The Casbah' for later US single release, and also to record a DJ-style remix entitled 'Mustapha Dance' for inclusion on the B-side of the 12-inch single. Work took place at New York's Power Station immediately prior to the US tour. Bob Clearmountain engineered, and this time Mick refused to hide behind either a pseudonym or a collective Clash credit. Coupled with 'Long Time Jerk', the original album version of 'Rock The Casbah' was released that June as the second single from the album in the UK. Don Letts hastily arranged a mid-tour video shoot of the band playing in front of an oil well in the Texas desert. To play up the supposed Middle Eastern theme two extras capered about dressed as an Arab and an orthodox Jew. These roles were taken by Bernie Rhodes (the Arab) and long-time band buddy Mark 'Frothler' Helfont for the single sleeve.

The Pop Star Army Fatigues look was by now at its most exaggerated and an aura of macho determination prevailed throughout the touring party. Recently recruited roadie Digby recalled the ambience when talking to the *NME*'s Steven Wells in 1991: 'We were all dressed in black combat gear and everybody got out of the way when we came through; *everybody*.' At the tour's opening-night party, Kosmo had turned up with a mohican-style haircut. This was partly in tribute to his enduring hero, Travis Bickle, but also a response to the more recent movie *The Road Warrior* (1981). The film is a futurist, post-apocalyptic nightmare set in the Australian desert, and the villains are a scavenging tribe of punk-*coiffured* hell's angels.

Kosmo's was hardly an original fashion statement. The years 1979–80 had seen the emergence of a fourth wave of UK punk bands. Incensed, like Garry Bushell, by the progressive and arty tendencies of so much post-punk/indie music, the likes of the Exploited, the UK Subs, the Cockney Rejects and Discharge proudly declared 'punk's not dead' and attempted to prove it with music that was even more basic and angry than that of the first wave, in spite of being highly derivative. Impressed by the *Road Warrior* outlaws' daring juxtaposition of leathers and crazy-coloured mohican cuts, many of these bands had already picked up a few fashion tips from the film, lending the punk look of the early Eighties a decidedly cartoonish aspect. Nevertheless, Joe was so taken with Kosmo's new hairstyle that, by the time the Clash came to shoot the 'Rock The Casbah' video, he too was sporting a red-dyed mohican. Refusing to be left behind in the weirdness stakes, Mick had a cowboy-style handkerchief mask obscuring his face for much of the shoot, and continued to affect it for the subsequent live dates.

Unintentionally or not, the band were giving off worrying signals. The militaristic Rat Patrol image suggested camaraderie and teamwork, but

Robert De Niro had decided to adopt the mohican cut for *Taxi Driver* after reading that stressed-out US soldiers in Vietnam sometimes cut their hair that way when convinced they were about to die. Certainly, the gang members in *The Road Warrior* were hardly wholesome role models. In view of Joe's recent, somewhat desperate behaviour, his adoption of such an extreme image did not bode well for his state of mind, and he later admitted that his intention had been to make himself look as ugly as possible. Meanwhile, Mick's mask indicated just how withdrawn from proceedings he had become.

It was a tour of ups and downs. In Atlanta, a local communist group attempted to distribute some literature outside the Fox Theatre, and a mini-riot ensued. 'They pulled the police guns out on us in Atlanta,' Joe told Dave McCullough. Fourteen people were arrested and charged with battery or disorderly conduct. In Hollywood the Clash sold out five consecutive nights at the 23,000-capacity Palladium, a feat made all the sweeter by the knowledge that the Jam had struggled to sell out just one night. Joe was even more pleased to learn that Bob Dylan had come to see them. 'He's said to have been recording rock'n'roll again the very next morning,' he crowed.

The first single culled from the album in the US was 'Should I Stay Or Should I Go', which, between 10 June and 20 July 1982, was released with no fewer than three different B-sides ('Inoculated City', 'Cool Confusion' and 'First Night Back In London') and in three different sleeves (one with a picture of Ronald Reagan). This blatant hard sell did not prevent it from stalling at number 45.

'Rock The Casbah' peaked in the UK before the Clash returned home to commence the tour that had been postponed when Joe disappeared, but despite the lack of live promotion and another bad review from the *NME*, it still managed to reach a respectable number 30 in the charts. The tour itself, which began at the Fair Deal in Brixton on 10 July, was rechristened the Casbah Club. The idea was that, in the absence of the permanent club they had been promising for years, the Clash would offer a peripatetic one in the tradition of Bernie's original Club Left. A statement read: 'The club will take over halls for the night as a celebration of low life and Clash fans. As well as the Clash playing, there will be guest appearances by celebrities, public figures and other attractions.'

Richard Cook paid those other attractions no attention in his *NME* review of the opening Fair Deal show, but the Clash could hardly complain at that: 'Every one of perhaps 20 songs was dealt out with a surly, scorched-earth bravado, spilling accents of suspicion and untempered wrath: purpose in every turn,' declared Richard. 'The Clash have learned to channel sound as never before. What the bungling theatre of sores that now calls itself British punk cannot grasp is this definition . . . the sound of punk shouldn't be the spluttery sprawl of mud-clogged feedback over Chad Valley drums, it should be this steeled rush, this fluorescent razor's edge! . . . The Clash have rediscovered something that rock is supposed to have forgotten: its grip on exhilaration . . . I say we need this anger, no matter how romantic it may be. I say this antidote to romantic *despair* is necessary. The Greatest Rock'n'Roll Band In The World. I guess that doesn't sit so badly, after all.'

Following the UK tour's completion early in August 1982, the Clash hardly had time to pause for breath before commencing the second month-long leg of the US tour on the 11th of that month. The venues were large and the receptions more enthusiastic than ever, but, inevitably, pressures were building. 'Terrible tensions,' recalls Terry Chimes. 'The tensions when I'd been in the band before had been flying around in all directions, but it had been mostly me versus everybody else. When I rejoined the band, they never argued with me about the politics or anything any more. This time, it was very much Mick versus Joe and Paul, and I felt that Kosmo was very anti-Mick as well. I'm not saying whether he deserved it, I'm just saying that's how it lined up. The record kept selling like crazy, and it seemed like we could do no wrong that year. And yet the tension was mounting and mounting.'

The tour's second leg was originally supposed to run down early in September, but then the band were offered a support slot on eight gigs on the Who's October retirement tour at stadiums holding 50,000 to 80,000. These included two consecutive nights at Shea Stadium in Queens, New York, as famously played by the Beatles in 1965. Seeing it as an opportunity to reach a new, even larger audience, they accepted. In the *NME* a disgruntled T-Zers entry wondered, 'Still steering that steady course straight to hell?' It was a question worth asking. Aside from a couple of charity shows and festivals, the Clash had always refused to support anyone, let alone dinosaur acts like the Who. What had happened to 'No Elvis, Beatles or the Rolling Stones' now? And *stadiums*: one of the central tenets of punk had been that rock'n'roll should be played in venues where audiences could see the whites of the band's eyes. Just a year earlier, the Clash had lined up seven nights at Bonds – extended to 16 – rather than play one night at the 16,000-capacity Madison Square Garden . . .

It was all justified in the name of breaking through, the only alternative, or so the Clash claimed, to remaining a cult attraction, just scraping by, forever at loggerheads with their record company. Rather than apologise for this change of policy, the band decided to flaunt it. Don Letts was lined up to film their performance on the first Shea night, with the intention of making a live-style video for the UK release of 'Should I Stay Or Should I Go'. Footage was shot of the Clash riding to the show in an open-topped car, playing at rock stars. Irony was doubtless intended, but the band were by now relying on such none too convincing double-bluffs to maintain their integrity. With the Clash debt having been settled months before, there was no reason for accepting the Who supports other than the blatant lining of their own pockets.

Another, less tarnished opportunity for exposure was offered by a 9 October live performance slot on the popular NBC TV show *Saturday Night*

Live. Here the Clash performed 'Should I Stay Or Should I Go' and 'Straight To Hell', which had coincidentally been released on 17 September as a UK double A-sided single. Adrian Thrills approved heartily of the latter track on behalf of the *NME*, while acknowledging that the less adventurous former song would probably receive most attention. This did, in fact, prove to be the case: the single climbed to number 17, the band's best domestic showing since 'Bankrobber'.

In late October, the second single release in the US was Mick's remixed version of 'Rock The Casbah'. Thanks partly to the exposure generated by their own tour and the Who gigs, and partly to the video's heavy rotation on the by now established cultural phenomenon of MTV, 'Rock The Casbah' climbed to a startling number eight in the US charts. This in turn helped the album climb to number seven in the US charts on its way to selling over a million and a half copies. To paraphrase Joe, one should not be frightened of the word 'irony': the Clash enjoyed their biggest ever US single with a song written and almost exclusively played by their recently departed drummer; and much of this success was due to a video in which they mimed to the song, shown on a station that, at that time, had much less of a personal touch and live feel than the reviled and boycotted *Top Of The Pops*.

On 27 November 1982, the Clash played the Jamaica World Music Festival in Montego Bay. 'We did that because it was like a little holiday at the end of all this, because we'd worked very hard in America,' says Terry. Through favouring the sizeable reggae element in their repertoire they won over the local crowd and finally gained some acceptance in the country that had inspired them but also spurned them for so long. As Richard Grabel's *NME* review summed up, 'The Clash took their chance and made it mean something.'

The upswing in the band's fortunes was continued by the end-of-year polls. *Creem*'s review of *Combat Rock* might have been less than complimentary – Richard Meltzer had dismissed it as a 'RELATIVE PIECE OF SHIT' – but the magazine's readership refused to be directed, awarding the Clash third best album, best single and sixth best single, third best tour, third best band and third best live band. (Most of the third places were after the departing Who and poodle-haired rockers Van Halen.) The *NME*'s readers still placed the Jam (also retiring that year) at the top of most categories, but the Clash claimed third best band, second best album, third best songwriters and third best live act: their best showing for years.

After a heavy year of live activity, it had already been decided to take a few months' holiday. Having enjoyed playing for the band, Terry would not have objected to staying on this time, but found it hard to envisage a long-term future while the relations between the others remained so strained. 'Although we could play gigs, I couldn't see how we were going to get into a studio and do anything creative while there was all that bad feeling going on,' he says. 'I had a private conversation with Joe and Paul, in which they said, "We don't know if we've got a band any more." That is, they didn't know what was going to happen with Mick. And I found it a bit irritating. I had other plans. I didn't want to spend six months sitting there while they argued about whether there was a band or not, so I got involved in other things.' He worked with Billy Idol for a while, joined Hanoi Rocks and made a drumming video. 'And then I decided the time had finally come to do medicine, or else I'd never get around to it.' In 1987, he began five years of training as a chiropractor. He now also practises acupuncture, and continues to drum in his spare time.

Over the few months following Terry's departure, band-related recording activity was limited to one recording session, a debt of gratitude to the no longer incarcerated Janie Jones. Joe wrote 'House Of The Ju-Ju Queen' for her, and on 28 December 1982, produced a session at Wessex during which both that song and a version of James Brown's 'Sex Machine' were recorded for a proposed single. Mick played guitar, Paul bass, Mickey Gallagher keyboards and fellow Blockhead Charley Charles drums. The single would eventually be released in December 1983 on Big Beat under the name Janie Jones and the Lash.

By February 1983, rumours about a Clash split had begun to circulate once more. Little happened to convince people that they were unfounded. On 17 March, Joe appeared in the *Sun*, posing in a T-shirt bearing the trashy tabloid's logo, along with Kenny Lynch, Lennie Bennet and two other members of a team intending to run the London Marathon in aid of Leukaemia Research. The general consensus was: nice cause, shame about the sponsor. Sporting another mohican cut, Joe completed his third marathon in as many years. May saw the *Sun* reporting that Paul had married Pearl Harbour in a New York register office. Meanwhile, Mick's relationship with Ellen Foley finally hit the skids.

The Clash were not entirely inactive during this period. They were attempting to write new material, and to this end had moved back into the warehouse building that had formerly housed Rehearsal Rehearsals, since refurbished and turned into a somewhat more salubrious rehearsal-cum-recording studio. The lack of live appearances could be attributed to the band's drummerless state, but, it appeared, this situation was not going to be allowed to drag on indefinitely. The classifieds section of the 23 April 1983 issue of *Melody Maker* carried the following large, but anonymous, display ad: 'YOUNG DRUMMER WANTED. Internationally successful group. Recording and concert appearances immediately.' After auditioning, or so they claim, in excess of 300 applicants, the Clash finally decided on 23-year-old Pete Howard, formerly of Bath band Cold Fish.

Appropriately enough, his Clash career threw him straight in at the deep end. In late May, the band played a few dates in the south-west of America in preparation for a scheduled appearance on the 28th of that month at the second annual Us Festival in Glen Helen Regional Park, Los Angeles. The three-day festival was the brainchild of Apple computers magnate Steve

Wozniak, and its title derived from the banner under which it was organised, Unuson, an acronym for Unite Us In Song.

The Clash had been offered a staggering $500,000 to headline the opening New Music Day, but shortly before they were due to go on, the band held a press conference denouncing what they now considered to be a complete charade. They said they had been informed that ticket prices would be pegged at $17, instead of the $20 to $25 plus parking that was being charged. As a consequence, they were refusing to take the stage until the promoters agreed to donate $100,000 to a southern Californian summer camp for disadvantaged children. This flagrant act of blackmail resulted in Unuson agreeing to hand over between $32,000 and $38,000 (different sources reported different figures). Not content with this, the Clash then cornered several other acts on the bill and insisted that they too donate a portion of their inflated fees to worthy causes. They finally went on two hours late to play an 80-minute set, throughout which Joe openly jeered at the audience. Banners behind the band read: 'SEX STYLE SUBVERSION' and 'THE CLASH NOT FOR SALE'. After the gig, the Clash brawled with event security and crew members. Kosmo punched the DJ in the nose and Paul sprained his thumb.

Their behaviour raised a number of questions in music press reports of the festival. If the Clash found the idea of the event so abhorrent and were indeed 'not for sale', why had they accepted so much money to play? Some cynics noted that the band had only begun complaining when they discovered Van Halen were getting a million dollars for *their* headlining spot on Heavy Metal Day (which drew 350,000 people as opposed to New Music Day's 140,000). How could a band who prided themselves on treating their audiences fairly justify keeping them waiting for so long, and then insulting them from the stage? Last but not least, instead of resorting to the blackmail ruse, why hadn't the Clash simply donated part of their own fee to the summer camp?

The Clash offered no explanation until the following year. 'We have to deal with the music industry, and that weekend, the whole industry was looking at the festival as *the* state of rock'n'roll,' Joe told *Creem*'s Bill Holdship. 'So we had to go in there and show them that we wouldn't be pushed under the carpet. Our second purpose was to spoil the bloody party, because I'm not going to have some millionaire restaging Woodstock for his ego gratification and tax loss in his backyard and get away with it . . . Don't tell me you can recreate Woodstock in the Me Generation of cocaine California in 1983 . . . On the Van Halen day, somebody got clubbed to death over a drug deal.' He did concede that the press conference had perhaps not been the best of ideas. Regarding the band's own fee, he told *Record*'s John Mendelssohn that they had originally earmarked it for the long-promised Clash-owned club: 'We needed it for London. If Wozniak wants to be a sucker and give us half a million dollars, we'll take it.'

Upon their return to the UK, arguments over just what the money should be used for added to the tensions in the Clash camp. No more was heard from the band until 10 September 1983, when the *NME* news pages carried the following statement: 'Joe Strummer and Paul Simonon have decided that Mick Jones should leave the group. It is felt that Jones had drifted away from the original idea of the Clash. In future, it will allow Joe and Paul to get on with the job the Clash set out to do from the beginning.' Mick's response, carried in the same issue, was: 'I would like to state that the official press statement is untrue. I would like to make it clear that there was no discussion with Strummer and Simonon prior to my being sacked. I certainly do not feel that I have drifted apart from the original idea of the Clash, and in future I'll be carrying on in the same direction as in the beginning.'

Although news of the split was not without impact, it hardly came as a surprise. The animosity that Joe and Paul had bottled up for the best part of two years spilled out during the next year in almost every interview they, and especially Joe, gave. There had been very little live work in 1983 because Mick had wanted to take six months off the road. To anyone else, this might have seemed a reasonable enough request following 1982's hectic schedule and bearing in mind that the only breaks Mick had taken in the two years prior to that had been those enforced by Joe's walk-outs. But Joe was now a man with a mission who believed the Clash should be following up on their American breakthrough by getting out on the road and, in his words, 'out-working' their heavy metal and AOR competitors.

Although playing the older material with Terry Chimes had been a move born of necessity, it had reminded both Joe and Paul – as well as critics like Richard Cook – how direct and hard-hitting the Clash had once been. They had wanted their new material to pursue a back-to-basics angry punk direction. Mick, on the other hand, had grown increasingly bored with both his and the band's traditional role, and wanted to persevere with hip hop and groove music. His demos for new songs used drum machines, synthesizers and samples. 'I was going, "Come on, let's dance"' was how he summed the situation up to the *NME*'s Paolo Hewitt in 1986. 'And they were saying, "No, let's riot!"' 'I had to beg him to play guitar, and he's supposed to be the Clash guitarist!' an exasperated Joe claimed in 1984. 'It was like dragging a dead dog around on a piece of string. Insane! Better to take a dive and never be heard of again than to carry on with that ridiculous performance. I'd rather go back to busking and be a nobody than carry on like that.' Mick's refusal to take what he considered to be a retrogressive step and the others' refusal to bend to his will meant that the summer of 1983 had been one prolonged Mexican stand-off.

Joe's version of the final straw received several airings. 'Mick eventually said, "I don't mind what the Clash does, as long as you check it with my lawyer first,"' he told Richard Cook in February 1994. 'I sat back and thought . . . hang on! And I said, "Go and write songs with your lawyer. *Piss off!*"' Mick, to his credit, refused to enter into any tit-for-tat bickering, or even to tell his side of the story in any detail, as long as the Clash existed in any form. In early 1985, however, he did tell *Rolling Stone*'s Bill Flanagan that, despite all ongoing rhetoric to the contrary, the Clash's original ideals had been shattered by the time of his sacking, thus making a split inevitable: 'We all knew that we were just doing it for the money. We couldn't face each other. In rehearsals we'd all look at the floor. It was the worst.' Joe had come to the same conclusion. 'I couldn't believe we'd turned into the people we'd tried to destroy,' he said in spring 1984. 'We'd turned into . . . *Pop Stars!*'

14... DEATH OR GLORY

With Mick Jones out of the way, the Clash were determined to heed the warm public and press response to 1982's gigs with Terry Chimes, and forge a music which, to paraphrase Richard Cook's Brixton Fair Deal review from July of that year, put the fourth wave Punk's Not Dead groups in their place with its sharpness, anger and bravado. Although the last plot to replace Mick had involved Steve Jones, the former Sex Pistols guitarist was not considered this time round. That he had since joined Topper on the heroin casualty list may have played some part in disqualifying him, but it had also been decided that the new Clash should not be some kind of punk supergroup. 'Who needs the old pals act?' Joe demanded in spring 1984, before – somewhat cheekily, bearing in mind the stadium support gigs that had done so much to break the Clash in America – doing his best to distance his band from the likes of the Who: '"Keith Moon's dead, so bring in Kenny Jones." That's not the way to do it; it doesn't work. Get some lunatic in off the street!'

In order to get back to the Spirit of the Clash, the now traditional anonymous advertisements were placed in the music press in the autumn of 1983. The classifieds pages of the 1 October issue of *Melody Maker* carried a large display ad reading: 'WANTED. YOUNG HARD GUITARIST who can hold his own. Immediate studio and live work.' Efforts were obviously being made to put more emphasis on the 'sex' in the 'SEX, STYLE, SUBVERSION' promised by the band's Us Festival stage banner, but unfortunately the innuendo was worthier of a *Carry On* film than a cutting-edge rock'n'roll band. It certainly failed to attract the kind of person the band had in mind, because two weeks later, a second ad was run requesting a 'YOUNG ROCKIN' GUITARIST UNDER 25, OVER 5'9". For international live work and recording.' By 5 November, what was required was simply a 'Wild, young GUITARIST. Must look good, play good, under 25. . .' etc. By this time, Joe had decided to concentrate more on singing, so the ads were in fact fishing for two new band members, which might go some way to explaining why the selection process was taking so long. The following week's ad took a different tack entirely, seeking a 'YOUNG UNSIGNED GROUP FOR FILM PART. . .' Either Bernie had another project in the works or the Clash were so desperate they were slyly hoping to poach people from existing bands.

The auditions required the hopefuls to play along with tape recordings of three new songs. Standing out amongst the supposed '300 heavy metal guitarists' who turned up (300 having by now replaced 204 as Clash-ese for 'a lot') were Nick Sheppard and Vince White, who were duly hired. Vince thought he was auditioning for Tenpole Tudor. Nick caught on slightly sooner, though little about the auditioning process itself gave the game away. 'A couple of friends of mine said, "Look, here's an advert, here's a number,"' he reminisced early the following year in a rare interview with his home-town local radio station, Radio West. 'I figured out pretty quickly who I was auditioning for. The first one was up in Camden, in the Electric Ballroom, and there was about 60 other guitar players there. We played along to a backing tape in front of the other 60. I had to do another audition after that in a studio, but I didn't meet the band because they didn't want people to play to form. If everyone had known it was the Clash, they'd have all got their hair cut and played what they thought they ought to.'

The new recruits' identities were not made known to the music papers until January 1984. According to the Clash camp's press release, Nick, 23, had formerly been in Bristol punk band the Cortinas, while Vince, also 23, and a native of Finsbury Park, was previously untested. Not revealed at the time was that Nick had more recently played in a Latin American-flavoured covers band going under the somewhat dubious name of the Spics. The T-Zers page of the 28 January issue of the NME told the world a little more about Vince: 'Actually, "Vince" White is in fact Greg White, a one time native of fashionable Southampton, not Finsbury Park. Greg arrived in London in 1979 to study physics and astronomy at University College London.' It seemed that street credibility was to be as highly prized an asset in the new Clash as it had been in the old.

The band's plan to 'out-work heavy metal bands', put on hold during the wrangles with Mick, was implemented with a vengeance in early 1984. The new line-up was broken in with a few small late January gigs in southern California: a deliberate return to the scene of the Us Festival, intended to illustrate how live rock'n'roll should be experienced.

In 1983, for the first time since 1977, the Clash had made no show in the NME end-of-year readers' poll, but tickets for the eight mid-February 1984 dates played in Eire and the UK under the banner Out of Control quickly sold out. Previously used for a 1977 jaunt, the tour title was another statement of intent. It was certainly borne out by the set lists. Although they included a handful of new Strummer compositions – 'Three Card Trick', 'Sex Mad Roar', 'Are You Ready?' and 'This Is England' among them – they also drew heavily on material from the Clash's first three albums. At first Nick was required to sing 'Should I Stay Or Should I Go', but he was never wholly comfortable with stepping so blatantly into Mick's shoes, and the song was soon dropped from the set. Funk and reggae excursions were rare, and Sandinista! was almost completely ignored.

From the UK, the tour moved straight on to Europe, finishing in Paris on 1 March. By this time, a second UK leg had been pencilled in, beginning in Edinburgh on the 3rd and ending with five nights at the Brixton Academy (formerly the Fair Deal) supported by Shane MacGowan's band the Pogues. Intrigued by Richard Cook's February 1984 *NME* interview with the new band – or, rather, Joe and Paul – the paper's Gavin Martin went along to see them with an open mind, but was disappointed. 'This new Clash are no big departure, they are still entangled with all the old faults. The new young bloods in the pack haven't brought fresh drive and commitment, they've merely grown into and expanded the idea of the Clash as posed-perfect rebels.' Gavin failed to see any evidence of a 'return to the primal elements of real rock shock', noting instead that 'the massed light banks, three prong guitar chunder, and video screen backdrop' made for 'the heaviest and most orthodox rock show I've ever seen the Clash play. The callisthenics, the heroic posturing, the riot scenes and war footage are all still there. For a group so against the machinations of violence, they still get an awful lot of mileage from its imagery.'

During the January 1984 US dates Mick Jones had contacted promoter Bill Graham to tell him the band he was booking was not the Clash. He had teamed up with Topper, and was planning to bring the *real* Clash over himself. Other than penning the identity-asserting anthem 'We Are The Clash' in response, Joe had brushed this aside. Time proved that Mick's threat was no more than a wind-up, as Mick himself later admitted. Joe had similarly attempted to ignore the writs directed at the new Clash by Mick, again backed up by Topper, but this time with less success. The band's assets had been frozen, including the profits from *Combat Rock* and the Us Festival. This not only meant that any last vestiges of hope for a Clash club had finally been killed off, but also put a question mark over the new line-up's recording future. 'I don't know if he's trying to make his lawyer a millionaire or something, but he's going the right way about it,' an exasperated Joe told *Jamming* magazine's Ross Fortune immediately prior to the band's second visit to the US. 'We were willing to give him his share of the dosh, but he never even asked for it. He just got his lawyer out and slapped an injunction on us.'

Back in February, Joe had assured Richard Cook that the new members would be having an input: 'We don't want a slave syndrome!' But it was plain to all that the Clash's musical and political direction had already been determined long before their recruitment. So had the image, an updated punk style consisting of a retro jumble of 1982 era Clash Pop Star Army Fatigues, Fifties leather motorcycle jackets and 1977-vintage punk T-shirts and accessories. Nick Sheppard even posed for one publicity photo in Bernie's 1974 'What side of the bed' T-shirt design. The opinions of the band's new boys were not heard in interviews. The Voice of the Clash was the voice of Joe Strummer, with occasional support from Paul or Kosmo, and it was a confrontational, angry, meandering rant that made some interviewers fear for his sanity.

He had points to make, though. Television was out of favour once more. 'Get up off your chair, turn off the TV, go outside and deal with real life,' Joe lectured *Creem*'s readership via his interview with Bill Holdship. After a four-year spell of having – at worst – ambivalent status, America was back on the Strummer shit list. 'I don't like it,' he told Ross Fortune. 'I don't like the food there, I don't like the way everything looks the same. I don't like the signs all over the place. I don't like the plastic buildings. I don't like the imitation muzak dribbling out of the speakers, and I don't like the way they let the government get on with things.' Body-consciousness, the band's work ethic and the decision that the last couple of albums had been overly self-indulgent had resulted in the outlawing of all drugs. 'If you take drugs, wear a kaftan,' Joe instructed the *NME*'s readers via Richard Cook. 'Be honest. Wear a bell round your neck. I've smoked so much pot I'm surprised I haven't turned into a bush.' DIY was back on the agenda. 'Anybody can do it,' he told Bill Holdship. 'The fact is, we play three or four chords. On a good day, we might hit five. But dammit to hell, I challenge anybody not to be able to learn five chords in three weeks. God, I could get a penguin to do that!'

The distilled essence of this long-winded proselytising, in Joe's own words, was 'You've got to feel like you can get involved' and 'Vote. Take some responsibility for being alive.' Yet even more than in 1976–7, when the punk era had at least provided an appropriate context, the often admirable points he made were nullified by the hectoring manner of their delivery. The year 1984 was a world away from '1977', whatever the countdown at the end of the latter song might have attempted to suggest to the contrary. The music scene had developed and splintered beyond recognition. There were fourth wave punk bands in the UK, and a hard-core scene in the US, true, but at the time these were little more than cults. Richard Cook made the comment that in rejecting both fun-loving New Pop youngsters and post-punk pale and interesting intellectual types, the Clash were in danger of talking themselves out of any kind of an audience at all.

In fairness to the Clash, despite their intention to present a sexy image, they were taking their impression of the mood of the times not from *Smash Hits* and *The Face*, but from newspapers and news programmes. The effects of economic recession and the government's reaction to it had dramatically increased the number of unemployed to a figure three times greater than that of ten years earlier. The north, traditionally home to the bulk of the UK's heavy industry, was especially hard hit. Comparisons with the still relatively untroubled, affluent south led to talk of a North–South Divide: Britain had broken into two economically disparate factions which, bearing in mind the history of the American Civil War, made the English Civil War Joe had sung about in 1978 seem distinctly possible.

It was more than just something in the air. The riots of summer 1981 had been a reaction both to rising inner city poverty and to the government's and the police's heavy manners response to the resulting disquiet. After the lull of the Falklands War, which had to some extent succeeded in externalising the nation's aggression, the spring of 1984 saw the conflict come to the surface once again in the shape of the Miners' Strike. The government had already made clear that it was prepared to use the most Draconian measures available in order to gain and retain control, even if that meant undermining civil rights and the country's industrial infrastructure, resorting to violence in the short term and forcing whole communities into a long-term poverty trap. The miners were making their stand not only for their own rights, jobs and communities, but also in order to provide a rallying point for the rest of the country's disaffected workers and unemployed. The most memorable image of the conflict comes from the pitched battle between pickets and mounted riot police at Orgreave in May 1984: a photograph of a mounted policeman at full gallop, leaning out to take a baton-swing at an unarmed female spectator. The Clash of '76 had managed to generate a righteous anger and capture the imagination of the nation's youth on far less fuel than this.

For all their anti-American remarks and renewed interest in the political situation in Britain, the Clash were still determined to follow up their late 1982 success in the States. A second US tour began at the end of March 1984 and ran through until the end of May, but with no new record to promote, the band's ability to draw started to slip and not all the venues sold out.

Back in London, preparation for a new album became a priority. Nick, Vince and Pete had been taken on as hired hands, rather than made fully-fledged band members, and were being paid a weekly wage. Although hardly true to the Spirit of Punk Joe had talked so much about trying to regain, this was perhaps understandable, given that they were unknown entities and that the band's funds were frozen. The point at which the set-up began to look dubious was when the songwriting sessions commenced that summer. On interviewing Nick and Vince for his 1994 *DISCoveries* Clash retrospective, Ralph Heibutzki learned that the three newcomers had been required to turn up at rehearsals on a daily basis to work on tapes of basic chord structures given to them by Joe. After these had been 'arranged' into more recognisable songs in his and, often, Paul's absence, Joe would then take them away to add lyrics. It might not have been outright exploitation, but it came perilously close. It certainly had little to do with the 'we're all in it together' vibe Joe had tried to establish in the media. 'I don't want to actually record until we've got the group as a unit,' he had told Ross Fortune. 'In my mind, I liken us to a new platoon,' he had told Bill Holdship during the second US tour. 'We're going to go out and crawl right in front of the enemy lines, get fired upon, and then look at each other to see how we're bearing up. Can I rely on this guy when my gun jams? We're under fire, and we're sharing that experience. And that's what's going to make our record great.'

Aside from this strange and decidedly un-Clash-like approach to composition, there was little other activity for the rest of 1984, something that was blamed on Mick's injunction. The band played four Italian dates in

September in support of that country's Communist Party and two benefits at the Brixton Academy on 6 and 7 December in support of the Miners' Strike Fund, but those were the full extent of their public showings. This remained the case until May 1985, when local radio and BBC2's *Whistle Test* (whose name had been shortened to slough off the old grey image) reported the unlikely news that the Clash had been seen busking in several northern towns over the weekend of the 11th.

It transpired that this was true: the band were hitching from town to town armed with only acoustic guitars and, in Pete Howard's case, drumsticks, and setting up in a variety of gathering places to play for loose change. They were even sleeping on fans' floors. *NME* stringer Paul Syrysko overheard Joe say, 'If anyone from the *NME* talks to you, just tell 'em we've gone stark, raving mad.' It might have been the last thing one would have expected the average big-name rock'n'roll band to do, but it made perfect sense in the context of Joe's previous remarks about getting back to basics: he was revisiting not only his own pre-Clash roots, but also the early days of rock'n'roll, blues and folk, when music was made with the most primitive of equipment. In addition to mostly old Clash songs – though new compositions 'Movers And Shakers' and 'Cool Under Heat' were also given an outing – the leather-clad band busked standards like the Monkees' 'Stepping Stone', the Beatles' 'Twist And Shout' and Gene Vincent's 'Be-Bop-A-Lula'.

The busking tour took the Clash from Gateshead station to Sunderland Carlton Bar Drum club to Nottingham, where they played outside the Garage club and in the Old Market Square, and to Leeds, where they played outside Le Phonographique nightclub. They stayed on for an extra day there in order to entertain customers queuing to see Clash-influenced band the Alarm, a performance that was disrupted first by the band's bouncers and then by an irate audience member who threw a balloon full of red paint at Joe in protest at CBS's involvement in South Africa. There followed a half-hour show in the Faversham pub. The Clash moved on to York, and the next day, busked outside York Minster to 600 people gathered to celebrate VE day. On Tuesday, the 14th, they turned in a set at Edinburgh's Coasters disco, playing to 1,300 people without a PA, and also visited reformed hard man Jimmy Boyle's Gateway centre for young people, especially those with drug-related problems.

'We'd play anywhere, morning or night,' Joe reminisced fondly to *Musician*'s Bill Flanagan in 1988. 'We played under canal bridges, in precincts, bus stops, nightclubs, discos.' Apart from the paint-throwing incident, reactions to the decidedly rough-and-ready performances ranged from the bemused to the ecstatic. Certainly, enough fans turned up with tape recorders to provide bootleggers with the raw material for several 'commemorative' albums. Had it been intended solely as a publicity stunt, the busking tour could have been deemed an unqualified success: it caught the public imagination in a way that the new Clash's bona fide gigs had failed to do, and even today is still the abiding memory most people have of the band's final incarnation.

The *NME* report announced that the Clash were 'still recording' their new album at that time, but nothing more was heard over the coming months. All thoughts of working harder than a heavy metal band seemed to have been forgotten as the Clash made just three more conventional live appearances over the summer of 1985, all at large European festivals: the Roskilde in Denmark on 29 June, the Rockscene at Quenne in Finland on 13 July and on the second night of a two-day event at the Antic Panathinaikon in Athens on 27 August.

The next development came as something of a surprise: the late September 1985 single release of 'This Is England', backed with 'Do It Now' and, on the 12-inch version, 'Sex Mad Roar'. At the *NME*, the Clash were unlucky enough to encounter Gavin Martin once again: 'Still determined to slay the totems, bare the social ills, attend the wake of our crumbling banana republic, Strummer's rant bears all the signs of agit rocker well into advanced senility: voice rambling and cracking over syn-drums flutter, football chants and ugly guitar grunge.' In other singles and albums reviews 'This Is England' was afforded considerably more respect and, in retrospect, it stands up as the last great Clash song. It failed to make any impression in the US, but reached a respectable enough number 24 in the UK charts.

The news pages of the 19 October issue of the *NME* carried the following unattributed statement from the Clash camp: 'As legal difficulties over the name the Clash have forced the band off the road, the group known as the Clash hope to play some shows in the UK and Europe before the end of 1985. The long-awaited album will be released in early November, and the Clash will start touring under a temporary name until this dispute is resolved.' What it didn't explain was how, if they were unable to play live as the Clash, the band would be able to release further records under that name. It made no sense. The paper also reported that rumours were circulating regarding a possible reunion of Joe and Paul with Mick and Topper.

The album, entitled *Cut The Crap*, turned up as promised. It was reviewed for the *NME* by Mat Snow, who provided some not unsympathetic historical context to the Clash's attempt at a punk revival before ripping the album apart. He described the sleeve as 'a marketing director's idea of Ye Style Punke' and poured scorn upon the inner sleeve 'communiqué', which reads: 'Wise MEN and street kids together make a GREAT TEAM . . . but can the old system be BEAT??. no . . . not without YOUR participation . . . RADICAL social change begins on the STREET!!. so if you're looking for some ACTION . . . CUT THE CRAP and Get OUT There.' On to the contents. As far as Mat was concerned, the band had succeeded in shaking off their global dabblings only to come up with a sound strongly reminiscent of Sham 69 and, in the case of 'We Are The Clash', the Sex Pistols: 'snub nosed guitars bullying the troops and railing at the bastions of privilege whilst full-throated terraces (that's us, remember?) roar their approval'. He noted that Joe's lyrics were hard to make out, and the few examples on the sleeve indicated that this was probably for the best. 'Where's his knack of a pungently well-turned phrase?'

At *Melody Maker*, the album was reviewed by Adam Sweeting. If Mat Snow was moved to sarcasm, then Adam was personally offended: 'Guess what? IT'S CRAP! And it doesn't cut it. Football chants, noises of heavy meals being regurgitated over pavements and carpets and a mix that Moulinex would be ashamed of. Who the hell does Joe Strummer think he is? . . . Ugly? It's painful.' Over at *Sounds*, bizarrely enough, Jack Barron liked it enough to give it four and a half out of five stars. 'Subtlety dies, but it was worth the wait for me, anyway,' he wrote. 'The Clash don't miss Mick Jones, and the band have finally managed to lucidly stitch together their love of ethnic musics with gut-level rock. The collisions of R&B, electro, funk, Tijuana horns and whatever are often splendid on a *sonic* level.' He conceded that the lyrics were not all they could be, but ventured the following justification: 'Joe Strummer has never been a poet: he deals in propaganda with broad slashes of filmic imagery.'

Back in 1984, Joe's stated aim had been to make an album that would have the same impact and stand up as well as the Clash's début. *Cut The Crap* is not that record. It would appear that the hip hop inflections were intended to serve the same function as the reggae ones did on *The Clash*, but in this case they fail to broaden the cultural base or to raise the music above the level of bog-standard punk. The album is one non-stop aural barrage, with too much going on, and everything louder than everything else; except, that is, Joe's vocals. The result is like straining to hear something shouted from an active construction site across a busy main road in the middle of rush hour. The stripped-down sound of *The Clash* might have been so raw that some people found it difficult to listen to, but this is real cacophony. To be fair, buried underneath are the faintest traces of at least five halfway decent tunes; but there are 12 tracks on the album.

As well as being largely incoherent, Joe's lyrical vision is arguably at its most flawed since *Give 'Em Enough Rope*. 'Dictator' is such a hackneyed character sketch of a US-funded Central American despot that it is impossible to take the intended political point seriously: it has more in common with 'Rock The Casbah' than with 'Washington Bullets'. Knee-jerk rhymes and empty sloganeering also drive the 'globally conscious' war song (listed here as) 'Are You Red . . . y?'

Far too many tracks are nothing more than 'punk' rallying cries. However stylised it might have been, *The Clash* captured the flavour of life for disaffected youth in the inner city. *Cut The Crap*'s punks live somewhere else entirely. They stay cool on the street in 'Cool Under Heat', coolly bum cigarettes in 'Life Is Wild', coolly pick up chicks at the hop in 'Fingerpoppin'' and coolly cruise cars in 'Dirty Punk': on the whole, more *American Graffiti* than British lowlife. As for 'We Are The Clash', neither Mott the Hoople nor Bo Diddley would want to claim parentage of this defiant and defiantly yobbish football chant. 'Play To Win' is largely indecipherable, but seems to consist of an exchange of xenophobic insults: terrace chauvinism to go with terrace harmonies, something that the Clash of '76 tried much harder to avoid. What increases the wince-factor is knowing that the man singing these songs is 32 years old.

The lyrics which genuinely try to address the state of Britain in 1984–5 are undermined by inapposite romanticism. 'Three Card Trick', 'Movers And Shakers', 'North and South' and 'This Is England' are all rooted in the national turbulence and division caused by the recession as managed by Margaret Thatcher, drawing particularly on the Miners' Strike and the North–South Divide. One might have expected such events to be truly inspirational to Joe Strummer of all people, but the results are at best mixed. 'Three Card Trick' is crammed with overblown, almost gothic imagery: 'Patriots of the wasteland torching two hundred years . . .' 'Movers And Shakers' is an attempt to promote the DIY ethic among Britain's disadvantaged and downtrodden, but it again suffers from ridiculous images – 'The boy stood in the burning slum' – and, as well as encouraging creative self-expression, suggests washing car windscreens at traffic lights as a viable career opportunity. The Clash work ethic? Is this really preferable to the factory or dole queue options derided in earlier songs?

'North and South' looks at the plight of the northern workers whose lives have been thrown on the economic scrapheap. At times genuinely affecting, it is marred by Joe's apparent inability to tell a tale without resorting to hyperbole. He raises the stakes just a little too high for credibility to stay the course with his dire warnings of internecine familial strife. In the context of the album 'This Is England' is also gratingly melodramatic, but – a more localised 'Straight To Hell' – its heartfelt compassion does win through. The cornered, world-weary tone is appropriate to the times, and it does not take too great a leap of the imagination to transpose the massed vocal choruses to a mining community's male voice choir.

Overall, it would appear the 'political' material is aiming for a futurist vision not dissimilar to that of *The Clash*. Whereas the band's début album borrowed from urban models by Ballard, Orwell and Kubrick, however, *Cut The Crap*'s post-industrial wasteland is suggestive of that depicted in George Miller's *The Road Warrior*. Certainly, Joe himself had continued to sport his red-tinged mohican for much of the past two years, and a similarly shorn leather-jacketed punk is pictured on the record's front cover. The film may even be the source of the album title. When a battered and broken Max volunteers to lead the escape by driving the tanker in the climactic chase sequence, doubts are expressed about his physical condition. 'Cut the crap!' retorts Our Hero. 'I'm the only real chance you've got.' The fact that this cartoon vision was totally inappropriate to the Britain of 1984–5 serves merely to illustrate how far from reality Joe's filmic obsession had taken him. One is reminded instead of the Comic Strip's satirical film *Strike!*, in which the miners' conflict is given the full Hollywood treatment to 'unintentionally' ludicrous effect.

Anticipation of a new Clash release allowed the album to climb to number

16 in the UK charts, though it faded away quickly thereafter; in the US it reached no higher than number 88. The 23 November 1985 issue of the *NME* carried a news report that Nick, Vince and Pete had left the band. Whether they were being treated as scapegoats for the album's poor reviews and sales or whether the other two were making way for the mooted reunion of the former Clash line-up was not made clear. No other statement was forthcoming, and that was how matters remained. Gradually, it dawned that this was the way the Clash were going to end: not with a bang, but with a whimper.

It would be several more years before the truth behind the last year of the new band's existence emerged, and it would take nearly as long for the machinations which had led to the former Clash's demise to be revealed.

Last things first. Ronald Mellor, Joe's father, died just before the March 1984 UK tour, leaving, as Joe himself put it, 'a lot unsaid'. By the time Joe came home from the US visit in June, his mother, Anna, had become ill. 'She spent all year doing chemotherapy and radiation treatments because she had a form of cancer,' he revealed on Channel 4's *Wired* in 1988. 'I spent most of the next year [1985] visiting her, and she died after the end of that year.' Not all was so bleak: in 1984, Gaby gave birth to a baby girl, named Jazz Domino in honour of Charlie Parker and either Fats Domino or the Van Morrison song as performed by the 101ers.

The arrival of a first child usually reinforces the awareness of family, and facing the loss of his parents at a time when he was only just beginning to understand what it meant to be a parent himself was especially hard for Joe. As he later admitted, it required him to do a lot of thinking about all areas of his life. He had to reassess not only his personal relationships, but also how he felt about the Clash. For all his interview rhetoric, he had never been wholly sure that he was doing the right thing with the new band. His own doubts were strengthened by those of others. Ex-roadie Johnny Green came to see one of the March 1984 Brixton Academy gigs, and he told Joe that what he was doing was rubbish. 'I know' was the forlorn reply.

This is why there were very few gigs after the subsequent US tour, why preparations for the album were so desultory and why Joe kept his distance from the new boys during that period. He also travelled separately from them on September 1984's Italian jaunt. Nick, Vince and Pete began to suspect there was more troubling Joe than bereavement and his mother's illness only in January 1985, when recording sessions were arranged in Munich – out of the public eye – and the three newcomers were not initially included in the plans.

It would appear that Paul was also losing interest, because, along with Mickey Gallagher, Norman Watt-Roy was drafted in to help out. Percussion, both acoustic and electric, was handled by Michael Fayne. Although, as Ralph Heibutzki revealed in *DISCoveries*, first Nick and then Vince were eventually brought in, their input was limited and they managed to gain no adequate overview of the project. Pete was not involved at all. Strangely, for someone who had expressed an interest in getting back to the fundamentals of punk-style rock'n'roll, Joe was allowing his songs to be constructed piece by piece, using the very programmed percussion and synthesizers to which he had so strongly objected when employed in Mick Jones's last demos for the band.

The paradoxes, dichotomies and contradictions that had been the raw stuff of Joe's life for so long had finally spun out of control. He was not making the album he wanted to make. Instead, Bernie was in residence behind the mixing desk and was making the album *he* wanted to make. Joe finally came to realise that he had not been in the driving seat for any part of the Clash's development over the past four years. Appropriately enough, it was a realisation that hit him with all the power of Kurtz's final glimpse into his own heart of darkness. Following a last blazing row with Bernie about the turkey they were basting in the name of the Clash, Joe walked out on the project and severed all ties with him. Shortly afterwards, he also fell out with Kosmo.

The May 1985 busking tour was an idea originated by Joe. It was partly a genuine attempt at last to capture that sense of unity and comradeship he had talked about in the previous year's interviews, but – bearing in mind the comments he had made following Mick's sacking, that he would 'rather go back to busking and become a nobody' than carry on with a band that was not working out – it was also an acknowledgement that the Clash were on their last legs. It was little more than an enjoyable outing. The three festivals the band played over the summer of 1985 were undertaken simply to earn money to cover basic bills. After the last of them Joe faced up to the fact that the farce could not continue any longer. Nevertheless, he still hedged his bets, neglecting to tell the new boys about his plans to render them obsolete when he and sometime roadie Terry McQuade went off in search of Mick. Joe prostrated himself at his former partner's feet, begged forgiveness and asked him to come back, with Topper, and re-form the real Clash.

Mick accepted Joe's apology, agreed to bury the hatchet and then turned down his offer. He had spent two and a half years putting together his new band, Big Audio Dynamite, and recording their first album. He was now playing exactly the music he wanted without having to fight anyone to get it recorded, and had no intention of giving that up. Joe listened to the rough mixes of the album and, not wholly graciously, according to the interview he gave Gavin Martin in 1986, informed Mick, 'It's the worst load of shit I've ever heard in my life. Don't put it out, man, do yourself a favour.' Then he went home.

At the expense of causing his new colleagues a good deal of uncertainty and discomfort, Joe continued to stall for time, keeping his options open as long as possible. He hoped either that Mick might change his mind or that the music press and general public's reaction to BAD might change Mick's mind for him. Meanwhile, Bernie had continued to work on the Clash album without Joe, bringing in engineers to help him remix it drastically. The first Joe knew of this was when 'This Is England' was released as a single, a track that was barely recognisable as the one he had left behind in the recording studio. The statement 'from the Clash' claiming that they were temporarily off the road for legal reasons was, of course, a Rhodes–Vinyl smokescreen to obscure the real reason for their reclusiveness. Dates had indeed been pencilled in for the coming year, but the management team's hopes were resting on the possibility that a positive reaction to the album would bring Joe back to his senses and back to the fold.

Neither Joe's nor Bernie's hopes were to be realised. Joe was astounded when the Clash album came out and he discovered that *it* was now the biggest pile of shit he had ever heard in his life. He'd had no say in the trite title, the tasteless packaging (which was exactly what Mat Snow suggested it was) or the risible inner sleeve 'communiqué'. Worse, his songs – some of which had been half-finished demos – had been buried under a cacophony of synthesizer, sampled voices, overblown massed backing vocals, brass and electronic percussion. One or two had been varispeeded into different tempos. The songs selected for the album were not necessarily the best of those stockpiled or those recorded: played live on various occasions but unreleased to this day are 'Glue Zombie', 'Thanks, Chief' and the ballad 'In The Pouring, Pouring Rain'.

Even worse still, whereas the single had been credited to Strummer & Co, Bernie had taken it upon himself to credit the tracks on the album to Strummer–Rhodes. 'He sort of served as a sounding board for me, but I thought it was a bit cheeky, all the same,' Joe told Bill Flanagan. 'That's not to say he didn't write *anything*, but I wouldn't have said that it was half and half.' Worst of all, Bernie had attributed the production to Jose Unidos, a nod to the band's earlier imaginary Puerto Rican helper Pepe Unidos. Although a pseudonym for Bernie, the 'Jose' had been deliberately chosen to suggest Joe as a means of legitimising the project. 'It wouldn't have been so bad if Bernie had just got the blame, but that was unbearable,' Joe told Gavin Martin in 1986.

The reviews of the album appeared in the 9 November 1985 issues of the music press. The following week's papers carried reviews for *This Is Big Audio Dynamite*. The *NME*'s reaction was only marginally kinder than it had been to *Cut The Crap*. John McCready totally missed the point of BAD's hip hop and rock collision when he described it as 'an occasionally engaging mess which consists of eight dub-singed middle eights stretched, at times, to transparency'. Other critics were more receptive, and became increasingly so as further singles were pulled from the album. Then the general public joined in, and responded surprisingly quickly to Mick's ground-breaking new sound by taking 'E=MC²' to number 11 in the UK charts, which equalled the best showing by the Clash to date.

Much of this humiliation was still in the future when Joe invited the three new boys to his Notting Hill flat and told them that the Clash were over. By this time, they had all had enough and were relieved to be able to admit it and go their separate ways. Nick played briefly in a band called Head and the others faded from the music scene. 'I think about those guys sometimes and hope it didn't fuck up their lives too much,' Joe told the *NME*'s Sean O'Hagan in 1988. 'Because they were good people in a no-win situation.'

The official announcement of their departure did not firmly shut the door on the Clash's continuing in some form, but as far as Joe was concerned, this was now dependent on Mick's changing his mind. All the same, it was an effective end to the band, which at last freed its former members to talk about its disintegration with an unprecedented openness.

Topper had released a single cover version of the Gene Krupa track 'Drumming Man' in June 1985, and had already begun to tell his version of events in the associated promotional interviews; he would continue to do so in the interviews accompanying the January 1986 release of his solo album *Waking Up*. The formerly close-mouthed Mick also felt justified by Joe's apology, the success of his new band and the dissolution of the new Clash to speak his mind, which is what he did in interviews pertaining to BAD releases and Clash reissues, and following his near-fatal illness in 1989. Joe felt he had more to get off his chest than anyone, and unburdened himself in interviews relating to his various film soundtrack recordings, his acting ventures, his solo album and Clash reissues. Paul absented himself from the picture for much of the rest of the Eighties, and, as he had not been a major player in the drama of the Clash's demise, had relatively little to say even when he eventually returned to the public eye in 1989 with his new band Havana 3 a.m.

The key to understanding what brought about the end of the longest-lasting and best-known version of the Clash is to be found in the discrepancy between what appeared to be going on – even to observers close to the band – and what was going on. (As it was in the beginning, so it was in the end.)

Early in 1981, Joe brought Bernie back because the Clash had lost direction. That he took this decision unilaterally, imposing his will on the others, made it all too easy to take at face value his subsequent domination of the Clash's media appearances and seeming dictation of musical direction and band policy. From 1981 onwards, nearly all music press reviews – for albums, singles and live shows – referred to the Clash as 'Strummer's band'. Certainly, on the early 1982 New Zealand visit journalists and tour managers alike were left in no doubt that Joe was calling the shots. When *Rolling Stone*'s Malcolm McSporran approached a band roadie named Jerry and asked him about Bernie's influence at that time, he received the following reply: 'The Clash have grown up. *Before*, he had four boys. *Now*, they're four world-weary hardened men. You can't tell them anything.' Returning to the Clash fold that May, Terry Chimes received much the same impression. 'There was a difference with Bernie,' he says. 'He was less powerful. He couldn't tell people what to do.'

In fact, Bernie had learned a salutary lesson from his first stint with the band. He was astute enough to realise that the now older and more experienced Clash would not stand for overtly authoritarian behaviour, but he had always been at his most effective when taking an indirect approach anyway. The mask only slipped once in public. On the summer 1982 US tour *Sounds'* Dave McCullough asked a drunken Rhodes what his role with the Clash was this second time round and received the indignant answer, 'I OWN THIS GROUP!' Otherwise Bernie was content to remain in the background and play what amounted to a brothel-creepered and bespectacled Iago to Joe's pale Othello.

On his return as manager, Bernie's first priority was to make the Clash viable again, which meant getting the band out of debt. All other considerations were secondary, even artistic integrity. It was Bernie who started the grumbling about radio-unfriendly ragas, and while it was Joe who announced the band's intention to deliver a slick AOR full-price single album then tour hard behind it to make it sell, it was Bernie's agenda. It was definitely Bernie who brought in Glyn Johns to transform *Rat Patrol From Fort Bragg* into *Combat Rock*. Joe told *Wired* in 1988 that the original idea for his April 1982 disappearance scam came from Bernie, but the motive was not, as he claimed, solely to awaken interest in tour tickets or the forthcoming album. The idea was also to reinforce the singer's dominance so that he could be Bernie's agent in bringing about Topper's dismissal, which, as already established, was pre-planned. Remember, back in September 1981, it had been Bernie who instigated the debate – the one Robin Crocker found so irritating – about Topper's condition and the obstacle it represented to the Clash's success.

Although Joe claimed sole responsibility at the time for that decision, in 1986 he gave *Record Mirror*'s Jim Reid a somewhat different account of the drummer's sacking: 'We were in Simonon's basement flat. It was dark and raining outside. We told Topper he was falling apart and he had to go. He split the flat, devastated. He walked around the block in the rain, and he came back. That's when my heart went *ping*, y'know. It just rose up in me to say, "Look, he's come back. That's enough isn't it?' What more do you want? Let's work with him. Let's help him!" Instead, I just shut my mouth, like everyone else in the room. Mick, me, Paul, Kosmo and Bernie.' Joe was trying to spread the blame around equally, but his repudiation of the notion that he himself was the instigator of the decision effectively points the finger at Bernie instead. In interviews he gave in 1985–6 Topper made it quite clear that he blamed Joe *and* Bernie for ousting him.

Up to the release of *Combat Rock*, the Clash were making money to pay off their debts, but from the 1982 dates with Terry Chimes onwards – especially the Who stadium supports and the 1983 Us Festival – they were, as Mick claims, simply making it for the sake of making it. This was un-Clash-like behaviour and, no matter what his detractors might say to the contrary, it was not even particularly typical of Bernie. In 1980, the manager had attacked the Clash for betraying their original punk audience, but it is hard to imagine a more complete selling out of that audience than the events of 1982–3. Terry was certainly convinced that, whatever might have been said from the stage or in interviews, politics were no longer an issue behind the scenes. But then the change back to angry rebel rock and political rhetoric following Mick's dismissal proved him wrong. In retrospect, the only explanation for the band's activities in the two years immediately prior to that upheaval is this: anticipating the showdown with Mick, Bernie was building a financial buffer to prepare for its impact, knowing that, after Mick was gone, he would be able to get on and do what he *really* wanted to with the Clash.

As early as December 1982, Joe and Paul gave Terry to understand that Mick was already heading for the sack. With the benefit of hindsight, Mick himself believes that part of the thinking behind Topper's dismissal in May of that year was to make his own expulsion easier for the remaining members of the band to countenance: the old McLaren–Rhodes principle of divide and rule in action. In 1986, talking to Lisa Robinson for *Hard Rock Video* magazine, he acknowledged that he had been difficult throughout the period following Bernie's return. 'I was right to be difficult,' he asserted. 'Because they were being run by the manager.' Lisa expressed amazement that anyone could take what Bernie said seriously. 'Well, I didn't listen that much, so that's why I stood out, right? But once he threw Topper out, and we all went along with that, he kind of knew that he had a free way. People were expendable. Basically, what happened was that Bernie wanted to sit where I was sitting in the group. The good seat, the comfy seat, the best seat in the house.' What about Joe? 'I think he sort of sat by and let it all happen.'

Mick's account of the sacking differs somewhat from the 'go and write songs with your lawyer' version Joe favoured in 1984. According to Mick, when the situation came to a head in August 1983 and Joe said he didn't want to play with him any more, Mick countered by telling Joe and Paul that he believed Bernie was a destructive influence and that they might be able to make it work again if the manager left. 'I asked the band who they wanted, me or Bernie,' he told the *NME*'s Paolo Hewitt in 1986. 'The group said they wanted Bernie, and then just looked at the floor. I couldn't believe my ears. I stood there for about ten seconds, stunned. Then I just picked up my guitar and walked out.' Reminiscing for the BBC2 programme *That Was Then, This Is Now* three years later, he said, 'I was set up, really. Bernie came running out after me with a cheque in his hand – you know, like a gold watch – which added insult to injury. But I took it anyway.'

'Sometimes I feel that I've only been a pawn in the game between Mick and Bernie,' Joe told *Record Mirror*'s Jim Reid in 1986. 'If you wanna look at the Clash story, the Titans in the struggle have been Mick and Bernie. They put it together, and then Mick said, "Let's get rid of Bernie", so we got rid of him. Three years later, I said, "Let's bring him back", so we brought him back. And then Bernie said, "Let's get rid of Mick", so we got rid of him.' This overview casts Joe in a strangely passive role for someone with so much natural charisma. That Lisa Robinson asked Mick how anyone could take

Bernie seriously prompts the question, why did Joe take him seriously? 'What you must realise is that a large percentage of people like me are idiots,' Joe explained to Gavin Martin, also in 1986. 'I sit in a room and write ditties while others are selling stocks to Malaysia on the vodaphone. It's easy to manipulate people like me. What I do best is write doggerel, so part of me must be very childish. I gave Bernie a little too much. Bernie sort of coerced me into thinking that Mick was what was wrong with the scene. That wasn't hard because, as Mick will admit now, he was being pretty awkward.' Just in case that admittedly scathing self-criticism still suggested he was opting out of responsibility for his actions, he went on to acknowledge his own ruthless streak: 'Plus my ego – a bad thing an ego – was definitely telling me, "Go on! Get rid of the bastard!"'

Looking back, it is hard to believe that the five-piece Clash's new direction could have been the brainchild of anyone but Bernie: the confrontational interviews, the retreaded punk rhetoric, the vitriolic denunciation of Mick and the revisionist overhaul of the band's recent history all had a tell-tale Stalinist odour to them. Evidence of brainwashing at work: in August 1980, before rejoining the band, Bernie told the *NME*'s Paul Rambali, 'the group has betrayed the mandate they were given by their fans to represent their interests and causes'; in February 1984, Joe told Richard Cook, 'The Clash were elected to do a job and it hasn't been done'; in November of that year, while delivering *Cut The Crap* to the *NME* offices, Kosmo Vinyl told Mat Snow, 'We're representing the audience. That's the ticket we were elected on, representing the audience!'

'Bernie's idea was to see if the original ideal of the Clash would still stand up in the Eighties,' Joe explained to Sean O'Hagan in 1988. 'I thought the idea was impressive, but it didn't work in practice. I didn't realise his full motives until it was too late and the whole thing had gone too far. It was too late to stop.' Then, when it came time to record the album, Bernie's game plan changed yet again. 'In the final dying moments of the Clash,' Joe told Gavin Martin, 'all he became interested in was, could you take elements like songwriting, rock'n'roll – that strange thing they call creativity – and package it like it was canned tomatoes? I was an unwilling part of the experiment to find out if it was possible.' Keeping up with Rhodesian logic has never been a task for the faint-hearted, but it's worth noting that Bernie's experiments were not without precedent. Two years previously, his great rival, Malcolm McLaren, had released his 'solo' album, *Duck Rock*, in fact a cross-pollination of other people's musical efforts complete with samples, scratching and beat box adornments: not a million miles from what Bernie attempted with *Cut The Crap*.

Thus, Bernie did end up sitting in Mick's seat: he not only took over his producer's chair, but, according to the album credits at least, also usurped his place as Joe's co-songwriter. Joe himself was already somewhat disoriented by his family troubles, but Bernie exhibited no more respect for or interest in the finer feelings of his supposed henchman than he had with either Topper or Mick. 'I had a terrible time with Bernie Rhodes in the end,' Joe told Sean O'Hagan. 'In a nutshell, in order to control me, he destroyed my self-confidence.' All he felt able to do was run away. Nor did Bernie's ambition come to a halt with the bad reviews for 'his' album and Joe's subsequent dismissal of the new band members. Back in 1984, justifying firing Mick, Joe had told *Creem*'s Bill Holdship, 'I'd hope that if I started to act funny *I* would be fired, and the Clash would continue to roll on without me.' Two years later, it looked as though Bernie and Kosmo might be preparing to take him at his word. In July 1986, *Record Mirror*'s Jim Reid told Joe about the rumours. 'I'd say that was possible,' came the reply. 'Only because I am au fait with the insanity behind the lines. It wouldn't surprise me.'

Thankfully, it didn't happen. Kosmo eventually came to his senses and split from Bernie. He set up in PR in New York, and, by the end of the Eighties, had made friends once more with the former members of the Clash. He became Joe's manager and started to act as a sort of unofficial custodian of Clash affairs, taking charge of putting together the compilation box set *Clash On Broadway* (1991). Bernie also departed for New York, where he discussed opening a club with who else but Malcolm McLaren, which, perhaps unsurprisingly, came to nothing. In a 1990 *NME* retrospective interview with Stuart Bailie he also claimed to have started up the hugely influential hip hop label Def Jam with Russell Simmons before Rick Rubin took over: 'I gave Russell the idea to start the label.' Returning to the UK in 1989, he tried to set up his own label, Sacred, via RCA. One of the projects was a single with Glen Matlock, who says their relationship ended in some acrimony because he found Bernie was now impossible to work with. The label duly folded.

Bernie – the man for whom managing the Clash meant never having to say he was sorry – remains unreconciled with most of his former charges to this day. In the 1990 *NME* retrospective he called Mick a cry-baby and Joe a coward, adding, 'They're such squares, the Clash. They've gone back to how they really are.' Three years later, though, when asked by *Q* magazine whether the band should re-form, he initially said no, but seemed to be in two minds. As well as repeating the claim previously aired in the *NME* feature, that he had written the lyrics to the band's first album, he offered the following insight, in which the more astute reader may well notice the faintest trace of unintentional irony: 'We had a great institution in punk rock English-style and we ruined it. But that's the music industry: see something good, sign it up, fuck it up. The kids end up feeling *molested*. If the Clash get involved with me again, then they can play for the right reasons.' Ladies and gentlemen, Bernie Rhodes has left the building. He was beaten to the exit by Messrs Headon, Jones, Simonon and Strummer . . .

In their different ways, Topper, Mick, Joe and Paul did feel molested by the lead up to and immediate aftermath of their various departures from the Clash, and have all since admitted that they took a long time to get over the experience. Topper's situation was complicated by denial related to his inability to come to terms with his heroin problem: in the interviews he gave during 1985–6, he professed to feel no bitterness towards the other members of the band, but not everything he said supported this claim. He occasionally even refused to accept that his drug use had been a factor in his sacking. For their part, Mick and Joe agree that things were never the same after Topper left.

Although Bernie ended up with the bulk of the blame, both Mick and Joe realised that making him the sole scapegoat would deny them the sturdy foundation they needed to rebuild their own relationship. Mick acknowledged that his petulant withdrawal had not only contributed to an impossible situation, but had robbed him of many potentially rewarding experiences. 'I missed a lot of the Clash because I was so self-involved,' he confessed to Paolo Hewitt in 1986. 'Like when we toured, I'd get on the coach, and I wouldn't look out of the window. I was so far up my own arse. The change now is, I know what I'm doing. If I'm rude to someone, then I know why I'm being rude. And if I'm doing something fucked up, I know I'm doing something fucked up.' Speaking to James Brown in 1991, he said, 'It was a shame how communication broke down. It got too big. We couldn't take the pressure.' Two years earlier, musing about the effects of success on *That Was Then, This Is Now*, he said, 'You become a different kind of arsehole.'

These were sentiments with which Joe heartily concurred, his most frequently quoted comment on the split being 'we fell to ego'. As early as 1984, when the five-piece Clash were trying to find their feet, he had already developed a fatalist attitude towards the previous incarnation of the band: 'We have fallen into each and every pitfall that you can possible fall into as a group starting from nothing and becoming something. We've probably invented a few new ones along the way. And there is no way around those pitfalls. You just do not get issued with a map. Every young group that starts is going to fall into them. I'm talking, specifically, about the success-goes-to-your-head pitfall, the ego-trip pitfall. You think you're musicians, you think you're artists, you think you're geniuses, you become drug addicts, you make over-indulgent records, you over-produce everything, you overdub the sound of ants biting through a wooden beam: all these things. We've gone through every damn one of them. We didn't even manage to shortcut one. I think it's inevitable. In fact, you can even say that one person cannot tell another person; it has to be learned by the actual pain of real experience. That's when you learn your lesson, living it. I remember reading advice like, "Don't sign anything", but you have to sign something sometime. There was no way of avoiding those things we fell into.'

Better communication might have helped avoid some of them, but – right from the start – relationships within the band had been established along adversarial lines. Dressing up like an outlaw gang or an army platoon, or even playing regular football matches, is not enough to bring a group of mutually reliant creative people to an understanding of true team spirit. Maybe

Topper ought to have helped himself, but maybe the others ought to have helped him too. Maybe Mick ought to have been less sulky, but maybe the others ought not to have pushed him into a corner. Maybe Joe ought not to have delivered ultimatums, but maybe the others ought to have taken more responsibility. Maybe Paul ought not to have taken sides, but maybe he ought not to have been put in a position where he felt compelled to do so.

Talking to Gavin Martin in 1986, Joe expressed his amazement that Mick had accepted his overtures of friendship. 'I did him wrong. I stabbed him in the back. Really, it's through his good grace we got back together and we're going to write together in the future.' They did indeed write together again – in 1986, for BAD's second album, *No 10 Upping Street* – but it was not to be an ongoing partnership. In his enthusiasm, and his occasionally acknowledged hope that a reunion might one day come about, Joe at first overlooked one other significant contribution to the inevitable break-up of the Clash: he and Mick had grown apart musically.

He faced up to it in 1988 when speaking to Harold De Muir of the *East Coast Rocker*: 'You go on for ten years, and it gets to a point where the other guy's taste is so far from yours that you think it stinks. People can start out as apprentices and sooner or later they want to become masters. People *grow*, y'know?' Having had longer outside the group to think about it, Mick was quicker to accept that the Clash's time was over and that the creative rift between himself and Joe might never be healed. Lisa Robinson interpreted the decision to dissolve the Clash as a tacit acknowledgement that Mick had been in the right with regard to the tussle over musical direction. She asked him if he derived any satisfaction from that. 'No, I think it was a great shame,' he replied. 'It was a bloody great shame and it was too late. So I don't get any satisfaction whatsoever from that.'

15... THE COOL OUT

Since they had made film appearances and flirted with both movie imagery and movie-derived images during their time together, it is perhaps not surprising that, in one way or another, the paths followed by the former Clash members have continued to traverse this alternative reality.

The movie Topper has lived is not one that he or anyone would have chosen for himself: *The Man With The Golden Arm*, Otto Preminger's 1955 film starring Frank Sinatra as a gifted jazz drummer destroyed by heroin addiction. Topper's sacking in May 1982 left him feeling depressed and directionless, and even more susceptible to taking refuge in his painkiller of choice. Towards the end of that year, though, he found himself involved in a sort of post-punk supergroup with, among others, Pete Farndon, who had been sacked from the Pretenders that June due to his own drug problem. On 14 April 1983, Pete Farndon was found dead in his bath, having overdosed on a mixture of heroin and cocaine. Instead of shocking Topper into cleaning up, this merely propelled him further into his addiction. The Who's Pete Townshend, who had agreed to produce some demos for the band, had recently recovered from addiction himself, and recognised the signs. He paid for Topper to undergo the Black Box treatment in Los Angeles. Within a matter of weeks, the drummer had succumbed to temptation once more, and the group fell apart.

So began the pattern that was to characterise the rest of the Eighties for Topper. Over Christmas 1983, the recently sacked Mick Jones approached him and invited him to drum with his new band on condition that he undertake an electro-acupuncture cure at Mick's expense. The collaboration did not last long. Topper's excuse was that he was unhappy with the emphasis on technology and sampling in Mick's new music, but really the break-up was over the not unrelated issues of money and drugs.

There followed another lengthy lay-off during which Topper worked his way through the substantial royalty cheque he had finally received from the Clash. He then gathered together a bunch of his old Dover cronies, including Steve, Gary and Bill Barnacle, to record a big-band single version of Gene Krupa's 'Drumming Man' at Wessex. Having been let go by CBS, Topper used it to secure a recording deal with Phonogram. Former Clash engineer

Jerry Green suggested that the drummer record an album in an R&B style, and put himself forward as producer and project co-ordinator. Mickey Gallagher, vocalist Jimmy Helms (best known for his 1973 Top Ten solo hit 'Gonna Make You An Offer You Can't Refuse') and several other experienced soul and R&B musicians were drafted in to record what became *Waking Up*.

Released in January 1986, shortly after both *Cut The Crap* and *This Is Big Audio Dynamite*, it received relatively favourable reviews. Nevertheless, there is little about the music it contains that is challenging or new, and Topper's lyrics are frankly dire. At least some of them seemed to be facing up to his heroin problem, and he went out of his way to assure music press interviewers that he had cleaned up his act. But the pressures of promotion proved too great for him to handle, and when he turned up to a couple of local radio interviews too far gone to talk, it marked the beginning of the end. The band toured behind the album, but it failed to sell. In denial, Topper strained his relationship with Phonogram by blaming the record company. Although they continued to gig for the remainder of the year, his highly professional band gradually lost all respect for him as his habit once more eroded his talents. By the end of 1986, he was reduced to selling off his Clash gold discs and collection of instruments to pay for drugs.

Whether his musical career could have continued much longer under the circumstances became a moot point early in 1987. On 16 February that year, Topper and his girlfriend, Catherine Belben, appeared in Dover Magistrates Court charged with 'supplying heroin to another between 7 and 10 February', and were remanded on substantial bail. Their case was put back several times during the course of the year, and the final reckoning did not occur until late November. In the mean time, fearing the worst, Topper and Catherine got married. Details of the case emerged only at the trial. The couple had gone out for the night in Dover with one Barry Waller and returned to his house for a fix from Topper's supply of heroin. The following day, Waller had been found dead from an overdose. The police had originally wanted to try Topper for manslaughter, but both he and Catherine contended that Barry had taken no more of the drug than had they, and – as he had also been a regular user – insisted that that amount could not have killed him without killing them too. The autopsy confirmed that Barry had almost certainly taken a further, ultimately lethal dose from a supply of his own. Nevertheless, first offender Catherine was given three months for possession and Topper was given 15 months for supplying.

While Topper was in prison, CBS put out the first instalment in their Clash reissue campaign: a single version of 'I Fought The Law' . . . His release came after he had served ten months, on 16 September 1988. He phoned Jerry Green from the Swiss Cottage Holiday Inn and invited him over. 'He'd booked himself a suite. God, it was a disaster: there was every drug under the sun.' Jerry finally lost patience with him, as Gary and Steve Barnacle and Joe Strummer already had. 'Everybody's tried talking to

Topper, but the guy just doesn't want to listen,' an exasperated Joe had told the *East Coast Rocker*'s Harold De Muir at the end of 1987. 'He's had all the cures in the book. It's not like he's a ghetto kid in Glasgow who's addicted to smack and will never have a chance to be cured of it. If you want to beat junk, you've gotta not have any drug at all, except coffee and cigarettes. Not even a beer. That's the only way to beat it. I've quit worrying about him, but I always think of him.'

Topper moved to France to join Telephone, but only lasted six months. Thereafter, there were occasional news snippets in the music press about his going back to work, but nothing came of them. In January 1989, it was announced that he was to play drums for Paul Simonon's Havana 3 a.m., but the post was instead filled by Travis Williams, with no explanation offered or required. Former Clash roadie Terry McQuade had by this time involved himself in the management of Flowered Up, touted as London's answer to Happy Mondays, and Topper's occasional attendances at rehearsals and dalliances with the bongos led to otherwise unfounded speculation that he might be about to join that band.

Other reports, including one attributed to Paul Simonon's manager Tricia Ronane, said that he was driving a minicab for a living. In a 1991 interview Joe mentioned that Topper had just come out of rehab again. In 1993, during the early research for this book, some sources commented on the appalling state he had been in last time they saw him. Other sources revealed that Mick and Joe had recently chipped in to fund yet another detox and rehab programme.

No single movie could adequately sum up the kaleidoscope of images, steals, references and personal dramas that have made up the work and life of Mick Jones post-Clash. BAD's 1986 breakthrough single, 'E=MC^2' celebrates the films of cult director Nic Roeg, but the contents, cover and title of *This Is Big Audio Dynamite* recall the spaghetti westerns of Sergio Leone. Whereas the Clashworld of *Combat Rock* brought the Vietnam movie experience to New York, the BADworld of the band's first and most of their subsequent albums takes independent, mainstream and arthouse movies from all over the world – and even trashy UK television – and brings them back home to Notting Hill, an area Mick likes to call the Wild West End. The music he has made attempts to filter the whole history of rock'n'roll through cutting-edge dance music, and to convey an equally contemporary view of the world via the multi-media junk-cultural images that once inspired his art school collages.

Initially, locale-specific references were just one of the ways in which he set out to prove that *he* was the one remaining true to the True Spirit of the Clash. Another was through the various names he considered for his new outfit: Top Risk Action Company (TRAC) was very *Rat Patrol From Fort Bragg*; the next choice, Real Westway, was a pun on football team Real Madrid and 'the real Sound of the Westway'; and the final choice, Big Audio Dynamite, as well as providing a convenient acronym – BAD as in bad-ass,

BAD meaning good – also captured the confrontational, in-your-face overtones of the Clash: a band that would explode off the stage.

According to Mick, his competitive spirit and determination to prove himself – the same motivating forces that had spurred him on to each new incarnation of the London SS – had him making plans for this new band a matter of a few weeks after his sacking, despite the blows to his self-esteem. In truth, the beginnings of Big Audio Dynamite were considerably more tentative, and Mick was so unsure of what he should do next that he even took acting lessons for six months. Shaky, he surrounded himself with close friends and known associates, which provided the watching music press with a few red herrings: not least when he helped out behind the mixing desk at live shows by Tony James's new band, Sigue Sigue Sputnik, a favour that Tony would later return for BAD.

Having already begun recording demos, Mick started to assemble his own band late in 1983, a process which echoed the formation of the Clash. The first recruit was Leo Williams, formerly Roxy barman, Slits roadie and Basement 5 bassist, with whom Mick had remained in contact via Clash video director Don Letts. Don himself was a non-musician, and had never thought about performing. Even so, Mick found he was increasingly using him as a sounding-board for his new plans. Thinking, as ever, in terms of image, he liked the idea of a skinny white guy standing between two big, beefy Dreads, and appreciated the advantage of having an in-house film-maker in what he was already thinking of as a highly visually oriented band. For his part, Don was growing bored with being a pop-promo man for hire, and recognised an opportunity similar to the one that had inspired him to pick up a camera in the first place. In addition to operating as a toasting second vocalist-cum-occasional lyricist, it was decided that Don should take charge of live sound effects. To this end, Mick taught him rudimentary keyboard skills, and Don put stickers on the appropriate keys just as Paul had once painted the notes on his bass.

It was at this point that Topper was invited to join. Mick recognised he was a great drummer and was also motivated by a sense of loyalty, and even of guilt, but it should not be overlooked that bringing his fellow sackee into TRAC, as it was then known, gave added credibility to his bid to represent the True Spirit of the Clash. Topper's later defection led to the end of another Clash connection for Mick. Throughout 1984, he continued to send Jerry Green tapes of his works in progress, looking for feedback, but also keeping the engineer abreast of developments so that the two of them would be on the same wavelength when it came time to record for real. When Mick learned Jerry was planning to produce Topper's solo album, however, he saw this as yet another betrayal. 'What Mick said was, "Do you want to work with Harold Robbins, or do you want to work with Tolstoy?"' laughs Jerry.

Topper's replacement was recruited in the time-honoured fashion of placing an ad in the music press. Greg Roberts was the successful applicant, partly because he seemed keener than anyone else, and partly because Mick thought he looked like Richard Gere. A few low-key support gigs, beginning in October 1984, featured Don liberally dosing the band's extended dance grooves with movie dialogue samples and Tony James indulging in some off-the-wall dub effects at the mixing desk. 'Tony's role is to take the group and rip it apart and make it something different every night,' Mick told *Rolling Stone*'s Bill Flanagan early the following year. 'It's like producing a new 12-inch single every time.'

Early in 1985, BAD continued honing their live sound as anonymous support on a European tour by U2. During the spring and summer, Tony James returned to his Sigue Sigue Sputnik duties and BAD worked on new material with a greater contribution from Don, who supplied effects and samples and studied as what he termed 'Mick's lyrical apprentice'. Any hopes Mick might have had of freeing himself from his CBS contract and starting afresh somewhere new were dashed, but in the US he switched from Epic to the company's other label, Columbia. With experienced dub remix producer Paul 'Groucho' Smykle as Jerry Green's replacement (an association that would last for three albums), BAD went into the studio in late summer to record *This Is Big Audio Dynamite*.

When it came time to take pictures for the album cover and inner sleeve – the latter was posed near Portobello Road with Trellick Tower in the background as another locale-specific reference – the band brought in photographer Dan Donovan, son of famous Sixties photographer Terence and former assistant to David Bailey. During the sessions Dan let slip that he played keyboards, though had never been part of a group. He was promptly invited to audition, and duly added to the line-up in order to help re-create the album's sound live. The multi-media band now had an in-house stills photographer to go with their video director.

Reviewing the album for the *NME*, John McCready wrote: 'at times this BAD travelogue turns the world and its problems into a well-meaning pop video script . . . I hope we're meant to laugh.' Well, exactly. While some underlyingly serious issues are addressed – South African apartheid in 'A Party' being the most obvious – all the tracks evince a wry, even satirical, upbeat take on the world. Mick believed BAD were continuing the Clash's policy of providing a social commentary, while managing to avoid both dogma and melodrama. 'It's very important not to be too preachy, to be bumming people out,' he told *Rolling Stone*'s David Fricke in 1986. 'Everybody knows how shitty it is out there. It's important to say those things, but the tactical problem is how to say them.'

BAD began playing headlining gigs early in 1986, but reviews of their shows and subsequent singles remained more negative than positive. Public reaction was another thing entirely: the band's sound caught the mood of the times, and the April UK tour was extended into May by demand once 'E=MC²' climbed to number 11 in the charts. Celebrating their status as a multi-media band, and perhaps indicating that his previous band's boycott of the programme had been a policy with which Mick personally was not in accord, BAD appeared on *Top Of The Pops* to promote it. In spite of having been dismissive of that single, the *NME*'s Neil Taylor had the grace to eat his words and admit it was 'utterly brilliant' when also praising the album's third single, 'Medicine Show'. This peaked at number 29 in the charts. Although the album from whence the singles came reached no higher than number 27, they managed to help keep it in the charts for an impressive 27 weeks.

Following the tour, it was time for BAD to go back into the studio and record their second album. The healing of the rift between Mick and Joe was by now public knowledge. During 1986, it leaked out that Mick had both played guitar on and produced Joe's début solo single, 'Love Kills', and that Joe had been responsible for suggesting a cover version of Prince's '1999' for what turned out to be BAD's hardy perennial live encore. Both Joe and Paul provided visual evidence of reconciliation when they turned up as extras – playing policemen – in the video for 'Medicine Show'. By August, news was starting to emerge that Mick and Joe were writing together once more.

The collaboration was not planned, and came about because Don bumped into Joe in the street one day and invited him along to the studio in Soho. He never left. Following several of the 36-hour recording sessions, he even slept under the piano. In the end, although he did not play or sing on the album, he co-produced it with Mick and co-wrote the music and lyrics to two songs with Mick alone, and three more with Mick and various permutations of the other BAD members. The remaining four song credits went to Jones–Letts. It was also Joe's idea to mix the album in New York, a process which proved to be so long drawn out and damaging to the BAD bank balance that it qualified as (admittedly inadvertent) revenge on his part for Mick's insistence on recording *Combat Rock* there.

Released in late October 1986, *No 10 Upping Street* – Joe's title, and supposedly the home of the alternative *funky* Prime Minister – was generally considered to be a disappointment. In places Joe's influence had given it a more rock'n'roll sound, and yet the album as a whole lacked much in the way of a rock'n'roll dynamic. The *NME*'s Danny Kelly identified the Strummer–Jones pounding rock'n'rap guide to inner city London, 'Sightsee MC', as the only track that successfully realises BAD's 'Great Idea . . . the rest are either doodles, sketches, blueprints, models or prototypes'.

Joe brings a touch of *Sandinista!* period Clash to BADworld with his lyric for 'Limbo The Law', which sits comfortably next to Mick and Don's 'Sambadrome': both songs draw heavily on cinematic images (particularly *Scarface*, Brian De Palma's 1983 film starring Al Pacino, a still from which graces the album's inner sleeve), to tell tales of drugs, bandits and economic expediency in South, Central and North America. As Joe notes in his song, and Tony Montana proves in *Scarface*, modern-day gangsters, like modern-day rock stars, learn how to behave from the movies. Joe's remaining contribution is to 'V 13', a song which builds a strange *1984*-like futurist vision on the deliberately banal foundations of the theme tune to TV soap *EastEnders* and the opening snatch of dialogue from *The Chain*, the 1984 removal film set in London. There is nothing remotely cosy about this world. There is a crack epidemic, post-Chernobyl radiation pollution in the rainwater and foodchain, and news censorship. The only release to be found is in vague nostalgia for the good old days. Conforming more to the upbeat brief of the first album, the rest of the songs are less glum, but ultimately far less interesting.

The album and its singles failed to match the success of BAD's earlier material. Although *No 10 Upping Street* reached number 11, it stayed in the charts just eight weeks. It was aided by neither 'C'mon Every Beatbox' nor 'V 13', both of which stalled in the lower reaches of the singles charts. Towards the end of 1987, though, the band finally got a good live review in the *NME*. Richard North described them as 'a million dollar, diamond-encrusted skyscraper designed by Fred Astaire'.

Recorded early in 1988, *Tighten Up Vol 88* found the Strummer association over, but it also – due to Joe's lingering influence or otherwise – found Mick moving away from technology and grooves towards more traditional instrumentation and song structures. He rejected the synth guitar – 'It looks like a Dalek's handbag, doesn't it?' – in favour of his collection of trusty old Gibsons, and was equally scathing about the role of computers in recording, telling *Blitz*'s William Shaw, 'Why do you think they call what computers have "software"? Because it's not *hard*, is it?' Neither is the resultant album. Mick's renewed interest in more traditional musical forms, which led him to make a pilgrimage to Nashville and Memphis immediately after the sessions were completed, was, in part at least, indicative of a loss of enthusiasm for contemporary music. In July, he admitted to William Shaw that he now spent most of his time listening to Elvis and Hank Williams. 'I'm a bit out of touch, to be truthful. I see it all as a load of rubbish, really. I'm not that interested.'

A taste of what was to come was provided by the single 'Just Play Music', released that May. Light, breezy, confident and punctuated with stirring soul brass, it has all the requirements of a summer hit. On first listening, its lyric seems to be suggesting something along the lines of 'don't worry, be happy'. On second listening, it is revealed to be a rejection of all rock'n'roll's attendant paraphernalia: 'I can't play your interviews / I can't hear your photographs.' This from a man whose entire career had been built on image and attitude as portrayed through the media, and who, even three years earlier, had extolled the virtues of recruiting people for the way they looked rather than for how they could play. It seemed the loss of plot had been both sudden and total. Once again, the single failed to trouble the upper reaches of the charts.

Tighten Up Vol 88 was released in June 1988, with a cover painting by Paul Simonon depicting an open-air blues party in the lee of the Westway and Trellick Tower. Sadly, the cover is the only remote connection with the Spirit of the Clash. The album is frustrating in many ways. It contains some of Mick's most varied guitar playing for years, and probably his most assured vocals ever. There are memorable melodies, and clearly defined song structures for those who moaned about the 'extended middle eights' of previous BAD grooves. But . . . the overall effect is lacklustre. The writing credits are shared around more evenly, which could have indicated a developing sense of band identity, yet here merely illustrates the loss of interest on Mick's part. BADworld is no more. The cinematic references so essential to the sound and vision of previous albums are conspicuous by their absence, as is any associated wide-screen world-view. Whether deliberate policy or a consequence of the fact that Don is responsible for the bulk of the lyrics, this album deals with the quotidian, the stuff of soap operas.

Q's Lloyd Bradley noted the move towards conventionality, but took this as a good sign: 'The BAD boys, it seems, are growing old not only gracefully, but with nothing less than a flourish.' He awarded it a perplexing four out of five stars. In the *NME*, which had by now also introduced an albums rating policy, John Tague gave it just six out of ten, concluding with an all too appropriate and, as it turned out, nearly prophetic paraphrase of a quote from *Heart Of Darkness*: 'The inspired zealot who stalked the Clash, the innovative shamen of "E=MC²", or the street-wise rhythm stealer of "C'mon Every Beatbox", *that* Mr Jones, he dead.' The album made it to number 33, and spent just three weeks on the chart.

Back in 1984, Mick's girlfriend, Daisy Lawrence, had given birth to a baby daughter, Lauren Estelle; the middle name was presumably intended as a version of Stella, after Mick's nan. Immediately before BAD's July–August 1988 UK tour, Lauren contracted chicken pox. In the last week of the tour, Mick also began to exhibit symptoms, only instead of manifesting itself as the usual skin rash, the disease attacked his throat and lungs. He developed a high fever and was rushed to St Mary's Hospital in Paddington. While there, he contracted pneumonia, went into a coma and had to be hooked up to life-support machines in intensive care. He was unconscious for 15 days, and for one eight-hour period hovered on the brink of death. When he came round, the nurses were very encouraging. 'They gave me so much psychological help,' Mick told the *NME*'s James Brown in 1991. 'They didn't let me know I was dying until after. They don't tell you until you're fully recovered in case you die of shock.' Recovery was to be some time away: while still recuperating, Mick caught a hospital virus and had to be isolated on the AIDS ward. 'The day I finally got dressed for the last time, and left the hospital, it gave the rest of the patients such a buzz to see someone getting out. I hadn't the heart to tell them I didn't have AIDS.'

They could have been forgiven for believing otherwise: the already skinny Mick lost 50 pounds in hospital and suffered considerable nerve damage. 'When I got out of the hospital, the first thing I did was to pick up a guitar and see if I could still play it,' he told *Melody Maker* the following year. 'When I found I could, I cried.' Work on his vocal cords took longer. He had to have speech therapy just to be able to talk properly, which he promptly followed up with singing lessons. The full process of recovery took nine months. Towards the end of that period, on 23 March 1989, the 89-year-old Stella Marcus died in Charing Cross Hospital, Fulham.

As soon as Mick felt well again, BAD went straight back into the studio, bringing in former Clash associate Bill Price to co-produce. The result, released in early September 1989, was *Megatop Phoenix*, an album which as its name – courtesy of Mick's friend Pete Wylie – suggests, represents a double, and doubly good, rebirth. His near-death experience and the loss of his nan had given Mick renewed enthusiasm for both life and music. While convalescing, he had read the posthumous compilation of Lester Bangs's writing, *Psychotic Reactions And Carburetor Dung*, and been especially fired up by Bangs' excitable 1977 *NME* feature on the Clash. He had listened to all the music that had made him fall in love with rock'n'roll in the first place and, perhaps more importantly, he had also been introduced to De La Soul's 'daisy age' psychedelic rap album *Three Feet High And Rising*, Happy Mondays' acid house-influenced rock and a considerable amount of acid house itself. 'We're talking thousands of kids getting together and dancing,' he enthused to *People Weekly*'s Steve Daugherty that November. 'It's all about freeing up yourself and dancing and getting loose. The authorities don't know what's going on. They have no control. It's just like punk was.'

All this and more is evident in the album. Arranged like the De La Soul record, with the 'real' tracks interspersed with bizarre collages of found sounds, it maintains a dance pulsebeat throughout. It also has a much tougher mix, helped considerably by Mick's gung-ho rock'n'roll guitar, and samples of countless other people's gung-ho rock'n'roll guitar. 'Rewind' sets the scene by submerging early BAD interview snippets in the mix and making lyrical allusion to being both part of a 'troop' – 'gonna kill 'em with sound' – and living in a movie: 'We'll ride off into sunset . . .' 'House Arrest' celebrates the acid house culture. The message is that BAD are moving forward in order to get back to what they were originally supposed to be about.

The attention to everyday details and emotions survives from the last album, but the movie wide-screen is also there to provide an added dimension. 'Contact' is about making human contact, but suggests a spy liaison. 'Around The Girl In 80 Ways' rivals the 'Mick's A Hippie Burning' snippet as the album's most appalling movie title pun, and yet makes the simple point that so many conventions of romance are really just communication-avoidance exercises. 'The Green Lady' is described like some mysterious Hollywood fantasy woman from the Orient, but is in fact the subject of a mass-produced framed print that hangs above many a sideboard, as it once did at 111 Wilmcote House.

In his review of the album for *Q* Graeme Kay believed it to be 'continuing the themes laid down on their three previous works', but noted the shift away from Mick's guitar 'to Don Letts and Dan Donovan's FX and keyboards' and the prevailing 'healthy Balearic beat'. He gave it four stars. At the *NME*, the album was reviewed by James Brown, almost a generation younger than

Mick Jones, but an unabashed fan of all things Clash. Awarding it eight out of ten, he wrote: '*Megatop Phoenix* has a profound sense of place, and as we tipple through the end of the decade and into the Nineties, it's proof that Big Audio Dynamite can make music as cosmopolitan and contemporary as possible . . .' James touched on something significant there: the album came closer to capturing the mood of the times than anything else Mick or his former colleagues had released since *The Clash* 12 years earlier.

US and UK dates followed immediately, but despite good reviews there were no hit singles and the album failed to catch the public's imagination. It climbed to 26, and remained on the charts for just three weeks. At least part of the reason it fell down the cracks was that yet another disaster was waiting to befall Mick: early in 1990, Don, Greg and Leo announced they were leaving the band. 'That wasn't particularly amicable' was the extent to which Mick would be drawn on the split – even four years later and on the other side of the world – by Graham Reid of the *New Zealand Herald*.

Mick's chief error had been in continuing to talk about the band as his underlings when they believed the compositional and musical contributions they had made to the last two albums warranted more equal status. Their sense of being taken for granted was exacerbated by Mick's doing nearly all the press, which meant that critics and members of the general public alike assumed Mick did everything else as well. Also, as the insecurity he had felt following his dismissal from the Clash began to recede, there were too many signs of the old Jones complacency and aloofness returning in his personal dealings with the others. Following the schism, the absconding trio formed their own band, Screaming Target (named after a Big Youth album), and teamed up with Paul 'Groucho' Smykle once more to record the 1991 Island album *Hometown Hi-Fi*. Co-written and mostly played by the three core members, it is largely an insipid affair which, ironically, says more about Mick's contribution to BAD than their own. It includes the song 'This Town', sung by Chrissie Hynde, which would appear to be an attack on their former bandmate: 'The wild one's selling jeans' was a reference to the Jones-sanctioned use of 'Should I Stay Or Should I Go' in a Levi's commercial. Screaming Target broke up soon afterwards, but the core of the band continue to make dance music under the name Dreadzone.

Around the same time as he lost the bulk of his band, Mick split up with Lauren's mother, Daisy. Typically, instead of succumbing to the emotional battering, within a matter of weeks, he had started work on putting together BAD II. Again, he turned to friends and established contacts for the personnel, but this time they came as a complete package. Already playing together in a local Notting Hill band were bassist Gary Stonadge, former Sigue Sigue Sputnik drummer Chris Kavanagh and second guitarist Nick Hawkins. All were in their early to mid twenties. The original intention was for Dan Donovan to stay as keyboard player. He co-wrote and played on 'Free', a track commissioned for the soundtrack of the unremarkable 1990 film *Flashback* and named after its hippy-child protagonist, but afterwards left the fold. He contributed to some tracks on the Screaming Target album, then – in a move not without a certain symmetry – joined the re-formed Sigue Sigue Sputnik.

While the band were rehearsing, writing and recording new material, Mick managed to remain in the public eye thanks to an unlikely collaboration with Aztec Camera's Roddy Frame. During his illness Mick had drawn strength from the Aztec Camera song 'Working In A Goldmine', and he told Roddy as much when the two happened to meet the following year. Roddy was subsequently moved to write 'Good Morning Britain' in such a blatant plagiarism of BAD's style that he felt honour-bound to invite Mick to sing and play on it as well as appear in the video. Its release as a single in September 1990, and near-immediate climb into the Top 20, could not have been better timed, coinciding as it did with the public emergence of BAD II.

For their début live performance the band chose the Town and Country Club's fifth-birthday celebrations, held on 10 August at the Alexandra Palace, Muswell Hill. The four-man line-up was augmented at the soundboard by DJ Zonka, who not only supplied the samples and effects previously provided by Don, but also played about with the mix as Tony James had in the original band's early days. The first gig was soon followed by the first album, released in October 1990. Produced by Mick with Olimax and DJ Shapps (Mick's cousin, Andre Shapps), it was recorded at Tony James's Sputnik studios and entitled *Kool-Aid*. It was a strictly limited edition, and a 'proper' album was scheduled to follow the next year. This perplexing concept certainly rubbed the *NME*'s Stuart Bailie up the wrong way: he noted that 'this sounds like a demo, and I wish it had stayed that way', awarding it just four out of ten. Over at *Q*, Ian MacMillan took a more considered approach, describing the album as 'a refreshing auditory experience . . . After one listen, several of the songs are in your head as firmly as a Christmas number one on Boxing Day. Perhaps the only common denominator is, oddly, the Clash: there are echoes of, in particular, *London Calling* all over this album . . . BAD will be hard pressed to surpass this in future.' He gave it four stars.

Even before the setbacks represented by his illness and the demise of the band's previous incarnation, Mick had rued BAD's failure to follow up on their 1986 commercial breakthrough in the UK. The limited edition idea was obviously a marketing device, and rushing something into the shops in time to benefit from the success of 'Good Morning Britain' also smacked of barefaced opportunism. Yet there was also a genuine impatience to get on with things. Stuart Bailie's dismissal of the project did not do it justice: it may be a record of a period of transition, but, as Ian MacMillan claimed, it is a fascinating one. Not least because all of the lyrics were written by Mick at a period of emotional turmoil, and are consequently some of the most nakedly autobiographical he has ever recorded.

The sense of hurt and loss he felt following the break-up of BAD and his relationship obviously opened other, older wounds, because the ghost of the

Clash also stalks *Kool-Aid*. It is not easy to tell where one ache stops and another starts. 'Can't Wait' expresses Mick's sense of frustration at having to return to square one yet again, but it also clearly harks back further than the last two years: there are references to mindgames, being told what to say and having something precious taken away. Similar sentiments are voiced in 'When The Time Comes' and 'In My Dreams'. An overview of Mick's life to date provides the raw material for 'Change Of Atmosphere', which ruminates on mistakes made and hearts broken; its main thrust comes from the chorus's identification of a 'situation no win' and expressed determination to 'rush for a change of atmosphere'. The opening lines revisit a sentiment already explored in the previous album's 'Baby, Don't Apologise', but here stated in the far more aggressively defiant first person: 'If I had my time again, I would do it all the same.'

The comparisons Mick had made a year before between the acid house and punk movements had been based on shared DIY music-making techniques and capacities to annoy the establishment. 'When The Time Comes' could be musing about contemporary police restrictions on raves or local government's interference with punk in 1976, or both. Unlike punk, however, acid house had no real voice of protest, something which Mick was evidently beginning to find disconcerting. Track titles like 'On One', 'Kickin' In' and 'Kool-Aid' might give the initial impression that at least part of the album is an unquestioning celebration of acid house culture. Nevertheless, first impressions would be wrong. 'On One' is a tough-minded and violently worded – 'I'd kill you if you weren't already dead' – attack on drug overkill, reinforced by a sample of William Burroughs, the cadaverous junky Beat author, croakily intoning 'feels so good you could just swim in it forever'. 'Kickin' In', a reworking of 'Free', is in this context a meditation on the illusion of the freedoms created by Sixties drug culture. 'Kool-Aid' describes people burning themselves out with endless partying, and hints at the apathy and withdrawal from the real world that underlie the rave scene's superficial sense of community.

The feeling that this album is as much about coming to terms with the Clash and the legacy of punk as it is about contemporary youth culture and Mick's private life is strengthened by a hard guitar sound, real, raw bass and drums and the odd sample of his old band. Which is not to say the record is retrogressive or even relentlessly angry. The dance beats might be harder, and played by what is evidently a rock'n'roll band, but they are still present. So are the samples and effects, which are relied upon to provide an otherwise unhappy collection of songs with a sense of humour, however black it might be. There is much use of the vocoder, giving parts of the album a robotic, futurist mood picked up by the cover artwork: garish lettering, computer grid images and a photo of the band clad in designer tracksuits and lit up to resemble characters in a video game (as in the 1982 film *Tron*). Although London landmarks are reproduced in the background of the front cover and the back cover map depicts London as the centre of the world, the usual locale-specific references are missing from the songs themselves. So, for the most part, are the usual cinematic allusions. Instead, the overall impression is of a self-created cyberpunk futureworld: an alien and somewhat unsettling environment. The album showed up in the charts for one week only, at number 55, thus becoming BAD's second lost classic.

Edited, remixed and revised by Mick and Andre Shapps, it was given a full release in July 1991 in a new cover and under the new title *The Globe*. BAD II were now on the Columbia label worldwide, as Sony had taken over CBS in late 1988 and had gradually phased out the label of that name. *Q*'s Dave Henderson offered the opinion that BAD's previous releases had normally failed to live up to the band's initial promise: 'But not any more. BAD II sees new mates with Jones, and the result is bizarre and sometimes breathtaking . . . Song phrases reappear in other songs, instrumentation is kept simple, the lyrics are tongue-in-cheek and strangely poignant . . . BAD II have taken new technology and redefined the process of putting an album together. A triumph against all the odds.' After that appraisal, the three stars he gave it seemed a little miserly. At the *NME*, Tim Southwell was impressed enough to award it seven out of ten, and comment, 'Like a trippy cartoon strip with a thousand central characters performing cameo roles, *The Globe* is quite ridiculous: ridiculous and utterly memorable.'

In truth, the changes between *Kool-Aid* and *The Globe* are hardly extensive enough to explain the three-point difference between Stuart Bailie's and Tim Southwell's *NME* evaluations. Most of the tracks are fundamentally the same, though the survivors have all been trimmed in length. 'Change Of Atmosphere' has been retitled 'Rush', and 'Can't Wait' replaced with a spunkier live version from the 10 August 1990 Alexandra Palace gig. The running order is little changed: 'Kickin' In' is replaced by 'I Don't Know' and 'The Globe', and 'On One' by 'Green Grass'; 'The Tea Party' is appended to side two.Two of the new songs reinforce the mood of the earlier version of the album. The title 'Green Grass' is open to several interpretations, and the lyric draws on most of them. It takes a journey through the mind to confront the self, and talks of coming to terms with 'what you are' rather than 'what you want to be'. The robotic bleeps and ragged guitar of 'I Don't Know' epitomise the album's sound, and its lyric, again about apathy and lack of communication, is openly accusatory.

In another echo of the past, BAD II made an arrangement with the *NME* similar to the one the Clash had made for the *Capital Radio* EP: a sticker was enclosed with the first pressing of *The Globe* and a coupon was printed in the 10 August 1992 issue of the paper; the first 2,000 people to return both together were sent a nine-track live album of BAD II's August 1990 Alexandra Palace show. The tracks were given approximate titles, in typical bootleg fashion, but, with the exception of Prince's '1999', were all drawn from previous BAD albums.

February 1991 had seen the re-release of 'Should I Stay Or Should I Go' precipitated by the Levi's ad. Rather than put it out with its original B-side,

Mick, whose song it was, had pulled off yet another marketing scam by insisting it be released as a double A-side single with BAD II's 'Rush'. 'With all the CD re-issues, new music doesn't have as much of an outlet as it should have, and I think of BAD II as a new band,' Mick explained to James Brown later that year, adding, less convincingly, 'I'm doing it for all the new bands to get in there.' In the event, all the airplay was afforded to the Clash song, but at least some of the people who bought it must have given 'Rush' a spin; having two of his compositions on the record certainly bumped up Mick's royalty cheque.

Despite these promotional efforts and an autumn tour, *The Globe* flopped in the UK, chalking up just one week in the charts at number 63. Thereafter, BAD II moved straight on to a US tour supported by the Farm. It was a jaunt with more than its fair share of ups and downs. One night, the car in which Mick was a passenger crashed and rolled over four times. Although he emerged unhurt, he was badly shaken by yet another brush with death. The tour was successful enough to take the BAD II album to number one in the US college radio (alternative) charts, and it went on to sell 250,000 copies. In Australia 'Rush' went to number one in the singles charts.

Surprisingly, given Mick's track record to date, no attempt was made to consolidate these breakthroughs with new material during the following year. In fact, the band appeared to go into hibernation. A long-form video compilation entitled *BAD I And II* was released in May 1992. The new band's only UK date in 1993 was supporting U2 at Wembley Stadium on 12 August. *BAD II* contributed two previously released songs to the soundtrack of rites of passage hoodlum movie *Amongst Friends*. Mick supplied a further two solo tracks, the reflective 'Long Island' and the mood piece 'No Ennio', both unremarkable. In September 1993 there were reports that recording had begun for a new BAD II album, originally set for January 1994 release. In November, the band – now officially including DJ Zonka and Andre Shapps on keyboards – accompanied U2's Zoo TV Tour to Australia. 'These big gigs are an opportunity to be heard by people who wouldn't normally ever see us,' Mick informed the *New Zealand Herald*'s Graham Reid. When he added, 'Anything below 50,000 and we're not really interested', he was ostensibly joking, but it did appear that he had grown tired of struggling on the lower rungs of the ladder to success. He also told Graham that he no longer listened to much music, and that he and his girlfriend, Lou McManus, preferred to spend most of their time watching rerun soaps on cable TV. All this sounded worryingly reminiscent of the interviews preceding the lacklustre *Tighten Up Vol 88*. An Antipodes-only 'greatest remixes' compilation album, pointedly entitled *The Lost Treasure Of BAD I And II*, was released to tie in with the visit. It included just one new track, the deeply uninspired-sounding 'Looking For A Song'. The sense that Mick had lost interest and direction was exacerbated by the delay in the new album's release.

Further band activity was limited to another name adjustment – to Big

Audio – and an appearance on 29 April 1994 at the Hammersmith Apollo memorial concert for Mick's erstwhile hero Mick Ronson, who had died from liver cancer exactly a year earlier. Ian Hunter was also on the bill. The following week, MTV carried news reports that Mick Jones had died of pneumonia. Perhaps taking the hint that he should get out more, he was often seen about London in the latter part of 1994, ligging and jamming with everyone from St Etienne to Primal Scream. He also contributed to the single project against the Criminal Justice Bill, 'Repetitive Beats', released under the name Retribution. This return to a more active role in popular culture came too late to gee up the long-in-the-pipeline album *Higher Power*, finally released in November 1994. It features yet another representation of Trellick Tower on its front cover and a song celebrating the main road running past Wilmcote House, 'Harrow Road', but for the most part it is twee, insipid and dull. More than one reviewer noted how appropriate it was that the 'Dynamite' had been dropped from the band's name.

Mick still insists that all he has ever wanted is to be in a band – and the inclusion of Andre Shapps means that at least part of his band now really is family – but one has to wonder how long a middle-aged man with a diminishing interest in contemporary music can continue to produce convincing work in the context of a set-up as self-consciously modern as Big Audio (Dynamite) (II). Most other successful creative artists of his age have endeavoured to free themselves from the image and genre restrictions that Mick still seems intent on embracing.

Bearing in mind his chiselled good looks, his interest in film and that he was given his first movie role in 1980 while still with the Clash, one might have expected Paul Simonon to be the former band member most likely to move into acting. This was not to be, but, as with Topper, there have been times in Paul's post-Clash life when he has appeared to be living a movie: his Los Angeles biking days, in particular, invite comparison with the Marlon Brando film *The Wild One* (1954) or the Dennis Hopper movie *Easy Rider* (1969). In truth, however, his interests have continued to combine the macho – motorbikes and bullfighting – with the creative – music and, especially, painting – and a true filmic portrayal of Paul's life would more closely resemble a James Dean biopic.

During the last years of the Clash, Paul began to regret having abandoned art so completely upon joining the band, and took it up again. Finding it as difficult as the others to adjust to the split in late 1985, he spent much of the following two years painting in his London flat or in New York. By 1988, though, he was beginning to miss playing in a band. The enthusiasm for rockabilly he had begun to develop at the beginning of the Eighties had flourished into a love of the full spectrum of Fifties rock'n'roll. Offsetting this essentially retro taste were his enduring fondness for reggae and a more recent interest in Tex-Mex and other Latin American musics he had been exposed to in his wanderings around Notting Hill and New York.

Paul had remained good friends with Nigel Dixon (formerly of occasional Clash support band Whirlwind and, briefly, Pearl Harbour's backing band) and decided Nigel's Gene Vincent-influenced rock'n'roll vocal style would be perfect for a new group combining all his musical interests. He lured him away from the band he was rehearsing with at the time by inviting him on an extended holiday-cum-ambience-research trip to El Paso, on the Texas side of the Mexican border. There, the two of them divided their time between writing songs and riding along the border on a couple of Harley-Davidson motorbikes they bought in town. Before long, they got caught up in the biker lifestyle, and decided to take an extended road trip to Los Angeles. 'We met up with Steve Jones in LA. We had the same bikes, so we decided to ride together,' Paul told the *NME's* Mary Ann Hobbs in 1991. 'It started out as three people and built up quite quickly to 30. I enjoyed the glamour of it.' Other members of this somewhat superannuated motorcycle gang were Billy Idol, Mickey Rourke and the Cult's Ian Astbury.

Steve Jones proved to be a useful contact. He had recently been touring with a hard rock backing band including guitarist Gary Myrick, who immediately clicked with Paul and Nigel: not only was he a versatile guitarist, having played with Stevie Wonder and Jackson Browne, but he was also Texan, a songwriter, a motorbike enthusiast and a painter. Together, the three worked up songs which reflected their part-real, part-fantasy world with titles like 'Joyride', 'Blue Motorcycle Eyes', 'Death In The Afternoon', 'Hey Amigo' and 'Blue Gene Vincent'. After some deliberation, they named themselves Havana 3 a.m. after an album by Cuban bandleader Perez Prado. They graduated from being the motorcycle gang's house band to playing gigs in Texas and north California with a friend of Gary sitting in on drums.

After a while, Paul began to grow tired of his new lifestyle. He was concerned because the motorcycle gang were being infiltrated by hell's angels, but there were other reasons. 'I got sick of the sunshine, and sick of people petting me,' he told Mary Ann Hobbs. 'I couldn't find anything I wanted to paint in LA, either. I got back to London and it was pissing down with rain, gloomy, freezing, and I was thinking, "God, this is lovely!" I went straight down the canal with a canvas and me brolly.'

Nigel and Gary moved to London with him, and – Paul having been let go by CBS – they began looking around for a record deal. After dropping the idea of bringing in Topper to sit in the drum seat, they ran the usual advertisement and held auditions. Travis Williams was hired in time to go out on the road supporting Big Audio Dynamite, and also for Havana 3 a.m. to headline their own shows in September and October 1989. A January 1990 gig at London's Borderline was reviewed by the *NME*'s Stephen Dalton, who noted that the band's stew of rock roots musics was essentially a variation on a theme outlined by the Clash on *London Calling*: 'Easily tonight's strongest offering is "The Hardest Game", a swirling Latino ghetto story and the finest slice of rock'n'roll mythologising since (pulling a name out of a hat) the Clash. Close behind comes ['Hey Amigo'] a chiselled instrumental slab of country-reggae-funk shot through with gunslinger guitar straight out of Sergio Leone.' These were the highlights. Stephen Dalton also noted that much of the rest of the set was made up of 'anonymous Gene Vincent-style workouts', and that 'Simonon's wired, wiry charisma and electrifyingly elegant movements' were the only things saving Havana 3 a.m. from being 'just another middling pub-rock outfit'.

Although there seemed to be no hurry to sign up the band at home, their cool rock'n'roll sound and image struck a chord with the West-obsessed pop market in Japan. A contract was offered by Portrait records, and Havana 3 a.m. recorded their eponymous album in Tokyo. It was released in Japan in December 1990 and promoted with a short tour. In February the following year, the album was issued in the UK by IRS. Reviewing it for the *NME*, Simon Williams wrote: 'At their best, the Havanas grab Tex-Mex culture by its neck and drag it round the dancefloor on the spaghetti western film set of life.' Again, though, he felt the highs did not justify the lows, describing the rockier songs as 'hamfisted' and 'punctuated by the kind of guitar histrionics that make Gary Moore suddenly seem like a decent bloke'. He awarded it five out of ten, summing it up as 'a lovingly-created tribute to past heroics which suffers only from a surfeit of utter banality'. At *Q*, Mat Snow enjoyed Paul's pursuance of the Clash's interest in 'global rockabilly', but asked for a little more ambition in future. He awarded the album three out of a possible five stars.

Together, the critics got it about right: 'Death In The Afternoon', 'The Hardest Game' and 'Hey Amigo' are all quality songs, but they take the Havana 3 a.m. concept's novelty value to its limits. Even the album cover is a pastiche, a photo of a reclining sultry young Latino woman superimposed on a fiery, explosive painted background, sharing the space only with a black and white photo of a Fifties motorcycle gang and excitable period lettering.

In fact, the woman is Tricia Ronane, former BAD PR agent and now the band's manager and Paul's wife. His previous marriage to Pearl Harbour having been dissolved, Paul married the 26-year-old Tricia in the Roman Catholic St Pius X Church, St Charles Square, Kensington, on 28 July 1990. (Objecting to the attendant pomp and circumstance, Joe Strummer boycotted the ceremony.) In late 1991, Tricia gave birth to a boy, Louis, and Paul bowed to family tradition by passing on the middle name Gustave. As early as February 1991, Paul admitted to Mary Ann Hobbs that his commitment to Havana 3 a.m. was at best sporadic. 'Painting is the number one thing for me these days,' he said. 'What can I say? I'll give the music a couple more years, and that's it.' The reaction to the album was hardly encouraging – none of Havana 3 a.m.'s records made the charts – and, although the band limped on for a while longer, the arrival of his son gave Paul yet another diversion, and the 'couple more years' were forgotten.

For all his supposedly wild youth, Paul was always the most stable member while the Clash were still together, and it would appear that he has adjusted best to life beyond the group. The need to 'strut his stuff' on-stage is no more. He has an alternative creative outlet, a family, and would appear to feel both realised and content with his lot.

Joe Strummer might not have been born with Paul Simonon's matinée idol looks, but his natural charisma and dramatic Clash stage persona suggested that, given the chance, he might come over well on the silver screen. He certainly made no secret of his love for the movies while with the band. Nor were the Clash's movie projects and his movie-influenced lyrics the sole means of expression for his enthusiasm. Following his contribution of two versions of 'Heartbreak Hotel' to the soundtrack of Diego Cotez's 1978 film *Grutzi Elvis*, he had attempted to make a 16 mm black and white film of his own in early 1983. Entitled *Hell West End*, it was a cops and robbers saga in which Paul Simonon played a street hoodlum in a poor boy cap, Mick Jones a slick hustler in a James Bond-style white tuxedo and Joe an armed British uniformed policeman with a moustache. Shot without a script, its director deemed it a disaster and was not too upset when it met a similar fate to Don Letts's *Clash On Broadway* film: the laboratory that held the negative went bankrupt and destroyed all the stock. The year 1983 also saw British director Stephen Frears offering Joe the role of the young hitman in *The Hit*, alongside John Hurt and Terence Stamp. Having just seen the play *Made In Britain*, though, Joe felt compelled to turn the offer down and instead point Stephen in the direction of the compelling young actor Tim Roth, who duly got the part.

While the Clash were still operational, Joe always put them first. The dissolution of the band and the commencement of his cinematic career were almost simultaneous, but it would be wrong to interpret this as a conscious plan. Perhaps more than any other former member of the Clash, Joe found it hard to come to terms with the band's demise, not least because he carried an extra burden of guilt. His confidence had been shattered by Bernie's manipulations, and he was also devastated by the death of his father and his mother's illness. 'I had to disassemble myself and put the pieces back together,' he explained on Channel 4's *Wired* in 1988. 'I'd lost my parents, my group. You want to think about things. You become a different person.' In 1986, not long after the death of his mother, Joe and Gaby had a second daughter, called Lola Maybellene (the former name possibly from the Kinks record, the latter certainly from Chuck Berry's first ever single). 'Imagine 20-odd years spent interested in yourself and your own ego, and suddenly there's a little bundle going, "Help me!"' Joe told the *NME*'s Gavin Martin shortly after Lola's birth. 'You get time to think about your own childhood, and watching my youngest girl, I've understood so much of what it is to be born and to live and to die.'

Thus, feeling at his most vulnerable for many a year, Joe was in no particular hurry to throw himself back into the spotlight, be it via music or via film. All his post-Clash activities have been low-key; whether in the field of music or cinema, or both, most of them have been bit parts or supporting roles and have allowed him to hide behind some guise or other. In 1988, *Musician*'s Bill Flanagan suggested to Joe that by taking small acting roles, composing music specifically for films, co-writing and producing for BAD and playing guitar for the Pogues, he had been avoiding expressing himself directly. 'That's true,' Joe acknowledged. 'It's a dead giveaway.' Bill went on to suggest that he was deliberately keeping his ego in check, and doing penance for past misdeeds. The feature was entitled 'The Exile Of Joe Strummer: In Which Our Vagabond Hero Roams The World, Taking Odd Jobs And Running From The Memory Of The Terrible Things He's Done'. Joe thought the latter part of the interpretation was taking things a little too far, but it has a certain romantic, cinematic – and, let's face it, Strummeresque – logic to it, recalling the Alan Ladd movie *Shane* (1953) or the Jack Nicholson film *Five Easy Pieces* (1970).

Following the Clash split, Joe allowed his activities and pursuits to be dictated by the random, by what came his way. It was initially a matter of coincidence that what came his way were opportunities to act the parts of rock'n'roll layabouts and gunslingers, and to compose and record basic rock'n'roll or Latin-tinged spaghetti western-style soundtracks; opportunities which, one cannot help but think, he probably would have accepted even if he had been taking a more active role in steering his own career. The gateway to this world of casual opportunity was an appropriately chance meeting with Alex Cox, who not only made a direct offer of work, but also furnished Joe with numerous further useful contacts. Once he plugged into this alternative network of independent film-makers and left-field musicians, Joe found himself part of a creative set-up that might have been larger, looser and more varied than the Clash, but was none the less another sort of group. The same names and faces were to pass in and out of his orbit in various permutations for at least the next seven years.

Originally from Liverpool, Alex Cox attended UCLA film school in Los Angeles on a Fulbright scholarship. He announced his arrival on the movie scene in 1984 with his wonderfully bizarre *Repo Man*. It was shot just outside LA and enhanced considerably by a soundtrack performed by local punk bands, among them the Circle Jerks, whose guitarist Zander Schloss also took an acting role. Alex's follow-up film was a typically off-the-wall version of the story of Sid Vicious and Nancy Spungeon entitled *Love Kills*. The chance meeting with Joe occurred before Christmas 1985. Having just wrapped up the latter film's English shoot, Alex was throwing a party at the Portobello Basin for the actors and crew. Joe and a friend decided to crash it, and Alex demanded a song for the film as price of admission.

Given that the movie was set in the heyday of punk, concerned a now deceased friend and was coming under regular attack from the former Johnny Rotten, Joe quite understandably had his doubts about the project. Even so, after finally giving in to Alex's repeated requests to go and see a rough-cut, he was impressed enough by the film's energy to agree to contribute. He composed an eponymous song for the closing credits and also supplied the track 'Dum Dum Club'. Mick Jones produced and played guitar on both songs. Alex maintained the LA punk connection by commissioning a song from the Circle Jerks. Former Pistol Steve Jones (now resident in LA) provided another, and Glen Matlock played bass for the film band's versions of the Sex Pistols' canon. Several more tracks came from the Pogues, for whose single 'A Pair Of Brown Eyes' Alex had recently directed a strange and controversial video. Nevertheless, Alex still did not have enough music and was running out of money. So Joe volunteered to write a few incidental pieces. CBS had allowed him to donate the original two songs to the film on the understanding that they retained the rights to release them as a single. As the soundtrack album was to be released on MCA, the terms of his contract forbade him to contribute further on an official basis. Thus, for the same reason as Mick's efforts were totally anonymous, Joe supplied this incidental music under an assumed name. Five pieces, including one entitled 'Garbage Kills', are attributed to the pen of the mysterious Dan Wul and performed by the equally elusive Pray for Rain.

The simultaneous release of the single 'Love Kills' and the film and soundtrack album in late July 1986 should have kicked off Joe's solo musical career in fine style, but circumstances conspired against him. Firstly, the title of the film and album had been changed at the last minute to *Sid And Nancy*, substantially diminishing the recognition factor. Secondly, the critical reception of both was hostile. In her review of the album for the *NME* Deanne Pearson claimed that neither the film nor the record caught the essence of either punk or Sid, and dismissed the music as a failed spoof. Denied an easy ride on the back of the movie, Joe's single might still have stood a chance of making it on its own terms. Alex Cox had even returned a favour by shooting a video for Joe in Tabernas, near Almería, where Sergio Leone had shot most of his spaghetti westerns. For some reason, the clip was denied general exposure, and even two years later, *Night Network* were unable to find a copy for broadcast. 'I hear it's in a bar in Durango on the video jukebox,' remarked Joe, drily.

One would not have received the impression that 'Love Kills' is a memorable, if basic, rock'n'roll song from Steven Wells's *NME* singles review. A former teenage punk still bearing a grudge towards the Clash for betraying their punk roots, he dismissed it as 'weak and pitiful' and offered the following career advice to Joe: 'It's time for the gold watch. P'raps you could get a job making tea at the BBC or something.' The single flopped, climbing no higher than number 69 in the UK charts. If Joe had briefly entertained thoughts of returning to the musical arena with an album project of his own, this would have been enough to dissuade him.

By the summer of 1986, however, he had already signed up for two further collaborations with Alex. Although mischievous provocation and dark, surreal humour are evident in all his work, much of the director's determinedly left-field approach to film-making is attributable to his somewhat more serious political agenda. In addition to cross-breeding and spoofing several different movie genres, *Repo Man* also attacks Ronald Reagan's America: a land without culture, opportunities or morality. Throughout the film overheard TV bulletins and conversational asides make reference to US interference in Central America. Alex's next film project was to be a more direct exploration of this issue, a biopic of William Walker.

Born in 1824, Walker was an adventurer and a firm adherent to the US's mid-19th-century concept of Manifest Destiny: namely that it was the God-given right of the American people to dominate the western hemisphere. Sponsored by trading magnate Cornelius Vanderbilt, he invaded Nicaragua in 1855 with a force of 55 mercenaries known as the Immortals, and set himself up as president. Within two years, he went from being a liberal to being, in Alex's words, 'a totally corrupt dictator'. Neighbouring countries defeated Walker in battle in 1857. He was forced to beat a retreat, but twice attempted to reinvade before the US Navy deported him to Nashville. He was eventually executed on 12 September 1860. Talking to Graham Fuller for an *NME* feature later that same year, Alex put Walker's apparently outrageous behaviour in context: 'He had a very real belief that he could just go and take a country. Because the US had recently seized or acquired New Mexico, California, Arizona, Colorado and Utah from Mexico, and he had no reason to doubt that he would become the ruler of Central America.' The parallel with the Reagan regime's covert and not so covert activities in the same area was not lost on the director. The temptation to make an allegorical film based on Walker's life proved irresistible. 'I want to look at him in terms of what's happened more recently, sorta saying that the 20th century's just around the corner . . .'

For Joe, the connection with his own *Sandinista!* era interest in Central American politics was too great to ignore, and he committed himself to an as yet unspecified involvement in the project. The other Cox venture he took on at this time had a more complicated genesis. Partly as background research for the William Walker film and partly as an adventure, Alex had suggested that Joe, the Pogues and recent Pogues producer Elvis Costello travel to Nicaragua to play a few gigs, while he accompanied them and made a video documentary of the trip. The artists all agreed, and duly kept August 1986 free. Unfortunately, Alex found it impossible to raise the £200,000 he needed to fund the project. Strangely, however, he was instead offered £900,000 by Island Pictures to follow through on a far flakier idea.

Along with Alex's friend Dick Rude and cameraman Tom Richmond, Joe had accompanied the director to the Cannes Film Festival earlier in the year to promote *Sid And Nancy*. The morning after an extended drinking bout, Alex looked at his three companions suffering by the hotel pool and was inspired to suggest – as a joke – making a film about three hopelessly incompetent, drunken hitmen. The others picked up the idea and ran with it. They envisioned a tacky B movie filmed in the style of a spaghetti western on the same set where Alex and Joe had shot the video for 'Love Kills', and where Alex had been going on occasional visits to pay homage to his spaghetti western director heroes since he was a schoolboy. Carried away with the idea, Alex and Dick committed themselves to writing a screenplay in just three days. To give the project a name, they appropriated a suitably melodramatic title from the Clash's back catalogue: *Straight To Hell.*

It was to realise this half-baked venture that the money men were prepared to furnish the best part of a million pounds. By far the biggest selling point was the inclusion on the cast list and provisional soundtrack credits of Joe, Elvis Costello and the Pogues, all of whom had nothing better to do with their Augusts after the cancellation of the Nicaraguan trip. Joe's 'method' preparations for his first sizeable acting role as one of the hitmen, Simms, goes partway to explaining his insistence on sleeping under the piano while helping co-write and produce BAD's *No 10 Upping Street.* Joe's involvement with that record also explains, indirectly, how Jim Jarmusch came to direct the video for BAD's 'Sightsee MC': Alex brought in fellow maverick director Jim to play a bit part in *Straight To Hell.* Also agreeing to come along on the 'working holiday' for a deferred share of the profits were numerous familiar faces from Alex's previous two movies, including Kurt Cobain's wife to be Courtney Love as 'pregnant white trash' Velma, Zander Schloss as Karl the Wiener Man and Sy Richardson as Norwood, the leader of the three hitmen.

The necessarily rapid shooting schedule, heavy and prolonged post-shoot drinking sessions and the absence of training or ambition among most of the amateur members of the cast did not bode well for a masterpiece of contemporary film, but no one could accuse Joe of failing to take his role seriously. During their work together on the *Sid And Nancy* soundtrack Alex had noticed that he wore the same clothes day after day (which Joe later claimed was indicative of how unhappy and confused he had been during that period) and had written this into the script as one of Simms's many unsavoury personality quirks. In his efforts to get into character and stay there, Joe refused to change or even remove his clothing for the duration of the shoot; slept on set most nights in a broken-down old car; used sugar water to persuade flies to walk across his face during takes; combed his hair with a knife dipped in petrol; went out drinking in local bars wearing his gun and holster; and practised twirling said weapon until his fingers were so sore they had to be taped up.

The fact that the film involved several of the music scene's leading figures attracted considerable interest from the music papers, many of which sent journalists to conduct interviews on set. Most of them found Joe's method approach not a little disconcerting. 'I'm a poseur,' he – or rather, Simms – informed *Q*'s Simon Banner. 'I can twirl a gun great, but I can't shoot for fuck. I'm a heap of trash. I'll bang any woman and kill any man, and I'll think nothing of it. I'm bad energy, man.' Stepping outside the role for a few moments, he admitted that he thought about acting 24 hours a day and indicated that he intended to make a full-time commitment to the craft. 'It's what I want to do, to be an actor. Not an ac-*tor*, though. I'm not going to go to drama school. I've discovered that there's a lot more to acting than just learning the lines. I've had an intense life, so I've got a lot of experience to draw on.'

While on set, Joe co-wrote with Zander Schloss and Miguel Sandoval the song Karl sings in praise of his Disco Wiener Haven (or, more precisely, his hot-dog stand), 'Salsa Y Ketchup'. Back in the UK, Joe, Elvis and the Pogues all wrote songs for the soundtrack. For the usual contractual reasons, Joe's official performances, backed by the Bug Out Gang, were limited to the Ennio Morricone pastiche 'Ambush At Mystery Rock' and the melodramatic ballad 'Evil Darling', the second of which made it to the album but not the film. Nevertheless, Dan Wul and Pray for Rain came up with a further 12 instrumental pieces, including one called 'Love Swells' (a reference to Velma's condition).

When the financial backers got to see the result of their investment, they were unanimously underwhelmed. The critics agreed, and the film sank without trace. If nothing else, this at least spared the world the proposed sequel, a Foreign Legion spoof entitled *Back To Hell*. Nor did the soundtrack album make enough money to spare anyone's blushes. Released on the Hell label, through Stiff, it proved difficult to find, let alone like. Reviewing it for the *NME*, Jane Solanas dismissed it as a substandard pastiche of Ennio Morricone's soundtrack work and offered a feminist perspective on the whole sorry shambles of the *Straight To Hell* project: 'I find the idea of grown men acting out schoolboy fantasies of guns, death, tits and rape – all that macho cowboy garbage – a bit sad; and I certainly don't want to have to *pay* them for it.'

If the truth be told, Joe's acting in the film leaves a lot to be desired, and his eventual death at the hands of Velma comes as something of a relief. The 'method' stylisations served only to make everything he does look . . . acted. All the same, he was offered another role immediately after completion of work on the soundtrack. Alex Cox had hired Rudy Wurlitzer – responsible for the scripts for cult road movie *Two-Lane Blacktop* (1971) and *Pat Garrett And Billy The Kid* (directed by Sam Peckinpah, 1973) – to write the script for *Walker*. In late 1986, Rudy co-directed a project of his own, entitled *Candy Mountain*. A rock'n'roll road movie set in Canada, it already had several other musicians, including Tom Waits, David JoHansen and Dr John, in the cast. Joe was offered a bit part as a security guard and member of an awful rock'n'roll band. 'It was very frustrating that Joe had only a small part, because he was very exciting,' Rudy Wurlitzer told Graham Fuller for *Film Comment* in 1987. 'One wanted more of him. He could be a great star, a major leading man. Somebody will have to give him a big romantic role soon, and I'm sure somebody will.' *Candy Mountain* itself was not to be Joe's ticket to stardom: it was late December 1989 before it was released in the UK, and it received mixed reviews and only limited distribution.

The eight and a half week shoot for *Walker* commenced in the Nicaraguan city of Granada in January 1987. This time Alex had a budget of $5 million, enough to bring in a couple of name actors for the leading roles, Ed Harris and recent Oscar-winner Marlee Matlin. Many of the lesser roles went to Alex's usual repertory company, however, and Joe found himself sharing accommodation with Dick Rude, the Pogues' Spider Stacey and Zander Schloss, among others. His own part was the relatively small one of Immortals dishwasher Faucet who, like Simms before him, was destined to be shot and killed by a woman. Even so, he underwent typically extensive preparations, growing his hair and beard, elaborately embroidering his waistcoat and using damp sand to protect his skin instead of anachronistic sun block.

Towards the end of filming, the shoot was visited by Graham Fuller, who subsequently filed reports for both the *NME* and *Film Comment*. Joe proved a reluctant interviewee. He seemed to be undergoing a crisis of confidence about his acting, despite the fact that his completed roles had yet to be thrown to the critics. 'This is the beginning of the end,' he said. 'It's too difficult.' The extent to which he was expressing his true feelings came into question later that year when he admitted to *Melody Maker*'s Ted Mico that his diffidence was a form of self-protection: 'I'm trying to underplay the acting bit at the moment. My secret ambitions may be another matter, but I don't want to set myself up by saying I want to be a great actor. Pop stars have a lot to live down in that field.'

The sense of disorientation he conveyed to Graham Fuller seemed genuine enough. Making reference to his involvement with the BAD album, he conceded, 'I don't know what to do for myself. I don't know whether to go back to rocking or not.' Some of the ambivalence he expressed can be attributed to the fact that *Walker* was providing more of an opportunity for him to stretch himself musically than it was as an actor. Prior to leaving the UK, he had been offered the job of composing the entire movie soundtrack. Intending to write in Nicaragua so as to capture the ambience accurately – more method – he had crammed a tiny Casio synthesizer and a large 4-track Fostex 250 tape recorder into his suitcases. A ten-day break mid-shoot allowed him to make use of a piano in the house where Alex was staying, but most of the composing was done following completion of filming. Played on the Casio and a guitar he picked up while in Nicaragua, his ideas were demoed on the Fostex. When with the 101ers, and for much of his time with the Clash, Joe's ability to compose music had been limited to sketching out some rudimentary chords. For those who were unaware of his attempts at occasional music for Alex's previous two films, Strummer the Versatile Musician and Imaginative Arranger was to come as something of a surprise.

Joe admitted to *Musician*'s Bill Flanagan that soundtrack composition offered a certain freedom that being part of a rock'n'roll band did not. 'You're suspended for a moment from the rules of rock'n'roll. I really like that. You can say, "Hey, the jazzy number fits a scene, that's why it exists." You're not saying, "*I* think this is hip": that's a burden.' During an interview with US radio station KCRW he – not wholly seriously – attributed the soundtrack's strong Latin feel to having lived in Mexico City as a child and revealed: 'The key for me was finding the Mexican harmony. Once I found that, I could hear the trumpet part in my brain. That was the first thing I had. Somehow it was in that rhythm, and it didn't work in any other rhythm.' Joe made efforts to come up with appropriate lyrics for most of the tunes, but after some consideration, he decided that not all of them worked in context. Of the 14 tracks selected for the soundtrack album, just three have lyrics, and two of these do not even appear in the film: by this stage Joe was keen for the record to stand as an interpretive piece of work in its own right.

Recording sessions took place at Russian Hill Recording in San Francisco. 'It was a lot of pressure because you're spending their money, and there's a lot of people waiting for you, and there's nobody to fall back on if you end up with a tattered pile of tape and there's no music for the movie,' Joe told the *East Coast Rocker*'s Harold De Muir. 'Movie people seem to operate on the edge of desperation constantly – everything's a crisis – and you just accept that and go along with it.' Joe hired no fewer than 15 Bay Area session musicians and got straight to work. He was so impressed with the musicians' playing that he insisted their names be printed prominently on the album's back cover. Zander Schloss is credited with guitar and numerous other stringed instruments, as well as for the guitar arrangements. Dick Bright, brought in to play violin, is credited along with Joe for the string and horn arrangements. Aside from writing and producing, the only other credit Joe took for himself was for singing 'The Unknown Immortal', 'Tennessee Rain' and 'Tropic Of No Return'. In fact, as he revealed to Bill Flanagan, he also played piano, guitar or marimba on almost all the tracks. Again, his reticence in this area had more to do with contractual constraints than modesty. The album was due to be released on Virgin's Movie Music label; the terms of his contract with CBS – now taken over by Sony – allowed him to write and produce for any project, but to sing or play on the album required a special deal, and, although Sony had agreed to the three vocals, Joe did not want to push his luck any further.

Released in February 1988, the album's cross-pollination of numerous folk and Latin idioms won unanimous acclaim. In the *NME* Gavin Martin – a man with something of a track record for puncturing the Clash's pretensions – gave it eight out of ten: 'You may be a little stunned and staggered at first (I was) to find the man with the demon bark and three chord bite has composed every note here. But from lustrous samba percussion, through flamenco horns and country inflections, it's all gorgeously effective and superbly detailed . . .' For *Q*, Charles Shaar Murray awarded the album four out of five stars, stating that it 'should finally erase any lingering impression of the old Clash man as some kind of wonderful loose cannon who is only effective when aimed and steadied by Mick Jones or some other comparatively lucid, cool-headed type. . .a remarkably elegant, loose-limbed and accomplished set of ersatz Latin themes spiked with delicate country touches.' He made special mention of 'an astonishing finale where the Latin and C&W motifs are combined for a symbolic reconciliation', before concluding: 'If the movie turns out to be rubbish, it certainly won't be Joe Strummer's fault.'

Whether or not the movie was rubbish was something some people would have to wait another year to find out, and many more would never be afforded the opportunity to discover for themselves. As CSM noted, a movie score is by definition part of a larger event. It is rare for largely instrumental movie soundtrack albums to be hugely commercially successful even in the most ideal of circumstances and, left to fend for itself, the *Walker* soundtrack album made little impact. When talking about working with Alex Cox to Sean O'Hagan, Joe likened his spirit and creative approach to that of the Clash. The director also seemed doomed to enjoy a similar kind of relationship with the business side of commercial arts. *Walker* raised the hackles of its Universal Pictures backers, and US critics found its oddball mixture of comedy and tragedy confusing. Alex believed that it was because he was 'perceived as a mad tool of the Sandinistas' in the US that 'the film played for about a week in six cities in six back street cinemas and was then removed by the distributor'. In the UK it was March 1989 before Universal's subsidiary could finally be persuaded to give it even a limited release. Reviews were not kind. 'Cox should get his act together, and stop making half movies,' wrote the *NME*'s David Quantick.

Walker's poor reception in the US may well have been at least partly politically motivated, but the less partisan UK reviewers were correct in suggesting that it is a film not without artistic flaws. Nevertheless, Alex firmly believed that his political leanings were to blame for the difficulties he found in raising funding for later projects. After the creative whirl of the mid-Eighties, he hit the doldrums in Hollywood, and went off to make films in Mexico City. He also presents BBC2's cult film slot, *Moviedrome*.

Following completion of work on the soundtrack in the summer of 1987, Joe returned to the UK. Exhausted, and intending to take some time off, his only planned activity was appearing on an edition of the Irish RTE television programme *The Session* that was devoted to the Pogues, on which he and the band performed 'London Calling'. In late November, a call came out of the blue asking him to stand in for Pogues' guitarist Phil Chevron (whose ulcer was playing up) on a month-long tour of America. He agreed, and after a few brief lessons from Phil and a warm-up gig at the Electric Ballroom, the band departed for the States.

Although the Pogues' tricky chord changes and full-tilt approach challenged Joe's still somewhat limited guitar technique, it was a relatively unpressured return to live performance, and he enjoyed it immensely. He spent most of his time in the background and made it clear that he had no desire to upstage Shane MacGowan, but he was allowed two vocal features, on 'London Calling' and 'I Fought The Law'. He gave his last performance as official deputy for Phil at another UK gig, at the Glasgow Barrowlands in late December, but was called back to repeat his guest spot at the Pogues' traditional St Patrick's Day bash on 17 March 1988. The gig was filmed and released later that year as the Virgin long-form video *The Pogues Live At The Town And Country: St Patrick's Night.*

By this time, Joe had already begun work on his next project. Director Marisa Silver's second film, entitled *Permanent Record* and starring Keanu Reeves, examines the impact of the suicide of a gifted, highly strung schoolboy on his friends and classmates. When asked to write the soundtrack, Joe was not keen to revisit the tensions of the *Walker* sessions quite so soon, but he attended a screening and, being the brother of a teenage suicide, found himself deeply touched by the film's subject matter. He took the commission. His brief was wider than might have been expected, and covered the full extent of the American high school experience: driving and party sequences as well as lonely bedroom musings. The music and lyrics had to reflect that the film was set in the American Midwest, but there was no need for foreign, historical or movie genre references, which gave him even more freedom.

Joe was encouraged and enthused by the critical reaction to his *Walker* soundtrack, with what CSM referred to as its combination of Latin and C&W motifs, and had been inspired by Paul Simon's 1986 album *Graceland,* which combined various African musics with American R&B, rock'n'roll, cajun and country. Of course, the Clash had made their experiments along similar lines on 1980's *Sandinista!,* and Joe had recently been playing various folk hybrids with the Pogues. Also, he had long been intrigued by the New Orleans group the Meters: 'The key to New Orleans music is that it is rock'n'roll, but it's also mixing with Latin styles of music,' he explained on US radio station KCRW later in 1988. 'If you investigate Professor Longhair, he was putting rumba and samba into the 4/4 blues. So New Orleans does have that salsa to it, although it's more hidden. It's called a second line rhythm.'

Joe wanted to begin writing some uptempo rock music again, but he was keen to pursue what had felt like a natural progression of Latin musical stylings through his last two soundtrack projects, despite the fact *Permanent Record* makes no sort of reference to Latin culture. With this in mind, he put together a band called the Latino Rockabilly War, featuring Zander Schloss on guitar, the Untouchables' Willie MacNeil on drums, jazz player Jim Donica on bass, Tupelo Joe Altruda on jazztone guitar and keyboards and – from the Poncho Sanchez Octet – Poncho Sanchez on congas and percussion and Ramon Vanda on timbales and percussion. The Latin musicians were 'to supply me with something to war against'; in other words, to create Joe's own version of a second line rhythm. Thus, wholly coincidentally or otherwise, Joe and his fellow former Clash member Paul Simonon both arrived at a similar sort of musical crossover at approximately the same time.

Recording took place at Baby O Recorders in Los Angeles. Joe's production standards were deliberately rough-and-ready in order to capture what he described as 'the sound of musicians struggling with their instruments'. As with *Walker*, he recorded more tracks than were absolutely necessary, with the intention of releasing an album that, though complementary to the film, could stand as a piece of work on its own. As it was to be released on Epic – his American label – there were no contractual limitations to his involvement in the project. He composed a total of 12 tracks, six of which had Strummer vocals.

In the event, whether it was because the results were deemed a little *too* rough-and-ready or because Epic wanted to make the most of tracks commissioned from other artists for the film, Joe's work was confined to side one of the album. Only half a dozen tracks are used – most of them fleetingly – in the film itself. The record features 'Trash City', 'Baby The Trans', 'Nefertiti Rock', 'Nothin' 'Bout Nothin'' and 'Permanent Record', the latter being the only instrumental and the film's main theme. Strangely, it is not listed in the film credits, though the other tracks are, along with another Strummer vocal, 'Cholo Vest' (subsequently made available on the B-side of the 12-inch version of Joe's October 1989 single, 'Island Hopping').

On 18 June 1988, 'Trash City' was released as a UK single on the Epic label. The *NME* review announced, 'Resurrection blooooooody Joe! . . . There might not be a riot goin' on, but there sure as hell is a small hooley arockin'! Nobody makes the pulse race better . . .' It was followed by the album in mid-July. 'Joe is pushing off on his solo adventures with an increasing sense of purpose now,' wrote Stuart Bailie for the *NME*. 'Mr Morricone will hardly feel threatened by his efforts, but there is a bigness afforded in this area, a facility for the indulgent sweep that fits in so ably with Strummer's own widescreen vision.' He noted the ongoing Latin references: 'But while the previous exercises made out with melancholy atmospherics and a flamenco twang, this time he's going for an upbeat basement rattle.' The hit-and-miss production provoked comment, as did the fact that Joe seemed to be coasting rather than pushing himself creatively. '"Trash City" has a few special moments, but there is nothing in the way of spacey textures to match the moody tracks on *Combat Rock*.' What the reviewer did not know, of course, is that any tracks answering to that description had been left off. He gave the album as a whole six out of ten.

Joe himself described the four vocal tracks on the album as 'rockabilly hymns to the problems of urban living'. Lyrically, they appear to be either composed of fragments taken from typical American teenage conversations or just plain stream-of-consciousness nonsense. 'Nothin' 'Bout Nothin'' touches vaguely on the kind of nihilism that can feed teen suicide, something which Joe voices more forcefully in the absent 'Cholo Vest': 'Nobody ever really, really thinks about you when you're gone.' Whereas none of the songs would make a top ten of his best compositions, the unusual musical stylisation does nothing to diminish their potency, though this may well be because, as repeated listenings reveal, 'Trash City' owes a clear musical debt to the Clash's 'Spanish Bombs', and 'Nothin' 'Bout Nothin'' to 'North And South'.

The film was released in the US in April 1988, where its topical subject matter struck a chord and made it extremely popular: the late Eighties and early Nineties saw something of an epidemic of ennui and disaffection among (chiefly) small town, Midwestern adolescents, and the most extreme manifestation of this syndrome was an increase in youth suicide. *Permanent Record* examines the devastation experienced by people left behind and attempts to promote a positive, optimistic response. Inevitably, however, the dramatic impact of the central tragedy serves to romanticise it and works against the main thrust of the film. Released much later in the UK, it had too few shared reference points with British culture to repeat its American success; like the previous film projects with which Joe had been involved, it quickly disappeared from the public eye.

An indication that Joe intended Latino Rockabilly War to be more than just a one-off movie project came in July 1988, when the band headlined a UK tour under the banner Rock Against the Rich, set up by Hackney-based anarchist squatters' organisation Class War. While nobody took exception to an event Joe played for Amnesty International at the same time, concern was voiced in the media about Joe's association with Class War, an organisation in favour of violent struggle. 'When people feel like that, they feel like that,' Joe told the *NME*'s Danny Kelly. 'You can either acknowledge it or pretend it isn't there. People in this place, from what I can see, might well feel violent from time to time.' Danny also suggested that it might be considered just a little hypocritical for someone as wealthy as Joe to take part in a tour entitled Rock Against the Rich. 'The issue isn't how well off or otherwise Joe Strummer is; they just needed some kind of frontman.'

Most considered his involvement to be a misjudged romantic gesture on a par with wearing the Brigade Rosse T-shirt ten years earlier, an indication not so much of his political commitment as of how far out of touch he was. Class War themselves tried to rectify this position by including an interview with him in their eponymous news sheet. Joe's retort to the press was 'They're scared that their cushy, middle class jobs might be at risk. They can handle stuff like Mandela or Amnesty, because it's about things going on in faraway places. None of those things are about people trying to change things here.' In an approximately contemporary interview published in Amnesty International's newsletter Joe's support for Class War was considerably more guarded. He confessed that he wished the words *against* and *anti* were not so prominent in their promotional literature, claiming that he was more interested in offering positive support to the various local organisations to which the tour would be donating money, promoting debate amongst young people and standing up for the freedom of speech. The following year, he revealed more about his own motives to the *NME*'s Stuart Maconie: 'After so long away, I just couldn't go out again to the heartland of Britain simply for the money. I didn't want anything like a Joe Strummer star trip. There had to be another reason.'

The Latino Rockabilly War played a set covering Joe's entire career to date: his first composition for the 101ers, 'Keys To Your Heart'; Clash favourites like 'I Fought The Law' and 'Police And Thieves'; 'Love Kills'; some of the songs he co-wrote for BAD, among them 'V 13' and 'Sightsee MC'; a couple of Pogues numbers, including 'If I Should Fall From Grace With God'; selections from the *Permanent Record* soundtrack; and a cover version of Nicky Thomas's 1970 reggae hit 'Love Of The Common People'. In her review of the Electric Ballroom gig Jane Solanas responded to this eclecticism thus, 'It may be let's-be-nice-to-Joe-Strummer time, but what he's doing with the Latino Rockabilly War is no different to what he did with the 101ers or the last incarnation of the Clash: pedestrian pub rock . . .'

The tour had been brought forward from August 1988 at short notice because Joe had another film commitment that month: a substantial acting role in Jim Jarmusch's latest project, *Mystery Train*. Set and filmed in Memphis, Tennessee, it consists of three separate, but overlapping, storylines touching in some way on the legacy of Elvis Presley. Since the Clash split, Joe had been affecting a Fifties rocker style not a million miles from that of his 101ers days, and in the film he was hardly cast against type as a displaced English rocker called Johnny, but nicknamed Elvis.

Not only was Joe on friendly terms with Jim via the *Straight To Hell* and BAD projects to which they had both contributed, but he was also a fan of Jim's work, having named him and Spike Lee among his favourite young directors early the previous year. Like Alex, Jim was fond of using amateur actors, many of them musicians. Tom Waits, whose path had crossed with Joe's on *Candy Mountain*, had taken one of the lead roles in his last film, *Down By Law*, and was to provide a DJ voice-over for *Mystery Train*. The new film also featured Screamin' Jay Hawkins and Rufus 'Walkin' The Dog' Thomas. On his arrival in Memphis, Joe found a team atmosphere not unlike the one he had enjoyed on Alex's shoots. Although Jim's style was very different, he and Alex had similar attitudes to the film business. That said, *Mystery Train* represented a step closer towards commercial viability for Jim, being shot in colour rather than his hitherto preferred black and white.

Released in the UK in December 1989, the movie was hailed as a minor masterpiece, but it could not be claimed that this was in any way due to Joe's contribution. As in his previous sizeable role, he *looks* as though he is acting, putting too much effort into his expressions and reactions. In interviews given prior to the film's release Joe made the same self-deprecating noises he had while filming *Walker*. '*Mystery Train* is a good, funny film, and I only spoil the last bit,' he told Stuart Maconie. 'But I wouldn't want to overplay the film stuff. Films were a respite, they were a nice place to go when I needed to get away from rock'n'roll. But they're not important to me, making records is what matters. And if you're going to do that properly, you don't have time to piss about in any other medium.'

Jim Jarmusch's friend and long-standing musical collaborator John Lurie provided the incidental music for the soundtrack. On one hand this was perhaps disappointing for Joe, whose own enthusiasms were very much in tune with the film's setting and subject matter. On the other hand, however, it meant there was nothing to divert his energies away from making music for himself. Straight after the completion of the filming schedule he returned to Baby O Recorders in Los Angeles to commence work on his first bona fide post-Clash rock'n'roll album. The Latino Rockabilly War had gone their separate ways after the UK tour, but Joe retained his old collaborator Zander Schloss for the sessions, and Willie MacNeil shared the drumming with former Red Hot Chili Peppers man Jack Irons. Making up the basic four-man group was new bassist Lonnie Marshall.

Joe had already written 12 of the 14 songs that would be included on the album. During the rehearsals Zander and Lonnie arranged their own guitar and bass parts, and with Joe, they also co-wrote 'Boogie With Your Children'. The remaining selection was a cover of C. Campbell and the Tenners' reggae song 'Ride Your Donkey'. Extensive rehearsals were necessary because Joe wanted to persevere with the basic production values employed on *Permanent Record* and, indeed, *The Clash*: 'We did it without a safety net. No click track in the drummer's ear, or any of that,' he told Stuart Maconie. 'All the time we were rolling tape, burning up time. We used a Neve desk, valve amps, and open mikes. You can't separate the channels, the sounds are overlapping all over the place, so you can't remix them. It's like a house of cards, pull out one piece and it all comes down.' Overdubs were usually limited to guitars, keyboards and vocals.

While Joe was resident in Los Angeles, the city experienced two minor tremors which prompted him to call the record *Earthquake Weather*. Its release, in October 1989, coincided with a San Franciscan quake measuring 6.9 on the Richter scale. The first single from the album, 'Gangsterville', emerged the preceding August. No one had told the *NME*'s Steven Wells it was be-kind-to-Joe-Strummer time, and he dismissed it as 'too busy and low key by half'. In his album review for the same paper Andrew Collins wrote: 'this album is a minefield of duff moments . . . mostly due to Joe being soppy in his old age. When he sounds hard, he can pull freight trains with his teeth, but when weaknesses like his penchant for weedy Latino tinkling come to the fore, it's all a bit of a comedown . . . Lyrically, Strummer's a poor Xerox of Tom Waits . . . He drops American references like a paper trail for us to chase.' He awarded it just five out of ten.

Musically, *Earthquake Weather* offers up a predictable enough gumbo of hard-driving rock'n'roll, hard funk, relaxed reggae and positively comatose Latin and jazzy noodlings. What is perhaps more surprising is how much variety Joe manages to coax from the predominant staccato 'Clampdown'-style uptempo rock template. The warm, analogue sound is ideally suited to the rootsy style of the music, but while the lyrics add to the ambience, they attempt little more; and it is this which is the album's main failing.

After his visits to both Almería and Granada, Joe was full of what he had learned from those cultures and how they had changed his opinion of British society. Later in 1989, he told Channel 4's *Rapido* programme, 'I want to grow up with my audience. I want to make music for the people I've grown up with. I'd like to keep their attention. I don't expect to be getting through to the younger pop crowd. I learned that from Paul Simon.' What Joe's audience might have expected, then, were songs reflecting his experiences since the break-up of the Clash: the struggles he had seen poor people going through, his thoughts on society, environment and culture, and some of the insights he had acquired from the traumas in his personal and professional life. That is not what his audience got. It is difficult to determine anything but the most general gist of meaning from many of the lyrics. One song that is all too straightforward, however, has Joe adopting the persona of a lazy Hemingwayesque sailor to contemplate going out 'Island Hopping' around the Caribbean. A long way from 'Garageland', 'Cheapskates' and Rock Against the Rich.

It would perhaps be unfair to expect him to remain true to the sentiments he expressed while with the Clash for the rest of his life, but Joe's best work has always been direct, passionate and/or compassionate, and he does himself a disservice when he ignores these strengths. 'Gangsterville', a tale of shady dealings in the Third World is – unlike, say, the Clash's 'Dictator' – given added clout by its first-hand observations of life in Granada. A few more like it would have made for a much more memorable album. Nearly all the songs on *Earthquake Weather* are too wordy, packed with cryptic references and in-jokes; the lyric sheet even includes a glossary. Although some of the obscure terms are British – for example, the Del-Boy-isms of 'Shouting Street', Joe's paean to dodgy market traders – and others are from a personal lingua franca picked up on his travels around the world, by far the bulk of the argot is American. The lyrics continue the tradition of the *Permanent Record* tracks by name-dropping US locations, consumer products, leisure pursuits and popular culture icons. The overall impression is that, scared to tackle anything more demanding, Joe has once more escaped into the mythical land of his teenage imagination. What's more, as Andrew Collins suggested, he has borrowed someone else's voice to do so: that of Tom Waits.

This is perhaps best illustrated by the numerous Beat-style references to jazz heroes: Mezzrow, Bird, the Pres, Dizzy and Cannonball Adderley are all namechecked at some point. Joe may have called his first daughter Jazz and have been in love with the *idea* of the music, but his previous musical output and 'anyone can do it' rhetoric would hardly have led the general public to believe it was one of the abiding passions of his life. Talking about be-bop on WHFS radio following the album's release, he admitted, 'It takes a lot of listening to know it, and I really don't know anything about it.' Several Clash albums had faked their own world too, but, with the exception of *Cut The Crap*, they did so with conviction. *Earthquake Weather* contains a few evocative images and occasional witty turns of phrase, but on the whole, Joe's constructions are cluttered and grammatically uncomfortable, stumbling over the rhythm and often even failing to scan.

In October, November and December 1989, he and the band played dates promoting the record in the UK, Europe and the US, but it still flopped badly. Perhaps because he had been away too long, or perhaps because they didn't recognise him in his new incarnation, Joe failed to regain and hold his peer group's attention. In the UK *Earthquake Weather* went into the charts at number 58; the following week, it disappeared for good.

Despite his claims to have given up on acting following *Mystery Train*, Joe signed up for another film project in spring 1990. Aki Kaurismaki had established himself as Finland's answer to Alex Cox and Jim Jarmusch. He made his début in 1983 with *Crime And Punishment*, Dostoevsky's novel transplanted to a Helsinki slaughterhouse. In 1990, his most recent work was *Leningrad Cowboys Go America*, about a terrible rock band with foot-long quiffs setting out to give the US a taste of Finnish cultural imperialism. His new project was 'an Ealing studio-style comedy' called *I Hired A Contract Killer*, about a Frenchman living in London who decides to commit suicide by putting out a contract on his own life, then changes his mind when he meets Margi Clarke. Like Alex Cox and Jim Jarmusch, Aki had something of a track record for using musicians to flesh out his cast list, and he hired Joe along with Nicky Tesco, formerly of the Members. Joe's role was the minuscule and undemanding one of a pub entertainer, but once again this offered him the opportunity to contribute to the soundtrack. No album emerged, though two Strummer songs were released as a promotional-only single on the Finnish Villealfa Film Productions label.

Both 'Burning Lights' and 'Afro-Cuban Be-Bop' are performed by Joe on his old black-sprayed Clash Telecaster accompanied by a solitary congo player, under the guise of Joe Strummer and the Astro-Physicians. Back in 1975, Joe had picked up a few tips from Bruce Springsteen the performer. In 1988, after mentioning that Springsteen's output around the time of *The River* (1980) owed more than a little to the Clash, Joe had joked to Bill Flanagan that he was going to 'rip some of *his* stuff off. *Alaska*: the new 4-track album with furry boots.' The two songs on this single bring the exchange of influence full circle: they are indeed strongly reminiscent of Bruce's *Nebraska*. Not only is the instrumentation minimal and the tone mournful and reflective, but both songs use car imagery to evoke dreams of escape and rootlessness.

'Burning Lights' was inspired by lights seen while driving through a desert, inevitably bringing to mind 'London's Burning'. Although it is a thousand miles away from the Clash song in terms of location, mood and message, the later composition draws on those very differences for its sense of profound melancholy: 'Some dreams are made for children / But most grow old with us . . .' 'Afro-Cuban Be-Bop' continues Joe's love affair with the notion of jazz, but its chorus line 'the house just wants to rock' goes all the way back to his earliest compositions with the 101ers. Almost as downbeat as the A-side, it at least contradicts that song's suggestion of fading confidence: 'I am a man to remember / Not to take no overdose.'

In the summer of 1990, Joe was brought in at the last minute, after several other people had turned the project down, to produce the Pogues' new album, *Hell's Ditch*. Method acting again, he attempted to inject a little Guy Stevens-like unpredictability into the recording process. He sported a Nicaraguan cowboy hat for the duration, and his volcanic personality soon earned him the nickname Strumboli. 'What I learned was to use whatever it takes, whether it's being polite and gentle or angry,' he told *Q*'s Phil Sutcliffe. 'The Pogues understand the emotional level's got to be up there.' Released in September 1990, *Hell's Ditch* was greeted as a return to form, with Joe receiving his fair share of the credit. The *NME*'s David Quantick, admittedly a long-time Pogues fan, awarded it nine out of ten.

During the following year, Shane MacGowan lost interest in the band, and the problem grew so pressing that, in September 1991, the rest of the Pogues were finally obliged to ask him to leave, much to his subsequently expressed relief. Unfortunately, they had just committed themselves to a six-month world tour and could not afford to cancel. As on previous occasions when faced with a personnel crisis, the band turned to Joe and asked him to help out. What was more surprising, on the surface, was that Joe agreed at just three days' notice. It meant stepping into Shane's shoes, something that, back in 1987, he had sworn he would never try to do. Singing the MacGowan songbook would be a form of acting and a challenge, but Joe's reputation as a performer had always been founded on highly charged, highly personal, communication. Another related, and not insignificant, issue was the fate of his own solo career: his stint with the Pogues would require him to put that on hold for the best part of another year. To anyone not conversant with the story behind the scenes, it was a decision that bordered on the perverse.

Joe had his own reasons for getting involved. He had spent the earlier part of 1991 preparing material for a new solo album, and had been on the point of booking a studio when Sony advised him not to as this would 'trigger the next phase of his contract': after the commercial failure of *Earthquake Weather*, they were not sure he was worthy of future investment. 'So the Pogues was a chance to get away from my own frustrations,' he told Phil Sutcliffe. It was also an opportunity to keep himself in the public eye as a performer at around the same time as Sony released *Clash On Broadway* in the US: which two events might serve to convince either Sony or, if not, then someone else that there was still some mileage left in his solo career.

As both he and the Pogues had something to prove, most of the live shows were both energetic and warmly received, but many reviewers found the arrangement to be a peculiar one. A news report in February 1992 claimed that Joe and the band had started writing together for a new album, but Joe left the Pogues that March, on schedule. He has maintained a low profile since completing the tour, even moving out of London in favour of a Home Counties dormitory town for a while. On 16 April 1994, he made his first live appearance for years in Prague, joining local band Dirty Pictures at a Rock for Refugees benefit gig to raise money for people fleeing the former Yugoslavia. Another 25 local bands played to an audience of just over a thousand in the Repre Club. Joe's set was made up entirely of Clash songs.

Suggestions that he was working on a solo album have been made every now and again, most recently in July 1994 by Joe himself, who said he 'hoped to have something out before the end of the year'. At the time of writing, it has yet to emerge. It seems the delays in releasing new material are still related to business decisions regarding his recording contract; other than that, his silence continues to be largely voluntary. 'When the *NME* ring up looking for an interview these days, I know they're gonna stick Joe Strummer on page 20. That's the way it goes. Things move on,' he told Sean O'Hagan as long ago as 1988. 'I don't mind stepping back. I *know* I'm a good writer, a good musician and I know that, these days, I'm a page 20 guy. It's cool.' Predictably, the paper ran the interview on page 20.

16... LOST IN THE SUPERMARKET

The break-up of the Clash occurred on the eve of the tenth anniversary of the London punk scene. Whatever the individual aims of the bands and other names and faces involved, in general terms punk – like the Clash – had been determined to make an impression. Over the years following the anniversary, while the former Clash members attempted to come to terms with the ultimate failure of their band, it became possible to assess the achievements of the movement as a whole.

Did punk actually change the world in any way? Certain bands and individuals who came out of the punk movement could be said to have had a direct influence in the political arena, and several more to have had an indirect effect by influencing the thinking of their followers. Many were quick to align themselves with the Anti-Nazi League after the Clash and the Tom Robinson Band led the way with the massive April 1978 Victoria Park gig. Subsequently, Rock Against Racism found many supporters among artists and fans alike.

Although it would be misleading to suggest the punk movement in any way started the trend – George Harrison's 1971 Concert for Bangladesh is but one of many earlier examples – it certainly helped establish the playing of benefit gigs and espousal of causes as a commonplace activity: a sort of moral dues-paying. The most famous of such ventures, the Band Aid and Live Aid projects, started out as a personal response to news footage of starving children in Ethiopia by Bob Geldof, the leader of a third wave punk band. The July 1985 Live Aid concert ushered in a new era of caring and sharing among new wave and old wave alike. Sometimes this 'we're all in it together' pally-ness was a little too saccharine to bear, as with the Prince's Trust concerts. Elsewhere, committed artists continued to support causes they believed in, and supporters of Artists Against Apartheid played no small part in raising consciousness about the issue, which in turn helped bring about Nelson Mandela's release and the establishment of a democratic South Africa. In addition to being supported by the annual Glastonbury Festival, CND received money from individual band benefits. The likes of Paul Weller and Billy Bragg lent their support to the pro-Labour Party group Red Wedge. In the late Eighties, it became *de rigueur* for big new wave bands to align themselves with a pet political or environmental cause. U2, Simple Minds and Sting all played shows on behalf of Amnesty International, Sting set up the Rainforest Foundation and R.E.M. took Greenpeace on tour with them.

One of the knock-on effects of punk was the raising of the standard of debate in the music press, and especially the *NME*. For much of the Eighties, it was no longer enough to talk about drugs, groupies and guitar solos; musicians, whether representatives of new bands or established artists, were expected to have *opinions*. As a result, 'the kids' were given the strong impression that a degree of social and political awareness was a virtue.

Unfortunately, a reaction seemed to set in at the end of the decade, when the loss of belief in a better tomorrow engendered by long-term unemployment and the general dampening effect of the recession encouraged an outbreak of the kind of apathy the Clash had warned about in 1976. The UK's rave culture was all about getting blissed out. Picking up on its influence, bands like the Stone Roses and Happy Mondays established the late Eighties Madchester scene and portrayed themselves as amoral, apolitical hedonists. In the US grunge bands helped both create and reflect a depressive, self-obsessed environment. Their followers and contemporaries were characterised as slackers, or – thanks to the already much-used title Douglas Coupland borrowed for his 1991 book – 'Generation X'. The general picture was of a generation living a morbid, uninformed, insular existence, supposedly numbed to all positive thought and action by media overload and the meaninglessness and mendacity of modern society: life sucks, pass the drugs.

As already established, many of the first wave of punk bands and a fair proportion of the early punk fans had preferred to adopt a negative attitude to life too; but it had been something of a pose, and there had invariably seemed to be at least some sense of anger or mischief behind it. Far more knowing in many respects than 'the kids' of the punk era, the slackers of today, whether they live in the UK, US or elsewhere, seem to have been seduced by soap-standard melodrama. Some have so disengaged themselves from life that they have become truly hopeless. Cynicism and negativity are fetishised. As an extreme example of where this kind of ennui can lead: in Budapest there is a goth-derived cult which prizes wrist-slashing scars as badges of otherness. Successful suicide attempts are a regular occurrence.

This is about as far from the Jekyll strain of punk influence – energy, creativity, protest – as it is possible to travel, but not all the signs are bad. The early Nineties heralded the advent of a wave of angry young radical women musicians and writers under the name riot grrrls, the most visible UK band being Huggy Bear. In 1993 came another movement embracing back-to-basics angry rock'n'roll, spearheaded by S*M*A*S*H and Those Animal Men. Owing an even more direct debt to the political punk of 1977, it was consequently branded the New Wave of New Wave. In the US a less political, but equally energetic and enthusiastic, movement began pulling together in the wake of Green Day.

The early Nineties in the UK witnessed another intriguing development: a wave of multiracial bands, like Cornershop and Echobelly, and multi-genre bands, like Senser, Fun-Da-Mental and Credit to the Nation (who crossed over hip hop, rock, funk, rap and more besides), made their opinions heard on a variety of issues, including racism. Less politically vocal, but showing plenty of social awareness and punk attitude was the mid Nineties guitar band movement usually referred to as Britpop, featuring the likes of Elastica, Sleeper, Blur, Supergrass and – especially – the rumbustious Oasis.

In the US the only other genre that can compete with massive sellers like country and grunge is rap. As a predominantly black, urban and aggressive musical form, its across-the-board success represents something of a triumph in itself, but rap has not been without its own crushingly negative impact: at various times (sometimes the same time) it has tended to be sexist, homophobic, extremely violent, pro-gang-warfare, drug-obsessed, gun-obsessed and racist (anti-white, anti-Jew, anti-Korean). Although Public Enemy have been known to cross one or two of those lines, they have consistently offered informed, positive comment and advice to what they consider is their true audience: the inner city black community. Arrested Development and the Disposable Heroes of Hiphoprisy have taken a less manic, more reflective approach to much the same issues. The latter outfit (now defunct) emerged from the ashes of radical black punk band the Beatnigs. Their 1992 – and only – album, *Hypocrisy Is The Greatest Luxury,* is one of the most wide-ranging and sustained dissections of contemporary society and culture ever recorded.

History may reveal that the *NME* indulged in a little wishful thinking in trying to establish riot grrrls and the New Wave of the New Wave as the Great New Hopes of rock just a few years before punk's 20th anniversary. In fact, they may be guilty of being too literalist in their definition of punk. As is suggested by some of the other artists the paper has championed over recent years – the UK crossover bands, and the more concerned and responsible rappers among them – the punk spirit of protesting about social ills can survive transmutation and even transmigration: it doesn't have to be three chords played fast on cheap guitars by skinny white boys (or girls).

Since the mid-Eighties, cheap sampling, programming and recording technology has been employed to make hip hop, acid house, techno and jungle music in garages and spare rooms. This amateur-hour approach has also extended to self-financed labels: true independents which, as they are offshoots of music cultures truly at street – or, at least, club – level, can keep their fingers on the pulse of the new trends much more effectively than the less pliable majors, and thus make regular and successful forays into the mainstream charts. Such dance records have kept the indie sector alive. They are also have-a-go DIY ventures, through and through. 'It's like punk, in a way,' Mick Jones told the *New Zealand Herald*'s Graham Reid in 1993. 'You don't need much, just a sampler and some records. It's that whole *Sniffin' Glue* thing. Get into the basement and form a band. But you still need an idea.' The addendum is an important one. In music, recording, writing, photography, design, film-making and any other creative endeavour it may be true that anyone can do it, but it is not quite as true as punk sometimes seemed to suggest that anyone can do it *successfully*, or in a way that is appreciated by others. The key point is that, without determination and application, talent and ideas are just unrealised potential. That lesson, there for anyone who wishes to learn it, is perhaps punk's greatest legacy.

Did punk change its own, more immediate world, the music business? In some ways yes, in others – the most important – no. Some of the third wave punk bands went on to become the most commercially successful major rock'n'roll names of the late Eighties: the Cure, Simple Minds and U2. Punk took a more indirect route into the mainstream in the US, but it eventually percolated through via first the localised hardcore scene and then the back-to-basics Trad Rock Renaissance of the mid-Eighties. Most of the early Nineties' big US bands display and acknowledge a strong punk influence, from Guns'N'Roses (who in 1994 released an album of punk covers entitled *The Spaghetti Incident?*) to R.E.M. to Nirvana and Pearl Jam. In 1993, when venerable New York noiseniks Sonic Youth released a video document of their European tour with Nirvana two years previously, the title they chose for it was not wholly ironic: *1991: The Year Punk Broke*. Nevertheless, packing stadiums and shifting units by the trailer-load were not the goals to which punk originally professed to aspire. Although such successes are in one way a vindication of a musical genre, in another they help maintain the music business establishment in fine style. In so doing, they represent a betrayal of the original – admittedly poorly articulated and confused – ideology that at least seemed to want to overthrow that establishment. Certainly, punk and its immediate aftermath shook up the music business in the late Seventies, but it rallied all too quickly.

One of punk's apparent triumphs was breaking down what Simon Humphrey, engineer on *The Clash*, calls the 'old school' studio system with its stuffy rules and firm distinctions between producer and engineer. 'Punk spawned a whole generation of producers who came from engineering,' he says. 'Steve Lillywhite [Simple Minds, U2], Hugh Padgham [the Police]. Well, the new wave did, really: punk didn't have any production. But within a year or so there were all those acts like XTC who got into it. Prior to that, the whole recording scene was different. The new wave came up with this whole group of producers who came up through the ranks. I mean *I* started producing. I did a few punk and new wave acts after the Clash, and that set me off.' To an extent this momentum has been maintained, with some musicians insisting on the right to produce their own material and dance music DJs making names for themselves as producers via their own self-financed recordings. It is worth noting, however, that whenever a band's or artist's popularity wanes, or their choice of producer is deemed to have made a hash of things, their record company will not hesitate to insist upon a name producer of their choice taking over.

At first, it looked as though the glut of independent labels appearing on the market in the late Seventies might pose a threat to the status quo, capturing most of the vital new talent while the majors were left with their redundant long-haired, flared-trousered dinosaur bands. This was not to be. Independents usually operated on a hand-to-mouth basis, and even those with the most successful roster of artists were often only one bad record or distribution hitch away from bankruptcy. Plus, the majors quickly learned to turn predator. Why take a chance on an untried artist when they could monitor the indie charts, and move in to poach a dead cert? Few independent labels could compete with the kind of financial incentives, publicity and distribution guarantees offered by the majors. Those that did became like little majors themselves, often with all the disadvantages and few of the advantages.

There were other tactics. Rough Trade set up its own distribution network, and in the Eighties various other independent labels and record shops got together to form a collective named the Cartel, but it was a losing battle. It was rare for even the most determinedly left-field bands to put the interests of an independent before their own. The Smiths stuck with Rough Trade for the duration of their career, though not always happily. New Order stayed with Factory until it went bust in 1992. But these bands were the exception rather than the rule, in terms of both loyalty and commercial success, and when their labels eventually ran into trouble, the rights to the bands' back catalogues were, inevitably, snapped up by majors.

Some of the independents that survived compromised their status by arranging distribution deals through majors or accepting part-finance from them. Also, because the independents' association with alternative music gained them considerable kudos, majors began inventing their own pseudo-independents: subsidiary labels with a specialised function – set up either for a particular sub-genre of music or for the use of one particular band equally desperate for credibility by indie-association – but with all the power of the major behind them. By 1992, when concern about this state of affairs led to an attempt to reform indie chart criteria, it was as difficult to define an independent label as it was to define indie music. Overall, with the benefit of hindsight, the best answer to Mark Perry's criticism of the Clash for signing to CBS in preference to releasing independent records is: what's the difference, and how do you tell? Which is not to say that the independents have given up: the mid-Nineties equivalent to the Cartel is the Network.

Nor did punk's new broom achieve much when it came to changing the majors from within. The famous 'artistic freedom' clause demanded by the Clash and other punk and new wave bands was shown to be worthless as soon as the issue of finance reared its head: they who control the purse strings control everything. The few skirmishes the majors were forced to fight in order to defend their position made them more contract-canny than ever before. If anything, the average artist's position is now considerably worse than it was immediately prior to punk.

In the mid-Eighties, Geffen records sued no less a legend than Neil Young for delivering 'unrepresentative' recordings: that is, not giving them exactly what they thought he should be giving them. In 1985, the similarly revered Eric Clapton was required by Warner Brothers to re-record a third of *Behind The Sun* with more 'commercial' material, including a cover version chosen by the record company themselves. In 1994, an expensive court case established that George Michael was indeed trapped in a contract with Sony (who had taken him over, along with the Clash, when they bought out CBS in 1988) that he defined as 'professional slavery'. Even for the most powerful of established stars, there are only two ways round this problem. One is to negotiate – from a position of strength that is, admittedly, not easy to attain – a licensing deal with a record company which allows you to retain the rights yourself. Paul McCartney does this with EMI through MPL productions. The other is to kill yourself off and come back under another guise. After an argument with his record company Warner Brothers over the release of his latest album, Prince ceased to exist in 1993. His contract required him to deliver several more albums under that name, which he threatened to take care of with material already in his vaults. He, meanwhile, would shop around for a new deal trading under the bisexual gender symbol he had adopted as his new identity. While he waited for the matter to be resolved, he wrote the word 'SLAVE' across his face each morning.

The Eighties recession caused a general slump in record sales, and singles were hit particularly hard. Record shops began to narrow the range of their stock, sticking to safer bets. All of this affected the (non-dance-oriented) independent labels most of all. They were singles-led, had no real promotional budget with which to push their product into the public consciousness and could not rely on large, steadily selling back catalogues to keep their businesses ticking over. The majors found it easier to adapt. They began releasing singles in a bewildering array of formats, with complex permutations of alternative mixes and B-sides, requiring ardent fans and collectors to buy multiple copies of a record. As singles were no longer important in their own right, they were released as trailers or advertisements: often four tracks – and occasionally more – were culled from an album for this purpose. Artists were increasingly required to help promote one album over three years and build it into a commercial monolith, rather than record new material that would require commencing a new campaign from scratch. The result has been an across-the-board epidemic of arrested creative development.

The cassette had already put up a challenge to vinyl by the end of the Seventies, and the introduction of the CD in the early Eighties sounded the death-knell for the traditional single and album medium of the vinyl disc. Some shrinkage in its share of the market was to be expected, but vinyl was certainly deliberately helped on its way to extinction by the majors. Any new format is initially expensive, but by 1990, it was only marginally more expensive to manufacture a CD than an LP – approximately 90p, as opposed to 70p – and yet the CD was still being retailed for anything up to two thirds as much again, making it a good deal more profitable. Vinyl soon accounted for less than ten per cent of the market. It was kicked while down by the mainstream record retailers, who deemed it to be a minority interest and stopped stocking it altogether. As well as hitting the consumer in the pocket, the switch from vinyl to CD again stuck the knife into the independent sector, which had always been vinyl-oriented.

Any sophisticated new technology has a certain status symbol value, and CD was no exception. Together, the gadget pioneers, hi-fi buffs and upwardly mobile poseurs got the format off to a good start, and word of mouth about its supposedly heightened sound quality soon spread. Before long, news reached former popular music fans who were now in their thirties and forties, and had record collections long since ruined by dust and scratches or banished to the attic. Those with disposable income were tempted to investigate. As youth unemployment was running high, there followed a shift in the record buying demographic away from youth cult-related artists and ground-breaking new acts towards fondly remembered back catalogue classics and newer records by established name artists. Golden Oldie radio shows and even an adult version of MTV, entitled VH-1, have ensued. It was the revenge of the Boring Old Farts, artists and consumers both.

The trend was a recession lifeline for the majors. The recording costs had already been met on the back catalogue product, years before, and here they were able to sell it again, often to the same customer, at a considerably inflated price. And not only in its original format: it became standard practice to release multi-disc CD boxed-set career retrospectives featuring several hours' worth of music. As the contracts with the back catalogue artists contained no clauses pertaining to the then non-existent medium of CD, the record companies could also get away with paying them minuscule royalties.

Although the punk principle of VFM took a real battering during the CD revolution, that revolution was not without its positive side-effects. Firstly, it dispensed with much of the knee-jerk ageism, propagated by teen pop, hippy and punk cultures, which said there was something wrong with you if you still liked rock'n'roll (or wrote about it) once past the age of 30. It created an environment where 40-plus artists like Neil Young, Paul Simon, Leonard Cohen and Lou Reed, instead of feeling they had to write for 'the kids', felt free to create something for people their own age without resorting to MOR platitudes. It also – perhaps for the first time ever – encouraged the mass of consumers to think of popular music in historical, cultural and sociological terms that were not purely to do with nostalgia or kitsch. Previously, too much emphasis had been placed on the disposability of pop, and punk had been particularly guilty of dismissing the past out of hand rather than choosing more specifically deserving targets for its venom. Efforts were now made to put rock's rich tapestry in context for a new market, not least with the publication (and success) of overview magazines like *Q*, *Vox* and (a little later) *Mojo*, aimed at the older, less fad-oriented music buyer.

The inkies were predictably unimpressed. Having themselves suffered during the recession – circulations fell, and *Sounds* folded in 1991 – they were both unhappy to see the competition and, especially in the case of the *NME*, annoyed by the climate that had engendered it. And they had a point. The CD boom not only further squeezed the independent sector, it also threatened new music of any kind. With guaranteed revenue from back catalogues and name artists, the majors were under no pressure to find and develop new talent. A&R departments went hungry, even closed down. Fewer new bands got deals. Rather than being nurtured for several years, those who did were expected to deliver straight away. Those who couldn't deliver, or who failed to build on or maintain initial commercial success, were simply let go, whatever their artistic status. It was a case of hit, and keep hitting, or get off the pot.

Q was not without a sense of humour – occasionally biting – but compared to the *NME*'s iconoclastic savagery, it tended towards the deferential, particularly for the first few years of its existence. And as far as the leading inky was concerned, a music scene that seemed to be hell-bent on returning to the smug, stagnant days immediately pre-punk was a music scene that needed its butt kicking on a regular basis. Thanks to the preservative powers of CD, many of the names reviled during the punk era were still dominating the charts with their risible tripe: Genesis and the solo Phil Collins, Yes (under that or any other name), the rump of Pink Floyd. By the beginning of the Nineties, some of the people who had at first set out to take their heads had instead joined them, both on the stadium circuit and in the extent of their pomp and pretension: Simple Minds, the Cure and U2, this means you.

The summer of 1994 saw Boring Old Fart acts like the Rolling Stones, Pink Floyd and the Eagles charging up to $60, $75 and $125 respectively for tickets on their stadium tours of America. In an effort to uphold the standard of VFM, latter-day punks Pearl Jam, who have also done their bit to keep vinyl alive, attempted to set up a tour at a far more reasonable $18 a head. They found it impossible to book dates without the assistance of the Ticketmaster booking agency, who insisted on between $5 and $8 for themselves as a handling fee. As a consequence, the band were forced to cancel.

In conclusion, then, one would have to say that the music business has left more of a mark on punk than punk has left on the music business.

These changes in the music business, its product and its target market in the few years preceding and the decade following the Clash split help explain much about the band's own posthumous reissue and compilation programme. Awareness of the changes, as well as of the more straightforward and predictable rose-tinting effect of nostalgia, contributes to an understanding of the post-split reversal of the music press and general public's attitude to the band; something which enabled the Clash Myth not only to re-establish itself, but also to increase in stature.

The untidy nature of the break-up and the poor quality of the final album meant that the band ended its life as an object of ridicule, seemingly unloved by critics, original fans and the wider record buying public alike. Once the Clash no longer existed as a performing or record making unit, however, the process of rehabilitation was free to commence. More and more, as time passes, we have colluded to forget or overlook the embarrassing moments, the mistakes, the musical filler, the petty squabbles and the unfulfilled promises. Instead, we take only selected highlights from the archive – the best songs, the most flatteringly posed photographs, the most passionate live video clips, the warmest memories, the most memorable quotes – and from them we construct a near-perfect rock'n'roll band, a Hollywood version of the Clash.

The well-deserved trashing handed out to *Cut The Crap* by the *NME*'s Mat Snow in November 1985 was offset by his acknowledgement that the band were once worthy of far greater respect. Three weeks later, the paper proved his point when it ran a chart of its contributors' Top 100 all-time favourite albums, and *The Clash* came fourth to Marvin Gaye's *What's Going On*, Van Morrison's *Astral Weeks* and Bob Dylan's *Highway 61 Revisited*: exalted company indeed. Both the generation of music writers who had been around since the late Seventies and the new generation, most of whom had reached adolescence during the heyday of punk, were more than a little disappointed that rock had failed to throw up anything to match it since. The tenth-anniversary celebrations of January and February 1986 gave them the opportunity to hold forth about the good old days.

ZigZag devoted an entire issue to punk, in which former editor Kris Needs provided a six-page survey-cum-update on the subsequent careers of the movement's leading lights. *The Face*, which had not been around in 1976, had already celebrated the fifth anniversary of punk back in 1981 – Jon Savage had supplied a three-page overview, peppered with extracts from his punk period diary (a dry run for his 1991 book *England's Dreaming*) – and all it needed to do now was recycle. The *NME* ran punk retrospectives over three issues, covering all aspects of the movement, its roots and its legacy. Danny Kelly – future editor of the paper and of *Q* – volunteered his appraisal of the Clash (a rehearsal for the essay he contributed to John Aizlewood's 1994 book of fan reminiscences, *Love Is The Drug*): 'It wasn't always like last year. *Cut The Crap*, that reflexive twitching of a corpse, the slackened muscles allowing a final, fetid evacuation of the bowels, wasn't typical. The Clash weren't always a wretched travesty, a grotesque waste of time and vinyl, a joke . . . Later, it became pantomime parody, but . . . for nearly 18 months, the Clash were the greatest rock'n'roll band in the world.'

The London punk movement had not had quite the same direct impact in the US, but *Rolling Stone* journalists were given their opportunity to wax nostalgic in August 1987, when the magazine celebrated its own 20th anniversary with its contributors' Top 100 albums of the last 20 years. *London Calling* appeared at number 14, and *The Clash* (UK version) at number 27, in the wake of a top three comprising the Beatles' *Sgt Pepper's Lonely Hearts Club Band*, the Sex Pistols' *Never Mind The Bollocks* and the Rolling Stones' *Exile On Main Street*. Three months later, the *NME* responded with its readers' all-time Top 100. *The Clash* made number 11 and *London Calling* number 28 behind a somewhat flavour-of-the-month-ish top three comprising the Smiths' *The Queen Is Dead*, the Jesus and Mary Chain's *Psychocandy* and Joy Division's *Unknown Pleasures*.

The next round of reappraisals accompanied the March 1988 release of *The Story Of The Clash, Volume 1*. Sony had been pressing for a 'best of' compilation since Mick's dismissal in 1983, and were even keener to tap into the nostalgia market following the band's split. The dissolution of the Clash and the reconciliation of its previously warring former members cleared the path for the project. In 1987, the task of compiling the album was taken on by Mick Jones and BAD PR agent Tricia Ronane: Topper had other worries at the time, and both Paul and Joe were prepared to take a back seat as a gesture of apology to the guitarist.

The 28-track double CD or LP, originally entitled *Revolution Rock*, was put on the release schedule for the end of 1987, but was eventually held over until the following year. The new title was less twee, avoided confusion with *Combat Rock* and gave the project a more grandiose, definitive feel. The bias of the album is towards singles – no fewer than 16 of the tracks having been previously released in that format – and towards the earlier part of the band's career: *Sandinista!* supplies just two songs, *Combat Rock* three, and *Cut The Crap* is not represented at all, whereas the original freebie version of 'Capital Radio' is included. Less understandable is the bizarre track sequencing, courtesy of Mick. Hopping about all over the place though it undoubtedly does, if any approximate trend is to be discerned, it is one that, perversely, moves *backwards* from 1982 to 1977. Thus, the 'story' the compilation tells is an elliptical one not too concerned with beginnings, middles or ends.

Joe was given the material for some last-minute tweaking. As well as the humorous memoir of 'band valet Albert Transom' – almost as random in approach as the album itself – he is also responsible for the subtitle, *Volume 1*. When he appeared on *Night Network* later in 1988, he said this was 'because I knew there'd never be a Volume 2', a remark which caused no little bemusement at the time and makes no more sense today. What Joe was really doing was refusing to acknowledge that the Clash was over and done with. Dressed up in a Pennie Smith photograph and a sleeve by long-time Clash packaging designer Jules Baulm, the album was released in March 1988 (still on the CBS label in the UK, Epic in the US), having been preceded earlier in the month by the single 'I Fought The Law'.

When reviewing the latter in the *NME*, Steven Wells might have been expected to unleash his powers of invective once more, but even he seemed to have succumbed to the warm glow of nostalgia. 'Too many spliffs and not enough haircuts knackered this "greatest band in the history of blah, blah, blah", but not before they had hammered out some classic rock'n'roll.'

Subsequently taking on the album, he indulged himself in some memories of his initial exposure to punk rock. Much as he loved *The Clash* and the early singles – retrospectively acknowledging the lyrics' previously overlooked humour – and prepared though he was to forgive *Give 'Em Enough Rope* its sins, he still dismissed the band's later work as 'sloppy, muso ramblings studded with flashes of the old spunk'. This view was reflected in the not wholly serious marks he awarded each of the four sides of the LP, ranging from zero for the muso ramblings to 'ten to the power of a thousand million' for the punk period tracks. 'The Clash were the catalyst that made (makes) punk such an intensely political "youth culture",' he concluded. 'They were the first to break away from the pretentious hippyness of punk's London roots: putting anti-racism firmly on the top of the agenda, making 1977 the year of Rock Against Racism as opposed to 1976's Rock Against Being Bored In Art School. And this is a package put out by a subsidiary of a Japanese multinational. That's not ironic, it's just one of rebel rock's silly little contradictions.'

At *Melody Maker*, Paul Mathur shared a similar perspective. 'It starts with the end. Ironically, but inevitably, the Clash's most commercially cherished moments came when they strapped on their funk fakery . . . empty music, drenched in the now familiar self-aggrandisement, but bereft of anything that even thinks of rhyming itself with irony . . . The second half of the double album is the Clash at the heart of your darkness . . . It's a great story.' *Rolling Stone*'s Elliot Murphy supplied the American angle. Although he awarded the album just three and a half stars, his impassioned tribute suggested that he had swallowed the Clash Myth more completely than his British counterparts: 'The Story of the Clash is a story that ended too soon . . . As this collection clearly shows, the Clash's political concerns remained in the forefront even as the band's musical influences moved beyond the Pistols to reggae and rap . . . the Clash's brand of rock, while commercially accessible, was truly revolutionary . . . We need this band more now than we did then.'

Coinciding with the album's release, *Sounds* printed a retrospective-cum-discography, the *NME* a retrospective interview with Joe and *Melody Maker* a track-by-track breakdown by Joe and Paul under the title 'The Last Gang In Town'. Aside from the last-minute comment Steven Wells made in his review, no one seemed prepared to spoil the celebrations by raising the obvious issue: that the repackaging and reselling of the Clash's recorded history represented a capitulation to the record company's commercial motivations – especially as its main purpose was to tap into the growing CD reissue market – and was therefore the latest in a long line of sell-outs of the band's original principles.

In the wake of 'No Elvis, Beatles or the Rolling Stones / In 1977', surely we had the right to expect no Sex Pistols, no Damned and especially no Clash in 1988? Back in 1979, in conversation with *Creem*'s Dave DiMartino, Joe had made sneering remarks about Americans' preference for repackaged nostalgia over contemporary music. And following his declaration that same year, 'THERE WILL BE NO SIX QUID CLASH LP EVER', even allowing for inflation, surely a double CD retailing for £22.99 (at the time of writing) was straying just a little too far from the band's VFM policy? At least the *Night Network* programme required Joe to defend himself. 'The LP is dead,' he said. 'Don't blame me that it's come out on CD. *I* don't have a player yet. It's just a retrospective: you can buy into it if you want, or just ignore it.' Quizzed about the amount of money he himself might expect to garner from the half-million copies already sold, he grew evasive. 'No idea, but not as much as if it'd been on vinyl record. All groups are shafted on CD royalties.'

'I Fought The Law' climbed to number 29 in the UK charts, which was respectable enough to prompt a second single re-release in late April 1988, this time of 'London Calling'. These two songs, it should be noted, were the ones Joe had performed during his autumn 1987 to spring 1988 stint with the Pogues, and would again perform later in 1988 with the Latino Rockabilly War. The *NME*'s singles review column afforded Adrian Thrills the opportunity to add his two penn'orth: 'With their more extravagant claims now a part of history, the myth of the Clash seemed to have been well and truly debunked . . . Then came *The Story Of The Clash, Volume 1*, one of the most playable records of the year, and a testimony to the lasting appeal of the band at their best.' 'London Calling' reached only number 46, but the album that spawned it climbed as high as number seven, and remained in the charts for ten weeks.

The ground thus prepared, in late April 1989, Sony re-released the band's entire album back catalogue on mid-priced CD. Retailing for approximately the same as a full-price LP (at the time of writing, they are available at £7.99 for *The Clash*, £10.99 for *London Calling* and £13.99 for the double CD *Sandinista!*), this hardly represented VFM. In the UK the albums appeared as they had in their original vinyl versions, with one crafty anomaly: the version of *The Clash* that emerged was the US one. The excuse given was that 'technical delays' had held up the UK version, which would now not be available until later in the summer. (In the event, it did not become available until October 1991.) What this meant in real terms, of course, was that the record company had finally managed to sidestep the band's 1979 objections to making the US album available in this country.

Reviewing the reissues in the *NME*, Stuart Bailie claimed he preferred the American version anyway, deemed it 'altogether orgasmic' and awarded it nine out of ten. *Give 'Em Enough Rope* was dismissed as 'gaseous trad rock' and given six. Stuart was obviously also in accord with the American vision of the Clash when it came to determining their greatest album, naming the single CD *London Calling* 'the most fluent rock music of the decade' and awarding it the full ten. Whereas he was prepared to concede that *Sandinista!* was occasionally worthwhile, he still believed the double CD contained 'too many dodgy reggae mixes and cooked-up fillers' and gave it six. He felt *Combat Rock* also suffered from inconsistency, but this time it was the uptempo numbers that were 'a little perfunctory' while 'the truly resonant tracks involve Strummer and his spacey beat poetry', and were afforded an extra dimension of eeriness by the hi-tech CD format, earning the whole eight. *Cut The Crap*, dismissed as 'mostly a work of lunacy', was given four. 'They weren't exactly the Right Stuff, and maybe they weren't the best rock'n'roll band ever,' concluded Stuart, 'but the Clash still knock the shit out of anything that's come along since. Remember them this way.'

Over at *Q*, Mat Snow was, for the most part, very much in agreement. He took issue with the 'imposter' version of the first album, also making the valid point that 'the wilfully crude recording – especially of Joe Strummer's even more wilfully crude voice – benefits not a jot from digitalisation'. Nevertheless, he still gave it four out of five stars. Being an unashamed rockist, he was not prepared to bend to the general consensus about *Give 'Em Enough Rope*, going so far as to attach the phrase 'sumptuously soaraway sound' to Sandy Pearlman's production and awarding it four stars. *London Calling* was again given full marks. *Sandinista!* was described as 'a double CD endurance test', but even so merited three stars. *Combat Rock* managed to bring New York streetsounds into the mainstream, but was not convincing enough to warrant any more than three stars. Mat detected 'Strummer's gift for the tersely addictive musical and lyrical phrase' under the 'huffing and puffing' of *Cut The Crap*, but felt it was buried too deep to earn the album more than two stars.

That November, *Rolling Stone* magazine ran a feature celebrating the Top 100 albums of the Eighties, as selected by the magazine's editors. *London Calling*, released in the US in January 1980, and therefore qualifying for consideration by the skin of its teeth, was voted number one. Again, there was evidence that the magazine had taken the Clash Myth at face value in its description of the London of late 1979 as a place 'where there was ample evidence of impending apocalypse (racial tension, rising unemployment, rampant drug addiction). Strummer's catalogue of disasters in the title track, scored with Jones' guitar firepower, sets the tone for the record. But that fear and urgency was also very real to the band . . .' Mick was deeply flattered by the honour. 'It was brilliant, because they voted [Martin Scorsese's] *Raging Bull* the best film, which I totally agree with,' he told the *NME*'s James Brown in 1991.

Aside from spawning the numerous rebel rock bands that had followed in their footsteps over the years, the Clash also made a more direct and involuntary contribution to less likely areas of popular music. In February 1990, Beats International, a loose dance music collective formed by ex-Housemartin Norman Cook, released 'Dub Be Good To Me', which married the SOS Band's 'Just Be Good To Me' to the bassline from 'Guns Of Brixton'. At the time of release, Norman openly admitted the source of the sample in interviews, telling the *NME* that it was an 'affectionate tribute to the Clash. It's like tipping my cap to them, because they were a huge influence on my growing up, both musically and politically.' The single reached number one, and remained there for several weeks during its 13-

week residency in the charts. When Paul Simonon approached Norman Cook for what he believed was his fair share of the royalties, however, Norman changed his tune (or, at least, its source), claiming he had lifted the bassline from an obscure ska track. The matter was eventually sorted out without recourse to legal action. In the meantime, Paul came up with another way to cash in, commissioning DJ and former Haysi Fantayzee member Jeremy Healy to remix the original 'Guns Of Brixton' for single release in July 1990. The *NME* made it single of the week, announcing, 'Purists need not be alarmed. This version retains Simonon's vision of urban menace as well as updating it.' By this time, though, 'Dub Be Good To Me' had used up most people's stock of affection for the bassline, and the Clash release stalled at number 57.

Mick's opportunity to exploit the Clash legacy came the following year. In an attempt to preserve their credibility, the band had always turned down approaches from advertising agencies wanting to use their music in commercials. When British Telecom changed London telephone numbers from 01 to 071 and 081, they had been refused permission to use 'London Calling' in their ad campaign. Yet when Levi's jeans asked if they could use 'Should I Stay Or Should I Go' in a 1991 UK TV commercial, the response was somewhat different. The original approach was made to all the Clash members, but as it was Mick's song, the others left the decision up to him. He agreed. His excuses were that this was not one of the band's more 'political' songs, and therefore there was no risk of its original meaning being undermined. Also, Levi's were one of the more enduring rock'n'roll accessories, and not a product to which anyone could object on moral grounds. 'Everyone's got a pair of Levi's,' Mick told James Brown. 'They're all right.'

The real issue, as Mick well knew, was whether an anti-establishment band like the Clash, who had always made a stand for creativity and idealism over commercial exploitation, should involve themselves with any kind of advertising at all. Even if Levi's jeans were an acceptable product in themselves, there was no getting round the fact that the Clash were doing it for the money and the exposure: all previous Levi's ad songs had resulted in re-release hit singles. Mick's decision to include 'Rush' on the single when it was issued on Columbia in February 1991 certainly smacked of opportunism. Paul, who had not been particularly keen on the idea of the ad in the first place, was not consulted about the use of the BAD II track. A 'spokesperson' told the *NME*, 'Paul felt Mick added insult to injury by putting "Rush" on. And that led to a few arguments.'

In March, 'Should I Stay Or Should I Go' became the first Clash single ever to reach number one in the UK charts. Joe was fixing his 1955-vintage Morris Minor at the time. 'I had my head under the bonnet, fucking with the fuel pump, and somebody came by and said, "Why don't you just go and get *another* one?"' he told Stuart Bailie. 'It's kinda weird that you didn't have to lift a finger. It wasn't as if you were at the height of your touring and all that hard work, and you'd feel, "Ah, we did it!" It took a trouser advert to take it there, and it was very peculiar.' In the wake of the single's success Sony re-released *The Story Of The Clash, Volume 1*; this time, it climbed to number 13, and spent a further nine weeks in the charts.

The band's first number one prompted another round of reappraisals. The seventh, April 1991 issue of *Vox*, IPC's answer to *Q*, ran a two-page portfolio of Pennie Smith's photographs of the band, accompanied by a two-page Mal Peachey retrospective interview with Mick entitled 'Remote Control'. 'Since they were the last great British rock'n'roll band, the four members of the Clash must live with an ever-increasing myth about a part of their lives which will not be forgotten,' wrote Mal. The *NME*, now edited by Danny Kelly, gave the front cover of its 9 March issue over to Pennie's famous photograph of Paul smashing his bass and the headline assertion 'THE CLASH: *Still The Greatest Rock'n'Roll Band In The World*'. Inside, illustrated with yet more Pennie Smith photographs, was James Brown's two-page retrospective interview with Mick, a page of 'tributes' from other artists and Stuart Bailie's two-page retrospective on the band's recorded legacy, in which he expanded but essentially reiterated his review of 1989's CD re-releases. The following week's issue offered 'Over 56 Things You Never Knew About The Clash'.

There is no statute of limitations on integrity. As well as causing rifts between the former Clash members, the advertisement and single release tie-in was the last straw for many long-term Clash fans who had always believed that, even if the band sometimes let themselves and others down, at least their hearts were in the right place. It was a point of view eloquently stated by Billy Bragg when approached for comment by the *NME*: 'I came to terms with the fact that the Clash's pose was nothing but a sham years ago, but it still grieves me to see that advert. At least it's a song from their Parody Period. It could be worse. Imagine "White Levi's / I want some Levi's / White Levi's / Some Levi's of my own." As Joe Strummer sang in "Death Or Glory", "He who fucks nuns will later join the church."'

The Clash's relaxation of principles for the project reiterated what previous post-split commercial endeavours had already signalled: considerations like respect for the music and the fans no longer obtained. Sony had already begun to exploit the Clash's back catalogue, but from 1991 onwards, their exhaustive and repetitive reissue and compilation programme attested to their belief that they had a licence to be as blatant and shoddy as they liked.

'Should I Stay Or Should I Go' was followed by the late March 1991 reissue, again on Columbia, of its fellow *Combat Rock* veteran 'Rock The Casbah'. The *NME*'s Stuart Maconie believed it 'exudes all the glamour and righteous menace of the boys at their peak'. It climbed to number 15 in the charts. To cater for this rekindled demand, in May 1991, Sony re-released *Combat Rock* itself. On to a good thing, Sony then re-re-released the original two singles from *The Story Of The Clash, Volume 1*: 'London Calling', which reached number 64 in June, and then 'I Fought The Law', which failed to show two months later. In late October, these were followed by 'Train In Vain', which also bombed.

The record releases were preceded at the end of March 1991 by a similarly opportunist long-form video, *This Is Video Clash* (CMV), which ran for just 30 minutes, and had a box cover recycling Caroline Coon's sleeve photo for the 1977 'White Riot' single. At *Q*, Adrian Deevoy seized the chance to deliver his tribute to the band, but at least paused to point out the video's shortcomings: 'Stitched together swiftly, one suspects, to capitalise on the current trouser commercial, *This Is Video Clash* is something of a tease. In fact, the nostalgia bud-tweaking "White Riot" jacket leads the potential buyer, a little naughtily, up punk's garden path. What you expect is wobbly hand-held footage of "Garageland" live at the Screen on the Green . . . What you get is a rather slick, not to mention short, compilation that starts with '78's "Tommy Gun" and ends in '82 with *Combat Rock*'s singles promos.' Nevertheless, Adrian believed the collection 'serves as a reminder of what a truly magnificent band these Ladbroke Grovers were'. He gave it three stars, clearly more in honour of the band than the artefact itself.

This Is Video Clash is an extremely lazy piece of work. As Adrian Deevoy said, it includes no material from 1977, which is an unforgivable omission. Sony had CBS's Dunstable video versions of 'White Riot', '1977' and 'London Calling' to hand; alternatively, had they been intent on using solely Don Letts material, they could surely have included some of the footage he shot at the March 1977 Harlesden Colosseum gig. A more enterprising project might have included a few TV spots, or some of the extensive live footage available from all stages of the band's career. Rush-releases like *This Is Video Clash* are doubly offensive: they not only represent the squandering of an opportunity in themselves, but they also spoil the market for future, potentially more inspired projects.

In October 1991, Sony finally got round to issuing the original UK version of *The Clash* on mid-price Columbia CD. By this time, of course, anyone who wanted the album on CD had given in and bought the 1989-released US version; die-hards would now buy this one as well. To accompany it on the schedules Sony also issued *Black Market Clash* in the UK. As with the UK release of the US version of *The Clash* two years earlier, this went against the band's wishes as expressed at the time of the record's original release. Reviewing them together in *Q*, Charles Shaar Murray gave the band's début – 'as raw, heartfelt, exhilarating and in-yer-face immediate as anything British rock has ever produced' – the full five stars, while the 'ragbag' compilation got just three.

November 1991 saw the UK rush-release on Columbia of a CD compiling the band's A-sides. Although dressed in a cover illustrated by Pennie Smith's photographs, it betrayed little in the way of thought or imagination, and bore no evidence of co-operation or collaboration from any member of the band. Witlessly entitled *The Singles*, it was yet another attempt to milk the success of 'Should I Stay Or Should I Go'. *Q*'s Jimmy Nicol served notice that the udder was nearly dry: '*The Singles* is a literal-minded collection of 45s, from "White Riot" to that Levi's song and is a barometer of a very ragged career indeed . . . This compilation is brutally frank: why else include the insanely bad "Hitsville UK"?' The album climbed no higher than 68, and spent just two weeks in the charts.

The US had seen little Clash-related activity since the release of *The Story Of The Clash, Volume 1* and the reissue of the band's back catalogue on CD. There had been two strange compilations on Relativity that claimed to be issued under licence from CBS: 1989's *The Clash Collection*, which brings together a fairly arbitrary selection of ten album tracks, and 1990's *A Collection Of Rare Tracks And B-Sides*, which combines the four tracks present on the UK, but not the US, version of *The Clash* with six assorted B-sides. The clumsy, unimaginative choice of material and titles gives the releases an at best semi-legitimate feel, and they certainly failed to have much impact on the wider record buying public.

While the success of 'Should I Stay Or Should I Go' precipitated a greedy smash-and-grab raid on the UK's Clash marketplace, the lack of activity in the US allowed an on the whole more considered and impressive project to get under way. Epic was just one of several major labels working through their lists to feed the demand of the CD generation for the recording world's equivalent of coffee-table books: boxed-set retrospectives.

Kosmo Vinyl, now resident in New York, was given the job of overseeing a Clash boxed set. No one could question his dedication or enthusiasm. He unearthed all the documentation relating to the Clash's recording career and tracked down masters for unreleased, obscure and, in some cases, forgotten tracks. He short-listed songs for inclusion and discussed their relative merits with the band members. He collected together lyrics for nearly all the tracks, and had them printed up as a CD-sized booklet. He assembled another, larger 66-page booklet which included: a variety of photographs, mostly by Pennie Smith and Bob Gruen; a specially commissioned essay on the Clash and America by rock writer and former Patti Smith guitarist Lenny Kaye; extracts from Lester Bangs's epic 1977 *NME* Clash feature as reprinted in *Psychotic Reactions And Carburetor Dung* (and probably suggested by Mick Jones); a discography; and, last but not least, a band history-cum-track by track breakdown consisting of excerpts from interviews Kosmo had recently conducted with the Clash, Bernie, former crew members and associates. The only thing he didn't do was produce the compilation, a task handled by Don De Vito and Richard Bauer.

Everything possible was done to make it feel like a bona fide Clash project. The title Kosmo gave it, *Clash On Broadway*, recycles that of the abandoned Don Letts film. The contentious 'Remote Control' is not included. An unlisted extra track, 'The Street Parade', has been snuck on to the end of the last disc, as on *London Calling*. The boxed set matches *Sandinista!*'s supposed folly in including three discs, but instead of 36 tracks features a total of 64: adding up to over three and a half hours' worth of music, or the equivalent of approximately five standard albums. A possibly unintentional point made by the set: with their track skipping and random selection mechanisms, CD players had succeeded in changing the way people consumed music, something that the Clash had attempted, but failed to do with *Sandinista!* 11 years previously; as a result, such a gigantic archive of material as *Clash On Broadway* was no longer considered as overbearing and unwieldy as the relatively petite triple album had seemed in 1980.

Not that the world was deemed ready for a wholesale re-evaluation of that album's highlights. Other than its collectors' selling points – a few rare B-sides and alternative live versions, two of Guy Stevens's Polydor demos and the three previously unreleased tracks, 'One Emotion', 'Every Little Bit Hurts' and 'Midnight To Stevens' – *Clash On Broadway* takes a predictable enough and near-chronological tour through the band's back catalogue. Although not necessarily in their original versions, it includes: 13 tracks from *The Clash* (that is, everything except 'Remote Control', making its exclusion even more of a statement), plus '1977'; all the singles, plus most of the key B-sides, 'Capital Radio' and the entire *Cost Of Living* EP except 'Capital Radio Two'; just five tracks (out of 10) from *Give 'Em Enough Rope*; 11 tracks (out of 19) from *London Calling*; just nine tracks, one of them unlisted, (out of 36) from *Sandinista!*; only five tracks (out of 12) from *Combat Rock*; and nothing at all from *Cut The Crap*, which the discography too conspires to write out of history.

Clash On Broadway is clearly a labour of love, but it is far from perfect. A true perspective on the Clash's career has been sacrificed for collectability, the motive behind the inclusion of the alternative versions, unreleased and rare tracks. A cynical ploy to tempt people who already have the band's albums and/or *The Story Of The Clash, Volume 1* (the contents of which are repeated in their entirety), it also throws the set's balance out of whack. Whereas the early B-sides deserve to be present on their own merit, later ones like 'Stop The World' are much less worthy than many of the omitted album tracks. Typically, the inclusion of these interesting, but inconsequential, oddities not only damaged the current project, but also compromised any future rarities compilation.

In addition to over-stressing the Guy Stevens connection, the boxed set's other failing is the overtly American bias of the packaging. Lenny Kaye and Lester Bangs's writings concentrate on the American perspective, as does the title *Clash On Broadway*. While the track selection concedes the pre-eminence of the punk years, the packaging pretends that the American campaign, as well as being the most important thing to the band,was also the most significant thing about them. This book has detailed the complicated and confused motivations behind the Clash's decision to concentrate on breaking the US from mid-1979 onwards, but even if one allows that it was wholly a matter of choice, it is important to remember that the band never pandered to America during its lifetime the way this compilation does posthumously. The Bonds residency was a great publicity coup, but hardly a triumph in itself. Perhaps it is more significant to note that Kosmo Vinyl joined the Clash camp only at the beginning of the American campaign – The Quest – which must inevitably have affected *his* perspective. In fairness to Kosmo, the former Clash members were involved in the project, and could have said if they were unhappy with any aspect of it. They must have known that, although commissioned by their American record label for the US market, *Clash On Broadway* would be their one and only chance to construct such a weighty memorial to their band, and that, sooner or later, it would be released all over the world ensuring that the American vision of the Clash it presents would become the general vision of the Clash.

The boxed set was released in the US in November 1991 as part of Epic's Legacy series, and helped along by a slick MTV *Rockumentary* which combined archive footage and contemporary talking head interviews with Mick, Paul and Joe. Despite being so openly courted by the project and remarking that 'the power and ambition of the Clash went well beyond the time-capsule limitations of punk, with a go-for-the-throat urgency that rock has lost in the years since', *Rolling Stone*'s Don McLeese still found it ironic that 'the band that railed against "turning rebellion into money" now finds itself repackaged as pricy punk nostalgia'. He gave the project three and a half stars.

The UK would have to wait two and a half years for the Americanisation of the Clash, *The Singles* having spoiled the market for the immediate release of the compilation boxed set. Not that all was quiet in the meantime. In 1992, the US version of *The Clash*, *Give 'Em Enough Rope* and *Combat Rock* were issued together as one in a series of Columbia mid-price boxed sets (it currently retails at £22.99). In February 1993, Columbia issued a five-track mid-priced CD entitled *Twelve Inch Mixes*, the sound of barrels being scraped. Evidence that it is not a group-originated project is provided by the inclusion of the new Clash's 'This Is England'. When he reviewed it for *Q*, David Hepworth was surprisingly generous: 'Perhaps the Clash will ultimately be remembered not as a punk rock combo or even as rock'n'roll classicists but as a dance band.' He gave it four out of five stars.

In November the same year, it was followed by yet another compilation. *Black Market Clash* had collected the Clash's oddities and B-sides up to August 1980, and it was now decided to update the project so that it covered their entire career; or, rather, up to 1982, which was when the Clash now chose to pretend the Clash had ended. This time Kosmo Vinyl took the role of compilation producer, while project direction was taken care of by Gary Pacheco. Again, efforts were made to give it the feel of a bona fide Clash release: entitled *Super Black Market Clash*, it employs a colour-tinted version of the earlier album's Rocco Macauley cover photograph; 25 tracks are packed on to the single CD, but the compilation was also made available as a triple 10-inch vinyl album, a nod to both the original 10-inch release and to *Sandinista!*; and a vintage Pennie Smith photograph appears on the inner sleeve. In addition, there are concise, but informative, sleevenotes detailing each track's place and time of recording.

Once more, though, the album suffers from a number of shortcomings. It was designed principally for the US market, where it was released on Epic. From an American point of view: while there are ten obscure tracks, including several late period B-sides, the instrumental 'Listen' from the *Capital Radio* EP and the original *Black Market Clash*'s main attraction, 'Time Is Tight', the other 15 all appear on *Clash On Broadway*. This time, the compilation was simultaneously released on Columbia in the UK, where *Clash On Broadway* had yet to appear. From a British point of view: it is irritating because it is so obviously oriented towards America, and includes the four tracks already available on the UK version of *The Clash* (but not on the US version). Also, the CD update is not cheap (currently retailing at £14.29).

In his review in *Q* John Aizlewood took the now customary opportunity to state, 'there's a reasonably strong case for arguing that the Clash were the greatest British rock band', before going on to find fault with this latest recorded testimonial: 'It's far from the treasure trove it could have been . . . There's little to recruit new converts and the whole exercise suggests a missed opportunity, but equally there's little that dispels the Clash's awesome aura.' He gave it three stars. It failed to chart. *Super Black Market Clash* would become even more redundant in the UK when *Clash On Broadway* was finally given a release. As John Aizlewood suggested, the former could have been more of a treasure trove: if its larger, sister compilation had stuck to more conventional material, then it could have rounded up all the obscurities and oddities for those really interested in such things. One also has to question why it failed to make room for the *Rat Patrol From Fort Bragg* outtakes. One possible answer might be that there are further half-assed compilations in the pipeline. Talking to *Vox* in 1994, Kosmo said not, insisting, 'There's nothing worth releasing.' As if *that* would ever be a consideration.

Clash On Broadway emerged in the UK, still on the Epic-Legacy label, in June 1994. It retailed for £33.49, hardly a give-away in itself, but by this time almost everyone keen enough on the band to buy it had given up on a UK release and paid closer to £50 for it on easily available import. The flurry of re-releases over the previous three years had used up much of the UK music papers' patience. The *NME* ignored it altogether. *Q* contented themselves with a review. Apparently not a fan of uptempo music, Tom Hibbert found some of the band's 'punky posturings' and 'politico nonsense' somewhat 'silly and dated': 'But when they slowed down, took a little control of themselves, they could be marvellous.' He deemed the previously unreleased material to be 'slightly disappointing', but overall found both packaging and contents 'rather splendid'. 'Don't play it all at once,' he concluded, before giving it four stars. 'It'll do your head in.'

Vox devoted two and a half pages of their *Record Hunter* supplement to Mike Pattenden's review-cum-overview, and another half a page to a brief interview with Kosmo Vinyl. Mike's reappraisal of the band's career, again under the title 'The Last Gang In Town', broke little new ground: 'The Clash were the quintessential punk band . . . Strummer, the middle-class, public school dropout, raged at the sort of issues with which every kid in cement-grey, high-rise Seventies Britain could identify: unemployment, urban boredom, racism, the rise of the Right, police brutality. . . and he made it sound fierce, noble and romantic in the best tradition of rock'n'roll.' Compared with Kosmo's bland assertion that it was 'done for recognition and overview. It was always important for them not to be ghettoised', however, Mike's reservations about the boxed set as an artefact came as a welcome breath of fresh air. He began his article, 'Now, with the belated arrival of *Clash On Broadway*, Epic's reverential three-CD boxed set, the Clash achieve record industry canonisation', and finished it in similar style: 'The deep irony of a jeans advert bringing them their only number one in 1991 was not lost on those who grew up with the Clash . . . They deserved better, but the suits could never swallow the real Clash. They were too jagged, too fucking unpalatable: like all great rock'n'roll. For that reason, a Clash boxed set can't but seem an incongruous monument.'

Back in November 1993, *Q* publishers Emap Metro had launched a new magazine called *Mojo*. It was intended not to compete directly with *Q*, but to complement it by taking a more in-depth, slightly academic approach to music, loosely targeting people in their mid-thirties and upwards. *Mojo*'s forte is the multifaceted career retrospective, and *Clash On Broadway* provided the magazine with an excuse to devote the bulk of its ninth issue (August 1994) to the band. Slightly disappointingly, the magazine also took its cue from the boxed set when it came to focus and approach. Although the heading accompanying the cover photograph of the band announced 'The Clash: FROM WESTWAY TO BROADWAY', the Westway element consisted of a six-page portfolio of Jonh Ingham's 1976 snapshots, only one of which was of the band. Equally tenuous – at least, more so than the boxed set would have the world believe – was the Guy Stevens feature tacked on to the end.

The rest of the epic feature was devoted to the Clash's American campaign. Ray Lowry supplied pen and ink drawings and a page of reminiscences from the second 1979 tour; Pennie Smith and Bob Gruen were chief among the photographic illustrators; Chris Salewicz provided a three-page reminiscence about the Clash's Bonds season, and interviewed Joe for a further page and a half of his recollections about America; and American correspondent Mark Coleman provided a two-page essay on the country's reaction to the Clash. 'In America, the Clash didn't break down any barriers; gradually, they crept in through a side door labelled New Wave,' he wrote, noting that the band had already modified their punk sound into something softer and more musical by the time they reached the US. He ended: 'The stridency and raw power of the Clash's pure punk roots certainly left a mark on America, but it's the controversial and "compromised" eclecticism of their New Wave phase that still rings in our ears.'

The problem with *Mojo*'s coverage was that it encouraged British people to think of the band in the same way; whereas, between 1986 and 1989, most UK commentators had held up *The Clash* as the band's shining moment and major contribution, it now appeared that increasing historical distance from the impact of the punk movement was bringing them around to the American point of view: namely that *London Calling* was the peak of the band's achievements. It was left to Will Birch to redress the balance in his review of the boxed set, hidden away at the back of the same issue of *Mojo*. As the former drummer with pub rock band the Kursaal Flyers, whom the Clash had supported on their fifth gig and whom punk had quickly rendered obsolete, Will might have been expected to take the opportunity to settle an old score. Far from it.

Recalling the Roundhouse gig, he wrote: 'The minute they walked in the building I knew it was all over. To me, their sound mattered not one iota: they had the look . . .' As far as Will was concerned, it was the band's first two albums and handful of singles that provided the foundation for the Myth. *London Calling*'s acceptance in America only served to launch 'the great trash-and-Vaudeville, coast-to-coast fancy dress party that culminated in Pennie Smith's epic photo album, *Before And After*'. Nevertheless, he concluded: 'The all-too brief career of the Clash is well represented and documented on this superb three-CD retrospective, and despite some dodgy moments their legend remains intact.'

In the years since the band broke up, parallel to these media re-examinations of their impact and legacy (most of which have served to enhance rather than damage the Myth) has run ceaseless speculation about the possibility of a re-formation. The lack of an official statement about the band's demise left the door open, and rumours that Mick Jones was about to return to the fold – keeping BAD as a sideline – began to circulate in May 1986. The release of *The Story Of The Clash, Volume 1* brought the band members back into the same orbit, and some believed its release was a prelude to a reunion that might eventually provide Volume 2. Announcing the split of the first incarnation of BAD in January 1990, the *NME*'s news pages posed the question 'CLASH FROM CHAOS?'

In early September 1991, a matter of months after the success of 'Should I Stay Or Should I Go' and around the same time as the band members were involved in putting together *Clash On Broadway*, the paper's news pages carried the following story: 'Sources claim that Mick Jones has been approached by American promoters bidding £10 million for a one-off US Clash tour, and the offer has received serious consideration from Jones and Strummer.' In July 1993, Rick Sky's *Daily Mirror* pop column reported, in typically circumspect tabloid style, 'Punk kings the Clash are getting back together for a massive £50 million world tour after a ten year break. The four-piece group have signed up with a top American manager and are currently lining up a string of dates: starting with a huge stadium tour of the US.'

Why would the Clash re-form? The obvious answer – especially in view of the figures mentioned above – is for the money. Although the band's attitude had verged on the mercenary between spring 1981 and the summer of 1983, prior to and following on from that period money had only been a factor when lack of it had prevented the Clash from pushing forward and doing what they wanted to do. Since the split, the reissue programme has seemed determined to wring every last penny from the band's assets, but that kind of behind-the-scenes greed can always be blamed away on to other parties. A reunion would be a more flagrant money-grabbing exercise, especially if it took the form of a stadium tour: not only would it net millions in itself, but yet more millions would come from merchandising (which these days can be more profitable than record sales), the live video, the live album and the inevitable compilation tie-ins.

'I don't think any of us would do it for the money,' Mick told *Vox*'s Mal Peachey in April 1991. 'I don't think we'd do *anything* just for the money.' Topper has not been earning as a musician since 1989; Paul has been painting full-time since 1992, and has a child to support; however worthy or satisfying, none of Joe's post-Clash projects has done much to swell his coffers, and he has two children to support; BAD were in debt even at the height of their success, and Big Audio now seem unlikely to take off in spectacular enough fashion to keep Mick in the rock star style to which he has become accustomed. With the exception of Topper, the re-releases and compilations have made the Clash members wealthy men – whatever they might claim to the contrary – but the money will not keep coming in for ever. There must be a temptation to pre-empt the possible humiliation of being forced to re-form out of financial necessity.

Maybe they would re-form because of a renewed enthusiasm for the idea of working together? No matter how guilty they might feel about the way they treated Topper, the others see him rarely. Mick and Paul do not get on and do not socialise. Joe remains friendly with both Paul and Mick, but they all have their own circles of friends and hardly live in one another's pockets. Paul now puts all his energies into his art, and no longer plays or writes music. Joe and Mick broke the ice on their songwriting partnership in 1986; the opportunity to repeat the venture has been there ever since, but they have chosen to ignore it. Save for the odd nod to Ennio Morricone, their respective musical paths have now diverged so widely it would take a great deal of compromise to bring them together once more; and even if they were prepared to make the effort, it is hard to see how either of them could feel wholly satisfied with the result.

They might get back together purely for reasons of status. As the Clash, they were Big Shots; as ex-members of the Clash, to greater and lesser extents, they are has-beens. Joe seems to feel he is unworthy of solo success.

After the best part of a decade in the wilderness, being treated with the mixture of pity and irritation reserved for the chronic junky, Topper would almost certainly relish the opportunity to be part of a name band again. In the early days of BAD, Mick's main drive was to prove himself with his new band. As time has gone on, however, and for a variety of reasons – many of them attributable to plain old bad luck – BAD's popularity has slipped, he has shown himself to be less and less prepared to slog round the medium-sized gig circuit. Playing support for U2 has also been difficult for him to take. As early as 1988, following BAD's first stint opening for the band, he told *Blitz*'s William Shaw, 'I used to sit around backstage and feel a bit jealous. Every time U2 went on stage, I used to think, "Oh fuck, man. I know where we went wrong." The Clash could have been there, know what I mean?'

Inextricably linked with the issue of status is the knowledge that the Clash went out with a whimper, scorned both critically and commercially. A high-profile reunion might provide a more appropriate Big Bang. The above quote would seem to suggest that Mick would be susceptible to this line of thinking. Paul views it somewhat differently: he understands that, with a little help from slanted compilations and a posthumous number one single, time has rewritten the Clash story so that it ends not with the embarrassment of *Cut The Crap*, but with the breakthrough 1982 US tour and the success of 'Rock The Casbah'. With his intuitive grasp on the importance of image, he recognises that it would not be becoming for men of 40-plus to dress, pose or work the stage the way the Clash did in their heyday. 'I want to retain my dignity,' he told the *NME*'s Mary Ann Hobbs in 1991. 'And I want to move on.'

For his part, Joe understands that, even if they seldom played the kind of arenas U2 play and sold nowhere near the same number of records U2 sell, the Clash still manage to hold their own. 'The modern definition of "made it" is filling the 100,000-seat stadiums. U2 do five a week,' he told *Musician*'s Bill Flanagan in 1988. 'But [back when the Clash were together] there was still some vestige of true underground feeling. You saw us in arenas, but we were at our finest with 3,000 in an old theatre . . . if you look at our record sales, nothing sold until *Combat Rock* and "Rock The Casbah". I'd say we sold a *speck* overall to what U2 sell now. We made it, but in another way. We made it in the culture.'

Nevertheless, it is one thing to know that the Myth is best served by leaving well alone, and another to walk away from it and accept effective retirement at such an early age. Paul appears to be genuinely content to immerse himself in painting instead. Joe has also tried to take a different tack with his acting and soundtrack work, but for him this does not seem to have been quite enough. The truth is that rock'n'roll has always been Joe's *raison d'être*, as it has been for Mick. While they were still with the Clash, both recognised the band's significance for them personally: that it was their one true shot, their life's work. Following his sacking, Mick has tried to transfer that commitment to BAD, but occasionally lets slip remarks which make it clear he knows his new band is not quite the same thing. Expressing his frustration with his UK record label to James Brown in 1991, he said, 'I think they want BAD II to fail so maybe I'll have to do the Clash again': as though re-forming the Clash were his only other option.

Has a re-formation ever seriously been on the agenda? Sort of. When filming *Walker* in 1987, Joe told Graham Fuller that he believed the Clash was finished, but on several occasions since he has expressed his willingness to have another go. An obvious opportunity came in 1988, with the release of *The Story Of The Clash, Volume 1*, but the possibility was ruled out first by Topper's jail sentence (which might explain why Joe went on record to express his impatience with the drummer at that time) and then by Mick's lengthy illness. It is perhaps not insignificant that Joe made his only bona fide solo album to date during this period. The next chance came in January 1990, with the break-up of the original BAD, but by this time Paul was committed to Havana 3 a.m. The Clash's posthumous UK number one single seemed like the ideal cue, but Mick had now got BAD II off the ground. Also, his insistence on including 'Rush' on the B-side of 'Should I Stay Or Should I Go' badly strained his relationship with Paul; again, it is perhaps not wholly coincidental that it was at this time that the latter declared he had no intention of being party to a Clash reunion.

The first public acknowledgement that substantial offers had been tabled came in April 1991, in Mick's interview with *Vox*'s Mal Peachey. That September, while the *Clash On Broadway* boxed set was being compiled – so the possibility of it being a publicity stunt should not be discounted – Mick told *Rolling Stone* that he would not rule out a Clash reunion at some future date. A few days later, having named the figure offered as £10 million, the *NME* phoned Tricia Ronane for comment on behalf of Paul – whom she was now managing – and was told the rumours were unfounded. 'The band certainly aren't in conference discussing re-formation at the moment . . . The Clash haven't had any serious offers from promoters recently. But if there is an American promoter willing to put £10 million on the table, I'm sure the band would consider re-forming. In fact, tell them to call me!'

If we can take Topper's willingness (as opposed to fitness) for granted, then there were now no obstacles other than immediate commitments, something which Joe confirmed to the paper in early October 1991: 'There have been offers for sure, but really to answer the question, I'd have to get all the boys in one place at one time and we'd have to discuss it. I think we will. But Mick's on tour right now in America, Paul's just had a son and he might be going off with Havana 3 a.m., and I'm off around the world for the next six months with the Pogues, so it sounds a bit unlikely for the immediate future.'

From March 1992 onwards, all three of them disappeared from the limelight, and their at best desultory efforts with their respective post-Clash projects served only to fuel the rumours that a reunion was imminent. The sole problem seemed to be Topper's condition, and it is tempting to read more than generosity of spirit into Mick's and Joe's joint funding of his rehabilitation programme at that time, and the fact that Kosmo subsequently agreed to manage his affairs. Whether or not a similar reading of the circumstances was the source of Rick Sky's July 1993 claim that the band had accepted an offer for £50 million, had management and were currently lining up a huge stadium tour, it certainly stirred things up again. *Q* followed up the story, and were met with denials on behalf of Paul and Joe and Mick. The belated November 1994 emergence of a new Big Audio album suggested that the waiting game would continue for some time.

Entering into the spirit of the debate, the December 1993 issue of *Q* included a two-page feature under the title 'The Big Question: Should The Clash Reform?' Twenty-three assorted former punks and Clash associates, record industry spokesmen and current name performers were asked to pass their verdict. Predictably, the money men, thinking purely in terms of gain, said yes, as did the members of other re-formed bands intent on justifying their own actions. Those with no vested interest said no.

No other re-formation has ever been 100 per cent successful, creatively and commercially. Admittedly, the now re-formed Buzzcocks and Sham 69 never had quite the same importance as the Clash, so their slide into relative obscurity second time round is hardly surprising. The Damned have re-formed so many times it hardly signifies: splitting up is their equivalent of taking a break between albums or tours. Television were met with the same kind of apathy that precipitated their first split. The Velvet Underground re-formation was eagerly awaited, but was something of an anticlimax and ended in bad feeling. Madness overstayed their welcome when they reappeared, and began to feel like a rip-off. The Eagles 1994 US tour was an even more blatant money-grabber. Bands who have got back together specifically for album projects, like the Small Faces, the original Animals and the Mark II incarnation of Deep Purple, have all succumbed to the same ego battles, petty squabbles and musical differences that caused them to break up in the first place.

There is also the now quite possibly irrelevant fact that the stadium dinosaur tour epitomises everything punk set out to eradicate from rock'n'roll. The Clash Myth would probably survive it; but all that establishes is how hollow the Clash Myth has become.

The last question on this subject is, *will* the Clash re-form? Providing that nobody dies, on past evidence, the answer has to be yes; if only because they have already made every *other* mistake in the book . . .

As Joe says, the Clash are now part of the culture. Not just because their music is sampled on other people's records, or because it is used to soundtrack jeans advertisements. In 1989, Panama's General Manuel Noriega rigged an election in order to hold on to power. Although it had previously been supportive, the US government now turned against him, accusing him of trafficking drugs to America. In December, it responded in that most American of ways, and sent in the troops. Noriega went to ground in Panama City's Vatican embassy. The troops besieged the building and fixed up loudspeakers to play high-volume rock'n'roll music at him day and night in an effort to encourage his surrender. The most popular tune – with everyone, that is, except Noriega – was 'Should I Stay Or Should I Go'. Following Saddam Hussein's order for Iraqi troops to invade Kuwait, the international community rallied behind the US's decision to reclaim the nation's oil for the free world. Allied troops began to gather in Saudi Arabia in October 1990, preparing for the following year's Gulf War. The first record played on the allied forces radio network was 'Rock The Casbah'. The Clash might be given pause to wince at such perversions of their original intention – the US's self-appointed role as the world's policeman being a long way from the sentiments expressed on *Sandinista!* or even *Combat Rock* – but in effect they were soundtracking significant historical events in much the same way as the Doors and Jimi Hendrix had soundtracked Vietnam and continue to soundtrack Vietnam movies.

In 1992, after receiving a letter seeking guidance from former Transvision Vamp singer Wendy James, Elvis Costello replied by writing her an album's worth of songs he felt were suited to her persona. One of them, released as a single the following spring, was entitled 'London's Brilliant', and included the line 'Still digging up the bones of Strummer and Jones'. It is a celebration-cum-satire of the people who, like Wendy herself, have flocked to the Ladbroke Grove area over the years in pursuit of the Clash Myth. Its greater truth is that, when the generation who grew up with the Clash think of Notting Hill, they think of the band, just as the previous generation automatically associate Liverpool with the Beatles.

The Clash have found acceptance in the most unlikely of places. The National Sound Archive is a branch of the British Library, and therefore the establishment's record of the nation's musical culture. The front cover of the leaflet currently advertising the pop archive features not, as might be expected, a picture of the Beatles, the Rolling Stones or even the Who, but Pennie Smith's *London Calling* photograph of Paul Simonon in the act of smashing his bass.

As time takes us ever further away from punk's cultural context, it seems that the Clash – thanks in no small part to *Rolling Stone*'s 1989 poll and the signals given off by the *Clash On Broadway* package – are to be remembered the way America sees them, as a classic rock'n'roll band. Until such a time as a reunion allows reality to intrude, they will doubtless continue to be thought of as a conflation of *London Calling*, the Bonds residency, the video clip of 'Should I Stay Or Should I Go' live at Shea Stadium and the black and white American outlaw chic as preserved in Pennie Smith's *Before And After* photo-book. Altogether it adds up to Chris Salewicz's memorable 1978 description of them as being 'like Peckinpah's vision of the Western outlaw in *The Wild Bunch*, the loners whose high moral sense is one of the last relics of another time'. There they are in any number of Pennie's photos: the central characters approaching the final shoot-out in some elegiac western, freeze-framed at the very moment they step out of time and into legend. The Last Gang In Town.

There are those of us whose lives were touched and attitudes altered by punk, and especially the Clash, who would prefer to remember them – in all their confused and contradictory glory – as a conflation of *The Clash*, the late 1976 London gigs, their clips from Don Letts's *Punk Rock Movie*, and the Pollock/Pop-Art/Lettrist/urban-guerrilla looks as preserved on Sebastian Conran's Xeroxed gig flyers. Back when they said and did everything they would subsequently fail to live up to and fail to live down. Back when they claimed they had come not only to shake up rock'n'roll, but also to change the world. Back when it still seemed both reasonable and possible for representatives of a youth culture to do that. Back when we were 'the kids'; or, maybe, to paraphrase Paul Simon on *Graceland*, back before you were even born, kid.

Both views are too one-sided, too reliant on the Clash Myth. Perhaps more important is the fact that the Clash inspired the kind of belief that we don't have in these cynical, withdrawn, post-modern times. Some of it was misguided, yes, and the band's failure to deliver to those who showed faith is one of the reasons they were given such a rough ride while still in existence (and also in this book). But at least they tried to live up to expectations for most of their career, and it is for that as much as for the music and the cool rock'n'roll image they left behind that they deserve their place in the folk memory and the pop culture history books.

THE END?

INDEX

782.4216
GRAY, MARCUS
LAST GANG IN TOWN

$25.00

DATE		